Contents

How to use this book   4
Introduction: AS/A Level History   6

Germany and West Germany, 1918–89   8

Introduction   8
Political and governmental change, 1918–89   10
Opposition, control and consent, 1918–89   36
Economic development and policies, 1918–89   62
Aspects of life in Germany and West Germany, 1918–89   88
How far was Hitler's foreign policy responsible for the Second World War?   114
Preparing for your exams   139

The rise and fall of fascism in Italy, c1911–46   166

Introduction   166
The liberal state, c1911–18   168
The rise of Mussolini and the creation of a fascist dictatorship, 1919–26   192
The fascist state, 1925–40   216
Challenges to, and the fall of, the fascist state, c1935–46   240
Preparing for your exams   265

Spain, 1930–78: republicanism, Francoism and the re-establishment of democracy   284

Introduction   284
Creation and destabilisation of the Second Republic, 1930–36   286
The Spanish Civil War, 1936–39   310
Establishing Franco's dictatorship, 1938–56   334
Dictatorship remodelled and the transition to democracy, 1956–78   358
Preparing for your exams   383

Index   402
Acknowledgements   406

How to use this book

STRUCTURE

This book covers Route G of the Edexcel A Level and AS Level History qualifications. Route G consists of three papers which are linked by the theme 'Nationalism, dictatorship and democracy in 20th century Europe'.

- Paper 1: Germany and West Germany, 1918–89
- Paper 2a: The rise and fall of fascism in Italy, c1911–46
- Paper 2b: Spain, 1930–78: republicanism, Francoism and the re-establishment of democracy

To take Route G, you must study Paper 1, plus **one** of the two Paper 2 options. You do not need to study the other Paper 2 topic for your exam, but you might like to read it for interest – it deals with similar themes to the topics you are studying.

If you are studying for A Level History, you will also need to study a Paper 3 option and produce coursework in order to complete your qualification. All Paper 3 options are covered by other textbooks in this series.

AS LEVEL OR A LEVEL?

This book is designed to support students studying both the Edexcel AS Level and A Level qualifications. The content required for both qualifications is identical, so all the material in the papers you are studying is relevant, whichever qualification you are aiming for.

The questions you will be asked in the exam differ for the two different qualifications, so we have included separate exam-style questions and exam preparation sections. If you are studying for an AS Level, you should use the exam-style questions and exam sections highlighted in blue. If you are studying for an A Level, you should use the exam-style questions and exam sections highlighted in green.

AS Level Exam-Style Question Section A

Was the work of Gustav Stresemann the main reason for the Weimar government's ability to overcome the challenges it faced between 1919 and 1929? (20 marks)

Tip
Think about the challenges the government faced and how they were dealt with before and during Stresemann's term in government.

A Level Exam-Style Question Section B

How accurate is it to say that Hitler's rise to becoming a dictator was achieved by legal means? (20 marks)

Tip
The question expects you to consider evidence to support and argue against the proposition.

The 'Preparing for your exams' section at the end of each paper contains sample answers of different standards, with comments on how weaker answers could be improved. Make sure you look at the right section for the exam you are planning to take.

FEATURES

Extend your knowledge

These features contain additional information that will help you gain a deeper understanding of the topic. This could be a short biography of an important person, extra background information about an event, an alternative interpretation, or even a research idea that you could follow up. Information in these boxes is not essential to your exam success, but still provides insights of value.

EXTEND YOUR KNOWLEDGE

Rationing
The system for rationing was set up at the start of the war and allowances varied depending on age and the kind of work that people did. For example, someone doing very heavy work was allowed 4,200 calories a day compared to the 2,400 calories allowed to an office worker. People were given colour-coded ration cards each month. The ration varied within years as well as by year, but the following figures give a yearly average. In 1939, an adult doing normal work was allowed, for example, 9.6 kg of bread, 2 kg of meat and 4 eggs. In 1942, it was 8 kg of bread, 4 eggs and 1.2 kg of meat. By 1945, they were allowed 6.8 kg of bread, 150 g of meat and no eggs.

Knowledge check activities

These activities are designed to check that you have understood the material that you have just studied. They might also ask you questions about the sources and extracts in the section to check that you have studied and analysed them thoroughly.

> **ACTIVITY**
> **KNOWLEDGE CHECK**
>
> **Challenges to the Weimar government**
>
> 1 Explain how the nature of the Weimar government exposed it to opposition.
>
> 2 List the four main points that a right-wing opponent of Weimar would make in a speech against the government.

Summary activities

At the end of each chapter, you will find summary activities. These are tasks designed to help you think about the key topic you have just studied as a whole. They may involve selecting and organising key information or analysing how things changed over time. You might want to keep your answers to these questions safe – they are handy for revision.

> **ACTIVITY**
> **SUMMARY**
>
> **Understanding political and governmental change**
>
> 1 Draw up a table showing the main features of government in the Weimar Republic, Nazi Germany and the FRG. Include, for example, structure of government, role of elections, nature of the civil service and other institutions, etc.
>
> 2 Identify and colour code similarities and differences between the three periods.
>
> 3 Give three examples of what the table cannot show you about the political structure of each period, and explain why they are significant.

Thinking Historically activities

These activities are found throughout the book and are designed to develop your understanding of history, especially around the key concepts of evidence, interpretations, causation and change. Each activity is designed to challenge a conceptual barrier that might be holding you back. This is linked to a map of conceptual barriers developed by experts. You can look up the map and find out which barrier each activity challenges by downloading the conceptual map from this website: www.pearsonschools.co.uk/historyprogressionapproach.

conceptual map reference

> **THINKING HISTORICALLY**   Evidence (3b)
>
> **It depends on the question**
>
> When considering the usefulness of a piece of evidence, people often think about authenticity in the case of artefacts, reliability in the case of witness statements, or methodology and structure in the case of secondary accounts. A better historical approach to the usefulness of a piece of evidence would be to think about the statements that we can make about the past based on it. Different statements can be made with different degrees of certainty, depending on the evidence.
>
> Work in small groups and answer the following:
>
> 1
>
>   a Write three statements that you can reasonably make about the Berlin Wall based solely on Source 11.
>
>   b Which of the statements can be made with the greatest degree of certainty? Why is this? Which statement can be made with the smallest degree of certainty? Why?
>
>   c What else might you need to increase your confidence in your statements?
>
> 2 Source 11 is an artefact and Source 12 is a witness statement. Which is more useful to the historian studying the impact of the Berlin Wall?
>
> 3 Look at Extract 5. How would the historian have gone about constructing this piece? What kinds of evidence would they have needed?

Getting the most from your online ActiveBook

This book comes with three years' access to ActiveBook* – an online, digital version of your textbook. Follow the instructions printed on the inside front cover to start using your ActiveBook.

Your ActiveBook is the perfect way to personalise your learning as you progress through your AS/A Level History course. You can:

- access your content online, anytime, anywhere
- use the inbuilt highlighting and annotation tools to personalise the content and make it really relevant to you.

Highlight tool – use this to pick out key terms or topics so you are ready and prepared for revision.

Annotations tool – use this to add your own notes, for example links to your wider reading, such as websites or other files. Or, make a note to remind yourself about work that you need to do.

*For new purchases only. If the access code has already been revealed, it may no longer be valid. If you have bought this textbook secondhand, the code may already have been used by the first owner of the book.

Introduction
AS/A Level History

WHY HISTORY MATTERS

History is about people and people are complex, fascinating, frustrating and a whole lot of other things besides. This is why history is probably the most comprehensive and certainly one of the most intriguing subjects there is. History can also be inspiring and alarming, heartening and disturbing, a story of progress and civilisation and of catastrophe and inhumanity.

History's importance goes beyond the subject's intrinsic interest and appeal. Our beliefs and actions, our cultures, institutions and ways of living, our languages and means of making sense of ourselves are all shaped by the past. If we want to fully understand ourselves now, and to understand our possible futures, we have no alternative but to think about history.

History is a discipline as well as a subject matter. Making sense of the past develops qualities of mind that are valuable to anyone who wants to seek the truth and think clearly and intelligently about the most interesting and challenging intellectual problem of all: other people. Learning history is learning a powerful way of knowing.

WHAT IS HISTORY?

History is a way of constructing knowledge about the world through research, interpretation, argument and debate.

Building historical knowledge involves identifying the traces of the past that exist in the present – in people's memories, in old documents, photographs and other remains, and in objects and artefacts ranging from bullets and lipsticks, to field systems and cities. Historians interrogate these traces and *ask questions* that transform traces into *sources of evidence* for knowledge claims about the past.

Historians aim to understand what happened in the past by *explaining why* things happened as they did. Explaining why involves trying to understand past people and their beliefs, intentions and actions. It also involves explaining the causes and evaluating the effects of large-scale changes in the past and exploring relationships between what people aimed to do, the contexts that shaped what was possible and the outcomes and consequences of actions.

Historians also aim to *understand change* in the past. People, states of affairs, ideas, movements and civilisations come into being in time, grow, develop, and ultimately decline and disappear. Historians aim to identify and compare change and continuity in the past, to measure the rate at which things change and to identify the types of change that take place. Change can be slow or sudden. It can also be understood as progressive or regressive – leading to the improvement or worsening of a situation or state of affairs. How things change and whether changes are changes for the better are two key issues that historians frequently debate.

Figure 1 Fragment of a black granite statue possibly portraying the Roman politician Mark Antony.

Debate is the essence of history. Historians write arguments to support their knowledge claims and historians argue with each other to test and evaluate interpretations of the past. Historical knowledge itself changes and develops. On the one hand, new sources of knowledge and new methods of research cause *historical interpretations* to change. On the other hand, the questions that historians ask change with time and new questions produce new answers. Although the past is dead and gone, the interpretation of the past has a past, present and future.

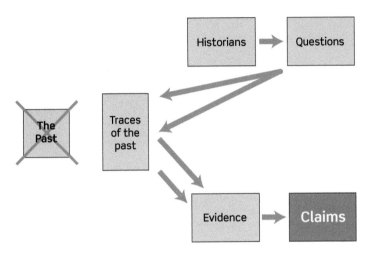

Figure 2 Constructing knowledge about the past.

THE CHALLENGES OF LEARNING HISTORY

Like all other Advanced Level subjects, A Level and AS Level history are difficult – that is why they are called 'advanced'. Your advanced level studies will build on knowledge and understanding of history that you developed at GCSE and at Key Stage 3 – ideas like 'historical sources', 'historical evidence' and 'cause', for example. You will need to do a lot of reading and writing to progress in history. Most importantly, you will need to do a lot of thinking, and thinking about your thinking. This book aims to support you in developing both your knowledge and your understanding.

History is challenging in many ways. On the one hand, it is challenging to build up the range and depth of knowledge that you need to understand the past at an advanced level. Learning about the past involves mastering new and unfamiliar concepts arising from the past itself (such as the Inquisition, Laudianism, *Volksgemeinschaft*) and building up levels of knowledge that are both detailed and well organised. This book covers the key content of the topics that you are studying for your examination and provides a number of features to help you build and organise what you know – for example, diagrams, timelines and definitions of key terms. You will need to help yourself too, of course, adding to your knowledge through further reading, building on the foundations provided by this book.

Another challenge is to develop understandings of the discipline of history. You will have to learn to think historically about evidence, cause, change and interpretations and also to write historically, in a way that develops clear and supported argument.

Historians think with evidence in ways that differ from how we often think in everyday life. In history, as Figure 2 shows, we cannot go and 'see for ourselves' because the past no longer exists. Neither can we normally rely on 'credible witnesses' to tell us 'the truth' about 'what happened'. People in the past did not write down 'the truth' for our benefit. They often had clear agendas when creating the traces that remain and, as often as not, did not themselves know 'the truth' about complex historical events.

A root of the word 'history' is the Latin word *historia*, one of whose meanings is 'enquiry' or 'finding out'. Learning history means learning to ask questions and interrogate traces, and then to reason about what the new knowledge you have gained means. This book draws on historical scholarship for its narrative and contents. It also draws on research on the nature of historical thinking and on the challenges that learning history can present for students. Throughout the book you will find 'Thinking Historically' activities designed to support the development of your thinking.

You will also find – as you would expect given the nature of history – that the book is full of questions. This book aims to help you build your understandings of the content, contexts and concepts that you will need to advance both your historical knowledge and your historical understanding, and to lay strong foundations for the future development of both.

QUOTES ABOUT HISTORY

'Historians are dangerous people. They are capable of upsetting everything. They must be directed.'

Nikita Khrushchev

'To be ignorant of what occurred before you were born is to remain forever a child. For what is the worth of human life, unless it is woven into the life of our ancestors by the records of history?'

Marcus Tullius Cicero

Germany and West Germany, 1918–89

NATIONALISM, DICTATORSHIP AND DEMOCRACY

The Europe that emerged after the First World War (1914–18) was not the same as pre-war Europe. Two great empires, the Russian Empire and the German Empire, had been torn apart. Russia was caught up in a civil war between the communist government and forces that wanted to overthrow it. Britain and France had suffered during the war but retained their old empires and their democratic systems of government – although the growth of communist groups in both countries worried their governments. Italy and Spain were both run as democracies immediately post-war; however, both had significant economic and social problems. The political situation in Italy and Spain was also precarious – their democratic governments faced strong opposition from right-wing parties and they also feared the growth of communism. What about the German Empire?

The new Germany, set up in 1918, ended up following the pattern of Italy and Spain. There was a period of democracy, followed by a takeover by a right-wing dictatorship. The dictatorships in Italy, Spain and Germany were in power when the Second World War broke out; they all fought on the losing side, and they were all replaced by democracies when the war ended. This unit considers the key political and governmental changes in Germany between 1918 and 1989, including the systems of government, the opposition it faced and how it controlled it, and how changes in the economy and society affected the various governments and were changed by them.

SOURCE 1

Adolph Hitler driving through Danzig shortly after German troops occupied it in September 1939. The banner behind him reads: 'One People, One Empire, One Leader!'

1918

11 November 1918 – Armistice Western Front: Germany and Western powers

1930

14 September 1930 – 107 Nazis elected to the Reichstag

1934

30 June 1934 – Night of the Long Knives

2 August – Hindenburg dies: Hitler becomes führer

1949

May 1949 – FRG set up

7 October 1949 – GDR set up

1989

9 November 1989 – Fall of Berlin Wall

DIVISIONS IN GERMANY

Adolf Hitler, dictator of Germany from 1934 to 1945, often referred to Germans as 'one people' and talked about the importance of the German nation. He talked of unity, but Germany had always had geographical, cultural and political divisions that could cut across each other and influenced behaviour right through to 1989. The various divisions were as follows:

- **Regional**: Inhabitants of one state often had a prejudiced view about another. For example, some states saw Bavarians as stupid. The regions had **Länder** that were allowed to make their own education, social welfare and other policies as long as those policies did not conflict with federal law.

- **Religious**: Religious conviction significantly influenced everyday life. Church organisations could tax their parishioners a percentage of their income tax payment (three percent in the 1930s, ten percent in the 1960s) and also received government grants. Members of the Länder were predominantly Catholic in the south and Protestant in the north, reflecting the religious make-up of the Land. Socially, people tended to divide along '**confessional**' lines. For example, most schools were confessional. In some places it was unusual for friendships to be made across the confessional divide.

- **Gender**: The gender divide was deep. Girls were expected to become wives and mothers, and there were gender-specific associations for everything from hiking to going to the opera.

- **Rural/urban**: In the late 19th and early 20th centuries, towns and cities had expanded rapidly because of industrialisation. By 1910, 150 German cities contained more than 100,000 citizens, with more, and bigger, towns and cities in the more industrialised north. Many Germans stereotyped rural life as an idyllic dream, while regarding cities as dirty and dangerous.

- **Class**: German class divisions were similar to those all over Europe, from the rich landowners down to the poor begging in city streets. However, class was more significant in the German army, which also had a powerful influence in politics. Most army officers also took part in local government.

- **Race**: The German word '*Volk*' translates as 'the people'. In early 20th-century Germany, the *Volk* were all people of German ancestry, no matter where they lived. The idea of being tied to other people by a common ancestry created a strong feeling that people from other races were inferior. There might be regional differences, but as far as the Germans were concerned any German was better than a Pole.

HOW PRE-WAR GERMANY WAS GOVERNED

While Prussia dominated the **Reich** (the kaiser who ruled the empire was the king of Prussia), the states kept some powers. The Reich had a common currency, tax system, transport and communication system, and foreign policy. Germany was governed for the Kaiser by a chancellor, a **Bundesrat** and a **Reichstag**. The Bundesrat had committees to run federal matters and voted on laws to bring to the Reichstag. The Reichstag had to approve laws and taxes.

Timeline

1919

Spartacist Rising
19 January 1919 – First Weimar Republic elections
28 June – Treaty of Versailles signed
31 July – Weimar Constitution passed

1933

30 January 1933 – Hitler becomes Chancellor of Germany
24 March 1933 – Enabling Act passed

1945

7 May 1945 – End of Second World War in Europe. Germany and Berlin divided into Allied zones

1961

12–13 August 1961 – Berlin Wall goes up

KEY TERMS

Länd
The regional governments of Germany, with a parliament and ministries for specific things such as education or culture.

Confessional
A faith-based association such as a school, business association or social club.

Reich
Empire.

Bundesrat
A federal council of representatives from each state with the kaiser as president.

Reichstag
A parliament that was elected by all men over the age of 25.

1.1 Political and governmental change, 1918–89

KEY QUESTIONS

- Why did the Weimar Republic surmount so many political challenges in the 1920s only to collapse by 1933?

- How did the business of government operate within the Nazi dictatorship in the years 1933–45?

- How far did the leaders of the Federal Republic of Germany create a stable political state in the years 1945–89?

INTRODUCTION

When Germany went to war in 1914 it was already under political strain. The parties in the Reichstag, which represented many different political views, had made a political truce to support Kaiser Wilhelm II and his military high command. However, the kaiser was not a capable war strategist and the military high command, led by Paul von Hindenburg and Erich Ludendorff, began to run Germany as a military dictatorship. The Reichstag still met, but the high command ignored it. They took Germany almost to the point of collapse, both economically and militarily, in the face of growing social unrest and political discontent. When US troops and supplies poured into Europe when the USA joined the war against Germany in October 1917, Ludendorff suggested to the kaiser that unrest might be calmed by a change in government. The rather cynical '**Revolution from Above**' was put in place. The army leadership stepped down. A new government, led by Prince Max of Baden, was formed from the majority parties in the Reichstag. It inherited a country that had huge economic difficulties and was closer to losing the war than anyone other than the German military high command realised. It also, for all its democratic airs, still had a Kaiser.

This change was the first of several government changes that took place between 1918 and 1989. Each government in turn had to try to resolve the problem of the conflicting desires of the politicians and those who voted for them in relation to the direction that the government should take – German unity or regionalism? A strong government that imposed decisions, so restricting political debate, or a government that allowed for political debate but could then get bogged down in this debate and fail to make decisions quickly enough? Each government was aware of the problems faced, and created by the previous ones, and each saw itself as needed in order to address those problems and avoid making the same mistakes.

KEY TERM

Revolution from Above
The name given to the new government that the kaiser and the military high command introduced in Germany in 1917 to stop a revolution of the people 'from below'. It was led by Max von Baden.

1918 - 11 November: armistice Western Front: Germany and Western Powers

1930 – 14 September: 107 Nazis elected to the Reichstag

1934 – 30 June: Night of the Long Knives
2 August: Hindenburg dies; Hitler is Führer

| 1915 | 1920 | 1925 | 1930 | 1935 | 1940 |

1919 - 4–15 January: Spartacist Revolt
19 January: first Weimar Republic elections
28 June: Treaty of Versailles signed
31 July: Weimar Constitution passed

1933 - 30 January: Hitler becomes chancellor of Germany
24 March: Enabling Act passed

1938 - 9 November: Kristallnacht

The Treaty of Versailles

The Treaty of Versailles was the treaty that officially ended the war between Germany and the Allies who had fought against Germany. It was signed on 28 June 1919. It cast a huge shadow over German politics for the next 21 years and helped to sweep Europe to war again. Indeed, even as the Treaty was being drawn up, people were saying that they feared this would lead to another war. The main terms of the Treaty were as follows.

Lost land

Germany lost land in Europe and all of its colonies. The land it lost in Europe was:

- all the land gained at the Treaty of Brest-Litovsk

- Upper Silesia

- Alsace and Lorraine (on its border with France)

- Eupen and Malmédy (on its border with Belgium).

European land taken from Germany included areas rich in coal and iron. Germany was forbidden to unite with Austria (a union referred to as the *Anschluss*), even if both sides wished it.

Military consequences

- The Rhineland became a demilitarised 'buffer zone' for France; it remained German, but German troops could not enter it.

- The German army was limited to 100,000 troops that could not leave Germany. It was not allowed tanks or heavy artillery.

- The German fleet was not allowed to have any warships over 10,000 tonnes and could not have any submarines at all.

- Germany was not allowed an air force.

Other terms

Germany was forced to accept responsibility for damage caused to the Allies. It had to agree to pay **reparations** to help rebuild in the Allies' countries after the devastation. There was much arguing over the amount that Germany should pay; in 1921, it was fixed at 132,000 million gold marks.

Figure 1.1: The new countries of Europe, drawn over the old ones. This shows land lost by Germany at Versailles, including land taken by Germany by the Treaty of Brest-Litovsk.

Key:
- Austro-Hungarian Empire 1914
- German Empire 1914
- Russian Empire 1914
- land gained by Germany and Austria-Hungary at Treaty of Brest-Litovsk

KEY TERM

Reparations
Compensation paid by a defeated country for the damage it caused when at war with other countries.

1949 – 22 May: FRG set up
7 October: GDR set up.

1989 – 9 November: fall of Berlin Wall

1945 — 1950 — 1955 — 1960 — 1965 — 1980 — 1985 — 1990

1945 – 7 May: end of Second World War in Europe
Germany, and Berlin, divided into Allied zones

1961 – 12-13 August: Berlin Wall goes up

WHY DID THE WEIMAR REPUBLIC SURMOUNT SO MANY POLITICAL CHALLENGES IN THE 1920s ONLY TO COLLAPSE BY 1933?

The creation of a republic, 1918–19

On 3 October 1918, Prince Max asked the Allies for an **armistice**. While the Allies discussed this (Britain and France were willing; the USA wanted to march to Berlin and force a surrender), German politics moved on. The end result of the political turmoil in Germany during the years 1918 and 1919 was the creation of the Weimar Republic.

Would Germany have a communist revolution?

Prince Max's government made some constitutional reforms. It extended the vote to all men. It made both the ministers and the army responsible to the government, not to the kaiser. These were significant changes. Yet unrest and talk of revolution continued. On 28 October 1918, the government's official inauguration day, the navy refused to sail against the British fleet. This set off strikes and mutinies across Germany. Some saw the reforms as a cynical fake. Others focused on what was unchanged: the country was still at war, the kaiser still ruled. Others, like the **Spartacists**, wanted a revolution like that in Russia. Workers' and soldiers' **councils** were set up. Some shared the communist ideals of Russian **soviets**. Others were less radical, but all wanted change. Prince Max was urged to press the kaiser to **abdicate;** the kaiser refused. On 8 November, Bavaria broke from Germany, declaring itself a republic. The kaiser could not ignore his empire breaking up. He abdicated and fled to Holland. Prince Max's government had to resign. It had lasted less than a month.

The Council of People's Representatives

On 10 November 1918, a new government was set up – the Council of People's Representatives – led by the socialist groups that held power in the Reichstag. The most significant were the Social Democrats (SPD), led by Friedrich Ebert, and the Independent Social Democrats (USPD), led by Hugo Haase. Ebert became chancellor with a cabinet of SPD and USPD members. The new government faced all of the problems of the previous one, worsened by a month of disruption and unrest. These problems forced Ebert to make the Ebert-Groener Pact with the army. The army would support the government as long as the government opposed the more left-wing ideas of parties in the Reichstag. The SPD and the USPD could not agree, let alone gain the wholehearted support of smaller parties. Ebert wanted to arrange for elections as soon as possible and leave any significant changes to the newly elected National Assembly that would write the new constitution. Haase wanted to start social and economic reforms at once, and wanted nothing to do with the army without reforming it first. What steps did the government take? Their first move was to stop the war. On 11 November, Matthias Erzberger of the German delegation signed the armistice on behalf of the government. The Allies then told the Germans they could not take part in treaty negotiations. In the shadow of this humiliation, parties began to form and reform, trying to gain enough votes to have a voice in the new Reichstag. The government also made some social reforms in the hope of improving the unsettled political and economic situation. It set an eight-hour working day, allowed independent trade unions, set up help for ex-soldiers to find work, and widened health and unemployment benefit. On 19 December, it fixed elections for 19 January 1919. Meanwhile, the rift between the SPD and the USPD over how radical their policies should be became so great that its council members resigned. Many USPD members joined the German Communist Party (KPD).

The Spartacist Revolt

The KPD was a new party, set up in December 1918. Many Germans were petrified of the 'Red Plague' of communism spreading from Russia, and the **_Freikorps_** had units specially recruited to fight in the East against possible communist invasion. KPD political meetings came under attack from the private armies of other political parties. The political atmosphere was so violent that when a Spartacist-led uprising broke out in Berlin in January 1919, Ebert moved the government to the small town of Weimar for safety. The _Freikorps_ were asked to deal with the Spartacists leaders and the results were brutal. Both Liebknecht and Luxemburg were captured, beaten, then murdered, and the rising collapsed.

A frightening time

Many political parties in 1919 had their own private armies. Returning soldiers, unemployed and bitter about the signing of the armistice, refused to return their military equipment. They set up private armies, the biggest of which were the *Freikorps* (Free Corps). Even the SPD had its own group, the *Sozi*. Electioneering was a violent business, people were regularly injured and killed. Between 1919 and 1922, there were 376 political murders in Germany; 356 by right-wing extremists from political paramilitary organisations. In October 1919, Hugo Haase, the USPD leader, was shot outside the Reichstag. One, group, *Organisation Consul*, was involved in the murder of two important Weimar government figures who were also associated with the Treaty of Versailles: Matthias Erzberger (August 1921) and Walter Rathenau (June 1922).

SOURCE 1

From *Through Two Decades*, written by Theodor Wolff in 1936. Wolff was a political journalist on a major German newspaper from 1906 to 1933. Here he is discussing being asked to form a new political party – the German Democratic Party (DDP) – in 1918 for the 1919 elections.

The middle class is frightened and at its wits' end, not knowing what to do or where to turn; most of them are fluttering like birds who have fallen out of the nest and do not know where to go. They must be found another nest, and those who are simply asking all the time 'What is to happen now?' must be given the courage that comes to them only with being in a numerous company and having something to lean on. For a new free state it is possible so far to count on the Social Democracy and the Centre [a moderate, mainly Catholic, party], and that is numerically a great deal, but not enough. The Social Democracy and Catholicism are incontestably two forces of immense importance and at present the two of the greatest importance. But Germany is Germany, and anybody with his eyes open and able to look ahead cannot accept these two strong pillars as enough in the long run to give the needed support to a republic – for the Republic has become the only possible thing.

SOURCE 2

This poster for the 1919 elections for Wolff's DDP party encourages people to see the party as sowing the seeds of freedom, peace and work. While the DDP focused on encouraging hope, other party posters played on people's fears. The Centre Party, for instance, showed pictures of the threat that communism posed to people's lives.

The creation of the Weimar Constitution

The government was still in Weimar for the 19 January election. To an extent, this election was a success: 82.7 percent of electors voted; people clearly wanted to take part in choosing the government. However, the SPD did not get the majority it had hoped for and could therefore only govern by forming a coalition with other parties. The SPD formed a coalition with the Centre Party and the German Democratic Party (DDP). Other parties had seats in the Reichstag (and therefore a vote) but were not part of the government.

The major parties and what they wanted

- The most right wing of the major parties was the German National People's Party (DNVP). It was created from older conservative parties and was conservative, nationalist and monarchist. It did not want social reform and disliked the idea of a republic, only grudgingly accepting it. It supported the army. A large number of its members were wealthy landowners, and many of its members were anti-Semitic.

- The other significant right-wing group was the German People's Party (DVP). This was a moderately conservative group, a new party restructured from the older National Liberals in 1919, under the leadership of Gustav Stresemann. It accepted, without really supporting, the republic. Its members were mostly the wealthy industrial middle class who were not in favour of social reform but who wanted the economy to be fixed quickly so that business could go on. It was nationalist and supported the army.

- Between the two main right-wing groups and the four main left-wing groups sat the Centre Party. This was a long-established party, largely Catholic, and included defending the Church in its policies. It drew in people from many social groups. It had conservative values but did advocate social reform. However, it was firmly against left-wing policies and fanatically opposed to communism. Its election posters tended to show the horrors that communism would bring, and urged voters to vote so as to guard against communism.

- The German Democrats (DDP) was a newly formed party (see Source 1) of liberal, educated professionals who supported the idea of the republic as well as a more representative constitution. It was often part of a government coalition. Its members believed in social reform, including regulating industry to give workers a better deal, and in reforming the army.

- The Social Democrats (SPD) was the largest party in the Reichstag from 1919 to 1929. It was a long-established party that, despite its name, was not anti-monarchist before the war. However, in a split in 1917, the SPD shifted to a republican stance to keep its members, who increasingly favoured a republic. It was the party at the head of the new post-war government. SPD members believed in the republic and in moderate social reform, but not revolution. Immediately after the war, it attracted many workers' groups. However, it also had a liberal, middle-class following of people who wanted moderate reform. It was hampered in its desire for some social reforms by the high number of union members it needed to please.

- The Independent Social Democrats (USPD) split from the SPD in 1917. The party wanted a more radical system than the republic – Rosa Luxemburg and Karl Liebknecht were members of the USPD before forming the Spartacists. They stood for social reform that included creating a more equal society.

- The German Communist Party (KPD) was set up in 1919. It wanted a workers' revolution and the establishment of a communist state with the abolition of private ownership. It mainly attracted the young, poor and unemployed – holding out to them the promise of a future that was far better than any of the other parties had to offer.

SOURCE 3

Results of Reichstag elections, 19 January 1919 and 6 June 1920. The shading runs from dark blue (extreme right-wing views) to dark red (extreme left-wing views).

Party	Seats in 1919 (% of votes)	Seats in 1920 (% of votes)
German National People's Party (DNVP)	44 (10.3)	71 (15.1)
German People's Party (DVP)	19 (4.4)	65 (14.0)
Centre	91 (19.7)	85 (17.9)
German Democrats (DDP)	75 (18.6)	39 (8.3)
Social Democrats (SPD)	165 (37.9)	102 (21.6)
Independent Social Democrats (USPD)	22 (7.8)	84 (17.9)
German Communists (KPD)	none	4 (2.1)

ACTIVITY
KNOWLEDGE CHECK

Major political parties in 1919

1 Draw a spider diagram to represent the major political parties in 1919.

2 For each party, briefly summarise their aims and how right wing or left wing their politics were.

3 Explain the problems of forming and maintaining a coalition in terms of leadership and policy-making.

The structure of the Weimar Constitution

On 7 February 1919, Ebert gave a victorious speech to the new assembly proclaiming victory for democracy. On 11 February, he was elected first President of the Republic by 277 votes to 51. The government, however, was still meeting in Weimar as it felt that returning to Berlin was too dangerous. Now the constitution had to be written. Although the result was always going to be a compromise, it was not hastily written or badly thought out. The Weimar Constitution was finally passed by the National Assembly on 31 July 1919 (see Figure 1.2).

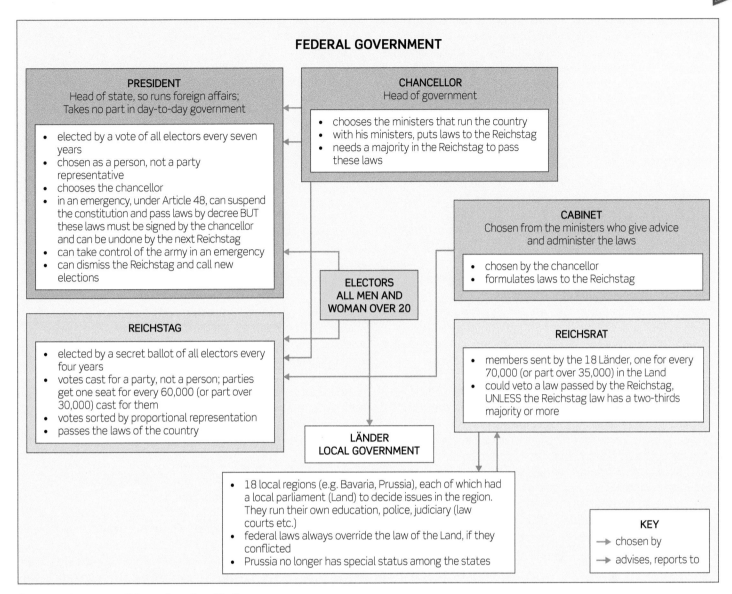

Figure 1.2: Structure of the Weimar Constitution.

Setting up the Republic

1 Explain why the kaiser's government set its 'Revolution from Above' in motion.

2 List the factors that meant the Revolution from Above failed and the Weimar Republic came to be seen as the answer.

Overcoming challenges to the constitution, 1918–29

On 28 June 1919, the German delegation from the Weimar government signed the Treaty of Versailles. They had no choice but to sign. However, it made the government hugely unpopular because resentment of the treaty was widespread and many Germans thought that the war could have been won. The elements of the Treaty that were most deeply resented were the fact that Germany was not allowed to take part in the negotiations, it was forced to accept responsibility for starting the war and it had to pay huge reparations.

So, from the start, the government had to battle its own unpopularity as well as challenges from other political groups and the weaknesses of the constitution itself. Opposition groups are discussed more thoroughly in Chapter 2, but it is important to realise that all through the 1920s and 1930s, political opposition was shown by voting, debate and violence. The end of the war had released large numbers of trained soldiers who were recruited by almost all of the political parties to form private armies. The political situation in which the Weimar government was elected was so unstable that they remained in Weimar until early in 1920 rather than return to Berlin. However, unlike Prince Max's government, the Weimar government managed to stay in power. A significant factor in this was that the most likely alternative to its rule was a more left-wing government. This meant that many right-wingers, who really wanted the return of an imperial government, supported the Republic, even if only in a lukewarm way, rather than run the risk of opposing it and ending up with a more left-wing government.

Challenges

The constitution allowed for a Reichstag with many political parties – it took only 60,000 votes to gain a seat. This was very democratic but it did not take into account that the more parties there were, the more difficult it was for the Reichstag to work effectively. The voting tables (see Sources 3, 4 and 5) show the parties that captured a significant amount of the vote. However, there were far more parties than this; on average, there were 29 different political parties in the Reichstag during the 1920s. Another problem was that members moved between parties and some parties split altogether. For example, in 1920, the USPD split over policy and about half the party left to join the KPD. Such shifts confused some voters. Adolf Hitler made the point early in his political career that voters needed a simple slogan, often repeated, and posters targeting particular groups to steer them through the minefield of voting. This was one reason his political party, the National Socialist German Workers' Party (NSDAP), won as many votes as quickly as it did. In addition to the sheer number of parties, there were other problems with the constitution:

- The method of proportional representation meant that people voted for a party in one of 35 large electoral areas rather than for a particular person in their area, as they had done before the war. Their representative in the Reichstag was then chosen from the party list. If a member died or resigned, there was not a by-election to replace them. The next person on the list took their place. To many, it began to feel as if there were a lot of politicians but none specifically interested in them.

- It was almost impossible for any party to have a majority in the Reichstag. All Weimar chancellors had to form governments from coalitions of parties. Between 1919 and the end of 1923, there were nine different short-lived coalitions and each party was focused almost entirely on what they could get out of the coalition, not how best to work together to govern. The different coalition parties did not have the same aims, so all governments spent a lot of time arguing out policies, even before laws could be presented to the Reichstag. When coalitions broke down, the chancellor had to ask the president to use **Article 48** to rule by decree. As this was only intended for emergencies, it made it look as though the government was in constant crisis.

ACTIVITY
KNOWLEDGE CHECK

Challenges

1
  a) Use Source 3 to explain the ways that the voting alignment changed from 1919 to 1920.

  b) Make notes for a meeting between the members of the Weimar coalition government to consider the election results. List at least three different problems that the voting pattern in Source 3 shows and explain why these need to be discussed.

2 Explain how the Weimar Constitution differed from the previous government in its voting requirements, its structure and the responsibilities of each body.

Overcoming the challenges

Despite its problems, the Weimar government stayed in power, and between 1924 and 1929 it seemed to be overcoming its challenges. The Reichstag kept meeting and there was no need to resort to government by decree, despite the fact that some right-wing politicians had been pressing for this ever since Paul von Hindenburg had been elected as president. Hindenburg had been in the military high command during the First World War and had been a strong supporter of the Kaiser and imperial rule. Despite his swearing an oath to uphold the Constitution when elected, he really favoured a more authoritarian system of government.

Between 1924 and 1929, the German economy recovered and Germany reached agreements with other countries that began to restore its position abroad and undo some of the terms of the Treaty of Versailles, for which the Weimar government was still being loudly and regularly blamed. This was largely due to the work of Gustav Stresemann, leader of the DVP, who was also one of the few politicians who urged parties to work together and managed to achieve this. Stresemann had initially been against the republic, but he changed his position when he saw the damage that party infighting was doing to Germany. He spoke against the 'trust no one, betray everyone' attitude between parties and was convinced that Germany needed a 'great coalition' of parties prepared to follow moderate policies despite their political differences. He also believed that economic recovery and peaceful relations with other countries were important for the stability of Germany's political system – this was one of the reasons he was foreign minister for most of his time in government.

Stresemann was chancellor during 1923, then foreign minister until 1929. He managed to hold together a coalition of the DVP, the Centre Party, the SPD and the DDP for much of that time by forming working relations based on trust with the leaders of these parties (for example, Wilhelm Marx of the Centre Party, who was chancellor 1923–25 and 1926–28) often despite significant opposition from the more extreme groups in all parties.

KEY TERM

Article 48
The Article in the Weimar Constitution that allowed the president to suspend the Reichstag in an emergency and rule by decree.

As the economy improved, so social conditions stabilised and political violence died down. Between 1924 and 1929, no major political figures were assassinated. The Weimar government had been in power for long enough for many people to accept that it was now the political system in Germany – as long as things continued to improve. Support for extremist parties (both left wing and right wing) reduced between May and December 1924 (see Source 4) although the communists and the Nazis started to gain ground again by 1928 as economic conditions worsened. Coalition governments were still the norm, although they changed less often; between 1924 and 1929, there were just six different coalitions. Stresemann's influence was vital to this. However, none of the weaknesses of the constitution had been resolved. In 1929, Stresemann died.

SOURCE 4

Results of Reichstag elections 1924 to 1928. The shading runs from dark blue (extreme right-wing views) to dark red (extreme left-wing views).

Party	Seats on 4 May 1924 (% of votes)	Seats on 7 Dec 1924 (% of votes)	Seats 20 May 1928 (% of votes)
National Socialist German Workers' Party (NSDAP), the Nazis	32 (6.6)	14 (3.0)	12 (2.6)
German National People's Party (DNVP)	95 (19.5)	103 (20.5)	73 (14.2)
German People's Party (DVP)	45 (9.2)	51 (10.1)	45 (8.7)
Centre	81 (15.6)	88 (17.3)	78 (15.1)
German Democrats (DDP)	28 (5.7)	32 (6.3)	25 (3.8)
Social Democrats (SPD)	100 (20.5)	131 (26.0)	153 (29.8)
Independent Social Democrats (USPD)	0 (8.0)	none	none
German Communists (KPD)	62 (12.6)	45 (9.0)	54 (10.6)

AS Level Exam-Style Question Section A

Was the work of Gustav Stresemann the main reason for the Weimar government's ability to overcome the challenges it faced between 1919 and 1929? (20 marks)

Tip
Think about the challenges the government faced and how they were dealt with before and during Stresemann's term in government.

Collapse of democracy, 1930–33

The Weimar system might have survived the death of Stresemann, despite the weaknesses to do with party formation and coalition, if several other factors had not come into play.

- **Public feeling about the Weimar government**: The public had long disliked the association of the government with the Treaty of Versailles. From 1925, one of the ways it showed this dislike was in electing Paul von Hindenburg as president of the Republic. Hindenburg was the first to voice the 'stab in the back' theory about the Treaty of Versailles. This theory, which he must have known to be false, was that the German army could have won the war, but was stabbed in the back by the **November Criminals** (those who signed the armistice and later the Treaty). This theory contributed to the unpopularity of the Weimar government. Hindenburg was now part of that government, but his public popularity was due to his pre-republic position. His commitment to the government was lukewarm at best. He was likely to favour government by decree and sidelining the Reichstag.

- **Economic problems and the government's failure to deal with them**: In 1929, the US economy was having problems when the Wall Street Crash in the USA led to a full-blown depression. The USA had been lending money to many countries in Europe to help them recover economically from the effects of the war. US loans had helped to put the German economy back on its feet. Now the USA was calling in all of its loans and not lending any more. Europe and other parts of the world were also dragged into the Depression. Prices rose rapidly, as did unemployment. Meanwhile wages fell. The government failed to agree a policy to help the economy and as it argued and the situation worsened, support for extremist political parties rose. The parties that benefited most were the most extreme – the communists and the Nazis.

KEY TERM

November Criminals
This term was first applied to those who had negotiated the armistice and the Treaty of Versailles, but it was increasingly used against the Weimar government as a whole by opponents such as Hitler.

- **Coalition failure**: Hindenburg was not inclined to keep chancellors who could not get an agreement on policy, but changing chancellors made government even more haphazard. Parties found it harder and harder to work together and the SPD refused to take part in any more coalitions. Hindenburg was forced to fall back on governing by decree under Article 48; from July 1930 until the elections of 1932, 109 laws were created by the chancellor, Brüning, using his presidential decree and only 29 laws were passed by the Reichstag. There were three chancellors and several elections in an attempt to find a government that would work.

The rise of Hitler and the Nazi Party

The first blow came with the September 1930 elections, when both the Communists (KPD) and the Nazis (NSDAP) made gains. Support for the Nazis in elections was boosted by the **Sturmabteilung (SA)** and its attacks on political opponents. Neither was in the government, but both were a significant force in the Reichstag.

EXTRACT

From *A History of Germany 1815–1945*, written by the historian William Carr and published in 1969.

> The Nazi landslide merits closer examination. During the lean years the hard core of Nazi support came from the 'white collar proletariat' – clerks, small shopkeepers, teachers and people on the lower fringes of the professions – a discontented and frustrated class in any advanced industrial society. It is no coincidence that almost all the Nazi leaders stemmed from this *milieu* [background]. But only when the middle classes as a whole abandoned their traditional political allegiances, under the impact of the depression, did the Nazis become a mass party. The Populists [DVP] lost over one million votes in 1930 and by 1932 were reduced to quite insignificant proportions, as were the Democrats [DDP]. The heaviest losses were sustained by the German nationalists [DNVP], who lost nearly two million votes – over half their total support – to the Nazis. In addition, four million more Germans voted than in 1928, almost half of them new voters. Some young electors were attracted by Communism; the vast majority were drawn to the Nazis. … The young voters and the disillusioned older voters who flocked to the Nazis were political flotsam and jetsam, men and women without a coherent philosophy of life – it is significant that the Socialist and Centre vote remained fairly constant, for Marxism and Catholicism both represented a way of life to their respective supporters. National Socialism [the Nazis] had much to offer the disorientated middle classes. It combined rigid hostility to Marxism with blistering attacks on all the republic stood for. Of all the parties only the Nazis held out the prospect of a new order of society where strong government, leadership, discipline and national pride would come into their own again.

The Nazis were not part of the government, but they had a sizeable standing in the Reichstag. When the presidential elections came round, in April 1932, Hindenburg, now 84 years old, wanted to retire but was persuaded to run again, to keep Hitler out, as it was feared Hitler would stand. Hitler did stand. Hindenburg won, by 19.4 million votes to Hitler's 13.4 million votes. However, he really needed a chancellor who would pull together a coalition that would work well in the Reichstag and gain the support of the people. The chancellor he appointed, Franz von Papen, was not a success because he was unable to get significant support from the Reichstag. He had to rule by decree. Then came the 1932 Reichstag elections.

EXTEND YOUR KNOWLEDGE

The 1932 presidential election
The 1932 elections nearly did not happen. Brüning, the chancellor at the time, suggested a two-year extension of Hindenburg's presidency, postponing the election because of the political unrest. Both Hitler and Hindenburg refused to accept this. When the election came there were four contenders: Hindenburg, Hitler, Ernst Thällmann (leader of the KPD) and Theodor Düsterberg (of the DNVP). In the first round there had to be a clear majority winner. There was not; the most votes went to Hitler (11 million) and Hindenburg (18 million). In the second vote, between Hitler and Hindenburg, a clear winner was all that was needed. Hindenburg won.

The Nazis now had the most seats in the Reichstag; traditionally, the head of this party was asked to be chancellor. Instead, Hindenburg offered the post of chancellor to an old army friend, Kurt von Schleicher, because he did not want to work with Hitler. He offered Hitler a place in the cabinet instead. Hitler refused the cabinet post, insisting he would only take the post of chancellor. Hindenburg called new elections. While the Nazis did not win as many seats, they were still the biggest party in the Reichstag. Hindenburg refused to carry on governing by decree when von Schleicher said that was the only way he could control the Reichstag. Von Papen suggested that if they made Hitler chancellor and von Papen vice-chancellor, Hindenburg and von Papen could control Hitler and Hitler could control the Reichstag. On 30 January 1933, Hindenburg grudgingly appointed Adolf Hitler chancellor, setting him on the path to becoming dictator of Germany by August 1934.

SOURCE

5

Results of Reichstag elections in 1930 and 1932. The shading runs from dark blue (extreme right-wing views) to dark red (extreme left-wing views).

Party	Seats on 14 September 1930 (% of votes)	Seats on 31 July 1932 (% of votes)	Seats on 6 November 1932 (% of votes)
National Socialist German Workers' Party (NSDAP), the Nazis	107 (18.3)	230 (37.4)	196 (33.1)
German National People's Party (DNVP)	41 (7.0)	37 (5.9)	52 (8.8)
German People's Party (DVP)	30 (4.5)	7 (1.2)	11 (1.9)
Centre	87 (14.8)	98 (15.9)	90 (15.0)
German Democrats (DDP)	20 (3.6)	4 (1.0)	2 (1.0)
Social Democrats (SPD)	143 (24.5)	133 (21.6)	121 (20.4)
Independent Social Democrats (USPD)	none	none	none
German Communists (KPD)	77 (14.3)	89 (14.6)	100 (16.9)

THINKING HISTORICALLY   Causation (3c&d)

The complexity of causes

1 Work on your own or with a partner to identify as many causes of the collapse of democracy in Germany by 1933 as you can. Write each cause on a separate card or piece of paper.

2 Divide your cards into those that represent:

   a) the actions or intentions of people

   b) the beliefs held by people at the time

   c) the contextual factors (that is, political, social or economic events)

   d) states of affairs (long- or short-term situations that developed in particular ways).

3 Focus on the intentions of some of the key people, or groups of people, in the run-up to Hitler's appointment as chancellor. For each person (for example, Hindenburg, Hitler, the people), draw on your knowledge to fill in a table, identifying:

   a) their intentions

   b) the actions they took to achieve these

   c) the consequences of their actions (both intended and unintended)

   d) the extent to which their aims were achieved.

Make sure you use detail to back up your statements.

4 Discuss the following questions with a partner:

   a) Did the Weimar government intend to alienate the voters?

   b) How important are people's intentions in explaining the collapse of democracy in Germany by 1933?

ACTIVITY
KNOWLEDGE CHECK

The collapse of democracy

1

a) List five reasons for the collapse of the Weimar government.

b) Separate your reasons into social, economic or political causes by underlining them in three different colours.

c) Put an 's' next to short-term causes and an 'l' next to long-term ones.

2 Which cause do you think was the most significant? Explain your reasoning, being careful to explain why you rejected the other causes as well as why you chose that particular cause.

KEY TERMS

Führer
A German term that means 'guide' or 'leader'. Hitler chose this as his title to show his supreme command over the German people and government. The common phrase used during Nazi rule was *Ein Volk, ein Reich, ein Führer* (One People, one Empire, one Leader).

Putsch
An attempt to overthrow a government by force.

HOW DID THE BUSINESS OF GOVERNMENT OPERATE WITHIN THE NAZI DICTATORSHIP IN THE YEARS 1933–45?

Establishing a dictatorship, 1933–34

In January 1933, Hitler was chancellor of Germany but he still had to operate within the Weimar system – and von Papen was still convinced that he could manage Hitler. By August 1934, Hitler was in complete control of the German political system, with no chancellor or president – just Hitler as **Führer**, leading a one-party government. He managed this by a combination of persuasion, intimidation and moving rapidly. Having learned the lesson of the failure of the Munich **Putsch** dealt with in Chapter 2, he could also argue that he had achieved this legally.

TIMELINE – ESTABLISHING A DICTATORSHIP, 1933–34

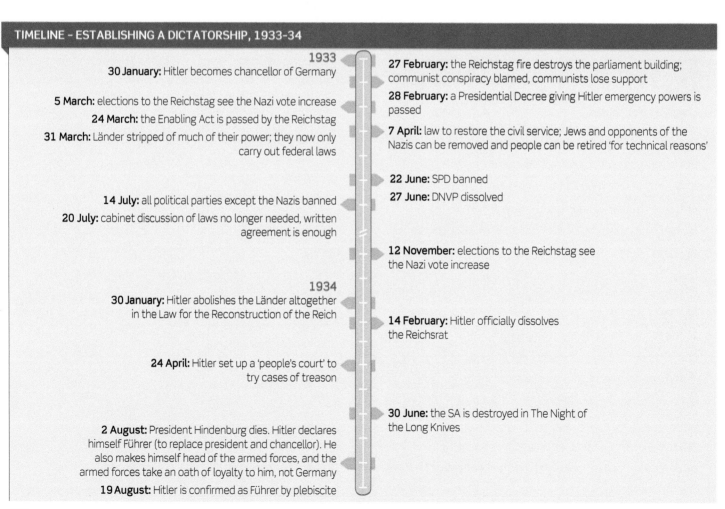

1933

30 January: Hitler becomes chancellor of Germany

27 February: the Reichstag fire destroys the parliament building; communist conspiracy blamed, communists lose support

28 February: a Presidential Decree giving Hitler emergency powers is passed

5 March: elections to the Reichstag see the Nazi vote increase

24 March: the Enabling Act is passed by the Reichstag

31 March: Länder stripped of much of their power; they now only carry out federal laws

7 April: law to restore the civil service; Jews and opponents of the Nazis can be removed and people can be retired 'for technical reasons'

22 June: SPD banned

27 June: DNVP dissolved

14 July: all political parties except the Nazis banned

20 July: cabinet discussion of laws no longer needed, written agreement is enough

12 November: elections to the Reichstag see the Nazi vote increase

1934

30 January: Hitler abolishes the Länder altogether in the Law for the Reconstruction of the Reich

14 February: Hitler officially dissolves the Reichsrat

24 April: Hitler set up a 'people's court' to try cases of treason

30 June: the SA is destroyed in The Night of the Long Knives

2 August: President Hindenburg dies. Hitler declares himself Führer (to replace president and chancellor). He also makes himself head of the armed forces, and the armed forces take an oath of loyalty to him, not Germany

19 August: Hitler is confirmed as Führer by plebiscite

How 'legal' was Hitler's creation of a dictatorship?

Hitler rose to power using the problems inherent in the Weimar Constitution. In January 1933, he was in a strong position, but far from sure of success. The Nazis were the largest single party in the Reichstag, but they only had about one-third of all Reichstag seats, not a majority. Hitler was chancellor, but Hindenburg still had all of his presidential powers and he distrusted Hitler. Only two of the 12 cabinet members were Nazis. People were expecting Hitler to settle in, to work to get more Nazis into the cabinet, to take a long-term view of the situation. Instead, he took advantage of the dramatic events of 27 February and moved fast.

On 27 February, the Reichstag was deliberately burned down. A young Dutch communist, Marinus van de Lubbe, was caught by the Nazis supposedly carrying evidence that he had set the fire. It is possible that he had done this, but it is also possible that it had been set by the Nazis, and that van de Lubbe was the scapegoat. What is certain are the huge benefits the fire created for the Nazis.

- The Nazis got the credit for catching the arsonist.

- The Nazis were able to stir up anti-communist propaganda.

- The Nazis gained not only from political but also from financial support; German industrialists contributed generously to Nazi funds as their fear of communism rose.

- Hitler persuaded Hindenburg to declare a state of emergency. This meant he gave Hitler control of the police and the power to govern Germany by decree without the Reichstag (with Hindenburg's consent to the measures). His Decree for the Protection of the People and the State suspended the civil rights of German citizens, so he could now legally arrest political opponents and ban opposition newspapers.

- Hitler persuaded Hindenburg to call an election for 5 March. Thanks to his (legal) use of his emergency powers to arrest some opponents and to the violent (illegal) campaign tactics of the Nazis, the Nazis' 17.5 million votes won them 288 seats in the Reichstag. Hitler used his emergency powers to ban the 81 communists from taking their seats. The support of the DNVP (52 seats) gave the Nazis a majority.

The Nazi management of the March election shows how they used the law to get what they wanted, but running alongside this was a violent, illegal elimination of opponents. This became increasingly visible as the Nazis legally acquired power and no longer needed help to keep it.

The Enabling Act

Hitler and Hindenburg opened the Reichstag together on 21 March 1933 in a ceremony at the Potsdam Garrison Church where the army and the SA formed the military guard together. This, and the audience of Nazis and members of the old government, under both Nazi swastikas and flags of the old empire, was meant to stress Hitler's acceptance by the old members of government and the continuity between the Nazi Party and earlier governments. It made the Nazis look respectable in the eyes of the people and in the eyes of the Reichstag members.

On 24 March, the Reichstag passed the Law for the Removal of the Distress of the People and Reich (the Enabling Act) by 444 votes to 84 (all of the SPD voted against it). This gave Hitler the right to pass laws without the Reichstag (in theory, only for four years). It was renewed in 1937 and after that it was ignored because Hitler's dictatorship was clearly established. The Act tore up the Weimar Constitution. In theory, Hindenburg might still have stopped Hitler at this point, but he was old, ill and able to see that even if he did stop Hitler's rise it would only be temporary. Hitler used his power to get rid of parties in the Reichstag, one by one, until on 14 July 1933 a law banned all remaining parties and made the country a one-party state. When Hindenburg died, Hitler was legally able to combine the roles of president and chancellor into that of führer, and the **plebiscite** he held to confirm this made Hitler's action more acceptable abroad.

KEY TERM

Plebiscite
A vote on a single issue, by all who can vote in elections.

The Night of the Long Knives

Alongside the 'legal' process of removal ran the violent, illegal, ruthless elimination of opponents. These included not only obvious political opponents but also prominent Nazis. Ernst Röhm and the SA had helped Hitler to power. But the SA had always been seen as thugs so they were bad for the Nazi image, and they were loyal to Röhm who was increasingly critical of Hitler's 'conciliation' of the old government, the army and industrialists. Hitler, having the **SS** and the **Gestapo** to do his bidding,

KEY TERMS

Schutzstaffel (SS)
The Schutzstaffel ('Protective Squad') began in 1925 as Hitler's black-shirted elite bodyguard, but later took over more and more of the 'political' policing of the Nazi state. Deeply committed to national socialist ideology and the commands of Hitler, the SS carried out many of the atrocities associated with the Nazis in occupied Europe. Its leader, Heinrich Himmler, became enormously powerful.

Gestapo
The Nazi secret police, who were allowed to arrest and imprison people without trial.

A Level Exam-Style Question Section B

How accurate is it to say that Hitler's rise to becoming a dictator was achieved by legal means? (20 marks)

Tip
The question expects you to consider evidence to support and argue against the proposition.

did not need the SA any more and he feared Röhm might try to seize power. On 30 June 1934, Röhm and other senior SA officers were arrested in what became known as 'The Night of the Long Knives'. They were shot the next day. Over the next few days, several hundred people were murdered by the SS. Many were SA members, but the dead included General von Schleicher (the ex-chancellor) and his wife. The SA continued working after 1934, but in a reduced form. Many people were quite relieved that Hitler had tamed the SA because their brutal tactics meant they were widely hated. It was not until later that the full extent of the killings was made clear.

SOURCE

6 These two photos were taken outside the chancellor's offices in Berlin on 19 August 1934, after Hitler had won the plebiscite. Each gives a very different view of his route to power.

THINKING HISTORICALLY Causation (4a&b)

Inevitability
Nothing that happens is inevitable. There are causes of change that did not have to develop as they did. Something could have altered or someone could have chosen differently. What actually occurred in the past did happen, but it did not have to be like that.

Work on your own and answer the questions below. When you have answered them, discuss the answers in groups.

Perceived reasons for Hitler's rise to become a dictator

State of affairs	Event	Development	Event	Trigger
Rise of the Nazis; Hitler becomes chancellor, 30 January 1933	The Reichstag fire	Hindenburg and Emergency Decree rule	Enabling Act passed	Death of Hindenburg

1 Consider the Reichstag fire and the political feeling at the time.

   a) How did the fire help Hitler in his rise to power?

   b) If there had not been a fire, would the Nazis have lost power?

   c) What other aspects of the situation existing in 1932 would have been affected if there had been no fire?

2 Consider the emergency decree and the election that followed.

   a) How important was Hindenburg and his behaviour in Hitler's rise to power?

   b) What effect did the granting of emergency powers to Hitler have?

3 What other consequences came about as a result of the information in the table above? Try to identify at least one consequence for each.

4 Choose one factor. How might Hitler's rise to power have developed differently if this factor had not been present?

ACTIVITY
KNOWLEDGE CHECK

Establishing a dictatorship

1

    a) List four important steps in Hitler's rise to dictatorship.

    b) Choose the one you consider the most important. Explain your reasoning.

2 Consider the photos in Source 6. Explain, with detailed reference to the photos, the impression they give of Hitler's rise to power.

The nature of Nazi government, 1934–39

The Nazi one-party state solved the problem of election majorities and coalitions at a stroke. The Reichstag remained, but it only passed seven laws between 1934 and 1945. The Nazi government made and enforced laws. However, Hitler kept much of the existing bureaucracy of government. The civil service had been purged of Jews and opponents in 1933. Many clerks had been Nazis even when there were other parties to choose from. Hitler also kept ministers who were not Nazis before the one-party system. They provided a useful level of continuity; officials and citizens felt they understood the system. However, this was illusory. Not all ministries had the same amount of power. For example, Hitler kept the foreign minister and many German ambassadors after he came to power. However, from 1934 the Bureau Ribbentrop operated alongside the foreign ministry and it was either Ribbentrop or another loyal Nazi who was entrusted with important foreign diplomatic missions as 'special envoy'. Hitler set up several other ministries and 'authorities'. Some took over the responsibilities of established ministries, others were entirely new (for example, the Reich Propaganda Ministry, headed by Joseph Goebbels). Whether deliberately (as some historians suggest) or because detail bored him and he delayed decision-making hoping things would sort themselves out (as other historians suggest), Hitler often left the details of who was responsible for what vague – this could create a good deal of overlap, duplication of work and confusion. If deliberate, it could have been done to introduce a spirit of competition among various ministries and departments – keeping people on their toes and reminding them they should not feel too settled in their position and that they owed their situation, ultimately, to Hitler.

EXTEND YOUR KNOWLEDGE

Joseph Goebbels, 1897–1945

Joseph Goebbels was a friend of Hitler as well as a loyal Nazi and an early member of the Nazi Party – he joined in 1922. At first he was not impressed with Hitler. In the leadership struggle between Hitler and Gregor Strasser after Hitler's release from prison in 1924, Goebbels initially sided with Strasser. However, he was won over by Hitler at the Bamberg Conference of 1926, where Hitler re-established control of the Nazi Party, and was a loyal follower ever after. He held the vital post of Minister of Propaganda. In this post he helped to shape Nazi government policy and laid down the way that Nazi policy was presented to people in the media. When Hitler committed suicide in 1945 he left orders appointing Goebbels as chancellor, but Goebbels also committed suicide soon afterwards.

What were the key features of Nazi government?

The Nazis worked on the principle of *Volksgemeinschaft*, the fact that the whole nation would work together for the common good. There were other basic features, too.

Leadership: Hitler, as Führer, was the leader of the nation and had ultimate power, 'Führer power' as it was sometimes called. The whole Nazi state operated on the policy of the *Führerprinzip*, a strict hierarchical order, where every area of life had someone in charge to tell the people what to do. This was essential in order for people to work together and not make their own decisions; initiative was frowned upon. It was important to work as a nation and think only of the good of the nation (as outlined by the Nazi official in charge).

KEY TERMS

Volksgemeinschaft
This means literally the 'people's community'; the German nation as a racially united body working for the good of the nation. Individuals were expected to obey the Nazi government and make sacrifices for the nation.

Führerprinzip
This German word means 'leadership principle'. The idea was that, at each level of government from Hitler down, there was one person who was clearly in charge – the leader. This person had power over everyone else on their level. They took responsibility for any problems at their level and reported to someone at the next level up.

SOURCE 7

From *Constitutional Law in the Greater German Reich*, a book explaining the Nazi state and the position of the Führer written by Ernst R. Huber, a Nazi supporter and constitutional theorist, in 1939.

The office of Führer has developed out of the National Socialist movement. In its origins it is not a State office. This fact must never be forgotten if one wishes to understand the current political and legal position of the Führer. The office of Führer has grown out of the movement into the Reich, firstly through the Führer taking over the authority of the Reich Chancellor and then through his taking over the position of Head of State. ... The position of Führer combines in itself all the sovereign power of the Reich; all public power in the State as in the movement is derived from the Führer power. If we wish to define political power in the *völkish* Reich correctly, we must not speak of 'State power' but of 'Führer power'. For it is not the State as an impersonal entity which is the source of political power but rather political power is given to the Führer as the executor of the nation's common will. Führer power is comprehensive and total; it unites within itself all means of creative political activity; it embraces all spheres of national life; it includes all national comrades who are bound to the Führer in loyalty and obedience.

Decision-making: It was impossible for Hitler to make every decision involved in running the country. Indeed, he hated paperwork and left most of it to others. However, everyone needed to be aware of the broad principles of what Hitler wanted and to run their sphere accordingly, 'working towards the Führer'. Those who were loyal to him and got the results he wanted were often given more power and more responsibility. In this way, trusted individuals such as Goebbels in the Ministry of Propaganda could become very powerful. Hitler did his best to stop groups of people working together to form policy as this made it easier for opposition groups to form. For example, he kept the cabinet of ministers from the previous government. However, he abolished cabinet meetings. Ministers worked individually and sent draft laws and policies to each other on paper.

Administration: This was still largely done by the civil service under their new minister Wilhelm Frick in the Ministry of the Interior. However, as part of the Nazi state it operated within Nazi ideology and ran on the *Führerprinzip* (although the existing civil service had a similar operating principle anyway). Although technically 'reformed', Frick's civil service frequently came into conflict with the Reich Special agencies (see Figure 1.3) and other ministries as well as Nazi party officials, despite a slew of Nazi 'policy clarifications' that insisted that the Nazi Party would only intervene in civil service matters where there were gaps in the civil service provision. Civil service decisions, taken after a significant amount of planning, were regularly overruled by 'Nazi principle' or whatever was seen as the prevailing opinion of the time.

One nation: The Nazis were against the division of Germany into Länder (see Figure 1.2). They wanted a centralised state, with a centralised administration. As early as March 1933, the Länder were stripped of many of their powers. On 30 January 1934, the Law for the Reconstruction of the Reich officially terminated them, saying that the German people now had a unity that overrode regional differences, so the Länder were no longer needed. The civil service structure that had separate services for federal business and the Länder was to be reorganised, with Frick, the minister of the interior, running regional and local government. This was never, entirely, achieved. In reality, Frick's civil service frequently came into conflict with the Gauleiters (see Figure 1.3) who were in charge of regional party organisation.

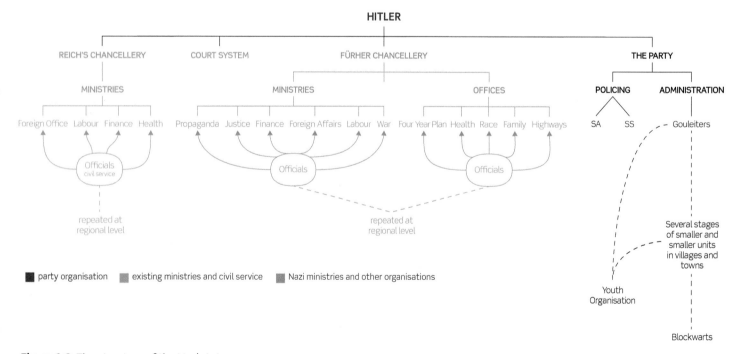

Figure 1.3: The structure of the Nazi state.

EXTRACT
2
From *Nazism 1919–45*, written by the historians J. Noakes and G. Pridham in 1984. Here, they are discussing the organisation, and lack of it, provided by the Nazi state.

This relative normality in State and society was increasingly liable to be breached at any moment by an intervention from the sphere of 'Führer power'. This would characteristically take the form of an assertion of the overriding importance of 'political priorities', enabling, for example, the Gestapo to consign anyone to a concentration camp without right of appeal even if he had just been found not guilty by the courts. At the same time, there was a progressive seepage of Nazi ideology into more and more spheres of life, including the interpretation of the law, and an insistent claim by Nazi party organisations to take over more and more of the activities hitherto covered by the state and local government. ... In place of the old image fostered by Nazi propaganda of the regime as a coldly calculating, ruthlessly efficient machine, research over the past twenty years has revealed the Third Reich to have been a labyrinthine structure of overlapping competencies, institutional confusion and a chaos of personal rivalries. The fields of propaganda and cultural policy, for example, saw permanent internecine warfare [conflict within the same group, supposedly with the same aims] between Goebbels as Reich Minister of Propaganda, Rosenberg as the agent for the supervision of the Nazi *Weltanschauung* [world view, national outlook], Otto Dietrich as the Nazi Press Chief, Bernhard Rust as Reich Minister of Education and Philipp Bouhler as head of a censorship office – among others!

Control: The Nazi state also established tight levels of control over 'political' matters by using the Gestapo – the secret police set up under Goering on 26 April 1933. The Gestapo was taken over by Himmler's SS in 1936, although the SS and Gestapo were still run as separate groups. Control of its citizens was an important feature of the Nazi state, as we shall see in Chapter 2. The Gestapo and the SS developed, and extended, their own judiciary that ran alongside the existing court system for 'political' offences, and Gestapo-controlled **concentration camps** were set up to manage political prisoners. Just as civil servants could find that the Nazis had overridden their decisions, so the courts could find that people they had freed were at once arrested by the Gestapo and put in concentration camps, where they could be held indefinitely without trial.

KEY TERMS

Concentration camp
A prison camp outside the established judicial system, used at first to imprison opponents of the Nazis. The first three camps – Dachau, Buchenwald and Sacherhausen – were set up in 1933. These camps soon took other kinds of prisoners, those that the Nazis considered socially undesirable, especially after the outbreak of war in 1939. Many more camps were set up and they often had several labour camps attached to them.

Volkssturm
The Nazi Home Guard, formed in October 1944 as a last-ditch defence against invasion. Boys, old men, those seen as physically unfit for the army and even women and girls were recruited.

Lebensraum
Literally 'living space' – land taken from other countries to provide Germany with the farmland and natural resources that the Germans needed.

ACTIVITY
KNOWLEDGE CHECK

The Nazi state in operation

1 List the key features of the Nazi state.

2 Explain how Nazi ideas about leadership and nationalism affected the way its government was organised.

3 How far do you agree that the Nazis simply ignored the existing government systems when they came to power, even though they left them in place?

Government in wartime, 1939–45

The Nazis had been gearing up for war from the moment they took power. The coming of war saw an escalation of the drive to war and some social changes. For example, women, who had been discouraged from working, were urged to take on war work. The SS took over more of the government administration. Anyone who worked for the government, in any capacity, had to join the Nazi Party or lose their job. The Gestapo and the SS stepped up their control of the population. SS numbers rose from 240,000 in 1939 to over a million in 1944. The SS ran Hitler's 'racial policy' of getting rid of non-German races from the Reich, through expulsion, isolation, forced labour and murder. Meanwhile, 13 'military districts' were formed from the German regions, and their *Gauleiters* were made Reich Defence Commissioners (RVKs). As such, they ran all the Home Front activities in the local areas, including civil defence, rationing and the ***Volkssturm*** (Home Guard).

New ministries and a new Council for Defence

The structure of government grew, with new, sometimes short-lived, bodies being set up at all levels. Each of the armed forces was given its own ministry to co-ordinate supplies, troops and so on. Their work was co-ordinated by the new high commander of the armed forces, Wilhelm Keitel. It was a thankless task as each of the armed services competed for the biggest budget for their needs. On 30 August 1939, the Ministerial Council for the Defence of the Reich was set up. It was supposed to co-ordinate domestic affairs to support the war effort. This seemed to be a significant change in direction. Hitler was not on the Council, although it reported to him. It was chaired by Hermann Goering and its members were very important Nazi officials: Frick (minister of the interior), Walther Funk (minister of the economy), Wilhelm Keitel (high commander of the armed forces), Rudolf Hess (deputy Führer) and Hans Lammers (secretary). This Council, however, did not last long, falling victim to Hitler's dislike of group meetings as a way of governing even among his trusted officials. The Council was disbanded in November 1939, although Frick, Funk and Keitel met infrequently as the 'Group of Three'.

Problems of the growing Reich

As the German army marched east it took over more and more land in its quest for ***Lebensraum*** (living space). While the SS was in charge of clearing out so-called undesirables in this newly claimed land, the task of allocating the land to incoming Germans and of running it as part of Germany became the job of 11 new

Reichsgau (regional governments) run by Reichsstatthalter. The most heavy-handed of these Germanisation programmes was undertaken in Poland as the army swept through. Firstly, Hitler made it clear that all Poles were untrustworthy and were to be used for hard labour only. Polish leaders were to be shot so that they did not become a focus for resistance. Southern Poland was treated as a 'colony' (not part of the Third Reich) called the General Government, administered by Hans Frank, its governor general. It was used as a dumping ground for all Poles and undesirables from other parts of the Reich, most of whom lived in appalling conditions and were used as slave labour. Other parts of Poland were absorbed into the Third Reich and **Germanised**. Over half a million ethnic Germans, mostly from Baltic countries and the USSR, went to the Warthegau area of Western Poland, while a similar number of Poles were deported east to make room for them.

Germany's growth meant there was much more land to govern and centralised government became harder. *Gauleiters* became increasingly powerful. From 1942, following the start of British bombing raids, they were given control of all civil defence measures, including firefighting, bomb damage clearance, rehousing and rationing, using various Nazi Party organisations such as the NSV welfare organisation. In August 1944, the decree 'For the Implementation of Total War Mobilisation' gave Gauleiters control over the local bureaucracy, not just Nazi Party officials, and gave them significant powers over local businesses.

Losing control

On 22 June 1941, Germany turned on her ally, the USSR, and invaded. It was a huge mistake. When the Soviet Red Army and people did not collapse as the Nazis had assumed they would, the German army had to fight a war on two fronts. Then, in December, the USA joined the war. From this point on, the German forces were badly overstretched and Germany began to suffer. Boys as young as 16 were conscripted in large numbers by 1944 – there were some soldiers at the end of the war that were as young as 12. Rationing became tighter – at first Germans had been shielded from shortages because food, fuel and other necessities were brought in from captured lands (for example, France). The policy of 'total war' meant that shops that did not contribute to the war effort were banned (for example, cake shops and sweet shops), as were professional sporting events. Children were evacuated from the cities. As it became harder to convince people that the army was invincible, and as German families lost their men and struggled with more difficult living conditions, the government lost support and resistance grew.

In June 1944, the Allies landed in Normandy and Allied troops moved towards Berlin from the east and the west. Hitler moved to a safe bunker in Berlin with trusted members of staff, his lover Eva Braun and the Goebbels family. He and Braun married then committed suicide on 30 April 1945; Goebbels and his family committed suicide the following day. Many other Nazis committed suicide either just before or just after capture by the Allies. The German government had collapsed.

Rationing

The system for rationing was set up at the start of the war and allowances varied depending on age and the kind of work that people did. For example, someone doing very heavy work was allowed 4,200 calories a day compared to the 2,400 calories allowed to an office worker. People were given colour-coded ration cards each month. The ration varied within years as well as by year, but the following figures give a yearly average. In 1939, an adult doing normal work was allowed, for example, 9.6 kg of bread, 2 kg of meat and 4 eggs. In 1942, it was 8 kg of bread, 4 eggs and 1.2 kg of meat. By 1945, they were allowed 6.8 kg of bread, 150 g of meat and no eggs.

KEY TERM

Germanise
To be forced to conform to German culture, but in terms of the Nazis this meant moving non-German people out of an area and moving people with pure German blood into it.

A Level Exam-Style Question Section A

How accurate is it to say that the system of government in Nazi Germany in the years 1933–39 was significantly different from that of the Weimar Republic? (20 marks)

Tip
This is a question about change and continuity. Remember to look at things that stayed the same as well as things that changed. Start by thinking about the different parts of the government.

HOW FAR DID THE LEADERS OF THE FEDERAL REPUBLIC OF GERMANY CREATE A STABLE POLITICAL STATE IN THE YEARS 1945–89?

Creation of the Federal Republic of Germany, 1945–49

Unlike the First World War, the Second World War ended with a carefully orchestrated Allied takeover of Berlin. On 7 May 1945, Germany signed the final surrender. Allied armed forces (from the USA, Britain, France and the USSR) took joint control of the German government. There was broad agreement between the Allies that 'democracy' should be restored in Germany, but less agreement as to what 'democracy' was and how it should be put in place. From 17 July to 2 August 1945, the Allies held a conference at Potsdam, just outside Berlin, to plan German reconstruction. Germany was divided into four zones to be run by the USSR, France, the USA and Britain (see Figure 1.4). Berlin, its capital (in the Soviet zone), was also divided into four zones. The Allies set up the Allied Control Council to make decisions across zones to keep 'Germany' intact for reunification.

Unfortunately, now that Germany was defeated, the differences between the Allies, especially the communist USSR and the other Western nations, grew. East and West became suspicious of each other's motives and actions and this affected how Germany developed. To begin with, because of the existing communication and transport systems, Germany was to be treated as a single economic unit and the Allies would work to the same system in their zones to get the country ready for a new government. The Potsdam Conference focused on disarming and demilitarising the country, decentralising it and de-Nazifying it.

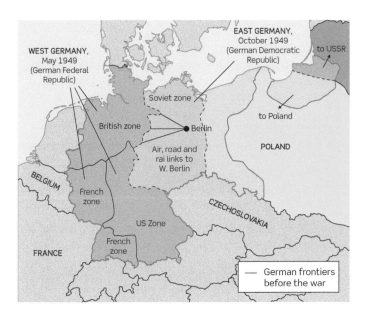

Figure 1.4 Allied zones in occupied Germany.

Setting up political parties

Political parties were set up in Germany from early June 1945; many were in Berlin at first, to allow communication across zones. However, from the start there were different leaders in the Soviet and Western Allied zones. The first party to announce itself, on 11 June, was the KPD, which had kept going outside Germany when the country was under Nazi control. Interestingly, the party's aims were not the creation of a soviet-style system. Indeed, the political message of all parties in the 1950s and early 1960s was one of moderation, of controlling extremism. The KPD stressed they wanted 'German socialism' not capitalism, with land reform, a new education system and a democratic government. It accepted Allied plans for reconstruction.

On 15 June, the SPD re-formed. Many SPD members, including its leader (Kurt Schumacher) had been in concentration camps under Nazi rule. The SPD had a moral advantage and used it to urge the Allies to allow Germans a greater say in the establishment of their government. The SPD's policies were more radical than those of the KPD – nationalisation of banks, land and key industries and significant social welfare systems were to be provided according

to their proposals. The Centre Party tried, unsuccessfully, to re-establish itself. However, two significant church-based groups were set up in 1945: the Christian Democratic Union (CDU) and the Christian Social Union of Bavaria (CSU). There were many smaller faith-based parties, formed with a sense of relief that faith was no longer regarded as suspect by the government. The groups all had a Christian outlook but they had a variety of other aims, although the idea of social support for the poorest was common to most of them. There were also a number of liberal groups, the biggest of which was the Liberal Democratic Party. These political groups had learned something from the Weimar government. They realised that by having a number of parties with similar aims, voters spread their votes over the different parties and their power was reduced. To this end, the faith-based and liberal parties in the Western zones negotiated to create single parties. These unions did eventually come about. In 1947, the liberal groups formed the Free Democracy Party (FDP), while most faith-based groups (excluding the CSU) joined the CDU in 1949. By this time, they were campaigning for elections in a new Germany – the Federal Republic of Germany (FRG), the western half of a now-divided nation.

A permanent division

Relations between the USSR and the West rapidly developed into the **Cold War.** Mutual antagonism was not helped as countries occupied by the USSR in its march to Berlin rapidly became communist (sometimes after carefully managed 'free' elections). Between 1945 and 1947, Yugoslavia, Albania, Bulgaria, Hungary and Poland all became communist states. The West, at the urging of the USA, then set up the **Marshall Plan** to give economic help to European countries that might otherwise take Soviet help and become communist (for example, Turkey and Greece). The tension showed itself most in Germany, for it had obvious points of conflict. The formation of political parties soon followed a different pattern in East and West Germany. In April 1946, the KDP and the SPD formed a single party – the Socialist Unity Party of Germany (SED). This became the most significant party in the Soviet zone, whereas West Germany retained the party system outlined above.

KEY TERMS

Cold War
When two hostile sides try to defeat each other by using political propaganda, economic restrictions and agreements, and military intervention in other wars, but not direct conflict between the countries concerned. Such a state developed between the East and the West, specifically the USSR and the USA, after the Second World War.

Marshall Plan
The economic aid plan for European countries set up in 1947. It provided supplies (for example, food, railway carriages) and money to help post-war recovery, and it provided aid to prevent the USSR from gaining influence.

EXTRACT

3 From *Germany Since 1945*, written by the historian Pól O'Dochartaigh and published in 2004.

Political life was thus re-established in two very different ways in the eastern and western parts of Germany, despite the creation of ostensibly similar party structures. In the West a multi-party democracy was created with parties of the left, right and centre and elections based on real choice. In the East the same parties were initially created, but the two big parties of the left were forcibly amalgamated as early as 1946 and the other parties were forced to toe the Soviet line. The contrast is a clear indication of the division that was rapidly being created in Germany after 1945.

Steps to separation

Given their political differences, it is possible that the Allies could never have agreed a single system government for all of Germany. They saw Germany as a country to be dismantled to make it politically powerless and a buffer zone between the communist East and the capitalist West. For these reasons, it was always likely that the country would be divided even though, at first, this was not what the Allies said they intended. In many ways, the most evident steps to separation were taken by the Allies in the West, although they claimed the Soviets were moving too slowly, or being obstructive, forcing them to act. In October 1946, elections were held across Berlin. The communists won in the Soviet zone (where the SPD had been forced to join the KPD, so providing many KPD votes) but they did badly in all of the other zones (where the KDP and the SPD were still separate parties). The timeline shows how things went from bad to worse from then on.

The Federal Republic of Germany (FRG)

The Parliamentary Council that was set up on 1 September 1948 to draw up a temporary constitution for the FRG announced this constitution, the Basic Law, on 23 May 1949. It was ratified in the week

TIMELINE – WORSENING ALLIED RELATIONS, 1947–49

By 1947
The Western zones have set up Länder with freely elected parliaments. There are elections for Länder in the Soviet zone, too, but there SED wins heavily in all of them and there are doubts as to how 'free' the elections have been

1947
29 May: the USA and Britain, who want unification, tire of waiting for the USSR and France. They unify their zones to form 'Bizonia'

14 June: the Soviet zone sets up the German Economic Commission in response to the formation of Bizonia

1948
February: the USSR tire of waiting for communists to come to power in Czechoslovakia and take over

1 March: Bank of German States is created in the Western zones to administer the Marshall Plan. This creates a single economic unit (breaking the agreement for economic unity across *all* of the zones).

20 March: The USSR leaves the Allied Control Council

20 June: Bizonia announces a new currency (the Deutschemark or DM) to be used in Western-controlled Germany

23 June: the Soviets introduce a different currency in their zone and announce that the Mayor of Berlin should force its use across the city, as it was supposed to be run as a single economic unit. The West responds by introducing the DM in their sectors

24 June: USSR closes all road, rail and canal links to Berlin, marooning the Western zones in Berlin inside the Soviet zone

1 September: a Parliamentary Council is set up to draw up the constitution for a new country: West Germany, composed of all parts of Germany not in the Soviet zone

June 1948 to May 1949
The Berlin Airlift: Western planes fly millions of tonnes of supplies to the Western zones of Berlin. In May 1949, the Soviets lift the blockade

1949
22 May: the Western zones of Germany become the Federal Republic of Germany (FRG)

7 October: the Soviet zone officially becomes the German Democratic Republic (GDR)

of 16–22 May 1949 by the parliaments of more than two-thirds of the Länder. It seemed to outline a very free and liberal democracy, while allowing for the fact that it was a constitution that would be rewritten when Germany reunited. The new German government had, in some ways, been handed a clean slate for its work. The Weimar government had to work against pressure from the army, trade unions and the monarchists of the aristocracy. These groups no longer had significant power bases from which to oppose a government. The Basic Law promised:

- equal rights to German citizens, regardless of sex, race, political views or religion

- free speech, the freedom to form unions or other groups, free assembly and no censorship

- a state education for all, although private schooling was allowed.

However, it also had clauses that suggested it could be used to be more repressive. For example, it was possible to ban political parties if they seemed to undermine the FRG or its democratic principles. Nervousness about extreme political groups was still apparent.

SOURCE 8

Extracts from the Basic Law for the FRG, 23 May 1949. The Basic Law was changed over time to allow for events such as the creation of the European Economic Community (EEC) in 1958.

ARTICLE 20

(1) The Federal Republic of Germany is a democratic and social federal state.

(2) All state authority is derived from the people. It shall be exercised by the people through elections and other votes and through specific legislative, executive and judicial bodies.

(3) The legislature shall be bound by the constitutional order, the executive and the judiciary by law and justice.

(4) All Germans shall have the right to resist any person seeking to abolish this constitutional order, if no other remedy is available.

ARTICLE 21

(1) Political parties shall participate in the formation of the political will of the people. They may be freely established. Their internal organisation must conform to democratic principles. They must publicly account for their assets and for the sources and use of their funds.

(2) Parties that, by reason of their aims or the behaviour of their adherents, seek to undermine or abolish the free democratic basic order or to endanger the existence of the Federal Republic of Germany shall be unconstitutional. The Federal Constitutional Court shall rule on the question of unconstitutionality.

FEDERAL GOVERNMENT

LEGISLATURE
Law-making body

BUNDESTAG
Elected by a secret ballot of all electors every four years.
Electors vote for a regional representative BUT also vote for a party:
Votes are sorted by proportional representation
Party needs at least five percent of the vote to gain a seat
Pass the laws of the country

BUNDESRAT
Representatives from the Länder; chosen by the Länder from those elected to the Länder

EXECUTIVE

Chancellor

MINISTERS
Administrate the laws and advise.

CIVIL SERVICE
Administrates the law

HEAD OF STATE

PRESIDENT
Elected by a Federal Convention every five years; Convention made up of all Bundestag members and an equal number of Bundesrat members

JUDICIARY

Federal Courts

REGIONAL GOVERNMENT

LEGISLATURE
16 Länder elected by voters in their region

EXECUTIVE
CIVIL SERVICE
Administrate the laws

JUDICIARY
Enforces and interprets laws
Regional courts

LOCAL GOVERNMENT

Local government varies, reflecting the way that the original state government varied when each state was set up. Each state is divided into counties and these counties run their own local services (water, power, rubbish collection, etc.) and local officials have some power over local planning. Cities have their own municipal government as do some, but not all, towns. Local officials get their powers from the state, but are elected by the people in their district.

Figure 1.5 The structure of the FRG.

Elections

The first elections to the Bundestag took place on 14 August 1949, and it first met in Bonn on 7 September 1949. The need for coalition governments had not been avoided, even with the consolidation of faith-based parties and liberal parties before the elections. Small parties still took up enough of the vote to ensure that there was not a majority party. The CDU/CSU party (the most right wing) won 31 percent of the vote, while the SPD (the most left wing) won 29.2 percent. The FDP/liberal coalition won 11.9 percent of the vote, so they held the balance of power. The first FRG chancellor was Konrad Adenauer, leader of the CDU. The USSR responded to the creation of the FRG by setting up the German Democratic Republic (GDR), announcing its constitution on 7 October 1949. The SED was the majority party. Neither republic ruled out unification. The fact that there were different governments with different political parties and different constitutions meant that the political situation became harder to overturn as time passed and the two systems took root in their respective areas, which had two different names (and so different identities in the eyes of the rest of the world).

ACTIVITY
KNOWLEDGE CHECK

The political system of the FRG

1 List the similarities and differences between the governments set up under the Weimar Constitution (page 15) and the Basic Law.

2 Prepare an information sheet for a member of the FRG ahead of a radio interview about the new government. Think of four problems the Weimar government faced that the new government might also face, and think of ways in which the new government might avoid them.

Consolidation under Adenauer and Erhard, 1949–65

From 1949 into the 1950s, both the FRG and the GDR still spoke about, and negotiated in relation to, unifying the country. However, as time passed, they developed an increasing number of economic and political bonds that tied them to the West and the USSR respectively, as the Cold War hardened.

TIMELINE – THE FRG AND THE GDR TAKE SIDES

1949

January: Comecon, the Council for Mutual Economic Assistance, set up between the USSR and its satellite states

4 April: NATO (North Atlantic Treaty Organization), an anti-communist alliance of Western countries, is set up

14 August: first elections to the Bundestag, the FRG is governed separately from the Soviet zone

7 October: GDR announces its own constitution and holds elections

1950
September: the GDR joins Comecon

1951
The FRG is allowed to make its own foreign policy rather than being under the control of the Allied High Commission

FRG joins the European Coal and Steel Community, with France, Italy, Belgium, the Netherlands and Luxembourg setting up preferential trade links between these countries

1955

9 May: the FRG joins NATO and all Allies withdraw; the FRG is officially self-governing. In this year, the Hallstein Doctrine says that the FRG represents all of Germany in world affairs and will not have diplomatic relations with countries that recognise the GDR as a government

14 May: the Warsaw Pact of communist countries is set up to oppose NATO. The GDR is a member

1957
25 March: FRG is one of the founder members of the European Economic Community

1961
Night of 12/13 August: the GDR erect the Berlin Wall, separating East and West Berlin, and cut off the rail links between the two sides of the city. The Wall, originally made of barbed wire and blocks, becomes a series of concrete walls with checkpoints and crossing points. Willy Brant of the SPD protests about the Wall the next day. It takes nine days for Adenauer to respond to the situation, despite the fact that many families were left stranded either side of the Wall

EXTEND YOUR KNOWLEDGE

The Hallstein Doctrine of 1955
Walter Hallstein (Adenauer's undersecretary of state in 1955) was responsible for the development of the Hallstein Doctrine, which hardened West Germany's attitude to East Germany. The Doctrine refused to recognise the legality of East Germany as a separate country. In 1955, the FRG announced that it spoke for the whole of Germany in world affairs, including the 'Soviet zone' (East Germany), which had not yet been absorbed into West Germany. It refused to accept the GDR as a lawful government and so said it would no longer have diplomatic relations with any country that had diplomatic relations with the GDR. It acted on this twice, cutting off relations with Yugoslavia in 1957 and Cuba in 1963.

How far did Adenauer create a stable political base for the FRG?

Konrad Adenauer, who had been mayor of Cologne under the Weimar government, became the most significant politician in the FRG, often seen as the father of modern Germany because he was chancellor when West Germany emerged from Western control. He was chancellor of West Germany from 1949 until 1963. His critics, for example, the SPD and the FDP, objected to his authoritarian style and forceful management of the Bundestag. Some even called his leadership a 'Chancellor democracy', suggesting he had more power than the Basic Law allowed. Until 1955, he controlled foreign and domestic policy as chancellor and foreign minister. He was also criticised for appointing weak ministers (Ludwig Erhard, the economics minister, was an exception), whom he treated as advisers not political equals. The benefit of his forceful personality was that he kept FRG coalitions working together until 1957, when the CDU/CSU won a majority for the first time. They remained the majority party in the Bundestag and the chancellor was always from this party until 1969.

On 20 September 1949, Adenauer set out his policy agenda in the Bundestag, concentrating on the domestic economy and foreign policy. The goals he set included uniting Germany and working for closer European integration. Many people pointed out that the second point worked against the first – closer ties with the West would hold back German unification. The SPD was especially critical of Adenauer's focus on the West. For others, this seemed the fastest route for the FRG to become self-governing and accepted as a part of Europe and the quickest way to rebuild the economy. Past history showed that Germany's economic problems soon led to political ones. Adenauer worked to exclude political opposition, especially left-wing opposition, in a way that reminded some people of Nazi policy in 1933. In 1953, changes to vote allocations and seats in the Bundestag made it harder for small parties to gain a seat. In 1952, the extreme right-wing Socialist Reich Party was banned, while in 1956 the KPD was declared unconstitutional in their attitude to democratic government. All KPD members of the Bundestag were stripped of their seats and the party was banned. In 1957, seat allocation changed to limit small parties even more. The moves were stabilising, but they resulted in a Bundestag that was a three-party house, with shifting coalitions that all supported the status quo. More and more people came to see this as a stability that ran counter to the democratic spirit of the Basic Law.

SOURCE

Results of Bundestag elections 1949, 1953, 1957 and 1961. The shading runs from blue (right-wing views) to red (left-wing views) although all major parties expressed democratic views.

Party	Seats in 1949 (% of vote)	Seats in 1953 (% of vote)	Seats in 1957 (% of vote)	Seats in 1961 (% of vote)
Christian Democratic Union and Christian Social Union (CDU/CSU)	139 (31.0)	243 (45.2)	270 (50.2)	242 (45.3)
Free Democratic Party (FDP)	52 (11.9)	48 (9.5)	41 (7.7)	67 (12.8)
Social Democrats (SPD)	131 (29.2)	151 (28.8)	169 (31.8)	190 (36.2)
German Communists (KPD)	15 (5.7)	none (2.2)	none	none

Restoring the civil service and government

Many Germans at the time, especially younger Germans, felt that, in his haste to build a federal and regional civil service, Adenauer allowed too many ex-Nazis into the government. Part of the problem was that in 1939 all government workers had to join the Nazi Party or lose their jobs. Adenauer and others argued that letting ex-Nazis work within the democratic system was the quickest way to move on and the only way to rapidly establish an effective civil service. The idea of 1945 as 'year zero' and no questions asked was born. The same argument was applied to the judiciary. On 11 May 1951, Article 131 was added to the Basic Law, officially allowing ex-Nazis to work in the civil service. Many people felt this went too far and hinted at Nazi sympathies in the CDU. A 1952 Bundestag report named four ex-Nazis working in the foreign ministry, saying this could damage the FRG's reputation abroad. In 1953, the League of Expellees party (BHE, led by ex-SS officer Waldemar Kraft) won enough seats to be part of the coalition government. It broke up in 1954, and many of its members joined the CDU. When the FRG began to establish its own army in 1955, it faced similar problems with Nazi Party membership and solved them in the same way, by accepting ex-Nazis.

Adenauer's moves against political opponents had been open to question. He worked to limit freedom of speech in a way that caused concern about a shift away from democracy and the Basic Law. This concern was voiced by the SPD in the Bundestag and by many others in West Germany as a whole. The SPD gained support when, after meeting at Bad Godesberg in 1959, it revised its policies, including supporting the idea of a **free market economy**. In January 1961, Adenauer tried to set up a government-controlled television station, realising that television was going to play a major part in the next election campaigns. On 28 February, the Supreme Court ruled it unconstitutional because the executive branch was interfering with the legislative branch (through elections). Worse followed. In October 1962, the magazine *Der Spiegel* published an article criticising the performance of West German troops in recent NATO exercises. Adenauer supported the arrest of the journalists involved on the orders of Franz Josef Strauss, Minister of Defence. FDP ministers resigned in protest and Adenauer only managed to get an SPD coalition by promising to resign in 1963.

After Adenauer

There were two more CDU chancellors after Adenauer: Ludwig Erhard (1963–66) and Kurt Kiesinger (1966–69). Both led coalitions where the newly re-formed SPD (with a more liberal, less left-wing policy programme) was gaining influence. Meanwhile the CDU/CSU was splitting between 'Atlanticists' (who wanted

to carry on working with the West, especially with the USA and Britain) and 'Gaullists' (who were prepared to work with France, but wanted to shift the focus to co-operation with East Germany). Erhard followed Adenauer's Atlanticist policies and also tried, increasingly often, to introduce an emergency law to tap phones, search homes, open mail, etc. in times of 'serious political tension'. The SPD refused to support these measures, but the measures were seen as another example of CSU conservative reaction to criticism. In 1966, Erhard introduced a budget that included such heavy taxation that the FDP ministers resigned. Erhard could not form a coalition, so he resigned. In the negotiations that followed, a CDU/CSU/SDP 'Grand Coalition' formed with Kurt Kiesenger as chancellor but the SPD leader (Willy Brandt) as vice-chancellor and foreign minister.

EXTRACT 4

From *A Concise History of Germany*, written by the historian Mary Fulbrook and published in 1990.

The economic recession of 1965-6 precipitated the collapse of Erhard's CDU government, the weak successor to Adenauer, and the CDU, under Kurt Georg Kiesinger as Chancellor, went into a 'grand coalition' with the SPD. The student movement in particular articulated a sense of protest and unease, and there was a perceived need for 'extra parliamentary opposition' with the lack of any real opposition in parliament. ... This period also saw the rise of active right-wing movements, with the highly nationalist NPD gaining representation in several Land parliaments, although failing to gain national representation. But in 1969 a new period in West Germany history was inaugurated when the SPD managed – after considerable post-election bargaining – to form a coalition with the now more liberal FDP, and to become, for the first time in the two decades of the Federal republic's history, the dominant party of government.

Maintaining political stability under Brandt, Schmidt and Kohl, 1965–89

The Grand Coalition formed at a point when the German economy was in a downturn and there was growing political hostility towards the government, some of it violent. Opposition came from small extremist political parties, such as the neo-Nazi National Democratic Party, and from other groups such as students and the German Federation of Trade Unions. This pushed the government to be more repressive. For example, the SPD had strongly objected to the idea of an emergency law, but they voted with the CSU to introduce one on 28 June 1968. The coalition hoped that a shift towards *Ostpolitik* (rejecting the Hallstein Doctrine and working with the GDR) would win the government support again. Kiesenger was the first CSU chancellor to support this policy. In 1969, the

FRG got its first SPD chancellor, Willy Brandt. From 1969 to 1982, the government was an SPD/FDP alliance with SPD chancellors Willy Brandt and Helmut Schmidt.

A new political alignment

Willy Brandt was younger than Adenauer and his generation of politicians. Brandt had spent the war in Norway and was one of those who had been critical of Adenauer's policy of ex-Nazi assimilation. Brandt pushed ahead with the policy of *Ostpolitik* and this remained policy for all chancellors until 1989, even though not all members of the government, especially the regional governments, supported this. Brandt's commitment to *Ostpolitik* met with serious opposition in the Bundestag, as did several more liberal measures his government put through, for example, the decriminalisation of homosexuality and reducing the voting age to 18. The CSU found it hard to accept that they had less political power, and they worked hard to undermine the SPD/FDP coalition.

Brandt's struggle to survive

In October 1970, several significant FDP politicians joined the CDU, and in March 1972, several SPD members also joined the CDU. They then forced a 'constructive vote of no confidence', naming Rainer Barzel of the CDU as the replacement chancellor. The vote failed by just two votes. Brandt responded by calling an early election in November 1972. It was, in effect, a vote of confidence on Brandt and *Ostpolitik*. In the highest turnout ever, the SPD won the most seats. However, in 1974, it was discovered that one of Brandt's advisers was a GDR spy. Even when it was shown that he knew nothing of this, he felt compelled to resign on 24 May 1974, despite the support of his party and others in the Bundestag, because he felt he should have known about, and removed, the spy.

Helmut Schmidt and the challenges of the 1970s

Helmut Schmidt, the new SPD chancellor, faced a period of economic and domestic upheaval. He won the elections of 1976 and 1980 mainly because there was no viable CDU candidate and he was careful not to introduce policies that rocked the political boat. Indeed, he was accused of adopting economic measures, for example, high taxation and welfare cuts, that made him as conservative as members of the CSU. He faced growing opposition for his failure to push through economic policies and he also faced growing opposition from a new political force – the Green Party. On 1 October 1982, a 'constructive vote of no confidence' in the Bundestag forced him to resign and he was replaced by the CDU's Helmut Kohl.

EXTEND YOUR KNOWLEDGE

The Greens

Environmental issues were of growing concern through the 1970s and 1980s. Smog, nuclear power plants and other environmental issues attracted a growing number of protesters of all ages and classes. For example, in March 1977, about 15,000 people protested against the building of a nuclear reprocessing plant in Lower Saxony. In July 1978, the first national 'green' party, Green Action for the Future (GAZ), was set up. In January 1980, the 'Greens' national political party was set up. From 1983 on, it steadily gained a share of the vote (see Source 10).

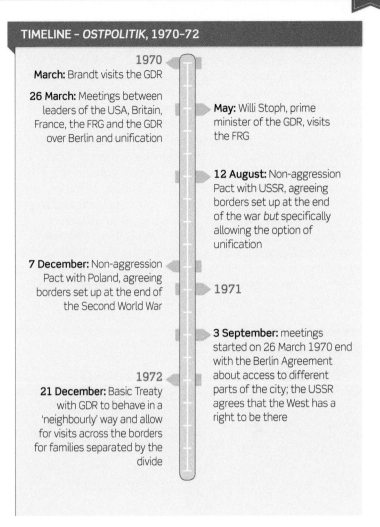

TIMELINE – *OSTPOLITIK*, 1970–72

1970

March: Brandt visits the GDR

26 March: Meetings between leaders of the USA, Britain, France, the FRG and the GDR over Berlin and unification

May: Willi Stoph, prime minister of the GDR, visits the FRG

12 August: Non-aggression Pact with USSR, agreeing borders set up at the end of the war *but* specifically allowing the option of unification

7 December: Non-aggression Pact with Poland, agreeing borders set up at the end of the Second World War

1971

3 September: meetings started on 26 March 1970 end with the Berlin Agreement about access to different parts of the city; the USSR agrees that the West has a right to be there

1972

21 December: Basic Treaty with GDR to behave in a 'neighbourly' way and allow for visits across the borders for families separated by the divide

SOURCE 10

Results of Bundestag elections 1976, 1980, 1983 and 1987. The shading runs from blue (right-wing views) to red (left-wing views) although all major parties expressed democratic views.

Party	Seats in 1976 (% of vote)	Seats in 1980 (% of vote)	Seats in 1983 (% of vote)	Seats in 1987 (% of vote)
Christian Democratic Union and Christian Social Union (CDU/CSU)	243 (48.6)	226 (44.5)	244 (48.8)	223 (44.3)
Social Democrats (SPD)	214 (42.6)	218 (42.9)	193 (38.2)	186 (37.0)
Free Democratic Party (FDP)	39 (7.9)	53 (10.6)	34 (7.0)	46 (9.1)
Greens	none	0 (1.5)	27 (5.6)	42 (8.3)

Helmut Kohl and the fall of the Wall

Helmut Kohl started his leadership as an unelected chancellor, so he called early elections on 6 March 1983. These brought the CDU/CSU 48.8 percent of the vote and so validated his position, although he faced opposition in the Bundestag from Greens on the left and the Republicans (set up in 1983) on the right. He also had to manage a parliament where the media was uncovering corruption scandals that affected politicians in every party but the Greens. He promised continuity, and his economic policies and *Ostpolitik* policies followed those of earlier governments. He also faced a sustained outbreak of terrorism directed at other governments and German institutions (for example, the bombing of both the US airbase in Rein-Main and Frankfurt Airport in 1985), so it is no surprise that his focus was stability. Kohl was working for unification with East Germany, but this still seemed a distant prospect despite the changes in Soviet policy that gave greater freedom to communist Eastern Europe. The East German government had not welcomed the changes.

In 1989, Hungary opened its border to the West and lifted travel restrictions across it. East Germany was under increasing pressure to open its borders. On 1 January 1989, it relaxed its travel restrictions. By the end of September, 161,000 people had applied to emigrate (32,000 fewer than applied in the previous 17 years). In August, Austria abolished visa requirements for citizens from Hungary and East Germany; about 3,000 East Germans had fled West via Hungary and Austria by the end of the month. From September, Hungary allowed East Germans to cross any border, not just return to East Germany. Thousands of East Germans made their way to the FRG. Demonstrations calling for the border to be opened and, as significantly, for change to the political system, spread across the cities and hundreds of thousands of people eventually took part. On 9 November, a government official announced that travel restrictions were lifted. People flooded through the Berlin Wall checkpoints and Germany, physically reunited, faced a new political future.

SOURCE 11

The Berlin Wall being dismantled in 1989.

EXTRACT 5

From *Germany Since 1945*, written by the historian Pól O'Dochartaigh in 2004. Here, O'Dochartaigh is describing events on Thursday 9 November 1989.

No one, either in the GDR or in West Germany, was prepared for the events as they unfolded on the evening of 9 November 1989. Helmut Kohl was on a trip to Poland at the time. Demonstrations continued in regional centres while West German politicians, including Johannes Rau, Minister President of North Rhine-Westphalia, visited the GDR. That evening, at a press conference called at the end of the two-day meeting of the Politburo, Günter Schabowski announced new travel regulations which would allow all GDR citizens, with few exceptions, to apply for and receive a visa for travel to the West. The full import of his words was not entirely clear. When asked when the new regulations would come into force, Schabowski shuffled his papers looking for a date. He seemed uncertain as he said 'immediately'.

Within a few short hours thousands of people had gathered at the various border crossings demanding to be allowed to go across to West Berlin. Eventually, the border guards simply opened the checkpoints, and tens of thousands of East Germans streamed into West Berlin. There were scenes of jubilation as they were greeted by West Berliners.

EXTEND YOUR KNOWLEDGE

An unexpected event
The fall of the Berlin Wall took politicians on both sides of the Wall by surprise, although they were negotiations for future unification. Helmut Kohl had to break off a trip to Poland to return to Germany when the Wall fell. Many historians were also surprised. One history of the FRG, published in 1989, spoke of the fall of the Wall as something that was bound to happen at some time in the future, not knowing that events would overtake the sentiments expressed in their book in the same year.

SOURCE 12

Astrid Benner worked as a waitress in the Café Adler, next to Checkpoint Charlie in the Wall, on the West Berlin side. She was interviewed by Christopher Hilton about the night of 9 November. In 2001, Hilton wrote about people's experiences of both sides of the Berlin Wall. Quoted in Christopher Hilton, *The Wall: The People's Story*, 2001.

I thought to myself [when she heard the border was about to open] 'What will I do now? I am by myself here.' I called my boss, the owner of the café at his home. 'Hell,' I said, 'you have to get here because I am totally alone and thousands of people may be coming at any moment. This is the first place they'll reach.' ... His [the first man to arrive] eyes were wide open, he thought it was all a mistake, all a kind of dream and at any moment he would wake. I gave him a glass of beer and he drank. We gave free beer to the first twenty, thirty that came in. After ten minutes the café was completely full. People were calling out 'I'm from the East and I'm really here' and people were crying.

THINKING HISTORICALLY — Evidence (3b)

It depends on the question

When considering the usefulness of a piece of evidence, people often think about authenticity in the case of artefacts, reliability in the case of witness statements, or methodology and structure in the case of secondary accounts. A better historical approach to the usefulness of a piece of evidence would be to think about the statements that we can make about the past based on it. Different statements can be made with different degrees of certainty, depending on the evidence.

Work in small groups and answer the following:

1
a) Write three statements that you can reasonably make about the Berlin Wall based solely on Source 11.

b) Which of the statements can be made with the greatest degree of certainty? Why is this? Which statement can be made with the smallest degree of certainty? Why?

c) What else might you need to increase your confidence in your statements?

2 Source 11 is an artefact and Source 12 is a witness statement. Which is more useful to the historian studying the impact of the Berlin Wall?

3 Look at Extract 5. How would the historian have gone about constructing this piece? What kinds of evidence would they have needed?

ACTIVITY
KNOWLEDGE CHECK

Brandt, Schmidt and Kohl

1 Explain why Brandt, Schmidt and Kohl did not have the same control of the Bundestag as Adenauer.

ACTIVITY
SUMMARY

Understanding political and governmental change

1 Draw up a table showing the main features of government in the Weimar Republic, Nazi Germany and the FRG. Include, for example, structure of government, role of elections, nature of the civil service and other institutions, etc.

2 Identify and colour code similarities and differences between the three periods.

3 Give three examples of what the table cannot show you about the political structure of each period, and explain why they are significant.

A Level Exam-Style Question Section B

How significant was the contribution of Adenauer in the establishment of a stable political base in the FRG in the years 1949–89? (20 marks)

Tip
The question expects you to consider evidence to support and argue against the proposition.

WIDER READING

Fulbrook, M. *A Concise History of Germany*, Cambridge University Press (2004)

Hiden, J. *The Weimar Republic*, Seminar Studies in History, Longman (1996)

Kitchen, M. *A History of Modern Germany: 1800 to the Present*, Wiley-Blackwell (2011)

Lee, S.J. *The Weimar Republic, Questions and Analysis in History*, Routledge (2009)

You can find footage of the building of the Berlin Wall on the internet if you search 'building Berlin Wall'.

1.2

Opposition, control and consent, 1918–89

KEY QUESTIONS

- How effectively did opposition express itself in the years 1918–89?
- How successfully did Germany's governments control the German people in the years 1918–89?
- To what extent did Germany's governments rule by consent in the years 1918–89?

INTRODUCTION

In the previous chapter we saw how the way that Germany was governed changed from 1919 to 1989, and how German politics shifted, changed and realigned. All German governments between the years 1918 and 1989 faced opposition, some of it political, some of it not. Governments applied different methods of control at different times, both in trying to manage the political institutions in place at the time and by suspending those institutions altogether.

Running alongside the more conventional forms of opposition there was always a thread of violent opposition, sometimes muted. The Kapp Putsch of March 1920, the July Plot of 1944 and the terrorist activities in the FRG in the 1970s and 1980s (for example, the murder of the economic minister for the Hesse region on 11 May 1981) were all a violent show of opposition that set off a violent government response. These violent opposition movements failed to change the government. But does the fact that they happened at all show that the government at the time was deeply unpopular? Or was it just unpopular with a small group of extremists? Was the fact that the attacks happened at all a sign that the government at the time was failing – failing to meet the expectations of the German people and failing to control opposition groups? These are the questions we will consider in this chapter.

Not everyone in Germany opposed the government; it is possible to find levels of government support at any point during the years 1918–89. Sometimes it is difficult to decide how far the support was, in fact, a sign of tight government control or actual support – this is most obviously the case under the Nazis. On the other hand, a significant amount of opposition to the Weimar government was made possible by its liberal determination not to control the expression of opposition.

1919 – Spartacist Revolt
19 January: first Weimar Republic elections
28 June: Treaty of Versailles signed
31 July: Weimar Constitution passed

1934 – 2 August: Hindenburg dies, Hitler becomes führer

1945 – 7 May: end of Second World War in Europe

Germany and Berlin divided into Allied zones

| 1915 | 1920 | 1925 | 1930 | 1935 | 1940 | 1945 | 1950 |

1920 – March: Kapp Putsch

1923 – November: Munich Putsch

1933 – 30 January: Hitler becomes Chancellor of Germany

February: Decree for the Protection of the People and the State suspends civil liberties

1949 – 22 May: FRG set up

HOW EFFECTIVELY DID OPPOSITION EXPRESS ITSELF IN THE YEARS 1918–89?

The impact of the Treaty of Versailles on German politics

The Treaty of Versailles (see Chapter 1) influenced the political agenda in Germany and was a campaigning point for politicians. It was also a cause of political discontent and a spur to opposition. Many Germans felt that the Weimar government were traitors to the country for arranging the armistice and signing the shameful Treaty of Versailles. Opponents of the government regularly used this to criticise it, but it is important not to forget that there was very real anger and resentment throughout Germany about the Treaty. This was partly as a result of misinformation. The German people had no idea of how badly the war was going for Germany. They believed the ideas put forward by many newspapers that Germany could have won the war if the Weimar government had not been cowardly and betrayed the country. At best, they blamed the revolution that had toppled the Kaiser and the military high command; and while not everyone in the Weimar government was part of the revolution, they certainly were in office as a result of it.

One of the significant effects of the imposing of reparations was that it enabled resentment against the Versailles Treaty to continue. It did not matter that Germany did not pay back a significant amount, or that loans from the USA to help rebuild the German economy far outweighed any reparations payments that Germany made. The USA brokered two agreements in the 1920s (the Dawes Plan of 1924 and the Young Plan of 1929) that greatly reduced reparations and extended the time for repayment. That did not have much effect on resentment either. The fact the reparations existed at all was enough.

EXTRACT

1 From the book *From Versailles to Pearl Harbor*, written by the historians Margaret Lamb and Nicholas Tarling and published in 2001.

One of the serious consequences of the settlement [Treaty of Versailles] on internal German developments was that the signing of the peace treaty was a political albatross around the neck of the moderate left-wing parties in the new republic. In their determination to continue the fight to obtain modifications of the treaty, successive governments emphasised its harsh aspects without a corresponding emphasis on the extent of Germany's military impotence at the time of its signature. In so doing they played into the hands of those opponents of the Weimar regime who claimed that the politicians who had signed the armistice and the treaty had betrayed Germany. Germany's losses under the treaty were undoubtedly considerable in territory, manpower and economic potential. Compared, however, with the terms of the treaty of Brest-Litovsk [imposed by Germany on Russia when Russia withdrew from the war in 1917] and the terms which it is now known Germany was intending to impose on the rest of Europe had it emerged victorious from the war, Versailles was not draconian. Germany remained far superior to France in the size of its population and, while it retained the Rhineland and Upper Silesia, it possessed far greater economic resources.

1968 – May: emergency law passed to allow police and secret service wider powers

1989 – 9 November: fall of Berlin Wall

| 1955 | 1960 | 1965 | 1970 | 1975 | 1980 | 1985 | 1990 |

1972 - September: terrorist massacre of Israeli athletes, Munich Olympics

SOURCE
1
From a 1933 English translation of *Mein Kampf,* written by Adolf Hitler. Here, Hitler describes his feelings when he heard about the German surrender in 1918 (while in hospital, having been gassed at the front).

So all had been in vain. In vain all the sacrifices and privations, in vain the starvation and thirst for many endless months, in vain the hours we spent doing our duty, gripped by the fear of death, and in vain the death of two millions of men!

But – was this the only sacrifice that we should be called on to endure? Was the Germany of the past worth less than we thought? Had she no obligations owing to her own history? Were we worthy to clothe ourselves in the glory of the past? In what light could this act be presented for justification to future generations?

Miserable, depraved criminals!... There were horrible days and worse nights to follow. I knew that all was lost. In those nights my hatred arose against the originators of that act. ... I resolved to become a politician.

SOURCE
2
From the statement made by Hindenburg (who had been a member of the military high command during the war) on 18 November 1918, to the committee set up by the Weimar government to investigate the loss of the war.

The intentions of the command could no longer be executed. Our repeated proposals for strict discipline and strict legislation were not adopted. Thus did our operations necessarily miscarry; the collapse was inevitable; the revolution only provided the keystone.

An English general said with justice: 'The German army was stabbed in the back.' No guilt applies to the good core of the army. Its achievements are just as admirable as those of the officer corps. Where the guilt lies has clearly been demonstrated. If it needed more proof, then it would be found in the quoted statement of the English general and in the boundless astonishment of our enemies at their victory.

That is the general trajectory of the tragic development of the war for Germany, after a series of brilliant, unsurpassed successes on many fronts, following an accomplishment by the army and the people for which no praise is high enough. This trajectory had to be established so that the military measures for which we are responsible could be correctly evaluated.

THINKING HISTORICALLY Evidence (3a)

The value of evidence
Read Sources 1 and 2, then work through the following tasks.

1 Write down at least three ways in which each source is useful for establishing attitudes about why Germany lost the war.

2 Compare your answers with a partner, then try to identify at least two limitations of each source for establishing attitudes about why Germany lost the war.

3 Discuss with a partner whether you think Source 1 or Source 2 is more useful for establishing these attitudes.

4 Now consider how the sources might be used to answer the question: 'Were the German people responsible for Germany's defeat?' Complete the diagrams below to show the usefulness and limitations of Sources 1 and 2 for answering this question and two questions of your own.

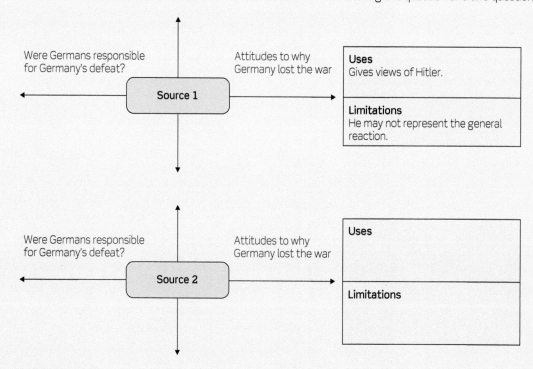

The impact of the Treaty of Versailles

1 Explain three ways in which the Weimar government was hampered by the point in German history at which it came to power.

2 Explain how opponents could criticise the Weimar government for:

  a) trying to get changes made to the Treaty of Versailles

  b) not trying to get changes made to the Treaty of Versailles.

Political extremism and crises, 1918–33

The Weimar government came into being after a violent upheaval in Germany. Germany after the war was full of men of all ages trained in war, many of them unemployed. Some formed private armies for political groups. This added to the violence that surrounded the new government, which was forced to leave Berlin in both 1919 and in 1920 when threatened with violent overthrow. The government was opposed by extremist groups on the left and the right for its:

- involvement in the Treaty of Versailles

- liberalism and democratic principles

- failure to produce a strong, decisive government and a strong leader

- failure to unite Germany.

The most significant left-wing opposition came from communist groups. These were especially active in the years immediately after the war. On 4 January 1919, the government dismissed the popular police chief in Berlin, Emil Eichorn, a radical USPD member. This brought the government into open conflict with the workers' councils. The Spartacists, members of the USPD and local union officials united to overthrow the government. On 6 January 1919, thousands of armed workers took over key buildings, such as the newspaper offices. This was how the Russian Revolution had started just over a year before, and the reason why Chancellor Ebert moved the government to the small town of Weimar for safety. The Freikorps crushed the rebellion and executed its leaders. Left-wing opposition tactics also included attempts to take over individual German states and establish communist governments. The most significant of these attempts were made in Bavaria in March 1919 and in Saxony and Thuringia in 1921. In all cases, the communist governments did not have enough popular support and were put down by the army. The government found it easy to get the army to put down left-wing opposition. However, the army was far less willing to suppress right-wing rebellion.

The DNVP opposed the Weimar government at first and so did not want to be part of it, preferring to act as an opposition party in the Reichstag. Later, it tried to work within the Reichstag, hoping to produce a more settled political environment.

More severe opposition came from various extreme right-wing groups that aimed to restore the empire and overturn the Treaty of Versailles. Right-wing opposition came from wealthy landowners, the army and industrialists as well as people in conservative groups, for example, those who worked in schools and universities. The Weimar government might never have won over the monarchists, but they did not try hard enough to convince the teaching profession of the benefits of the new system of government, so it was not passed on to students. It was hard to convince people of the virtues of a democracy when parties were unable to work together in the Reichstag. The most significant right-wing extremist actions were the Kapp Putsch of 1920 and the Munich Putsch of 1923.

The Kapp Putsch

This was an attempt to overthrow the government by Wolfgang Kapp and *Freikorps* leaders Walther Lüttwitz and Herman Ehrhardt. The putsch had the support of Eric Ludendorff, who had been a general in the First World War. They took over Berlin on 12 March and the government fled. Most of the army did not join the putsch, but would not fight the rebels. With the government gone, Kapp looked to be in a good position. The leaders proclaimed themselves the new government, dissolved the National Assembly and said the Weimar Constitution was no longer in force. For a few days it looked as if Germany had a new government. Then the trade unions called a general strike, demanding an end to the putsch and a new government with the SDP in control. The general strike was almost universal. Four days after the strike began, the Kapp government fell. The Weimar government returned to Berlin thanks to the strike rather than anything it or the army had done. Kapp died in prison, awaiting trial; the other ringleaders were given short prison sentences.

The Munich Putsch

In 1922, the Italian **fascists**, led by Benito Mussolini, held 'The March on Rome', a military show of force that brought Mussolini to power. Hitler decided to mount a similar Nazi takeover of Germany, starting from Munich, where he thought he could gain the support of local politicians and citizens. On 8 November, the SA surrounded a large beer cellar in Munich, where Gustav von Kahr and other important officials were in a meeting. Hitler then crashed into the hall and announced that the government of Bavaria, and the national government, were deposed and that he and Ludendorff were to form a new government. He locked them in and he and Ludendorff spoke to the crowd. But one by one the prisoners escaped and organised resistance to the putsch. When the Nazis attempted to start their march on Berlin in the morning, they were taken prisoner after a short battle with the police.

KEY TERM

Fascist
A term for an organisation that was right-wing and believed in the power of the state over all its people.

TIMELINE – CRISES FOR THE GOVERNMENT, 1919-33

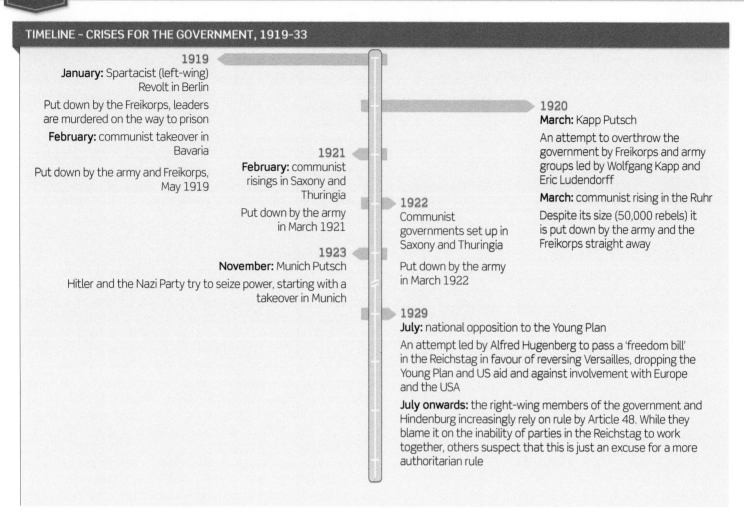

1919

January: Spartacist (left-wing) Revolt in Berlin

Put down by the Freikorps, leaders are murdered on the way to prison

February: communist takeover in Bavaria

Put down by the army and Freikorps, May 1919

1921

February: communist risings in Saxony and Thuringia

Put down by the army in March 1921

1923

November: Munich Putsch

Hitler and the Nazi Party try to seize power, starting with a takeover in Munich

1922

Communist governments set up in Saxony and Thuringia

Put down by the army in March 1922

1920

March: Kapp Putsch

An attempt to overthrow the government by Freikorps and army groups led by Wolfgang Kapp and Eric Ludendorff

March: communist rising in the Ruhr

Despite its size (50,000 rebels) it is put down by the army and the Freikorps straight away

1929

July: national opposition to the Young Plan

An attempt led by Alfred Hugenberg to pass a 'freedom bill' in the Reichstag in favour of reversing Versailles, dropping the Young Plan and US aid and against involvement with Europe and the USA

July onwards: the right-wing members of the government and Hindenburg increasingly rely on rule by Article 48. While they blame it on the inability of parties in the Reichstag to work together, others suspect that this is just an excuse for a more authoritarian rule

---

Although the putsch seemed to have been a failure, it was really a success for Hitler. The trial enabled him to give a speech about his beliefs that was widely reported and increased his fame. In the tradition of milder punishments for right-wing groups, Hitler's sentence was five years in prison, with the possibility of early release. He used the time in prison to think through his political ideas and write *Mein Kampf*. The putsch, too, pushed him into an understanding that he should try for power by legal means, getting Nazis into the Reichstag.

Opposition and dissent in Nazi Germany, 1933–45

Opposition and dissent were very dangerous in Nazi Germany. By August 1933, it was not possible to oppose the Nazis in the Reichstag – all opposition parties were illegal and many members of parties such as the KPD and the SPD had either left the country or were in concentration camps built to hold political prisoners indefinitely without trial. The problem was how to protest. Public meetings were not possible. However, particularly in the early 1930s, various groups worked against the Nazification of Germany: political groups and trade unions; church groups; student and youth groups and members of the army. They risked discovery and punishment, and had to overcome the feeling they were being disloyal to Germany by secretly conspiring against the government. Members of the army also faced the fact that they had sworn a personal oath of loyalty to Hitler and broke it by opposing him and the Nazis. What they were trying to do became increasingly impossible as the Nazi grip on the country tightened and people began to think that protest and dissent was not possible, that politics was not for ordinary people and that any form of protest or appeal was not just dangerous – it was useless.

A Level Exam-Style Question Section A

How far do you agree that opposition to the Weimar government in the years 1918–32 was rooted in a hatred of the Treaty of Versailles? (20 marks)

Tip
Questions beginning 'How far do you agree…' are asking you to give a balanced assessment, supplying evidence for and against the statement, and then give your judgement on the proposition.

ACTIVITY
KNOWLEDGE CHECK

Challenges to the Weimar government

1 Explain how the nature of the Weimar government exposed it to opposition.

2 List the four main points that a right-wing opponent of Weimar would make in a speech against the government.

EXTEND YOUR KNOWLEDGE

Hindenburg opposes Hitler

There were very few people who could openly stand against Hitler, but, in the early days of his chancellorship, President Hindenburg did try. On 4 April 1933, he wrote to Hitler about the proposed law to dismiss non-Aryan (primarily Jewish) members of the civil service. He pointed out that many lawyers, judges and other civil servants who were Jewish had fought and been wounded in the First World War. He urged Hitler to reconsider a law that would punish people such as these. Hitler wrote back saying that the Jewish monopoly of these jobs had to stop, but that he would tell the minister of the interior of Hindenburg's reservations. The law was passed on 7 April. There were no exceptions.

How did people express opposition and dissent?

- **Anti-Nazi campaigns**: In the early 1930s, the KDP, SPD and trade unions printed pamphlets and other anti-Nazi literature. For example, in 1933 the SPD group Red Shock Troop, working mainly in Berlin, published the newspaper *Red Shock Troop* about every ten days and built up a membership of around 3,000. Then, in December, the leaders were arrested and sent to concentration camps and the group folded. Other SPD and KPD groups sprang up, but by 1938 it was clear that it became so easy to trace groups by their publications that it was like sending the Gestapo a list of people to arrest. After this, the KPD and other groups did much of their work by word of mouth and tended not to form organised groups. The SPD outside the country (SOPADE) then turned mostly to gathering information about public opinion in Germany to pass on to the Allies. Once Germany invaded the USSR in Operation Barbarossa in June 1941, communist groups revived. The Uhrig groups leafleted factories and put up posters urging workers to acts of sabotage. The Red Orchestra was a group of mainly government employees who, while not necessarily communist, passed information about the German war effort to the USSR.

- **Sabotage**: Workers sabotaged the Nazis in a variety of ways. They held lightning strikes that usually only lasted a few hours. In 1936, for example, the workers who built the autobahns held a lightning strike. Workers also sabotaged production by working slowly, damaging machinery or reporting in sick when they were not. All of these actions could lead to arrest if they were reported. However, workers were in great demand, especially once war broke out, so actions like these – and even more subversive actions such as not giving the Nazi salute when there were Nazi officials present – were often overlooked. If groups became too organised, or too successful, then the Gestapo stopped turning a blind eye and arrested its members. For example, members of the Anti-Fascist Workers' Group were arrested in 1944. Once Germany was at war, various resistance groups, some with help from Britain and other Allies, worked against the Nazis in increasingly violent ways such as blowing up bridges or railways lines.

- **Disobedience**: Some young people, usually from the affluent middle class, deliberately did not join the **Hitler Youth**. Instead, they went to clubs to listen to 'cool' music such as swing

SOURCE 3

This anti-Nazi poster was printed by the KPD for the March 1933 elections. Its slogan is 'Comrade, help me and together we will defeat them!' and it shows the KDP and the SPD fighting the Nazi snake.

and jazz. They also dressed in clothes that were as similar to fashions in the West as possible; some even set up their own bands. After 1940, these clubs were declared illegal and went underground. The Nazis made occasional arrests, but mostly they left these groups alone. While they were not conforming to what the Nazis wanted, they did not express actively anti-Nazi sentiments. The same was not true of the Edelweiss Pirates. The Pirates, a largely working-class movement, were actively anti-Nazi, although to varying degrees. Many Pirates wore their own uniform, a deliberate statement that they were not members of the Hitler Youth. Their activities varied from area to area. Some simply ran their own activities, such as hiking and camping. Others painted anti-Nazi slogans on walls or collected anti-Nazi leaflets dropped by Allied planes and posted them through letterboxes. Some went even further and worked with resistance groups. If caught, they were executed. A different

KEY TERM

Hitler Youth
The name for the various Nazi youth groups for boys and girls (separate organisations) aged 6 to 18 years.

group, made up of students at the University of Munich, was the White Rose Group. This group operated in secret, distributing anti-Nazi material urging sabotage and exposing the Nazi murder of Jews, while urging non-violent resistance to the Nazis. They were caught and executed. It was not only young people who practised disobedience. One of the most widespread ways of opposing the Nazis was to help those the Nazis wanted to arrest – whether for their race or their political beliefs. Some people who did this acted alone. Others were part of a more organised escape line (the Protestant Church ran one). It is difficult to estimate how many people (Jews, political opponents and, later, Allied prisoners of war) escaped this way, but it was many thousands. Some worked within the Nazi organisation. Hans von Dohnanyi worked in the Nazi justice system, but he worked with his brother-in-law Dietrich Bonhoeffer, a Protestant pastor, to help escapees. They were both arrested and sent to concentration camps in 1943.

- **Attempts to assassinate Hitler**: From July 1921 to July 1944, there were about 15 known attempts to assassinate Hitler. Of these, the seven made after 1939 were by army members or groups led by army members. The army, when Hitler became führer in 1934, had to swear an oath of loyalty to Hitler, not to Germany. Despite this, Hitler always had his own military groups such as the SS, and many army members disapproved of the more extreme Nazi beliefs and actions, especially the murder of Jews and other '**undesirables**'. All plotters who were caught were executed immediately. Investigations then went on to find others involved in the plots who, if caught, were also executed or sent to concentration camps. The most serious plot was the July Plot of 1944. It was an attempt by the German army to take over the government and negotiate the end of the war with the Allies. On 20 July, Lieutenant Claus von Stauffenberg left a bomb in a briefcase in a conference room where Hitler was going to meet military aides. He made an excuse to leave the room and when the bomb went off he believed reports in the confusion that Hitler was dead. While four people were killed, Hitler survived with only minor injuries. As it became clear that Hitler was not dead, one of the plotters, Freidreich Fromme, arrested the chief plotters to prove his loyalty. They were either shot or committed suicide. Investigation led to the arrest, trial and execution of about 200 other people who were said (rightly or wrongly) to have been involved in the plot. Fromme was one of these – he did not save himself by betraying the others.

- **Church opposition**: Hitler was well aware of the power of religious beliefs. He wanted the loyalty of the German people to be directed to him alone. He moved carefully, firstly setting up a Concordat with the pope in which he promised to leave the Catholic Church alone if it did not interfere in German politics. He then developed a Nazi-influenced 'People's Church' with a Reichsbishop in control as a branch of the biggest Protestant church organisation, the German Evangelical Church. Many church members were soothed by Nazi nationalism, conservatism and anti-communist stance, as well as by point 24 in the Nazi *25-Point Programme* of 1920 (see Source 4). However, by 1933 the 'People's Church' had clearly become less Christian and more Nazi, even displaying Nazi banners in its churches and demanding the removal of the Old Testament from the Bible as it was 'Jewish'. This caused a reaction and the formation of the Pastors' Emergency League (PEL) that developed into the Confessing Church in May 1934. It condemned the People's Church for obeying the state, being anti-Semitic and even encouraging atheism. Many members of the Confessing Church were arrested and some were executed.

SOURCE

From the Nazi *25-Point Programme* policy document, written by Hitler and other Nazi leaders in 1920. The document formed the basis of Nazi Party policy even after they came to power in 1933.

24 We demand freedom for all religious denominations in the State, provided they do not threaten its existence nor offend the moral feelings of the German race.

The Party, as such, stands for positive Christianity, but does not commit itself to any particular denomination. It combats the Jewish-materialist spirit within and without us, and is convinced that our nation can achieve permanent health only from within on the basis of the principle: The common interest before self-interest.

Spontaneous protests

While the Nazis were firmly against opposition, they did pay attention to more informal reactions by groups of people, such as when large groups protested publicly against a particular Nazi action. For example, when the Nazis imprisoned two bishops (Hans Meiser and Theophil Wurm) for speaking out against the Nazis in October 1934, there was a public outcry and people took to the streets to protest. The Nazis, who were moving very cautiously against both Protestant and Catholic churches at this time, backed down and released the bishops. As another example, when Hitler was considering invading Czechoslovakia in 1938, he ordered military processions in Berlin. Instead of cheering and waving, Hitler was told that the people on the street were unenthusiastic. It was one of the reasons that prompted Hitler to work with Chamberlain at the Munich Conference to reach agreement over the land he was claiming in Czechoslovakia rather than going to war.

ACTIVITY
KNOWLEDGE CHECK

Opposition and dissent in Nazi Germany

1 Draw a spider diagram of dissenting groups in Nazi Germany. Colour code them by shading in the groups whose objections were mainly political, moral or social. If you think a group had more than one *main* focus, use more than one colour.

2 Explain what happened to many of the groups under discussion and how far the same thing would have happened in Weimar Germany.

THINKING HISTORICALLY   Causation (3a&b)

The human factor

1 'Our lack of control'. Work in pairs.

Describe to your partner a situation where things did not work out as you had intended. Then explain how you would have done things differently to make the situation as you would have wanted. Your partner will then tell the group about that situation and will say whether they think that your alternative actions would have had the desired effect.

2 'The tyranny of failed actions'. Work individually.

Think about the Kapp Putsch.

a) Write down three ways that Kapp could have acted differently.

b) Now imagine that you are Kapp. Write a defence of your actions. Try to think about the things that you would have known about at the time and make sure that you do not use the benefit of hindsight.

3 'Arguments'. Work in groups of between four and six.

In turn, each group member will read out their defence (from 2b above). Other group members suggest ways to reassure the reader that they were not a failure and that, in some ways, what happened was a good outcome.

4 Think about Hitler and the Munich Putsch.

a) In what ways were the consequences of the Munich Putsch not anticipated by Hitler?

b) In what ways did the Munich Putsch turn out better for Hitler than the intended consequences?

5 Think about Stauffenberg and the July Plot. Answer the following questions.

a) In what ways were the consequences of the plot not anticipated by Stauffenberg?

b) In what ways did the situation turn out worse for Stauffenberg than he intended?

6 To what extent are historical individuals in control of the history they helped to create? Explain your answer with reference to specific historical examples from this topic and others you have studied.

Political dissent and active challenge, 1949–89

The FRG, established in 1949, was set up to be a democracy. Its constitution was devised to try to avoid some of the problems that the democratic Weimar government had in making coalitions and forming policy, but the Basic Law that became its constitution was very clear about the fact that there should be free speech, freedom of the press and no censorship. This meant that opposition had a voice again in Germany, both within the political system and inside the country as a whole.

In the 1950s, the FRG was trying to establish itself. Political dissent and active challenge were less important than the bigger issues of the time:

- rebuilding the government, working together in useful coalitions to avoid the problems that the Weimar government had had

- building a sense of identity while leaving room for reunification with East Germany

- rebuilding the economy and physically rebuilding the country

- establishing the FRG as a viable, moderate member of Europe; even the newly re-established communist party stressed it wanted German Socialism, not a revolution.

This does not mean that there was no political dissent. It is not surprising that the coalition that emerged from the first elections in August 1949 had as its largest party the Christian Democratic Union (CDU) and that the party with the most radical political agenda (the SDP) was not part of the government, because there was a feeling among voters that they wanted parties that trod a moderate line. The SDP became the group that voiced what political opposition there was in the 1950s. It argued against several moves by Adenauer, the chancellor, such as his 'year zero' approach to past membership of the Nazi Party and his desire to align the FRG with Europe, thereby making reunification with East Germany less likely.

Demonstrations and marches in the 1950s

The government did clamp down on certain political groups, using a clause in the Basic Law that said that political parties could exist as long as they did not threaten the constitution or the principles of democracy. This clause was used to ban the right-wing Socialist Reich Party in 1952 because it was expressing views that were too reminiscent of those of the Nazi regime and therefore were a threat to democracy. The KPD, having been unable to win enough seats in the Bundestag to feel represented there, began to organise communist demonstrations in the cities. In Munich in 1953, about 6,000 communists clashed with the police and the police used water cannon to disperse the marchers.

Changes in the 1960s

By the 1960s the FRG had found its political feet in Europe and, by what was referred to as an 'economic miracle' (see Chapter 3), had an astonishingly strong economy as well. People were more confident and a younger generation, growing in numbers due to the post-war baby boom, was getting caught up in the feeling of youth protest all through the West. This wave of youth protest showed itself in the FRG in several ways.

- Young people who objected to the 'year zero' principle that had helped Adenauer rebuild the civil service and the army wanted to confront Germany's Nazi past. They especially objected to ex-Nazis in positions of political power. They adopted the slogan 'What did you do in the war, Daddy?' in a knowing reversal of the British recruitment poster for the First World War that had used this slogan to urge soldiers to join up to fight. The slogan was used by many to taunt the older generation, but some young people genuinely felt dislocated by the widespread lack of family history that was the result of 'year zero' behaviour.

SOURCE 5

Many demonstrations in the 1950s were not about politics, as such, but about issues such as peace. This poster from 1958 (the year the German Campaign Against Nuclear Death (GCND) was set up) urges 'No Experiments No Nuclear Armament' The GCND organised demonstrations and strikes to protest against Germany producing or housing nuclear weapons.

- There were protests against the FRG's military – its involvement with the West through NATO and the possibility that it might start to build and store atomic weapons, or allow other NATO countries to store nuclear weapons in the FRG.

- Young people joined the rising discontent with the way the USA was conducting the war in Vietnam. For many young people, the USA became the face of money-grabbing, repressive capitalism.

The APO

There were many groups in the 1960s that had, as their core membership, left-wing intellectuals, many of them students or young professionals. The Ausserparliamentarische Opposition (the Extra-Parliamentary Opposition, or APO) came about partly because of the distrust of young intellectuals for the established, conservative government and partly because there were no left-wing parties to absorb them after the KPD was banned and

The Vietnam War (1954–75)

The Vietnam War began when the French were driven out of the country by communist Vietnamese rebels in 1954. The United Nations organisation, formed after the Second World War to deal with international disputes, intervened to divide the country into a communist North and a democratic South. Unfortunately, Ngo Dinh Diem, the elected leader, was corrupt and his government was seen by many as almost as bad as the communist regime. The friction between North and South meant that the USA, who had helped to elect Diem, spent the 1950s giving South Vietnamese troops training, advice and supplies. The first troops were sent in by President Kennedy in 1961. From then on, the war escalated and became more and more unpopular. The USA was fighting a guerrilla war, where it often could not distinguish allies from enemies, and their destruction of civilian communities (which might or might not have been helping the enemy) shocked people around the world.

the SPD revised its policies to be less radical in 1959. While the revised policies got the SPD more power in government, it left people on the left wing (especially students and trade unionists) feeling unrepresented. Violent political protest, never far from the surface in Weimar Germany, began to gather force again. The APO had a strong university membership, many of whom supported radical theories about how to oppose government, theories that saw action as more important than argument, and saw student protest as a key method of protest. Films such as *Viva Maria!* (released in December 1965) showed a radical, revolutionary lifestyle with the use of bombs and guns for social revolution.

EXTRACT

2 From an analysis of student politics in the 1960s, in *Germany: 1933–1990*, written by the German historian Heinrich August Winkler and published in 2007.

The effects of the student movement were contradictory and, to a great extent, unintentional. The activists of the APO were bitter opponents of what they called 'US imperialism'; however, by adopting 'sit-ins', 'go-ins' and other forms of protest from the American student movement, they helped further westernise and 'Americanise' German society. They fought against pluralism, believing it to be an ideology to disguise capitalist class rule, but helped to make Germany more pluralist than ever before after 1968. They attacked the parliamentary system with radical leftist-democratic rhetoric, but their practice showed that their own model amounted to the manipulation of an 'unenlightened' majority by an 'enlightened' minority. They drove forwards the critical reappraisal of the National Socialist past and, at the same time, stretched the term 'fascism' so far that it could be applied to the 'late capitalist' West German state as easily as to the Third Reich.

The SDS

The German Socialist Student Union (SDS) had been part of the SPD, but it broke away in 1961 because it felt the party was becoming less and less radical and no longer represented its feelings, over rearmament, for example. Much radical protest in the 1960s, and the even more violent terrorism of the 1970s, was not always directed at political issues in the FRG – it was

directed at various human rights and moral issues in the world as a whole. The SDS, for example, protested about the Vietnam War and nuclear weapons. That said, the SDS also protested about former Nazis holding office in the government (it called them the Auschwitz generation after the infamous death camp, see Chapter 4) and the FRG's involvement in NATO. From 1965, the SDS leader was Rudi Dutschke, who some hold responsible for the escalating violence of student demonstrations. In 1967, during demonstrations against the human rights record of Iran during a visit from its shah, conflict with the police escalated and a student, Benno Ohnesorg, was shot. This led to an increase in the membership of the SDS but also to a split regarding how violent demonstrations should be. Gudrun Ensslin, one of the protestors, said after the shooting that violence was the only way to answer violence and that there was no arguing with the Auschwitz generation.

In April 1968, Rudi Dutschke was shot by a right-wing fanatic who read criticisms of student protests in newspapers published by the conservative newspaper owner Axel Springer. The 'Easter riots', a series of attacks on offices of the Springer Press all over Germany, followed. The riots died down and the SDS took part in the last major demonstration on 11 May 1968 in Bonn against the Emergency Law (see page 32). About 80,000 people from many different groups protested together against what they saw as a violation of the Basic Law's human rights principles. The law was passed anyway. It allowed the government powers of arrest and surveillance that led to a change in student protest.

EXTRACT

3 From an article in the *German Law Journal* written in 2008 by a number of contributors, all students or lecturers in law at Washington University.

On 30 May 1968 the West German Bundestag passed by the requisite two-thirds majority vote an amendment to the German constitution, the Grundgesetz (Basic Law), entitled the 'Seventeenth Law To Supplement the Basic Law.' The amendment was enacted in order to create a 'new constitutional organ' with responsibilities and procedures in both peacetime and wartime. Among the new powers given to the German government under the amendment was the authority to enact 'surveillance of written and oral telecommunications for security purposes... reinforce civilian police manpower, establish extensive administrative regulation... and radically centralize the federalist distribution of powers.'

The decision to enact this amendment, which functioned as an emergency constitution, was a catalyst for the student uprisings of 1968 as well as a reactionary measure by the government to the events of that year. The emergency laws were a clear example to the students of the so-called 'fascist tendencies' that had existed in Germany since before World War II. The laws were also a direct pushback by the German government against the anti-authoritarian movement sweeping the youth of Germany and other European countries. Not only did the emergency legislation contemplate legitimate necessary government action for times of war but it also established a basis for firm, centralized government control and action during times of national 'stress.' As the date for the passage of the emergency laws approached, student protests in Bonn and in the universities of West Germany increased, signifying that the amendment was in direct opposition to the growing counter-cultural movement of 1968.

Challenges in the 1970s

Government pressure on protest and dissent via the emergency laws and police control reduced the amount of protests by many groups. However, it had the effect of making some groups feel more marginalised and so increased the level of violence by resorting to terrorism. At first, the police and the government were thrown off balance by the terrorists' refusal to work through conventional protest. Later, they developed hard-line policies to deal with them, including putting up posters of wanted terrorists, appealing to the public to turn them in. Terrorist groups were fluid; groups formed, joined each other, changed their names, split, then fell apart all the time. Despite being constantly on the move, terrorists were in and out of prison – sometimes their arrests provoked terrorist attacks. There were regular gun battles with the police, sometimes several times a month, as terrorists tried to avoid arrest. In 1971, for example, one of the leaders of the West Berlin Tupamaros was shot by the police. The other leader was in prison, and so its members disbanded and moved on to other groups. Terrorism was accompanied by articles and pamphlets about what they wanted and why they were terrorists.

One of the most long-lived terrorist groups was the Baader-Meinhof Gang. Set up in early 1970, its first known action was the bombing in Dahlem in May 1970. It was named the Baader-Meinhof Gang by the press; it called itself the Red Army Faction (RAF). The group was influenced by Carlos Mirighella's *Minimanual for the Urban Guerrilla*, published in June 1969. It advised getting training, and the group went to Jordan to train with Palestinian terrorist group, the PLO. The first significant publication by a West German terrorist group was *The Concept of the Urban Guerrilla* published in 1971 by the Baader-Meinhof Gang. By the end of 1970, most of the gang's leaders were in prison and they called for hunger strikes. In November, Hoglar Meins, one of the hunger strikers, died in prison. This resulted in bombings of the homes of several lawyers and judges involved in the trials that sent the gang members to prison. However, by 1975 all of the Baader-Meinhof Gang were arrested and some were placed in solitary confinement. There were bombings in Stockholm, Paris and other cities to show support for them, but then terrorist activity in the FRG slowed, partly due to government activity and partly to a feeling that this form of protest was not achieving anything. There were still bombings throughout the 1980s, but they were not a regular occurrence.

ACTIVITY
KNOWLEDGE CHECK

Development of dissent, 1945–89

1 List three different types of dissenter in the years 1949–89 and explain how they would have expressed their dissent.

2 Explain how the way that people expressed their dissent changed over this period, giving reasons for the change.

AS Level Exam-Style Question Section B

How far do you agree that anti-government protest changed completely between 1933 and 1989? (20 marks)

Tip

This is a question about change and continuity. Consider both similarities and differences in methods of protest and remember to cover the whole period.

TIMELINE – TERRORIST ACTIVITY IN THE FRG, 1968–75

1968

2 April: Andreas Baader, Gundrun Ensslin, Horst Söhnlein and Thorwald Proll plant bombs in two department stores in Frankfurt. They are caught and imprisoned

1969

November: West Berlin Tupamaros formed; they set off a series of bombs in West Berlin

Members of the Kommune I groups (formed in the late 1960s) try to bomb a motorcade containing the US president, Richard Nixon, on a state visit. The bomb is discovered and the groups arrested

1970

May: a group of terrorists attack the Dahlem Institute for Social Research, there is shooting and a staff member is killed. The press name the group the Baader-Meinhof Gang (after two of its members)

September: the Baader-Meinhof Gang and a group that becomes the Movement 2 June group some time in 1971 rob three banks

1971

January: Baader-Meinhof robs more banks

February: Socialist Patients Collective (SPK) try to plant a bomb on a train that the president of the FRG is on. They miss the train. By July the members have been absorbed by the Baader-Meinhof Gang

December: Baader-Meinhof robs a bank, shooting a police officer

1972

February: Baader-Meinhof robs a bank

May: Baader-Meinhof bombs the headquarters of the US Army in Frankfurt and a US army base in Heidelberg, police stations in Augsburg and Munich, the Hamburg headquarters of the Springer Press and the car of the judge who signed most of the warrants for the arrest of Baader-Meinhof members

September: Black September Palestinian guerrillas take Israeli hostages at the Olympic Village during the Munich Olympics

1974

October: the five Baader-Meinhof leaders go to trial

February: Movement 2 June kidnap the CDU candidate for mayor of Berlin, Peter Lorenz

HOW SUCCESSFULLY DID GERMANY'S GOVERNMENTS CONTROL THE GERMAN PEOPLE IN THE YEARS 1918–89?

Attempts to control extremism, 1918–32

The Weimar government's problems controlling extremist groups stemmed from both conditions at the time and the fact they were setting up a liberal democracy. The government had come to power through a revolution and many people wanted a revolutionary government – not the old empire and not a compromise democracy. But there were not enough of them to sweep the country into revolution. The Weimar government was a theoretical democracy with left-wing opponents who thought it was not radical enough and right-wing opponents who wanted a strong, authoritative government that would return Germany to something very like the old system. It gave people freedom of speech and assembly; it also gave the press freedom to print what it liked. This meant that criticism of the government was open and it spread. There was no knowing if this government would last any longer than Prince Max's had – and this uncertainty meant that the various political groups still felt they had a lot to play for, that they could still change the government to make it more to their liking. The fact that the government was forced to leave Berlin and spend its first days in Weimar during the Spartacist uprising (see page 12) and its aftermath just underlined its precarious position.

What the government needed to do was to provide stability and to show it had support. It needed to reform the army (Reichswehr), the civil service, the educational system and the judiciary to make sure of support in these key areas of society. It also needed to rein in revolutionary ideas. However, it was not really strong enough to do either, at least not without taking sides and using one group to control the other. Without support, the government was not going to be strong enough to deal with opposition. Ebert saw this and met with the army and the trade unions, offering concessions for their support.

Making concessions

On 10 November 1918, Ebert had agreed the Ebert-Groener Pact with the new leader of the army. Their agreement was that the army would support the new government as long as it opposed the more left-wing ideas of parties in the Reichstag. On 15 November, Ebert reached the Stinnes-Legien Agreement with the leader of the labour unions, Carl Legien, and the industrialist Hugo Stinnes. For their support, Ebert offered legislation on hours of work and on adequate union representation.

Neither the army nor the representatives from industry knew about the agreement with the other at first. However, there were half-hearted alliances on all sides and the government often had to turn to the *Freikorps* to restore order if the army refused. When both refused (for example, the Kapp Putsch), the government was in a very difficult position.

SOURCE 6 Part of a letter from Groener to his wife, dated 17 November 1918, explaining the army 'support' for Ebert and the new government. His last sentence refers to the revolution that led to the Kaiser abdicating.

The Field Marshall [von Hindenburg] and I intend to support Ebert, whom I estimate as a straightforward, honest and decent character, as long as possible so that the cart does not slide further to the left. But where is the courage of the middle class? That a tiny minority could simply overthrow the whole German Empire together with its member states, is one of the saddest events of the whole history of the German nation. During four years the German people stood unbroken against a world of enemies – now it permits a handful of sailors to knock it down as if it were a dummy.

EXTRACT 4 From *A Concise History of Germany*, written by the historian Mary Fulbrook and published in 1990.

What developed in Germany in 1918–19 was a series of fudges and compromises, satisfying neither left nor right, and embodying a set of legacies that were to prove liabilities for Germany's first attempt at democracy. These compromises were already symbolised in arrangements made in the first few days after 9 November. While apparently stabilising in the short term, they tended to paper over, rather than resolve, tensions which erupted all the more powerfully in the longer run. Furthermore, the so-called revolution of 1918 in effect amounted to little more than a political and constitutional revolution, from Empire to Republic, but it – crucially – failed to effect radical changes in the socioeconomic structure of Germany, nor did it reform key elites. Army, bureaucracy, judiciary, educational and religious establishments, retained their positions of power and influence – and used them to speak and act in the main against the new Republic.

Regional disruption

The Weimar government had varying control in each of the regions of Germany, all of which were having their governmental struggles as rulers followed the Kaiser and abdicated, some willingly some less so. They did all eventually adopt the Weimar Constitution, but not all at the same time. For example, Thuringia did not hold elections until the end of June 1920. This added to the uncertainty and meant that, in some places such as Bavaria and Saxony, it was possible for the communists to set up a government of their own. The Weimar government used the army and the *Freikorps* to restore order in these places using a system of *Reichsexekution* – a takeover by the federal government and the army until the Weimar constitution and the Weimar system of government could be put back in place.

> **EXTEND YOUR KNOWLEDGE**
>
> *Reichsexekution*
> This was when the federal government removed the state government as a threat to the republic. It then put in place a military government, headed by a civilian governor appointed by the government, to restore order. This is how the government dealt with the establishment of communist governments in both Saxony and Thuringia in 1922. Troops marched in and broke up the meetings in each Land. There were arrests and imprisonment and the army was particularly heavy-handed with groups of workers – there were riots in which workers were shot.

Lopsided control

The Weimar government was forced to rely on the army to manage extremist threats (for the most significant threats, see the timeline on page 40). It was noticeable all through the period that the reaction of the *Reichswehr* and the judiciary to these threats was different, depending on whether they came from left-wing groups or right-wing groups. Left-wing problems were dealt with quickly, and often brutally, by the army. Those brought to court were sentenced harshly. On the other hand, the army sometimes did not act against right-wing groups at all, for example, against the Kapp Putsch, and the judiciary were noticeably less harsh on right-wingers who came to trial, for example, the Munich Putsch. This made its left-wing opponents more angry. It made its right-wing opponents more confident. Also, as Hindenburg became president, chancellors changed rapidly and the economy went into a depression, it made its right-wing opponents increasingly confident that people wanted a strong, right-wing government, not the Weimar. Eventually, the people voted in sufficient numbers for the Nazis to gain a foothold in government and rapidly replace the democratic Weimar government.

ACTIVITY
KNOWLEDGE CHECK

Controlling extremism, 1918–32

1 Explain what Source 6 suggests about the army as a means of control for the Weimar government.

2 What other information do you have that bears this out?

3 Explain how each of the following would have allowed the Weimar government to exert control in Germany:

　a) the judiciary

　b) the civil service

　c) the education system.

4 Explain how regionalism might make government control harder.

How did the Nazis use censorship and repression from 1933 to 1945?

The Nazis believed in a strong, centralised government and an obedient people. They used violence against their political enemies or, as in the Night of the Long Knives (see pages 21–22), enemies within the Party. They used censorship and repression to create a situation where ordinary people were, in the main, too scared to oppose the Nazis. The Decree for the Protection of the People and the State (28 February 1933) allowed the Nazis to ban publications and also suspended civil rights; the Nazis could search homes and workplaces and take people into 'protective custody' without then taking them to trial. This supposedly short-term emergency measure was never lifted.

Censorship

The Nazis were quite clear that all forms of communication were subject to Nazi control. On 25 March 1933, Goebbels (minister of propaganda) told all of the controllers of German radio that radio stations served the government, so they had to express Nazi ideology and follow government instructions about what to broadcast. Not only was the content of radio programmes controlled, the staff were purged to get rid of Jews, half-Jews and people married to Jews as well as people who had belonged to the communist KPD or the socialist SPD.

The press was also censored, although this was harder (radio was a newer medium with far fewer people to control). Germany had more daily newspapers than the USA; they were national, regional and even printed for cities and towns. On 4 October 1933, Hitler issued a decree that made the content of any paper the responsibility of the editor and made it a crime for the editor to publish anything that might weaken the Third Reich, at home or abroad, or harm the German economy, culture or people. It established a Reich Association to compile a list of 'accredited' journalists. Many journalists (those with Jewish connections or who were 'politically unsuitable') did not make the list.

At the end of 1932, there were 59 Nazi newspapers with just over 780,000 readers. At the end of 1933, the Nazis had 86 newspapers and over three million readers. In December, a state-owned press agency was set up and all newspapers were expected to pick up their news stories from the agency, with guidelines on how to report the stories. It also issued lists of stories that were not to be reported. These lists were incredibly detailed, ranging from not reporting the arrests of certain people to not publishing photos of Nazi leaders sitting at tables with several bottles of alcohol on them.

Repression

Nazi repression began with banning all political parties but the Nazi Party. This made forming a political party a crime, and the Nazis set up a series of concentration camps to hold political prisoners. Between 1933 and 1945, over 500,000 non-Jewish people were sent to these camps for political crimes. The first, at Oranienburg in Prussia, opened in 1933. Imprisonment in these camps was a severe deterrent to political protest.

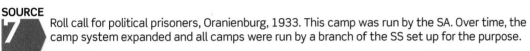

SOURCE 7

Roll call for political prisoners, Oranienburg, 1933. This camp was run by the SA. Over time, the camp system expanded and all camps were run by a branch of the SS set up for the purpose.

Policing and the courts

The Nazis also ran their own security system alongside the existing police and judicial system, despite the fact that these underwent the same 'co-ordination' (purging) as the civil service and the media.

- The Gestapo, the secret police, was set up in April 1933 by Hermann Goering. It inaugurated its own legal system and operated independently of the existing legal system. Gestapo agents were in all parts of Germany and spread as Germany spread. The Gestapo's brief was to weed out enemies of the state, and people could be arrested by the Gestapo for anything from plotting to kill Hitler to telling jokes about the Nazis in a bar. Unlike the SA and the SS, the Gestapo did not wear uniform and it encouraged people to think that any stranger they met might be a member to make people very careful about what they said.

- The SS (*Schutzstaffel*) began as Hitler's bodyguard of 240 men. It was a political police and, after removing most of the SA in 1934, ran the concentration camp system. As SS numbers grew, so did its responsibilities. By 1936, about 240,000 SS were in charge of the Gestapo with their own economic branch to run labour and concentration camps.

- The People's Court was set up in Berlin in 1934 as a court specifically to try people accused of being traitors to the Third Reich. It had two judges and five other members chosen from the Nazi Party, the SS and the armed forces. The trials were not publicly held and it was not possible to appeal against the verdict. Tens of thousands of people had passed through the Court by 1945.

- Nazi Party officials, from those who ran a region or *Gau* down to the Bloc Wardens (*Blockwarts*) who ran individual apartment blocks, were all assumed to be watching for the smallest infringement of Nazi rules. People listened to banned music with the volume down low and their ear against the radio. Conversations edged round and round and seldom strayed into political matters. It was hard for people to be frank with anyone about dissident views in case people who they thought would agree with them, even old friends, reported them to the Gestapo.

SOURCE 8

Jacob Zorn, who was a member of the KPD in Cologne 1933, was interviewed after the war by the historian Dirk Gerhard for his book *Antifascism*, published in 1976. Here, Zorn discusses the state of resistance to the Nazis in late 1933.

At that time the organisation was working really well. All the city wards [KPD units in Cologne] were intact. In other words the whole organisation was intact and ready to go, right down to the smallest unit. The Communist Party, if I remember rightly, was really the only party which managed to offer organised resistance – that is resistance on a broad basis. By 'organised resistance,' I mean getting money for the organisation, distributing leaflets, making contacts abroad, all these things. We hardly saw anything of the SPD at this time.

SOURCE 9

From a report by Gestapo headquarters to the SS in 1936, discussing the organisation of the SPD after the first rounds of arrests and releases in 1933.

They promote energetically the so-called whispering campaign which, for the time being, represents the most effective illegal work against the State, against its institutions and activities, and against the Party. The main subjects of discussion are price increases, low wages, economic exploitation of the people, freedom, shortage of raw materials, corruption, nepotism [favouritism], gifts at the nation's expense and so on. Since many of the SPD and trade union officials are now commercial representatives and travelling salesmen, such catchwords will spread comparatively quickly into the furthest parts of the Reich. Despite the extent of these subversive activities it had not yet been possible to catch a single one of these persons in the act and bring him to trial.

THINKING HISTORICALLY Evidence (4a&b)

Evidence in context

Sources 8 and 9 could be used by the historian to build up a picture of the state of the SPD in Nazi Germany in the 1930s.

1 Explain why Sources 8 and 9 offer two views of the state of SPD resistance in Nazi Germany in the 1930s. How might this affect their value as pieces of evidence appraising the event? Explain your answer.

Discuss the following in groups:

2 Suppose the historian had ten more accounts that agreed broadly with Source 8 and only four that agreed with Source 9. What would that tell them about the event?

3 How far should the balance of evidence play a role in constructing written history? What else must the historian consider about the evidence being used before drawing conclusions?

ACTIVITY
KNOWLEDGE CHECK

Censorship and repression, 1933–45

1 Write an outline for a spokesman from the Ministry of Propaganda who is going to give a speech at a meeting of Nazi officials in 1933 to explain what the Ministry is going to do to control the media and how it will help.

2 Explain why Hitler felt the need to have a Nazi system of police and legal systems in place, running alongside the existing ones.

The constitutional and legal responses to political extremism, 1949–89

Political extremism in the FRG became very severe, turning to terrorism in the 1970s. In some ways the increase in the extremity of the protests was linked to the government responses to these protests. It is interesting that, while people did not turn to terrorism in large numbers, there was a surprising level of sympathy for terrorist groups in the early 1970s. A public poll in 1970 showed that one in five Germans felt some sympathy for the Baader-Meinhof Gang and five percent of them would be willing to let a member of the group stay in their house for a night if that person was on the run. This suggests that government action against these groups did not always get a positive reaction from members of the public, which could be seen as a lack of success. The government was in a difficult position in that it wanted to uphold democracy and free speech, but it did not want this democracy overthrown by groups from either side. As it turned out, rather like the Weimar government, it came down more heavily on left-wing extremists, although it could be argued that these were the groups that posed more of a threat – certainly terrorist groups in the 1970s were left wing.

Policing the people

The government took a number of steps to control political extremism between 1949 and 1989. The Bundesamt für Verfassungsschutz (BfV, set up in 1950) and the Bundesnachrichtendienst (BND, set up in 1956) were both entitled to investigate people they suspected of working against the Basic Law. The BfV worked only inside Germany and reported to the minister of the interior. The BND reported directly to the chancellor and it conducted investigations abroad as well as in Germany. Both organisations were hampered by the civil liberties granted to people under the Basic Law: they were forbidden to open mail, search homes or monitor phone calls. The government tried to pass a law to supplement the Basic Law to allow the BND to use measures such as these, and to have wider powers of arrest and detention, in what was described as 'moments of political tension'. The government tried to introduce such a law in 1960, 1962 and 1965. It was finally passed in 1968 (and called the Emergency Law) as protests by students, unions and other groups became more violent (see page 32). The passing of the Law certainly led to a drop in the number of open protests and a significant number of arrests. However, while some groups were silenced, others decided that underground, violent opposition (terrorism) was the only way. This was an unintended, and unwelcome, consequence.

The Emergency Law allowed police activity that could track down terrorists even though they kept on the move. It was much more successful after the introduction of Beobachtende Fahndung (BEFA), a system that gave the BND centralised access to all police information in the FRG. By the end of the 1970s, there was much less terrorist activity in the FRG, which could be seen as a success for the government, but this needs to be set against the possibility that it was the government's actions that had encouraged the rise of terrorism in the first place. After the shooting of Israeli athletes at the Munich Olympics in 1972, Grenzschutzgruppe *9* (GSG-9) was set up as a special operations unit to act against terrorists. It had close links with the British SAS and the US Army's Delta Force, which were trained for similar missions. It operated worldwide. On 17 October 1977, a team successfully rescued hostages on a plane that had been hijacked on its way to Frankfurt and ended up in Mogadishu, Somalia. It also took part in some arrests of Baader-Meinhof members.

People management

The government's attempts at policing extremism met with a good deal of criticism; so did its other tactic against extremism, which was to restrict the work that known extremists could do. There had been employment restrictions in government from 1949 on. This Berufsverbot (employment ban) was initially aimed at specified political parties that might be thought to pose a threat to democracy, including the KPD and parties with aims similar to those of the Nazis. It was very seldom applied – fewer than 100 people lost their jobs between 1950 and 1972 – although it is impossible to estimate how many people were not employed because of their political views. Adenauer eventually passed Article 131 in May 1951, to allow for the employment of ex-Nazis in the civil service. However, the ban was still in place and was occasionally used. With the rise of extremist protest, much of it coming from universities, the government introduced the Radikalenerlass (Anti-Radical Decree) in January 1972. This allowed for political vetting of everyone applying for a state job, from teachers to postmen to civil servants. The protests against it usually labelled it the Berufsverbot, confusing the two.

TIMELINE – LAWS PASSED BY THE FRG TO CONTROL OPPOSITION

1950

December: the Bundesamt für Verfassungsschutz (BfV; Federal Office for the Protection of the Constitution) set up

The employment ban, Berufsverbot, introduced

1956

April: the Bundesnachrichtendienst (BND; Federal Information Service) set up to deal mostly with information-gathering abroad, but also some in the FRG

1968

30 May: the Seventeenth Law to Supplement the Basic Law (the Emergency Law) is passed to give the federal government powers in a 'national emergency', giving them greater powers inside the states and allowing them to use the army inside the country

1972

28 January: the Radikalenerlass (Anti-Radical Decree) allowing vetting of people applying for jobs in the public sector is passed

Grenzschutzgruppe 9 (GSG-9 anti-terrorist special forces) is set up

1977

A central police surveillance system (Beobachtende Fahndung, BEFA) is set up to provide computerised access to the same police information all over the country

---

ACTIVITY
WRITING

The language of change

Which of the following phrases do you think best defines the introduction of the Emergency Law amendment to the Basic Law by the government of the FRG in May 1968? Make your choice and then write a justification of your choice. Choose from:

- a significant change of policy

- an adaption to changing methods of protest

- a radical change of policy

- a long-term shift in government thinking

- a violation of the Basic Law.

THINKING HISTORICALLY   Change (4b & c)

The bird's-eye view

The event	Medium-term consequences	Long-term consequences
The Emergency Law becomes part of the Basic Law.	Protest against invasion of privacy, fears of increasing repression. Extremists detected by the newly allowed surveillance measures; arrests. Rise of terrorism. Laws used to catch and prosecute terrorists.	Decline of terrorism. The government did not become increasingly invasive and repressive.

Imagine you are looking at the whole of history using a zoomed-out interactive map like Google Maps. You have a general view of the sweep of developments and their consequences, but you cannot see much detail. If you zoom in to the time of the Emergency Law amendment to the Basic Law in May 1968, you can see the event in detail but will know nothing of its consequences in the medium or long term. If you zoom in to look at the medium- or long-term consequences, you will know about them in detail but will know very little about the event that caused them.

Look at the table above and answer the following questions:

1 What were the immediate consequences of the event?

2 In what ways are the medium-term consequences different from the long-term consequences?

Work in groups of three.

Each student takes the role of the teacher for one of the above (the event, medium-term consequences or long-term consequences) and gives a short presentation to the other two. They may comment and ask questions. After each presentation, the other two members of the group write a 100-word paragraph showing how the presentation links to their own.

Answer the following questions individually:

3 What happens to the detail when you zoom out to look at the whole sweep of history?

4 What are the advantages and disadvantages of zooming in to look at a specific time in detail?

5 How could you use the map in order to get a good understanding of history as a whole?

ACTIVITY
KNOWLEDGE CHECK

Controlling extremism, 1949–89

How successful was the FRG in controlling extremism between 1949 and 1989? Consider the methods used and the reaction they produced, and explain your reasoning.

TO WHAT EXTENT DID GERMANY'S GOVERNMENTS RULE BY CONSENT IN THE YEARS 1918–89?

The nature of support for the Weimar Constitution, 1918–32

The Weimar government had a huge number of problems and faced a good deal of opposition. It is easy to fall into the trap of thinking that the Weimar Constitution itself did not have much support, or that the support it had was entirely half-hearted. However, it is possible to find evidence of significant support for the idea of a democracy where the people have a real say in the elections. One of the most notable signs of support was that a significant number of people turned out to vote at every election. This suggests that they were in favour of the democratic process because they were prepared to go and vote.

SOURCE 10

Turnout of voters in Reichstag elections from 1919 to November 1932, given as the percentage of all people registered to vote who actually voted.

	1919	1920	May 1924	December 1924	1928	1930	July 1932	November 1932
Turnout (%)	83.0	79.2	77.4	78.8	75.6	82.0	84.0	80.6

SOURCE 11

This election campaign poster for the SPD, from 1930, shows that it saw itself as the upholder of democracy and the enemies of democracy as Nazism, communism and militarism. It also shows that it expected that campaigning under the banner of 'democracy' would win votes. The SPD won 24.5 percent of the vote in 1930. From 1918 to 1930, it was consistently the biggest party in the Reichstag.

Which political parties supported the constitution?

The SPD consistently supported the Weimar constitution. The other more moderate parties that often played a part in forming a coalition also supported the constitution, although to different degrees (the DVP was the most lukewarm, despite the fact that its leader was Gustav Stresemann, the person who produced the more settled economy between 1924 and 1929). These moderate parties were the Centre Party, the German Democrats (DDP) and the German People's Party (DVP). The problem lay in the fact that supporting the constitution and the idea of a democratic government was not enough. The parties had to be prepared to work together and try to negotiate policies that would help the government to function properly – and they could not do that. However, if we think about the support that these parties got, it should suggest the people who favoured the constitution. These were, in the main, middle-class business people, Catholics and the professional classes.

Percentage of votes for major pro- and anti-constitution parties in Reichstag elections from 1919 to November 1932.

	1919	1920	May 1924	December 1924	1928	1930	November 1932
Pro-constitution (SPD, DDP, DVP and Centre) (%)	80.5	57.5	48.8	56.0	57.7	43.9	35.2
Anti-constitution (KPD, USPD, Nazis) (%)	17.9	35.1	32.9	29.8	27.4	31.4	58.3

EXTEND YOUR KNOWLEDGE

Smaller parties
The number of smaller parties standing in the elections from 1919 to 1933 varied. In 1919, there were 18 parties and eight of them won no seats at all. The biggest number of parties standing in this period was in 1932, when 51 parties stood (including one called For Hindenburg and the Pope – it got over 27,000 votes). The smallest number of parties was 14 in March 1933, showing the success that the SA (Hitler's stormtroopers) had in suppressing political parties.

Popular support for the constitution

It is noticeable that many people welcomed the Weimar Constitution when they were presented with something they liked less. For example, in 1923 the people of Saxony welcomed the *Reichsexekution* and the removal of the communist government, which had not been elected but had imposed itself on the region. The American ambassador in Dresden said the troops were greeted with cheers as if they were an army of liberation. It is likely that the Weimar Constitution had more supporters, as a template for democratic government, than the actual government had. Critics at the time often criticised what the government was or was not doing, not the ideas behind the constitution. For example, many people wrote angrily about the various parties in the Reichstag failing to make coalitions work.

When the government did get things right, there was a rise in support. So from 1924 to 1929, as the government seemed to be making the economy work and getting Germany accepted as a power in Europe again, the constitution and the parties that supported it got more support. In 1924 the SPD, the face of the constitution, won 131 seats in the Reichstag. This rose to 153 in 1928, surely a sign of approval. However, when the government failed, democracy swung into action again. A right-wing president was elected by popular vote and then the Nazis won a rapid rise to power in the Reichstag, again with voters exercising their democratic rights. Once there, they dismantled the Weimar Constitution.

ACTIVITY
KNOWLEDGE CHECK

Support for the Weimar Constitution, 1918–32

Prepare notes for a debate on the statement: 'The Weimar government and its constitution were doomed from the start because Germans were not interested in democracy.'

Think of at least three points in favour of the statement and three points against it.

Read the statement carefully and note that it discusses both the government and the constitution.

Support for the Nazi regime and the use of propaganda, 1933–45

The Nazis certainly had enough support to win sufficient seats in the Reichstag to take part in government. In the same way that it is difficult to judge the level of opposition to the Nazis, it is also difficult to judge the level of support for them. You cannot believe Nazi propaganda on the subject and you cannot necessarily believe the photos of hordes of people cheering and waving – the Nazi system of control meant many people would smile and wave even if inwardly they did not support the Nazis. However, there were people who supported the Nazis, and when these were added to the people who withdrew from politics and got on with their lives, it was quite easy for the Nazis to give the impression that the whole country was behind them. Complete support was a vital concept for the Nazis. Hitler stressed the importance of actual support, not just the appearance of support, for the war he knew was coming. One way the Nazis gained support was to make Hitler into a national hero, a god-like figure who could do no wrong. The 'Führer myth' that the Nazis created made people willing to make sacrifices when Hitler asked them to.

EXTRACT

5 From *Nazism 1919–45*, written by the historians J. Noakes and G. Pridham and published in 1984.

The image of German society conveyed by Nazi propaganda in newsreels and the press was of mass enthusiasm and commitment. However, in trying to understand what Germans really felt during these years the historian is faced with serious problems. Not only were there no opinion polls but it was impossible for people to express their views in public with any freedom: the result of elections and plebiscites were rigged; the media were strictly controlled. Newspapers are of limited value as a source, since the editors were subject to detailed instructions from the Propaganda Ministry on what to print and were severely disciplined if the stepped out of line. In short, an independent public opinion did not exist in the Third Reich.

Winning support

The Nazis used a variety of methods to win the support of the people, all of them carefully targeting a particular group, as they had done with their election propaganda.

- The Nazi's use of propaganda was very sophisticated. As early as the 1920s, Hitler was saying that people could be won over to almost anything if it was presented as a simple idea, with a single slogan or image repeated over and over again. For example, 'One People, one Reich, one Führer', or the image of a Jewish person as an ugly dark man with a huge hooked nose. Nazi control of the media enabled them to manipulate what people saw and heard from very early on. For example, they made sure a Nazi reported the reaction to Hitler's appointment as chancellor. He reported huge, cheering torchlight processions in Berlin, with a mass of people chanting 'Sieg Heil!' (the Nazi chant, 'Hail Victory!'). So everyone listening to the radio was immediately convinced of Hitler's huge popularity. The Nazis made sure that the cheapest and most widely available radio was the People's Receiver. In 1939, over 70 percent of the population owned a radio; by 1943, one-third of all radios were People's Receivers. These had a limited range and, unless the owners lived close to the German border, they could not pick up foreign radio stations.

- From 1933 on, the Nazi propaganda machine manipulated the news and other information to make people think that Nazi policies were working, or that Nazi prejudices were right. For example, Nazi propaganda told people that Jewish people were greedy, dirty, subhumans. After 1939, the Nazis crowded all the Jewish people they could into **ghettos** where food, water and electricity were only sporadically available. Selected images of Jews living like this then reinforced the anti-Semitic propaganda.

- The Nazis punished opposition, but they made sure to reward conformity as well. Mothers were rewarded with medals for having babies. One mother, Anna Klein, remembered that she loved the way that she was valued as a mother. It was all she had ever wanted to be and no mothers in her parents' generation had received the extras she got just for doing what she wanted: a 1,000 mark loan on marriage that was reduced by 250 marks for each child (so four children cleared the loan); regular check-ups and vitamins while pregnant. In 1939, the Nazis introduced a series of medals of honour for having more than four children. It was not just women who were rewarded

KEY TERM

Ghetto
An area of a town or city, fenced off (or walled off) from the rest of the city where all the members of a particular group of people live.

for conformity. For example, workers were rewarded with free trips with the Kraft Durch Freude (KDF, Strength Through Joy) programme.

- The Nazis were popular with people whose prejudices they shared. There were people who hated Jews, gays, Gypsies, communists and other groups seen by the Nazis as 'undesirable'. For them, it was a pleasure to see these groups victimised by the Nazis. The support ranged from informing on people in their apartment building who were listening to banned foreign radio broadcasts to running Hitler Youth groups or acting as an official of the DAF, the Nazi 'trade union'.

- The Nazis had the support of people who benefited from their rule. These ranged from the wealthy industrialists (who benefited from the banning of the KPD and trade unions) to the middle classes (who found their savings had value again) to people who applied to 'Germanise' an area. Those who were accepted were given homes and farmland on which to live. They were usually people who would not have owned their own farms without having been given the chance to Germanise by the Nazis. They were therefore prepared not to think too hard about how, exactly, the land they were taking over had been acquired. They were told that the owners were part of a move eastwards and were starting new lives on farms there.

- Support also came from those Germans who saw the Nazis as reversing the losses of the Treaty of Versailles and asserting the power of Germany in Europe. They were people who failed to see how Stresemann had managed, with his careful work in Europe, to improve reparations and gain other reversals of Versailles because he had done so by working with 'the enemy'.

Support during the war
While many Germans were initially lukewarm about going to war, many changed their mind when the German army started to sweep through Europe and the East. The 'Führer myth' kept support going even when the Nazis made the mistake of invading the USSR and began to struggle to keep advancing. This support varied from collecting for the various charities organised by the Nazis to joining the special murder squads that took part in the mass murder of Jews, Poles and Slavs as the German army swept through Poland and then the USSR. However, while there were always some people predisposed to support the Nazis, it was far harder for them to retain the support of the majority of ordinary people during the war as their living conditions deteriorated and Allied bombing devastated the cities.

AS Level Exam-Style Question Section A

Was the main reason for popular support for the Nazis in the years 1933–45 the party's use of propaganda? Explain your answer.
(20 marks)

Tip
This question asks you to consider how propaganda helped to generate support for the Nazis. However, 'main reason' means you need to find and assess other reasons as well as propaganda.

EXTEND YOUR KNOWLEDGE

Strength Through Joy (KDF)
This organisation was set up by the Nazis as part of the Deutsche Arbeitsfront (German Labour Front; DAF) that was the only trade union allowed under the Nazis. Strength Through Joy officials organised after-work activities, weekend activities and holidays for workers and their families. Activities were either free or provided at a very favourable rate compared to what similar holidays and trips would cost if a family went on its own. This was because the activities were heavily subsidised by the government (23 million marks for the year 1933). All DAF activities were full of opportunities to push various Nazi propaganda messages, although they were promoted as a sign of the government caring for workers by offering them wider cultural opportunities.

EXTRACT

6 From *Backing Hitler*, written by the historian Robert Gellately and published in 2001.

We are used to ignoring the subsequent elections and plebiscites under Hitler's dictatorship, but they tend to show that a pro-Nazi consensus formed and grew. In October 1933 Hitler withdrew Germany from the League of Nations and called a national plebiscite to ask Germans if they agreed. The results were 95 per cent in favour. Hardly less spectacular were the results of the election he called for November, held along with the plebiscite. The results were that Hitler and his party received almost forty million votes (92.2 per cent of the total). Hardly less remarkable was the turnout of 95.2 per cent of those eligible. We can hardly take the election at face value, because all other political parties were outlawed. Nearly three and a half million people spoiled their ballot, presumably to show their opposition. Still, the vast majority voted in favour of Nazism, and in spite of what they could read in the press and hear by word of mouth about the secret police, the concentration camps, official anti-Semitism and so on.

ACTIVITY
KNOWLEDGE CHECK

Support for the Nazis, 1933–45
1 List the points Gellately makes in Extract 6 to show that Hitler had support in 1933.

2 Think of counter-arguments to as many of these points as you can.

3 The League of Nations was an international organisation set up by the Allies after the First World War and written into the treaties that ended the war. Germany had initially been excluded, but was allowed to join in 1926. Why might leaving the League be a particularly popular decision?

The de-Nazification policies of the Western Allies, 1945–49

At the end of the war, the German people had to face defeat, huge economic problems and the division of their country by the Allies into zones of influence. The Allies were all agreed that one of the first things that had to happen in Germany was de-Nazification.

This did not simply mean finding all Nazis, especially those who had taken part in the **Holocaust** (see Chapter 4) and prosecuting them – although they wanted to do that. It did not even mean just making people face up to the more extreme Nazi policies, for example, marching them past the piles of dead bodies in concentration camps, although they also did that. What they wanted to produce was a changed culture, a changed political outlook. The national identity that had been hammered into them by the Nazis had to change, as did the racial and cultural ideas that had also been imposed over the years.

> **KEY TERM**
>
> Holocaust
> This is the name given to the Nazis' attempt to wipe out the Jewish race. Other groups that the Nazis saw as 'inferior' were also caught up in the Holocaust.

The Nuremberg Trials

These war crime trials, held in Nuremberg (where Hitler had held yearly mass rallies), were of those Nazi leaders who had neither committed suicide nor escaped. The first trial began on 18 October 1945. Of the 22 defendants, 12 were sentenced to death, three to life imprisonment and three were acquitted. The remaining defendants went to prison. Surveys at the time showed that the trials were accepted by most Germans as a necessary part of losing the war, although there was also a feeling that there should be an end to the pursuit of Nazis. The 'Führer myth' changed for many people – Hitler became the person to take all the blame. Now he was dead and many of the most famous Nazi leaders had been dealt with, many people felt they should be allowed to get on with rebuilding their lives, without too close an examination of what they had done before 1945, which should be allowed to become 'year zero'. This policy was firmly supported by many right-wing politicians (for example, Adenauer, who was to become chancellor of the FRG) and many of those who had lived through the war as adults.

De-Nazification policies

Different Allied zones pursued de-Nazification differently, although thousands of people were arrested in all of the zones: about 250,000 were arrested by the end of 1946. However, there were problems with classifying who was a Nazi. Many people had joined the party to keep their jobs, but they did not really have Nazi sympathies. It was possible for more involved Nazis to remove themselves from the record. There were also problems with the sheer scale of the process. Inevitably there were injustices in all zones at all levels. The problems with this was that the process came to look bungled and corrupt – and this did not encourage people to welcome the democratic process set up by the same Allied authorities.

The Western zones, having seen the effect of the Hitler Youth movement and Nazi propagandist education, set out to re-educate the young. They faced an uphill battle because the young were most likely to have been indoctrinated. In May 1946, the Allies banned Nazi schoolbooks, films and slides that taught Nazi racial theory. They also banned books that used such theories as examples, such as the school textbook that asked how many

marriage loans could be paid from the cost of keeping one disabled person alive over a year. Teachers were vetted to weed out Nazis at universities and teacher training institutes. Libraries and librarians had to go through a similar process. The problem was that Nazification had been so thorough that de-Nazification meant there were not enough people to do many of the key jobs, not only in education but in government as well. This was something that the Allies had to adapt to, as well as the FRG government; there was not a single uniform policy. The USSR was most ruthless in its weeding out of Nazis; the British were most pragmatic in accepting that they would have to employ some ex-Nazi Party members in order for government to work.

Reactions to de-Nazification

Reaction to de-Nazification was a two-stage process. Immediately after the war, as the Allies pressed for de-Nazification, Germans reacted in a combination of the following ways.

- **Resigned acceptance**: They had lost; the Allies were bound to want to punish Germany and do their best to eradicate Nazism. This was especially widespread between 1945 and 1949, when US opinion polls suggested that between half and two-thirds of those asked thought that de-Nazification was necessary. However, after 1949 (and the withdrawal of Allied troops) the number of people saying this fell to under a quarter in 1951.

- **Indignation**: The Allies had dropped atomic bombs on Hiroshima and Nagasaki in Japan, they had bombed Dresden to bits, and Soviet troops had wiped out German villages on the push to Berlin. Why should only the Germans be punished for war crimes? Also, the Allies were censoring the press, vetting teachers and so on. Yet they had been critical of the Nazis doing the same thing.

- **Avoidance**: Those who had supported the Nazis, even if they had not taken part in any war crimes, wanted to avoid too close an examination of who did what during the war.

- **Cynicism**: Some people pointed out that, apart from the Nuremberg Trials, the prosecution of ex-Nazis was patchy. All of the Allies were guilty of allowing ex-Nazis with useful skills to leave Germany and start a new life in their country (about 1,600 ex-Nazi scientists and doctors avoided prosecution by agreeing to work for the USA, including the rocket scientist Werner von Braun).

- **Desire to move on**: These people believed in the 'year zero' theory and many people in the new government of the FRG wanted to follow this pragmatic course. The quickest way for the government to rebuild the country's structure (for example, schools, hospitals, the civil service) was not to look too closely at the past of those who were qualified to do the work. By 1947, more than 85 percent of the school teachers in Bavaria who had lost their jobs through de-Nazification were back at work. In other cases, teachers banned in one zone moved and applied for work in another zone, and were taken on without question. The same was true in the universities and many other places. This meant that the education system that had been meant to work hard towards distributing democratic ideas was, quite often, slow to do so. In 1961, only one-third of all students in the University of Frankfurt believed in the future of democracy.

By the 1960s there was a new reaction to de-Nazification. Many of the young who had grown up in the new Germany were impatient with the 'year zero' policy. They wanted to know what their families had done in Nazi Germany, they wanted to clear the air. They were angry at the way de-Nazification had been sloppily applied. While some accepted that it might have been necessary to allow those who had been Nazis only in name to keep their jobs, they were unhappy that more prominent Nazis had been allowed to take quite significant jobs in the government (see page 32). Some students were unhappy at the numbers of ex-Nazis among the older teaching staff, members of staff who encouraged the formation of right-wing student groups that had distinctly Nazi policies, including anti-Semitism.

EXTEND YOUR KNOWLEDGE

Too successful?

In some areas, de-Nazification was too successful. The fact that national pride became so closely associated with the Nazis meant that it became hard for people in the FRG to express a sense of national pride. This was complicated by the fact that the separation of the FRG and the DRG, which was not supposed to be permanent, meant that the FRG saw itself as temporary – even the Basic Law was set up as a temporary expedient. These things contributed to an uncertainty about national identity, which had carried on even beyond unification. In 2001, the general secretary of the CDU said he was proud to be German. It sparked off a huge debate, with people trying to define exactly what part of being German could, or should, make a person proud.

EXTRACT

7 From an article in the *German Law Journal* written in 2008 by a number of contributors, all students or lecturers in law at Washington University.

In the newly constituted Federal Republic, much of the government structure retained the authoritarian outlines of the previous regime. The Allies' early efforts to purge the judiciary of former members of the National Socialist party failed to achieve even moderate success, as in some counties up to 95% of all jurists were former Nazis. The program of de-Nazification was eventually abandoned in the interest of maintaining law and order within the new Federal Republic, and many former party members were pardoned and allowed to re-enter the civil service. Former judges and prosecutors, themselves involved in the drafting or enforcement of the Race Laws, were assigned to posts in the new government. In some cases they had responsibilities for hearing the grievances of those they had persecuted during the war.

Because many of the former Nazi jurists were absorbed back into the system, often into high-ranking positions, they lacked any incentive to make amends for the past. The ease of their reincorporation into the legal system perhaps sent the signal that they had nothing for which they needed to make amends. They felt their involvement was justified or even necessary. For instance, Erich Schwinge, formerly a presiding judge at the Military Court in Vienna, became a law professor and in 1977 published a study defending the roles of military courts entitled *Military Justice in the National Socialist Era.*

Unsurprisingly, the judiciary of the new Republic was responsible for upholding a number of laws reminiscent of the old National Socialist era. The Law for the Prevention of Hereditary Diseases, which led to the sterilization of 350,000 people, was not repealed until 1974. The Federal Law on the Defence of the State, which sought to punish intentions to endanger the State was also upheld. This statute was broad in scope and encompassed strikes, protests, and any affiliation with the Communist party. A conviction of having 'intent to endanger the State' could have prevented an individual from the right to drive a car, receive a high school diploma, or to be admitted to college exams.

The nature of support for democracy in the FRG, 1949–89

At the end of the war, the German people had been living in a dictatorship since 1933. The penalties for having political opinions of their own had become increasingly severe during the period. Obedience and conformity were the safest options. The Nazis had told the German people that they did not matter as individuals, the German nation was all that mattered and they had to sacrifice themselves for it. They had been taught to see democracy as weak. At Potsdam, the Allies (even the USSR) agreed they wanted to return the country to democracy, although the ideas of each of the Allies about exactly what they meant by that were different. Not only that, but Germany's only experience of democracy had been under the Weimar government – and few people thought that had turned out well. For the first few years there was genuine concern that, despite its constitutional differences, the new government would be another Weimar, and it would fail as Weimar had.

The level of support for democracy in the FRG, as in Weimar Germany, can in some ways be seen in the turnout figures for elections, for they show whether people wanted to participate in the democratic process. The figures show a high level of turnout. The only time it was less than 84 percent was in 1949, when voting happened for the first time and some people were still stuck in old attitudes and nervous of the democratic process. In Britain over the same period, voter turnout was always lower, only going above 79 percent twice. Using this as a measure, there was a significant level of support for democracy between 1949 and 1989. Research by the Allensbach Institute (set up in 1947 to conduct surveys of public attitudes) showed that the number of people who believed that members of the Bundestag represented the public interest doubled between 1951 and 1964, while in the same period the number of people who believed that a monarchy should be restored fell from one-third to one-tenth. By the 1960s, surveys showed that the majority of Germans felt that the FRG represented the best time in German history and that most people believed that democracy was the best kind of government.

EXTEND YOUR KNOWLEDGE

Research institutes in the FRG
The Western Allies, especially the USA, wanted to set up public opinion research to measure, among other things, the attitudes of the German people to the democratisation process. The Americans provided training for researchers, even giving them grants to study market research in the USA. One of the first German research institutes was set up by Karl von Stackelberg in 1945: the Emnid Institute in Bielefeld. The Allensbach Institute was set up by Elizabeth Noelle and her husband Erich Neumann, who also trained in the USA and followed the research procedures just being worked out by George Gallup (Gallup Polls are still the most influential in the USA). Both research institutes are still in business. Some people mistrusted the findings of these institutes to start with. It was not until the 1960s that representatives from these institutes took part in televised debates before elections.

SOURCE

Turnout of voters in Bundestag elections from 1949 to 1987, given as the percentage of all people registered to vote who actually voted.

	1949	1953	1957	1961	1965	1969	1972	1976	1980	1983	1987
Turnout (%)	78.5	85.5	87.8	87.7	86.8	86.7	91.1	90.7	88.6	89.1	84.3

A Level Exam-Style Question Section B

How accurate is it to say that the years 1918 to 1933 and 1949 to 1989 gave Germans two very different experiences of democracy? (20 marks)

Tip
This question requires you to consider 'how accurate' and therefore produce evidence to support the statement and to oppose it.

Other measures of support

People in Germany in this period showed support for the idea of democracy in other ways. There is a distinction here, as in a consideration of the support for the Weimar government and the Weimar Constitution, between support for the idea of democracy and support for the particular government that this democracy has brought to power.

- People demonstrated against some of the changes that the government wanted to make that would restrict democracy and the civil liberties that they had under the Basic Law. For example, many people demonstrated against the Emergency Law that the government wanted to introduce all the way through the 1960s and even after it was made law in 1968. People were beginning to demand that the country live up to the ideals of democracy that were set up in the Basic Law.

- They marched in support of democracy and against repressive regimes in other countries, for example, the military junta that ruled Greece after 1967, and against their government having diplomatic or trade relations with these regimes, for example, South Africa under apartheid.

- They protested against the shift to *Ostpolitik* (see page 32) if it meant establishing relations with the USSR, because of the repressive communist regime in that country. This was a difficult issue for supporters of democracy because they were often in favour of reunification with the GDR and also in favour of helping to establish democracy in Soviet satellite states. So they approved of a realignment eastwards. However, they found it difficult to accept that such a realignment, at least at first, had to include the USSR, because of their influence in the GDR.

In the case of both Weimar Germany and the FRG, it is clear that there was support for the idea of democracy that was seen as a separate issue from support for the government in power, which was supposedly democratic.

ACTIVITY
KNOWLEDGE CHECK

Support for democracy in the FRG, 1949–89

1 List the ways that people supported democracy in the FRG between 1949 and 1989.

2 Explain how it was possible to support democracy in the democratic FRG at this time and yet not support the government.

ACTIVITY
SUMMARY

Attitudes to democracy

1 'Germans 1918 to 1989 were happier with a strong authoritarian government and did not care about democracy.'

a) Make a list of points you could make to support this statement.

b) Make a list of points you could make to oppose this statement.

In both cases, make sure that your examples cover Weimar Germany, Nazi Germany and the FRG.

c) Write a paragraph summing up your judgement of the accuracy of the statement.

Controlling opposition

2 Draw a diagram with three boxes labelled: 'Violent means', 'Persuasion', 'Legal control'.

a) For each box give at least one example of the use of these means of controlling opposition in Weimar Germany, Nazi Germany and the FRG.

b) Explain whether each example given is representative of the general nature of control by each government.

 WIDER READING

Carr, W. *A History of Germany 1815–1990*, Hodder Arnold (1991)

Lee, S.J. *Hitler and Nazi Germany*, Routledge (2009)

Williamson, D. *Germany: From Defeat to Partition 1945–63*, Routledge (2001)

You can find footage of British newsreels of the Kapp Putsch protest marches in the FRG if you search the internet using the terms 'Kapp Putsch' or 'Protest West Germany' plus a date (for example, 1968).

1.3 | Economic development and policies, 1918–89

KEY QUESTIONS

- How successfully did the Weimar Republic respond to economic challenges in the years 1918–32?

- How far did the Nazis control the economy in the years 1933–45?

- What effect did the creation of a 'social market' economy have on the Federal Republic in the years 1945–89?

INTRODUCTION

Between 1918 and 1989, the German economy was far from stable. It had to deal with the effects of two world wars and various international economic crises. Different governments had different economic policies that varied according to the current economic theories but also on the government of the time. Political theories and the domestic and foreign policies that the government was practising also affected its policy towards the economy. The following events seem unconnected, in time and place, but this chapter will show how they all had a part to play in the development of the German economy.

- In 1919, at the end of the First World War, the German economy was in a bad way. **Inflation** had made the currency – the mark – virtually worthless and many people were starving.

- In 1929, the US economy sank into the Great Depression.

- In 1933, the Nazis came to power in Germany and signed an agreement with I.G. Farben industries to subsidise the production of synthetic fuel.

- In 1937, Germany had full employment.

- In 1945, at the end of the Second World War, the German economy was in a bad way. Food was rationed and people were starving.

- In 1973, the Arab oil-producing states cut off trade with any country that had a pro-Israeli foreign policy.

- In 1979, the **European Monetary System** came into operation among members of the **European Economic Community**, in an attempt to control a worldwide financial crisis.

1919 - 28 June: Treaty of Versailles signed

31 July: Weimar Constitution passed

1924 - 30 August: Rentenmark replaced by new currency, Reichsmark (RM)

1933 -
30 January: Hitler becomes chancellor of Germany

1935 - Unemployment down to just over two million (ten percent of the population)

| 1915 | 1920 | 1925 | 1930 | 1935 | 1940 |

1923 - Hyperinflation causes the value of the mark to fall rapidly

15 October: Rentenmark Decree replaces the mark with the temporary Rentenmark. Confidence in money begins to rise again

1932 -
Unemployment reaches over 5.5 million (30 percent of the population)

1934 - 2 August: Hindenburg dies; Hitler becomes führer

HOW SUCCESSFULLY DID THE WEIMAR REPUBLIC RESPOND TO ECONOMIC CHALLENGES IN THE YEARS 1918–32?

In 1918, the German economy was in trouble. The war, and circumstances surrounding it, had hit the economy hard. The government had spent all of its gold reserves on the war, and had been printing more and more money. In June 1914, there were just over 6,300 million marks in circulation; by December 1918, this had increased to just over 33,000 million, causing severe inflation. At the end of the war there were 150 printing firms with 2,000 printing presses running day and night to make enough new banknotes. This meant that wages, and savings, lost value as prices shot up. Some people became less willing to spend money as their wages were worth far less. This was bad for trade. Trade all over Europe had been disrupted by the war, which meant businesses suffered and people lost their jobs. This was made worse when the war ended and the production of war goods, such as ammunition, ended with it. Farm production had dropped by about 20 percent during the war and industrial output had almost halved. The loss of both agricultural and industrial land as a result of the Treaty of Versailles slowed the economy. During the war, a **black market** had developed as inflation shot up and goods became scarce. Immediately after the war, with the turmoil of strikes and political unrest and the changes of government (see Chapter 1), the economy spiralled out of control. The economy had three main phases between 1918 and 1932: 1918 to 1923, 1924 to 1928 and 1929 to the end of 1932.

Economic crises and government response, 1918–23

From 1918 to 1923 was a period of rising inflation in Germany. The cost of everything went up with increasing speed, the worst period being during 1923. However, the economy is not just about prices. Wages, savings and employment are also highly significant, as is the value of money itself. Between 1918 and 1923, the economic downturn, the ending of war production and soldiers leaving the army drove up the number of unemployed and many employers (in an effort to stay in business, or simply to make as much money as possible) reduced wages. So wages dropped, and the value of wages, savings and payments, such as pensions, also dropped.

What were the crises and how did the government try to deal with them?

- **Social welfare**: After the war the government set up retraining schemes for those who had fought in the war, and it provided loans to help those leaving the army until they could find work. It also set up pension payments for the wounded, widows and orphans. The Weimar government was a liberal one and so made efforts to make adequate provision, with national committees to oversee care in the Länder. Both the federal government and the Länder provided layers of support. There were a variety of social welfare programmes for different groups. For example, at the beginning of

KEY TERM

Black market
Illegal trade. People who buy and sell on the black market trade illegally, avoiding government taxes and price regulation. Black market trade is often carried on as barter (exchanging goods) and a black market often favours well-off people who have valuables to exchange for scarce goods.

1949 – 22 May: FRG set up
7 October: GDR set up

1989 – 9 November: fall of Berlin Wall

| 1945 | 1950 | 1955 | 1960 | 1965 | 1990 |

1945 – 7 May: end of Second World War in Europe
Germany and Berlin divided into Allied zones

1961 – 12–13 August: Berlin Wall goes up

1920 there were an estimated 1,537,000 disabled veterans and 1,945,000 survivors not classed as disabled. The government looked after them with a mixture of lump sum payments and pensions. By 1924, the government was still supporting about 768,000 disabled veterans, 420,000 war widows with 1,020,000 children, and 190,000 parents of dead soldiers. About ten percent of the population were receiving federal welfare payments and many more were on regional poor relief. All of these payments had to be made by a government (whether at federal or regional level) that had to go into debt to make them.

- **Debt and reparations**: The government had borrowed heavily during the war; by 1918, it owed about 150 billion marks (three times what it had owed in 1914). To add to this debt, the policy of reparations laid down by the Treaty of Versailles (see page 11) put the government even deeper into debt. At first, the government tried to meet the payments, and carried on borrowing and printing money. If the government had tried to change this economic policy, it would have been unable to make any payments at all. From 1921 on, Germany was entangled in negotiations with the Allies about how much it should pay, how much it could pay, and when payments could and should be made. The Allies, especially France, felt that Germany was deliberately trying to avoid any payments at all. They argued that the German economy had problems, but so did other European countries, especially France. Until 1924, reparations were paid in kind, for example with coal, wood and railway carriages.

- **The Ruhr**: In January 1923, Germany failed to deliver its reparation payments in full. When it fell behind in 1921, the London Ultimatum of the Allies had been that payments should be met or the Allies would occupy the Ruhr, which was vital to the German economy because of its coal and the industries based there. In 1923, the French did just that with the aid of Belgian troops. The government instantly stopped all reparation payments to France (but not to the other Allies), told all German officials not to accept orders from non-Germans and urged the workers in the Ruhr to passive resistance, for example, working slowly, strikes and sabotage. The French replied by cutting the Ruhr off from the rest of Germany by setting up a border, patrolled by armed forces, and taking control of the postal and telegraph services. They then tried to solve the problems of worker resistance by using force or bringing in their own workers. Neither France nor Germany benefited from the situation. In 1923, the new German coalition government called for a stop to passive resistance tactics and began negotiations with the French.

EXTEND YOUR KNOWLEDGE

The occupation of the Ruhr

The occupation of the Ruhr by French and Belgian troops diverted German distrust away from the government and towards the occupiers. The behaviour of the French was certainly harsh; but then they had been treated harshly under German occupation and most were convinced that Germany was deliberately avoiding paying the reparations that were due. German resistance to French occupation did not improve the attitude of the French.

In 1923, a series of reports of the behaviour of the occupiers were published, based on 90 testimonies made under oath and supported with photographic evidence. It suggested the occupiers were guilty not only of a callous disregard to the living conditions of workers, for example, providing very little in the way of food and shelter, but that they also committed murder and rape.

- **Hyperinflation**: The crisis in the Ruhr escalated inflation into hyperinflation – inflation that spiralled out of control. Prices were going up several times a day. A newspaper that cost one mark on 1 May 1922 cost 100,000 marks by 1 September 1923 and 700 billion marks by 17 November of that year. People lost their faith in money entirely and came to rely increasingly on barter and the black market. As more and more people used the black market, it could not supply enough for everyone, and its prices (which were always high) rose so much that only the rich could afford to 'buy' on it. The economy was doing badly, the government was floundering, but those with goods to sell on the black market made huge profits. As well as the black market, towns, regions and even businesses began to issue their own Notgeld or 'emergency money'. Even the government cut back on staff; about 750,000 federal and regional government employees lost their jobs. All those on fixed payments, including social welfare, suffered as these payments lost their value. Although the poor were worst hit because they had nothing to fall back on, well-off families also suffered. The head of the von Lingans family, who owned significant amounts of land and had a large number of servants, had to close the house, sack the servants and move to Berlin to take a job in the offices of a factory that made ball bearings. His family was not starving, but it had suffered a significant loss of both wealth and prestige.

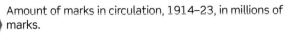

SOURCE 1

Amount of marks in circulation, 1914–23, in millions of marks.

Year	June 1914	Dec 1918	Dec 1921	Dec 1922	June 1923
Number of marks (in millions)	6,323	33,306	122,963	1,295,228	17,393,000

SOURCE 2

This photo shows a woman lighting her stove with marks in 1923. There was a point when marks became a cheaper fuel than coal or firewood.

A change of government

In August 1923 the crisis was at its worse. The government collapsed. The new coalition government, with Gustav Stresemann of the DVP (see Chapter 1) as chancellor, benefited from the Emergency Decree of 10 August which gave his government powers that included postponing Reichstag meetings and governing by decree if necessary. Possibly the most significant policy decision of the new coalition was the use of emergency decrees to avoid tying up decision-making in the Reichstag. Using decrees, the government could act more rapidly and decisively than any coalition in the past, because it did could take decisions without the need to negotiate among the various coalition members.

ACTIVITY
KNOWLEDGE CHECK

Economic crises, 1918–23

1 Draw a spider diagram to show all of the factors that led to the hyperinflation of 1923. Colour code them according to whether they are economic factors, social factors and political factors.

2 Decide which factor you think had the greatest impact and explain your choice.

Policies for recovery, 1924–28

Stresemann was chancellor and foreign minister in August 1923. This coalition government only lasted until November 1923, but Stresemann was also asked to serve as foreign minister in the next government. He was a stabilising force in the government, urging compromise on political ideals to work together to solve Germany's problems.

Making money work

Stresemann's first significant policy measures were undertaken to regain control over money. The almost worthless mark was withdrawn and, as a temporary measure, the Rentenmark took its place in October 1923. People who still had savings objected to the Rentenmark because it had such low value against one gold mark. The various forms of 'emergency money' were banned.

The introduction of the Rentenmark was overseen by Hjalmar Schacht, who was made president of the Reichsbank in December 1923. The currency change had the effect of restoring faith in the German currency, both at home and abroad. Germans changed their hoarded foreign currency and 'emergency money' for the Rentenmark and prices settled. The government also used emergency decrees to control rents, wages and prices, which also helped to stabilise the currency. Schacht later oversaw the change to the Reichsmark (RM) in August 1924.

TIMELINE – POLICIES OF STRESEMANN AND THE GOVERNMENT THAT AFFECTED THE ECONOMY

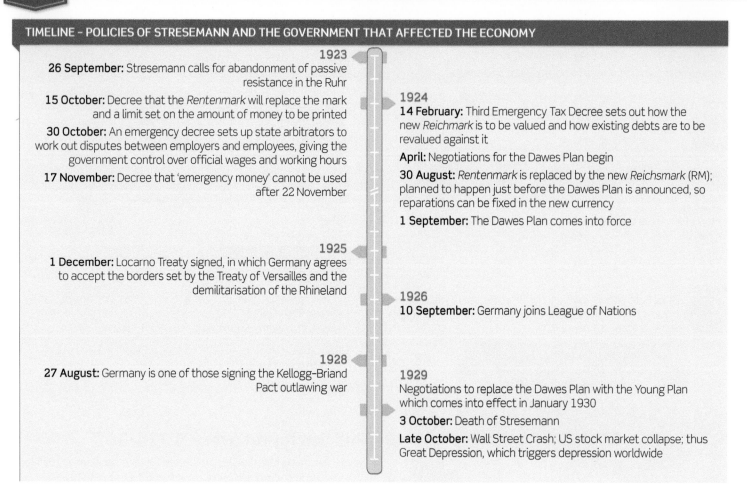

1923

26 September: Stresemann calls for abandonment of passive resistance in the Ruhr

15 October: Decree that the *Rentenmark* will replace the mark and a limit set on the amount of money to be printed

30 October: An emergency decree sets up state arbitrators to work out disputes between employers and employees, giving the government control over official wages and working hours

17 November: Decree that 'emergency money' cannot be used after 22 November

1924

14 February: Third Emergency Tax Decree sets out how the new *Reichmark* is to be valued and how existing debts are to be revalued against it

April: Negotiations for the Dawes Plan begin

30 August: *Rentenmark* is replaced by the new *Reichsmark* (RM); planned to happen just before the Dawes Plan is announced, so reparations can be fixed in the new currency

1 September: The Dawes Plan comes into force

1925

1 December: Locarno Treaty signed, in which Germany agrees to accept the borders set by the Treaty of Versailles and the demilitarisation of the Rhineland

1926

10 September: Germany joins League of Nations

1928

27 August: Germany is one of those signing the Kellogg–Briand Pact outlawing war

1929

Negotiations to replace the Dawes Plan with the Young Plan which comes into effect in January 1930

3 October: Death of Stresemann

Late October: Wall Street Crash; US stock market collapse; thus Great Depression, which triggers depression worldwide

Why was foreign policy vital to the economy?

Stresemann is often called the architect of Germany's economic recovery, yet he was chancellor for only a brief period, then he was foreign minister. However, foreign policy was vital to the economy's recovery. The **Dawes Plan** and the **Young Plan** made reparations more manageable and provided loans to rebuild the economy. Also, Stresemann's other foreign policy moves (see the timeline above) made Germany an acceptable foreign power again, so other countries were happier to lend Germany money and make trade agreements. While this helped to produce stability, and stability was vital to recovery, it meant that the economic recovery was based on loans, many from the USA. Other European countries, for example, France and Britain, were also rebuilding their economies with the help of US loans – the US was called 'the world's banker'. However, that did not make the level of borrowing any less dangerous should the USA want to call in the loans.

The recovery of business

The government also helped businesses to make changes that made them more efficient and profitable. Big businesses were more able to ride out economic problems. In the early 1920s, however, many small businesses collapsed; in 1924 there were more bankruptcies than in the previous five years altogether. The surviving big businesses began to form **cartels** whose fixed prices helped to stabilise the economy. Some cartels organised themselves into associations of shared interests. The biggest was I.G. Farben, set up in 1925, which united various chemical-based cartels that made everything from rayon to dynamite and fertiliser. Many factories were rebuilt with the latest mass-production assembly lines and 'time and motion' thinking that was taking hold in the USA. By 1925, the chemical industry was producing one-third more than in 1913, and almost two-thirds more by 1930. However, recovery did not mean that all was well in business. There were significant levels of dispute between business owners and workers all through the Weimar period, with workers pressing for better conditions and owners trying to cut wages and extend working hours. Strikes and lockouts were common. There were fewer of both in the more prosperous years of 1926–27, but they never went away despite the government setting up state arbitration in October 1923.

KEY TERMS

Dawes Plan (1924) and Young Plan (1929)
Agreements made between Germany and the Allies that reduced the amount to be paid in reparations and extended the time in which to pay it. The plans also included US loans to help Germany's economic recovery.

Cartel
A groups of businesses in the same industry or retail sector that made agreements to set and control prices. This provided some stability because it stopped prices moving as much. However, it also meant that cartels could fix higher prices than they would have charged if they had operated as separate, competing businesses. In the mid-1920s, there were 2,500 cartels.

EXTEND YOUR KNOWLEDGE

State arbitration

The government arbitration boards, set up in October 1923, marked a significant change from the agreement made by Ebert with industry and the trade unions (see Chapter 1). This agreement had fixed working hours at eight hours a day but had left the negotiation of wages and the management of disputes to those involved. Now, the government was to settle wages and any other matter under dispute. Between 1924 and 1929, 60,648 cases were taken to the arbitration boards. At first the boards tended to favour the employers, but after 1924 they tended to make compromise rulings. The rulings were usually accepted, but in 1928 industrialists in the Ruhr refused to accept a compromise ruling and locked their workers out of the factories. Eventually they offered the workers a compromise themselves.

Trade recovery

At first it was difficult for Germany to establish trade links, especially with Britain and France, because of bad feeling after the war. There was a shifting in trade worldwide (set off by the US policy of **isolationism**) that led to many countries introducing **tariffs** on foreign goods, and Germany suffered from heavier tariffs initially as part of the reaction of many countries to Germany's part in the war. However, Germany was producing steel and chemicals that other countries needed. With Germany's admission to the **League of Nations** and the other international agreements that Stresemann set up (see timeline, page 66), German exports were back to their 1913 levels of ten billion marks by 1926, and by 1929 exports were 34 percent higher than in 1913.

Agriculture

Farming was still a significant employer in the 1920s; between a third and a quarter of all workers were agricultural workers. Like the businesses, the bigger farms managed better than the smaller ones. They could invest in new machinery and farming techniques. Many small farmers were heavily in debt and could not afford to pay the interest on their loans or even, in some cases, their taxes. Big landowners, such as President Hindenburg, had political influence that enabled them to block farming reforms where they did not work in their interest, such as the 1918 Reich Settlement Law that made landowners sell land to the government to be redistributed among their poorest tenants. They simply strung out the negotiations over the land sales. The influence of the wealthy landowners also allowed them to press for high grain subsidies that benefited most those with big farms.

Government spending

The new economy was built on foreign loans, many of them short term, with the expectation that they would be renewed as the world economy improved. As well as borrowing heavily, the government also spent heavily. It subsidised grain production, it subsidised industry and it spent heavily on social welfare, providing housing and benefits for the poorest. It funded this by borrowing and taxation. Even with economic recovery, though, most ordinary people were not as well off as they had been before the war, so they paid less tax and resented the idea of tax rises. In 1913, the lowest tax band was made up of 47 percent of taxpayers; this hit 62 percent in 1926 and was 55 percent in 1928. This meant that the government had to borrow money it might otherwise have made by raising taxes. This was another way in which the economic recovery was flawed. Not only was it built on foreign borrowing, but it was kept afloat by government support. The government even had its own bank to provide federal and regional funding; this helped businesses for only as long as the government could keep lending them money. A final problem was that industrial expansion and production was damaged by the constant disputes between businesses and workers, which affected productivity and drove wages up until 1930, when the depression led to such high unemployment that people were willing to work for any wage at all.

ACTIVITY
KNOWLEDGE CHECK

Economic recovery?

1 Draw a spider diagram with a leg each for agriculture, trade, industry and money. For each one show a way in which it recovered in the years 1924 to 1928, and a way in which it still had problems.

2 Describe the most significant problem that the recovery had, giving reasons why you see it as the most significant.

KEY TERMS

Isolationism
Interacting as little as possible with other countries, politically and economically.

Tariff
Tax on foreign goods that makes them more expensive and so encourages people to buy goods made in their own country.

League of Nations
An international organisation set up by the Allies after the First World War to work for international co-operation and peace. All of the signatories of the peace treaties that ended the war had to agree to join the League, but Germany was excluded and was not asked to join until 1926.

A Level Exam-Style Question Section A

How accurate is it to say that the years 1918 to 1929 were a period of economic disruption followed by a period of stability and consolidation? (20 marks)

Tip
'How accurate' is asking you to consider evidence to support the statement and evidence to contradict it. Be sure to provide both.

What impact did the Great Depression have on the Weimar Republic, 1929–32?

The impact of the worldwide depression on Germany

In 1929, the US economy collapsed and US banks not only stopped renewing short-term foreign lending, but also called in loans from abroad. All of the countries it was lending to were hit hard and in similar ways (see Figure 3.1).

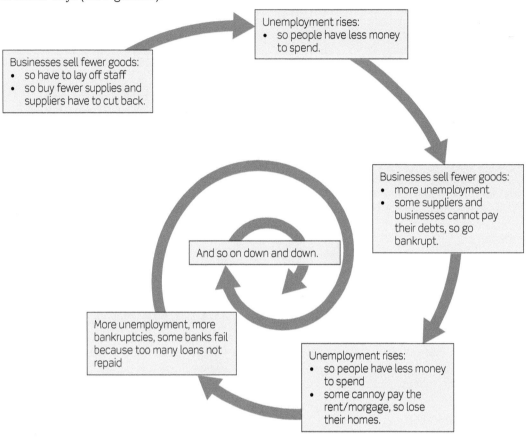

Figure 3.1 The downward economic spiral of the Depression.

SOURCE 3 Unemployment figures (in thousands) and percentage of workforce unemployed, 1921–33.

Year	Unemployed (in thousands)	Workforce unemployed (%)
1921	346	1.8
1922	215	1.1
1923	818	4.1
1924	927	4.9
1925	682	3.4
1926	2,025	10.0
1927	1,312	6.2
1928	1,391	6.3
1929	1,899	8.5
1930	3,076	14.0
1931	4,520	21.9
1932	5,603	29.9
1933	4,804	25.9

In Germany industrial production fell, slowly at first, then more rapidly. By the end of 1932, it was about half its 1928 levels. Unemployment rose in the same period (see Source 3) and wages fell by 20–30 percent. However, because prices also fell, real wages only fell by about 14 percent. The parties in the Grand Coalition government (see Chapter 1), without Stresemann, were arguing not co-operating. The government failed to cope with the Depression because it could not make decisions or act quickly, and President Hindenburg was resistant to more government by emergency decree. The coalition collapsed and was replaced in 1930 by one led by Chancellor Brüning, who suggested cuts in government spending (especially on social welfare), wage cuts and higher taxes. These policies were rejected by the Reichstag. Reluctantly Hindenburg, who agreed with Brüning's policies, went back to government by decree in July 1930 in order to put Brüning's policies into practice.

EXTRACT 1

From *Modern Germany*, written by the historian V.R. Berghahn and published in 1987.

The sudden recall of large sums of American money had quickly caused the collapse of the loan-induced prosperity of the late 1920s. The victory of the Nazis in September 1930, which alarmed many foreign investors, accelerated this process. Since many German banks and industrial enterprises had used short-term credit to finance long-term investment programmes, the withdrawal of loans quickly caused a cash-flow crisis. Soon holders of German accounts also rushed to their banks to draw out their money. Some institutions were forced into bankruptcy and the international banking system was in complete disarray. In their attempt to stave off disaster, many firms began to shed parts of their workforce. Those who were unable to solve their liquidity [cash] problems in this way and who found demand collapsing around them were forced into liquidation [closing down], thus throwing more people out of work.

Brüning believed that the best way of combating economic collapse was to adopt a policy of deflation. Above all, the budget had to be balanced. If state revenue declined, state expenditure had to be cut. If social security contributions fell because of unemployment, benefits had to be reduced. Civil servants and teachers who had tenured [guaranteed] positions and could not be dismissed had their salaries cut.

Did government policies work?

Brüning's policies brought **deflation** but avoided devaluing the currency, which he feared would bring inflation, or even hyperinflation, as in 1923. One of the few benefits of his policies was that, as Germany's depression deepened, it was clear to all countries that it would not be able to meet any reparation payments or even repay loans from other countries. On 1 July 1931 the Hoover Moratorium, an international agreement, suspended the need for Germany to pay back loans, or to pay interest on them, for a year. In December 1931, leading German trade unionists suggested a plan for job creation, as in the USA, to boost the economy. Others suggested **devaluing the currency**. Brüning's response was another emergency decree that introduced wage cuts, rent cuts and tax rises. It also said reparations would not be paid for the next year. Brüning's policies in the years 1930–32 did not work; they simply deepened the recession.

Industrial production fell, prices fell and exports fell, all by around 50 percent. Unemployment rose to its highest level ever in 1932.

In late May, Brüning was replaced by von Papen who introduced some tax concessions and subsidies for businesses that created new jobs and produced some economic improvement. However, the government was by now caught up in political problems that made it hard to focus on the economy and produce a coherent policy. In December 1932, the chancellor changed again. The new chancellor, von Schleicher, appointed a Reich Commissioner for employment who drew up a list of public works to be financed by the government in order to create employment. He was given a budget of RM500 million, but he had not put anything into effect before the Nazis came to power and changed the system of government entirely in a very short space of time.

The fact that coalition government had failed, and government was increasingly by decree, made the Weimar government look a failure. The policies imposed by decree were hard on the German people and also did not seem to be working, making this system of government, which had been intended only for emergencies, very unpopular. President Hindenburg stayed popular; the ever-changing chancellors and ministers were held responsible for the problems. The government's unpopularity led to a rise in the popularity of more extreme parties, which led to the rise of the Nazis and Hitler (see Chapter 1).

Changing living standards, 1918–32

During the First World War there were severe shortages. It was hard to farm productively when all of the horses had been requisitioned for the Front. Much of the food produced also went to the Front. Allied blockades of ports stopped supplies getting into Germany. Food shortages meant 'alternative foods', such as 'K-brot' bread made from potatoes, oats and sometimes even straw, were common. Infant mortality and stillbirths, often due to the poor health of the mothers, were high. Malnutrition was common. For example, in one district of Berlin, 90 percent of all children aged between two and six years were undernourished. So the Weimar government inherited a country where the standard of living, especially for the poor, was very low. The war government also had to cope with the need to support a large number of war veterans and dependents of those who had died in the war (see pages 63–64).

Living standards vary widely at all times depending on social class, wealth and social setting, for example, town or countryside. The factors by which the standard of living is judged are also complex. Wages are complex because of the need to consider other factors, such as the benefits a job provides. For example,

KEY TERMS

Deflation
Keeping prices low by reducing government spending.

Devaluing a currency
This means reducing the value of a currency against another currency (usually the US dollar). It makes goods from the devaluing country more attractive to other countries because they cost less.

is a farm worker's home tied to the job? Are wages backed up by savings? What do the wages have to cover, for example, does the family pay rent? From 1919, the German government ran an analysis of the standard of living in Germany based on the cost of a basket of goods for a family of five. To allow for comparison all through the period, the standard of living sections here will take a more detailed look at the cost of living survey against wages, before considering other economic effects on the standard of living in each period. When considering food, it must be remembered that for many of the poorest, food was mainly bread, potatoes and other vegetables. Meat (a small piece of sausage or some bacon) was possible once a week at most.

The Weimar government provided benefits for the poorest. It regulated pensions. It did its best to cope with the large number of people who had been dependent on those who died in the war. Immediately after the war, these measures meant that the standard of living improved, more people were employed and wages rose. However, as inflation galloped away, it was impossible for the standard of living to do anything but drop sharply. As unemployment rose, especially long-term unemployment, many people scraped by, by doing badly paid jobs with long hours. Women, especially single parents, often had to take in home-based work, which had no hours at all but was paid by the 'piece'. For example, a woman who covered metal buttons with fabric for the fashion trade would be paid a set amount for every 50 buttons. To make any money at all, even if their children helped, these women often had to work all day and some of the night. Even in factories, which were more regulated, the eight-hour working day, established in 1918, had all but disappeared by 1924. While it was still the law, workers could not afford to press for it and employers had never wanted it.

EXTRACT

2 From *Rethinking the Weimar Republic*, written by the historian Anthony McElligott and published in 2014.

These living conditions were tied to whether or not one had regular work. For many working people under the republic, employment *insecurity* was the norm, and not vice versa. Apart from 1922 and 1928 when there was full employment, most workers regularly experienced bouts of unemployment (between 1925 and 1928, the level of unemployment doubled from 3.4 per cent of the working population to 6.3 per cent and peaked in 1926 at 10 per cent), and these periods got longer for certain sections of the labour force in the second half of the 1920s (even before the mass unemployment of the early 1930s). ...

One man's recollection of life in Hanover between the wars reveals the constant money worries of a working-class family suffering from chronic penury [poverty]. His father had become unemployed in 1931 and remained unemployed for four years. After paying the rent from the weekly unemployment benefit of 17.50 RM, the family had barely ten marks left over for food and other necessities. The worry over money prematurely aged his mother, and it blighted his early childhood, even after his father found work in 1935. Even then, money remained scarce.

SOURCE

4 Wages, the cost of living and real wages 1913–33 (1928 = 100; statistics before and after vary in relation to this so are a percentage of 1928 values). Real wages are wages with the changing cost of living built in.

Year	Wages (as % of 1928)		Cost of living (as % of 1928)	Real wages (as % of 1928)
	Hourly	Weekly		
1913	53	61	66	93
1924	No data	No data	86	n/a
1925	77	75	93	81
1926	82	78	93	84
1927	90	88	97	89
1928	100	100	100	100
1929	106	103	101	102
1930	103	95	97	97
1931	95	84	89	94
1932	80	69	80	86
1933	77	71	78	91

Many families lived in cramped housing with shared toilets and washing facilities. The poorest shared one room and had no running water at all. In Berlin in 1925 (population just over four million), there were 130,500 people who were lodgers and 44,600 who just paid to sleep in a bed, with none of the other facilities of a lodger. The situation was similar in 1929. Children were often expected to give up their bed to a lodger.

Skilled workers and low-level clerical workers also experienced rising unemployment and many ended up spending all of their savings and having to claim benefit. Although the number of clerical workers expanded rapidly in the 1920s, men still lost their jobs in this sector as many businesses preferred to employ women, who were paid significantly less. Some small family businesses managed to scrape by, especially if they had savings to fall back on. Many did not and ended up losing their business and sometimes their homes too. Everyone suffered from the hyperinflation, even the very rich, except those who exploited the situation. For example, black marketers; people who bought up property and crammed tenants into it while providing few, if any, amenities such as running water; industrialists who could afford to buy up small businesses and exploit workers who feared losing their jobs. These people could do well and were used as targets by political opponents of the Weimar government.

TIMELINE – MAJOR SOCIAL LEGISLATION, 1918–32

1920

May: Reich Pension Law regulates pensions, especially those paid to war veterans, war widows and parents of dead soldiers, and is linked not to the rank of the soldiers (as previous pensions were) but to the jobs before they joined up

1922

February: Labour Exchange Law sets up government offices to provide training and help find work for the unemployed; it puts forward the idea that people have a right to work

1924

February: Economic Enabling Law restructures unemployment benefit and sets rates for employers' contributions

Reich Social Welfare Law pulls together all of the different post-war benefits and relief systems, federal and regional (for example, poor relief, maternity care), and sets up municipal welfare offices to administer them

1927

July: Unemployment Insurance Law introduces unemployment insurance to give benefit to all those out of work, not just those temporarily unemployed due to sickness

THINKING HISTORICALLY Causation (5a)

Interrelations

Causes never simply come one after another. They are often present simultaneously and have an effect on one another. Sometimes new causes develop and interact with existing ones.

Think about the following causes of the collapse of the Weimar Republic:

- the problems of coalition government
- economic problems, 1918–23
- the way rebuilding the economy was financed
- the problems that never went away
- the Depression and its effects
- the rise of extremist parties.

Work in groups to produce a diagram of causes and the links between them.

- On an A3 piece of paper, write all of the causes of the collapse of the Weimar Republic. Write these in boxes, the size of which will reflect how long they were a relevant factor. For example, if you argue that 'the problems of coalition government' had been an important factor since the end of the war, then it will be quite a big box, whereas 'the rise of extremist parties' would be a lot smaller. Spread these boxes over the page.

- Make links between all of the causes. Draw lines between the boxes and annotate them to explain how the causes are connected and in what ways each affected and altered the other. For example, between 'the Depression' and 'the way rebuilding the economy was financed' you could write something like: 'The Depression meant the USA called in loans it had made and Germany could not repay the high level of loans it had from the USA to finance rebuilding.'

Answer the following questions:

1 How do the causes differ in their nature? (Think in terms of events, developments, beliefs, states of affairs.)

2 How do the causes differ in the roles they played in causing the collapse of the Weimar government? (Think about whether each cause created the right conditions, was a trigger for events, or acted in some other way.)

3 Write a 200-word paragraph explaining how important it is to recognise the relationships between causes. Give examples from your diagram. Try to include connective phrases such as: 'this created conditions conducive to…', 'this triggered an immediate reaction…', 'this made the development of that situation more/less likely'.

EXTEND YOUR KNOWLEDGE

The cost of living survey
The survey was of 560 local authority districts all over Germany, 497 of which were towns with more than 10,000 inhabitants. At first surveys were taken monthly, then (from 1922) twice a month, then (from March 1923) weekly, then (at the height of inflation) twice a week. The fact that the intervals reduced so rapidly shows how unstable the economy was in 1922–23. The cost of living was measured against prices in 1914 for a basket of goods for a family of five: two adults and three children aged 18 months, 7 years old and 12 years old. The survey covered food, heating, lighting and accommodation. From April 1922, clothing was added. However, furniture, transport, school and recreational spending (on newspapers and cigarettes, for example) were never in the survey. This is significant when the price of a one-mark tram ride in Berlin doubled between 1918 and 1919, was seven marks in July 1920, ten marks in July 1921, 40 marks in July 1922 and 10,000 marks in July 1923.

ACTIVITY
KNOWLEDGE CHECK

The standard of living
1 What does Extract 2 suggest about living standards for the poorest in the years 1918–33?

2 Use Sources 3 and 4 to write a description of how real wages moved between 1925 and 1933 and how, if at all, it relates to the unemployment statistics.

HOW FAR DID THE NAZIS CONTROL THE ECONOMY IN THE YEARS 1933–45?

How did the Nazis attempt economic recovery in the years 1933–36?

The Nazis came to power promising economic recovery and they wanted to achieve it as soon as possible. They did not have to face the issue of reparations; in 1932, Brüning had said Germany could not pay and, at a conference in Lausanne, the Allies agreed that the Depression made reparation payments impossible. While this was good for the economy, although Germany had always been paying as little as possible, Hjalmar Schacht (one of the Weimar government officials that the Nazis kept as president of the Reichsbank) still had to pay the government debt on foreign borrowing and fell behind on this. In 1934, Germany failed to pay its US debts and trade with the USA collapsed. This did not matter as much to the Nazis as it had to previous governments – the Nazis were not intending to rely on foreign trade. Schacht drew up a 'New Plan', making trade treaties with other countries, such as Hungary and Yugoslavia, which involved exchanging goods rather than paying for imports.

The Nazis' first priority was securing political security (see Chapter 1), but they still announced their first Four-Year Plan on 1 January 1933, with the aim of achieving **autarky** as soon as possible. Their most important targets were unemployment and agriculture.

KEY TERM

Autarky
Economic self-sufficiency without the need to rely on imports in any area of life, from food to petrol to electricity.

Creating employment
Work was one of the major economic issues and the Nazis soon had an impact on employment statistics.

How did the Nazis have such an effect on unemployment statistics? Firstly, the Depression had hit its lowest point and turned around. Businesses were employing people again. Second, the Nazis manipulated the statistics. The definition of 'workforce' changed dramatically as Jewish people were no longer allowed to work in the civil service or in other occupations. This took them out of the workforce statistics. Women were discouraged from working and married women who left work, or were sacked, did not count in the workforce statistics either. Third, the Nazis created work and

SOURCE 5 Unemployment figures (in thousands) and percentage of workforce unemployed, 1930–36.

Year	Unemployed (in thousands)	Workforce unemployed (%)
1930	3,076	14.0
1931	4,520	21.9
1932	5,603	29.9
1933	4,804	25.9
1934	2,718	13.5
1935	2,151	10.3
1936	1,593	7.4

SOURCE 6 RAD workers on the autobahns and other building projects did manual labour and were deliberately provided with the minimum of equipment to toughen them up and make the work last longer. This photo was one of many in a book published in several languages intended as a souvenir of the Olympic Games in 1936.

encouraged businesses to do the same, especially temporary work for the long-term unemployed. Reichsarbeitsdienst (Reich Labour Service, or RAD) schemes for unemployed men and women provided manual work, often for less pay than unemployment pay, with very basic food and accommodation in labour camps that were either tents or barracks. Their road-building schemes, tied to increased car and truck manufacture, created work and improved communications, which helped to move goods and raw materials more efficiently.

EXTEND YOUR KNOWLEDGE

Building the autobahns
Nazi propaganda stressed the autobahn building scheme's role in ending unemployment. The Nazis wanted a new, efficient road system to move goods around the country more easily (to support other industries) and also, later, to allow the army to move around more rapidly. The project was slow to get going and did not produce as many roads as intended. Between December 1933 and January 1935, the maximum number of workers on this project at any one time was 84,000 – there were often fewer. But the road and vehicle building did help business. Between 1934 and 1936, 126,000 trucks were built. Only 15,700 went to the army.

Managing agriculture
Agriculture was important to the Nazi desire for autarky, so agricultural reforms were part of the first Four-Year Plan. In his first weeks in office, the minister of agriculture, Alfred Hugenburg, increased import tariffs on agricultural produce, making German produce cheaper; he banned banks repossessing farms from farmers in debt, to keep them farming; and he made margarine manufacturers put butter from German farmers in their margarine. Hugenberg resigned in May 1933, so it was his replacement, Richard Darré, who set up the Reichsnährstand (Reich Food Estate, or RNS) to regulate food production and distribution of farm produce, as well as setting prices and farm wages. The RNS could fine people up to RM100,000 for not conforming. It also set up Reich agencies to control the importing of farm produce. Work creation schemes sent people, especially young women, to work

on farms as well as on building projects. Government control of food and prices was not welcomed by everyone. Not all farmers wanted to be told what to produce and what price to sell it for. However, the measure had an effect. In 1928, German farmers provided 68 percent of all farm produce in the country; by 1934, this was 80 percent.

Managing business and the workers
Some big businesses, such as the iron and steel industry and I.G. Farben, supported the Nazis. Others, for example those depending on exports, were less happy. Some suffered due to measures to help small businesses. So, some department stores made 80 percent less in 1934 than they had in 1929 because the 1933 Law for the Protection of Retail Trade stopped the building of new stores and banned the expansion of existing ones. Nazi propaganda discouraged using department stores because small businesses had supported Hitler. Most owners of big stores had not.

Unions had been a problem for big business in the Weimar Republic; there had been wage disputes, disputes over hours, strikes and lockouts. Such actions meant the loss of millions of working days, from 1,222 million (the least) in 1926 to 36,198 million (the most) in 1924. Many of these businesses, including I.G. Farben, had backed Hitler and were expecting him to act decisively to cut the unions down to size. On the other hand, many workers had voted for the Nazis, too, and had hopes that the Nazis would provide not only work, but good working conditions and wages. The Nazis did not contradict them, even making 1 May, a traditional Socialist workers' festival, an official holiday in 1933. On 6 May, they announced that there was now only one union – the Deutsche Arbeitsfront (German Labour Front, or DAF). Joining the DAF was 'voluntary', but it became increasingly difficult for non-members to get work. The DAF, and its organisation of working conditions, made it possible for big businesses to exploit workers more – they could set their own working conditions. The Reich Trustees of Labour were a last resort and usually sided with the employers. The DAF became a powerful force, as part of the 'rewards' system of controlling the people (see Chapter 2).

The crisis of 1935–36

Schacht's shifting of Germany's trade to south east Europe and his use of exchanging goods meant that trade initially improved. By 1935, however, many countries were demanding cash, not an exchange of goods, for their goods. For example, Bulgaria began to demand cash not goods for their oil. Germany was still not completely self-sufficient, and rearming and work creation meant that it still needed to import raw materials. Worse still, it also needed to import food – there were growing shortages of fats and meat. In 1935, Schacht, who wanted to keep borrowing as low as possible, had to choose between food and raw-material imports. This was a significant crisis. Increasing exports went against Nazi policy. The alternative was to cut consumption, without introducing unpopular rationing, and press for higher production. This was the basis of the new Four-Year Plan of 1936.

ACTIVITY
KNOWLEDGE CHECK

The Nazi economic recovery

1 Explain the ways in which Nazi policies to create employment and rebuild industry and agriculture were similar.

2 Explain how the following would affect the economy:

   a) the Law to Reduce Unemployment (1933)

   b) the creation of the Reichsarbeitsdienst

   c) conscription and rearmament.

3 Explain why the Nazis dealt with foreign trade and debts differently to trade and debts within Germany.

Creating a command economy, 1936–39

A command economy is one where the state, not business or agriculture, decides what and how much to produce. The Nazis worked towards this from the start, setting up state control over industry and agriculture as they rebuilt the economy. The first Four-Year Plan ran for just three years, until 1936. In 1936, the state had high foreign debts because of raw-material imports for rearmament and work creation.

TIMELINE – NAZI ECONOMIC LEGISLATION, 1933-36

1933

6 May: Deutsche Arbeitsfront (German Labour Front, DAF) a Nazi trade union is set up, all other unions banned; workers reorganise on 7 December along Nazi Party lines

12 May: Law for Protection of Retail Trade bans new department stores and the expansion of existing ones

19 May: Reich Trustees of Labour set up, 12 for the whole country, to regulate working conditions under the Minister of Labour

13 September: Reichsnährstand (Reich Food Estate, RNS) is set up

21 September: Second 'Reinhardt Programme' to provide employment gives businesses tax concession for providing work projects, as well as government loans for them

Reich Entailed Farm Law sets up about 700,000 farms of at least 7.5 hectares to be given to German farmers to be farmed by them and their families and passed down to the eldest son (rather than being split)

1935

16 March: Conscription to the military and rearmament is announced

1 June: Law to Reduce Unemployment, the first 'Reinhardt Programme' to provide employment is drawn up by Fritz Reinhardt in the Ministry of Finance. Becomes the Reicharbeitsdienst (RAD, State Labour Service); gives women a marriage loan (in vouchers to spend on household goods) if they leave work when they marry

Debt Regulation Law restructures agricultural debts to reduce or write them off

22 June: law to build autobahns expands a pre-Nazi work creation scheme of road building

24 October: DAF is given responsibilities for 'Strength Through Joy' (see page 57) and 'Beauty of Labour' (to persuade employers to provide good working conditions)

29 November: Law for Construction of German Craft Trades says skilled workers have to be properly trained and members of a Nazi-run trade guild

26 June: the RAD is made compulsory for young people between the ages of 19 and 25, who then have to work on a RAD project, usually living in state labour camps

The second Four-Year Plan

The new Four-Year Plan had a tight focus on autarky and preparing for war. Hermann Goering was in charge of the plan and had control of all business and agricultural production. His Office of the Four-Year Plan had six departments: raw material production; agricultural production; distribution; labour; prices; and foreign exchange matters. The raw materials Germany could not produce were replaced, as far as possible, with German-manufactured synthetic alternatives. For example, rubber was replaced by the synthetic 'Buna'. This sometimes meant building new factories. Consequently, results were not as rapid as was hoped and, because the processes were new, there were technical difficulties at first. It took six tonnes of coal, needed for many industries and to heat homes, to produce 1 tonne of synthetic fuel. The synthetic fuel, however, was essential to military transport, so it was prioritised.

EXTRACT

3 From *Nazism 1919–1945*, written by the historians J. Noakes and G. Pridham and published in 1984.

The Four-Year Plan, then, was initiated because Schacht's New Plan had failed to solve the problem of providing sufficient raw materials to sustain the rearmament drive as well as tolerable levels of consumption. Although it marked a watershed in German economic policy in a number of ways, it was not in fact a comprehensive and well co-ordinated plan but rather a collection of individual measures in particular areas. It inaugurated a period of tighter controls on prices – a new Reich Price Commissioner was appointed in 29 October with extensive powers – on wages, and on the labour and finance markets. Above all, however, it represented a reorientation of the economy in the interests of manufacturing synthetic raw materials and an increase in the production of Germany's own sources of raw materials, such as coal and iron ore, even where these were uneconomic compared to the price levels of the world market.

SOURCE

7 Output in major industries, 1936–42, under the Four-Year Plan (which ran for longer than four years).

Commodity	Actual output (in thousands of tonnes)			
	1936	**1938**	**1942**	**Target set by Four-Year Plan**
Oil (including synthetic petrol)	1,790	2,340	6,260	13,830
Buna (rubber)	0.7	5	96	120
Explosives	18	45	300	223
Steel	19,216	22,656	20,480	24,500
Iron ore	2,255	3,360	4,137	5,549
Coal	319,782	381,171	411,977	213,000

Guns or butter?

Germany had a constant problem reconciling the needs of rearmament and the needs of the people for food, fuel and other necessities. Although Hitler was continually saying, in public speeches and in meetings with Nazi officials, that rearmament was the most important concern, this did not make the situation simple. Hitler also believed that it was vital for the Nazi state to have the support of all the people, and it was clear that if rationing was introduced, for instance, to try to control food consumption, the state would become very unpopular. Too many people remembered the rationing of the war, the starvation diets many were on for years and the shortages during the Weimar years. The Nazi election promise had been 'Work and Bread' and they felt the need to provide both in order to remain popular. So the choice between spending on guns or spending on butter was a hard one. The Office of the Four-Year Plan was an attempt to have a central control for everything to balance these needs. The Nazis also tried to 're-educate' people to consume less, especially less meat and fat, with propaganda aimed at changing their eating habits and at getting them to consume less to be patriotic.

EXTEND YOUR KNOWLEDGE

The 'guns or butter' debate
Historians have debated how early Hitler was planning for a war economy, as we will see in Chapter 5. This 'guns or butter' debate is complicated because coal, steel and other 'war' materials can also be used in non-military ways. However, Hitler's speeches were, from the start, focused on rearmament and war, so some historians have argued that he exploited this ambiguity to seem more butter focused in the early 1930s to avoid too early a conflict. For example, he could argue that conscription and rearmament reduced unemployment and boosted the clothing trade due to the need for more uniforms. However, it seems clear that war was the focus after 1936. Schacht resigned in 1937 because he disagreed with the focus of the Four-Year Plan and because his Ministry of Economics had virtually no power once the Office of the Four-Year Plan was created.

The situation in 1939

By 1939, the Nazis had tight control of the economy. Farming and industry did not always meet the Four-Year Plan targets set by the command economy, but some targets were unrealistic. For example, by 1938–39, Germany was still importing 17 percent of its agricultural needs. This was an improvement on 1934, when the figure had been 20 percent, but it was not as great an improvement as had been hoped. Propaganda was churned out to persuade people to switch from eating meat to eating fish, and to eat jam with their bread, not sausage. It had some success, for example, jam consumption trebled between 1928 and 1938, but again, this was less successful than had been hoped. The shift to a command economy had also made the Nazis unpopular with several groups that had previously supported it but resented Nazi levels of control, for example big industrialists and manufacturers of consumer goods. In terms of readiness for war, the country was not as ready as it would have been if the Nazis had been able to focus entirely on war production without also keeping the food supply topped up with imports. Even so, rearmament had been significant and had been achieved without pushing up prices or wages and without provoking widespread public protest at having goods that factories might otherwise be making, such as toys or electrical goods, in short supply.

SOURCE
8

Self-sufficiency in basic foods, 1927–28, 1933–34 and 1938–39, as a percentage of the amount of the foodstuff that was consumed.

Food	1927–28	1933–34	1938–39
Bread grains	79	79	113
Potatoes	96	100	100
Vegetables	84	90	91
Sugar	100	99	101
Meat	91	98	97
Fats	44	53	57
Eggs	64	80	82

ACTIVITY
KNOWLEDGE CHECK

Establishing a command economy

1 Study Source 7 and add together the outputs of each industry.

   a) Which came closest to meeting its targets?

   b) Did any overproduce?

   c) Which did least well at meeting its targets?

   d) Explain why the nature of the industries made these results likely.

2 Study Source 8. What evidence do you have about Nazi statistics that might lead you to question them?

3 Make notes that a member of the Office of the Four-Year Plan can use to write a report to Hitler about how close the country is to having a command economy.

Changing living standards, 1933–39

SOURCE
9

Wages, the cost of living and real wages, 1930–39 (1928 = 100, statistics before and after vary in relation to this, so are a percentage of 1928 values). Real wages are wages with the changing cost of living built in.

Year	Wages (as % of 1928)		Cost of living (as % of 1928)	Real wages (as % of 1928)
	Hourly	Weekly		
1928	100	100	100	100
1930	103	95	97	97
1931	95	84	89	94
1932	80	69	80	86
1933	77	71	78	91
1934	79	76	80	94
1935	80	77	81	95
1936	81	80	82	97
1937	83	83	82	101
1938	86	87	83	105
1939	89	90	83	108

The standard of living in Germany between 1933 and 1939 became increasingly sharply divided between that of conformist 'pure Germans' and that of people the Nazis saw as 'undesirable'. The Nazi approach to ethnic minorities is considered in Chapter 4. However, there were other 'undesirables' in the Nazi state.

- On 18 August 1939, all doctors, nurses and midwives had to report any babies and children under three years of age that showed signs of physical or mental disability. In October 1939, the Nazis mounted the T4 campaign to get rid of disabled children. Parents were offered the chance to send their disabled children to 'specialist clinics'. Here, they were killed. The programme expanded to cover all disabled children up to the age of 17. From January 1940, T4 was extended to other hospitals and institutions for the old, the mentally ill or the chronically sick. Over 70,000 people died under the T4 programme.

- Between October 1936 and July 1940, families that were 'asocial' (for example, they failed to pay the rent, failed to keep a job or were alcoholic) were sent for about a year to be 're-educated' at Hashude – a fenced-off housing estate for 78 families. Re-education included lectures and classes, living to set schedules and visits at any hours of the day or night by officials. Hashude was closed when housing became scarce.

The ordinary worker

For conformists, living standards initially improved under the Nazis. Unemployment dropped. Nazi statistics showed that real wages rose. However, there were issues. For example, wages were regulated, so people did not have too much spending money because industry was geared to war production, not consumables. So real wages only improved if a worker worked overtime. The 'Strength Through Joy' programme provided many extras. Some of these, such as the provision of loans, medical care and extra food and vitamins for 'suitable' mothers, were real enough. Others, for example, the chance to save for a Volkswagen, the new 'people's car', were not – only a few of these were produced before the factory began war production instead.

Social welfare

The Nazis said they were building a society where social welfare would be unnecessary. However, they realised that the economic circumstances they inherited meant they had to provide some form of social welfare. They inherited a social welfare programme, but in 1933 they set up the National Socialist People's Welfare (NSV), which divided the needy into those who 'deserved' help and those who did not. The NSV's aims were to create a healthy nation, not to care for the welfare of individuals. It was the NSV that ran the Mother and Child programmes and the crèches and kindergartens that the Nazis saw as their vital first chance to influence children's upbringing. By the end of 1938, there were about 10,800 of these. The NSV was also responsible for housing. By 1939, the NSV had over a million voluntary workers and about 500,000 block wardens who were responsible, depending on area, for 30–60 households. From 1933, it ran a yearly Winter Aid programme, distributing food and clothing parcels and running soup kitchens at emergency centres. Hitler announced its launch with a speech urging people to contribute, and by the next day

he could announce that RM2 million had been donated (some by Nazi Headquarters). However, from the start it was very hard to refuse to contribute when a blockwarden, often in SA uniform, appeared asking for donations. Some factories took a 'voluntary' donation from wages. Many people viewed the NSV officials and volunteers as Nazi 'snoopers' who were hoping to catch people breaking regulations, for example, listening to foreign radio broadcasts.

EXTEND YOUR KNOWLEDGE

The Volkswagen – just propaganda?
On 17 February 1939, Hitler presented one of the first Volkswagen cars to a motor show in Berlin. He gave another to his mistress, Eva Braun. By the end of 1939, about 270,000 people had entered a scheme where workers saved money, in a state-run bank account, towards buying one – in effect lending the state RM110 million. No one ever got a car (or their money back from the Nazi government savings account). The factory was converted to war production as soon as the first few cars had been produced.

AS Level Exam-Style Question Section A

Was the recovery of the German economy the main reason for the survival of the Nazi regime in the years 1933–39? (20 marks)

Tip
You will need to think about other reasons for the survival of the Nazi regime, including methods of controlling opposition and propaganda.

ACTIVITY
KNOWLEDGE CHECK

The standard of living
Write a description, in no more than 150 words, for a GCSE handout, describing the standard of living under the Nazis in the years 1933–39.

What was the impact of war on Nazi economic policies, 1939–45?

In 1939, when war broke out, Germany was more prepared for war than Britain and France, but not as ready or as self-sufficient as Hitler had hoped. The army, for example, wanted four months' worth of supplies of ammunition in store before going to war; in September 1939, there was six weeks' worth.

The war did not change Nazi economic policies; they had been geared for war before 1939. However, it did, eventually, change the way the war economy was run. The Office of the Four-Year Plan was not managing war production well, hindered by the fact the several different organisations were involved in organising war production: the Office of the Four-Year Plan; the economics ministry; the army, navy and air force (with separate, competing departments); and the war ministry. Goering was head of the air force as well as the Office of the Four-Year Plan, so he favoured the air force. People who understood the latest engineering and factory production techniques were ignored, while Nazi officials who knew much less were given power.

On 26 February 1940, Hitler made Fritz Todt minister of armaments and munitions with the task of organising industry to full production. However, Todt needed centralised control to make the industry as efficient as possible – and none of the other departments would accept that he had this level of control, especially not Goering, who carried on allocating more and more resources to the air force. On 3 December 1941, a memorandum from Hitler on simplifying and improving the armaments industry insisted on a policy of rationalising needs, updating factories and equipment to produce the most efficient weapons as efficiently as possible, and insisting that the army, navy and air force kept their demands as low as possible. However, he did not force the adoption of Todt's reorganisation and centralisation plans. On 8 February 1942, Todt died in a plane crash.

The new system

Todt's replacement, the architect Albert Speer, convinced Hitler that the armaments minister needed to be in full charge. Hitler's decree of 22 April 1942 set up the Central Planning Board to distribute raw materials, decide on whether to build a factory or extend an existing one, and to organise transportation. It had a variety of committees, made up of specialists and engineers, each with responsibility for a type of armament, for example, ammunition or tanks. Hitler specifically said that he was the only person who could override the Board's decisions. Firstly, each committee looked at all of the factories producing the same equipment. They closed many smaller factories, concentrating production into a few larger ones. Factory machinery was standardised, so there was only one model of each part, making construction and repair easier. Factories were adapted to the most efficient mass production techniques and machinery. Production had to become more mechanised as thousands of skilled workers were being conscripted into the armed forces and being replaced by less-skilled women and foreign workers (in 1929, 1.4 percent of the workforce was in the army; in 1944, this was 13 percent). It took time for these changes to happen, but when they did, the change was spectacular. During 1942, for example, the monthly production of 200 cm searchlights was 20. This rose to 80 by the end of 1943 and 150 by the end of 1944. Production in 1944 was almost three times that of 1940.

As the war dragged on, different equipment was needed. Before 1940, Germany seemed well on the way to winning the war. The tactic of *Blitzkreig* meant that the German army had marched through Belgium, Holland and France with stunning speed, and Britain was the only one of the Allies still fighting by July. In the first year of the war, then, it was important to produce planes, tanks and armoured vehicles. Then, when France fell on 22 June 1940, Hitler needed U-boats and longer-range planes for his conquest of Britain. Between July and September, the two air forces battled it out in the air over Britain, while Hitler planned to invade Britain and win the war before the end of the year. When Britain did not surrender and Hitler began Operation Barbarossa (in June 1941) against the USSR, he needed tanks and armoured vehicles again. All of this meant changes in factory production that the new system made easier, but which still caused delays.

SOURCE 10 Military spending, 1936–43 (millions of marks).

Year	Spending (millions of marks)
1936	10.8
1937	11.7
1938	17.2
1939	30.0
1940	53.0
1941	71.0
1942	91.0
1943	112.0

An overstretched economy

In 1945, the economy was severely overstretched and war production had been badly affected by:

- Allied bombing, which wiped out factories, mines, towns and transport links
- the loss of land that had provided raw materials, for example, Upper Silesia's coal
- damage to electricity, gas and water supplies
- sabotage by foreign workers, for example, deliberate 'mistakes' that damaged equipment and machinery.

Food production had also been affected by the loss of farm workers to the Front and the bombing of transport links. People were starving. The black market had taken over, as it did during and just after the First World War. As the army fell back or deserted and Allied troops advanced, the economy ground to a halt and Germany waited to see what would happen next.

EXTRACT 4 From *The German Economy, 1870 to the Present*, written by the historian Gustav Stopler in 1940 and revised by Karl Häuser and Knut Borchardt in 1967.

In the first half of 1944 alone, more bombs were dropped in Germany than in all four preceding years combined. One after the other the large cities were turned into rubble and ashes, while small towns, individual industrial plants, and transportation centres were also levelled through saturation bombing. Apart from destroying the towns, the Allied air forces tried to cripple all of Germany's industry, or at least her war industry, by selecting key industries. Thus first the few ball-bearing factories were hit, among them those in Schweinfurt, Steyr (Austria), Bad Cannstadt, Ekner, Leipzig, and Elberfield. After this the attacks singled out the submarine pens with their auxiliary industries and the docks; further targets were the airplane factories and the airfields, attacked in order to eliminate the Luftwaffe. Towards the end, oil refineries and storage facilities, plants to produce synthetic rubber, and all transportation centres became strategic targets of the enemy air forces.

Blitzkrieg
This means 'lightning war' and was a tactic that the very mobile army which the Nazis had been building up were perfectly placed to fight. It was a war of rapid movement. First, an area was attacked by bomber planes, to cause as much damage to the military as possible. They were followed by tanks that moved on through the area, tackling places where there was still resistance. Finally, the army followed. The planes and tanks pressed on, while some army units stayed to occupy the area.

ACTIVITY
KNOWLEDGE CHECK

The Nazi economy and war

Write a short paragraph on each of the following:

1 Why planning the war economy needed rationalisation.

2 Why planning the war economy needed centralisation.

3 How the creation of the Central Planning Board improved the war economy.

4 What the most important factor was in the economy's collapse?

A Level Exam-Style Question Section B

To what extent were attempts to create a command economy in Nazi Germany successful in solving the economic problems of the Weimar Republic? (20 marks)

Tip
You will need to be clear about the definition of 'command economy' in this question, as well as thinking about ways of measuring success.

WHAT EFFECT DID THE CREATION OF A 'SOCIAL MARKET' ECONOMY HAVE ON THE FEDERAL REPUBLIC IN THE YEARS 1945–89?

On 8 May 1945, Germany surrendered, just 27 years after it lost the First World War. Once more Britain, France and the USA were among the victorious Allies. Once more the German economy was ruined and its people were starving. However, there were differences. This war did not end with an armistice and people believing Germany might have won. It ended with a march to Berlin from east and west, the suicide of Hitler, and the occupation of the country by the victorious Allies. Between 17 July and 2 August 1945, in Potsdam, just outside Berlin, the Allies met to decide what would happen next (see pages 26–27).

How far was economic recovery achieved in the years 1945–55?

The Allies agreed it was important to rebuild Germany's economy. However, they also agreed that it was important that Germany did not start another war, so industries considered to be war industries (for example, munitions) were banned and others that were war-related (for example, chemical industries) had their outputs restricted. Reparations were to be taken in equipment and machinery from each zone. Considering the level of bombing, some places had very little of either. However, the French and the Soviets dismantled many remaining factories for reparations, undermining any chance of an economic recovery.

The fact that the Reichsmark was almost worthless was damaging to the economy too: the black market thrived (1 kg of sugar in 1947 had its price fixed at RM1; it could only be obtained on the black market, where it cost RM120–RM180) and it was hard to get workers when their wages bought hardly anything. Transport and communication links crossed the zones, hampering economic recovery. At first the Allied Control Council (see page 26) worked together to overcome these difficulties, but each zone was run by a military high command and the way they ran their zones varied, with the difference between the Soviet zone and the others widening.

The economic and physical devastation in Germany was so great, and the occupation so dislocating, that some Germans left and others chose not to return. For example, 160,000 German prisoners of war in France stayed there after the war rather than returning to Germany. However, these numbers were far exceeded by the influx of some ten million Germans who came as refugees ahead of the Soviet army, or were expelled from Eastern Europe under the reallocation of land and people agreed at Potsdam. These refugees, at first seen as adding to Germany's troubles, were to become one of the country's biggest assets. The Allies had to deal with the refugees and homeless Germans and were forced to introduce rationing.

The refugee problem
Some refugees were found work on farms as part of the rebuilding of Germany's agriculture. The rest needed housing and feeding. Many refugees were housed was in camps, some were even housed in Dachau, an ex-concentration camp (see Chapter 2). Adding to the movement of people around Europe were soldiers returning home and people from Nazi labour camps or concentrations camps (called 'displaced persons' or DPs) who had to be housed and fed until they could go home – about 4.5 million of them.

SOURCE 11

The photo shows Germans, mainly women, clearing the rubble of bombed Berlin in September 1945. The devastation in the cities was immense and there was a huge amount of work to be done to rebuild the economy. The war had killed far more men than women – even in 1950 there were three million more women than men in Germany.

Erhard and reform

Ludwig Erhard was appointed director of the economic administration in March 1948. He believed in the idea of a **social market economy** and worked to create one under the Allies and then as economics minister of Germany from 1949 to 1963. On 18 June 1948, he announced that the RM would be replaced by the DM on 21 June. On 24 June, the Economic Council gave Erhard the power to abolish almost all but the most essential rationing, such as bread and milk powder, and all price controls. Wages stayed fixed until November 1948 to allow businesses to establish themselves. The combination of the new currency and these measures meant that suddenly cakes, vegetables, butter and eggs were for sale in the shops, as were non-food items from stoves to stockings. People stopped hoarding goods and began selling them. Also, rather than buying anything that became available, they began to shop with a more careful concern for price and quality because they felt more confident that supplies would be less erratic. The currency reform only affected cash and monetary savings. The military government wanted a tax on all **assets**, the money to be used to compensate those who had lost everything. The system of compensation was complicated and took some time to work out, but in 1952 the Bundestag eventually passed the Equalisation of Burdens Act. The money raised and redistributed helped many people to start again.

KEY TERMS

Social market economy
This is a free market economy with elements of social support for the poorest built in – a 'socially responsible' free market economy.

Asset
Property or other valuable possession.

West Germany after 1949

Relations between the USSR and the West deteriorated rapidly, and the Cold War developed (see Chapter 1). One of the major factors in the separation was the economic aid (worth about $1.4 million) given to the Western zones under the Marshall Plan of 1948, which set off the creation of the Deutschmark (DM) to administer the aid. The new currency helped to stabilise the economy and break up the black market as the currency was backed by the Western powers. However, it led to the Soviet zone setting up its own currency because it was not included in the DM, and it made separation more likely. By the end of 1949, Germany had divided into the Federal Republic of Germany (FRG) and the German Democratic Republic (GDR).

SOURCE 12

From the OMGUS (Office of the Military Government, United States) report prepared for the US Military Command in the US zone, July 1948, discussing the effects of the currency reform.

Overnight the financial and commercial life of tens of millions of people was transformed. ... The new money has brought out of hiding a relatively large and well assorted supply of goods. Wages and salaries have again acquired genuine purchasing power. Job efficiency has risen and there are indications of increased output in almost all fields of manufacturing. The currency reform has created a psychological as well as a material revolution in German life. Psychologically it has introduced the hope of better times and of improved conditions. Cheer and optimism are taking the place of the scepticism and pessimism that previously prevailed.

EXTEND YOUR KNOWLEDGE

The currency reform
Every adult was given DM60 when the new currency was introduced. They could then exchange every 100 of their old RMs (which had no real value) for DM6.5. The confidence that the currency reform brought the people was the start of the revival of the economy because wages became worth something, people worked and saved and spent, allowing for higher levels of factory production, especially of consumer goods. There were some initial problems because the money supply was limited.

Erhard's reforms did not bring immediate economic recovery, for the problems that had to be overcome were great. Factories and businesses could start producing and trading again, but they had to replace machinery and train workers. Some businesses failed after the currency reform because they could not afford to pay wages. Other businesses managed to keep going, but they had to lay off some of their workers. Unemployment rose from 442,000 in June 1948 to 937,000 in January 1949. By 1950, it was as high as 1,800,000, but then it began to fall. In 1955, it was 1,000,000 and it continued to fall. Car production in 1959 was 4.5 times greater than in 1950. In the same period, steel production doubled, underlining Germany's new focus on consumer goods.

Opposition

Erhard had faced opposition, first in the Economic Council then in the Bundestag, for his policy of converting from a command economy to a social market economy. Britain had also opposed the idea, supporting the concerned labour union leaders who feared a social market economy would lead to exploitation of the workers by business owners. The USA, with a fairly positive experience of a form of social market economy under the New Deal, had supported Erhard. It was a gamble. Industrialists were not all supportive. The pre-command economy, with cartels and price fixing, was what many wanted back; Erhard wanted the cartels broken up and price fixing abandoned in favour of competition within industries. Socialists opposed the change not to support price fixing, but that was because they wanted to nationalise industries and use state control, not allowing a capitalist market to set its own levels. However, the combination of a capitalist market with a responsible government that provided a social safety net for the poorest won Erhard enough supporters in the Bundestag to continue his policies, allowing businesses tax concessions and removing wage restrictions, while encouraging the setting up of trade unions to make sure that workers had adequate representation in wage negotiations. All businesses had workers' councils, and in 1951 there was a policy of **co-determination** allowing for workers' representatives on managerial boards in industry.

ACTIVITY
KNOWLEDGE CHECK

Economic recovery

1 Explain whether each of the following would be possible in a social market economy:

  a) state control of the coalfields

  b) state control of rents

  c) state housing allowances to cover rising rents

  d) state wage regulation

  e) state taxation.

2 Write a brief explanation of the importance of the German currency reform.

The economic miracle, 1955–66

From 1955, the German economy improved so rapidly that some economists called the recovery an economic miracle. There were a variety of factors that contributed to this.

- **The Korean War**: In 1950, war in Korea sparked a need for war supplies. The FRG was banned from producing these, but its industrial goods, chemicals, steel and electrical goods were now in greater demand where other countries, such as the USA, had shifted to war production. In 1955, the FRG joined the North Atlantic Treaty Organisation (NATO), a Western military alliance, and was then allowed to re-arm and to start producing war materials, mainly as a result of the war.

- **New investment**: Many businesses had recovered sufficiently by the mid-1950s to be able to invest in new, more efficient equipment, even new factories. They concentrated on producing high-quality goods and kept their prices as low as possible to compete. The reputation of German goods improved and exports grew. As exports grew, so businesses could invest more and employ more workers. Manufacturers of consumer goods could also buy more raw materials.

- **Workers**: The influx of refugees immediately after the war meant there was a large pool of 'guest workers' for businesses to draw on. At first many of these needed training, but once that problem was overcome they provided an efficient workforce, and the fact that there was a large pool of workers kept wages low.

- During the 1950s, about 3.6 million more workers came to the FRG from the GDR, many of them young, skilled and highly educated (for example, doctors and engineers), all actively seeking work and also wanting to become part of the West German consumer culture, thereby helping the economy twice over. Most of them were employed on short-term fixed contracts. The government saved the money that would have been spent on education costs, training people in the FRG, and could use it elsewhere, for example, funding housing construction.

The photo shows a German housewife in her kitchen in the early 1960s. After the deprivations of the war years, the economic miracle was helped by a huge demand for consumer goods once people were earning enough money to spend and factories were producing these goods.

SOURCE
14

Exports and imports, 1950–70, in millions of marks.

Year	Imports (millions of marks)	Exports (millions of marks)
1950	11,374	8,363
1955	24,461	25,717
1960	42,700	47,900
1965	70,400	71,700
1970	109,600	125,300

SOURCE
15

Unemployment figures (in thousands) and percentage of workforce unemployed, 1950–71.

Year	Unemployed (in thousands)	Workforce unemployed (%)
1950	1,869	8.1
1955	1,074	4.2
1960	271	1.0
1965	147	0.5
1971	185	0.7

SOURCE
16

Real growth (adjusted for inflation, growth from the year before) in the German economy, 1951–66.

Year	Growth (%)
1951	10.4
1952	8.9
1953	8.2
1954	7.4
1955	12.0
1956	7.3
1957	5.7
1958	3.7
1959	7.3
1960	9.0
1961	5.4
1962	4.0
1963	3.4
1964	6.7
1965	5.6
1966	2.9

Possible problems

Erhard disliked the phrase 'economic miracle', preferring to see Germany's economic growth as the result of good economic planning and hard work by the German people. German businesses also did their best for the economy, putting profits back into businesses to expand old factories and build new ones. External factors, such as the Korean War and the influx of workers from the GDR, helped too.

There were possible problems, however. Growth could not keep going at the rapid rate of the 1950s and early 1960s. Once everyone had bought their consumer goods for the first time, demand fell to a lower level as people replaced these goods at different times. The Berlin Wall, put up in August 1961 by the GDR to cut it off from the FRG, stopped workers crossing from the GDR into the FDR and reduced the 'free' professionals that had helped the expanding economy.

ACTIVITY
KNOWLEDGE CHECK

The economic miracle
Prepare for a debate on the statement: 'The "economic miracle" could not last.' Develop at least three points in favour and against the statement. Consider the position of Germany in 1945, the currency reform, Germany's industry and trade, and any other factors you consider relevant.

How did the Federal Republic survive the economic challenges in the years 1966–89?

Between 1966 and 1989, the FRG experienced a number of economic challenges, and it rose to some of them more easily than others. Real economic growth (see Sources 16 and 17) had a tendency to vary significantly anyway, but after 1966, it tended to move at a lower rate. In 1966, the government, urged by the new economics minister Karl Schiller, began to accept that it had to intervene in the economy, with the Bundesbank managing the money supply and a new system of federal and regional budgeting. Running alongside particular crises and the measures taken to deal with them were rising levels of government spending, especially on social welfare. In 1965, for example, the government spent DM46.7 million on social welfare; by 1970, this was DM115.9 million. This happened despite various cuts to benefits. More encouragingly, the economy was helped by the fact that Germany's export figures stayed healthy thanks to continued demand and the fact that Chancellor Schmidt worked hard to persuade other world leaders not to introduce protective tariffs to limit world trade during the first oil crisis of 1973. The crises included the following.

- **The recession of 1966–67**. The FRG's first economic recession hit confidence hard – by this time West Germans saw themselves as economic leaders. Trade – domestic and international – reduced and unemployment increased. Many guest workers were on one-year renewable contracts, without social benefits. Guest workers had been vital to economic growth and they were also vital to managing the effects of an economic crisis. At the start of 1966, there were 1.3 million of these workers; by September 1967, there were 991,000. Productivity began to fall. Due to its social welfare policies, the government had been spending more and more – public spending was spiralling out of control. Erhard was chancellor. The economics minister, Karl Schiller, reorganised the government's approach to the economy. He increased government planning, intervention and control, for example, subsidies for agriculture and the coal industry. He also reintroduced cartels to stop prices rising. The 1967 Economic Stabilisation Law allowed for government intervention in times of economic crisis to limit regional spending and introduced a Five-Year Plan system for all government spending. In 1968, a provision was added to the Basic Law (see page 28) that said the federal government could move money around between Länder, using money from the wealthy ones to provide more social welfare in the struggling ones. Schiller's economic policies were regarded as having failed and he was replaced with Helmut Schmidt in 1972, just in time for the next crisis.

- **The oil crises of 1973 and 1978**. During the 1960s and 1970s, the FRG came to rely on oil rather than coal as a fuel, and car ownership pushed up petrol consumption. It was the same in many other countries. The oil-rich countries of the Middle East grew rich on oil sales, but they had so much oil that they sold it at an affordable price. In 1972, the FRG spent DM10.8 billion on 140 million tonnes of oil. This changed in 1973 when, in October of that year, the Fourth Arab-Israeli War broke out and OPEC (the Organization of Petroleum Exporting Countries) put up prices sharply in 1973 and again in 1978. The FRG got 40 percent of its fuel needs through OPEC: 140 million tonnes of oil cost DM32.8 billion in 1973 and DM49 billion in 1978. This contributed to an economic crisis and it hit the FRG in 1974–75. Unemployment rose sharply again, made worse by the fact that the FRG's **baby boomers** were just hitting the employment market. Again, foreign guest workers found that their contracts were not renewed and a ban was placed on recruiting guest workers. As before, this helped to prevent the crisis from becoming worse.

- In fact, the FRG was not hit as hard as some other countries as it was helped by its export income and, once again, the economy recovered rapidly. Oil consumption dropped, partly because of government measures such as encouraging 'car-free Sundays' and introducing speed limits on the autobahns in order to save fuel. Government propaganda pushed energy-saving tactics in homes and industry and the government also began to invest seriously in atomic power to reduce dependence on oil. The biggest push to the cut in consumption was that the government, unlike other governments such as that in the USA, did not subsidise oil prices, but just let them rise in line with their actual cost. This made it expensive and encouraged cutbacks. German industries converted to new fuels much more rapidly than in any other country. The government also brought in public spending cuts and higher income tax in 1975.

KEY TERM

Baby boomers
Between 1946 and 1964 there was a sharp rise in the number of births in many countries. The children of this generation became known as the 'baby boomers'. In West Germany, there was an increase from 69.4 live births per 1,000 women in 1954 to 86.8 live births per 1,000 women in 1964. In the USA, a similar baby boom took place earlier, with the birth rate beginning to drop after 1959. This does not mean that German soldiers returning home were any less keen to build a family and look to the future – but first they had to get home, find their families and repair the devastation that Germany had to cope with after the war.

EXTRACT

5 From *The Social Economy of West Germany*, written by the economist Graham Hallett and published in 1973.

The period from 1969 to 1972 was one of uneven recovery, characterised by higher rates of inflation than before. Boom conditions developed in 1969 and 1970, with profits rising, unemployment falling below 1%, and the number of unfilled vacancies once again far exceeding the number of unemployed. In 1970 workers became more militant in pursuing wage claims and using strike action if they were not met. Wage claims of 12-15% were submitted, and often conceded by employers as being less harmful to them than a strike.

Challenges of the 1980s

In the 1980s, the gap between the richest and the poorest widened in Germany. This created friction, for example, hostility towards guest workers. The FRG had ridden out the crises of the 1970s better than some countries, largely due to its healthy exports. In 1978, West Germany even exported more to OPEC countries than it imported. Even though much of the rest of the world was in recession, Germany's total exports continued to rise and stayed consistently ahead of imports. However, it never regained the economic heights of the 1960s, and real growth in the economy shrank as prices, which Germany had kept under control, began to rise with inflation. Unemployment hit 1.7 million in 1981, the highest since 1950 (although in 1975 it had been just over one million). This drove up the amount of spending on unemployment benefits and assistance for the long-term unemployed. The 1981 government cut public spending, including benefits and housing allowance, and was deeply unpopular, especially with those who felt Germany should return to a social market economy. There were arguments in the Bundestag about whether to create more work by reducing the working week, or setting up job-share programmes to get the unemployed back into at least part-time work.

Despite the need to help the unemployed, the government that took over in 1982 was determined to turn the economy around by cutting spending even more fiercely, saying that welfare support just created dependency, an idea that was being taken up by many countries experiencing recession, including the USA. Chancellor Helmut Kohl said that productivity levels were falling because of this dependency and because of the slack values of the baby boomers, and that people needed to be more independent in order to be energised to find and keep work. His government brought in even more cuts in social welfare spending, including maternity benefit. It also cut public holidays and reduced the retirement age to 58, urging people to take early retirement. The government also sold off shares in state-run institutions (for example, Volkswagen and the state airline Lufthansa), partially privatising them. These policies produced a slight but growing improvement, and by 1989 unemployment was at its lowest, while the economic growth rate had risen. Then the Berlin Wall fell and the economy of the FRG had to brace itself for reunification.

SOURCE 17

Real growth (adjusted for inflation, growth from the year before) in the German economy, 1966–84.

Year	Growth (%)
1966	2.9
1967	−0.2
1968	7.3
1969	8.2
1970	5.8
1971	3.0
1972	3.4
1973	5.1
1974	0.4
1975	−2.7
1976	5.8
1977	2.7
1978	3.3
1979	4.5
1980	1.8
1981	−0.2
1982	−1.0
1983	1.3
1984	2.6

ACTIVITY
KNOWLEDGE CHECK

Economic challenges, 1966–89

1 Draw a spider diagram of the causes of the economic slump of the mid-1970s.

2 For each decade choose a problem, then:

   a) explain it

   b) say how the government tried to deal with it

   c) say if it worked

   d) explain if it was in keeping with the policy of 'social market economy'.

3 Explain how Source 17 reflects what was happening in Germany at the time, pegging the data to an event where possible.

Integration into the European economy, 1949–89

The Allies included the Western zones of Germany in their organisations that were set up to try to rebuild Europe, for example, the OEEC (see the timeline opposite). From the moment the FRG was set up, Chancellor Adenauer was concerned to establish closer ties with Europe and be accepted as a part of Europe. Like Stresemann in the 1920s, he saw political and economic integration with the rest of Europe as vital for Germany's economic and political success. He was especially concerned to build a close working relationship with France. To this end he was far more concerned about establishing trade and other agreements with Europe than achieving unification with the GDR (see page 30).

EXTEND YOUR KNOWLEDGE

Germany and France

Adenauer was very concerned about establishing good relations with France. When he and the French prime minister, Charles de Gaulle, signed a Franco-German Friendship Treaty in the Elysée Palace in Paris on 22 January 1963, it was the result of 15 different meetings and a joint commemoration of the war dead of both countries in Reims Cathedral in 1962. Adenauer faced considerable opposition to his signing of the treaty from those Atlanticist members of the Bundestag who thought he should be forging closer ties with the USA and from those who thought that de Gaulle's firm rejection of Britain's request to join the EEC meant Adenauer should back down. He did not. Feeling was so strong on this matter that when the Bundestag ratified the Treaty, it added an introductory paragraph saying that Germany was keen for Britain to join the EEC and that the Treaty did not exclude Germany from close ties with the USA.

Between 1958 and 1969 FRG exports and imports to and from other EEC countries doubled. The FRG strongly supported the Basel agreement that linked European currencies to deal with changes to the US dollar exchange system, set up in response to the 1971 oil crisis, and continued to push for a common currency. During the 1980s it was the FRG and France who pushed for the Single European Act, which became law in July 1987, to tie the European economies closer together, easing the way to a single currency.

TIMELINE – STEPS TO JOINING EUROPE, 1948–79

1948
16 April: the Western zones of Germany form part of the Organisation for European Economic Cooperation (OEEC), set up to manage European economic recovery. It administers the Marshall Plan aid in Europe

1950
September: European Payment Union (EPU) set up by OEEC to manage economic co-operation across various national finances, including in FRG

1951
FRG joins General Agreement on Tariffs and Trade (GATT), set up in January 1948 to establish favourable trade agreements among its members

1952
13 August: FRG joins the International Monetary Fund (that began operations on 1 March 1947) which oversees the stability of world currencies

1951
18 April: FRG joins the Council of Europe (set up in May 1949)

FRG joins the European Coal and Steel Community (ECSC), with France, Italy, Belgium, the Netherlands and Luxembourg setting up preferential trade links between these countries (it comes into effect in July 1952)

1955
9 May: FRG joins the North Atlantic Treaty Organization (NATO), an anti-communist alliance of Western countries set up in April 1949

1957
25 March: FRG signs Treaty of Rome to become one of the founder members of the European Economic Community (EEC). Comes into effect 1 January 1958

1967
1 July: Brussels Treaty joins three different European groups to give them one Commission and one Council. The first president of the European Commission is a West German, Walter Hallstein

Germany and Europe

The Treaty of Versailles of 1919	The Dawes Plan of 1924 and the Young Plan of 1929	The FRG is a founder member of the EEC in 1957
Germany joins the League of Nations in 1926	The FRG joins the OEEC in 1948	The FRG joins NATO in 1955

Patterns of development consist of changes which, at given times, converge and have a bearing on one another and, at other times, diverge and have little in common. In the above example, the changes come together to form a pattern of development that tends towards Germany being part of the European community in 1989.

In groups, write each change on a small piece of paper and arrange them on a large A3 piece of paper as you think best. Then link them with lines and write along the line what it is that links those changes. Try to make sure that you think about how those links may have changed over time.

Answer the following questions individually or in pairs:

1 What impact did the Treaty of Versailles have on Germany's desire to be part of Europe?

2 How did the events before 1933 bring Germany closer to Europe?

3 What post-war changes brought Germany into Europe?

4 How was joining NATO a significant milestone?

Changing living standards, 1945–89

Living standards underwent a huge change from 1945 to 1989. In 1945, war damage meant that families were torn apart, people were starving and many people were homeless. About one-fifth of all housing had been bombed flat, and about one-third of that still standing was damaged. The refugee influx (see Chapter 2) led to even more pressure on housing. Housing and food were the most pressing issues of the late 1940s and first few years of the 1950s. A ministry of housing was set up to oversee rebuilding. Rents were frozen and the building industry was given tax concessions to build. Housing associations were set up to build homes. Some were state run for social housing and for workers in state-run industries such as Volkswagen. Others were privately run.

SOURCE 18

New homes (blocks of flats or houses) built in the FRG between 1949 and 1971.

Year	Total (in thousands)	Social housing (%)	Average floor area (sq km)	With central heating (%)
1949	222	69	not given	none
1952	461	69	54.8	none
1954	572	53	57.9	7
1960	574	46	70.4	31
1966	605	34	80.5	76
1971	553	27	84.0	96

Spending patterns

As the economy strengthened, so the standard of living rose and people began to spend their money on different things, mainly consumer goods. By 1963, 63 percent of homes had a fridge, 42 percent had a TV and 36 percent had a washing machine. By 1985, these percentages were 82 percent, 82 percent and 87 percent, respectively. All through the period, real wages kept ahead of prices, even though the extent by which they were ahead varied. By the 1980s, about 90 percent of all people were covered by benefits and healthcare. Pension reforms in the 1980s meant that most people received a state pension, which is just as well as people in 1980 lived, on average, 12 years longer than people in 1950. However, social inequality had deepened. Even in the affluent 1960s, when the economy was at its best, one percent of all households owned 35 percent of the wealth. In 1973, the top percent of all households owned 78 percent of the wealth while in 1988 they owned 45 percent of the wealth.

SOURCE 19

Patterns of spending (as a percentage of income) in the FRG between 1957 and 1985.

Year	Food	Clothing	Housing	Savings	Furniture/cars/ leisure/travel
1957	36.6	12.5	9.3	8.0	33.6
1967	29.3	9.4	13.5	11.7	36.1
1977	23.0	8.2	14.4	13.7	40.7
1985	17.4	6.5	15.6	12.7	47.8

EXTRACT 6

From *A History of West Germany*, Volume 2, written by the historians Dennis L. Bark and David R. Gress and published in 1989.

It should be noted, however, that despite the economic problems of the 1970s the personal incomes of Germans continued to rise, and in 1980, on average, real personal income was six times what it had been in 1949. From 1950 to 1978 the proportion of personal income needed by an average wage-earning household for basic necessities had fallen from 74 to 46 per cent. In 1973, only 51 households out of 100 had a telephone, but this number rose to 88 by 1983. In 1978, 416 of every 1,000 households lived in their own house or apartment. ... Except for a small minority, the main concern was no longer where the next meal was coming from, but how to manage one's life and finances over the long term, what sorts of domestic investments to make, what kinds of savings to have, and where to go on vacation. The effects of these changes on the temperaments and attitudes of the people were revolutionary. In the late 1940s most Germans feared political change, because they had experienced too much of it and longed for stability. In the 1970s they feared change because they had a lot to lose.

ACTIVITY
KNOWLEDGE CHECK

The standard of living

1 'The changes shown in Sources 18 and 19 show a rising standard of living.' Explain how far you agree with this statement.

2 Decide what is the most significant point made in Extract 6 about the standard of living in Germany from the late 1940s to the late 1970s and explain your choice.

ACTIVITY
SUMMARY

The German Economy, 1918–89

1 Draw a graph to show how you think the German economy moved from 1918 to 1989, with 'Doing badly' at the bottom and 'Doing well' at the top.

2 Choose one high point and one low point in the economy. Describe the factors that brought Germany to these points, and how far government control (or lack of it) helped to create the situation.

WIDER READING

Hallett, G. *The Social Market Economy of West Germany*, Macmillan (1973)

An internet search on 'German history in documents and images' will bring up a website that can be searched chronologically.

The Facing History and Ourselves website provides useful information about the economy of Weimar Germany, including personal accounts.

1.4 Aspects of life in Germany and West Germany, 1918–89

KEY QUESTIONS

- To what extent did the role of women and attitudes towards them change and develop in Germany in the years 1918–89?
- Why were educational and cultural developments often controversial in Germany in the years 1918–89?
- How far did attitudes towards ethnic minorities affect their status in Germany in the years 1918–89?

INTRODUCTION

The photos in Sources 1 and 2 were taken in Germany in 1923 and 1960. Clearly the women had very different lives. Was this because one was rich and the other poor? Was it because the woman in Source 1 came from an ethnic minority? Or was it because the woman in Source 2 had a better education? There are other questions to ask. Were their lives entirely different? They are, after all, both in kitchens, cooking. Was *Kinder, Küche, Kirche* the role of all women throughout the period 1918–89? Did German culture all through the period represent women as housewives?

This chapter addresses aspects of life in Germany and West Germany between 1918 and 1989, and will hopefully give these images some context and help to provide an understanding of the lives of both women.

> **KEY TERM**
>
> *Kinder, Küche, Kirche*
> Literally, this means 'Children, Kitchen, Church'. It was a phrase that was in common usage just before the First World War to sum up the role of women as homemakers and moral support for the family.

SOURCE 1

This photo shows a woman lighting her stove with marks in 1923. There was a point when marks became a cheaper fuel than coal or firewood.

1918 – 11 November: armistice

12 November: women get the vote

1919 – 19 January: first Weimar Republic elections

28 June: Treaty of Versailles signed

1933 – 30 January: Hitler becomes chancellor of Germany

1934 – 2 August: Hindenburg dies: Hitler becomes führer

1935 – 15 September: Nuremberg Race Laws

1945 – 7 May: end of Second World War in Europe

Germany and Berlin divided into Allied zones

1949 – 22 May: FRG set up

1915 1920 1925 1930 1935 1940 1945 1950

The photo shows a German housewife in her kitchen in the early 1960s.

1977 – Marriage and Family Law revised to give women equal status with men in marriage

1955   1960   1965   1970   1975   1980   1985   1990

1961 – 12–13 August: Berlin Wall goes up

1989 – 9 November: fall of Berlin Wall

TO WHAT EXTENT DID THE ROLE OF WOMEN AND ATTITUDES TOWARDS THEM CHANGE AND DEVELOP IN GERMANY IN THE YEARS 1918–89?

Before the First World War, the government's attitude towards women was summed up by the German Civil Code of 1900: women could not vote; single women could study for a profession, such as law, but could not take the exams to qualify and practise. Married women had no legal status at all; a man had to do any legal business on their behalf. Some liberal men and women campaigned for equality, but had little impact on the government and were dismissed as 'socialist'. A woman's role was seen as *Kinder, Küche, Kirche*. During the war, women took the place of men in factories, on farms and in almost every other sphere of life. In 1913, for example, the armament manufacturer Krupp had no women employees. In 1918, it had over 28,000. By the end of the war, 75 percent of women of working age were in work. The war also meant that 1.6 million men were killed, so women without men ('surplus women' who could never find husbands because there were not enough men) were now a significant part of the population.

Was there a change in the role and status of women in the years 1918–32?

The Weimar government's attitude to women was liberal in theory but far more traditional in practice. On 12 November 1918, even before the new constitution was established, the emergency government gave women the vote. This was unexpected, even after women's work during the war. Their status under the Civil Code meant the pre-war women's groups had fought for legal rights more than the vote. All of the political parties taking part in the election wanted women's votes and campaigned to 'educate' women on the issues. The turnout of women at the first elections was 90 percent and women took seats in local government and the Reichstag. In total, 112 women were elected to the Reichstag between 1919 and 1932.

So there were women in the Reichstag when the constitution was written. It said that 'in principle' women had equal rights (Article 109), marriage should be an equal union and women should be able to enter the professions. This seemed a huge step. However, this was what *should* be; it did not change the legal status of women under the Civil Code. The Reichstag was split on the matter. Some people, mostly SPD members, supported equality and women's rights. However, others thought women should return to being wives and mothers. The falling birth rate was a concern. It fell from 128 live births per 1,000 women in 1911 to 80 in 1925 and to 59 in 1933. The divorce rate was a concern, too. It had been 27 per 100,000 inhabitants in 1913, but it rose and stayed high to the end of the Weimar period (59 per 100,000 in 1920 and 65 per 100,000 in 1932). Of concern, too, was the campaign of some women's associations for free contraception and the right to abortion under certain circumstances, such as rape.

Women and work

Weimar government policy was that women should give up jobs to returning soldiers. By the first post-war census, taken in 1925, the percentage of the workforce that were female (36 percent) was almost back to pre-war levels (34 percent). However, work itself was expanding, so even if the percentage of the workforce was similar, the actual numbers of working women rose. While women were expected to give up jobs traditionally done by men, there were many more 'white blouse' jobs after the war – clerical and shop work traditionally done by women. In areas such as office work where men and women sometimes had the same level of job, women were, on average, paid about 33 percent less than their male counterparts. The idea of single women working was more accepted than that of married women working – and single women working was seen as a temporary activity until they married; they were not expected to pursue a career. This is one of the reasons that there was opposition to women entering the professions – professions required long-term training and provided a career. It was possible for single women to go further in education and in the professions than before, but the number of women in the professions was still very small by 1933. Women could qualify as lawyers (by 1933 there were 36) and the number of women working at the lower levels of the legal profession, as notaries or drawing up documents such as wills and contracts, rose from 54 in 1925 to 251 in 1933. In 1925, there were just over 2,500 women doctors; this had almost doubled by

1933. However, professional women faced hostility and discrimination from male colleagues. Married women had to face practical hurdles as well as opposition if they wanted to work – the school day was structured to end at lunchtime, so they had to find childcare or work from home or part-time. In 1925, over a quarter of a million women were doing poorly paid work from home because they could do this and look after the children. By 1935 (the nearest census to 1933) this figure had doubled.

Of the 36 percent of women working in 1925, over half were working in poorly paid manual jobs. In industry, trade unions were strong and male dominated. They opposed all women workers and also equal pay and conditions for those women that did work. They were especially hostile to 'double earners' (married women bringing a second wage into the home) because they were fighting hard for men to be paid enough to support a family.

New women

Women were changing, especially young, educated, unmarried women who had come of age during the war. They wanted independence, and many who found work, largely in 'white blouse' industries in offices and shops rather than manual or industrial labour, chose to abandon traditional female behaviour. They wore more revealing clothes, cut their hair short, smoked and drank, and behaved with the freedom of a man – very like 'flappers' in the USA. Many also took advantage of contraception to enjoy sexual freedom. These 'new women' were mostly city based and part of the racy city culture that emerged in the 1920s. Politicians and the media criticised these women, calling them immoral and urging them to marry and settle down. Despite this criticism, the advertising and film industries loved them, producing glorified images of emancipated, achieving, good-time girls that aspiring 'new women' were constantly trying to live up to. These images were blamed for seducing good girls to move to the city to chase the dream of becoming a 'new woman' rather than settling down and living a sensible, productive life. In real life, 'new women' faced wage discrimination and sexual discrimination. Many, in fact, did as expected and settled down to marriage. In doing so, they may have hoped for a more equal marriage than their mothers had, but they were unlikely to achieve it.

EXTRACT

1 From an article on 'new women' in Weimar Germany, written by the historian Rüdiger Graf and published in 2009.

Because of women's improved position in the workforce and their newly acquired rights as citizens in Weimar Germany, not only their position seemed to have changed but women themselves also seemed to have changed: many intellectual observers discerned the occurrence of a 'new woman.' According to their political and intellectual preferences, they described and evaluated the 'new woman' in various ways as promising or terrifying. After the war, in the mass media the older ideal of the new woman as an emancipated and autonomous human being became closely linked to changes in lifestyles and female fashion. Magazines such as *Die schöne Frau, Die Dame, Elegante Welt,* and the German *Vogue* helped to create an easily identifiable visual type of a 'new woman.' They presented a new generation of women that differed fundamentally from their mothers, having short haircuts (*Bubiköpfe*) and wearing shorter skirts, plain tops and sweaters, narrow hats, sportive clothes, and sometimes even decidedly male accessories.

EXTEND YOUR KNOWLEDGE

What was wrong with the new woman?
The 'new woman' faced criticism on several levels, from many different types of people and of differing levels of seriousness.

As described by Elsa Herrmann in a book called *This is the New Woman* (written in 1929) she was selfish, thinking of herself and of a career, rather than thinking of the future and future generations. She did not plan or save, but lived the good life in the present.

As described by the journalist Heinrich Jacob, she was wrong to try for economic equality, she was wrong to try to copy male independence because she would cause the downfall of society.

As described by the fashion designer Paul Poiret, she was wrong to take on a boyish manner and style – it was against nature; she should dress and behave in a womanly way.

The Depression

The Depression and the rise in unemployment (see Chapter 3) meant even more hostility towards working women, and even more desperation among those women who were the breadwinners in their families. Neither men nor women were able to press for reforms or better working conditions when jobs were scarce. Both men and women were hit by unemployment, but women actually suffered a less steep level of unemployment because they were cheaper to employ than men. In 1932, 46 percent of men were unemployed compared to only 33 percent of women, although the difference was almost entirely made up of women doing part-time work. On 30 May 1932, Chancellor Brüning passed a decree allowing for the dismissal of married women in government service if they had husbands who were earning. The same was happening in privately owned industry. Women, often the last hired, were the first to be fired.

ACTIVITY
KNOWLEDGE CHECK

Attitudes towards women in Weimar Germany

1 'The minute the war was over the role and status of women went right back to where it was before the war – they were back to the wife and mother role.'

How far do you agree with this statement?

2 Prepare for a radio talk about 'new women' in the Weimar Republic, covering:

a) what a 'new woman' is and why she is so noticeable

b) why many people were horrified by her

c) how she would justify her behaviour.

The impact of Nazi rule on women's lives, 1933–45

The Nazis' attitude towards women was not as clear-cut as it at first appeared. They adopted the slogan '*Kinder, Küche, Kirche*' to give their view of women a familiar feel. However, while they certainly wanted women at home in the kitchen, they were against church membership as it competed with their influence. As for children – they wanted the right women producing the right kind of children. They stressed the virtues of the family, saying women were equal to men but different, physically, so the family was their job. However, they really wanted women producing good Nazis for Germany. They saw family units as too individualistic and wanted family members to work for the good of Germany, not to support the family.

Women as mothers

As mothers, women were vital to the state. Work, and influence outside the home was another matter; politics was for men, the Reichstag emptied of women. Women had their own Nazi organisation, the National Socialist Womanhood (NS-Frauenschaft, or NSF). A wider-based movement called the German Women's Enterprise (Deutsches Frauenwork) organised activities for non-party members. The Nazis believed ideas about **eugenics** that were current at the time. They encouraged 'pure' German couples to breed, and passed laws to stop the 'wrong' kind of breeding (see the timeline below). Couples were given marriage loans to encourage them to marry, but only if they had a licence saying they were fit and racially acceptable. Help with school fees and transport fares were provided for families, but only after an interview eliminated the 'unsuitable'. 'Suitable' poor families were given grants of up to RM100 for each child. The Lebensborn programme, started in 1936 and run by a special branch of the SS, took things further. Its aim was to produce healthy, **Aryan** children. Selected men, usually members of the SS, were encouraged to mate with as many different 'racially pure' young women as possible, many from the **Bund Deutscher Mädel (BDM)**. The programme had its own hospitals, clinics and homes for the children born on the programme. The children were then adopted by 'fit' Germans who had trouble conceiving. Once the Third Reich started to expand, the Lebensborn programme took 'suitable' children from families in the lands they took over and put them into the homes.

KEY TERMS

Eugenics
The belief that controlling reproduction can produce a healthier population. The Society for Population Policy, set up in 1916, fed the growing interest in issues of heredity and genetics in its magazine *The Coming Generation*.

Aryan
To Hitler and the Nazis, Aryans were people of 'pure' German descent: blonde-haired, blue-eyed northern Europeans.

Bund Deutscher Mädel (BDM)
The League of German Girls, the older female Nazi youth group.

SOURCE 3

A copy of a painting of a farming family painted by Wilhelm Haller in the 1930s. It shows the perfect Aryan family: serious, conservatively dressed and obviously hard-working. Paintings such as this were copied and sold widely.

TIMELINE – NAZI POLICIES TOWARDS WOMEN

1931

31 December: SS Marriage Order states members of the SS can only marry Aryan women (amended in 1936 to say SS men married or not have to have at least four children by such a woman)

1933

1 June: Law to Reduce Unemployment includes an interest-free marriage loan to Aryan couples if the woman gives up her job (and promises not to work again as long as her husband has a job) and is passed as 'fit' to have children. The loan is reduced by a quarter for every child the woman has (so four children clear the loan)

30 June: All married women in the civil service with wage-earning husbands to be dismissed; wages of the rest are fixed lower

14 July: Law for the Prevention of Offspring with Hereditary Diseases makes it possible to sterilise those (male and female) with mental and physical disabilities, but it is also extended to women with several sexual partners or illegitimate children and to male and female alcoholics. It is secretly extended to cover racial 'undesirability'

1935

18 October: Law for the Protection of Hereditary Health of the German People is a fitness-to-marry certificate required to prove neither couple is genetically or racially 'impure'

1936

Women are excluded from working in the law, except in administrative posts

1937

Due to increasing war goods production, to be ready for war, women can work and still be awarded the marriage loan

1938

Marriage law extends the grounds for divorce to include infertility, having an abortion and refusing to have a baby

1939

May: the Mother's Cross introduced for mothers with four (bronze), six (silver) or eight or more (gold) children. It is awarded on Mother's Day, Hitler's mother's birthday in August

The impact of Nazi policies

One significant effect of Nazi policies was that large numbers of women, especially married women, lost their jobs. Single women still found work; usually domestic work, shop work, or as secretaries, but were excluded from the highest levels of work. Even highly skilled doctors were expected to work in 'suitable' jobs such as in maternity clinics or as GPs, rather than putting their skills to full use. Other single professionals were also sidelined. For example, teachers, who belonged to the largest female professional group, could only work at the lowest levels in schools; women who had taught secondary school had to teach primary school children. Civil servants had to work in a women's section of the government offices in which they worked.

Nazi social policies meant that women who were considered racially suitable and wanted to be wives and mothers found that they had a higher level of health care and a higher status in Nazi Germany than they had before. Mothers of soldiers who had died or were on active service were also given more support and honoured on occasions such as Mother's Day, which the Nazis made a national holiday. They were brought together in small groups for coffee and cake with local youth groups. On the other hand, expectations of mothers meant that there was a level of state policing, as well as care. A mother was expected to eat well, get enough exercise, not smoke. She was expected to be a good housewife and a faithful wife. The Nazis expected their various organisations to monitor mothers to make sure they kept to these standards.

EXTRACT

From the book *From Nurturing the Nation to Purifying the* Volk, written by the historian Michelle Mouton and published in 2009.

Almost from their first day in office, the Nazis inundated Germans with propaganda exalting motherhood. Government-sponsored advertisements and posters, carefully designed for shop-windows and for blitz campaigns, loudly and publicly proclaimed, 'The care of mothers and children is the holiest duty of the entire German *Volk*,' 'The future of a *Volk* is only secure when it is prepared to give the highest sacrifice for mother and child,' and 'Only a healthy and strong mother can give her *Volk* healthy sons and daughters.' When I asked whether she was aware of the state's pronatalist attitudes, one woman I interviewed (born 1916) claimed that there was an atmosphere in which motherhood 'was so self-evident, it hung in the air.' Another woman agreed, telling me: 'Yes, then, well, somehow we were all so "in" [the spirit of motherhood] that we all wanted to marry and also gladly have children. I don't even know whether we were aware of it [the propaganda]. It was just the general propaganda which influenced us.'

The impact of the Second World War on women in Germany

The Second World War changed life for German women in similar ways to the First World War. Men went away to fight in greater and greater numbers; millions did not come back. Food and other goods became scarce and the war dragged on. But there were also differences. War put extra pressure on production and, as more men were conscripted into the armed forces, it meant a shift in attitudes towards women working. Women were urged to join war work even if they were married. More childcare was provided. The NSV had 31,000 kindergarten and crèches by the end of 1942. Even so, the number of German women going into war work was far less than during the First World War (where the number employed went up 76 percent between 1913 and 1918). The total number of women in the workforce went up by 27 percent between 1933 and 1939, and just two percent between 1939 and 1944. In Britain, the increase was 50 percent over the war years. There were three main reasons for the smaller increase in German women entering the workforce:

- The Nazi propaganda machine had done its work well. Many women were reluctant to work and many organisations were reluctant to have them, telling volunteers who said they had children to go home.

- The government did not use women in all kinds of war work, preferring to have them replace male teachers or work on the land rather than in mines or heavy industry (work they were doing in Britain).

- Germany had the use of 'foreign labour' from the lands they had conquered, so their need to mobilise women in the workforce was nowhere near as great.

EXTEND YOUR KNOWLEDGE

Foreign workers

In 1944, about one-third of the workforce in agriculture and war production were foreigners – either people from captured land in the east who had been put into forced labour camps or prisoners of war (there were some British POWs in such camps). The foreign workers included women. Unlike 'pure German' women, these women were expected to work. These figures do not include the prisoners in concentration camps, although many of these people were also made to work in labour camps, for example, at the Monowitz work camp near Auschwitz that had a Buna rubber factory.

The war came closer to home. After 1940, the cities of Germany were bombed intensively as a response to the German Blitz on Britain. Women had to cope with being bombed out (often more than once) and living without electricity, water or even a roof. Supplies of food and essentials were patchy – different areas had shortages of different goods. Even substitutes, such as soap made from fish oil, could be scarce.

From October 1940, women were allowed to join the armed forces in women's auxiliary services doing clerical and support jobs to free up men to fight. Members of the BDM had to serve in the forces for six months, then they could choose whether they left or stayed. By 1941, there were not enough women in the auxiliary services and the Nazis introduced compulsory military service for women between the ages of 18 and 40. However, like other Nazi measures to get women into work, this law was not rigorously enforced (women could be excused for a number of reasons, including 'ill-health'). By 1944, the shortage of men was so severe that women were being trained to operate anti-aircraft guns and were sent to work in signal stations close to the front.

SOURCE

 4 Nazi control policies meant that people were put in situations where they could not express normal feelings. Hildegard Gratz, interviewed in 1989 for the book *War Wives*, explained how people could be fearful about sympathising.

The postmen came to dread their round if ever there were one of those black-edged letters [reporting a soldier's death] to be delivered. It wasn't just a question of witnessing grief and suffering. You could get drawn into conflicts. The official line was that women were bearing the news 'with proud grief', but many of the women in their despair screamed out curses on this 'damned war'. It was a risky business even hearing them, because you were supposed to report them to the police for 'undermining the spirit of defence'.

ACTIVITY
KNOWLEDGE CHECK

Women in Nazi Germany

'Women in Germany had a terrible shock when the Nazis took over, because attitudes towards them, and their role and status totally changed.' How far do you agree with this statement?

The role and status of women in the FRG

The defeat of the Nazis in 1945 brought a new period of struggle for women in Germany. Once again, there were many 'surplus women'; in 1948, there were 7.3 million more women in Germany than men. Once again, the country was devastated. People were brought face to face with the evidence of Nazi atrocities – the most shocking of which was the Holocaust. It is not surprising that many people wanted the start of the FRG to be 'zero hour' (see page 32) – a clean slate on a large scale but also on a small scale – so that families where husbands did come home could also start again. For many families, the dislocation and deprivation were too much. The divorce rate rose sharply in the late 1940s as couples realised their marriages could not work. At its highest, in 1948, the divorce rate was 80 percent higher than in 1946.

In the first few years after the war, the military government in each of the occupied zones (see page 27) worked not only to help rebuild the economy, but also to rebuild ideas suppressed by the Nazis, such as the idea that individuals and individual families mattered. At first, however, it was more important to rebuild the economy, and the size of the task and the loss of so many able-bodied men meant women had to work. They worked at anything and everything, from clearing the rubble to building and office work.

SOURCE 5

Grete Emde, interviewed in 1989 for the book *War Wives*, lived in the town of Düren, near Cologne, before the war. She and her two daughters were evacuated during the war. She returned when the war ended. He husband did not get back until 1947.

There were a lot of evacuees returning to Düren after the war. We got back [to Düren] in an open railway coal wagon and found the town nothing but ash and rubble. My children and I were given the numbers 221, 222 and 223, there were so many of us returning then. I had nowhere to live; we had no furniture, no clothes, except what we were wearing. They gave me two bomb-damaged attic rooms. There was no glass left in the windows and the roof was leaking. They told me to buy three paper sacks and ask a farmer for some straw that could be our beds. We were told we'd just have to manage as best we could. Eventually we were all issued with a box to store potatoes in. We were each supposed to have an allocation of 50 kilos, but I never got my share because I didn't have a carpet or clothes that I could give in exchange.

The status of women

Immediately after the war, women worked on many committees set up to organise a return to normal. Fewer of them got involved in politics; many of those who did had been politically active before 1933. Ingrained Nazi propaganda that politics was not for women hampered them at this point. The ideal woman, for many people and political groups, was still a wife and mother, a fact underlined by the setting up of a Ministry for Family Affairs in 1953 to provide wives and mothers with financial benefits. The government did little to make work attractive for women. The FRG's first chancellor, Adenauer, made speeches about the importance of making more jobs available to women, and making working conditions more equal, but the government did not make that happen. The Bundestag, just like the Reichstag, was split between supporters of equal rights (still chiefly the SPD) and others, such as the CDU, who did not want to encourage women to work by providing equal pay or working conditions. However, Article 3 of the Basic Law (the new constitution) did guarantee unqualified 'equality under the law' for all citizens – although many Reichstag delegates had wanted to add a version of Weimar's 'in principle' phrase to make it more theoretical. So women, and minorities that had previously faced discrimination, were theoretically equal. As groups that were guaranteed legal equality in many countries have discovered, the law is necessary, but it is not enough to make certain of actual equality. While politicians accepted the need to revise the Civil Code to give women legal freedom, this did not happen until 1958. Before this, married women still needed their husband's permission to go to work, and the husband got full control of the woman's property on marriage.

Women and work

It was not until 1977 that the Marriage and Family Law was revised to give women equal rights in marriage. It also overturned the Civil Code law that said women could only work if it did not interfere with the role as a wife and mother, which had been in force since 1900 and was a significant expressions of *Kinder, Küche, Kirche* thinking. Women's liberation movements in the 1960s and 1970s were constantly battling this ingrained thinking. In a 1982 survey, 50 percent of men and 54 percent of women said that a man's career was more important than his wife's, and 70 percent of men and 68 percent of women thought women should stop work on marriage. Seventy percent of men and women thought men should work and women should care for the home.

Women's liberation movements

Women's liberation movements were active in Germany in the 1960s and 1970s, as they were in many other countries. As elsewhere, the movements were most popular with students and radicals, and so they were city (mostly university) based. In 1967, some West Berlin students set up a commune to live on equal terms. The women ended up doing almost all of the cooking and cleaning and left after six months. In January 1968, the Action Council for Women's Liberation was set up in West Berlin. Unlike many of its counterparts in other countries, this feminist organisation began with practical action, setting up day-care centres and organising a campaign with nursery school teachers to get the government to change the way day care and schools were run. In September, Helke Sander of the group spoke to the Socialist German Students Federation (SDS) at its convention in Frankfurt, describing what they had done. However, by 1969, the group had split and the 'mother faction' had been shed as not being theoretical enough and not looking at women outside the family.

The more radical and woman-focused groups targeted **Paragraph 218** and abortion rights. The journalist Alice Schwarzer was one of the leaders of this campaign, whose tactics included putting 30 photos of women on the cover of the magazine *Stern* with the title 'We've had abortions!' Groups that started organising protests against Paragraph 218 also set up refuges for battered women, not just in the cities but also in small towns. They wrote magazines and published pamphlets explaining about women's health, including contraception. A largely city-based lesbian movement evolved, with its focus on West Berlin.

EXTEND YOUR KNOWLEDGE

Arguing for equality

There were only four women on the parliamentary council that drew up the Basic Law for the new government of the FRG. They were Elizabeth Selbert (SPD), Friederike Nadig (SPU), Helene Wessel (Centre) and Helen Weber (CDU). Of these, only Selbert pushed for an unqualified equality clause in the Basic Law, and she pushed for specific reference to women (which she did not get). The others certainly believed in equal pay and other equal rights – but they assumed they would naturally follow. Selbert also argued that the Civil Code needed to be rewritten quickly. Although women now had legal rights, the rights of fathers and husbands over their wives and children were still specifically upheld in the Code.

KEY TERM

Paragraph 218

Paragraph 218 of the German Penal Code, established in 1871, made it a crime for women to seek an abortion (or for doctors to perform one) unless there were strong medical reasons to do so.

What did not happen in West Germany but which happened in other countries was the development of women's groups that focused on actively campaigning for progress in equality in the workplace and laws against sexual discrimination (such as the National Organisation for Women in the USA).

EXTEND YOUR KNOWLEDGE

Women and abortion in Germany

Despite campaigns by some women from the late 1900s, most Germans were anti-abortion and so supported Paragraph 218. Indeed, campaigning against Paragraph 218 was one of the activities that led many women in the Weimar Republic to leave the various women's groups that pushed for it. *Kinder, Küche, Kirche* thinking and strong church influence meant that there was more widespread opposition to the idea in Germany than in other countries such as Finland. Pressure from women's liberation groups in the late 1960s and early 1970s led to the passing of a law allowing abortion in the first 12 weeks of pregnancy in 1974. However, there was a huge public outcry and the law was declared unconstitutional by the Federal Court in 1975 because it violated the rights of the foetus.

EXTRACT

 3

From an article by the historian Eva Kolisky in *The Cambridge Companion to Modern German Culture*, published in 1998.

Close to half a century after the constitutional promise of equality had been formulated, many obstacles remained in place. Women's pay for full-time employment was still one-third lower than that of men. Most married women had interrupted their employment for family reasons, often more than once. Only 17 per cent had worked without career breaks. Returning to the labour market often involved accepting lower-skilled and lower-paid work. Women with children faced the challenge of combining family roles and employment without significant institutional support. Less than 5 per cent of pre-school children in West Germany had access to full-time childcare (in the GDR over 90 per cent did), kindergartens opened for two to three hours in the morning or the afternoon, schools closed at lunchtime.

Women's role and status by 1989

In 1989, there was still a clear demarcation in thinking between 'mothers' and 'working women', which was highlighted when the two Germanys united in that year – women in the DRG had a very different, more equal status. In the DRG women were far more likely to work full-time. State crèches provided childcare for them to do so. On the other hand, women in the DRG were more likely to need to do so for the family to have a sufficient income. In the FRG, the fact that married women were still seen in terms of the family gave motherhood a higher status than in many other countries, and families had tax breaks and benefits to encourage mothers to stay at home at least for the first three years of each child's life. Only 50 percent of married women with a child under 15 living at home had a paid job, and half of these were working part-time. In part this was driven by the fact that school hours meant women needed to be at home in the afternoon if they had no childcare.

EXTRACT

 4

From an article on the changing role of women written by the journalist and author Viola Roggenkamp, for the German newspaper *Die Zeit* on 22 April 1977.

Civil society is becoming introspective. It has to deliberate awhile, because what is going on in its own ranks is breaking the rules. Lonesome – twosome: this word pair in its original meaning is starting to lose its significance. What is supposed to have a negative connotation, and what [is supposed to have] a positive one, is being turned upside down. The bond for life, the institution of the family, seems to attract people less and less. Although society and the state are doing all they can to make it as uncomfortable and difficult as possible for bachelors to do their own thing – as compared with tax gifts for families – the number of those who prefer the single life to tying the knot is still growing. And those who tied the knot are increasingly untying it and becoming single again.

It is women, in particular, who are declaring their independence, throwing in the dishtowel and leaving the reservation known as matrimony. Or they avoid it in the first place. 'We no longer want to be there just for society,' which to them means having and raising children. At least they don't want that right away. Society was, for a moment, speechless. And then it calculated what that meant: If this trend continues, then the 57.9 million citizens of today's Federal Republic will have reduced their numbers to 22 million by about the end of the twenty-first century.

THINKING HISTORICALLY   Change (4a)

Significance

1 In Extract 4 how does Viola Roggenkamp view the changes in the position of women?

2 Does she see the changes as significant?

3 In Extract 3 how does Eva Kolisky view the position in 1998?

4 Why do you think these views differ so greatly?

A Level Exam-Style Question Section A

How far do you agree that the Federal Republic saw a complete rejection of the traditional female role and stereotypes that had existed in Germany since 1918? (20 marks)

Tip
Begin by defining the traditional role and stereotypes of women in Germany, then work from 1918, consolidating what you know about the role of women from 1918 to 1989, and how much it and attitudes changed.

ACTIVITY
KNOWLEDGE CHECK

Women in Germany, 1918–89
Prepare notes for a debate on the statement: 'By 1989, attitudes towards women had changed significantly for the better compared to those in 1918.' Choose to argue for or against the motion, but be careful when making notes to think of arguments that could be raised against you and how you would counter them.

WHY WERE EDUCATIONAL AND CULTURAL DEVELOPMENTS OFTEN CONTROVERSIAL IN GERMANY IN THE YEARS 1918–89?

Education in the Weimar Republic

Before the war, some Länder provided kindergarten care for an hour or so in the morning for children aged three to five. Education was compulsory from six to 14. Children of upper-class parents went to fee-paying schools. Working-class children went to *Volkesschule* – schools with large classes (usually over 50), which taught basic reading, writing and numeracy, as well as 'respect your betters and your place in society'. Most schools were **confessional schools**. Social mobility was difficult. Most working-class children needed to work from the age of 14, if not before, and any education after the age of 14 was expensive. The education system supported the social status quo, with children from professional families entering the professions, and so on.

Changes to compulsory education

The post-war temporary government was socialist and wanted a new, fairer, education system of state schools with a mixed, not confessional, intake and no religious education. It set up compulsory Grundschule for all children aged six to ten. It stopped clerical inspections of schools and said parents could remove their children from religious education. Some people (usually living in towns and cities in the northern Länder) approved, but others (especially in the rural and southern Länder) objected. Education was a significant political issue because most Germans felt strongly about it; some wanted religion taught, some did not. Others valued teaching religion not for its own sake, but because it taught basic morality. When the Weimar government came to write the Constitution, the various parties in the Assembly could not agree. The education Articles were a compromise; the popular Centre Party fought to keep confessional schools and religion in the curriculum. The Articles kept the compulsory Grundschule for all children aged six to ten, run by the Länder but meeting the needs of parents locally.

The government said that Germany needed a federal education law that gave the Länder guidelines to work to, while meeting the needs of families in their region. Until this was passed, non-confessional state schools (**common or simultaneous schools**) were set up. Confessional schools could run as private schools. Without a national law, Länder provided a wide variety of education. The government tried to introduce a federal school law in 1921 and in 1925, but the Reichstag could not agree. In 1927, a new bill proposed that confessional, common and **secular schools** be set up on an equal footing as long as they were requested by the parents of at least 40 children. Children in common schools would have religious education in their own

faith. All over Germany, people supported the bill, for example, the Reich Parent's League. Others, for example, the Volkskirche Association for Evangelical Freedom, vigorously opposed it. Some were relieved at the level of educational provision, others wanted religion to be a matter of the religious bodies, not schools. The bill was sent to be revised by a committee, which could not agree. It never came back to the Reichstag. The education system of Germany stayed diverse, as set up by the Länder. In 1931, there were 29,020 Protestant schools, 15,256 Catholic schools, 97 Jewish schools, 8,921 common schools and 295 secular schools.

EXTRACT

From 'German evangelical churches and the struggle for the schools in the Weimar Republic', an article on schooling changes in the Weimar Republic, written by the historian Frank J. Gordon in 1980 in *Church History: Studies in Christianity and Culture*.

During the Weimar Republic, the Germans were a nation ideologically rent asunder, and no issue revealed this so clearly as the school question. Every society seeks to perpetuate itself by inculcating its values into its youth, and the means to this end is the school. The problem in Weimar Germany was that there was no consensus as to what the society's values were – or should be. Not only did different groups hold differing opinions; they held them passionately, and as each group sought to mould the future of Germany according to its own beliefs, the struggle for the schools went beyond political party programs and Reichstag debates. School strikes were not unusual as parents sought to force the issue at the local level. In 1927 alone, parents demanding secular schools struck in Sterkrade and Erfurt; in Osterode, Catholic parents used the strike in an attempt to force the establishment of a Catholic school; in Dortmund, it was the turn of Evangelical parents. Germans of all ideological positions were taking the education of their children very seriously.

Education beyond the age of ten

Education beyond the age of ten had to be paid for. Students went to a Hauptschule (five years' schooling, leading to pupils going into apprenticeships or trade), a Realschule (six years' schooling, leading to pupils going into business or technical training) or a Gymnasium (nine years' schooling, leading to pupils going to university). This meant a child's career was decided at the age of ten. It was also possible to study in a variety of private schools with different systems. All students who wanted to go to university had to pass the Abitur exam. A 1928 survey of the fathers of university students found that 45 percent were civil servants (21.2 percent of these were university educated) and only 2.3 percent were working class. The government hoped to reform the system. However, the Weimar Constitution principle of freedom of choice meant that universities carried on as before, so the rest of the school structure had fit in with them. Universities had their own 'corporations', which formed nationwide associations.

The 'duelling' corporations, where differences were settled by a swordfight, were popular with the sons of wealthy landowners. Non-duelling corporations were seen as socially inferior. In 1928, about 56 percent of students were members of a corporation, some of which excluded people by race or social class, for example, the German-Aryan Chambers. Membership was important because support, or the lack of it, from those who had been in the same corporation affected a person's career.

Cultural experimentation, 1918–32

Music, art, theatre, books, even fashions, sports and buildings are all part of a nation's culture. Hiking was a part of Weimar culture, as was going to the opera and listening to the radio. Culture in the years of the Weimar Republic is often portrayed as vibrant, experimental and, especially in cities, decadent. It must be remembered that this is based on the activities of a small part of the population in particular places – there were large parts of Germany that were untouched by cultural experimentation, or were horrified by it. However, the cultural experimentation, with its influence on technology, efficiency and a stress on the modern, had considerable influence inside and outside Germany. Influential movements included **Bauhaus** and **Neue Sachlichkeit** ('New Objectivity'). Weimar culture divided into separate strands.

KEY TERMS

Bauhaus
This literally means 'architecture house' and it was a design school set up by Walter Gropius in 1919. It saw beauty in technology, simple (unfussy) design and careful craftsmanship. The name spread to a way of thinking and designing, not just the design school.

Neue Sachlichkeit
The New Objectivity movement grew out of the 'modern' and 'expressionist' movements that had developed just before the First World War. It meant a matter-of-fact representation of life. For example, showing the squalor of poverty in art, books or film.

- **Art elite culture**: Artists, intellectuals, writers and those who supported them formed this group. They were the most experimental, using ideas, developing them and then moving on. At first they favoured the forward-looking modernism or expressionism, but they then gave it a darker twist with the new objectivity movement. These movements existed side by side, influencing art, music, literature, opera and theatre. This creativity was highly valued by some wealthy people who subsidised artists.

- **Government-subsidised culture**: The government subsidised theatres, orchestras, museums and libraries – bringing culture to even quite small towns. However, subsidies were small and social welfare projects took priority for both federal and state governments. The government also encouraged other cultural initiatives. Ufa, a government-organised film consortium of the biggest film studios, made most German movies, including Fritz Lang's famous silent film about the future: *Metropolis*. It was the first full-length film to have a science fiction subject and the most expensive movie ever made up to that point.

EXTEND YOUR KNOWLEDGE

Expressionism and modernism
Expressionism stressed that thoughts and feelings (especially those of the artist) were more important than accurate representation in art or conventional musical tones. For example, the composer Arnold Schonberg devised a system of atonal music (not written in one key as conventional music was) and then had to develop a different system of musical notation to write it down. Schonberg also painted expressionist paintings. Like a significant number of the influential people in the Expressionist movement, Schonberg was Jewish.

Modernism embraced the future. It saw beauty in technology, mass production and mass culture. It also rejected representational art or stylised fiction about rich landowners.

SOURCE

This poster for the Fritz Lang film *Metropolis* shows many of the features favoured by artists during the Weimar period: the future, mechanisation, city life.

- **Popular culture**: This was widely enjoyed and largely non-subsidised. It was also the most diverse. Some people, especially the young in urban areas, were heavily influenced by US trends such as a consumer culture, advertising and jazz. But traditional music and plays still had a wide following. Cinema took off in the Weimar period. The subjects of Weimar movies were often 'dark'; *Nosferatu*, the first vampire movie, was made in Germany in 1922. Clara Zetkin, the communist and women's rights campaigner, agreed with New Objective thinking when she said that film should show real life, not unrealistic or fantastic stories. However, she was hoping such films would spark social reform.

Reactions to experimentation

The Weimar Constitution said free speech was a right of citizens. While some people thought this meant no censorship, the Criminal Code still had Paragraph 184, allowing the banning of 'obscene' films, publications and so on, which had been widely applied pre-war. The Weimar government used censorship to protect those under 16 from pornography, but people could paint, sing or write far more freely. While this allowed Expressionism to flourish, it also allowed critics of both Expressionism and of the government to express their views, forcefully. Many right-wing people, from politicians (for example, the Centre Party) to farmers, worried about Weimar culture on several levels. They were worried about the decadence, the increasing number of influential Jewish writers, artists and musicians, and the increasing Americanisation of the culture, for example, jazz and the way 'new women' dressed and behaved.

ACTIVITY
KNOWLEDGE CHECK

Education and culture in the Weimar Republic, 1918–33

1 Choose three aims that the provisional government of 1919 had for education. Write a paragraph explaining how far these had been reached by 1933.

2 Decide what was the most significant obstacle to the achievement of these aims and explain your choice.

3 Choose three words to sum up culture in the years 1918–32 and explain your choice.

Nazis education policies, 1933–45

The Nazis saw children as a valuable resource to be educated to become good Nazis, so they changed what was taught and who taught it. The state school structure stayed in place, but private primary school education was abolished. Fee-paying secondary schools and universities remained (only for 'pure Germans'), but they emphasised physical fitness. Corporations became Nazi Comradeship Houses and students had to join the Nazi student union. On 20 April 1933, the Nazis opened three National Political Education Institutions (Napolas) – free boarding schools to train an elite group of boys as government administrators.

Teachers and the curriculum

The Nazis had set up a National Socialist Teachers League (NSLB) in April 1929. In January 1933, it had just 6,000 members. 'Undesirable' teachers were purged by the law of April 1933, the same law that purged the civil service. A decree of 24 September 1935 gave the Nazis control over appointments. By 1937, it was almost impossible to get a job if not in the union, and 97 percent of teachers had joined. It ran courses that teachers had to attend to absorb the ideas they were expected to teach. The Nazis valued schools as places to indoctrinate children, but, following Hitler's lead, the Nazis were anti-intellectual. Teachers were not shown much respect by the administration or even by their pupils. Teaching became less popular as a profession. In 1938, 2,500 new teachers qualified and there were 8,000 teaching vacancies.

The most important role of schools, for the Nazis, was to teach loyalty to Hitler and Germany, physical fitness (for fighting or childbirth) and racial purity. So they made significant curriculum changes. At first, these varied from state to state, following general outlines. From 1935, a stream of central directives covered all years in education and all subjects. There was a significant increase in the amount of sport for both sexes; it came to fill about 15 percent of the curriculum. History was to focus on creating a *Volksgemeinschaft*, a sense of nationhood. Textbooks were censored, some were burned, others were simply mutilated. Booklets were printed to support new areas of the curriculum, for example race studies, which taught that Aryans were a superior race, Slav races were inferior and Jews were the source of all of Germany's problems. Biology focused on race, eugenics and motherhood for girls. Even maths had propaganda built in, for example calculating how much money could be saved for marriage loans if the money for keeping the mentally ill in care was 'saved'.

EXTRACT

6 From *Hitler and Nazi Germany*, written by the historian Stephen Lee and published in 2013.

The role of indoctrination in schools was extensive. The Law of 20 March 1933 provided for the separate education of boys and girls, ended confessional schools and placed curbs on private education. Schools also experienced a radicalisation of the curriculum which saw the introduction of race study, eugenics and health biology, all used as vehicles for imparting Nazi ideology. According the Hitler in *Mein kampf*, 'No boy and no girl must leave school without having been led to an ultimate realisation of the necessity and essence of blood purity'. Conventional subjects, such as History and Mathematics were given a twist: they were geared, at every possible opportunity to enhance Nazism. According to Rust, the Minister of Education, the purpose of textbooks was 'the ideological education of young German people'. For example, 22 out of the 76 pages of the official Mathematics textbook contained ideological references such as calculations of the cost to produce lunatic asylums as opposed to workers' housing. Another radical departure from the past was the preparation of boys and girls for separate and obviously stereotyped roles; in the process, matriculation options for girls were restricted to modern languages or home economics, compared with the options for boys of modern languages, science or classics. Meanwhile, 'elite' schools were established to mould the future leadership of the *Volksgemeinschaft*. Particularly important were the *Nationalpolitische Erziehungsanstalten* (or *Napolas*) for the education of future government officials and military personnel; the Adolf Hitler Schools and the Castles of Order (*Ordensburgen*). Underlying all the changes was the emphasis on race and anti-Semitism. Jews were forced out of German schools and allowed only to attend Jewish schools – until these were abolished in 1942. Finally, the teaching profession was also carefully reorganised: the Nazi Teachers' League (NSLB) – established in 1929 – accounted for 97 per cent of the total teaching force by 1937, as compared with 25 per cent in 1935.

Outside school

The Nazis set up a Hitler Youth movement with separate groups for boys and girls. Boys joined the Pimpfen ('Little Folk') aged six, moved to the Jungvolk ('Youngsters') at ten and then joined the Hitler Jungend ('Hitler Youth') aged 14–18. In 1937, the Hitler Youth opened their first schools for future administrators, similar to the Napolas, but their physical training focus did not equip students to work as administrators. Girls joined the Jungmadel ('Young Girls') at ten and then joined the Bund Deutsches Madel ('Association of German Young Women', BDM) aged 14, moving to the Glaube und Schöneit ('Faith and Beauty') aged 17–20. These organisations hammered home the messages being taught in schools. Pamphlets were issued for the leaders of meetings and summer camps to teach issues from the unfairness of the Treaty of Versailles, to racial purity, to the importance of having strong healthy babies. Anyone who was a member of a Hitler Youth group was also expected to report on anything their teachers (or family) did that was against Nazi teachings.

ACTIVITY
KNOWLEDGE CHECK

Education in Nazi Germany, 1933–45

1 Make notes for a Nazi official who is going to lecture a group of new student teachers about the role of education in Nazi society and how the Nazis have improved on the Weimar system. Your notes should include:

a) the structure of the education system

b) the role of teachers

c) the availability of education

d) the purpose of education.

2 What do you think is the most important point to get across? Underline it in your notes and write a footnote to explain why you have chosen this point for the official who will be reading the notes and approving them, or not.

KEY TERM

Gleichschaltung
The policy of 'co-ordination' involved making sure that every aspect of life was controlled to meet the aims of Nazi policy – from maternity care to torchlight parades, from theatre performances to radio broadcasts.

Nazi cultural policies, 1933–45

The Nazi policy of *Gleichschaltung* (co-ordination) meant the Nazis wanted tight control over culture as well as education. They censored 'unacceptable' culture and created one of their own. Nazi propaganda stressed that Germans were the Kulturträger (culture-bearers) of Europe, but that they had been led astray by the over-intellectual, Jewish-led, corrupt culture of Weimar Germany.

Censoring unacceptable culture

On 10 May 1933, with the help of the Nazi student organisation, the Nazis organised the mass burning of about 25,000 books that were 'unsound', from textbooks to famous foreign authors such as Ernest Hemingway. Jewish authors were all seen as 'unsound'. Towns also held book burnings on various dates throughout 1933. Art, music and theatre were also censored, weeding out works that were by 'unacceptable' people (for example, Jews), of an 'unacceptable' style (such as Expressionist), with an 'unacceptable' message (for example, pacifism) or that were 'intellectual' (for example, works of philosophy). Almost anything that encouraged individualism or discouraged conformity was 'unsound'. Magazines, newspapers and radio were censored (see page 48).

> **EXTEND YOUR KNOWLEDGE**
>
> **Burning books**
> The Nazis used the book burnings as yet another propaganda exercise. Students were collecting books from 6 April until 10 May for burnings. The burnings were held in the big public squares of 35 cities and big towns at night for the firelight effect. The books were taken there in a torchlight procession. The press were notified beforehand and senior Nazis made speeches. Goebbels spoke in the Opernplaz in Berlin and there were about 40,000 people there to listen to him denounce the immorality of the books to be burned and the fact that the Nazis were returning Germany to morality and family values. These 'immoral' books included Erich Maria Remarque's *All Quiet on the Western Front* (its realistic portrayal of the horrors of the First World War made it anti-war) and the works of Helen Keller (who was deaf-blind and championed the rights of the disabled).

KEY TERM

Reichskulturkammer (RKK)
All artists and those who dealt with art, such as publishers and art dealers, had to be registered with the Reich Chamber of Culture, which had separate departments for music, literature, motion pictures and broadcasting. The Chamber could refuse to register 'degenerate' art and it laid down strict guidelines for what could be produced.

Promoting acceptable culture

On 22 September 1933, Goebbels set up the **Reichskulturkammer (RKK)** to control all of the creative arts, stopping culture being 'elitist' and bringing it to everyone: the right sort of culture with the right sort of message. Nationalist, approachable, realistic art was acceptable. Despite the fact that Nazis encouraged modern production techniques in factories and spent a lot of public money on large-scale urban building schemes, they idealised the simple, rural life and the simple, healthy farmer, and approved art often reflected this idealised view. Art they saw as 'degenerate', on the other hand, focused on urban life and was often impressionistic if not completely abstract. The Nazis promoted 'acceptable' culture in a variety of ways.

- To involve everyone in culture, there were 'Strength Through Joy' trips to the theatre, the opera and to art galleries and museums. Art exhibitions not only showed people 'acceptable' art, they also 'educated' them in the kind of art they should despise. In 1937, for example, there was a 'degenerate' art exhibition in Munich. The pictures had information boards explaining why the art on display was 'worthless' and 'corrupt'. Acceptable art was even displayed in factories and other workplaces, to saturate people with images that conveyed Nazi propaganda.

- Sport was encouraged, for everyone, to produce a healthy nation. Artists, particularly sculptors, were encouraged to produce art that showed strong, healthy, physically perfect Aryans. Various kinds of large-scale sporting displays were held, and hosting the 1936 Olympics was an opportunity to show off German sporting abilities. Germany won 89 medals, 33 of them gold. The USA had the next highest number of medals (56) followed by Italy (22). So Germany could count the games as a triumph, even though they did not always use their best athletes – they excluded Jewish athletes, for example.

- The calendar of festivals and holidays was rearranged around important dates in Nazi history. For example, Mother's Day became an official holiday celebrated on Hitler's mother's birthday. There were parades that people were expected to watch and cheer, which usually ended with propagandist speeches. In large cities, such as Berlin and Munich, some of these parades were increasingly military in character after 1935, with not just soldiers but also tanks and armoured vehicles parading through the streets.

- The Nazis had huge building projects in the cities. This was useful in creating work, but it also created the impression of the Third Reich as being powerful and established. The large-scale public buildings were hung with enormous flags that showed the Nazi swastika. The Reichssportfeld (sports complex) and Olympic Village that were built especially for the 1936 Olympics in Berlin are an example of this. The stadium itself could hold over 100,000 spectators and there was a special stand for Hitler and his guests. The Nazi Party Rally Grounds in Nuremberg was another example of large-scale building designed to impress. It was here that the Nazis held yearly rallies in late August or September from 1933 to 1938. They lasted up to a week and drew not only Germans but many foreign journalists. It was also here that many of the party leaders made long propaganda speeches.

A Level Exam-Style Question Section B

To what extent did the Nazi regime overturn the Weimar education system? (20 marks)

Tip
Identify the key features of the Weimar education system and discuss the changes the Nazis made.

ACTIVITY
KNOWLEDGE CHECK

Culture in Nazi Germany, 1933–45

1
- **a)** In what ways were the Nazi aims for culture similar to their aims for education?
- **b)** Were there differences?

2 What do you think was the most significant difference between Nazi culture and Weimar culture? Justify your answer.

Education in the FRG

In 1945, the Allies wanted to remove Nazi influence and educate children for a democratic society. They shut all schools as soon as they took over in order to de-Nazify both the curriculum and the teachers.

Post-war re-education policies

The Allies hoped not only to de-Nazify the curriculum, but also to prevent the reintroduction of 'confessional' education and to stop with the early selection of career paths at the age of ten. Allied reforms focused on pre-university education, although they weeded out Nazis in the universities. They removed Nazi teachers and textbooks. However, children still needed education in reading, writing and numeracy. So the Allies said that schools could reopen in the autumn of 1945. While the Allies pressed for a reform of the system, it had still not been changed by the time the FRG was set up.

EXTEND YOUR KNOWLEDGE

Schools in the zones
The Allies wanted primary and secondary systems to be the same for all. Thanks to US record-keeping, we know that in the US zone in 1945, there were 1,200,174 children aged six to ten. The zone had 6,477 schools and 14,176 teachers. This gave a class size of 85. There were 510,000 children of this age with no schools to go to; their old schools had been bombed or converted to other uses. The Americans brought in over five million textbooks and tried to introduce an American-style system, with elementary, middle and high schools leading to university. Britain and France wanted similar systems.

The Soviets also weeded out Nazi teachers and set up teacher-training courses. They soon had 40,000 teachers, all from working-class backgrounds (for the Soviets wanted to teach communist values too). They introduced a system of eight years of primary school followed by either three years of apprenticeship-style training or four years of high school leading to university.

Under the Basic Law, the Länder remained responsible for educational and cultural policy, so there were few secular schools in the south, while they flourished in the north. The curriculum varied widely between Länder. There were long-running disputes between and within Länder, for example, over history teaching. Nazi propagandist history had to go – but should the Nazi period be taught? How should the First World War be taught? Many Länder resolved these questions by dry, factual history teaching of mainly European, not German, history. The control the Länder had over education remained a stumbling block to reform. Even if the federal government could agree reforms, it had to convince the Länder to adopt them. All through the 1960s and 1970s, meetings at federal and Länder level discussed the need to make education available to all on a fairer basis, including the introduction of Gesamtschulen (comprehensive schools). A joint federal and regional committee (Bund/Länder Kommission) failed to agree on any policies. In 1971, the Brandt government tried to introduce a federal framework for restructuring schools that Länder would have to adopt. It included extra help for the disadvantaged, less streaming by ability, more mobility within secondary schooling and a reform of the university structure. The Bundestag passed it, by a narrow majority, but it did not get the majority it needed in the Bundesrat to become law. By the time it was passed, it simply restated the existing system. School restructuring did not happen.

EXTRACT

7

From *A History of West Germany*, written by the historians Dennis L. Bark and David R. Gress and published in 1989.

In the western zones it was abundantly clear, by late 1946, that the Germans were distinctly uninterested in major reform [in education], and saw little merit in tampering with the one area of German culture of which they were proud. Even some social democrats shared this pride and associated resentment at Allied interference, despite their conviction that the old system with its confessional schools, needed change. Adolf Grimme, the last social democratic minister of culture in Prussia in 1932, and the first postwar minister of culture in Lower Saxony, complained often that it was disgraceful to hear foreigners say 'do such and such, it has worked well for us,' when in fact some of the best ideas for reform were of German origin.

An educational crisis

In the early 1960s, there was concern that the university system was failing to serve Germany's needs. Student numbers had risen. Facilities such as lecture theatres and student accommodation were inadequate. Critics said the curriculum was too old fashioned, teaching neither technology nor economics, for example, and still only catering mostly for the children of academics, civil servants and the well off. There were calls to make university education more 'democratic'. The state provided free education up to the end of secondary school. Parents were encouraged to keep their children in secondary education; the number of children in Gymnasium rose from 853,400 in 1960 to 2,019,000 in 1980. More students went to university, from 239,000 students in 1960 to 749,000 in 1980. In 1971, the Federal Education Promotion Act provided a mixture of state funding and state loans to encourage students from working-class families to go to university.

Cultural and generational tensions in the FRG

Cultural tensions

Germans had traditionally seen their country as a leader of European culture and, after the war, many Germans, especially older Germans, wanted to find a way to regain that position. It was easy to remove Nazi controls and to reintroduce the 'degenerate' culture that the Nazis had banned. It was easy to re-establish a free press, although this ran alongside Allied-influenced newspapers that were urged to discuss 'democratic' themes. It was harder to retain culture such as the music of Wagner that the Nazis had approved of; many people found it easier to adopt the cultural offerings that the Allies flooded their zones with, for example, Hollywood movies in the American zone and Shakespeare in the British zone.

Not all aspects of culture divided the generations. From the 1950s, a growing number of social movements drew in people of all ages. The anti-nuclear movement and various ecological and alternative lifestyle movements are all examples of this. They shared a rejection of consumerism and a desire for a peaceful, more equal, society. They also shared a desire to change established society – some of them simply wanted this to create a better society, others felt this change was the only way to save society from destruction.

Film and the cultural divide

The development of cinema in Germany gives an example of the cultural divide that grew up during the 1960s. Until the 1960s, one of the most popular film genres was *Heimatfilm* ('homeland' film) – films about Germany. In contrast to the American films flooding the market, these were set in beautiful rural locations with escapist, romantic plots. They were a complete contrast to the bombed cities and economic and political problems of everyday life. Some historians have argued that their strongly regionalist character helped the FRG to develop a 'regional' culture in contrast to the strongly nationalistic Nazi one.

During the 1960s, however, younger film-makers developed new styles and new themes. *Das neue Kino* ('New German Cinema') was set up in 1962 and chose to focus on 'the unassimilated past' of Nazi Germany or the social problems of the FRG. For example, Alexander Kluge's 1966 *Abschied von Gestern* ('Yesterday Girl') looked at the problems of an East German female migrant worker in the FRG, while in the same year Volker Schlöndorff's *Der junge Törless* ('Young Törless') examined German persecution of Jews. After 1965, they had state sponsorship from the Board of Young German Film.

Generational tensions

During the 1960s, there were increasing generational tensions, with many of the older generation wanting to see 1945 as 'year zero' and many of the younger generation wanting to confront the past (see Chapter 1). This expressed itself in culture too, with older people, in the main, wanting a familiar, traditional German culture and also wanting a comfortable consumerist lifestyle after the shortages and upheavals of the 1940s. Meanwhile, many younger people, especially students, pressed for a less consumerist lifestyle and a culture that faced both the present and the immediate past rather than embracing the distant past or American culture. Not all people who argued for this were young. For example, the psychoanalysts Alexander and Margarete Mitscherlich had left Nazi Germany but returned there after the war. In their book *The Inability to Mourn*, published in 1967, they suggested that most Germans who lived through the Nazi era behaved as if Nazism had been like an infectious disease, something they had caught, recovered from and were not responsible for. The Mitscherlichs said Germany had to face its past. The book was widely read and hugely influential, and some Länder reformed their history teaching in schools and universities to include Nazi Germany.

ACTIVITY
KNOWLEDGE CHECK

Education and culture in West Germany, 1945–89

1 How far do you think the Allies achieved their aims for the education system in the new Germany?

2 Draw a flow diagram to show the education system in Weimar Germany, from kindergarten onwards. Annotate it with any changes made up to the FRG in 1989.

3 Choose three words to sum up culture in the years 1945–89 and explain your choice.

How significant was the period of Nazi rule in the development of cultural and generational tensions in the FRG? (20 marks)

Tip
Begin by explaining the tensions, then relate them to the Nazi period and other causes.

HOW FAR DID ATTITUDES TOWARDS ETHNIC MINORITIES AFFECT THEIR STATUS IN GERMANY IN THE YEARS 1918–89?

German nationalism, and the idea of *Volk*, meant that from 1871 onwards, ethnic minorities (Poles, **Gypsies** and Jews) in Germany were not regarded as equal, especially by elite groups such as the landowners or the army. However, in Germany other prejudices were at work too – there was Protestant prejudice against Catholics and there was prejudice between different regions. Before the war, ethnic minorities were partially integrated with Germans – businessmen did business together and people interacted in daily life. There was even a significant amount of intermarriage, especially in the big cities. In 1915, for example, about one-third of all married Jews were married to non-Jews. However, there were also clear areas of difference: ethnic minorities had their own exclusive clubs and associations, and Germans had theirs.

Gypsies
In Germany during the 1920s and 1930s, 'Gypsies' referred to Roma or Sinti travelling people who had their own language and traditions and who travelled across Eastern Europe.

The status of, and attitudes towards, ethnic minorities, 1918–32

Under the Weimar Republic, life for ethnic minorities varied widely, depending on where these minorities lived and who they were. In broad terms, ethnic minorities were mostly accepted, although there was low-level discrimination of the kind faced by women. They received lower wages, for example, and were less likely to be hired than a 'German' man. Elite, conservative groups – the landowners and the army – were less welcoming, and city-based liberals were more welcoming. Article 113 of the Weimar Constitution said that groups that spoke a different language could not be legally stopped from using this language or preserving their national identity in the way they ran their schools and daily lives. This was a liberal law, but it was not always implemented and did not control laws made by the Länder against minorities. All through the period, people seem to have differentiated between 'the Jews' or 'the Poles' as groups, and the people from these groups who were their neighbours. People were more accepting of people who settled and became familiar.

EXTEND YOUR KNOWLEDGE

Weimar and eugenics

There were a significant number of people in the Weimar Republic who believed in various theories of eugenics, and these theories led some to racist thinking. Some eugenicists concentrated on the hereditary nature of disease, but others did not. Also, the very way that eugenics brought scientists to think about people could lead to dangerous thinking. In 1920, the authors of a book called *The Release and Destruction of Lives Devoid of Value* recommended the 'mercy killing' by the state of 'defective' human beings. This theory was then adopted by some people and applied to racial groups.

Attitudes to Jews

The Jewish population was about one percent of the German population in 1918, and the falling birth rate meant it was only 0.76 percent in 1933 (about 500,000). A significant number of Jews lived in the cities (66.8 percent) and about one-third of them lived in Berlin, which many anti-Semites called 'Jew Berlin'. Jews had a huge influence on culture and some became politicians. Five Jews held cabinet posts in the Weimar Republic, including Walther Rathenau who became foreign minister in 1922. The appointments led to criticism of the government for appointing Jews. Rathenau was assassinated shortly after his appointment and this led to the government banning some anti-Semitic organisations. The most aggressive of these, the German Peoples Offensive and Defensive Alliance, had 25,000 members in 1919 and around 170,000 when it was disbanded in 1923. They said the Jews had conspired with the Allies and lost Germany the war. Many of them joined the Nazis when their Party was disbanded. Some conservative judges were anti-Semitic and made racist remarks with their judgments, in the way that they were also anti-communist (see Chapter 2). When the depression hit, people became more desperate and more likely to want someone to blame for their misfortune. In Weimar Germany, the government was given a good deal of the blame, but so were Jews and communists. Jewish organisations, such as the Reich Federation of Jewish Front Soldiers, were set

up to fight anti-Semitism. Their name stressed they had fought for Germany in the war – 85,000 Jewish soldiers had fought and 12,000 had died. As the depression worsened, however, more and more people turned to parties on the extreme left or right and many of these parties were extremely anti-Semitic.

EXTRACT 8 From an article on letters to the Nazi newspaper *Der Stürmer* before the Nazis came to power, written by the historian Dennis E. Showalter in 1983.

The letters published in *Der Stürmer* clearly suggest the breakdown in Weimar Germany of neutral zones – areas of interaction in which surface civility set the tone and religious or cultural backgrounds were discounted, if not always entirely ignored. Since the mid-eighteenth century the development of the German Jewish community had been heavily influenced by the existence of such neutral territory. But the same letters also show that Jews fought back on a day-in-day-out basis, refusing to back away from these zones, or abandon them entirely, without protest. Facing public challenges, they could frequently count on support from personal friends, opponents of National Socialists, and what at this distance in time can legitimately be described as decent people. Officials too were often more helpful than they are generally credited with being, even in Weimar's later years. A Nazi who accosted a girl in the Nüremberg municipal park and asked her how she could associate with a Jew promptly found himself answering the questions of a police constable. The writer might fume that in the coming new Germany, Jews who consorted with Aryan women would end in the penitentiary. Nevertheless in the Weimar Republic, he was the one faced with a fine for disturbing the peace.

Attitudes towards Gypsies and other minorities

Gypsies were discriminated against, despite Article 113, largely because they moved around and so did not contribute to the country by working, paying taxes or becoming involved in life outside their own community. While there was no federal legislation against Gypsies, there were several Länder – Prussia and Bavaria, for example – that passed laws to try to control them. In 1926, Bavaria passed a series of laws against Gypsies, mostly controlling their movement and aiming to get their children into schools and the adults into work. Various other states, such as Hesse, adopted these laws. Other states passed different laws to control Gypsies. In 1927, for example, Bavaria said all Gypsies should carry identity cards.

Immediately after the war, the border between Poland and Germany was redrawn, leaving people from each group on the wrong side of the border. Some moved, others stayed because they did not want to leave their homes just because the border had moved. In 1925, there were over 200,000 Polish speakers in Germany and another 500,000 who spoke both Polish and German and who were more integrated, often born in Germany and seeing themselves as German. There was significant hostility to Poles because they had fought Germany in the war, and between 1925 and 1933 about 30,000 left the country.

One very visible ethnic group that met with rising hostility after 1923 was black people. This was because the French army of occupation that took over the Ruhr in 1923 had black units from the French colonies. From 1923 on, about 500 mixed race children were born as a result of the arrival of these troops and they were denounced as 'Germany's shame'. Black adults who had lived in Germany before 1923 found that some areas became more hostile after the occupation, though musicians and writers were accepted in the cities.

ACTIVITY
KNOWLEDGE CHECK

Ethnic minorities in Weimar Germany

'Ethnic minorities in the Weimar period were, just like women, legally supported by the government, but actually not helped at all.'

How far do you agree with this statement?

Nazi racial policies

The Nazis wanted Germany to be racially pure – peopled by Aryan Germans. The pursuit of racial purity included getting rid of the elderly and disabled, even if they were pure-blood Germans. They believed in the eugenic theories current in Weimar Germany and quickly brought laws into force to control breeding, as well as pursuing the increasingly violent persecution of ethnic minorities.

On 1 January 1934, the Nazis began a compulsory sterilisation programme. Doctors and hospitals had to report those they saw as 'unfit' to breed to one of the hundreds of Hereditary Health Courts set up all over Germany, which decided who to sterilise. Sterilisation was supposedly for hereditary defects, but it extended to include Jews, Roma and Sinti (Gypsies), criminals, and black and mixed race people. The law was widened in June 1935 to allow abortion of the unfit. Far from being concealed, sterilisation was publicised in the press and at public meetings. It was even taught in schools, using pamphlets, books and films. While there are no official figures, it has been estimated that about 400,000 people were sterilised between 1934 and 1945. Almost all were sterilised against their will. At least 5,000 people are known to have died from the procedure, most of them women. There is no knowing how many died after leaving the clinics.

Making Germany 'Jew free'

The Nazis did not immediately start murdering Jews and other ethnic minorities when they gained power in 1933. Hitler's position was not strong enough in 1933 to begin the mass slaughter now called the Holocaust. The Nazis worked towards the 'Final Solution' to the 'Jewish problem' by degrees. Even before gaining power, their propaganda was anti-Semitic. Next, alongside the propaganda, they began to separate Jews from the community in two ways. Firstly, by legal separation – removing Jews from jobs and separating them from non-Jews in public spaces. Secondly, bans and boycotts – imposed with escalating violence – on Jewish shops and businesses. The first national boycott, on 1 April 1933, did not stop people from using the shops and businesses. However, SA members stood outside urging people not to enter, sometimes roughly. From then on, the SA and Hitler Youth organised attacks and boycotts all over Germany, and the violence to both Jews and their supporters escalated. During April 1933, a series of laws restricted the number of Jewish university students, banned Jews from athletic and sporting groups and

stopped people with 'Jewish names' from sending telegrams. By the end of the year, Jews were excluded from working on German newspapers or as financial advisers.

EXTEND YOUR KNOWLEDGE

Other victims of the Holocaust

As well as the millions of Jews murdered in the Holocaust (historians cannot tell the number accurately, even to the nearest million) the Nazis also murdered about 200,000 Roma and Sinti; about 200,000 elderly, mentally ill and disabled (mostly German); and millions of Polish and Soviet civilians and soldiers. The Nazis also persecuted, imprisoned and executed political opponents, religious groups and homosexuals. It is important to remember that, while there were only five death camps, people died in their tens of thousands in concentration camps and labour camps due to the poor conditions and brutality of the guards.

The Nuremberg Race Laws

The Nuremberg Race Laws of 1935 heralded a growing number of laws to exclude Jews from many areas of life. Anyone with three or four Jewish grandparents was 'Jewish'. So a Catholic nun whose parents had been Jewish but had become Catholic and brought the nun up as a Catholic was still counted as Jewish. Many different organisations had begun to exclude Jews ahead of the exclusion laws. Regional governments had their own anti-Semitic laws. A yellow star was displayed on Jewish-owned shops, encouraging random violence, such as window-breaking by the Hitler Youth or SA. Propaganda urged the idea of separation to prevent contamination: separate, yellow, park benches, tram cars, restaurants, concerts and swimming pools were to keep 'pure Germans' safe. It marked Jews as not just different, but also dirty, dangerous, less than human. The timeline on page 108 outlines Nazi measures, including *Kristallnacht*, important as one of the first large-scale organised acts of violence against Jewish people and their synagogues. The language the Nazis routinely used to describe the Jews never referred to them in human terms: 'sub-human', 'vermin', 'filth', 'vile polluters'. By the time the Nazis were transporting Jews to concentration or death camps, they were not even referred to as living things at all – they were called 'cargo' or '*stüke*' ('pieces', used for factory goods).

KEY TERM

Kristallnacht
The 'Night of Broken Glass' on 9 November 1938 when the Nazis organised concerted attacks on Jews across Germany. Over 260 synagogues were burned and Jewish-owned homes and shops attacked and looted. Over 20,000 Jews were arrested and taken to concentration camps; some were released some weeks later. Jews were then taxed a billion Reichsmark for repairs that were never carried out.

Getting away

At first the Nazis encouraged Jews to leave Germany and took a 'flight tax' of 30–50 percent of their wealth. Between 1933 and 1939, over 450,000 Jews emigrated. Some did not go far enough; those who settled in the Netherlands or France later found themselves in Nazi-occupied territory, often without time to get away because of the rapid German advance into these countries. However, emigration got harder as the Nazis became less willing to let Jews go and as other countries began to set quotas rather than accepting everyone who wanted to come. On 11 March 1938, the German army 'liberated' Austria. Immediately, it imposed the same restrictions on the 185,000 Austrian Jews as were already in place in Germany. They also introduced humiliating tasks – for example scrubbing the streets on their knees – to dehumanise the Jews more rapidly. They said Jews could leave – the flight tax this time was almost everything but a suitcase each. There were only about 60,000 Austrian Jews left when the outbreak of war put a stop to large-scale emigration and caused a shift in Nazi policy.

War and a change of policy

When Germany invaded Poland in 1939, special SS units called *Einsatzgruppen* were set up. Their official job was to root out Polish political and resistance leaders and kill them. The troops also killed Jews in increasing numbers by shooting or, for example, locking them in a synagogue and setting it alight. By the time the Nazis invaded the USSR in 1941, they were committing mass murder by rounding up Jews, forcing them to dig huge graves, making them strip and stand on the edge of the graves and shooting them. In very approximate figures, two million of the six million Jews murdered in the Holocaust were *Einsatzgruppen* victims.

TIMELINE – ANTI-SEMITIC MEASURES IN NAZI GERMANY

1933

1 April: official boycott of Jewish shops and businesses is called by Nazis. Local violence against Jews escalates (for example, storm troopers in Wuppertal torture then drown a Jewish dentist; four Jewish political prisoners murdered in Dachau)

7 April: Law for the Restoration of the Professional Civil Service excludes Jews and 'politically unreliable' people from government posts, including the civil service (federal and regional) and teaching (including universities)

1934
More exclusion of Jews from acting, working for the armed services, taking university or professional examinations

1935
15 September: Nuremberg Race Laws pull together and extend all the anti-Semitic legislation; laws also define a Jew as someone with three or four Jewish grandparents

Reich Citizenship Law deprives Jews of German citizenship

Law for the Protection of German Blood and German Honour forbids marriage, or sex, between Germans and Jews

1936
Jewish doctors cannot work in government hospitals and Jewish patients cannot use these hospitals (from 25 June 1938 no Jewish doctor can treat non-Jewish patients)

1938
5 October: all Jews must have 'J' stamped in their passports

9 November: *Kristallnacht*: burning of synagogues and other anti-Jewish violence, including the looting of shops and homes

3 December: all Jewish businesses and shops to be taken from the Jews and Aryanised

1939
1 September: Jews cannot be out after 8 p.m. in winter, 9 p.m. in summer and on 23 September radio sets are forbidden for Jews

September: *Einsatzgruppen* begin to murder political opponents and Jews

28 October: first Jewish ghetto set up in Poland

23 November: all Jews in Poland have to wear a Star of David

1940
12 February: first large deportation of German Jews to ghettos

1941
1 September: all Jews over the age of six have to wear a yellow Star of David with the word 'Jude' on it in black

8 December: an experimental death camp at Chelmno begins gassing Jews

1942
20 January: Wannsee Conference authorises the use of death camps

Ghettos

To the Nazis, the Poles were of an inferior race to Aryans, and Polish Jews even more so. Those that were not shot were rounded up into ghettos in towns and cities such as Warsaw. The first ghetto, in Piotrkow, was set up in October 1939. Ghettos were deliberately badly overcrowded and food and medical supplies were kept to a minimum. Often electricity and water were only available for a few hours each day. Nazi propaganda then stressed the fact that Jews were dirty and ridden with lice and fleas – a situation they had created. The 'Strength Through Joy' organisation ran bus trips through the Łódź ghetto, so people could see for themselves what a depraved race Jews were. This was another way to dehumanise them. Gypsies were also sent to the ghettos. About 5,000 were sent to the Łódź ghetto, for example, where there were already 160,000 Jews at the start, and over 40,000 more were sent there from Germany.

Concentration camps and the Final Solution

As well as being coralled into ghettos, Jews were sent to concentration camps. Sometimes they were sent straight to the camps, sometimes they were sent to the camps from the ghettos. The camps were full of a variety of groups that the Nazis saw as 'undesirable'. Everyone had to wear a patch on their clothes to show what their 'crime' was. From these camps people were sent to dig roads, work on the land or work in factories. The conditions were appalling and there was hardly any food. People died from starvation, dysentery or due to beating or other mistreatment by the guards. Most of these camps had a crematorium to burn the many people who died there. The Final Solution for the Jews was decided at a Conference held at Wannsee on 20 January 1942. Death camps were to be set up at Chelmno, Treblinka, Sobibor, Belzec, Majdanek and Auschwitz-Birkenau (see Figure 4.1). Here, if people worked, they only did so for a short while, while waiting to be gassed.

Figure 4.1 Map of concentration camps and death camps in Nazi-occupied Europe.

Complex change

Changes leading up to the Final Solution.

Strand	Explanation of how the strand links to the Final Solution
The Nazi 25-Point Programme says Jews cannot be German citizens	Makes Nazi anti-Semitic policies clear
The Nuremberg Laws and other exclusion laws	Defines who is Jewish Begins the separation of Jews from other Germans
Einsatzgruppen begin to mass murder	Begins the deliberate mass murder of Jews
The Wannsee Conference	Takes the decision to set up death camps

Make two copies of the graph below.

1 On the first, plot the individual strands against the *y*-axis. Use a different colour for each. You do not need to label it with the events.

2 On the second graph, plot a single line which is a combination of all four strands. (For example, at a given point, two of the four strands are plotted high up on the *y*-axis, while two are plotted lower. The combined strand would have to be plotted somewhere in the middle to represent a summary of those four individual strands.)

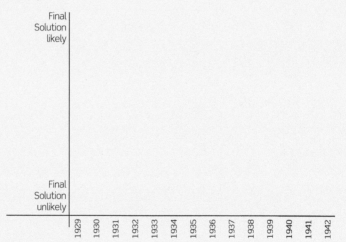

Answer the following questions:

1 How have the strands combined to make change less or more likely?

2 Why did the Final Solution begin in 1942 and not before?

ACTIVITY
KNOWLEDGE CHECK

Ethnic minorities in Nazi Germany

1 Draw a flow diagram to show younger students the way that Nazi racial policies to the Jews escalated towards the Final Solution. Keep the text as brief as possible, while covering the main points.

2 Were Nazi attitudes to minorities very different from previous attitudes?

3 Was the status of minorities in Nazi Germany very different from previously?

The status of, and attitudes towards, ethnic minorities in the FRG

At the end of the war, Germany became a country with millions of refugees and people on the move; some wanting to leave the country, some wanting to enter it and some just wanting to reach a different part of it. The administrations of the various Allied zones tried to manage this vast mass of people to the best of their ability – but it took until 1947 to produce a near accurate rough count. On 1 April 1947, there were about 10 million refugees and 'expellees' – Germans from parts of Europe that were no longer part of Germany. To begin with, these people were seen as a problem: they needed housing and feeding. However, it soon became apparent that they were important to the building of the economy (see Chapter 3).

The economic boom of the 1950s and 1960s

The economic boom in the FRG during the 1950s created a need for more workers. By 1955, there was more or less full employment, and the government wanted to recruit workers from abroad. At first, the unions disliked the idea. There was already a significant number of foreign workers in the country, and the unions feared that new foreign workers would force wages down and undercut existing workers by accepting less favourable working conditions. So the government guaranteed non-German workers the same wages, and agreed to give preference to German workers when hiring. A Federal Office for Labour Recruitment was set up in Nuremberg to run offices in the countries with which West Germany had labour recruitment treaties. People applied for work and had a physical examination to make sure they were fit to work. They then signed a contract for a particular job, which they could not leave, for just one year. The employer provided basic accommodation, often in dormitories near factories and outside towns, cutting them off from the community. The programme was stepped up after 1961, when the Berlin Wall was built (see Chapter 1) and West Germany lost its East German labour force.

The foreign labour programme favoured men of 20–40 years of age at first, and the work they were given was heavy manual labour. Rather than taking work from Germans, they were taking jobs that Germans were happy to leave for other work. Between 1961 and 1973, about three million German workers switched from industrial and agricultural work to white-collar jobs. Between 1961 and 1971, about 870,000 Germans left jobs in mining and 1.1 million guest workers took those jobs. From 1960, more female workers were recruited (43,000 in 1960; over 700,000 in 1973) at the request of some industries – electronics and hospitality, for example. The number of foreign workers kept rising and an increasing number of 'illegal' foreign workers arrived, without a work permit or a job. These people took the worst jobs possible for very low wages, and no accommodation or anything else was provided.

The new foreign workers became known as 'guest workers'. This name underlines the German attitude – they were guests, so their stay would be temporary. While they had guarantees under their contracts with their employers, they did not have the rights of German citizens. Even if their contracts were renewed (25 percent of workers in Germany in 1964 had been there over three years),

it was on a year-by-year basis. However, they kept coming, and many stayed. Some brought their families, hoping to settle and integrate in the community. The unions helped them to adjust to work, but they were less helpful about long-term assimilation, saying they had no desire to turn these workers into Germans. The guest workers had support from church organisations, for example, the Catholic organisation Caritas and the Protestant organisation Diakonisches Werk, and also from their own organisations. Tensions grew due to the hopes of the guest workers and the expectation of most Germans, and this came to a head during the 1966 recession (see page 83).

The recession did not last long, but it produced a significant amount of hostility to guest workers, especially those who did not speak much German or try to integrate. Many landlords refused to take guest workers as tenants, so helping to confine them to living among other guest workers in the poorest areas. The recession was over quickly, and guest workers were in demand again. However, hostility, especially from some right-wing groups, remained and it was made worse when guest workers began to organise and demonstrate for better working and living conditions.

EXTEND YOUR KNOWLEDGE

Welcoming the millionth guest worker

In 1960, the average number of guest workers was 270,000. Just four years later, the millionth guest worker arrived. The labour minister, Theodor Blank, made a speech to mark the occasion. He said that guest workers had been the foundation of Germany's success and that, as their labour pool was likely to go on shrinking (with only 22 percent of the German population under 15 years of age), guest workers would continue to be important. He said they were learning useful skills for their return home, but that the government was also working to help to make their lives in the FRG easier, including bringing families over. This was because they were keen for guest workers to extend their stay to make things more stable for them and also for their employers. This meant help with learning the language and with child benefits and other welfare help.

EXTRACT

9 From the *Encyclopaedia of Contemporary German Culture*, edited by the historian John Sandford in 2013.

The rapid growth of the West German economy from the early part of the 1950s meant that a constantly expanding workforce was needed. The return of more than 4 million prisoners of war, the influx of 4.7 million refugees and expellees of working age from former German territories in the late 1940s and early 1950s, and the 1.8 million migrants from East Germany up to the building of the Berlin Wall in 1961, ensured a constant supply of new workers for the expanding economy. But by 1960 unemployment had fallen below 1 percent and the influx had dried up. Therefore new sources of labour were required. From 1960 to the stop on recruitment in 1973 the number of foreigner workers grew from 280,000 to 2.6 million.

TIMELINE – LABOUR RECRUITMENT TREATIES

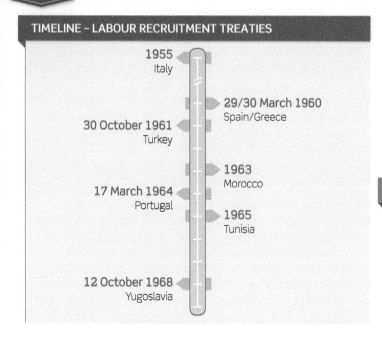

1955
Italy

29/30 March 1960
Spain/Greece

30 October 1961
Turkey

1963
Morocco

17 March 1964
Portugal

1965
Tunisia

12 October 1968
Yugoslavia

with no pre-school education and language help as much pre-school education was run by Christian, mainly Catholic, schools. Many groups set up their own national schools because children were not learning in state schools. However, this did not help integration. Koran schools attracted a lot of hostility. In the 1980s, there was a sharp rise in the number of refugees and asylum seekers applying to enter, and actually entering, the country. The Basic Law encouraged this.

Challenges in the 1970s and 1980s

During the 1970s, with the oil crisis and the sudden rise in unemployment, guest workers were again under pressure to leave jobs and Germany. This time, in November 1973, the government put a stop on hiring and banned permits for families of workers already in the country. The number of guest workers fell to just under two million. In 1974, Ford car works in Cologne offered guest workers 'voluntary severance packages' based on their time working at the factory. They said that mass layoffs were likely otherwise, and that many would not get their contracts renewed at the end of the year. Many workers accepted, not realising that, legally, workers had to be laid off according to a point system, so a German with two children, for example, would be laid off before a Turkish guest worker with four children. Many guest workers did not leave. In 1975, the government gave guest workers' children the same benefits as other children, because there were now unemployed guest workers. In 1977, the ban was removed and workers started coming in again. In 1978, the first Federal Commissioner for Foreigners' Affairs was appointed by Helmut Schmidt to work for the rights of foreign workers and to promote their integration. At the same time, a clear set of rules for applying for unrestricted residence, but not citizenship, was laid down.

One of the most serious problems was managing the education of children of guest workers. The government policy, as laid down in the Basic Law, was to provide 'democratic education': equal opportunity for all. They tried to persuade the Länder to provide mixed-culture learning groups with classes of Germans and of the children of guest workers, giving these children books in their mother tongue and books in German. The number of foreign children in schools rose from 165,000 in 1976 to almost 200,000 in 1983 and 60 percent of these were Muslim, so there were significant cultural problems with education provision. Most Muslim guest workers' children started school at the age of six

EXTEND YOUR KNOWLEDGE

Ethnic Associations

Guest workers often belonged to 'Ethnic Associations': groups of people who came from the same country as guest workers. West Germans were divided over these organisations. Some felt that they helped the newcomers to settle in, helping them to learn the language and understand cultural differences. Other West Germans felt that these associations slowed, or even stopped, the newcomers from integrating into West German life. In fact, both these things seem to have happened. The attitude of the associations themselves was vital. For example, Greek associations tried hard to work to integrate their members, while Turkish associations were more likely to try to preserve Turkish culture, especially in the Muslim communities. Integration was more difficult without a shared religion, or an understanding of, or sympathy for, the demands of a different religion by some West Germans.

While Ethnic Associations affected how guest workers were assimilated, the biggest help, or hindrance, to assimilation was the attitudes of West Germans themselves. Suspicions about guest workers' religion and their politics caused hostility. Language problems increased the lack of understanding. Also, while politicians and people generally continued to view guest workers as temporary residents, there was little incentive for either group to work for assimilation. Suspicions about their religion and their politics caused hostility.

ACTIVITY
KNOWLEDGE CHECK

Ethnic minorities in the FRG

1   To what extent is Source 7 representative of the experience of guest workers in the FRG between 1945 and 1989? Explain your answer.

2   Explain what you think was the most significant factor in changing attitudes to minorities in the FRG.

AS Level Exam-Style Question Section B

Was unemployment the main reason for the varying treatment of minorities in the FRG between 1960 and 1989? (20 marks)

Tip

Explain how the treatment of minorities varied and then analyse the reasons for these shifts, weighing them in importance against unemployment.

SOURCE
7   A photo of Turkish families in a West Berlin park on 1 May 1980, the May Day holiday.

ACTIVITY
SUMMARY

Life in Germany and West Germany, 1918–89

How far was Nazi Germany an aberrant period in the history of Germany in the years 1918–89, neither influenced by the Weimar Republic nor influencing the FRG?

Answer this question referring to the three themes of this chapter:

- attitudes towards women

- education and cultural developments

- attitudes towards ethnic minorities.

WIDER READING

Hiden, J. *The Weimar Republic*, Longman (1996)

Murphy, D., Morris, T. and Fulbrook, M. *Germany 1848–1991*, Collins Educational (2008)

Peukert, D.J.K. *Inside Nazi Germany*, Penguin (1993)

Williamson, D. *Germany: From Defeat to Partition 1945–63*, Routledge (2001)

Footage of the book burning in Berlin in 1933 can be found on the United States Holocaust Memorial Museum website.

Colour footage of the 1938 Nuremberg rallies can be found online, although the sites often also contain neo-Nazi propaganda.

1.5

How far was Hitler's foreign policy responsible for the Second World War?

KEY QUESTIONS

- How far did German history influence Nazi foreign policy?
- To what extent did Hitler shape Nazi foreign policy?
- Why did Germany invade Poland in 1939?
- To what extent did other nations contribute to the outbreak of war?

INTRODUCTION

How far was Nazi foreign policy responsible for driving the world to war? To what extent did 'Nazi foreign policy' mean 'Hitler's foreign policy' and to what extent did Hitler have, and follow, a master plan? Did Hitler intend war at all? These questions do not have simple answers. The answers rest on interpretations of history, which are affected by many things including the discovery of new evidence and trends in historical thinking.

Changing views of historians

Immediately after the Second World War a significant number of historians said that Nazi expansionist foreign policy, more specifically *Hitler's* expansionist foreign policy, took the world to war in 1939. It was widely accepted that Hitler always intended to go to war in order to build a German empire, although there were differing views about how far he had a step-by-step master plan to achieve this. Then, in 1961, two books were published that changed the way historians thought about the causes of the war. In Britain, A.J.P. Taylor's *The Origins of the Second World War* suggested that, while Hitler wanted a German empire, he did not have a master plan, nor did he necessarily intend to go to war in 1939. Taylor's view was that Hitler mainly reacted to events, at home and abroad. Meanwhile, in Germany, Fritz Fischer's *Germany's Aims in the First World War* drew connections between German aims in the First and Second world wars, suggesting that Nazi foreign policy continued a long-held German expansion policy rather than being a new policy. The interpretations caused outcry among many historians, some of whom said Taylor was 'excusing' Hitler.

1933 – 30 January: Hitler becomes chancellor of Germany

14 October: Germany leaves League of Nations and Disarmament Conference

1936 – 7 March: German troops re-occupy the Rhineland

17–18 July: Spanish Civil War begins

1 November: Germany and Italy announce the Rome-Berlin Axis

| 1933 | 1934 | 1935 | 1936 |

1934 – 26 January: Germany and Poland sign Non-Aggression Pact

25 July: Failed Nazi putsch in Austria

18 September: USSR joins League of Nations

1935 – 13 January: Saar plebiscite: people vote to join Germany

16 March: Germany introduces conscription

1935 – 2 May: USSR and France: Mutual Assurance Treaty

16 May: USSR and Czechoslovakia: Mutual Assurance Treaty

18 June: Britain and Germany sign Naval Agreement

Understanding Hitler

Hitler's foreign policy speeches and actions varied wildly. He could tell one set of people he wanted to make a diplomatic deal over a piece of disputed territory, for example with Poland over the Polish Corridor, while telling others there was no option but to go to war over that territory. This can be interpreted as an inability to make up his mind, cunning diplomacy (manipulating these groups by giving them different impressions of his aims) or shifts in thinking in response to variations in the political situation and which nations he saw as most dangerous/helpful to Germany at the time. It could be all of those things at different times.

This chapter works by approaching the build-up to the Second World War by way of a series of questions. Timelines provide a chronology. However, it is also important to keep the various causes of the war in mind when considering one aspect of them. Most historians agree that the war was triggered by Germany's invasion of Poland. Figure 5.1 summarises other, less immediate, causes for quick reference.

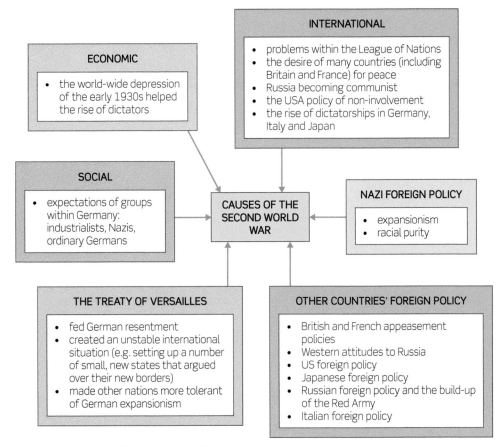

ECONOMIC
- the world-wide depression of the early 1930s helped the rise of dictators

INTERNATIONAL
- problems within the League of Nations
- the desire of many countries (including Britain and France) for peace
- Russia becoming communist
- the USA policy of non-involvement
- the rise of dictatorships in Germany, Italy and Japan

SOCIAL
- expectations of groups within Germany: industrialists, Nazis, ordinary Germans

CAUSES OF THE SECOND WORLD WAR

NAZI FOREIGN POLICY
- expansionism
- racial purity

THE TREATY OF VERSAILLES
- fed German resentment
- created an unstable international situation (e.g. setting up a number of small, new states that argued over their new borders)
- made other nations more tolerant of German expansionism

OTHER COUNTRIES' FOREIGN POLICY
- British and French appeasement policies
- Western attitudes to Russia
- US foreign policy
- Japanese foreign policy
- Russian foreign policy and the build-up of the Red Army
- Italian foreign policy

Figure 5.1 Causes of the Second World War.

1938 – 11–13 March: Germany takes Austria: Anschluss

29–30 September: Munich Conference: Germany, Italy, Britain and France

1939 – 15 March: Germany takes Bohemia and Moravia

23 March: Germany takes Memel

22 May: Germany and Italy: Pact of Steel

23 August: Germany and USSR: Non-Aggression Pact

| 1937 | 1938 | 1939 | 1940 |

1939 – 1 September: Germany invades Poland

3 September: Britain and France declare war on Germany

17 September: USSR invades Poland

Evaluating interpretations of history

Interpretations are a matter of opinion, but this does not mean we cannot evaluate them or should discard an interpretation that is clearly based on the historian's point of view. There is nothing wrong with historians having a point of view. What is important is that historians present the evidence to support that point of view and explain the methods they used to collect this evidence, arguing logically for their point of view.

The interpretations of historians who present no evidence and show no clear methodology will be less valid than clearly supported ones because we have no way of knowing, unless they show us, how they arrived at the interpretations. Bear the following considerations in mind when reading each of the extracts in this section:

- Is it giving an interpretation or just information?

- Is there evidence to support any interpretation given?

- Is there any sign of the methods used?

It is also important to realise that historians can have a point of view that you do not agree with and still provide clear and helpful analysis of aspects of a situation. It would be a mistake, for example, to not consider Taylor's analysis of the impact of the First World War on Germany just because you decide that you do not agree with his view of the extent to which Hitler's policies were new.

 THINKING HISTORICALLY | Interpretations (5a)

Historical methodology
Below are three descriptions of the perspectives of famous historians.

Herodotus	Leopold von Ranke	Karl Marx
• Research consisted of conversations • Identified that accounts had to be judged on their merits • Some believe that certain passages in his writing are inventions to complete the narrative	• Believed in an evidence-based approach and relied heavily on primary sources • Desired to find out the 'facts' and discover the connections between them • Stressed the role of the individual in shaping history	• Believed that history would go through stages leading to a state where everybody was equal • Believed that historical changes were ultimately determined by changes to the economy • Was often driven by political considerations and looked for evidence to support his point of view

Work in groups of between three and six. Each member or pair should take the perspective of one of the above historians and argue from that perspective. Work through the questions as a group and answer the last question individually.

1 Herodotus did not use written evidence to construct his history. Does this mean that his history is less useful than the others?

2 Ranke based his writing almost exclusively on primary sources from the time he was investigating rather than secondary sources. How might this affect his ability to see larger patterns in history compared with the other two?

3 Marx put his philosophy of history, and perhaps politics, first and research second. Would this make his history weaker than the others?

4 'Colourful' individuals populate the writing of Herodotus and Ranke, while Marx concentrates on the difference between classes. Write three historical questions that each historian might ask.

5 The three historians all had different methods and motivations and yet their writing has been valued ever since it was created. Explain how the prior knowledge that we bring to the history that we write does not invalidate it.

Interpretations of Hitler's foreign policy and the Second World War

The level of debate over the origins of the Second World War in Europe is possible because the various interpretations put forward by historians are just that, interpretations. No one argues whether or not there was a war. However, once historians move on to discuss the relative importance of each cause, and the intentions of various governments and people involved, dispute is possible. How far is it possible, even with documents to hand, to discuss the intentions of anyone? Should you believe what politicians say in their public speeches? Should you believe what they say to each other? There are records of talks between Hitler and politicians from other countries. His aims, and theirs, are often clearly stated. How much either side meant what they said is hard to know. Some historians move into the realms of 'what if?' history, also called 'counterfactual history', trying to answer questions such as: 'If Hitler had not come to power, would there have been a war?' and 'If Britain and France had acted against Germany earlier, could a war on the scale of the Second World War have been avoided?'

Figure 5.2 outlines the main positions in the historical debate over the Nazis and the causes of the Second World War. Some historians, both immediately after the war and now, interpret the situation using elements from both the intentionalist and the structuralist camps, while others put themselves very firmly in one camp.

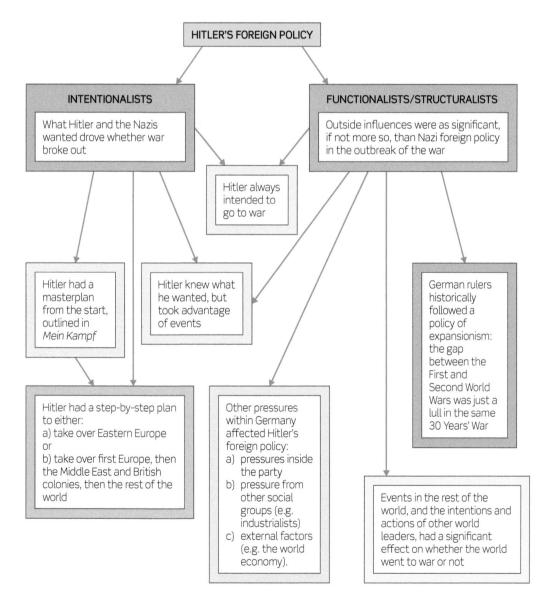

Figure 5.2 Historians' interpretations.

EXTRACT

1 From 'The origins of the Second World War', written by the German historian Georg Franz-Willing for the *Journal of Historical Review* in 1986.

The outbreak of the war of 1939 was caused directly by the conflict between Poland and Germany over the 'Corridor' and Danzig problems. Great Britain and the USA did not grant Germany fulfillment of her rights to self-determination: unification of Austria and the Sudeten region with the German Reich in 1938 had shifted the relations between the powers on the continent in favor of Germany – an event unacceptable for England's traditional policy of a 'Balance of Powers.' Equally unacceptable for America was the Europeans' independent decision at the Munich conference, excluding the United States and the Soviet Union. By means of a European war, both Roosevelt and Stalin intended to realize their dream of world rule according to totally different views and totally different aims. Thus Washington and Moscow staged a new European war, enabling both colossi to destroy and displace a Europe engaged in self-mutilation. The European order of the world was replaced by two 'super powers,' leading to a balance of terror. Thus, America lost her position as arbiter mundi ['world arbiter'] which she had attempted to exercise in 1919, and was forced on the defensive against an aggressive and expansionist Communism striving for exclusive world domination.

EXTRACT

2 From *The Origins of the Second World War in Europe*, written by P.M.H. Bell and published in 2007.

We started by examining the view that between 1914 and 1945 Europe passed through a Thirty Years' War, of which the so-called Second World War was only the final phase. This interpretation carries much weight, in two notable respects. First, eastern Europe emerged from the wreckage of the First World War and the ensuing settlement in a profoundly unstable condition, with potential conflicts lurking in half a dozen different areas. Moreover, in the period between 1919 and 1922 the countries of eastern Europe made very different assessments about the use of force than those current in the weary west. The Bolsheviks fought and won a civil war, and established their authority by force over much (though not all) of the old Russian Empire. The Poles defeated a Russian invasion at the Battle of Warsaw in 1920, and then reaped the fruits of victory by pushing their frontier eastward at the Treaty of Riga in 1921. They also seized Vilna and held it in defiance of Lithuania; while the Lithuanians for their part occupied Memel. Rumanian forces intervened in Hungary in 1919 to overthrow the Bolshevik government of Bela Kun and stake a claim to Transylvania. While in France and Britain men counted their dead and meditated on the futility of war, the peoples of eastern Europe counted their gains and losses and observed the efficacy of force. It is not wholly surprising that, some years later, war was resumed in eastern Europe.

THINKING HISTORICALLY | Interpretations (4b)

Method is everything

Bad history	Good history
• Based on gut feeling • Argument does not progress logically • No supporting evidence	• Based on an interpretation of evidence • Argument progresses logically • Evidence deployed to support argument

A spectrum of historical methodology

Historical writing can reveal much about the methods by which it was constructed. Read Extracts 1 and 2, and answer the questions below in pairs.

1 Look carefully at the spectrum of methodology.

   a) Where would you place each source on the spectrum of historical practice?

   b) What evidence would you use to support your choice?

2 Look at Extract 1. How would you change it to make it the same quality of historical writing as Extract 2?

3 Use a dictionary. Explain the following words in relation to historical writing: substantiation, deduction, inference, cross reference.

4 How important is it that historians understand and evaluate the methods used by other historians?

HOW FAR DID GERMAN HISTORY INFLUENCE NAZI FOREIGN POLICY?

In his book *Mein Kampf*, Hitler showed a significant interest in German history. Three main strands of his view of history, often far from accurate, influenced Nazi foreign policy. The first was a largely fictional 'racial history', which drove Hitler's very firm views on race (see page 107). The second strand was nostalgia for earlier empires and a sense that power and land were Germany's right. The third strand was the First World War and the effect of the Treaty of Versailles. These strands not only influenced Nazi foreign policy but were also used as propaganda to unite the German people behind Nazi policies. For this reason, accuracy was less important to the Nazis than propaganda impact.

How did Aryan racial theory drive foreign policy?

For Hitler, true Germans were Aryan, although he thought that some other countries in northern Europe (including Britain) also had Aryan roots. Hitler saw the Aryan race as superior to all other races – by which he meant ethnic groups such as black or Asian peoples, as well as Slavs in Russia and Eastern Europe, and especially Jews. He wanted Germany to be a great Aryan empire. He used the idea of **Pan-Germanism** to excuse this: uniting all German-speaking peoples in one country would mean capturing other countries and clearing them of 'inferior' people to give 'pure Germans' enough land to live on. These aims affected Nazi foreign policy because they led the Nazis to favour alliances with racially acceptable countries such as Britain. They also led the Nazis to favour German expansion eastwards, taking land from those who were racially inferior. However, their racial theory did not stop the Nazis from making alliances with 'inferior' countries to gain temporary advantage; these alliances were seen as a necessary evil.

KEY TERM

Pan-Germanism
The idea that all German-speaking peoples should be united and live in one country.

EXTEND YOUR KNOWLEDGE

Nazi racial theory
The Nazi 'Aryan' race was an invention, drawing on ideas circulating in the late 1800s that Nordic and Germanic races were superior. As believers in racial purity, the Nazis devised a series of spurious 'scientific' tests to measure racial purity by measuring what they saw as racially inherited characteristics such as eye or hair colour, or the shape or size of a person's nose. In 1933, when the Nazis began banning Jews from public places and certain jobs, they needed a quick, easily tested rule. The law banning Jews from the civil service specified three or four Jewish grandparents. However, in different areas officials interpreted the definition differently, for example, if the grandparents were practising Jews rather than just their ancestry. The 1935 Nuremberg race laws created categories of Jewishness including '*Mischling*' ('mixed race') and also assessed the race of the husband or wife of the person whose Jewishness was being assessed, and whether they were a practising Jew.

Why the Third Reich?

Hitler's Third Reich was meant to be a Germany returned to its rightful power and place in Europe. Unlike the Weimar politicians, the Nazis were not 'revisionists' who simply wanted to overturn the Treaty of Versailles and return to 1914. The Nazis wanted to overturn Versailles, but then to expand further, securing far more land in the east than Germany had held in 1914. They focused on two earlier German empires:

- the First Reich – the Holy Roman Empire of Charlemagne (800 to 1806)

- the Second Reich – the German Empire founded in 1871 by Otto von Bismark after Prussia defeated France. Bismark was prime minister of Prussia and the first chancellor of the empire. He died in 1898. By the time war broke out in 1914, the empire was beginning to fall apart.

Both empires had gained land, and kept it, by war and military strength. However, they had also worked hard diplomatically for acceptance by other nations, especially when first in power. The Second Reich had a series of carefully created alliances with other nations. It could be argued that, while Nazi propaganda focused on the glory of these empires, this strategy may also have influenced Hitler, because his foreign policy during his early years in power included stressing his desire for peace.

EXTRACT

 From 'Misjudging Hitler' an article by Richard Overy in *The Origins of the Second World War Reconsidered*, published in 1986.

German policy in the 1930s was rooted in the longer course of German history and did not represent a sharp rupture with the past. It can be clearly demonstrated that the main elements in Hitler's view of foreign policy derived in almost a straight line from the radical nationalism of the pre-1914 Reich. These elements were three: the pan-German longing for the territorial unity and independence of all racial Germans; the pursuit of *Lebensraum* (living space) in order to achieve the proper match between the territory and the economic needs of a people (with the strong implication that space should rightfully be allocated to people with superior cultures and forms of social organisation); the pursuit of *Weltpolitik*, or global policy, in which the united and enlarged state engaged in worldwide imperial politics.

Giving the Nazis credibility

Harking back to earlier empires was also a way of giving the Nazis credibility, appealing to Germans who wanted a political party with a history. They could stress that they were 'continuing' and 'restoring' a great Germany. They used other successful German rulers in their propaganda, especially if they had enlarged the nation. During their time in power, for example, one of the many propaganda postcards on sale at Nazi rallies showed the faces of Frederick the Great (ruler of Prussia, 1740–86), Bismarck, Hindenburg and Hitler, all facing the same way, with Hitler in front. The slogan read: 'What the King conquered, the Prince formed, the Field Marshall defended, the Soldier saved and unified.' It was, Hitler constantly said, the glorious past of Germany that made the loss of the First World War and the humiliating treaty that followed all the worse.

ACTIVITY
KNOWLEDGE CHECK

German history

1 List three different ways in which Nazi foreign policy was influenced by history.

2 For each of the three ways, write a short explanation of how it might influence Nazi foreign policy and how Nazis might use it as propaganda in Germany.

The effect of the First World War on Nazi foreign policy

More recent history also had a significant effect on Nazi foreign policy. The way the First World War ended was a bad beginning for the peace and the new German government: the overthrow and abdication of the German kaiser (Wilhelm II), the creation of a new German government and an armistice. There was no public surrender or open admission of defeat. Many German people, misinformed about how the war was going, believed Germany could have won had the kaiser stayed and the army kept on fighting. Many Germans felt that they had been 'stabbed in the back' by the 'November Criminals', the politicians in the new government who had negotiated the armistice and signed the Treaty of Versailles. So the new government started out under a cloud of unpopularity and protests against the signing of a treaty that, in fact, any government would have been forced to accept. Despite the fact that the army had privately advised the government that Germany could not win the war, members of both the government and the army publicly said the army could have won, so increasing German resentment over the Treaty.

EXTEND YOUR KNOWLEDGE

The legend of the 'stab in the back'

The idea that the German army could have won the war but were 'stabbed in the back' by the government that replaced the Kaiser, was introduced in a speech by General von Hindenburg in November 1919, when called as a witness at a Weimar government enquiry into why the war was lost (see Chapter 1). The phrase was taken up by many political groups, including the Nazis, to emphasise how unfair the end of the war was. The idea became so accepted that many Germans firmly believed the Treaty of Versailles had been forced on a country that had been betrayed, not defeated.

The effect of this belief was an increased hostility towards the government and also increased support for extreme right-wing and left-wing groups. The government, which was finding it difficult to govern effectively because of the scale of the problems that Germany faced and the difficulty of getting agreement in the Reichstag, found it difficult to win support for its policies in the face of this hostility.

EXTRACT

4   From *The Origins of the Second World War*, written by A.J.P. Taylor in 1961.

The peace of Versailles lacked moral validity from the start. It had to be enforced; it did not, as it were, enforce itself. This was obviously true in regard to the Germans. No German accepted the treaty as a fair settlement between equals 'without victors or vanquished'. All Germans meant to shake off at any rate some part of the peace treaty as soon as it was convenient to do so. They differed as to timing – some wanted to repudiate at once, others (perhaps the majority) wishing to leave this to a future generation. But the German signature in itself carried no weight or obligation. There was little respect for the treaty in other countries.

SOURCE

1   The photo shows demonstrators protesting against the Treaty of Versailles outside the Reichstag, Berlin, on 18 May 1919. The banner says 'Against the violent terms of peace'.

Hitler and the Nazi Party

Adolf Hitler, in his book *Mein Kampf*, outlined his political theories and wrote about his experiences as a soldier in the First World War, including how he felt when he heard about the armistice, the abdication of the kaiser and the replacement of the empire with a republic. He was in hospital at the time, recovering from a gas attack at the front. He said he felt that all the suffering and death of the war had been in vain. He raged against the politicians he felt had betrayed Germany. It was this that made him decide to become a politician. When he returned to Germany, he joined a small right-wing party called the Deutsche Arbeitserpartei (DAP). In April 1920, it changed its name to the Nationalsozialistische Deutsche Arbeiterpartei (National Socialist German Workers' Party, NSDAP, or Nazi Party). Hitler was one of its leaders and its 25-Point Programme contained many ideas about race and German expansion that Hitler had outlined in *Mein Kampf*.

Many other disillusioned soldiers joined paramilitary groups after the war, often associated with political parties. Between 1919 and 1923, there were 376 political murders, most committed by right-wing paramilitary groups. There were also two attempts to overthrow the government: the Kapp Putsch in 1920 and the Munich Putsch in 1923 (see Chapter 2). Both attempts failed, but they showed the government's weakness and the limited support the army was prepared to give it. The Munich Putsch was led by Adolf Hitler and the Nazis; its failure taught Hitler the problems of resorting to violence without enough force, or public support, to win. Hitler was sent to prison for his part in the putsch. It was here he wrote *Mein Kampf* and decided that his next takeover would not be a military takeover, but a parliamentary one – by a majority in the Reichstag.

The terms of the Treaty of Versailles

One of the most unarguable facts about the Treaty of Versailles between the Allies and Germany at the end of the First World War was that it was resented by almost everyone in Germany and that even some of the Allies saw it as unfair. 'The Big Three' (Britain, France and the USA) that contributed most to the terms of the peace, started with different aims. France, which had suffered most damage during the war and had most to fear from the outbreak of another war because of its proximity to Germany, had pushed for the severest measures. The British government had promised the British people to press for severe measures, but it did not want to force a treaty on Germany that was likely to cause resentment. President Woodrow Wilson of the USA, which had entered the war late and had lost least through it, had pressed the most for a reasonable treaty and the setting up of a system of international negotiation to prevent future wars – it was at his insistence that all those who signed the treaties that ended the war should join the League of Nations, an international organisation set up to promote harmony between nations.

The main causes for German resentment of the Treaty concerned those terms that led to it losing status in Europe, losing its ability to defend itself and to Germans feeling humiliated.

- Germany lost land (see Figure 1.1 on page 11). The loss of Danzig and the creation of the Polish Corridor were the most bitterly resented because they cut East Prussia off from the rest of Germany. However, all land losses were resented. Some 6.4 million Germans found themselves outside the new borders.

- Germany was told to disarm. It could have no submarines, no heavy warships, no tanks and no air force. It could no longer conscript soldiers for its severely reduced army of 100,000 troops that could not leave Germany. Germany's army had always been part of the political system as well as a defensive force, and its officers came from the wealthy landowning class.

- The German army could not enter the Rhineland, which ran along most of the border with France. It became a demilitarised 'buffer zone' for France.

- Germany had to pay heavy reparations – set at 132 million gold marks in 1921.

- Germany had to sign a clause that seemed to hold it responsible for starting the war, and it was not allowed to join the League of Nations and so was not accepted as an equal power in Europe.

- Germany had no say in the terms of the Treaty; it was a diktat, a *dictated* peace.

Effect of the Treaty of Versailles

Many historians argue, as did critics of the Treaty when it was drawn up, that the Treaty laid the foundations of the Second World War by its effects on Germany and on other countries. Even the Weimar government that had signed the Treaty worked against it. Members of the Reichstag privately agreed that a forced treaty did not have to be obeyed, and turned a blind eye to signs of rearmament. Politicians protested openly against the Treaty and foreign ministers worked for changes diplomatically, especially Gustav Stresemann (see Chapter 1), but the government also worked secretly to break some of the terms of the Treaty, for example, the requirement to disarm and the limitations placed on the size of the army. The army view was that it had not been defeated but undermined, so it could rearm. Secret rearmament agreements were made with the USSR, which allowed for German armaments to be made on Soviet soil, by Soviet companies. In 1926, a Russian tank-training school near Kazan began to train German soldiers, and by 1928 tanks for Germany were being built and tested in Russia. Some members of the army felt the Weimar government was not legal. Their argument was that the army was all that remained of the legitimate government, so it could make its own decisions.

EXTEND YOUR KNOWLEDGE

Secret rearmament

Germany's secret rearmament was known to the government – it was funded through a series of government projects. In 1927, for example, the Phoebus Film Company, set up in 1923 and one of Germany's most successful new film companies, had a secret fund of several billion marks that the army used to support rearmament. When the story finally came out in the press there was heated debate in the Reichstag, and the defence minister, Otto Gessler of the DDP, was forced to resign.

The Treaty of Versailles and Nazi foreign policy

The Treaty of Versailles affected Nazi foreign policy because opposing it made any political party popular, and the Nazis, like most Germans, rejected it as a matter of course. The war had created problems that could be blamed on the Treaty rather than the war. For example, the economic disruption in Europe, one such problem, added to Germany's problems with reparations imposed by the Treaty. All countries were finding it difficult to trade, and without trade Germany's economy could not recover quickly enough to cope with reparation payments (see Chapter 3). The war had also caused political disruption – no part of central and Eastern Europe in 1918 had the same government as in 1914. The small, **self-determining** states created by the Treaty were weak and often had ethnic divisions that made governing them difficult. Many had a sizeable German population. They squabbled among themselves over the borders they had been given, which were, in many ways, artificial constructs. The unintended consequence of creating these states was that their weakness made them desirable targets for the USSR, Germany, Italy and Poland.

Even some Allies saw the Treaty as being too harsh. The British Prime Minister, Lloyd George, made it clear that he felt the Treaty was so unfair that there would be another war in 25 years' time. French representatives, despite France's demands for harsh terms, said similar things. Guilt about the Treaty, and the fact that many nations desperately wanted peace, affected their reactions to both Weimar and Nazi foreign policy. For example, Germany complained about the problems that reparations caused, yet it never paid an instalment on time, either with money or goods. Other countries also turned a blind eye to secret rearmament. In 1935, Britain signed an Anglo-German naval agreement with the Nazi government setting naval sizes for both countries that broke the Treaty of Versailles' limitations on the German navy. While the Nazis only seemed to be reversing the losses of Versailles, many other nations did not fight to enforce the Treaty. Instead, they seemed to accept this reversal of 'unfair' terms, hoping not to have to fight another war. They hoped that when this was done, Germany would be satisfied and would not try to expand further. This encouraged the Nazis to expand Germany yet further and also gave them time to build a stronger military force.

ACTIVITY
KNOWLEDGE CHECK

The Treaty of Versailles

1 a) List the main reasons why Germans resented the Treaty of Versailles.

    b) Which term was being secretly disobeyed before the Nazis came to power?

2 Write a short explanation of how the way the war ended contributed to German resentment of the Treaty.

3 How might the policy of self-determination have created a situation that affected Nazi foreign policy?

TO WHAT EXTENT DID HITLER SHAPE NAZI FOREIGN POLICY?

Nazi foreign policy has been interpreted in very different ways. There are various questions to be answered. Was Nazi foreign policy a new departure for Germany, shaped by Hitler's **ideology**? Or was it, on the other hand, simply a continuation of earlier foreign policy which any other leader of Germany would have followed, even if not with the same ruthlessness? How far were Hitler's aims the only drivers of Nazi foreign policy?

KEY TERMS

Self-determination
The policy by which the newly created states in Eastern Europe were supposed to peacefully agree their borders and government.

Ideology
The linked ideas and beliefs that drive the behaviour of a person or a government. Dictatorships, for example, have an ideology of a single, strong leader; an obedient people; tight police control; a large army; and expansion.

SOURCE

From notes taken by General Liebmann (an infantry commander) at a meeting between Hitler and the commanders of the armed forces on 3 February 1933. Here, Liebmann's notes record Hitler's outline of goals for the country.

The sole aim of general policy: the regaining of political power. The whole State administration must be geared to this end (all departments!).

1 *Domestic policy*: Complete reversal of the present domestic political situation in Germany. Refusal to tolerate any attitude contrary to this aim (pacifism!). Those who will not be converted must be broken. Extermination of Marxism root and branch. Adjustment of youth and of the whole people to the idea that only a struggle can save us and that everything else must be subordinated to this idea. (Realised in the millions of the Nazi movement. It will grow.) Training of the youth and strengthening of the will to fight with all means. Death penalty for high treason. Tightest authoritarian State leadership. Removal of the cancer of Democracy!

2 *Foreign policy*: Battle against Versailles. Equality of rights in Geneva [in the League of Nations]; but useless if people do not have the will to fight. Concern for allies.

3 *Economics*: The farmer must be saved! Settlement policy! Further increase of exports useless. The capacity of the world is limited and production is forced up everywhere. The only possibility of re-employing part of the army of unemployed lies in settlement. But time is needed and radical improvement not to be expected since living space is too small for German people.

4 *Building up of armed forces*: Most important prerequisite for achieving the goal of regaining political power. National Service must be reintroduced. But beforehand the State leadership must ensure the men subject to military service are not, even before their entry, poisoned by pacifism, Marxism, Bolshevism or do not fall victim to the poison after their service.

How should political power be used when it has been gained? That is impossible to say yet. Perhaps fighting for new export possibilities, perhaps – and probably better – the conquest of new living space in the east and its ruthless Germanisation.

What was the ideology behind Hitler's foreign policy?

Hitler had several ideas that clearly drove his approach to both domestic and foreign policy. Some, but not all, of his aims overlapped with both those of the Weimar government and of the Kaiser's government that went to war in 1914. Hitler even deliberately allowed officials in the foreign ministry from before he came to power to keep their jobs as part of his policy of providing continuity (see page 23). His first aim was complete control in Germany and a build-up of Germany's military strength. This was the first step that was necessary in order for his ideology to be realised.

- **The Treaty of Versailles had to be overturned**: To achieve this, Germany had to rearm, lost land had to be regained, the Rhineland had to be reoccupied and reparations had to be left unpaid. Clearly, the kaiser's government, which collapsed after the war, had no view on the Treaty. The Weimar government was 'revisionist': it wanted to overturn the Treaty and return to Germany as it was in 1914, including the colonies it had lost. Hitler did not want a return to Germany as it was in 1914. He wanted the Third Reich to expand beyond its pre-war borders in Europe and he did not want the problems of managing colonies until Germany was fully established in Europe.

- **The Nazi Third Reich should be a large and powerful world power**: Hitler's expansionist policy aimed to create a large German empire in Europe. This was to be achieved by alliances, where possible, and war if necessary. Unlike the kaiser's government that took Germany to war in 1914, Hitler wanted alliances with countries that had an 'acceptable' ethnic mix. Britain was one of those countries; one he saw as having a suitable ethnic mix. This did not mean Hitler was not prepared to make short-term alliances with any country if it would benefit Germany – even Russia, which he often condemned for the racial inferiority of its people and the communism of its politics. The Weimar government did not openly discuss expansion beyond the borders of 1914, although it did want Germany to be a world power again. The kaiser's government had definitely wanted to extend its power in the world and saw war as a way to do that. However, it did not care about the ethnicity of its allies, or of the people in the lands it conquered.

- **The Third Reich needed *lebensraum* ('living space')**: Germany needed to expand, taking *lebensraum* not only to become a great nation, but also to meet the needs of its people – including its economic needs, for Hitler believed that Germany had a shortage of raw materials and farmland. Hitler said this much-needed living space should come from countries in the east with a high Slavic population and a significant German-speaking population. Both Germany and the land it took over should, as soon as possible, be cleared of all but 'pure' Germans, to allow the Germans to breed and flourish. Hitler's ideas about race were repeated often and publicly; earlier governments might have shared them, but they were never integrated into government policy. The kaiser's government had very similar ideas about the need to expand and the direction in which to expand, although, unlike Hitler, it also wanted to acquire a large number of colonies.

- **Europe was under threat from world Jewry and Bolshevism**: Hitler regularly repeated his conviction that there was a worldwide conspiracy of Jews to control governments which would, sooner or later, have to be stopped. He felt that there was a definite Jewish strategy to stir up anti-German feeling in other countries, especially the USA and Britain. As well as being anti-Semitic, Hitler was also anti-communist and often saw the two groups as being in league with each other. His opposition to these groups, added to his notion of *lebensraum*, led to a conviction that, sooner or later, Germany would have to go to war in Eastern Europe at the very least, to take land and to defeat communism. His concern was to delay war for as long as possible, so that Germany could rearm and make useful alliances to prevent attacks. His early foreign policy was, therefore, directed at convincing the Western powers that Germany wanted peace, nothing but peace, and the return of the land and people that were rightfully German, lost under the Treaty of Versailles. His real intentions were more expansionist.

SOURCE 3

From notes made by Joachim von Ribbentrop on instructions given to him by Hitler before he left for London to negotiate about Britain joining the Anti-Comintern Pact (anti-communist), set up by Germany and Japan on 25 November 1936.

Get Britain to join the Anti-Comintern pact, that is what I want most of all. I have sent you as the best man I've got. Do what you can... But if in future all our efforts are still in vain, fair enough, then I'm ready for war as well. I would regret it very much, but if it has to be, there it is. But I think it would be a short war and the moment it is over, I will be ready at any time to offer the British an honourable peace acceptable to both sides. However, I would then demand that the British join the Anti-Comintern pact or perhaps some other pact. But get on with it, Ribbentrop, you have the trumps in your hand, play them well. I'm ready at any time for an air pact as well. Do your best. I will follow your efforts with interest.

EXTRACT 5

From *The Origins of the Second World War*, written by A.J.P. Taylor and published in 1961.

He [Hitler] changed most things in Germany. He destroyed political freedom and the rule of law; he transformed German economics and finance; he quarrelled with the Churches; he abolished the separate states and made Germany for the first time a united country. In one sphere alone he changed nothing. His foreign policy was that of his predecessors, of the professional diplomats at the foreign ministry, and indeed of virtually all Germans. Hitler, too, wanted to free Germany from the restrictions of the peace treaty; to restore a great German army; and then to make Germany the greatest power in Europe from her natural weight. There were occasional differences in emphasis. Perhaps Hitler would have concentrated less on Austria and more on Czechoslovakia if he had not been born a subject of the Habsburg Monarchy; perhaps his Austrian origins made him less hostile originally to the Poles. But the general pattern was unchanged. This is not the accepted view. Writers of great authority have seen in Hitler a system-maker, deliberately preparing from the first a great war which would destroy existing civilisation and make him master of the world.

A Level Exam-Style Question Section C

In the light of differing interpretations, how far do you agree that Nazi foreign policy in the years 1933–39 was an area where Hitler 'changed nothing' (Extract 5)?

To explain your answer, analyse and evaluate the material in Extracts 5 and 6, using your own knowledge of the issues. (20 marks)

Tip

You must explicitly consider the ways in which Hitler's foreign policy was both a continuation of previous foreign policy and a change of direction.

EXTRACT

6   From *The Origins of the Second World War in Europe*, written by P.M.H. Bell in 2007.

It is not difficult to discern the similarities between the objectives of the Kaiser's Germany, and especially the war aims pursued by Germany in both east and west during the First World War, and the aims of Hitler's Germany... Against this strong evidence of continuity is the view that Hitler's personality, the nature and methods of his new regime, and the overriding demands of Nazi ideology constituted a sharp break in German policy, dated either in 1933, when Hitler came to office, or in 1938, when he finally broke the power of the conservative establishment in the Foreign Office and the General Staff. Even though some continuity with the past was maintained, the new elements were more important than the old. In particular, there is a strong case that by the 1930s the old-established German political and military leaders had grown cautious, and were by no means eager for a war of conquest. Hitler introduced a new way of thought, new men from far outside the old élites, and revolutionary new methods.

ACTIVITY
KNOWLEDGE CHECK

Hitler's foreign policy aims

1 Make a table showing the similarities and differences between Hitler's foreign policy aims and those of the Kaiser's government and the Weimar government.

2 Read Source 3.

  a) How could a historian interpret its language as showing that Hitler had clear aims in his policy towards Britain?

  b) How could a historian interpret its language as showing that Hitler had only vague aims in this policy?

THINKING HISTORICALLY   Interpretations (3a)

Differing accounts

Read Extracts 5 and 6, which give historical interpretations of the extent to which Hitler's foreign policy was a new departure in German foreign policy.

1 For each of the historians create a summary table of their views.

  a) Make a note of how they address/interpret the key issues outlined below:
- How far was Hitler's foreign policy a change from the policies of the kaiser's government and the Weimar government?
- To what extent did Hitler break from the past?

  b) Make a note of the evidence they give in support of their claims.

  c) Use your notes and knowledge to give evidence that supports or challenges their interpretations.

2 In pairs, discuss which historian's interpretation of Hitler's foreign policy seems to fit best with the available evidence – which seems the most convincing?

3 Make a note of any issues that made it difficult to compare the two interpretations directly.

4 Challenge: Seek out another historical interpretation of whether Hitler's foreign policy was a new departure and compare this to the views you have explored already.

Did Hitler drive Nazi foreign policy?

Historians give varying interpretations of how far those in the Nazi government agreed with Hitler's foreign policy aims. Some Nazis certainly tried to argue with Hitler on policy, but Nazi foreign policy followed Hitler's ideology as closely as possible. Hitler asked many different Party members for advice, but in the end he made his own decisions, and they often went against the requested advice. For example, Hitler faced opposition within the Nazi Party over his desire for an alliance with Italy – because it meant not trying to occupy parts of the Tyrol area which had a significant German-speaking population. Hitler pushed through the alliance, despite objections, because for him the alliance was more important, at the time, than the policies of overturning the Treaty of Versailles and *lebensraum*, both of which would suggest the reoccupation of South Tyrol.

The main features of Nazi foreign policy

Nazi foreign policy was ruthless in its pursuit of what it saw as Germany's 'rights'. In 1934, for example, Germany signed a non-aggression pact with Poland that was actually a cynical move to cut France off from its Eastern European allies. Poland was land that would be part of the Nazis' expansion eastwards, so the alliance was bound to be temporary. The main foreign policy features were:

- **Overturning Versailles** by spreading Nazi influence in those areas it wanted to reclaim (for example, Austria and Danzig) and, where necessary, by using military force.

- **Strategic alliances** to stop anti-German power blocs building up and make sure that, when it came to war, Germany did not have to fight a war on two fronts. These were made with individual countries wherever possible. This was to divide the other nations and made the treaties easier to break.

- **Expansion** by spreading Nazi influence, forming alliances and, where necessary, using military force.

- **Germanisation** by spreading Nazi racial ideas, oppression and removal of 'undesirables' in German-controlled lands.

How far did Hitler have a masterplan?

The dispute over how far Hitler was a step-by-step planner and how far he was an opportunist is, in some part, driven by the interpretation of the word 'plan'. It is possible to interpret much of the evidence in different ways. For example:

- Until 1936, Hitler kept many foreign ministry officials from before he came to power. This could be used as evidence that he did not interfere or impose a plan. It could also be said to show long-term planning. For example, Hitler wanted full control of Germany and far greater military strength before going to war. A show of continuity with a liberal government policy would make him seem more moderate.

- A comparison of Nazi land gains from 1935 to 1939 with the aims Hitler expressed in *Mein Kampf*, and in many speeches and meetings, could show planning if there was a significant match, as with the overturning of Versailles and the policy of *lebensraum*. However, it could be argued that these policies, such as eastward expansion, were simply broad aims, rather than a plan.

- An analysis of how prepared the Nazis were for each foreign policy move might use evidence of their unpreparedness as evidence that Hitler had not planned the move. However, it could be argued that, while the move was planned, it was brought on early by other factors. For example, his takeover of Austria happened earlier than he might have planned because of the actions of Austrian Nazis.

EXTRACT

From *The Road to War*, written by Richard Overy and Andrew Wheatcroft and published in 1989.

The opportunity to strike against Austria came sooner than expected, and was not entirely of Hitler's making. The agitation of the Austrian Nazi movement, fuelled by money and advice from Berlin, brought Austria to the edge of political crisis early in 1938. Italy was embroiled in Spain and was anxiously watching France in the Mediterranean. France was in the midst of a government crisis. The British Foreign Secretary, Anthony Eden, had just resigned. British intervention could be discounted. Hitler presented the Austrian Chancellor, Kurt Schuschnigg, with an ultimatum to accept Nazis into the Austrian government and co-ordinate foreign and economic policy with the Reich. The ultimatum was rejected and Schuschnigg organised a national referendum on the issue of union with Germany. Though there was widespread support for union in Austria beyond the confines of the Nazi movement, it was not clear that the referendum would go Hitler's way. Faced with all the risks of occupying Austria by force under the eyes of the League powers Hitler experienced a sudden loss of nerve. It fell to Göering to communicate German threats and instructions to Vienna on the night of 11 March; faced with domestic chaos, isolated internationally, Schuschnigg gave in and 'invited' German troops to restore order. The *Anschluss* was a fact. For the first and last time a state was conquered by telephone.

Historians agree that the evidence overwhelmingly suggests that Hitler was an excellent, almost hypnotic, speech-maker, in the flesh, if not on film or radio. There is evidence that he worked hard at speech-making because he believed, as he says in *Mein Kampf*, that effective speech-making was vital to controlling the population. Historians also agree that he seemed to be bad at personal relationships. However, how much of his bursts of out-of-control fury in speeches and meetings were real or stage-managed is open to question, as is whether he was more temperamentally suited to long-term planning or opportunism. His foreign policy shows signs of both, for example, his desire to expand eastwards and his invasion of Austria.

EXTRACT

8 From *The Foreign Policy of the Third Reich*, written by Klaus Hildebrand in 1973. Here, Hildebrand is discussing Hitler's autobiography, *Mein Kampf*.

Everyone, above all the foreign statesmen whom Hitler regarded as enemies, could have been familiar with the core of Hitler's Programme as published in *Mein Kampf*. Even Stalin, the leading statesman in that nation which Hitler had selected as his chief victim, was thoroughly acquainted with Hitler's thoughts after studying the Programme carefully, when Hitler came to power in 1933. ... Already in the first few days after the 'seizure of power', it became clear that Hitler was adhering to the aims drawn up in his Programme. In an address to the most senior officers of the Reichswehr [army], he expounded his views thoroughly in line with his Programme set down in *Mein Kampf*.

EXTRACT

9 From *How War Came* written by Donald Cameron Watt in 1989. Here, Watt is discussing Hitler's character, including his lack of perception and his desire for loyal followers.

This is the side of Hitler that is so difficult to relate to the Hitler of so many historians, filled with a vision of German dominance of the world, took successive steps which unfolded in a long-developed programme, which he set in action once he had achieved power. However, there is nothing in Hitler's previous record to show that he was capable of so long and sustained an effort of foresight and planning. Nor, despite the popularly-held beliefs to the contrary, is there anything in his one published work, *Mein Kampf*, which can be identified as a programme to which his later actions were to conform. *Mein Kampf* is an explanation of Hitler's political ideas and methodologies, not a programme in any meaningful sense of the word, and still less a 'blueprint' for aggression. Such programmatic elements as can be found in Hitler's foreign policy after 1933 were imposed upon him by external factors, not his own internal vision.

AS Level Exam-Style Question Section C

Historians have different views about how far Hitler's foreign policy was responsible for the Second World War. Analyse and evaluate Extracts 8 and 9 and use your knowledge of the issues to explain your answer to the following question.

How far do you agree with the view that Hitler carefully planned out Germany's foreign policy years before he came to power? (20 marks)

Tip

You must explicitly consider the ways in which Hitler's foreign policy was both a continuation of previous foreign policy and a change of direction.

SOURCE

4 This British cartoon from 8 July 1936 shows that there were some people at the time who were sure that Hitler had a step-by-step plan which had no boundaries – he would go as far as he was allowed.

STEPPING STONES TO GLORY.

TIMELINE – MAJOR EVENTS IN NAZI FOREIGN POLICY

1933
28 May: local Nazi Party wins elections in Danzig
14 October: Germany leaves League of Nations and the disarmament talks in Geneva

1934
26 January: Germany and Poland sign Non-Aggression Pact
25 July: Nazi Putsch fails in Austria

1935
13 January: Plebiscite in the Saar votes to rejoin Germany
16 March: Germany introduces conscription and announces it is rearming
18 June: Britain and Germany sign the Naval Agreement

1936
7 March: German troops reoccupy the Rhineland
1 November: Germany and Italy announce the Rome–Berlin Axis

1938
11–13 March: Germany takes Austria: *Anschluss*
1 October: Germany takes the Sudetenland

1939
15 March: Germany invades the rest of Czechoslovakia
23 March: Germany invades Memel
22 May: Germany and Italy sign Pact of Steel
23 August: Germany and USSR sign Non-Aggression Pact
1 September: Germany invades Poland

1940
9 April: Germany invades Denmark and Norway
10 April: Germany invades Belgium and the Netherlands

ACTIVITY
KNOWLEDGE CHECK

Nazi foreign policy

1 List the land Germany lost at the Treaty of Versailles (see page 11).

2 Work through the foreign policy events timeline above. Number the German takeovers from the first to the last and write that number next to an area on your list, if possible.

3 Write new areas of occupation under your original list and number them. Explain how this might support the theory that there was a plan behind Nazi expansionism.

EXTEND YOUR KNOWLEDGE

What kind of army did Germany build?

By the summer of 1939, Hitler had 103 infantry divisions of 15,000 to 18,000 men. This included about 3,000 tanks, mostly small and light, designed for rapid movement. The navy was small but powerful. The air force had grown from a few 'civilian' planes and pilots (secretly being trained to war) in 1933 to about 2,000 fighter and bomber planes and crews. There was a constant stream of conscripts and a well-established armaments industry. Many historians, looking at troop numbers and types of weapon and transport, feel Hitler was planning small, local wars – hard fought and over quickly. His generals developed the tactic of *Blitzkrieg* ('lightning war'): aircraft bombed an area, damaging airfields and other military targets, tanks moved in, infantry followed and stayed to make the area secure, the aircraft and tanks moved on to the next target.

Did Hitler always intend war?

Hitler built up an army from the moment he came to power; from 1935 he did it openly, defying the Treaty of Versailles. Conscription, forbidden by the Treaty, was reintroduced; tanks and other armoured vehicles, also forbidden, were built. As dictator, Hitler had no need for the Reichstag's permission to gear the economy for war. Source 2 (see page 122) suggests he had war in mind from before he became führer in 1934. Hitler's Four-Year Plan of 1936–39 stressed Germany's need to put militarisation first and to develop synthetic oil and other war materials, so Germany would not depend on other countries for these materials in wartime.

When Hitler spoke of rearming in the early 1930s, he stressed Germany's need to rearm for defence, not attack. In a speech to the Reichstag in 1933, he stressed his hopes of reversing Versailles by diplomacy. Privately, he told his generals that it would be a disaster to provoke a military attack until they had built up their armed forces to defeat such an attack, but that he intended expansion, not defence.

Figure 5.4 German expansion before the outbreak of war.

Could Hitler achieve his aims without war?

Hitler might have believed he could achieve his aim of making Germany a world power again without going to war, but he must have known he could not achieve *lebensraum* and expansion eastwards without war. However, he may have hoped to avoid war with Britain, if not France. *Blitzkrieg* warfare suited Hitler's troop numbers and weaponry, but it was not really designed for a long, drawn out war, which a world war was likely to be. Hitler certainly seemed to think Britain and France would not go to war with Germany over Eastern Europe. Germany remilitarised the Rhineland and took Austria by invasion without causing war. So Hitler did not expect military opposition to his next claim – the Sudetenland area of Czechoslovakia. This was not land taken from Germany at Versailles, but it had a high proportion of German speakers who wanted to be part of Germany. However, the Second World War nearly began in 1938, not 1939. France, Yugoslavia and Romania had signed a mutual aid treaty with Czechoslovakia. For a while it seemed that they would fight to honour it. War was averted at the Munich Conference, where Hitler agreed Germany's territorial expansion would stop with the Sudetenland (see Figure 5.4). Some historians have argued that Hitler really wanted war over Czechoslovakia. Others are less sure, even though he had set a date for the invasion and made speeches suggesting he was about to go to war, the last in Berlin on 26 September 1938. Six months later, Hitler took advantage of disputes between different parts of what remained of Czechoslovakia and stepped in 'to restore order'. Germany now had all of Czechoslovakia. Hitler had broken the promise made at Munich.

ACTIVITY
KNOWLEDGE CHECK

Preparing for war

Prepare for a debate on the statement: 'Hitler intended to go to war from the moment he took power.' List at least three points in favour of the statement and three points against it.

EXTRACT

10 From *The Origins of the Second World War*, written by A.J.P. Taylor in 1961.

Why did Hitler pause at the last moment? Was he shaken by renewed warnings from his generals? Did he surmise that the German people were against war? Was he taken aback by Mussolini's intervention [the Italian dictator asked Hitler not to invade Czechoslovakia, but to negotiate]? All these are possible explanations, on the assumption that he intended to go to war. But the implications are all the other way. Hitler's judgements before the crisis, his skill in keeping the door open for compromise – or rather for peaceful victory – suggest that he never lost control of himself. ... 28 September was the last moment when Hitler could call the war off. He could appear conciliatory and still collect his gains.

EXTRACT

11 From *Hitler: A Study in Tyranny*, written by Alan Bullock and published in 1952.

Hitler was genuinely undecided up to noon on 28 September, when he received the message from Mussolini, whether to risk war or not. The hesitation was not, as Chamberlain thought, between getting the Sudetenland by force or by negotiation, but between getting the Sudetenland and overrunning the whole of Czechoslovakia. Hitler had been impressed by the events of 27 September both by the evidence of German lack of enthusiasm for a war and by the urgent warnings from the Army and the Navy of the chance of defeat, but it was not until he received the message from Mussolini that he finally made up his mind to withhold the order for an attack on Czechoslovakia. For the message from Mussolini not only sought to persuade him of the advantages of such a course [negotiating at a conference in Munich], but implied, to Hitler's suspicious mind, that if he went on he would go on alone.

WHY DID GERMANY INVADE POLAND IN 1939?

Germany and Poland had a history of enmity. The Treaty of Versailles gave land to Poland, along with about 800,000 Germans. The Polish Corridor, created by the Treaty, with the 'free' port of Danzig on its coast to give Poland access to the sea, was bitterly resented by the Germans. Poland was in a difficult position. It had been dismembered and rebuilt, and this created problems ranging from the number of minority groups within its borders to the fact that the communication systems and railway lines did not interact across the country. The Polish government was very aware that both Germany and the USSR wanted some, if not all, of its territory. Therefore Poland could not trust its neighbours as allies; far from it. The growing Nazi military forces made Western powers look increasingly weak. Poland had a mutual assistance pact with France, made in 1925 at Locarno. France had made a similar pact with Czechoslovakia, but it had not gone to war because neither Britain nor the League of Nations would have supported such a war. Also, the Western powers were badly placed geographically to help Poland if Germany invaded (see page 11). On the other hand, it is important to remember that Poland was not a weak country, struggling to survive, as Allied propaganda portrayed it once the war began. It had its difficulties, but it was also fiercely independent and just as keen to take land as other Eastern

European countries. It went to war with the USSR over land in the Ukraine in 1920 and took Teschen from Czechoslovakia in 1938. It had a large army in proportion to its population. However, its army was not very mechanised – most of its heavy artillery was still horse drawn and it still had cavalry regiments. In 1939, it had just begun to build, and train crews for, light tanks.

Nazi relations with Poland up to 1936

It came as a shock in Germany when, in 1934, Hitler made a non-aggression pact with Poland, despite his many speeches about reversing the terms of Versailles. Nazi relations with Poland show evidence of Hitler's long-term planning, his fluctuating plans (or devious manipulation) and his acting opportunistically. In 1934, Hitler had not been in power long and wanted to make himself secure in Germany and build up his army before he did anything aggressive. He saw the USSR as the biggest threat to Germany, so Poland, which stood between Germany and the USSR, was a useful ally. The pact meant Poland could not join the USSR in an attack on Germany. This was so valuable that Hitler faced outspoken opposition within the Nazi Party and the Reichstag, even before he was secure in power, to make the pact. He wanted Danzig and the Polish Corridor back, but it was not the most important issue in 1934 – securely rearming was. Besides, by making the pact, Hitler diverted attention from the fact that the Nazi Party was very active in Danzig. In 1933, the Nazis won a majority in the town government. It was not enough of a majority to allow them to change the city's constitution and declare it part of Germany, but it was enough to establish Nazi control of the city. Danzig had long been an important German trading port with a largely German population (96 percent in 1914). Even the Allies had stopped short of giving it to Poland, creating instead a 'free city', run by the League of Nations, to which all nations had access. The Polish Corridor connected Danzig to Poland because one aim of Versailles was to give Poland access to the sea. The fact that it split East Prussia from the rest of Germany was inconvenient for Germany on almost every level: political, religious and social.

It is hard to tell whether Hitler would ever have been satisfied with Poland as a German satellite, but it is clear that this was his minimum requirement. He needed to be able to rely on Poland not to attack Germany. From 1935 on, the Nazis presented themselves to the Poles as wanting to sort out the problems of the Polish Corridor and Danzig by diplomacy, and wanting Poland as an ally. Between 1935 and 1937, there were various high-level meetings in which the Nazis pressed Poland to develop the non-aggression pact into an alliance that included military support in times of war. They floated the idea of a mutual war against the USSR, offering Poland a chunk of Ukraine if they won. They suggested that all they wanted, as far as the Polish Corridor was concerned, was the right to build road and rail connections to East Prussia. The Poles resisted, knowing the Nazis wanted Poland as a satellite state at the very least, and that a more developed alliance with Germany would damage relations with the USSR. Poland was still trying to maintain a balance where it was seen as a possible, valuable ally to both sides and therefore would be attacked by neither.

How did relations change after 1936?

When the Nazis remilitarised the Rhineland in 1936, the Polish government expected France to fight to drive the German troops out, so it offered military help under the terms of the 1921 Mutual Assistance Pact with France. However, the French did not send troops into the Rhineland, thereby changing the political situation.

- Poland had exposed itself as willing to fight Germany.

- France had shown itself as unwilling to fight, as did Britain and the League of Nations.

- Hitler became more confident about pressing for what he wanted by force.

However, Czechoslovakia was the next logical conquest, so Hitler continued negotiations with Poland rather than attacking it. Poland went as far as to make an agreement with Germany to guarantee the rights of Germans in Poland in return for a guarantee of the rights of Poles in German-controlled territory. However, it was still unwilling to become an obedient satellite of Germany, and German patience was running out.

The events that followed persuaded Hitler that he was not going to meet resistance to the use of force to get the land he wanted. In the case of both Austria (1938) and the remains of Czechoslovakia (1939), he exploited events in those countries to march in and take over, displaying opportunism about the exact moment of takeover, even if he had been preparing to use force. Hitler agreed to Poland getting Teschen when Czechoslovakia was divided up in 1939, but the alliance terms that he now offered Poland included Poland joining the **Anti-Comintern Pact**, something that would almost certainly have set off a Soviet invasion. The Pact was Hitler's litmus test of obedience. Hungary agreed to join and so remained an independent satellite. While Germany was technically offering a peaceful alliance to Poland, therefore, it was offering it on terms that Poland was likely to refuse.

The final pieces
Then Hitler signed two treaties that strengthened his position.

- On 22 May, the Pact of Steel between Italy and Germany committed both sides to close economic ties and mutual military aid. Hitler had previously feared that Mussolini would not support him militarily – it was probably one reason he did not invade Czechoslovakia when Mussolini urged him to negotiate in 1938. The Pact of Steel meant he could now rely on Italy's military support.

- The Nazi-Soviet Pact, signed on 23 August 1939, was seen by many politicians and ordinary citizens worldwide as a cynical alliance that would only last as long as it suited both parties. The press in Britain, France and the USA were especially dismissive of its sincerity – political cartoonists mocked the way that two politicians who had spent years criticising each other now acted as if it was possible to work together. However, both sides clearly thought it was worth making, even temporarily, and it shifted the balance of power in Eastern Europe by placing allies on both sides of Poland. What the signatories of the Pact did not reveal was the secret clause in which Germany and the USSR agreed to invade Poland and divide it between them.

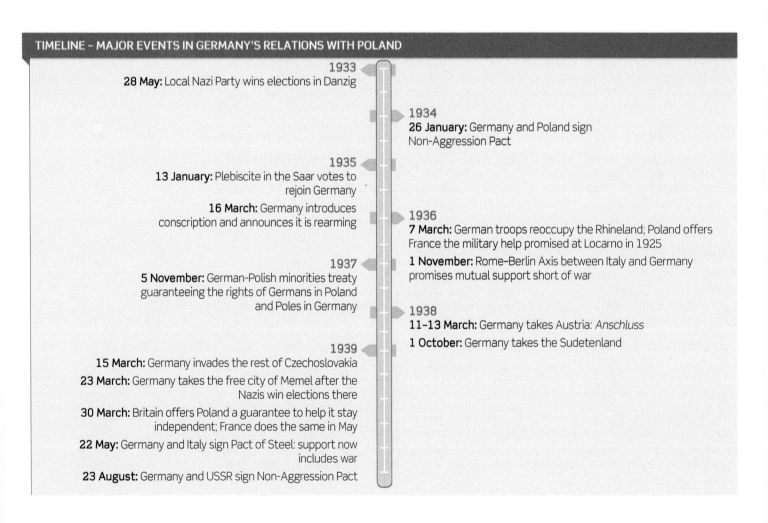

TIMELINE – MAJOR EVENTS IN GERMANY'S RELATIONS WITH POLAND

1933
28 May: Local Nazi Party wins elections in Danzig

1934
26 January: Germany and Poland sign Non-Aggression Pact

1935
13 January: Plebiscite in the Saar votes to rejoin Germany
16 March: Germany introduces conscription and announces it is rearming

1936
7 March: German troops reoccupy the Rhineland; Poland offers France the military help promised at Locarno in 1925
1 November: Rome–Berlin Axis between Italy and Germany promises mutual support short of war

1937
5 November: German-Polish minorities treaty guaranteeing the rights of Germans in Poland and Poles in Germany

1938
11–13 March: Germany takes Austria: *Anschluss*
1 October: Germany takes the Sudetenland

1939
15 March: Germany invades the rest of Czechoslovakia
23 March: Germany takes the free city of Memel after the Nazis win elections there
30 March: Britain offers Poland a guarantee to help it stay independent; France does the same in May
22 May: Germany and Italy sign Pact of Steel: support now includes war
23 August: Germany and USSR sign Non-Aggression Pact

Hitler did not believe the guarantee made by Britain and France to support Polish independence. Both countries had backed down when he invaded Czechoslovakia, why would they go to war to help Poland? Besides, there was no evidence of Britain and France rearming more rapidly, introducing conscription or transferring troops or equipment to Poland to prepare for war. If they had seriously intended to defend Poland, they should have been doing all of those things – especially the last, considering the geographical problems of reaching Poland without crossing Germany. On 1 September 1939, German troops invaded Poland. On 3 September, Britain and France declared war on Germany – too late to save Poland.

ACTIVITY
KNOWLEDGE CHECK

German–Polish relations

1 Make notes for a speech to be given by one of Hitler's aides about the signing of the non-aggression pact with Poland in 1934. Consider objections that might be made to the pact and how they might be countered.

2 'The Nazis were always going to invade and Germanise Poland.' How far do you agree with this statement?

Was the invasion of Poland a step in a move to world war?

Did Hitler intend to start a world war when he invaded Poland? After all, Britain and France had promised military aid to Poland if it was attacked. However, in speeches and in negotiations with Italy, he talked of being ready to fight a large-scale war in the early 1940s, when the newly acquired land in the east would be Germanised and Germany would have a larger military force. However, Hitler may have perceived the British and French promises as just bluff; failing to see that his increasing brutality towards Jews in Germany, such as *Kristallnacht* in November 1938, combined with him breaking his promise not to take more territory after the Sudetenland had led to a change of feeling in Britain and France.

Their policy of **appeasement** was neither keeping the peace nor keeping the new nations of Eastern Europe secure, although it had bought them time to build up their troops and armaments. Politicians, and the people, in France and Britain were swinging to a majority view that war was the only way to stop Hitler. Also, there is the possibility that Hitler was so buoyed up by his alliance with the USSR that he was prepared to fight a war in the West. With the USSR as his ally, he did not need to worry about a war on two fronts and he would have the Red Army to help in his fight. It is possible that, given the success he had and the fact that he thought Britain and France were spineless and weak, he felt the time was right to take them to war and win.

KEY TERM

Appeasement
The policy of attempting to keep the peace by giving in to someone's demands.

EXTRACT

12 From *War and Economy in the Third Reich*, written by Richard Overy and published in 1994.

The outbreak of a general European war in 1939 seems to have been the result of miscalculation on Hitler's part. He wanted to wage his major war three or four years later, when the economy and armed forces were ready. There is no doubt, of course, about his intention to have a local war in 1939 to destroy Poland, once it became clear that the Polish government would not agree to become a virtual satellite of the Reich. Hitler's planning involved a great risk, but a combination of what looked like favourable international circumstances, British and French hesitancy over Danzig, and intelligence sources which indicated western military unpreparedness, persuaded him that the risk was worth taking. His conviction that the western states would not seriously intervene to save Poland was based not on mere wishful thinking, but on what Hitler thought was a reasonable calculation of western strengths and weaknesses. ... The Polish campaign was part of a concerted German drive into eastern Europe. The timing was determined by international and military factors rather than domestic structural pressures.

EXTRACT

13 From *Germany, Hitler and World War II*, written by Gerhard L. Weinberg and published in 1995.

It was precisely because the German government of the 1930s understood both the hope for peaceful settlement of disputes and the unwillingness of Britain and France to acquiesce in the kind of massive reordering of the continent that Germany intended, that Berlin always waved off the British and French efforts at what was occasionally referred to as a 'general settlement'. Germany would take advantage of the hopes for peace, but it would do so in a manner designed to prepare the way for war, first against Czechoslovakia, then against England and France. That second war would be the big one; and once it had been won, then Germany could easily and quickly seize from the inferior and disorganised peoples of Eastern Europe, especially the Soviet Union, the vast reaches of *Lebensraum*, living space, that Hitler coveted for his nation. And even while these wars were in preparation and progress, Germany would build the 'blue-water' navy, and seize the intended bases for it, so that thereafter she could fight the United States.

THINKING HISTORICALLY Interpretations (4a)

The weight of evidence

Work in pairs. Read Extracts 12 and 13, then answer the questions below:

1 Use highlighter pens to colour-code copies of the extracts. Use one colour for 'evidence', another colour for 'conclusions' and a third for language that shows the historian is 'reasoning' (for example, 'therefore', 'so'). Alternatively, draw up a table with three columns headed 'Evidence', 'Conclusions' and 'Reasoning language' and copy the relevant parts of the extracts into the columns.

2 How do the extracts differ in terms of the way that the evidence is used?

3 Which of these extracts do you find more convincing? Which has the best-supported arguments?

4 What other information might you want in order to make a judgement about the strength of these claims?

5 Write a paragraph of 200 words explaining the importance of using evidence to support historical claims.

EXTEND YOUR KNOWLEDGE

Hitler's beliefs and intentions

In the months that followed Hitler's occupation of the remains of Czechoslovakia in March 1939, he made many speeches and had many meetings and conversations about invading Poland and how the West would react. He was probably genuinely wavering: certain one day that the West would not fight and certain on others that it would. However, he seems to have always tailored his opinions to fit the reaction he wanted to get out of the people listening to his speeches, or in his meetings. It is important to consider who Hitler is speaking to (or writing for) when reading what he said or wrote.

SOURCE

 5 From the official notes taken at a meeting between Hitler and the heads of the armed forces on 23 May 1939, four months before the invasion of Poland and two months after Britain's guarantee to Poland. Published in 1956.

Further successes can no longer be won without bloodshed. The delineation of frontiers is of military importance. The Pole is not a fresh enemy. Poland will always be on the side of our adversaries. In spite of treaties of friendship Poland has always been bent on exploiting every opportunity against us. It is not Danzig that is at stake. For us it is a matter of expanding our living space in the East and making food supplies secure and also solving the problem of the Baltic States... The problem of Poland cannot be dissociated from the showdown with the West. Therefore Poland is also a doubtful barrier against Russia. Success in war in the West with a rapid decision is questionable and so is Poland's attitude. ... We cannot expect a repetition of Czechia [if Germany invades Poland]. There will be war. Our first task is to isolate Poland. Success in isolating her will be decisive.

From invasion to war

1 Explain why Hitler may have thought that Britain and France would not help Poland. Give as much supporting detail as possible.

2

   a) What does Source 5 suggest Hitler's views were about whether the invasion would lead to war with the Western powers?

   b) Why might he say what he does and yet think something else?

TO WHAT EXTENT DID OTHER NATIONS CONTRIBUTE TO THE OUTBREAK OF WAR?

Foreign policy is, of its nature, interaction between countries, so many Nazi foreign policy aims could only be achieved if other countries shared those aims. During his early years in power, for example, Hitler tried to form an alliance with Britain, which he saw as a racially acceptable ally. Various British politicians visited Germany in the early 1930s and some spoke hopefully of his peaceful intentions. However, despite signing the 1935 Naval Agreement, Britain never made the alliance the Nazis wanted. International relations are also complicated by ideologies and past history. It was, for instance, hard for the Western powers to accept the idea of an alliance with the USSR because it was governed by a communist regime.

How did international politics influence the move towards war?

International politics influenced the move towards war by the conditions that it created. Immediately after the First World War, central and Eastern Europe was in a very unstable state. Borders, rulers and government systems had changed in most countries since 1914. The policy of self-determination set up in the treaties that ended the war had created new, small, independent states, such as Estonia and Lithuania, that were economically, politically and militarily weak. Many of them disputed the borders they had been given; in the 1920s, there were a series of disputes that threatened to spill over into war. This created an uneasy political atmosphere, although this was offset by a genuine desire for peace among many countries and a desire to do as much as possible to avoid war. This was very evident in the policies of the more established Western powers. Other international influences were the way that the League of Nations behaved and the way other countries behaved towards it, as well as the ideologies of individual countries and the ways in which these affected countries' interactions.

Ideological divides

At the end of the First World War, the most significant ideological divide was between communist Russia and the capitalist West. Russia set up Comintern, an organisation to spread the ideas of communism worldwide. There was significant post-war unrest after the war, communist party membership rose in the West and governments saw communism as a real threat. This affected international relations because, rather than making an alliance with Russia, the Western powers helped the 'Whites' to fight the communist 'Reds' in the Russian civil war (1917–20). By the mid-1930s, there was a new ideological divide. Three countries became dictatorships: Germany under Hitler, Italy under Mussolini and Japan under military leadership. While there were differences between the ideologies of these countries they were united by their anti-communist beliefs, a resentment of the Treaty of Versailles, a rejection of democracy and a belief in the importance of a strong military that could impose the will of the dictatorship by force. At first their anti-communist attitude appealed to Britain and France, who hoped they might destroy the USSR. As the dictatorships became more powerful and aggressive, Western democracies began to see them as dangerous. However the USSR now had a leader, Joseph Stalin, who ruled more and more as a dictator and was building up a significant Red Army. It would make a good ally against Germany, but the British politician Lloyd George summed up the problem with an alliance in 1939, saying that Britain needed the USSR, but did not want it.

From *The Origins of the Second World War in Europe*, written by P.M.H. Bell in 2007.

The role of ideology in the coming of the Second World War in Europe was significant, and any analysis which ignored it would be well wide of the mark. Ideology was a powerful force in international relations. Fascism, Nazism and communism offered ideas and systems which were attractive alternatives to liberal democracy, which faltered in the face of the political and economic challenges of the 1920s and 1930s. ... Ideological links and antagonisms made it difficult for governments to act solely on the basis of power politics and material interest. For example, France and Italy might well have made an alliance against Germany on power politics lines, but ideology stood in the way – fascist Italy was anathema [hateful] to French left-wingers, while Nazi Germany was in the same ideological camp as fascist Italy.

ACTIVITY
KNOWLEDGE CHECK

Ideological differences

1 Explain how the following ideological differences contributed to the outbreak of war:

a) communism and anti-communism

b) dictatorships and democracies.

The League of Nations

At the end of the First World War there was a strong desire in many countries for international co-operation and a way for countries to work together to avoid war (referred to as **collective security**). The League of Nations was set up to resolve disputes between member countries. All of the countries that signed the peace treaties ending the war had to agree to join the League. Its members agreed to take disputes to the League and accept its ruling rather than go to war. The League could act against a country that did not accept its ruling – economically or, as a last resort, militarily. It also ran a series of disarmament conferences to negotiate the gradual disarming of all member states. However, the League had serious weaknesses.

KEY TERM

Collective security
Co-operation between countries that agree to settle their disputes without resorting to war and to help each other if attacked.

Membership: Not all nations were part of the League. This made it weak as a worldwide organisation, as non-League countries did not have to work with it. Countries that had fought the Allies were not asked to join, nor was Russia. Germany was asked to join the League in 1925 when it signed the Treaty of Locarno agreeing to accept the boundaries set in the Treaty of Versailles. The US Congress refused to join, despite the fact that President Wilson had been the driving force behind the League's creation.

Bureaucracy: The League was slow to make decisions and members seldom agreed to economic sanctions, let alone military force. It needed the agreement of a significant majority of members, sometimes all of them, in order to act.

Enforcement: It did not have its own army; member countries had to agree to supply troops, which most were reluctant to do. Its failure to act quickly and use force made it seem increasingly weak. Most nations naturally act in their own self-interest and when it became clear that the League was not able to enforce decisions, there was less and less need to obey a ruling that was not in a country's self-interest.

All of this meant that countries, both in and outside the League, increasingly negotiated independently of the League. The League had some successes in the 1920s, for example in the dispute between Germany and Poland over Upper Silesia in 1921. It also had failures; Poland taking Vilna by force in 1920, for example. The more members ignored it (as when France took over the Ruhr in 1923), the weaker it seemed and the more nations acted without reference to it. It also meant that the Nazis did not see it as a force to contend with in foreign policy. Hitler took Germany out of the League and its disarmament conferences in 1933. The League had shown it could not protect its members, or get them to act against what they saw as their own national interest, including on disarmament. While Britain and France did disarm, as did the USA (although it was not a League member), most other states did not feel secure enough to do so.

EXTEND YOUR KNOWLEDGE

The League in the 1920s
League successes in the 1920s included setting up a plebiscite in Upper Silesia to solve the dispute over that territory between Germany and Poland, and settling a dispute between Finland and Sweden over the Aaland Islands (both 1921). In 1925, Greece invaded Bulgaria, but withdrew when the League told it to. On the other hand, the League did nothing when Poland took Vilna from Lithuania in 1920 and refused to withdraw. It could not persuade Lithuania to give back the 'free city' of Memel or Italy to leave Corfu, both of which were invaded in 1923. Even in the 1920s, when the League had most success, member countries made treaties and alliances of their own to prevent war. For example, the Washington Naval Conference of 1921 resulted in the Five Power Pact that limited naval expansion in Britain, France, Italy, Japan and the USA. The Nine Power Pact made at the same conference involved an agreement not to use poisoned gas in war and limited the use of submarines. It was signed by Britain, France, Italy, Japan, the USA, the Netherlands, Portugal, Belgium and China.

Major disputes involving the League of Nations after 1931

- **16 September 1931**: The Mukden Incident in 1931 led to the Japanese takeover of Manchuria, which it ran as a satellite called Manchukuo from 1932. The League of Nations protested, but Japan ignored the protests and withdrew from the League in March 1933.

- **3 October 1935**: Italy invaded Abyssinia (now Ethiopia) after a dispute that was taken to the League of Nations in December 1934. On 7 December, the League of Nations demanded that Italy left; Italy did not leave. On 9 December, the League imposed partial economic sanctions. News leaked out that Italy, Britain and France had a secret meeting and signed the Hoare-Laval Pact which gave two-thirds of Abyssinia to Italy. By 1936, Italy had all of Abyssinia; the League had done nothing, and two of its most powerful members had worked outside the League to agree on Italy's takeover.

- **1936**: Spanish Civil War – Spain had supported the League, but a civil war was not aggression from another country, so the League wavered. Germany and Italy accepted Franco as the new leader of Spain. In December, the League told them not to intervene; it did not intervene itself. By May 1937, there was clear proof of Italian troops on Spanish soil, but the League still did nothing.

- **1937**: China and Japan went to war over disputed territory. The League joined with other nations, including the USA, in condemning Japan's invasion; neither country was a League member and it had no effect.

- **30 November 1939**: The USSR invaded Finland. The League intervened, urging the USSR (still a member) to withdraw. It did not withdraw. The League expelled the USSR.

The USSR and the League of Nations

In 1919, the Western powers did not accept Russia's communist government, so Russia was not invited to join the League of Nations. Russia was dismissive of the League until 1934 when, worried by the way Germany and Japan spoke against communism, it decided it needed allies and asked to join the League. A majority of League members voted to allow the USSR to join, but relations were never easy; the USSR and the Western powers were too suspicious of each other, while the smaller states in Eastern Europe were concerned that the USSR wanted to take them over. The situation became more difficult after 1936, with Stalin's purges and increasingly dictatorial behaviour and the USSR's involvement in the Spanish Civil War (1936–39). Both Britain and France tried to negotiate independently of the League to end the USSR's involvement in the war. The result was that the USSR became yet another country that saw the League as too weak to police European politics. However, it did not leave the League, unlike Italy, Germany and Japan. The Nazi-Soviet Pact of 1939 put relations between the USSR and the League under even more strain. When the USSR invaded Finland on 30 October, the League met to discuss the situation and the USSR was asked to leave the League on 14 December 1939.

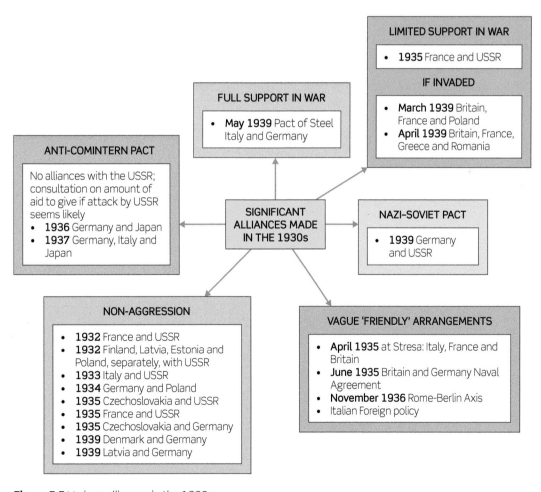

Figure 5.5 Various alliances in the 1930s.

How did the attitudes of individual countries influence the move towards war?

During the 1930s, various countries discussed possible alliances, non-aggression agreements and treaties (see Figure 5.5). Some of these meetings were successful, such as Germany's non-aggression pact with Poland in 1934 and its Naval Agreement with Britain in 1935. Other meetings failed to produce an alliance, such as Germany's attempt to form an alliance with Britain. Britain and France often seemed to simply be reacting to the actions of others. For example, the 1936 Anti-Comintern Pact led them to negotiate with the USSR, although they found agreeing terms so difficult that their indecision was one of the factors that drove the USSR into the Nazi-Soviet Pact in 1939.

Britain

Britain had an empire and a worldwide, not just European, focus. In the 1920s, it made no alliances and relations with France cooled. Britain's attitude to Germany until 1939 was to avoid an alliance, but to pursue a course of appeasement in the hope of keeping the peace and preserving the situation in Europe set up by the Treaty of Versailles. This attitude was driven by several factors. There was a genuine desire among politicians and the public not to go to war again because war, in any part of the world, would cause problems with the colonies and trade. Also, the government was doubtful that, after the losses of the First World War, its colonies would want to join another war. Indeed, in 1938, both Australia and South Africa made it clear that they would not go to war against Germany. Britain faced colonial unrest and pressure for greater independence from colonies such as India and Egypt. Both political and public opinion hardened after news of *Kristallnacht* in 1938 and Hitler's invasion of the rest of Czechoslovakia in 1939. Britain prepared for war, while still hoping for peace. Poland was the line in the sand. Britain's appeasement policy contributed to the war because it encouraged Germany, Italy and Japan to seize more territory.

SOURCE 6

From official notes taken at a meeting between Sir John Simon, the British foreign secretary, and Hitler in March 1934, and published in various collections of foreign policy documents after the war.

It was the object of British policy to serve peace by securing cooperation amongst all European countries. His Majesty's Government most earnestly wished that Germany should work with all countries for that object. They believed that the future of Europe would take one of two forms: it would either take the form of general cooperation for securing continued peace – and this is the form which His Majesty's Government earnestly desired. Or it would take the form of a division into two camps – isolation on the one side, and combination [forming alliances] (which might look like encirclement) on the other. The message he had to deliver on behalf of His Majesty's Government was that they were convinced that the future would develop in one of these two ways.

France

France's attitude to Germany until 1939 was one of resentment and anger because of Germany's failure to meet the terms of the Treaty of Versailles. The one French attempt at imposing its will on Germany by force, the invasion of the Ruhr in 1923, had ended in failure. So France turned to appeasement. However, unlike Britain, France had a very real fear of German invasion, which showed itself most openly in the Maginot Line defences on its border with Germany and its desire to make European alliances. Before the First World War, Britain and Russia had been strong allies. Now with Britain cooling and Russia a communist country, France felt isolated and it made a variety of alliances with the new European states, such as Czechoslovakia. It even made increasingly binding agreements with the USSR after 1932, such as its 1935 pact, and pushed Britain to join it. While France had a large army, it had lost a quarter of its young men between the ages of 18 and 27 in the First World War and the quality of the army and its equipment was variable. France faced political difficulties. It developed strong communist and fascist parties, just as Germany did. The government changed 11 times between 1932 and 1935, and there was trouble with colonial demands for independence. When a left-wing government came to power in 1936, it faced considerable criticism. All this, combined with economic problems, made France weak at home and abroad, and certain it could not win a war. As with Britain, its appeasement policy increased Hitler's confidence in his Eastern European aggression.

Italy

Italy and Germany were both dissatisfied with the Treaty of Versailles. They shared an anti-communist outlook, and a belief in autarky, strong government and military force. At first, their mutual interest in land on the Austrian border was an issue. When the Austrian Nazis tried to take over in 1934, Italian troops quickly moved to the border and made them back down. Hitler gave up all claims on the South Tyrol area of Austria to encourage an alliance. Italy and Germany both helped Franco's fascists in the Spanish Civil War, which led to the Rome–Berlin Axis agreement. However, Hitler and Mussolini found it difficult to trust each other and their foreign policy was not always compatible. Hitler refused military aid when Mussolini invaded Abyssinia, for example, saying his army was not ready, while Mussolini did the same when Hitler was about to invade Czechoslovakia in 1938. Even when united in the Pact of Steel, an agreement to provide instant military support, they kept some war plans secret, for example, Italy's invasion of Albania in April 1939 and Hitler's invasion of the rest of Czechoslovakia and then Poland in 1939. When war began in 1939, Mussolini told Hitler that he had expected a war in 1942 and could not join the war at once – despite the Pact of Steel. Indeed, until France fell in 1940, Hitler was still in contact with Britain, hoping to make an alliance and change sides. Once France fell, Germany seemed the stronger power and Italy joined the war on Germany's side. While Hitler never fully trusted Mussolini, the Pact of Steel was an encouragement to him to go to war.

The USSR

The USSR was isolated in Europe by its communist ideology. The fascist dictatorships and the democratic nations of Europe were anti-communist, and the USSR was open to attack from both east and west. Stalin wanted to build up the USSR's industry, agriculture and army to the point where the country was self-sufficient and safe from attack; he wanted to avoid war. In this respect, his aim was very similar to Hitler's. Knowing that any agreements made with any country were fragile, he reacted to the Nazi-Polish non-aggression pact by joining the League of Nations and supported the existing Spanish government, a League member, against the fascists supported by Germany and Italy. The USSR suggested a variety of pacts and alliances to the Western powers. France agreed to some (see Figure 5.5), but Britain dragged its heels, not wanting a communist ally. Stalin was humiliated not to be asked to join the Munich Conference in 1938, but even after that he held talks with the Western powers. However, he also held talks with Germany. From July to August 1938, the USSR was fighting with Japan on its eastern border. This made the USSR more likely to reach an agreement with Germany, otherwise it might have to fight Germany and Japan on two fronts.

The USA

In the 1920s and 1930s, the USA followed a policy of isolationism and also of disarmament. Indeed, by 1938 its army was smaller than Belgium's. However, this does not mean that its attitude to Germany and other fascist governments was not important. The USA was neutral over the Abyssinian crisis and the Spanish Civil War. However, it still exported arms to Italy and Germany, who were supplying arms to Franco. The USA did try to set up various meetings in the 1930s to work for world peace, and it did intervene to try to persuade Hitler to withdraw from Czechoslovakia in 1938. The very fact that the USA openly said it would not go to war in Europe, and produced a permanent Neutrality Act in 1937 to underline it, encouraged Hitler to go to war.

Japan

Japan, like Italy, was on the winning side in the First World War and joined the League of Nations. But, also like Italy, it was dissatisfied with the results of the treaties that ended the war and with its treatment in the League, where it was not treated as an equal by the other Allies. In 1931, Japan provoked China to war with the Mukden Incident. Over the next year it took much of Manchuria and some of northern China, creating a new state, Manchukuo, which it said was independent of China, Japan or the USSR. However, Japan chose Manchukuo's ruler. Only Germany and Italy recognised the new state. When the League finally ruled against Japan in 1933, Japan left the League and formed uneasy alliances with Italy and Germany. Although Japan and Germany were not enthusiastic allies, Germany was encouraged by the alliance in its aggressive policies because Japan was an enemy of the USSR, and it was useful for Germany to have an ally geographically on the other side of the USSR. Also, if the USA decided to enter the war, Japan would be able to act against the USA in the Far East. The Nazi-Soviet Pact came as a shock to Japan, but by that time, Italy and Germany were the only allies it had.

EXTRACT

15 From *From Versailles to Pearl Harbor*, written by Margaret Lamb and Nicholas Tarling and published in 2001.

The response of the other powers to the aggressor states [Germany, Italy and Japan] affected not only the timing of the outbreak of the war, but also the extent of the conflict when it ultimately occurred. Britain, France, the United States and the USSR, at different times and in different degrees, made concessions to the aggressors. By 1939, as a result, Germany had succeeded in removing all its grievances from Versailles apart from the German-Polish border. It had broken up the Czech state, struck a body blow at France's alliance system, and was in the process of a steady economic penetration of eastern Europe. German and Italian assistance had assured Franco of victory in the Spanish Civil War. Germany was once more the dominant power on the continent. In the Far East Japan without impediment from the other powers had resumed major hostilities against China. The extent of the concessions which had been made meant that when first Britain and France, and then the Soviet Union and the United States, decided to resist, Germany and Japan were considerably strengthened and had much greater forces at their command. The resulting war would inevitably be a major one.

ACTIVITY
KNOWLEDGE CHECK

Attitudes to Germany

Draw a summary diagram of the attitudes of Britain, France, Italy, the USSR, the USA and Japan to Germany. Give each country a separate box and sum up, as briefly as possible:

- their attitude to Germany (including any shifts)
- the reasons for that attitude
- how that attitude might contribute to war.

What other influences affected the move towards war?

There were other causes that contributed to the Second World War. One significant cause was the world economy. The Depression that began in the USA after the 1929 Wall Street Crash hit economies worldwide, creating problems that governments found difficult to deal with. The resulting discontent led to growing support for extreme left- or right-wing political movements and helped parties such as the Nazis take power. The depression also made countries more inward looking. They traded less; they could not afford to buy as much and sold less because other countries were in the same position. Britain set up favourable trade agreements with its colonies, which it kept when the economy began to recover. This meant it did not set up trade links with the new Eastern European countries, leaving them more likely to trade with Germany or the USSR.

Hitler's actions were influenced by more than his foreign policy and other aims. Third Reich expansion was vital to him, and he tied his domestic policy to it. However, some historians, such as Richard Overy, have argued that Hitler's foreign policy was also affected by his domestic circumstances. For example, rearmament helped the German economy to recover from the depression, although demands then grew so great that they produced economic strain. Hitler also had to meet the expectations of the German people and groups within it, such as industrialists and Nazi Party members. He also underestimated the effect that domestic anti-Semitism had abroad. *Kristallnacht*, for example, was significant in changing British public opinion towards war with Germany.

Hitler's foreign policy was certainly a significant factor in the outbreak of the Second World War. His invasion of Poland set the war going in 1939. How much that invasion was intended to start a wider war is still open to a debate, as is the extent to which he had a long-term plan or exploited opportunities as they came his way.

ACTIVITY
SUMMARY

Hitler's foreign policy and the war

There have been a variety of different interpretations of Hitler's foreign policy. Consider the following statements:

1 'Hitler always planned a world war.'

2 'Hitler simply took advantage of international circumstances such as the behaviour of Britain and France and the weakness of the League of Nations.'

3 'Hitler's foreign policy was simply a continuation of earlier German foreign policy.'

For each one, explain how far you agree with the statement, giving as many examples to back up your argument as you can. Consider points in favour of and against the statements.

WIDER READING

Bell, P.M.H. *The Origins of the Second World War in Europe*, Pearson Education Limited (2007)

Lang, S. and Kinloch, N. *Nazi Foreign Policy, 1933–39*, Philip Allan (2009)

Nicholls, D. *Adolf Hitler: a Biographical Companion*, ABC-CLIO (2000)

Overy, R. *The Origins of the Second World War*, Routledge (2008)

There is footage of some of Hitler's speeches on the internet, for example, if you search on 'Hitler speech Sudetenland'.

Preparing for your AS Level Paper 1 exam

Advance planning

1. Draw up a timetable for your revision and try to keep to it. Spread your timetable over a number of weeks, and aim to cover four or five topics each week.
2. Spend longer on topics that you have found difficult, and revise them several times.
3. Above all, do not try to limit your revision by attempting to 'question spot'. Try to be confident about all aspects of your Paper 1 work, because this will ensure that you have a choice of questions in Sections A and B.

Paper 1 overview

AS Paper 1	Time: 2 hours 15 minutes	
Section A	Answer 1 question from a choice of 2	20 marks
Section B	Answer 1 question from a choice of 2	20 marks
Section C	Answer 1 compulsory interpretations question	20 marks
	Total marks =	60 marks

You should familiarise yourself with the layout of the paper by looking at the examples published by Edexcel. The questions for each section are followed by eight pages of lined paper where you should write your answer.

Section A questions

Section A questions ask you to analyse and evaluate either cause or consequence. You should consider either the reasons for, or the results of, an event or development. You will be asked for coverage of a period of around ten years, possibly a little longer. For example, a question for Option 1G might be: 'Was the main reason for popular support for the Nazis in the years 1933–45 the party's use of propaganda?' Your answer should consider the reason(s) given in the question, then look at other relevant points and reach a conclusion.

Section B questions

Section B questions cover a longer timespan than in Section A, at least one-third of the period you have studied. The questions take the form of 'How far…', 'How significant…', 'To what extent…' or 'How accurate is it to say…'. The questions can deal with historical concepts such as cause, consequence, change, continuity, similarity, difference and significance. Again, you should consider the issue raised in the question, consider other relevant issues, and then conclude with an overall judgement.

Section C questions

There is no choice in Section C, which is concerned with the historical interpretations you have studied linked to the question 'How far was Hitler's foreign policy responsible for the Second World War?' You will be given two extracts totalling around 300 words (printed separately) and the question will take the form 'How far do you agree with the view that…?' There is no need to use source analysis skills such as making inferences or considering provenance for this Section C answers. You will need to use the extracts and your own knowledge to consider the view given in the question.

Use of time

This is an issue that you should discuss with your teachers and fellow students, but here are some suggestions for you.

1. Do not write solidly for 45 minutes on each question. For Section A and B answers you should spend a few minutes working out what the question is asking you to do, and drawing up a plan of your answer. This is especially important for Section B answers, which cover an extended period of time.
2. For Section C it is essential that you have a clear understanding of the content of each extract and the points that each extract is making. Read each extract carefully and underline important points. You could approach your answer by analysing the first extract, then the second, and then using your own knowledge before reaching an overall judgement. You might decide to spend up to ten minutes reading the extract and drawing up your plan, and 35 minutes writing your answer.

Preparing for your AS Level exam

Paper 1: AS Level sample answer with comments

Section A

These questions assess your understanding of the period in breadth. They will ask you about the content you learned about in the four key themes, and may ask about more than one theme. For these questions remember to:

- give an analytical, not a descriptive, response
- support your points with evidence
- cover the whole time period specified in the question
- come to a substantiated judgement.

Was the main reason for popular support for the Nazis in the years 1933–45 the party's use of propaganda? Explain your answer.
(20 marks)

Average student answer

The Nazis thought propaganda was very important to get the German people to think what the Nazis wanted them to think. This is what propaganda is all about and Hitler knew that all along – in 'Mein Kampf' he talked about how important propaganda was; that was when he was in prison after the Munich Putsch of 1923. So he was always very clear about its importance and how he wanted to use it to control people and get popular support. The Nazis used propaganda very effectively to get themselves elected, using powerful slogans such as 'Land, Work and Bread' and targeting particular groups of people, such as women. As soon as Hitler was in power he got the Ministry of Propaganda established under Goebbels, but even before that he was using Nazi newspapers to spread his views, such as his anti-Semitism. Under the Nazis, the ministry was very powerful and controlled the media, telling the newspapers what to print and so on.

Propaganda aims at getting people to believe certain things. Successful propaganda will produce support for the ideas that it is spreading. One important message of Nazi propaganda was its anti-Semitism. The German people were bombarded with information that told them that Jews were conspiring with communists, that they were 'subhuman', that they were 'degenerate' and that they would corrupt 'pure' Germans, the Aryans that the Nazis wanted to support them. So, to consider if propaganda got support for the Nazis you could ask: 'Did Germans become more anti-Semitic?' The answer is that some people did become more openly anti-Semitic: boycotting Jewish shops when asked to, or telling their children not to play with Jewish children who had previously been their friends. Indeed, the Nazis and their anti-Semitic policies made it harder and harder for them to support Jewish businesses or befriend Jewish people.

This brings us to one of the biggest problems with trying to measure support for the Nazis – how to tell the difference between support and enforced acceptance, considering the way the Nazis controlled people by only having one political party (so people had to vote Nazi) and having the Gestapo and Nazi officials watching what people did and said all the time. People had to be brave to act against Nazi policies, because the punishments were so harsh. You had to be really opposed to the Nazis to risk speaking out, more and more so as time went on. It was easier to go along with policies, and ignore what was going on, even if you did not actually support some of the policies, because you could be sent to concentration camps if you spoke out.

This is a weak opening paragraph because it mainly discusses events outside the given timeframe, even though the points made are accurate. The paragraph also focuses on the Nazis and their use of propaganda, not on popular support for the Nazis. It could be improved by keeping to the timeframe and addressing the question more directly.

There is a reasonable level of analysis here, but as yet there is no consideration of any other factors for support but propaganda.

This paragraph considers how you can assess support and has made a good point about the difficulties of judging 'support'. However, the question is not about how real support for the Nazis was – it is about what created that support. So consideration of support for and opposition and to the Nazis takes the answer down the wrong route.

Once they were in power the Nazis worked hard to retain popular support. Even when they were gearing up for war and putting a good deal of government money into war-related industries, Hitler said they had to make sure that the standard of living did not fall beyond a certain level – that there was enough food to go around, for instance, even though rationing was brought in early, in 1939. Also, and this was the issue that the Nazis addressed first when they came to power, they targeted unemployment which was a serious problem. They created work schemes, for example, building the autobahns to absorb some of the unemployed. They also encouraged women to leave work and start having families, and this meant that all of the jobs the women left could be taken by 'suitable' unemployed men. The Nazi's anti-Semitic policies meant that they forced Jewish people out of an increasing number of jobs as time went on and these jobs were also be filled by unemployed 'pure' Germans, the people whose support the Nazis wanted to gain. The Nazis were never trying to get the support of the various groups that they saw as 'undesirables', they wanted to get rid of them.

> This paragraph gives two more factors in popular support here, but more analysis is needed. The point about whose support the Nazis wanted needs to be developed further. The idea that reasons for support might shift over the given time frame has been mentioned before but has not been developed, and this also needs further development.

The Nazis got support from a variety of people for a variety of reasons. It is unlikely that most people looked at all aspects of Nazi rule and considered whether to support the Nazis or not on that basis. Most people who supported the Nazis focused on certain aspects of their policies – the need for a strong government, for example, or the desirability of introducing anti-Semitic policies such as taking businesses away from Jewish owners and giving them to non-Jewish people. Then there were people who had never really been political. They might not even have voted when there were many parties to vote for and now they only had the Nazis to vote for they saw politics as the business of politicians and ordinary people just had to get on with life and obey the law.

> This 'scattergun' list of support for the Nazis is undeveloped. It would be better to chose one or two examples and explain how the support was created.

There were some people who supported the Nazis because their own lives had improved under them, for example, the Nazis got support from men who had a job when they had been unemployed before, or from women who were made to feel special for being a mother. Some businessmen liked the profits they were making under the Nazis and also liked the cheap labour that they were increasingly able to draw on from the concentration camps that held political prisoners and 'undesirables' of various sorts.

Propaganda was very important in getting popular support for the Nazis, especially at the start, before they came to power in 1933 and in the first year or so when maybe they could have been pushed out of power. There were other factors, but it was propaganda getting many people to think the way the Nazis wanted them to that meant they came to power and stayed in power and so could take the other measures that helped to build up their support. So I think that makes it the main reason.

> This concluding paragraph has a judgement but does not clearly explain the reasons for arriving at the judgement, by tying together all of the strands of the argument.

Verdict

This is an average answer because:

- it has far more narrative than analysis
- it does not always back up points with evidence
- it does not come to a strong reasoned judgement.

Use the feedback on this answer to rewrite it, making as many improvements as you can.

Paper 1: AS Level sample answer with comments

Section A

These questions assess your understanding of the period in breadth. They will ask you about the content you learned about in the four key themes, and may ask about more than one theme. For these questions remember to:

- give an analytical, not a descriptive, response
- support your points with evidence
- cover the whole time period specified in the question
- come to a substantiated judgement.

Was the main reason for popular support for the Nazis in the years 1933–45 the party's use of propaganda? Explain your answer. (20 marks)

Strong student answer

It is difficult to judge levels of popular support for the Nazis because there was little room for opposition in the Nazi state – for example, people could not vote against them as they were the only political party. However, they were voted into power in 1933 with significant support and there was enough support up to 1945 for their control measures to work (people informing to the Gestapo or working hard in the factories). Propaganda was a significant reason for popular support for the Nazis but it is likely that propaganda was less effective in the last years of the war than in the early years of Nazi rule. Propaganda was vital in getting the Nazis to power. Once they were in power, popular support was the result of more than propaganda. The improvements the Nazis made in the economy, the strong government it provided, and its reversal of the Treaty of Versailles and early war time success also helped to win support.

Propaganda aims at getting people to believe certain things and behave in particular ways. We need to consider if propaganda actually gained the Nazis support. For example, Nazi propaganda urged people to support the Nazi state, to put Germany first – before family, friends and themselves. Hitler was portrayed as the leader and the father of the nation, the head of the family all Germans belonged to. The message was repeated and reinforced. Various Nazi organisations took people out of the family and into large group activities – for example, the Hitler Youth groups, hiking groups and so on. We know that after the war the Allies had to work to change ways of thinking ingrained in many people under Nazi rule. They found that people did not value individuals or families and were, at first, uncertain about taking part in politics. This suggests that propaganda did influence people.

However, support for the Nazis was not just a matter of people being brainwashed into believing their ideas. The Nazis gained support in other ways. Support for the Nazis was not a steady, fixed, thing. It shifted according to circumstances. It was probably strongest in the early years, when the Nazis made life easier for many Germans, especially those who were willing to conform to their demands, such as joining the Nazi 'trade union' which, rather than supporting the workers, simply made sure the workers obeyed the rules. The Nazis reduced unemployment – even if not as much as their manipulated statistics suggested. Organisations such as RAD provided work for thousands of men who had been unemployed. Much of the work created was manual work, such as building roads, but the projects provided work, a wage and often basic food and accommodation. Those who wanted to work to get a sense of purpose and pride again would be likely to support the Nazis for creating this work. After 1935, the reintroduction of conscription also absorbed larger and larger numbers of unemployed men, and munitions factories and other war-based industries also increased their labour force, and so helped to reduce unemployment.

> This strong opening paragraph addresses the question directly and outlines the main body of the argument that will follow.

> This paragraph discusses the success of propaganda in gaining support with a valid example.

> This paragraph provides a valid example and discusses it with accurate detail.

The Nazis worked to gain support from particular groups. Various organisations, such as 'Strength Through Joy', provided workers' benefits – including cheap or free holidays. Pregnant women and mothers with young babies received medical care and benefits. Mothers with more than four babies were even awarded medals – showing the government valued their role. Women who were mothers at the time said they were made to feel special and were given benefits their mothers never had. These policies probably gained the Nazis support from affected groups. In a more general way, the Nazis used the Gestapo and the police service to provide law and order, not just to spy on, arrest or imprison opponents and 'undesirables'. The government's firm treatment of 'asocials' (prostitutes, thieves and drunks) gained it support from those who felt that cities and towns had become dangerous places. Hitler told his ministers that, while their main aim was to prepare for war, it was important not to reduce the standard of living below a certain level. He said a nation satisfied with its standard of living was more likely to support the government. In this he was right. When the rations were cut more and more and when the British bombing of German cities (which began in 1940) caused appalling devastation in cities such as Dresden, support for the government fell, because the government was no longer providing for, or protecting, its citizens.

Support for the Nazis shifted when they failed to provide for or protect their citizens. It also fell as the Nazis did less well in the war. Their initial success in regaining land that had been lost as a result of the Treaty of Versailles gained them huge support because the Treaty had been deeply resented. The re-militarisation of the Rhineland and Anschluss with Austria were also approved of. However, when it seemed that Hitler might go to war over Czechoslovakia, approval dropped. One reason Hitler agreed to the Munich Conference was that a military parade he organised was not greeted with cheering, flag waving and other signs of support, which suggested that war did not have wide public support. Once the Nazis went to war their rapid success gained them support, reinforcing the propaganda of Germany as a great and powerful nation. As the Third Reich extended its borders into Poland and beyond it began to lose control over the land it held and it also made its ruthless racial policies plain, uprooting Slavic people to Germanise their land, creating ghettos and herding people into concentration camps simply based on their race, not for any crime or political opposition to the Nazis. These policies also affected support for the Nazis.

> These paragraphs develop and analyse the factors for and shifts in support for the Nazis, with detailed consideration and evidence.

Propaganda was important in gaining popular support for the Nazis, especially getting them to power in 1933 and in the first years of their rule, when they might have lost power. Support shifted during the years 1933–45. They had a lot less support towards the end of the war, when they were losing the war and running the country less well. Propaganda was a constant factor all through the period, but people also supported the Nazis because they improved individuals' circumstances, or made them feel safer, or gave them a sense of national or personal pride. However, I do think propaganda was probably the main reason for popular support, especially considering the way people at the end of the war had come to believe in working together for Hitler and the nation and abandoning their personal needs.

> The concluding paragraph picks out the key arguments and comes to a reasoned judgement.

Verdict

This is a strong answer because:

- it considers a number of factors in reasonable depth
- it analyses the question and focuses on the right time period
- it develops and explains the points it makes and makes links
- it comes to a strong reasoned judgement.

Paper 1: AS Level sample answer with comments

Section B

These questions assess your understanding of the course in breadth and will cover a period of 30 years or more. They will ask you about the content you learned about in the four key themes, and may ask about more than one theme. The questions will also require you to explore a range of concepts, such as change over time, similarity and difference, as well as significance. For these questions remember to:

- identify the focus of the question
- consider the concepts you will need to explore
- support your points with evidence from across the time period specified in the question
- develop the evidence you deploy to build up your overall judgement
- come to a substantiated judgement that directly addresses the question set.

How significant was the period of Nazi rule in the development of cultural and generational tensions in the FRG? (20 marks)

Average student answer

The cultural and generational tensions that emerged in the FRG had many causes and affected different people in many ways. However, it is true to say that the shadow cast by the period of Nazi rule did have a significant impact on the tensions and raised issues that were likely to spark debate that led to tensions. However, there were other reasons for these tensions that were not completely tied to Nazi rule but were the result of other factors. Younger people, for example, were more likely to reject traditional German culture in favour of a more Westernised culture. On the other hand some tensions cut across the generational divide and were more related to class and political divisions – and were not related to the Nazi period at all.

The subject of the period of Nazi rule was one of the most likely issues to create tension between generations. The older generation were likely to adopt the idea of calling 1945 'year zero'. They did this both in a broad sense, concerning Nazi rule generally, and on a personal level, to do with the activities of individuals during the war. The Nazis were responsible for the Holocaust and other atrocities and were widely seen as being responsible for the Second World War too. Although they had been badly bombed by the Allies during the war, the general feeling was that this happened in response to the German Blitz of Britain, and would not have happened otherwise, so the Nazis brought that on Germany too.

Many of the younger generation, on the other hand, wanted to confront their Nazi past rather than pretend it had never happened. They wanted to hear the German version of the stories of events such as the Holocaust that they heard about at second- or third-hand from other sources. They were also much more likely to see things in black and white – Nazis and their supporters were bad and should be found and punished. Not all young people felt this way, and among those who did, the extent to which they pushed the matter varied; some were much more confrontational about it than others.

Other tensions worked between the generations that were not tied to the Nazis. A significant number of young people, but not all, were keen to embrace Western culture, especially that of the USA. Those who embraced Western culture took on Western fashion of the time. They listened to Western pop music and tried to create a German version of it. This was significant because the 'alternative' culture they adopted rejected the values of the earlier generation, so this caused tensions between the generations that added to the tension created by differences about how to approach the Nazi period of Germany's history.

This first paragraph is too generalised, listing factors rather than addressing the idea of 'significance'. However, it shows an understanding that there were other factors creating these tensions, not only the existence of a Nazi past. It could be improved by giving examples with supporting detail.

This paragraph gives some reasons why the Nazi period created tensions, but it does not expand sufficiently – the answer is more narrative than analysis.

This paragraph gives another factor for tension and attempts to evaluate it. It could be improved by developing the reasons further and considering the cultural context.

In the late 1960s there was a turn against the USA among many young people because of the country's involvement in Vietnam, but until then, its culture was very influential. There was also a Western-influenced shift at about the same time towards a rejection of materialist culture and the values of those who had worked to rebuild Germany after the war: working hard and building up a comfortable lifestyle. However, it is important to understand that Western influence on culture was variable across Germany. It was much more likely to have an impact in cities and in the northern Länder, and was at its strongest in universities, among the better-educated young people whose families were better off. This was also true of the tensions raised by the Nazi period, but that affected more people.

> This paragraph gives a useful example of the variability of cultural tensions. It could be improved by pulling out how this applies to significance.

There were other cultural tensions at the time that, unlike the one discussed above, cut across the generational divide rather than running along it. Firstly, there were a growing number of people who rejected a society that was part of NATO (the Western Europe military defence organisation) because they disliked the whole idea of war and being tied up in a relationship with other countries that would drag you in to help them if they went to war. Secondly, others (sometimes also against NATO) disliked a culture that was extravagant with fossil fuels like coal and oil and wanted more conservation projects and policies. Thirdly, there were those who objected to nuclear power as a fuel and for weapons. Some protesters rejected some of the objections in this list, others embraced them all. Tensions grew between those who saw nuclear power and fossil fuels as the right energy choices and 'alternative' energy as impractical and unnecessary and those who campaigned against fossil fuel and nuclear power and in favour of 'alternative' energy solutions. The tensions grew from the 1950s to the 1980s, as those who campaigned for alternative energies and the banning of nuclear power grew and campaigners could not be derided as simply being a small group of better-off, liberal, well-intentioned but impractical people with policies that were impossible to achieve.

> These paragraphs outline and analyse cross-generational cultural issues, but there is still little consideration of how significant they were.

The rise of the Green Party was a cultural phenomenon of the 1980s that can be used as an example of the cross-generational divide in German society that also created tensions while not being related to the Nazi period of history. It was about what was going on at the time and would happen in the future. The fact that the Greens managed to establish themselves as a political party with a growing number of seats in the Bundestag during the 1980s came as a result of cultural change that led to Green ideas being more widely accepted by Germans. It was tied in with the idea of alternative and non-consumerist ways of living.

It seems to me that the period of Nazi rule and the way people reacted to it was a very significant factor in generational tensions in the FRG. However, I think it had less impact on the cultural tensions that emerged even though the Nazis did have clear ideas about culture and what was 'acceptable' culture and what was not. In the matter of cultural tensions, I think the influence of the West was more important.

> The concluding paragraph mainly restates points made earlier without analysing how they support the judgement made.

Verdict

This is an average answer because:

- there is too much narrative and not enough analysis
- it does not consider 'significance' enough
- there are no inaccuracies, but many points are made without development and explanation
- it does not come to a strong reasoned judgement.

Use the feedback on this answer to rewrite it, making as many improvements as you can.

Paper 1: AS Level sample answer with comments

Section B

These questions assess your understanding of the course in breadth and will cover a period of 30 years or more. They will ask you about the content you learned about in the four key themes, and may ask about more than one theme. The questions will also require you to explore a range of concepts, such as change over time, similarity and difference, as well as significance. For these questions remember to:

- identify the focus of the question
- consider the concepts you will need to explore
- support your points with evidence from across the time period specified in the question
- develop the evidence you deploy to build up your overall judgement
- come to a substantiated judgement that directly addresses the question set.

How significant was the period of Nazi rule in the development of cultural and generational tensions in the FRG? (20 marks)

Strong student answer

The cultural and generational tensions that emerged in the FRG had many causes and affected different people with varying severity. However, it is true to say that the shadow cast by the period of Nazi rule did have a significant impact on the tensions and raised issues likely to spark debate that led to tensions. Older people, who had lived and worked under Nazi rule, were more likely to want to draw a line under the period of Nazi rule and start again, not examining the past too closely. Younger people were more likely to demand that the older generation confront the past and deal with it. However, these tensions had other reasons that were not tied to Nazi rule. Younger people, for example, were more likely to adopt Western, especially American, culture. Some tensions, such as protests against nuclear power for weaponry and fuel, cut across the generational divide and were more related to class and political divisions – and not to the Nazi period at all.

> This is a strong first paragraph. It shows a grasp of the issues and an understanding that it is important to consider the significance of the influence of the period of Nazi rule.

The subject of the period of Nazi rule was the issue most likely to create tension between generations, because the older generation had lived through it and the younger generation had not. The older generation were likely to adopt the idea of calling 1945 'year zero', both in a broad sense, concerning Nazi rule generally, and on a personal level, to do with the activities of individuals during the war. It was not as simple as people wanting to hide Nazi sympathies, or participation in the brutalities of the regime. Many of those who had been in camps wanted to forget the brutality of that time. The shortages and desperate living conditions in the cities towards the end of the war drove people to do things that they would prefer not to discuss and both partners in a marriage might have things they wanted to keep secret when the husband returned from war. Many of the younger generation, on the other hand, wanted to confront their Nazi past. The period was not taught in schools, their parents and grandparents would not talk about it and so there was a black hole in the past. They wanted to hear the German version of events such as the Holocaust that they heard about at second- or third-hand. They were also more likely to see things in black and white – Nazis and their supporters were bad and should be found and punished. Not all young people felt this way, and among those who did, the extent to which they pushed the matter varied. Some simply wanted the subject be taught and talked about. Others protested, using slogans such as 'What did you do in the war, Daddy?', an ironic mirroring of posters used in Britain to encourage men to join up in 1914 to fight in the First World War.

> This paragraph analyses the reasons why the Nazi period created tensions.

There were other tensions between the generations that were not tied to the Nazis. A significant number of young people were keen to embrace Western culture, especially that of the USA. This was a rejection of not just the Nazi 'acceptable' Germanic culture, but also all German culture. It was a determination to look forward, create a 'new' culture in Germany, rather as in the Weimar period, which had also looked to the USA for inspiration and pressed for an examination of social issues in books and films. Those who embraced Western culture took on Western fashion – hairstyles, clothing such as jeans. They listened to Western pop music (including the Beatles from the UK) and tried to create a German version of it. They were satirised by opponents as demanding burgers and fries, not traditional food. This was significant because the 'alternative' culture they adopted rejected the values of the earlier generation, and so caused tensions. It was part of a wave of cultural tensions across the generations at the time that can be seen as part of the traditional cultural differences that spring up between generations all the time.

> This paragraph gives another factor for tension and evaluates it.

In the late 1960s, there was a turn against the USA among many young people because of the country's involvement in Vietnam, but until then its culture was very influential. There was also a Western-influenced shift at about the same time towards a rejection of materialist culture and the values of those who had worked to rebuild Germany after the war: working hard and building up a comfortable lifestyle. However, it is important to understand that Western influence on culture was variable across Germany. It had its greatest impact in cities and in the northern Länder, and was at its strongest in universities, among the educated young people whose families were well off. This was also true of the tensions raised by the Nazi period, but the latter were more widespread – those who had no interest in culture were still likely to have an interest in their background and past. This seems to be to be an important contributor to tension, but not as significant as the Nazi period.

> This paragraph gives a developed example of the variability of cultural tensions.

There were other cultural tensions at the time that, unlike those discussed above, cut across the generational divide rather than running along it. A growing number of people rejected a society that was part of NATO, that was extravagant with fossil fuels and that used nuclear power as a fuel and for weapons. The tensions grew from the 1950s to the 1980s, as more people campaigned for alternative energies and the banning of nuclear power, so they could not be derided as being a small group of better-off, liberal, well-intentioned but impractical people with policies that were impossible to achieve. Again, this was part of a wider movement in the USA and Western Europe. Some protesters embraced all these causes, others only a few. The rise of the Green Party is one cultural phenomenon that shows the cross-generational divide in German society. The Greens established themselves as a political party with a growing number of seats in the Bundestag during the 1980s (from no seats in 1976 to 42 seats in 1987) as their ideas became more widely accepted by Germans. Pressure from people with Green ideas led to changes in Germany, such as a high level of recycling and energy conservation drives in public buildings, even when those people did not to vote Green in elections.

> This paragraph outlines and analyses cross-generational cultural issues that provoked tension with accurate and detailed development.

It seems to me that the period of Nazi rule and the way people reacted to it was a very significant factor in generational tensions in the FRG. It was a very emotive issue for both those who lived through the period and those who did not, and tensions are at their worst when both sides are emotionally involved and less able to think clearly. I think it had less of an impact on cultural tensions, although you could argue that young people turning to Western culture was a rejection of the 'acceptable' German culture urged on the older generation by the Nazis.

> The final paragraph gives a conclusion supported by reference to the other possible influences.

Verdict

This is a strong answer because:

- it analyses the impact of the various factors throughout
- it considers 'significance' throughout

- there are no inaccuracies, and many points are developed and explained
- it comes to a strong reasoned judgement.

Paper 1: AS Level sample answer with comments

Section C

These questions require you to read and analyse two extracts carefully in order to develop a response which examines and makes an informed judgement about the different interpretations. The best answers:

- need to show an understanding of the extracts and identify the key points of each interpretation
- deploy own knowledge to develop the points emerging from extracts and provide necessary context
- develop a judgement after developing and weighing up different interpretations.

Study Extracts 8 and 9 (from Chapter 5, page 126) before you answer this question.

Historians have different views about how far Hitler's foreign policy was responsible for the Second World War. Analyse and evaluate the extracts and use your knowledge of the issues to explain your answer to the following question.

How far do you agree with the view that Hitler carefully planned out Germany's foreign policy years before he came to power? (20 marks)

Average student answer

The two extracts certainly seem to be saying different things. In Extract 8, Klaus Hildebrand states very clearly that he thinks that it is perfectly obvious that Hitler had a long-term programme for conquest – even Stalin had read it, so he should have seen that Hitler intended to invade the USSR and everyone else should have seen that he intended to expand eastwards into Czechoslovakia and Poland. Donald Cameron Watt, on the other hand, rejects the idea that Hitler had a programme that the Nazis followed. He thinks that Hitler was not capable of long-term planning – he just reacted to events as they happened. He thinks that what Hildebrand calls a foreign policy programme was really just a set of vague aims.

Extract 8 suggests that there is a clear foreign policy outlined in 'Mein Kampf'. This is the book that Hitler wrote in prison, when he was thinking out what to do and how to run the Nazi Party and gain political power once he was released. It is in print, and translated into various languages, so we can read it. It laid out several of Hitler's main ideas. Firstly, it said Germany needed to expand for the German nation to become more powerful and have enough land to be self-sufficient. It suggested that this land should be gained by reversing the Treaty of Versailles and taking back all of that land, then expanding eastwards into lands held by the 'inferior' races there. Secondly it wanted to get rid of the Jews and communists in Germany (and the land that Germany took over). In the book he seemed to think that it was not possible to do what he wanted without building up Germany's army and going to war, making alliances with racially suitable countries such as Britain.

Hildebrand (Extract 8) seems to have a point, then, when he says the book laid down a plan that Hitler followed when he came to power. The book itself seems to support this. Also, there is a record of the meeting that Hildebrand refers to and in this he talks about overturning Versailles, rearming, expansion and the need to fight. That all happened when Hitler came to power too. So what Hitler did when he came to power does look like trying to do just what he said he would do, not only in 'Mein Kampf' and the meeting referred to by Hildebrand, but also in lots of other meetings and speeches.

> In this first paragraph, some overall understanding is shown and reasonable use is made of the extracts. It could be improved by explaining the stances of the historical debate more clearly and tying the points more tightly to the question.

> These two paragraphs focus entirely on Extract 8. There is some own knowledge, but it is vague; more accurate detail is needed and it should be provided as evidence to support analysis – there is too great an emphasis on description rather than analysis in these paragraphs.

However, it is important to consider that the fact that Hitler outlined aims in 'Mein Kampf' and acted to make them come about is not necessarily 'carefully planned' foreign policy. It is not really detailed enough for that. Also there is evidence that Hitler was not able to achieve all his foreign policy aims – what he wanted did not drive foreign policy, because factors from outside meant things did not always go the way he wanted. An example of this is where Mein Kampf says that an alliance with Britain would be a good thing, but, although Hitler tried to make an alliance, the British would not agree. This had a significant effect on his foreign policy, but it was not something that he planned.

> This paragraph introduces ideas from Extract 9, but obliquely, without reference to the extract or its author. There is some attempt at analysing evidence to support/ contradict Hildebrand's argument. This could be improved by a more explicit reference to the second extract and the ideas Watt expresses in it. More analysis is also needed.

In Extract 9, Donald Cameron Watt suggests two things: that Hitler was not good at planning ahead and that his foreign policy was driven more by outside events and actions than by what he wanted to do. However, Hitler did have the ability to plan ahead. For example, when the Second World War started, earlier than expected, over Hitler's invasion of Poland, he was able to act quickly and put his Blitzkrieg plans into action to invade Belgium, France and other countries in western Europe. He would not have been able to do this without long-term planning to have the military equipment and the men trained to use the equipment and use the system (which was a new one) of bombing and moving on, leaving the infantry to occupy the land taken. So I am not convinced by the notion that Hitler could not plan ahead.

> These paragraphs discuss Extract 9, and correctly identify the two points made in that extract, but not in much detail. Own knowledge is used to provide evidence to analyse the interpretations, which, again, lacks detail.

I am more convinced by the second factor that Donald Cameron Watt suggests – the idea that Hitler's foreign policy was influenced by outside factors. As I said when discussing Extract 8, Hitler wanted an alliance with Britain, and hoped to be able to make one because Britain was very against the USSR because it was communist and Germany was not. Britain did make a naval treaty with Germany – this would have encouraged Hitler to think Britain might become an ally because it was working outside the Treaty of Versailles. Another reason to be encouraged was that Lloyd George (the British prime minister) had publicly said that he thought the Treaty had been too harsh. Also, several British politicians had openly praised the early Nazi government as being strong and capable and managing to improve the economy. But in the end, Britain did not become an ally, no matter what Hitler wanted. He had to change his foreign policy to allow for the fact that Britain was not going to be an ally so was probably going to become an enemy, instead, and an enemy that Hitler thought would pose problems, unlike the USSR, which he mistakenly thought would crumble when invaded because his ideas about race made him think that Slavs were weak and not good fighters.

Overall, it seems to me that the balance of the argument seems to lie with Watt's argument about external factors, although his assertion that Hitler was not able to plan for the long term is less plausible. I think Hildebrand is right in saying that Hitler had a plan that was outlined in 'Mein Kampf' and that he tried to make it the Nazi foreign policy. However, I think it is important not to say that Germany's foreign policy was entirely driven by what Hitler wanted. He had to change his plan, in both the short term and the longer term, as a result of external factors, such as Britain not becoming an ally.

> This is quite a good summing up. There is a decision about which argument is most reasonable and some reasons for that choice are given. It would be improved by expanding the supporting material.

Verdict

This is an average answer because:

- it is not rooted closely enough in the extracts and they are not linked effectively
- not enough context is given; however, there is no incorrect information and the answer tries to analyse the extracts in relation to the question

- it makes a judgement but it needs more substance; it lacks the necessary sense of argument for a strong answer.

Use the feedback on this answer to rewrite it, making as many improvements as you can.

Paper 1: AS Level sample answer with comments

Section C

These questions require you to read and analyse two extracts carefully in order to develop a response which examines and makes an informed judgement about different interpretations. The best answers:

- need to show an understanding of the extracts and identify the key points of each interpretation
- deploy own knowledge to develop the points emerging from extracts and provide necessary context
- develop judgement after developing and weighing up different interpretations.

Study Extracts 8 and 9 (from Chapter 5, page 126) before you answer this question.

Historians have different views about how far Hitler's foreign policy was responsible for the Second World War. Analyse and evaluate the extracts and use your knowledge of the issues to explain your answer to the following question.

How far do you agree with the view that Hitler carefully planned out Germany's foreign policy years before he came to power? (20 marks)

Strong student answer

The two extracts certainly seem to say different things. Hildebrand states clearly that Hitler had a long-term programme of conquest that was clearly outlined in 'Mein Kampf' and discussed with army leaders 'in the first few days' after coming to power. Watt, on the other hand, explicitly rejects the idea that Hitler had a foreign policy programme that the Nazis followed. He says the 'programme' that some historians (such as Hildebrand) talk of was simply an outline of Hitler's ideas and that Nazi foreign policy was significantly affected by external factors. He also suggests Hitler was incapable of long-term planning. These different interpretations do not disagree about the facts of Hitler's foreign policy. Their disagreement hinges on interpretations: of the word 'programme', of Hitler's character and of the importance of external factors.

'Intentionalist' historians, such as Hildebrand, see Hitler's intentions as the driving force behind Nazi foreign policy and the cause of the Second World War. Some believe Hitler had a master plan, some go further and believe he had a step-by-step plan for either European or world domination. Yet others believe he had a master plan but took advantage of events as to timing. 'Functionalist' or 'structuralist' historians, such as Watt, emphasise the role of external factors. They point out that foreign policy involves interacting with other countries. Events in other countries and domestic pressure in Germany exerted pressure on foreign policy decisions – it was not possible to follow a plan laid down years before. Some of them also see Hitler's foreign policy as simply a continuation of the German expansionist policies that led to the First World War, saying that the Second World War was simply a continuation of the First World War and implying that Germany would have gone to war whoever its leader was.

Hildebrand believes that 'Mein Kampf' and the meeting with the army leaders show that even before coming to power Hitler had foreign policy aims that he made reality as leader of Germany: overturning the Treaty of Versailles and expanding eastwards. There is evidence outside Extract 8 for early planning, as Hildebrand suggests. 'Mein Kampf' explicitly discusses the need for lebensraum to the east in 'Slav' countries (Poland and the USSR) and the right of Germans to claim this space, which will probably have to be taken by fighting a war. Notes exist taken at the 1933 meeting with army leaders showing that building up the country for war, overturning the Treaty of Versailles and 'conquest in the east' were discussed. Hitler made many speeches about the need for lebensraum. It does look as if Hitler had formed his aims for Germany by the time he wrote 'Mein Kampf', and still had them as aims in the 1933 meeting.

Side comments:

This opening paragraph focuses on the sources and identifies their key arguments, setting up the debate and suggesting a reason for the opposing views, also showing an awareness that it is foreign policy under discussion.

This paragraph outlines the intentionalist and structuralist debate and its various layers, introducing information from own knowledge and slotting the sources into place in their particular camps while suggesting reasons for their different views.

This paragraph analyses Hildebrand's interpretation, with contextual points drawn from own knowledge, well developed to show that there is evidence outside the extract to support Hildebrand's point of view.

Another piece of evidence to support Hildebrand's view of 'Mein Kampf' as an outline of the policies Hitler intended to follow when he came to power is the book's rabid anti-Semitism, which Hitler adopted as a domestic policy when in power.

Hitler wrote 'Mein Kampf' in prison following the failed Munich Putsch. He dreamed of coming to power, but he was not close to gaining it. Many politicians campaigned with the policies of overturning Versailles and German expansion. 'Mein Kampf' also contains evidence to support Watt (Extract 9) that external factors had a significant effect on Hitler's foreign policy. In the book, Hitler envisages Britain as Germany's ally. The British were, in his racial theory, almost Aryan and had built an empire, and kept it, with a ruthlessness that Hitler admired. When Hitler came to power he tried to make an alliance with Britain, sending von Ribbentrop to Britain several times. However, while Britain made a naval treaty that limited both navies it would not agree to an alliance. This stopped Hitler's foreign policy going the way he outlined in 'Mein Kampf'. This supports Watt's view that external circumstances affected Hitler's foreign policy. However, the fact that an alliance with Britain is in 'Mein Kampf' and he tried to achieve it when he came to power, suggests Watt is wrong in saying that Hitler was incapable of long-term planning.

There are other examples of external factors influencing Hitler's foreign policy that support Watt. Mussolini made it clear he would not give military aid if Hitler invaded Czechoslovakia in 1938. This, and the fact that an invasion did not have popular support in Germany (another factor outside Hitler's complete control) meant he went to the Munich Conference and negotiated. There is evidence that in his negotiations with Mussolini he was thinking of war in Europe in 1942 or 1943, when he and Mussolini had built up their military strength still further. However, he misjudged the reaction of the West to his invasion of Poland and war broke out in 1939. Hitler may have needed to adapt his plans to external circumstances, but he was not afraid to take bold steps and take advantage of events, even if it meant changing the plan. The takeover of Danzig was planned, but Anschluss with Austria was not; the timing was driven by the activities of Austrian Nazis. There is evidence that Hitler was a poor long-term planner. He changed his mind frequently. However, there is evidence that he could plan ahead. An example is the war itself. It came earlier than expected, but he reacted at once and his Blitzkrieg tactics, planned in advance, resulted in the rapid fall of Denmark, Norway, Belgium, the Netherlands and France. Another example is that when Hitler came to power he needed to be sure the USSR would not attack Germany as he built up its military strength. He formed an alliance with Poland, a traditional enemy of Germany. Under the plan outlined in 'Mein Kampf', Poland should have been taken for lebensraum; but Hitler adapted to Germany's circumstances and made it a temporary ally, a short-term change made for long-term gain.

Overall the balance of the argument seems to lie with Watt's argument about external factors, although his assertion that Hitler could not plan for the long term is less plausible. I think it is clear that Hildebrand is right that Hitler had clear aims for foreign policy in Germany well before he came to power, and that he outlined them in 'Mein Kampf'. However, it seems to me that Hildebrand overemphasises the power of Hitler's aims over world events. Hitler could not always pursue his aims and he had to react to external factors, as outlined above. He had a plan, but he had to change it in both the short term and the longer term as a result of external factors.

> These paragraphs introduce accurate recall to support Watt's interpretation that Hitler's foreign policy was not following a careful plan, but shaped by external factors, while querying the assertion that Hitler was not capable of long-term planning, also with use of detailed evidence from own knowledge.

> The concluding paragraph comes to a clear judgement based on the balance of the evidence.

Verdict

This is a strong answer because:

- it identifies and illustrates the arguments of the two extracts; it develops an argument that considers both interpretations and tries to provide balance

- it deploys a sound range of specific evidence to develop points emerging from the extracts; it provides a sense of the context
- there is a clear judgement.

Preparing for your A Level Paper 1 exam

Advance planning

1. Draw up a timetable for your revision and try to keep to it. Spread your timetable over a number of weeks, and aim to cover four or five topics each week.
2. Spend longer on topics that you have found difficult, and revise them several times.
3. Above all, do not try to limit your revision by attempting to 'question spot'. Try to be confident about all aspects of your Paper 1 work, because this will ensure that you have a choice of questions in Sections A and B.

Paper 1 overview:

AL Paper 1	Time: 2 hours 15 minutes	
Section A	Answer 1 question from a choice of 2	20 marks
Section B	Answer 1 question from a choice of 2	20 marks
Section C	Answer 1 compulsory interpretations question	20 marks
	Total marks =	60 marks

You should familiarise yourself with the layout of the paper by looking at the examples published by Edexcel. The questions for each section are followed by eight pages of lined paper where you should write your answer.

Section A and Section B questions

The essay questions in Sections A and B are similar in form. They ask you to reach a judgement on an aspect of the course you have studied, and will deal with one or more historical concepts of change, continuity, similarity, difference, cause, consequence and significance. The question stems that will be used will include 'To what extent…', 'How far…', 'How significant was…' and so on. You should consider the issue raised by the question, develop your answer by looking at other relevant points, and reach a judgement in your conclusion.

The main difference between Section A and Section B questions will be the timespan of the questions. Section A questions will cover a period of ten years or more, while Section B questions will be concerned with at least one-third of the period you have studied.

A Section A question for Paper 1G might read 'How far do you agree that opposition to the Weimar government in the years 1918–32 was rooted in a hatred of the Treaty of Versailles?' Your answer should consider how a hatred of the Treaty of Versailles might affect attitudes to the Weimar government and also consider other factors, such as the government's perceived inability to solve Germany's economic problems or its need to keep resorting to 'emergency' rule by decree, and how these produced opposition to the government, before reaching an overall judgement on the question.

A Section B question on the same paper will cover a longer period of time, but have a similar shape. For example, 'To what extent were attempts to create a command economy in Nazi Germany successful in solving the economic problems of the Weimar Republic?' Here you should consider how Nazi attempts to create a command economy helped to solve the economic problems of the Weimar Republic, but you should also consider other factors for recovery, for example, work creation schemes and social changes such as pressuring married women not to work, that produced an improvement in the economy. You should conclude by reaching a judgement on the question.

Section C questions

There is no choice in Section C, which is concerned with the historical interpretations you have studied linked to the question 'How far was Hitler's foreign policy responsible for the Second World War?' You will be given two extracts totalling around 400 words (printed separately) and the question will take the form 'How convincing do you find the view that…?' There is no need to use source analysis skills such as making inferences or considering provenance for this Section C answers. You should approach your answer by analysing both extracts separately, and then use your own knowledge to support, and to counter, the view given in the question, before reaching an overall judgement.

Use of time

This is an issue that you should discuss with your teachers and fellow students, but here are some suggestions for you.

1. Do not write solidly for 45 minutes on each question. For Section A and B answers you should spend a few minutes working out what the question is asking you to do, and drawing up a plan of your answer. This is especially important for Section B answers, which cover an extended period of time.
2. For Section C it is essential that you have a clear understanding of the content of each extract and the points that each extract is making. Read each extract carefully and underline important points. You might decide to spend up to ten minutes reading the extracts and drawing up your plan, and 35 minutes writing your answer.

Preparing for your A Level exams

Paper 1: A Level sample answer with comments

Section A

These questions assess your understanding of the period in breadth. They will ask you about the content you learned about in the four key themes, and may ask about more than one theme. For these questions remember to:

- give an analytical, not a descriptive, response
- support your points with evidence
- cover the whole time period specified in the question
- come to a substantiated judgement.

How far do you agree that opposition to the Weimar government in the years 1918–32 was rooted in a hatred of the Treaty of Versailles? (20 marks)

Average student answer

Between 1918 and 1932 there was certainly a widespread hatred of the Treaty of Versailles. The Weimar government was the government that had signed the Treaty, even if any other government that had come to power would have done the same thing. However, not all opposition to the Weimar government sprang from their involvement in signing the Treaty. Other reasons for opposition were: holding a different political viewpoint and disapproving of policies.

> This is a good opening paragraph that establishes both the timeframe and the focus of the question. It could develop its points more.

The Treaty of Versailles was regarded as humiliating and unfair by most Germans and even many of the Allies whose governments had imposed it. Many people said at the time that it was laying the foundations for another war – Lloyd George, the British prime minister, suggested it would be in 25 years and overestimated the gap. From a German point of view, the Weimar government lost a great deal of support in the country for having signed the Treaty. The government also lost support because of the belief at the time that Germany could have won the war if it had kept on fighting rather than asking for an armistice and then signing the Treaty of Versailles. The Kaiser and the Military High Command kept very quiet about how badly the war was going for Germany, so it was a huge surprise to many Germans when there was an armistice followed by a treaty that was harsh and humiliating and which Germany had not been allowed to take part in framing. Many Germans called the government 'the November Criminals' for signing the Treaty. So feelings ran high over the Treaty and the Weimar government was held responsible for it. All opposition parties in politics, from the most right wing to the most left wing, had overturning the Treaty as a political aim and used it as a focus for opposition.

> This paragraph focuses on the question. There is some analysis but much of it is narrative. It could be improved by developing the level of dislike, for example, by mentioning the 'stab in the back' theory.

However, there were other reasons for opposing the Weimar government. There were political parties who opposed the Weimar government for political reasons. They wanted the country run in a different way – they did not accept that democracy was the right way to govern. However, there were groups and individuals who opposed the Weimar government too – people who saw their pensions vanishing, for example. Many of the paramilitary groups that sprang up after the war were made up of ex-soldiers who believed the government had betrayed them and so opposed it. They were against the government for reasons to do with hating the Treaty of Versailles, but many of them then attached themselves to political parties so added a political element to their opposition and fought all opposition groups, not just those groups in the Reichstag who might become part of coalition governments. For example, the Nazis

> This paragraph gives reasons for opposing the Weimar government other than a hatred of the Treaty of Versailles, but it provides very little analysis.

fought most bitterly with the communists – so this was a case of right-wing extremists fighting left-wing extremists. They were, in fact, competing with each other for voters who opposed the government and wanted work, food and a strong government – both the Nazis and the communists promised to provide these things if they were brought to power.

The Weimar government was a democracy, but the way it was set up there were too many parties in the Reichstag and it resulted in coalition governments which found it had to agree. In turn, this made it hard for the government to act decisively, so it failed to act swiftly to solve problems such as unemployment and hyperinflation – both of these affected the lives of many Germans badly and so made them oppose the government. Government failure is not the same as the Treaty of Versailles, although people might be opposing the government for that as well. It is likely that a strong government would have faced less opposition than one that did not seem to be working and that used government by decree towards the end almost all the time – although it was supposed to be used only in emergencies. If you know that the government is ruling by an emergency measure much of the time then you think it is not working very well and you oppose it. You look for an alternative.

Gustav Stresemann reduced opposition to the Weimar government, because he managed to make coalition government work, and negotiated plans to reduce reparations that meant more money could be ploughed into the economy and there were US loans too. While this did not mean less opposition from political parties, it did reduce opposition among the German people, which suggests that if the Weimar government had been able to govern more effectively from the start they would have got more support from people, despite the hatred of the Treaty of Versailles. The party system was too fragmented and opposition parties were able to stir things up because of the free speech and free press that the Weimar government allowed.

These paragraphs make some good points, but in a jumbled fashion. These would be better addressed point by point with more development.

Unemployment and rising prices came back with the Depression and it was not coping with this that was the downfall of the government because opposition rose and people turned to other parties as prices and unemployment went on rising. Hindenburg was popular as a person, but his chancellors were not, and nor was government by decree of the measures that the government wanted to put in place in 1932 to solve the economic problems. The way the government managed things was a big factor in creating opposition; the Treaty of Versailles was not the only factor.

Between 1918 and 1932 the Weimar government faced a great deal of opposition, from political parties and individuals and groups outside political parties. The widespread hatred of the Treaty of Versailles was certainly a significant factor in opposition and it united all the opponents of the government no matter what the political stance of their opposition. However, other factors were the existence of parties with different ideas about how Germany should be governed – parties that thought democracy was not a good system and was not working in Germany under the Weimar government. There were also people and groups who thought that the government was not governing very well most of the time, with the exception of the Stresemann period.

The concluding paragraph simply restates points made earlier without reaching a reasoned judgement.

Verdict

This is an average answer because:

- there is too much narrative and not enough analysis
- there are no inaccuracies, but many points are made without development and explanation
- it does focus on the question
- it does not come to a strong, reasoned judgement.

Use the feedback on this answer to rewrite it, making as many improvements as you can.

Paper 1: A Level sample answer with comments

Section A

These questions assess your understanding of the period in breadth. They will ask you about the content you learned about in the four key themes, and may ask about more than one theme. For these questions remember to:

- give an analytical, not a descriptive, response
- support your points with evidence
- cover the whole time period specified in the question
- come to a substantiated judgement.

How far do you agree that opposition to the Weimar government in the years 1918–32 was rooted in a hatred of the Treaty of Versailles? (20 marks)

Strong student answer

Between 1918 and 1932, there was certainly a widespread hatred of the Treaty of Versailles. The Weimar government had signed the Treaty, and this provoked reaction against the government, although any other government in power would probably have done the same. However, not all opposition to the Weimar government sprang from its involvement with the Treaty. Some had a different political viewpoint, others disapproved of particular policies. Some opposition varied according to the circumstances: one reason for opposition was feeling the government was not solving Germany's problems. This was strong after the war and during hyperinflation, lessened as things improved under Stresemann then deepened with the increasing economic problems brought on by the Depression.

> This is a good opening paragraph because it establishes the timeframe, analyses the question and suggests a direction for the answer.

Most Germans, and many of the Allies whose governments had imposed it, saw the Treaty of Versailles as humiliating and unfair. The Weimar government lost support in Germany for having signed it and because of the prevailing belief at the time that Germany could have won the war. The kaiser and the Military High Command kept very quiet about how badly the war was going, so people did not realise Germany was on the edge of defeat. Hindenburg, an army leader, said the army had been 'stabbed in the back' by the government. He was popular and an important military officer who people trusted, so people tended to believe him. All opposition parties in politics had the overturning of the Treaty as a political aim. Even the Weimar government worked to overturn the Treaty – publicly, with its negotiations to revise its position in Europe and reparations, and in secret, with rearming, although its very secrecy stopped the government from being able to use it to gain popularity.

> The paragraph clearly explains why the Treaty of Versailles produced opposition to the Weimar government.

However, there were other reasons for opposing the Weimar government. The first broad reason was having different political aims. The government faced opposition from the far right: political parties such as the DNVP, which wanted to restore a monarchy. It also faced opposition from groups on the far left, such as the KPD, the communist party. Almost all of the parties in the Reichstag opposed some proposed government policies because they conflicted with that party's policies. This was one of the reasons that the Weimar government found it hard to govern effectively – it had to operate in coalitions and often found it very difficult to agree on policies. Even if the coalition government could agree, getting enough support in the Reichstag to pass the laws was never easy. This shows that political opposition was very significant and deep rooted. The Weimar government also faced opposition from other groups because of its democratic stance. It faced opposition from various paramilitary groups and even from the army at times – it would not put down the right-wing Kapp Putsch of 1920, although it had put down the Spartacist revolt the previous year. This was because the army tended to have

> This paragraph outlines political reasons for opposing the Weimar government and analyses their extent.

right-wing views and the Spartacists were very left wing: many joined the KPD after 1919. All this opposition, because it stemmed from political ideas, could be seen as being as deeply rooted as opposition based on a hatred of the Treaty of Versailles. However, political opponents would have hated the Treaty as well. The factors worked together and all politicians knew that expressing a hatred for the Treaty would gain public support.

Political opposition, being based on political ideas, was steady throughout the period. However, the Weimar government also faced opposition to what it did, or did not do, as well as its policies. Opposition from groups or individuals varied according to circumstances – especially economic circumstances. When the Weimar government came to power, the German economy was in a bad way. Unemployment rose, the mark lost value and kept losing it, hitting hyperinflation levels in 1923. The government's social policies, put in place to care for the poorest Germans and those wounded or widowed in the war, made the situation worse. The government had to print more money to cover the costs, worsening inflation. The fact that the government failed to deal with economic problems and people's earnings and savings lost almost all their value caused huge opposition to the government. Opponents included those with savings, the unemployed, those who were employed but whose wages were almost worthless – almost everyone. Support for political parties on the extreme right and left rose – showing that voters wanted a new government. However, the reforms introduced by Stresemann (including the currency reform that replaced the mark with the Rentenmark and then the Reichsmark) improved the economy. People became confident in the currency again, inside Germany and out. Stresemann's diplomacy meant foreign countries wanted to trade with Germany again, and this boosted the economy. As the economy improved, individual opposition to the Weimar government declined. This is shown in the way that, for example, the newspapers talked about the government. Fewer people voted for extreme political parties – instead they voted for parties that might be part of a government coalition. A swing back to extreme parties, including the Nazis, came when Stresemann died and the Depression hit, both in 1929. Either would have been bad for the economy, but both were a disaster because Stresemann was no longer there to hold coalitions together and push through economic and other changes and the Depression hit the economy hard, plunging Germany into unemployment and rising prices again. The government failed to deal with the situation, then there was a long period of government by decree that not only failed to solve the problems but created a feeling that the government could not cope, as it was constantly resorting to 'emergency' government.

> This paragraph outlines political reasons for opposing the Weimar government and analyses their extent. It also introduces the idea that opposition was not fixed, but shifted according to circumstances.

Between 1918 and 1932, the Weimar government faced much opposition, from political parties and individuals and groups outside political parties. I think the widespread hatred of the Treaty of Versailles was a significant factor in opposition and the factor that united all the opponents of the government no matter what their political stance. However, it is important to consider that political opposition is also very significant. Such opposition would have come whether the Weimar government had signed the Treaty or not, although the Treaty was a handy stick for the political opponents to beat the government. It is possible that the Weimar government would have encountered far less opposition if it had managed to deal with the problems Germany faced. The Treaty was one deep-rooted factor in the opposition, but not the only significant one.

> The paragraph restates the question and offers a supported judgement on the issue.

Verdict

This is a strong answer because:

- it analyses the question and focuses on the right time period
- it considers a number of factors in reasonable depth
- it develops and explains the points it makes and makes links
- it comes to a strong reasoned judgement.

Paper 1: A Level sample answer with comments

Section B

These questions assess your understanding of the course in breadth and will cover a period of 30 years or more. They will ask you about the content you learned about in the four key themes, and may ask about more than one theme. The questions will also require you to explore a range of concepts, such as change over time, similarity and difference, as well as significance. For these questions remember to:

- identify the focus of the question
- consider the concepts you will need to explore
- support your points with evidence from across the time period specified in the question
- develop the evidence you deploy to build up your overall judgement
- come to a substantiated judgement that directly addresses the question set.

To what extent were attempts to create a command economy in Nazi Germany successful in solving the economic problems of the Weimar Republic? (20 marks)

Average student answer

The economic problems of the Weimar Republic were to do with unemployment and rapidly rising prices, especially the hyperinflation of 1923. Then, just when things were getting under control, the Depression hit, set off by the stock-market Wall Street Crash in the USA and spreading to Germany bringing high unemployment, falling demand for goods and banks calling for the payment of many loans they had made. The Nazis came to power promising to solve these problems. Creating a command economy contributed to the drop in unemployment and a rise in factory production, because the government is in control in a command economy – the factories produce what the government tells them to produce.

A command economy is where the government is in charge of production. This means the government decides what should be produced and also sets the quantities, prices and wages – the USSR had a communist government and a command economy at the time. A command economy gives the government, not the factory owners, control and so this kind of economy had a lot of appeal for the Nazis because this meant they could make the factory owners produce the goods they wanted. The Nazis wanted to control production more to gear it to war than to solve the problems of the economy – although they also wanted to do that. They wanted factories to concentrate on producing war goods – although in their early years in power from 1933 they insisted that the war production was for defence, because Germany needed to be able to defend itself if attacked in the way that the French occupied the Ruhr in 1923. The Nazis also wanted a bigger output from the factories, and this meant hiring more workers and enlarging factories or building new ones.

The Nazi government's urging of industrialists for higher production created work. Factories expanded to meet the demands and so needed more workers and this had the effect of reducing unemployment. Some factories expanded and some industrialists built new factories. Coal and steel producers also needed more workers to produce more and the new industries that were working to create new kinds of fuel also created employment, they needed workers and they needed new buildings. This meant that there were also builders, plumbers and so on who found work because of the demands for higher production. A command economy meant that the government could set prices and fix wages. This, in its turn, meant that the government had a tighter hold on the economy. Fixing prices meant they were more likely to be able to control inflation and stop it spiralling out of control. Fears about hyperinflation, as there had been in Weimar Germany in 1923, were quite high when the Nazis came to power – because prices had started rising again with the economic problems cause by the Depression and people had begun to fear that 1923 would happen all over again. It was one of the reasons that the Nazis came to

This first paragraph addresses the economic problems of the Weimar government and the Nazi command economy, but without enough development in terms of detail or considering the idea of extent. It could be improved by covering these points, and introducing the argument of the answer clearly.

This paragraph explains how a command economy works and goes some way towards explaining why it was a system the Nazis wanted. However, it does not analyse why it might help the economy. It could be improved by tying the information more closely to the question.

This paragraph analyses how the effects of the Nazis trying to create a command economy might solve the economic problems that the Weimar government had faced. It could be improved by more accurate detail from own knowledge to support the points made.

power, that people had no confidence in the Weimar government's ability to prevent another period of hyperinflation. Nazi price control was able to stop a panic and loss of confidence in money and spending.

It was not only the government's attempts to move to a command economy that helped to solve the economic problems that the Weimar government had suffered. There were other factors that also helped to solve the problems. One such factor was that the government embarked on government building projects, such as its road systems, which employed men, usually young men, who would otherwise be out of work. They gave them work and often also gave them basic food and accommodation while they were working because they were often working in out-of-the-way places and so needed these things to be provided. Getting people employed was one of the most significant things that the Nazis could do to solve the economic problems that had existed under the Weimar government before the Nazis came to power. The work that was created under their job creation schemes was usually hard manual work with the lowest possible pay, but it was work. The work schemes set up by the Nazis were a real solution to unemployment. The Nazis also had policies that created work for some people by removing others from their jobs. In this way they were not increasing the number of jobs, but they were having an effect on the unemployment figures. For example, women were urged to leave work when they got married, and to concentrate on keeping house and raising a family. The Nazis encouraged them to do this by giving the women marriage loans that allowed them to buy things to set up their home. The jobs that these married women left could then be taken by unemployed men. It is also significant to note that the Nazis did not count married women as unemployed in their unemployment statistics.

Another factor in the improvement of the economy that had nothing to do with the Nazi attempt to create a command economy was a factor that had nothing to do with the Nazis at all. It was to do with the Weimar government's policies or, perhaps, to do with the way the world economy was behaving. In 1933, when the Nazis came to power, there were signs that the economy was already beginning to improve, while it was still being governed by the Weimar government. Unemployment had fallen from almost 30 per cent of the workforce to about 26 per cent of the workforce. This was a definite fall, and could be taken as a sign that the economy was beginning to pull out of the Depression. Also the cost of living had dropped slightly and real wages had increased slightly. This was not a huge difference, but putting all the elements together it did seem to indicate a general improvement of the economy while it was still under the Weimar government.

It seems to me that Nazi attempts to create a command economy did help to solve the problems of the Weimar government. It meant the government had a far more significant control over the economy and how business was behaving; it was not leaving factory owners and mine owners to set their production, wages and prices for their own benefit, it was making them do what the government wanted instead. Controlling prices was something that helped to prevent inflation from rising out of control into hyperinflation and the high production levels helped with employment. However, I think there were other factors involved that also improved the economy. These factors were things that the Nazis did, for example, setting up projects that created higher levels of employment that thereby caused the unemployment figures to fall. Another element to consider is that there were signs when the Nazis came to power that the economy was beginning to recover, and there were the other Nazi moves to help the economy, such as job creation schemes.

> These paragraphs give three factors other than the Nazi attempt to create a command economy that influenced economic recovery. Some own knowledge is deployed to support the points made. However, there needs to be more accurate detail and more analysis of the points made.

> The concluding paragraph is a recap of the points made in the answer, but it does not come to a judgement of extent. It simply produces a list of factors. It could be improved by reaching a clear judgement.

Verdict

This is an average answer because:

- there is too much narrative and not enough analysis
- it does not consider the full time range
- there are no inaccuracies, but many points are made without development and explanation

- it does not come to a strong, reasoned judgement.

Use the feedback on this answer to rewrite it, making as many improvements as you can.

Paper 1: A Level sample answer with comments

Section B

These questions assess your understanding of the course in breadth and will cover a period of 30 years or more. They will ask you about the content you learned about in the four key themes, and may ask about more than one theme. The questions will also require you to explore a range of concepts, such as change over time, similarity and difference, as well as significance. For these questions remember to:

- identify the focus of the question
- consider the concepts you will need to explore
- support your points with evidence from across the time period specified in the question

- develop the evidence you deploy to build up your overall judgement
- come to a substantiated judgement that directly addresses the question set.

To what extent were attempts to create a command economy in Nazi Germany successful in solving the economic problems of the Weimar Republic? (20 marks)

Strong student answer

By the time the Nazis came to power, the economic problems of the Weimar Republic had been made worse by the worldwide Depression set off by the Wall Street Crash of 1929 in the USA. Like many other countries depending on US loans, Germany in 1932 had high unemployment, falling demand for goods and a collapse of credit systems (such as bank loans) and confidence in money. The Nazis came to power promising to solve these problems. The creation of a command economy contributed to the drop in unemployment by producing a rise in factory production. A consideration of the extent of their success involves looking at how far the problems were solved and how far Nazi attempts to create a command economy contributed to the success. Other factors that contributed were work creation schemes and a Nazi racial policy that excluded Jews from both professions and the employment statistics.

A command economy is where the government is in charge of production. This means the government decides what is produced and also sets the quantities, prices and wages – the USSR had a communist government and a command economy at the time. The Nazis wanted a command economy, to control production to gear it to war and to solve the problems of the economy. When businesses controlled prices (in a free market economy) they worked for their own profit. A command economy made them work for the good of the government and, hopefully, the country. The Nazis wanted factories to concentrate on producing war goods – although in the early years they insisted this was for defence. They also wanted a bigger output, and this meant hiring more workers and enlarging factories or building new ones. All of this created work for the unemployed – either building or manning the factories to increase production. This helped to solve the unemployment problem. The Nazis also wanted industry to work towards autarky – self-sufficiency in all goods. This made sense in the economic climate. The Depression meant world trade had slumped. Many countries became more inward-looking, aiming for some self-sufficiency. Germany's trade had suffered, slowing production and contributing to unemployment. The Nazis focused not on food or domestic goods such as cars (as in the USA) but on goods they would need for war. For example, synthetic rubber (Buna) and oil were a priority because they were essential war supplies. Government urging production in these industries also created work. In the command economy, the government set prices and restricted consumer goods production to limit public spending. It wanted people to feel well-off but not dependent on consumer goods. Fixing wages controlled spending. Fixing prices stopped the economy spiralling into hyperinflation as it had in 1923 – something people had

This is a strong first paragraph. It shows a grasp of the timeframe and a realisation that it is important to consider the *extent* of success and the contribution of the attempts to create a command economy to it, as opposed to other factors.

This paragraph clearly explains how the command economy created work and prevented inflation, with accurate use of own knowledge to develop the points.

feared would reoccur in the early 1930s. This fear was one reason the Nazis came to power. The Nazis could also channel production in a command economy – for example, many government-approved radios were produced (that did not get foreign radio channels) and sold cheaply. This meant many people bought radios and listened to Nazi propaganda transmitted by the radios.

Other factors helped to solve the economic problems that the Weimar government had suffered. One such factor was the government building projects, such as the autobahn road system, the buildings for the 1936 Olympics and other public buildings such as airports and stadiums. All these employed men, usually young men, who would otherwise be out of work. The schemes had the bare minimum of machinery, so more people were needed to do the work and they took longer to do it. The Nazis kept the unemployment figures lower for longer and kept people in genuine employment, even though it was hard manual work with the lowest possible pay. Getting people working was one of the most significant ways of solving the economic problems that had existed under the Weimar government. Job creation was a real solution to unemployment. The Nazis also had policies that created work for some people by removing others from their jobs. They were not increasing the number of jobs, but were affecting the unemployment figures. This statistical manipulation makes it difficult to trust the government figures. For example, women were urged to leave work on marriage, encouraged by marriage loans (credit to buy goods such as furniture to set up their new homes). The jobs these women left were then taken by unemployed men. Meanwhile the Nazis did not count married women as unemployed. In this way they brought down the unemployment figures from two directions. The Nazis also, from 1933 on, removed Jewish people from an increasing number of jobs and from the unemployment figures. Another factor that improved the economy was a factor that had nothing to do with the Nazis at all. Some historians have pointed out that the economy had begun to improve in 1933 when the Nazis came to power. Unemployment had fallen from almost 30 percent of the workforce to about 26 percent – in a set of statistics that included all the workforce (women and Jewish people too). However, by 1934 it was down to about 7.5 percent. Even allowing for government-manipulated figures there must have been a significant improvement in the levels of employment. In 1933, the cost of living had dropped slightly and real wages had increased slightly. This was not a huge difference, but putting all of the elements together it did seem to indicate a general improvement in the economy while it was still under the Weimar government.

> This paragraph analyses three factors other than the Nazi attempt to create a command economy that influenced economic recovery. Accurate own knowledge is deployed to support the points made.

It seems to me that Nazi attempts to create a command economy did help to solve the problems of the Weimar government. Controlling prices helped to prevent inflation from rising out of control into hyperinflation and the high production levels helped with employment. It is difficult to judge the exact extent to which it was the command economy that solved the problems, however. There were other factors involved, and the Nazis did manipulate government statistics. Another element to consider is that there were signs when the Nazis came to power that the economy was beginning to recover. What we can be sure of, however, is that the attempts to create a command economy made the recovery more certain, and more rapid, than it would have been had the Nazis left the economy as a free market economy.

> The final paragraph gives its conclusion supported by reference to the other possible factors and is not afraid to suggest that there are some questions where a balanced judgement has also to be tentative.

Verdict

This is a strong answer because:

- it analyses the impact of the various factors throughout
- it uses the full time range for its examples
- there are no inaccuracies, and many points are developed and explained
- it comes to a strong, reasoned judgement.

Paper 1: A Level sample answer with comments

Section C

These questions require you to read two extracts carefully to identify the key points raised and establish the argument being put forward. For these questions remember to:

- read and analyse the extracts thoroughly remembering that you need to use them in tandem
- take careful note of the information provided about the extracts
- deploy own knowledge to develop the points and arguments that emerge from the extracts and to provide appropriate context
- develop an argument rooted in the points raised in the extracts and come to a substantiated conclusion.

Study Extracts 5 and 6 (from Chapter 5, pages 123–24) before you answer this question.

In the light of differing interpretations, how far do you agree that Nazi foreign policy in the years 1933–39 was an area where Hitler 'changed nothing' (Extract 5)?

To explain your answer, analyse and evaluate the material in both extracts, using your own knowledge of the issues. (20 marks)

Average student answer

Extracts 5 and 6 do seem to be presenting two different interpretations of Hitler's foreign policy, although they are not exact opposites. Extract 5, from a book by A.J.P. Taylor, suggests that there were things that Hitler did in his domestic policy that were big changes from previous foreign policies, but that in foreign policy itself he changed nothing, he followed the policy of German statesmen before him. Extract 6, from a book by P.M.H. Bell, suggests that, while there were similarities, there were also differences and that the differences were more important.

The differing interpretations do not mean that one historian is wrong. It is just that they are interpreting the facts and events differently, putting emphasis in different places and working on their different views of Hitler's character. For Taylor, in Extract 5, the thing that drives his interpretation is the similarity in the broad aims of foreign policy. He sees these as being the same as previous governments. Hitler wanted to overturn Versailles and many Germans did too. Hitler wanted to make Germany great and others had wanted that too. Looked at from this angle, his foreign policy does not seem new, in Taylor's view. In other places in the same book he says that Hitler was not good at planning and thinking ahead and so was unlikely to shape a new foreign policy.

Bell, in Extract 6, on the other hand, sees Taylor's point (he refers to 'strong evidence of continuity') but he thinks that it is more important to realise that Hitler's methods were very different and that his foreign policy differed, especially from that of the Weimar government, in its willingness to go to war. Bell sees this as most important, because being cautious about going to war would change foreign policy behaviour, whereas being willing to go to war would make Germany's leader more likely to take chances to expand and get more land to make Germany great.

There is some evidence to support the view, expressed in Extract 5, that Hitler had a view that his foreign policy was one of continuity. He was interested in the history of Germany and spoke of 'restoring' Germany to greatness. His racial theories were rooted in the past, too. Hitler's ideas about race revolved around a racial theory about an invented 'Aryan race' who were 'pure' Germans in the past and who should become the German nation again. 'Pure' Germans should not only rule Germany, but be the only people who were its citizens – everyone else should be driven out to keep the German race as pure as possible. Hitler called his Empire 'the Third Reich', not 'the New Reich', showing that he saw it as part of a continuing line of German

> The first paragraph explains the different interpretations in the extracts and refers back to the question, but it does not outline the argument that will follow. It could be improved by doing this.

> These paragraphs address the question and provide some vague analysis, but are almost entirely a précis of each extract. They could be improved by adding analysis and a clearer contest of the issues in the debate among historians.

Empires, and he used images of Bismark, Frederick the Great and Hindenburg alongside his own in his propaganda. All this shows nostalgia for a past, the glories of which Hitler wanted to recreate.

Taylor points out that overturning the Treaty of Versailles and rebuilding the army were not new aims but the aims of every politician after the Treaty was imposed. However, you need to balance against this the points that Bell makes about methods and the willingness to go to war. While the Weimar government wanted to overturn Versailles, they tried to do it diplomatically – Hitler did not. These are very different approaches and foreign policy is about methods as well as aims. So this counts against the idea that he changed nothing.

These paragraphs begin to balance points in Extract 5 against some own knowledge and points raised in Extract 6 to arrive at a balanced view. They could be improved by more detailed support and a tighter analysis.

Hitler wanted to expand eastwards. In this he had the same aims as Bismark and Kaiser Wilhelm who was ruler of Germany when the First World War broke out. They wanted to take parts of Poland and land held by what was then Russia and an empire. While there were areas along the borders of France that earlier German rulers had considered German and disputed, such as Alsace, German rulers did not claim all of France, or consider expanding westwards in preference to eastwards. However, when we look at what Hitler actually did at the start of the war, he took Poland and then turned west before he invaded the USSR. He occupied Belgium, the Netherlands, Denmark, Norway and France. This suggests that his expansionism was driven by his own, grander, aims, although it was also driven by his need to keep the USSR as an ally until Poland was secure and Germany could not be attacked from the west. It was not until Hitler was sure that he could not be attacked on both sides at once, a problem demonstrated by the First World War, that he turned on the USSR, despite his Nazi-Soviet Pact with it.

These paragraphs are not tied closely enough to the points in the extract and lose the focus of the question, but there is some relevant support with own knowledge. They could be improved by keeping to the question and relating the relevant points back to the extracts.

Hitler did keep on old officials from the Weimar Republic – ambassadors in foreign countries and also civil servants in the Foreign Affairs Ministry. This was partly to give an idea of continuity to Germans – the government was moving along with familiar systems in place. But Hitler did not always use these people. He did this at home too. He set up entirely new Ministries like the ministry of Propaganda, but he also set up new ministries running alongside the old ones. For example, he kept the existing ministry that dealt with economic affairs. However, he set up the Office of the Four-Year Plan too that he gave more and more powers for economic planning. So the old ministry, although he had not removed it, had less and less power. This was the case with the ambassadors and foreign ministry officials, too. They were overruled by new organisations and also by Nazi 'special envoys' that he sent to other countries to negotiate for him with the power to override any negotiating the ambassadors that had been left in place had done.

It seems to me that Hitler's foreign policy did not 'change nothing'. This is a very sweeping statement, the kind of statement that is hardly ever entirely right, because most issues in history are far from that clear-cut, and there were things in Hitler's foreign policy that changed. In terms of broad aims, Taylor is right to see continuity. However, if you move beyond aims and consider everything that goes into foreign policy – the methods and the people who ran it and the attitudes behind it – then you can see that Hitler might have been intending the same thing, but he set out to achieve it differently. So, in conclusion, he might not have changed the general aims, but he changed the methods and thinking, so he did change something.

The concluding paragraph comes to a clear judgement, but it could be improved by developing the basis of this judgement.

Verdict

This is an average answer because:

- it is not rooted closely enough in the extracts and they are not linked effectively
- there is not enough context given; however, there is no incorrect information and the response tries to analyse the extracts in relation to the question
- it makes a judgement but it needs more substance.

Use the feedback on this answer to rewrite it, making as many improvements as you can.

Paper 1: A Level sample answer with comments

Section C

These questions require you to read two extracts carefully to identify the key points raised and establish the argument being put forward. For these questions remember to:

- read and analyse the extracts thoroughly remembering that you need to use them in tandem
- take careful note of the information provided about the extracts
- deploy own knowledge to develop the points and arguments that emerge from the extracts and to provide appropriate context
- develop an argument rooted in the points raised in the extracts and come to a substantiated conclusion.

Study Extracts 5 and 6 (from Chapter 5, pages 123–24) before you answer this question.

In the light of differing interpretations, how far do you agree that Nazi foreign policy in the years 1933–39 was an area where Hitler 'changed nothing' (Extract 5)?

To explain your answer, analyse and evaluate the material in both extracts, using your own knowledge of the issues. (20 marks)

Strong student answer

Extracts 5 and 6 do seem to present two different interpretations of Hitler's foreign policy, although they are not exact opposites. Extract 5, from a book by A.J.P. Taylor, suggests that Hitler made big changes in his domestic policies, but that in foreign policy he changed nothing: he followed the policy of German statesmen before him. Extract 6, from a book by P.M.H. Bell, suggests that, while there were similarities in the policies, such as the desire to build an empire, there were also differences; there were things that Hitler changed, especially the way he carried out his foreign policy, which affected what happened.

The debate surrounding Hitler's foreign policy is the result of historians interpreting the facts and events differently, with different emphasis and with different views of Hitler's character. The debate over Hitler's foreign policy falls into two camps – the 'intentionalist' camp, which sees Hitler's wishes as driving foreign policy, and the 'structuralist' (or 'functionalist') camp, which sees Hitler's foreign policy as affected by external factors, such as the actions of other politicians or events outside his control. Historians adopt a variety of interpretations, also affected by their views of how far ahead Hitler could plan and whether he was able to adapt his planning to events as they occurred. Taylor seems to suggest that Hitler was just following the foreign policy path of many earlier German leaders, while Bell sees this point (he refers to 'strong evidence of continuity') but thinks it is more important that Hitler used different methods and his foreign policy differed, especially from that of the Weimar government, in its willingness to go to war.

There is some evidence that Hitler saw, or wanted Germans to think he saw, his foreign policy as one of continuity. He was interested in German history and spoke of 'restoring' Germany to greatness. His racial theories were rooted in the past, too – the invented 'Aryan race' were 'pure' Germans who had lived in Germany before. For various reasons, other races had mixed with them, 'corrupting' their racial make-up. Hitler called his empire 'the Third Reich', not 'the New Reich' and he used images of Bismark, Frederick the Great and Hindenburg alongside his own in his propaganda. All this shows nostalgia for a past, part real, part imaginary, the glories of which Hitler wanted to recreate.

As Taylor points out, the broad aim of overturning the Treaty of Versailles and rebuilding the army had been a Weimar aim too, and the aim of every political campaigner after the Treaty was imposed. Also, as Bell points out, he kept Weimar foreign office officials in place until 1938. However, balanced against this are Bell's points about methods and the willingness to go to war. While the Weimar government wanted to overturn Versailles, it tried to do it diplomatically – for example, Stresemann

---

Side comments:

An effective opening paragraph that focuses on the extracts and identifies their key arguments. It cites some of the evidence put forward and begins to set up the debate.

This paragraph unpacks the issues of the debate and places the extracts in this context.

These paragraphs analyse points made by Extract 5 and weigh them up against both own knowledge and the points raised in Extract 6 to arrive at a balanced view.

negotiated the Dawes and Young plans to revise reparations and his negotiations got the French out of the Ruhr. Hitler marched into the Rhineland and remilitarised it without negotiation, gambling that the Western powers would not go to war over it. These are very different approaches and foreign policy is about methods as well as aims. So this counts against the idea that he changed nothing. Also, Hitler may have kept on Weimar officials, but he also set up offices of his own, such as the Ribbentrop Bureau, to work independently of them.

Taylor talks of Hitler wanting to make Germany a great power again but, in Extract 5, he does not explicitly talk about the direction that Hitler wanted German expansion to take, although he may do this elsewhere. The direction Hitler wanted to take provides more support for Taylor's 'continuity' argument. Hitler wanted to expand eastwards. In this he had the same aims as Bismark and Kaiser Wilhelm who was ruler of Germany when the First World War broke out, so you could argue he 'changed nothing'. While there were areas along the borders of France that earlier German rulers had considered German and disputed, such as Alsace, German rulers did not claim all of France, or consider expanding westwards in preference to eastwards. However, when we look at what Hitler actually did at the start of the war, he took Poland and then turned west before he invaded the USSR. He occupied Belgium, the Netherlands, Denmark, Norway and France. This suggests that his expansionism was driven by his own, grander, aims, although it was also driven by his need to keep the USSR as an ally until Poland was secure and Germany could not be attacked from the west.

As Bell points out, a point against the idea that Hitler 'changed nothing' is the way that he introduced new thinking, new men from outside the old elites and new methods that Bell calls 'revolutionary'. An example of the new thinking is Hitler's racial theory. The fact that he saw other races as inferior affected his foreign policy and the methods he used when occupying a country. The hostility between Germany and Poland was long-standing: the Einsatzgruppen murder of political opponents was new. As for new men, Hitler set up systems running parallel to many of the old systems, including the army and the foreign office, that were run by Nazis he trusted. So the Bureau Ribbentrop ran alongside the Foreign Ministry and conducted many negotiations abroad, for example, with Britain over an alliance. The Office of the Four-Year Plan geared up the German economy for war production – not the economics ministry. An example of 'revolutionary' methods is the Blitzkrieg method of warfare that enabled the rapid conquests in Western Europe once Poland had been secured. This had been planned for and new technologies had been used to provide the right weapons and equipment for this rapid invasion and occupation strategy to work.

> This paragraph extends the analysis of the points in both extracts and supports the analysis with own knowledge.

It seems to me that Hitler's foreign policy did not 'change nothing' – this is far too sweeping a statement. In terms of broad aims, Taylor is right to see continuity. However, if you move beyond aims and consider everything that goes into foreign policy – the methods and the people who run it and the attitudes behind it – then you can see that Hitler might have been intending the same thing, but he set out to achieve it with a ruthlessness and a disregard for the rights and opinions of other nations that was a change. In conclusion, Hitler might not have changed the general aims, but he changed the methods and thinking.

> The concluding paragraph comes to a clear judgement based on the balance of the evidence.

Verdict

This is a strong answer because:

- it identifies and illustrates the arguments of the two extracts; it develops an argument that considers both interpretations and tries to provide balance

- it deploys a sound range of specific evidence to develop points emerging from the extracts; it provides a sense of the context
- there is a clear judgement.

The rise and fall of fascism in Italy, c1911–46

'I am the most hated man in Italy.' This was how the Italian dictator, Benito Mussolini, described himself to his secretary in 1943 as his dictatorship fell apart under the strain of the Second World War. It was a phenomenal decline for the man who at one time had been exalted by millions of Italians as the saviour of the nation, the leader who had reclaimed Italy's past glory and was building a new, united and powerful country that all Italians could be proud of. Twenty-one years previously, on 30 October 1922, the king of Italy, Victor Emmanuel III, had appointed Mussolini prime minister of Italy. It had been an incredible rise to power. The party Mussolini led, the Fascist Party of Italy, had only been founded in 1919 and had done quite poorly in the general elections it had fought. Now, however, Mussolini, the former journalist, soldier and socialist agitator, had become Italy's youngest prime minister at the age of only 39. It was a role he was to hold until his downfall and eventual execution during the Second World War. Mussolini is one of the most important historical men of the 20th century. From 1922 up to his death in 1945, Mussolini was a key world figure, his dictatorship fascinating foreign observers who marvelled at his ability as a statesman who had taken Italy from the ruins of the First World War and apparently transformed it into a modern, militarised nation that could challenge the balance of power in Europe. Mussolini's dictatorship introduced a new word to the world: fascism. This political ideology, with its emphasis on extreme **nationalism**, strict governmental control and military force, would have a profound effect on Europe and would lay a path to the Second World War and the most destructive war in history.

KEY TERM

Nationalism
A strong patriotic identification with ones' nation. This ideology began to emerge in the late 18th century, before which people tended to see themselves in terms of their family connections or place of birth. It was accompanied by the emergence of national symbols such as flags and anthems, which were meant to provide a shared identity for people of the same country. Nationalism has been one of the most important ideological movements of the previous 200 years and the strong belief that the Italian people should be united into one nation inspired those who fought to unite the country in the mid-1800s.

1860	1860 – Giuseppe Garibaldi conquers southern Italy, uniting it with the Kingdom of Piedmont in the north ruled by Victor Emmanuel II
1870	1870 – Italian forces conquer Rome and complete the unification of Italy
1892	1892 – Giovanni Giolitti becomes prime minister of Italy
1896	1896 – Italian troops defeated by Abyssinian forces at the Battle of Adwa
1915	April 1915 – Italy signs the Treaty of London and enters the war on the side of Britain, France and Russia
1918	October 1918 – Italy defeats Austria-Hungary at the Battle of Vittorio Veneto
1919	March 1919 – Benito Mussolini founds the Fasci di Combattimento June 1919 – Italy fails to make major gains at Versailles settlement September 1919 – Gabriele D'Annunzio seizes port of Fiume November 1919 – Socialist and Catholic political parties win over half the votes in the Italian election but fail to form a government
1923	July 1923 – Acerbo Law passed August 1923 – Mussolini achieves foreign policy success in Corfu
1925	January 1925 – Mussolini begins establishment of dictatorship
1929	February 1929 – Concordat with pope
1934	
1936	May 1936 – Victory proclaimed in Abyssinia July 1936 – Spanish Civil War. Italian troops support right-wing forces under General Franco October 1936 – Axis agreement with Nazi Germany signed
1940	May 1940 – Germany invades France. Italy declares war on France and Britain October 1940 – Italy invades Greece
1942	1942 – Italian forces face a series of defeats in Africa
1943	July 1943 – Allied forces land in Sicily. King dismisses Mussolini. Fascist Party of Italy falls from power September–October 1943 – New government under General Badoglio declares war on Germany. Germany invades Italy and installs Mussolini as head of the new Italian Salo Republic
1946	June 1946 – Following a referendum Italy is proclaimed a republic and King Victor Emmanuel III is forced to abdicate and leave the country

1861	1861 – New united Kingdom of Italy under Victor Emmanuel II established
1871	1871 – Rome established as the capital of united Italy; pope condemns the new state and refuses to recognise it
1895	1895 – Italian Socialist Party (PSI) established
1911	1911 – Italy defeats Turkey and gains Libya as a colony
1914	August 1914 – First World War begins – Italy chooses to stay neutral
1917	October 1917 – Italy defeated by Austria-Hungary at the Battle of Caporetto. Russian Revolution puts Bolsheviks in power
1920	1919–20 – Two years of socialist unrest known as the Biennio Rosso ('Two Red Years') – strikes and factory occupations
1921	May 1921 – Fascists win seven percent of the vote in the Italian election November 1921 – Mussolini establishes the National Fascist Party (PNF)
1922	October 1922 – Fascists seize control of many northern cities. Fascist members threaten to march on Rome to take power 30 October 1922 – King Victor Emmanuel appoints Mussolini prime minister November 1922 – Mussolini granted emergency powers for one year
1924	April 1924 – Fascists win 66 percent of the vote in national election June 1924 – Socialist leader Matteotti murdered, Mussolini faces serious challenge to his position as prime minister
1926	1926 – Mussolini able to establish law by decree. Strikes forbidden and opposition parties banned. Secret police (OVRA) established
1933	1933 – Adolph Hitler becomes chancellor of Germany
1935	October 1935 – Italy invades Abyssinia
1937	November 1937 – Italy, Germany and Japan sign the Anti-Comintern Pact which is aimed against the USSR December 1937 – Italy withdraws from the League of Nations
1938	July 1938 – Italy introduces anti-Jewish laws
1939	April 1939 – Italy invades Albania May 1939 – Pact of Steel committing Italy to a formal military alliance with Germany signed October 1939 – Germany invades Poland. Britain declares war on Germany. Mussolini declares Italy 'non-belligerent'
1941	June 1941 – Germany invades the USSR. Italy follows by also declaring war on the USSR December 1941 – Italy declares war on the USA
1945	April 1945 – Mussolini captured by Italian Communist partisans while trying to flee to Switzerland and is executed on 28 April Hitler commits suicide on 30 April bringing the Second World War to an end

SOURCE 1 Benito Mussolini. Dictator of Italy from 1922 to 1943.

While fascism tends to be associated most prominently today with Hitler and the Nazi Party, its origins actually lie in Italy and the ideas Mussolini promoted when he founded the Fasci di Combattimento in 1919. Mussolini was influenced by his experiences as a soldier in the First World War and he sought to create a system of government that would replicate the extreme nationalism and aggressive militarism that he experienced in the trenches, and which he believed would provide Italians with the sense of national purpose and unity they had been lacking since the country unified in 1861. Although fascism was an Italian creation meant to solve uniquely Italian problems, the overriding ideals of fascism would shape the Europe of the interwar period and influence a style of dictatorship that emerged not only in Germany, but also in countries such as Spain, Austria, Hungary and Croatia. Fascism would inspire millions of Europeans to die either to save it or to destroy it, and the effect it would have on the 20th century would be long lasting and significant. Thus, the study of Mussolini and Italian fascism is crucial in understanding the ideological trends that affected Europe after the First World War. Mussolini came before Hitler and the study of the ideology's foundation in Italy and its influence both in Italy and across Europe helps to build a better understanding of what fascism's key ideas were and why for a period it appealed to people across the continent and challenged the future of democracy. Mussolini's style of government, built on style over substance, charismatic leadership, enthralling speeches and an emphasis on nationalism, continues to influence politics today, and makes the study of this dictator's rise and fall crucial to comprehending one of the key political movements of the last 100 years.

2a.1 The liberal state, c1911–18

KEY QUESTIONS

- What were the key problems facing Italy in the early part of the 20th century?
- How did the government of Giovanni Giolitti shape Italy's political situation from 1911 to 1914?
- How successful was the liberal government in dealing with Italy's growing instability between 1912 and 1914?
- What was the impact of the First World War on Italy?

INTRODUCTION

In 1911, Italy held a series of events to celebrate the 50th anniversary of Italian unification. In Piedmont, the International Industrial Fair, a prestigious event demonstrating Italy's economic progress since unification, was opened with great fanfare at a massive new stadium filled with 70,000 cheering spectators.

In Rome, the celebrations reached their height when a new monument dedicated to the first king of a united Italy, Victor Emmanuel II, was unveiled to large crowds in June. Throughout the year, artistic and cultural events took place in the capital, emphasising Italy's excellence in art and fashion. These events were meant to highlight Italy's progress over the preceding 50 years, patriotically celebrating the achievements that Italian unification had brought about by bringing together the Italian people under one nation.

However, behind the façade of cheering crowds lay a darker reality that was hard to ignore. The Catholic Church boycotted the events and refused to celebrate Italian unification, while socialist

ACTIVITY
KNOWLEDGE CHECK

What impression of the new Italian nation do you think the Turin poster for the International Industrial Fair shown in Source 1 was meant to give?

SOURCE 1

Poster advertising the International Industrial Fair held in Turin in 1911 as part of the 50-year celebrations of Italian Unity.

1892
Italian Socialist Party (PSI) founded

1896
Italy defeated by Abyssinian forces at the Battle of Adwa

1898–1900
Italy experiences period of socio-political turmoil. On 29 July 1900 King Umberto I assassinated by anarchist

1903–1905
Giovanni Giolitti becomes prime minister for the second time

1906–1909
Giovanni Giolitti becomes prime minister for the third time

1910
Italian Nationalist Association (ANI) formed

1911
30 March – Giovanni Giolitti becomes prime minister for the fourth time
29 September – Italy launches invasion of Libya

1912
Greater suffrage introduced. Number of eligible Italian voters rises from three million to 8.5 million
July – Revolutionaries within the PSI take control of the party
18 October – Turkey surrenders Libya to Italy

1913
First elections under new suffrage law held in Italy. Socialists, radicals, Catholics and nationalists all make gains

1892   1896   1900   1904   1906   1908   1910   1912   1913

politicians asserted that the idea of a united Italian nation was meaningless. A deep divide between the north and south linguistically, economically and politically still existed. Italy had achieved partial unification in 1861, but had only been finally unified fully with Rome in 1870. Since then, Italy's politicians had failed to construct a real sense of patriotism that would bind the diverse elements of Italian society together. In 1911, Italy's prime minister, Giovanni Giolitti, would set out a programme that he hoped would inspire an Italian nationalism, thus uniting the Italian people, including the Catholics and socialists, within the framework of Italy's liberal political system. Giolitti's failure and the subsequent impact of the First World War would be key factors in both the foundation of Italian fascism and its popular appeal as the political movement that could finally achieve the dream of a united Italian nation, which the liberals under Giolitti had been unable to achieve.

WHAT WERE THE KEY PROBLEMS FACING ITALY IN THE EARLY PART OF THE 20TH CENTURY?

Unification

Italy had only become a nation in 1861 and fully unified in 1870. In the subsequent 50 years, political leaders had struggled to create an identity for this new country that could unite its citizens and encourage a sense of shared patriotism. Italy had been fragmented politically, economically and culturally since the Middle Ages and the idea of 'Italy' as a nation meant very little to Italians, who were used to identifying predominately with their local towns or regions. Instead, Italians were defined by *campanilismo*, a feeling of pride and belonging to their place of birth, which was much stronger than any sense of national identity. They were not even unified by language, with 99 percent of Italians speaking a regional dialect and unable to understand what people from other areas of Italy were saying. The official language 'Italian' was the dialect from Florence, but very few outside Florence or the educated classes spoke it. Even the king, Victor Emmanuel II, mostly spoke in the Piedmont dialect, meaning most Italians outside Piedmont could not understand him. This was a clear impediment to the creation of a unified nation of Italians under the figure of the monarchy that the leaders of the **Risorgimento** had dreamt of. The Italian politician Massimo d'Azeglio had famously written at the time of unification 'We have made Italy. Now we must make Italians', yet these hopes had not been realised by the time Italy celebrated 50 years of unification in 1911. In fact, in the last years of the 1800s people had questioned whether Italy could even survive as a unified nation. In May 1898, protests against Italy's political system and growing economic problems had been met by a brutal government crackdown and 100 protestors had been killed in Milan. On 29 July 1900, the king, Umberto I, had been assassinated by an Italian **anarchist** who wanted to avenge the protesters' deaths. Political and economic turmoil threatened to tear the nation apart. One of the key issues was Italy's political system.

KEY TERMS

Risorgimento
Means 'resurgence' or 'rebirth' and refers to the unification of Italy, which had concluded with the incorporation of Rome in 1870 and the creation of Italy as a new nation with its capital in Rome. Italy had not been united since the Middle Ages and had been little more than a geographical term, with the region being split into numerous differing states ruled by a variety of powers, such as the pope, the Austro-Hungarian Empire and the French–Spanish Bourbon royal family. Italians who had led the *Risorgimento* struggled to articulate a united vision for the nation they had fought to create.

Anarchism
A political ideology that believes in the violent overthrow of state authority and control (the government, police and military) and the establishment of a self-governing order where people would be free to live in a society without government rule or laws. It was particularly influential in Italy during the latter part of the 19th century where it was viewed by young intellectuals as an alternative to the restrictive liberal government and the only means of bringing about freedom for the impoverished Italian peasantry.

1915
26 April – Antonio Salandra signs Treaty of London and commits Italy to entry into the war in support of the Triple Entente of Britain, Russia and France
13 May – Parliament splits over decision to enter war. Salandra resigns and the king asks Giolitti to form government
16 May – Giolitti refuses to form government. Salandra reinstated
20 May – Parliament votes Salandra emergency powers
25 May – Italy declares war on Austro-Hungarian Empire

1917
24 October – Austrian forces launch major campaign at Caporetto. Italian forces in mass retreat. Boselli resigns and is replaced by Vittorio Orlando. Commander of the Italian army Luigi Cadorna is replaced by Armando Diaz

1914	1915	1916	1917	1918

1914
March – Giolitti resigns as prime minister after anti-clerical radicals withdraw support. Antonio Salandra becomes prime minister
August – First World War begins, Italy declares neutrality

1916
June – Austrian forces launch *Strafexpedition* against Italian forces. Salandra forced to resign and replaced by Paolo Boselli

1918
30 October – Italian forces launch successful offensive against Austrians and enter the town of Vittorio Veneto
4 November – Austro-Hungarian Empire surrenders, war between Italy and Austria ends with Italian victory

Figure 1.1 Map of Italy before 1870 showing how it was ruled by foreign powers.

The political system in Italy

The Italians who made up parliament were all drawn from the very narrow, predominately northern, professional, middle class and tended to represent the interests of their own class at the expense of the wider population. Italy's political development was also hampered by the attitude of the Catholic Church and the '**Roman Question**'. Pope Pius IX was angered at the capture of Rome in 1870 and the loss of the papal territory and refused to recognise the new Italian state. In 1886, the new pope, Leo XIII, formally forbade Catholics from either running for office or voting in national elections. While it is difficult to judge exactly what effect this had on the vote, in predominately Catholic Italy where the pope was revered, it robbed Italy of a potentially unifying symbol and questioned the legitimacy of the new nation. Many of Italy's politicians feared that challenging the Church would only further alienate the population. It also prevented the creation of a national conservative party based on Catholic values, which some Italian aristocrats and conservatives had wanted to pursue. This in turn meant that there was no parliamentary challenge to the liberal middle classes who ruled Italy due to the lack of popular political opposition and the fact that less than 25 percent of Italian men had the vote.

Italy's politicians shared the same liberal ideology and, unlike Britain or Germany, there were very few formal political parties. Instead, prominent politicians formed governments by offering key positions to other parliamentary members (known as deputies), who would then agree to support them as prime minister. Governments tended to be short lived, as politicians could simply withdraw their support for the prime minister if they were offered a better deal by another deputy. Success as a politician was therefore not due to the ability to attract votes through popular or successful policies, but instead rested on skill in forming political alliances by knowing how to buy the support of other deputies. This political manoeuvring was known as *trasformismo* and was characterised by corruption, frequent changes in government (there were 29 changes of prime minister between 1870 and 1922) and an inability to pass legalisation that might improve the lives of Italian citizens. As a result, although Italy frequently changed prime minister, this had very little, if anything, to do with the people of Italy and their opinions. The majority of the Italian population were disenfranchised and were seen by the liberal politicians as lacking in the political education required for electoral participation. Any protests against the government tended to be met with violent repression from the military. This attitude from the liberal elite simply reinforced the divide between 'real Italy' – the Italian people – and 'legal Italy' – the ruling classes. The inability of most Italians to voice their anger at Italy's politicians through the ballot box fuelled popular protest and the growing strength of more extreme revolutionary ideologies, such as anarchism.

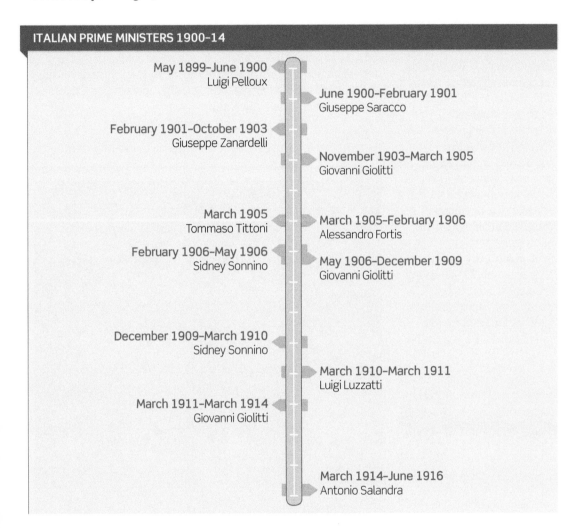

ITALIAN PRIME MINISTERS 1900–14

May 1899–June 1900
Luigi Pelloux

June 1900–February 1901
Giuseppe Saracco

February 1901–October 1903
Giuseppe Zanardelli

November 1903–March 1905
Giovanni Giolitti

March 1905
Tommaso Tittoni

March 1905–February 1906
Alessandro Fortis

February 1906–May 1906
Sidney Sonnino

May 1906–December 1909
Giovanni Giolitti

December 1909–March 1910
Sidney Sonnino

March 1910–March 1911
Luigi Luzzatti

March 1911–March 1914
Giovanni Giolitti

March 1914–June 1916
Antonio Salandra

Economic growth and social problems

The feeling of political alienation and anger at the ruling classes felt by many Italians was accentuated by economic and social problems. Between 1899 and 1914, Italy experienced considerable economic expansion and industrialisation focused in the north of the country. The iron and steel industries grew significantly, as did the newer chemical, mechanical and electrical industries. The Italian car industry was a great success, with companies such as Fiat, Alfa Romeo and Lancia established. At the same time, industrialisation and improved techniques helped increase agricultural production. Despite Italy's developing economic expansion, industrialisation did not provide benefits to the wider population and the living standards of both industrial and rural workers remained low. Protests against unemployment, food shortages and high taxation were common throughout Italy. Between 1901 and 1911, there were over 1,500 strikes involving nearly 350,000 workers. Industrialisation also accentuated one of Italy's most serious problems – the considerable division between the north and south. The economic and social divisions between the wealthier north and the more impoverished south had concerned Italy's politicians since 1861 and was viewed as one of major barriers in creating the unified nation they longed for.

North–south divide

Intellectuals and politicians grappled with the *questione meridionale* ('southern question'), focusing their work on an attempt to understand why the south had fallen into such poverty and what could be done to alleviate it. Theories regarding the south's poor economic structure, its geographical location, its history and its poor treatment by the richer north were all espoused as possible reasons for the situation there. Southern intellectuals called for greater economic investment and new fiscal policies but, despite several parliamentary inquiries into the question, very little was actually done. Italy's politicians tended to ignore the major issues facing the region, no Italian prime minister even visited the south until 32 years after unification. By 1911, the situation had worsened, as industrial economic expansion centred on the large northern cities, Milan, Turin, Genoa and Bologna, while the southern agriculturally based economy stagnated, leading to an increase in the south's already substantial rural poverty. In 1911, the government census showed that almost half of Italy's 2.2 million industrial workers were employed in the northern provinces of Lombardy, Liguria and Piedmont. This area was known as the 'industrial triangle' and focused around the three major industrial cities of Milan, Genoa and Turin. By contrast, the south was one of Europe's most impoverished areas, where the peasant population suffered from poor diet, malnutrition, a lack of clean drinking water and high rates of infant mortality, malaria and tuberculosis. Between 1910 and 1911, for example, 25,000 people died in Naples due to an epidemic of cholera caused by poor drinking water. More than half the entire population of the south were illiterate, five times the rate of Piedmont in the north. By 1911, income per head in the northern industrial area was double that in the south.

Politicians still viewed the *questione meridionale* as the most critical issue facing Italy, but their policies, such as trying to encourage

industrial investment in Naples, failed to make any noticeable difference in improving the lives of the southern peasantry and bridging the growing gap between north and south Italy. Instead, the only means of alleviating the pressure in the south was through emigration and millions of southern Italian peasants migrated overseas, predominately to the USA, in search of a better life. Between 1901 and 1913, around 200,000 southern Italians left Italy every year, including one million Sicilians out of a population of only 3.5 million. Three out of every four Italians who migrated to the USA came from the south and by 1910 there were around 600,000 Italians living in New York, making its Italian population as large as any city in Italy at the time. While this mass emigration did help to lessen the economic strains in the south, it failed to deal with the central, long-term issues facing Italy and was reliant on other countries' continual willingness to accept large influxes of poor, unskilled, Italian migrants.

SOURCE
2 Rural poverty in Calabria, a region in the south of Italy.

Italy as a 'great power'

Italy also tended to lag behind Europe's 'major powers' in foreign policy. Italy's industrial development was behind that of Britain or Germany, while geographically it was disadvantaged by the fact that the French and British navies dominated the Mediterranean. Italy was not an insignificant country in relation to Europe's balance of power, but tended to be viewed as 'the least of the great powers'. Italian foreign policy goals tended to focus on **irredentism**, the belief that Italy should reclaim the areas of Istria and the South Tyrol. Due to the fact that many of the population in these areas were ethnically Italian and spoke the language,

KEY TERMS

Meridionale
A term used to refer to the Italian south encompassing the regions of Abruzzo, Apulia, Basilicata, Calabria, Campania, Puglia, Molise, Sicily and Sardinia. Apart from Sardinia, all the other regions were part of the Kingdom of the Two Sicilies, which had been formed in 1442 and ruled by members of the Spanish and Bourbon royal families. *Meridionalismo* was an intellectual movement that developed after unification and focused on developing a serious understanding of the south's problems in order to encourage proper government reform. Southern Italy is also referred to as the *mezzogiorno*, which roughly translates into English as 'land of the midday sun'.

Irredentism
A movement that grew out of Italy's unification and gained popularity in the late 19th and early 20th centuries. It asserted that Italy's successful unification in 1870 should continue until all Italian-speaking areas were incorporated into Italy. This focused on numerous areas such as Corsica, Dalmatia, Istria, Malta, Ticino, Trentino, Trieste and Fiume. Most of the areas were under Austro-Hungarian rule and there was little the Italian government could actually do to claim this territory. The ideal of irredentism was to have a large influence in Italian politics up to 1945, as both the nationalists and the fascists who followed them popularised the concept and blamed the weakness of the liberals as the reason why these lands had not been taken as part of Italy.

the areas were viewed as rightfully Italian, but at that time fell within the Austro-Hungarian Empire. Italy did not have either the military power or the diplomatic means to reclaim the areas from the other powerful European nations. Italy also looked to gain overseas colonies, particularly in Africa, as colonisation was seen as essential for any nation wanting to claim a place as one of Europe's great powers. Here too Italy found itself in a weaker position in comparison with the other great powers. Italy had first focused on Tunisia, an area where it had particular economic and strategic interests, but in 1881 the French, with the diplomatic support of Britain, invaded Tunisia and claimed it for themselves. The resulting considerable anger within the Italian government led to the signing of a defensive alliance with Austria and Germany, known as the Triple Alliance, which was aimed predominately against France. The Triple Alliance, however, angered many Italians, as it allied Italy with Austria, its traditional enemy and the country that was seen as the barrier to the recovery of the *irredente* ('unredeemed') lands.

In 1884, the British government informed Italy that it would agree to Italian expansion in Abyssinia, but attempts to gain this part of Africa as a colony failed at the Battle of Dogali, where the Italian forces were defeated by the Ethiopian army and 500 Italian soldiers died. From 1894 onwards, Italy again sought to gain Abyssinia, but this attempt at claiming an Italian colony in Africa ended disastrously at the Battle of Adwa on 1 March 1896. In the worst defeat ever suffered by a European power in Africa, 5,000 Italian troops were killed and thousands more injured at the hands of King Menelik of Abyssinia's powerful army. The Italian prime minister at the time, Francesco Crispi, had hoped that colonisation in Africa would be a means of uniting Italians of all classes and regions in patriotic pride at Italy's powerful foreign expansion, but instead the humiliation of the Battle of Adwa accentuated growing anger towards Italy's political class and was the catalyst for the mass protests and riots that rocked Italy at the end of the 19th century.

SOURCE 3 Census figures from 1911 in the *Annuario Statistico Italiano*.

Illiteracy Rates Italy 1911

Northern Italy	Southern Italy
Piedmont 11%	Apulia 59.4%
Lombardy 13.4%	Basilicata 65.3%
Venice 25.2%	Calabria 69.6%
Liguria 17%	Sicily 58%

Figure 1.2 Map showing the *irredente* lands.

EXTRACT

From Martin Clark, *Modern Italy 1871–1995* (1996).

Far more important was the fact that most of the other 99 per cent spoke regional dialects and nothing else. This was true even among the upper classes: King Victor Emmanuel II himself nearly always spoke in Piedmontese, even to his Cabinet ministers. His famous remark on arriving at Rome, which the history books record as 'ci siamo e ci resteremo' (here we are and here we shall stay) was actually 'finalment i suma' (we're here at last) – said after a long and tiring journey!... Only in Rome, which had long been a centre of immigration for Italians from other regions, and in parts of Tuscany, where the Italian language had been created from the Florentine dialect, was 'Italian' spoken by the man in the street.

SOURCE

4

From the Italian philosopher and communist leader Antonio Gramsci, writing some time between 1926 and 1934.

The leaders of the Risorgimento said they were aiming at the creation of a modern state in Italy, and they in fact produced a bastard. They aimed at stimulating the formation of an extensive and energetic ruling class and they did not succeed; at integrating the people into the framework of the new state, and they did not succeed.

ACTIVITY
KNOWLEDGE CHECK

Study the census figures from 1911 (Source 3) and read through Extract 1 and Source 4.

1 In what ways do Source 3 and Extract 1 support Gramsci's argument (Source 4)?

2 What other evidence of Italy's development following unification supports Gramsci's assertion?

HOW DID THE GOVERNMENT OF GIOVANNI GIOLITTI SHAPE ITALY'S POLITICAL SITUATION FROM 1911 TO 1914?

The influence of Giolitti

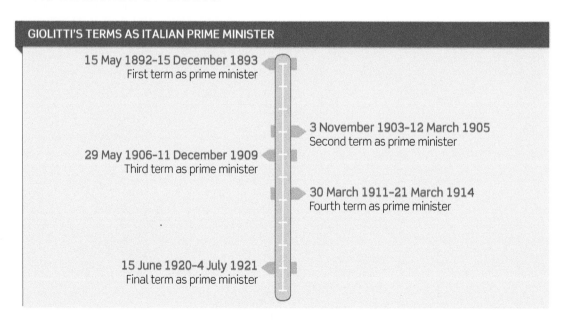

GIOLITTI'S TERMS AS ITALIAN PRIME MINISTER

15 May 1892–15 December 1893
First term as prime minister

3 November 1903–12 March 1905
Second term as prime minister

29 May 1906–11 December 1909
Third term as prime minister

30 March 1911–21 March 1914
Fourth term as prime minister

15 June 1920–4 July 1921
Final term as prime minister

SOURCE
5
Giovanni Giolitti, the most important and influential politician of the liberal era.

Giovanni Giolitti was the most prominent politician of the liberal era. He was prime minister of Italy on five separate occasions and his political ideas shaped Italy to such a degree that the period from 1901 to 1914 is generally known as the Giolittian Era. Giolitti was the master of *trasformismo* and he kept files on the weaknesses of every deputy in the Italian parliament, so that he had a specific understanding of exactly how to guarantee their support. He was fairly cynical about politics, believing that virtually all his opponents could be 'transformed' into political allies if the right deal was offered. In 1911, he became prime minister for the fourth time. His key policies varied little from his previous terms as prime minister and focused on the key goal of making Italy into a modern, industrialised, successful country where the masses were unified by shared values and a faith in the liberal ideals of parliament. His programme on achieving this focused on gaining the support of the three key oppositional forces to **liberal Italy**: the socialists, the Catholic Church and the nationalists.

KEY TERM

Liberal Italy
Refers to the period of Italian history from 1870 to 1922. It does not refer to one specific political party. Confusingly, there were no established liberal political parties, just an array of rapidly changing coalition governments. While there were numerous politicians who contested elections, the vast majority believed in the politics of liberalism, namely democratic and free elections, freedom of the press, freedom of religion, the right to private property and support for free trade. Despite these democratic ideals, the period was characterised by corruption, economic problems, social discontent and a lack of political development. The liberal era would eventually end in failure with the rise of fascism in 1922.

Giolitti and the socialists

The main focus of the 1911 Giolitti programme was the Partito Socialista Italiano (PSI), which had been formed in 1892 and had quickly developed into a powerful political institution. It was one of the very few formal political parties in Italy. In the general election of 1900, it had achieved 216,000 votes and 32 deputies out of the total of 508 parliamentary seats. By 1913, it had grown substantially, winning nearly a quarter of all votes cast and achieving 79 deputies in parliament. Socialism's growth in popularity mirrored Italy's industrialisation as the population in the major northern cities expanded considerably due to mass internal migration. Milan, for example, almost doubled in size between 1880 and 1914. This urbanisation transformed Italian politics: the peasants who moved to the city encountered a new modern world that was very different from the southern regions they had come from. Within the industrial centres the greater mixing of Italians from all over the country encouraged the dissemination of political thought and increased literacy, education and an awareness of political engagement, which in turn encouraged the growth of socialism as a means for working-class advancement. Led by Filippo Turati, the Italian Socialist Party was supported by a large number of academically educated intellectuals, who had lost faith in the ability of the liberal politicians to achieve the dreams of the *Risorgimento* and instead believed that only socialism could solve Italy's problems of political corruption, persistent rural poverty and the widening gap between the ruling classes and the masses. In contrast to the liberal politicians, the members of the Italian Socialist Party were active in taking their message to Italy's poor, holding public meetings, lectures, discussions and debates in the places where the working class and rural poor gathered, such as bars and cafés. They promoted education as the means by which Italy's poor could challenge the political order, working to encourage greater school attendance and providing books to workers.

Socialism grew rapidly; by 1902, 250,000 industrial workers had joined socialist national federations and there was a considerable amount of strike action in the pursuit of higher wages. In the agricultural sector, 218,000 Italians had joined the thousands of socialist agricultural cooperatives that had been formed by 1910. Although the success of the Italian Socialist Party alarmed many liberal politicians, Giolitti tended to view it as another oppositional force that could be dealt with through *trasformismo*. Giolitti's programme focused on 'absorbing' the socialist deputies, such as Turati, into the political system by offering a range of social reforms. These included compulsory accident insurance in industrial work paid for by the employer and a non-compulsory national insurance fund for health and old age (1898), the banning of the employment of children under 12 (1901), limiting the working day for women to 11 hours (1902), and the introduction of a maternity fund (1910). In 1913, further reforms, such as a state-subsidised sickness and an old age fund for the merchant navy, were introduced. Giolitti's most important concession to the socialists came in 1906 when he asserted a new policy of non-intervention in labour disputes and the establishment of arbitration courts that would look to settle pay disputes between employers and employees, thereby lowering the need for strike action. These courts were welcomed by Turati, who viewed them as a way of gaining better pay for workers without the need for violent strikes or confrontation with the police. In 1911, Giolitti's programme even went as far as to offer one of the key socialist leaders, Leonida Bissolati, a place in his cabinet, although this was eventually declined.

Giolitti's programme of placating the PSI by offering moderate social reform was partly successful, particularly with moderates like Turati, at least up to 1912, but he found it increasingly difficult to win over the entire PSI. The key issue was that the party was split between the reformists who were prepared to work with Giolitti to bring about gradual change for the workers and the maximalists who believed in revolution and the violent overthrow of the state. The maximalists, which included a young Benito Mussolini, despised the liberal state and opposed Turati's reformism, believing it would undermine the party and stop the chance of real reform taking place. Despite Giolitti's social policies, he was not able to win over this powerful radical element and this in turn undermined his key aim of *trasformismo* directed towards the PSI. His compromises with the PSI also brought him into considerable conflict with the two key ideological groups who opposed socialism – the Catholic Church and the nationalists.

Filippo Turati (1857-1932)
Filippo Turati was the leader and key figure of the *Partito Socialista Italiano* from its formation in 1895 up to the First World War. Born in 1857 in northern Italy, he was the son of a prefect and was well educated. He was a strong republican and believed that the original ideals of the *Risorgimento* had been betrayed by the corrupt liberal order. He originally pursued a literary career and wrote and published poetry, but later came to believe that the Italian nation's problems could only be solved by a radical transformation of Italian politics and society. He embraced the cause of socialism as the only means to achieve this aim. He helped form the PSI in 1892, was its first leader, and under his direction the party grew in support. Despite his belief in socialism, Turati was not radical in his politics and welcomed working with Giolitti if it led to better social policies for the Italian workers and peasants. He led the PSI in this strategy of compromise and cooperation up until the invasion of Libya in 1911, after which the more radical, anti-compromise wing of the party gained greater control of party policy.

Giolitti and the Catholic Church

Giolitti recognised the power and influence of the Catholic Church and was extremely careful in his dealings with this institution. His relationship with the Church in 1911 rested on previous policies that had been implemented since 1904. In 1904, he had pronounced that the Church and state were 'two parallel lines, which should never meet', clearly defining that there should always be a separation between the two institutions. Giolitti, however, was prepared to offer concessions to the Church in return for its support and in this sense he was successful up to point, being the first Italian prime minister to win the organised Catholic vote. This was achieved in a similar way to his 'absorption' of the socialists, by offering a series of policies and compromises that could gain the support of the Church. As prime minister in 1904,

he allowed a divorce bill, which had been close to passing before he took office, quietly to disappear from parliament and promoted Catholic interests in areas such as education. Concerned with the rise of socialism, the pope took the considerable step in 1909 of encouraging Italians to vote in around 150 constituencies where the socialists had a considerable chance of winning. When Giolitti became prime minister again in 1911, the cooperation between Catholics and liberals was most evident at a local level, where Catholics were part of the governing coalitions in Turin, Bologna, Florence and Venice. The Catholic Church had grown its political influence through youth movements and sports clubs that had expanded considerably from 1904 to 1911. Through these groups the Catholic Church held considerable sway over the popular vote, particular in the north. Giolitti was happy to use the Catholics to improve his parliamentary majority, but while he welcomed any support the Church provided, he was not prepared actively to court a greater link with the Catholic Church. Instead, he prioritised the support of the socialists and Turati, believing that this was key to encouraging the workers to support the liberal state, and he was not prepared to jeopardise this by offering concessions to the Church that might imperil his programme. He was also not prepared to give the pope any concession on Roman territory and therefore was unable to solve the 'Roman Question', which still festered at the heart of the tension between Church and state.

Giolitti and the nationalists

Despite his difficulties with the Church, Giolitti found that the largest threat to his programme came from a new, dynamic force that was growing in strength at the start of the 20th century – the nationalists. Organised Italian nationalism as a political force had barely existed in 1908, but through Giolitti's term from 1911 to 1914 it became a highly influential political movement. Nationalism was a powerful force across Europe in the early 20th century, where it tended to be more an ideological movement than organised political parties. However, in Italy, the supposed failure of the values of the *Risorgimento*, the humiliating defeat at the Battle of Adwa, the country's weakness as a world power and the shame felt at the fact that millions of Italians had to leave the country in the search for a better life meant the nationalist movement gained particular strength. The nationalists were antisocialist and antiliberal and believed that only through an aggressive foreign policy that looked to expand Italy's power in Africa and claim the *irredente* lands could Italy assert itself as a world power. This nationalist mission aimed to unite the differing classes of the Italian people within their patriotic love for Italy and sweep away the decadent liberal order that had failed to uphold the values and potential of the *Risorgimento*. The nationalist movement was supported in particular by the educated middle classes, who viewed it in terms of a force for national renewal which would undermine the rising popularity of socialism and destroy the cynical corruption of Rome, bringing about a new, more dynamic Italy. War and expansion would overcome domestic strife by linking the Italian people behind the nation. Liberal values, the nationalists believed, only encouraged selfish individualism; Italy could not be great until Italians understood that the nation was the superior ideal which stood above shallow, individual needs and were prepared to die for their country. Giolitti's attempts to work with the socialists were opposed and viewed as demonstrating the weakness and corruption of the liberal order.

In 1910, the nationalists inaugurated the Associazione Nazionalista Italiana (ANI), bringing the differing currents of nationalism into a more formalised organisation under the leadership of Enrico Corradini. Nationalism was a dynamic force which Giolitti found difficult to deal with. Unlike the socialists and Catholics who were prepared to work with parliament to an extent, the nationalists instead saw Giolitti and the liberal politicians as representing everything that was weak and corrupt about Italy and needed to be overthrown. Giolitti had at first attempted to boost Italian support for his leadership through a liberal programme of reform and economic modernisation, which he hoped would encourage Italians to view the liberals in a more positive light and therefore undermine the nationalist's growing support. This policy failed to halt the rise of nationalism. In a major part this was due to the fact that nationalism had a greater attraction than liberalism in its more passionate patriotic message, which promised to unite the Italian people under a powerful and assertive Italy. In 1911, Giolitti pursued a different path, this time attempting to embrace nationalism by expanding Italy's empire in North Africa through the invasion of Libya.

EXTEND YOUR KNOWLEDGE

Associazione Nazionalista Italiana (ANI)

The Italian Nationalist Association was formed in 1910 under the leadership of Enrico Corradini. Corradini was influenced by the ideas of nationalism and the struggle between nations that were current in Europe at the time. Unless Italy militarised and asserted its power through colonisation and annexation of the *irridente* lands it would be dominated by the more powerful nations of Europe. Only through the powerful force of nationalism could Italians be united and achieve the greatness that the *Risorgimento* was meant to establish. War would unite the classes and create an Italian nation that was not regionally divided. Corradini claimed that the nation should override any individual needs and that the greatest thing any Italian could do was to die for their country. Although never capable of overthrowing the liberal control of parliament, the nationalists did well in the elections they contested from 1913 onwards. After Mussolini became prime minister, the ANI was merged into the Fascist Party.

SOURCE

6 Giolitti writing on his policies concerning the working class during his time as prime minister. From Giovanni Giolitti, *Memorie della mia vita* ('Memories of My Life') (1922).

The elevation of the Fourth Estate (the workers) to a higher level of civilisation was the most pressing problem for us now. The exclusion of the working classes from both the political and administrative life of the country necessarily has the effect of laying them open to the influence of revolutionary parties and subversive ideas, for the apostles of these ideas have a formidable argument at their disposal when they see that the masses, on account of this exclusion, have no other means of defending themselves against the possible injustices of the ruling classes, whether particular or general, than with violence.

SOURCE

7 Cover of the magazine *L'Asino* from 14 May 1911 satirising Giovanni Giolitti as two faced: wearing parliamentary robes on the left side but dressed as a worker on the right.

ACTIVITY
KNOWLEDGE CHECK

1 Look at the portrayal of Giovanni Giolitti in Source 7. How far is this an accurate depiction of Giolitti's programme?

2 The picture was meant as a criticism of Giolitti. In what way does the magazine question Giolitti and his policies?

3 Using your own knowledge, how useful is this source in understanding criticisms towards Giolitti's programme in 1911?

AS Level Exam-Style Question Section A

Why is Source 6 valuable to the historian for an enquiry into Giolitti's policy priorities in 1911?

Explain your answer using the source, the information given about it and your own knowledge of the historical context. (8 marks)

Tip
Think about Giolitti's motivations for his compromise with the PSI and the social policies he introduced.

Foreign policy

Giolitti found Italy's foreign policy particularly difficult. The Triple Alliance with Germany and Austria-Hungary still held, but there were signs of strain by 1911. Most problematically, Italy's key interests in the Balkans clashed with its supposed ally Austria who also held the territory that many Italians believed was rightfully theirs. Nationalist forces pressured Giolitti to take a more aggressive stance towards Austria, although Giolitti resisted such moves. However, in 1911, Giolitti was prepared to placate the nationalists by expanding Italy's colonial empire. The war with the Ottoman Empire over Libya came about for several reasons. First, Italy had signed a deal in 1902 in which Italy would support French expansion in Morocco in return for the French backing Italian influence in Libya. In 1911, France began to consolidate its control over Morocco and Giolitti feared it was preparing to break the deal and expand into Libya as well. Another national humiliation such as the one that had occurred over Tunisia was unthinkable. Second, an invasion of Libya by the Italians would gain the support of the Catholic Church, who had considerable financial interests in Libya and had been encouraging the government to secure Libya as an Italian colony. Thus, an invasion appeared to Giolitti to be a way of gaining the support of both the influential nationalist and Catholic organisations and uniting the Italian people behind his liberal government.

In the short term, he was successful in this regard. The invasion of Libya on 29 September 1911, was greeted with an outpouring of national enthusiasm, even from socialist leaders such as Bissolati, who hoped that acquiring the colony could help provide land for Italy's poor peasantry. Italy's naval forces seized most of Libya's ports and coastal towns within only three weeks and the government committed 70,000 troops in its invasion. Giolitti had hoped that the Libyan population would greet the Italians as liberators from Ottoman rule but this did not happen, hampering Italy's attempt to gain control of the country. Instead, Giolitti looked to put pressure on the Ottomans elsewhere and Italian forces occupied 13 Turkish-held islands in the Aegean Sea. This move, alongside the fact that Turkey had begun a war with Montenegro, Serbia, Bulgaria and Greece in October 1912, meant that the Ottomans could not continue the war and, on 8 October, they formally surrendered control of Libya to the Italians. Italy was forced to keep 50,000 troops in Libya to pacify the Arab population and the war had cost around 3,500 Italian deaths. However, the colonisation of Libya was greeted as a resounding Italian victory that had overcome the shame of Adwa and demonstrated Italy as being a true European power. Giolitti's foreign policy had gained him considerable support, but he was to find that this success was to be very short lived.

By 1912, therefore, it appeared that Giolitti's programme had been successful. His social reforms had encouraged the support of the PSI deputies in parliament who were prepared to support his government and effectively act in coalition with Giolitti. The Catholic Church had become less antagonistic to the state and was cooperating with the liberals in several key areas. The victory in Libya appeared to galvanise nationalist support for the government. However, despite this apparent success, the Libyan War and the introduction of universal suffrage (the right to vote) were to have severe consequences for Giolitti's government.

ACTIVITY
KNOWLEDGE CHECK

1 Summarise Giolitti's particular difficulties with (a) the socialists, (b) the Catholics, (c) the nationalists and how he attempted to deal with each group.

2 Giolitti believed the priority was to 'absorb' the PSI even if it meant opposition from other political groups such as the Catholics. Using your own knowledge of Italy's social and political situation in 1911, why do you believe he saw this as his most important political task?

SOURCE 8

The liberal politician Giustino Fortunato writing a letter to his friend Pasquale Villari in December 1911.

I was fearful for the Tripoli expedition and continue to be fearful.* But I have one great, one immeasurable, consolation. For the first time since Italy was created amid the sea and beneath the sky, the southern peasants (and I know them well and they are not easily aroused to enthusiasm) are finally conscious of a duty to fight for a fatherland, their fatherland, and that this has a name: Italy. Yes, indeed, half a century of unity has not been wasted!

* Fortunato had been opposed to the Libyan War when it began in September.

AS Level Exam-Style Question Section A

How much weight do you give the evidence of Source 8 for an enquiry into support for the Libyan War in 1911?

Explain your answer using the source, the information given about it and your own knowledge of the historical context. (12 marks)

Tip

With this question you must go beyond the simplistic idea that this is only one individual's view so therefore can't be given weight. Consider how representative Fortunato's views may have been of most Italians, particularly in the south, in light of your knowledge concerning how the war was greeted in Italy.

HOW SUCCESSFUL WAS THE LIBERAL GOVERNMENT IN DEALING WITH ITALY'S GROWING INSTABILITY BETWEEN 1912 AND 1914?

Impact of the invasion of Libya

The Libyan War did not help Giolitti in his attempt to 'absorb' the nationalists; instead, the war not only increased support for the ANI, but also accentuated their opposition to the liberal government. The nationalists took credit for the war, claiming that Giolitti had only launched it under pressure from their movement. They denounced the liberals, blaming their weakness and lack of patriotism as the reasons why the Italian army had lost so many men during the fighting. More critically, the Libyan War destroyed Giolitti's cooperation with the PSI, which had formed the key basis for his programme of *trasformismo*. The PSI opposed the war as imperialist militarism. More radical socialists, who had been angered by the growing compromise with the liberals in parliament, expelled those members who had supported the war, such as Bissolati. The revolutionary wing of the party seized control and rejected further cooperation with Giolitti, with the more moderate members of the PSI isolated and unable to influence party policy. Benito Mussolini, a radical socialist and talented journalist, was appointed editor of the socialist newspaper *Avanti!*, which focused its campaign on the corrupt liberal order and militarists who had murdered workers both in Libya and Italy. Giolitti's attempts at absorbing the socialists into the liberal state had ended in failure.

Impact of the franchise extension of 1912

Giolitti's problems were accentuated by changes to the suffrage in Italy which he had made part of the government programme in 1911. Previously the vote was restricted to literate men over the age of 21, but it was now difficult to deny the vote to Italy's conscript soldiers who were fighting in Libya, many of who did not have the required literacy level to enable them to vote. Consequently, in 1912, a new law was passed that extended the vote to all men who had completed military service and all men aged 30 and over regardless of literacy. Despite the concern that now around 70 percent of Italy's voters were potentially illiterate, Giolitti hoped that increased suffrage would promote greater national unity, increase the popularity of the liberals and strengthen the vote in the rural areas, which tended to be more conservative than the industrialised cities where the PSI were popular. He also believed that increased suffrage would undermine the PSI, as with greater electoral representation the working class would be less inclined to support more radical ideologies.

Resignation of Giolitti

The first elections under the new suffrage took place in 1913 and demonstrated the overall failure of Giolitti's strategy. Liberal deputies won only 318 seats, a loss of 71 seats from the 1909 election, with the socialists, nationalists, radicals and Catholics making gains. However, the critical problem was the liberals' links to the Catholic Church. The president of the Catholic Electoral Union, Count Gentiloni, had secretly asked liberal candidates to agree to seven key points (mainly on religious education and divorce law) in return for the Catholic vote. Gentiloni boasted after the election that around 228 liberal deputies of the 318 elected owed their victory to Catholic support. Giolitti claimed that he knew nothing of the pact, but regardless of whether this was true or not, the liberal regime found themselves more and more reliant on support from the Catholic Church. Italy was becoming more ideologically polarised and Giolitti's attempt to unite oppositional

groups within the liberal system using *trasformismo* was now virtually impossible. His concessions to the Catholic Church angered both socialists and anticlerical liberals within parliament. In the spring of 1914, they withdrew their support for Giolitti following Count Gentiloni's claims concerning the pact and Giolitti chose to resign. This in turn infuriated the Catholics who felt that with the anti-Church faction in government gone, Giolitti could have formed a new pro-Catholic block that pursued policies in line with the Church's teachings.

Growth of nationalism and socialism

Giolitti's programme of deal-making and attempting to bring oppositional forces within the liberal parliamentary system floundered under the mass suffrage that he had been so eager to promote. Instead, mass suffrage meant mass parties and both the nationalists and the Catholics found the powers of religion and patriotism were the most dynamic forces in gaining the support of the Italian people. Giolitti was replaced by Antonio Salandra who believed he could revive liberalism by linking it more closely with nationalism. However, by June 1914, Italy was again in turmoil. The PSI proclaimed a national strike after three protestors were shot dead by police in Ancona. Anarchists, republicans and other radicals joined in and for a week most of northern and central Italy was in chaos as public buildings were torched, tax registers destroyed, railway stations seized and churches attacked. Hundreds of workers lost their lives in battles against authorities and Italy appeared to be on the verge of revolution. Eventually 'Red Week' ended after trade unions agreed to call off the strike, but the riots had demonstrated to Salandra the difficulty of achieving national unity. Instead, Italian society appeared more divided on class and ideological grounds than at any time since unification.

SOURCE 9 From *The Times*, 17 March 1914.

On succeeding to the Premiership he controlled General Election after General Election, conducting them through his prefects with the maestria [skill] of a Tammany [infamous corrupt town council in the United States] 'boss'. Then, with the power of socialism broken he played the conservative and even – as during the recent general election – the semi-Clerical... The parliamentary situation is his situation. He has made four Deputies out of every five, and knows how far each man has compromised himself in order to obtain his favour. He made a war and a peace, he spent 1,000,000,000 of lire, he renewed an alliance, he decreed a universal suffrage almost without consulting parliament or the nation. He leaves the finances of Italy compromised, the Chamber demoralised, the subversive forces strengthened and the Crown – to which he has, at this cost, guaranteed 13 years of tranquillity – without any serious indication as to the policy to be pursued. Under his dictatorship Italy has progressed materially and has revealed an economic resilience previously unsuspected but it is an open question whether such progress has not been clearly bought by the sacrifice of the ideals that guided her elder statesmen.

EXTRACT

2 From Paul Corner, 'State and society, 1901–1922', in *Liberal and Fascist Italy: 1900–1945*, edited by Adrian Lyttelton (2002).

Faced by mounting opposition on both left and right, the Giolittian 'system' built on mediation and compromise appeared by the end of 1912 to be in pieces. The increasing polarisation of politics was evident as economic crisis strengthened the appeal of revolutionary socialism and syndicalism, on the one hand, and the worsening international situation provoked ever more overt expressions of nationalism, on the other. Between 1912 and 1914, Italy was to witness some of the most bitter strikes in its short history, costing more than five million working days, with agricultural labourers and industrial workers expressing open hostility towards the state which had become synonymous with misery and repression. The circuit of violent protest and violent repression was resumed, but with a new ferocity. In the elections of 1913 – the first with universal male suffrage – Giolitti was able to gain a majority only through the massive intervention of the Catholics on his behalf... While Catholic intervention in 330 of the 508 electoral colleges helped to produce a majority for Giolitti, the price paid was high. The Radicals withdrew their support and liberal anticlericalism expressed its grave doubts about government's complicity with Catholicism. In March 1914 Giolitti resigned.

EXTRACT

3 From Martin Clark, *Modern Italy 1871–1995* (1996).

There were many reasons for the collapse of Giolittianism, beside the Libyan War and the introduction of semi-universal male suffrage. Giolitti was a good political juggler, but even he could not keep all the balls in the air at once. If he made concessions to the Socialists, he annoyed the Catholics. If he allied with the Catholics, he lost the Radicals. If he invaded Libya, he betrayed the Socialists... Political systems that rest on 'absorption' and 'concessions' are always faced with this 'me-too problem'; it is still a major issue in Italy today. It was particularly acute in the later Giolittian years, because economic growth had slowed down; there was simply not enough money available to keep everybody happy.

ACTIVITY
KNOWLEDGE CHECK

Read Source 9 and Extracts 2 and 3 concerning Giolitti's failures and his resignation in 1914.

1 Summarise their interpretations of Giolitti's leadership and decide how far they agree. What are their key disagreements?

2 Use your own notes and knowledge to give evidence which supports or challenges their interpretation.

3 Write your own summary on why Giolitti's programme failed and he was forced to resign in 1914.

The declaration of neutrality, 1914

In August 1914, Salandra was to face an even greater challenge, as war broke out in Europe pitting the central powers, Germany and Austria, against the entente of Russia, Britain and France. Italy had joined the Triple Alliance with Germany and Austria-Hungary in 1882. When the First World War broke out in August 1914, however, Italy did not have to join Austria as it had not consulted with Italy's government before declaring war on Serbia. This meant Italy's treaty obligations to Austria did not apply. Instead, Italy announced that it would remain neutral. This decision caused considerable splits within Italian politics. Many within parliament, including Giolitti, believed that Italy was not economically ready to engage in a major war, particularly so soon after the war in Libya, and he argued that Italy could gain by negotiating with both sides to stay out. Despite the anger of the nationalist press who pushed for intervention, it appeared that the majority of Italians had no wish to get involved in the European conflict and backed Giolitti and the other non-interventionist politicians.

EXTEND YOUR KNOWLEDGE

Antonio Salandra (1853–1931)

Antonio Salandra was a leading conservative politician. He believed that Italian unity could be achieved through nationalist missions that would promote patriotism among the people. He was prime minister in 1914 and pushed for Italian entry into the First World War, believing that the war and subsequent victory would unite Italy and inspire the Italian nationalism he longed for. He resigned in 1915 after a parliamentary revolt against the Treaty of London, which he had negotiated in secret, but was reinstated by the king later that year. He was prime minister until 1916, when he was forced to resign after the Austrian army launched the *Strafexpedition* in summer 1916 against Italy's forces (see below). He would later play a key part in Mussolini's appointment as Italian prime minister.

THINKING HISTORICALLY — Interpretations (5c)

Good questions/Bad questions

Below are approaches attributed to three famous historians. They are generalisations for the purpose of this exercise.

Herodotus	Leopold von Ranke	Karl Marx
He looks for the interesting story, the drama and the colourful characters.	He is interested in how great men use their influence to bring about change.	He is looking underneath the events to see what patterns there are over long periods of time and how ordinary people fit in.

Work in groups.

1 Devise three criteria of what makes a good historical question.

2 Consider what you know about Giolitti's period as prime minister from 1911 to 1914.

   a) Each write a historical question based on that subject matter.

   b) Put these in rank order, with the best question first, based on your criteria.

3 Using a piece of A3 paper, write the names of the three historians so they form a large triangle.

   a) Write your questions from 2a on the piece of paper so that their positions reflect how likely the historians are to be interested by that question. For example, a question about how far Giolitti was successful in his political aims would interest Herodotus and Ranke but not Marx and so would be somewhere between Ranke and Herodotus, but nowhere near Marx.

   b) Add some further questions about Giolitti. Try to think of questions that only one of the three would be interested in.

4 Take it in turns to try to answer the questions you have created in the style of one of the historians. See if the other members of the group can guess which historian it was.

Answer the following questions individually using the examples created by the above activity.

5 Does one method of constructing history lead to better reasoning than the others? Explain your answer.

6 Explain why all historians who deploy rigorous methodology are, to an extent, useful sources for the study of the past.

AS Level Exam-Style Question Section B

How far was the rise of Italian nationalism as a political force the main reason for the failure of the Giolitti programme?
(20 marks)

Tip

This question requires you to consider a range of factors and weigh up their relevant importance. Why did the Giolitti programme fail and what were the key reasons? Was the rise of the Italian nationalists the most important?

WHAT WAS THE IMPACT OF THE FIRST WORLD WAR ON ITALY?

The intervention crisis

Italy's declaration of neutrality in 1914 split the opinion of the liberals in parliament and set off a political crisis concerning Italy's possible intervention in the war. The prime minister, Antonio Salandra, argued that Italy should join the war, fearing that if Germany and Austro-Hungary won they would not be sympathetic to an ally who failed to come to their side at this critical time. On the other hand, if Britain and France were victorious and Italy had not assisted them in their efforts they would not be open to discussing Italy's ambitions in the Mediterranean. It was a difficult situation. Salandra also believed that the unique situation provided by the war would enable him to introduce more repressive legislation, which would offer an authoritarian solution to Italy's political problems. If Italy was victorious then it would be difficult to challenge Salandra's policies. At the start of 1915, Salandra and his foreign minister, Sidney Sonnino, began secret negotiations with the British and French governments as well as Germany and Austria. It was the Entente, however, which offered the best deal, promising that with victory Italy would gain much of the *irridente* lands – South Tyrol, Trentino, Istria, Trieste and much of Dalmatia. On 26 April 1915, Italy signed the Treaty of London pledging to support Britain, France and Russia. News of the treaty caused significant unrest in Italy. It had been conducted in absolute secrecy by Salandra and Sonnino and not even the army general staff had been informed. The PSI was firmly against intervention, as were most Catholics, including the pope, Benedict XV. In April 1915, the politicians who had won Italy's local elections, known as prefects, were asked to report on public opinion and overwhelmingly replied that most Italians in the provinces feared war and had little concern for irredentism or war against Austria.

In early May 1915, the crisis of Italy's possible intervention in the First World War grew considerably when Giolitti denounced the Treaty of London and 300 deputies announced their opposition to Salandra's decision. Those backing neutrality called on Giolitti to become prime minister again, but parliament was hopelessly divided. Massive crowds of supporters for the war held rallies in the streets where those backing neutrality were declared traitors. Mussolini, who believed that entry into the First World War was the best chance of creating revolution in Italy, was expelled from the Socialist Party for promoting intervention. Salandra resigned and the king asked Giolitti to form a new government, but he was worried by the fact that going back on the Treaty of London was now impossible; if he did so, then Italy would have betrayed both sides in the war. Most importantly, the king told Giolitti that he felt committed to the Treaty of London and might abdicate if it were not honoured. Given his previous position, Giolitti felt he could not support the treaty, but at the same time he certainly did not want to risk overthrowing the king, so he declined the offer to become prime minister again. Now the king turned to Salandra, who was reinstated as prime minister on 16 May and on 20 May was granted emergency powers by parliament. On 25 May 1915, Italy formally declared war on Austria, with Salandra proclaiming that only through national unity could Italy claim victory against its enemies.

Italy's entry into the war had been predominately due to both foreign and domestic political reasons and had little to do with the interventionist protests going on at the same time. However, the myth that the government had been forced into the First World War by the 'interventionists' would later play a strong role in Mussolini's political campaigns after 1918. Salandra had hoped that the war would bring the Italian nation together and unite them in a heroic cause. However, the majority of Italians still opposed intervention and even before a shot was fired, the debate over Italy's entry into the war had caused troubling divisions. Significantly, the PSI had voted against Salandra's emergency powers and at the time of Italy's entry into the First World War were the only far left wing party in Europe not to support their country's intervention in the conflict.

EXTRACT

4 From Thomas Row, 'Italy in the international system 1900–1922', in *Liberal and Fascist Italy: 1900–1945*, edited by Adrian Lyttelton (2002).

Throughout the spring of 1915 Italy struggled towards intervention. In the press and in the piazza the interventionist and neutralist force fought each other and fought for the soul of public opinion... Meanwhile and despite this turmoil, the key decisions about the war were being made in high places. On 26 April Italy signed the Treaty of London. This bound the country to enter the war on the side of the Entente against Austria-Hungary. Upon victory, Italy was to receive Trent and the Tyrol to the Brenner Pass, Trieste, Istria, Gorizia and much of Dalmatia... Italy's decision to enter the First World War marked a rupture in the country's liberal evolution. The decision was made against the backdrop of the great crisis of the international system and the weakening of Giolitti's reformist domestic programme. The key diplomatic choices had been made on the traditional basis of raison d'etat [a purely political decision] by Salandra, Sonnino and the King. But their choices were also conditioned by domestic policies, by the desire to re-establish the political hegemony [power] of the liberal political class against the perceived threat of the left and the advance of a Catholic movement... Despite the thunder of the interventionists, a majority of Italians had no desire to enter the world conflict. Italy went to face the supreme test of war, then, not united, but confused and divided.

ACTIVITY
KNOWLEDGE CHECK

1 What does Extract 4 argue were the main motivations for Italy's entry into the war?

2 Divide the reasons into domestic and foreign policy reasons. Can you make an argument that it was mainly due to either domestic or foreign policy motivations or are they equal?

EXTEND YOUR KNOWLEDGE

The young Mussolini: from radical socialist to pro-nationalist

Benito Mussolini was born on 29 July 1883 in the predominately left-wing town of Predappio. His father was a prominent socialist and Mussolini was named after Benito Juarez, a Mexican revolutionary. Mussolini had followed his father's political direction as a radical socialist and by 1910 he was editor of a small socialist newspaper, *La Lotta di Classe* ('The Class Struggle'), in the town of Forli. He preached revolution and condemned parliament, the Church and militarism. He was arrested in 1911 for attempting to stir up insurrection against the war in Libya. His work as editor and his growing prominence as a socialist radical saw him rise through the PSI and in 1912 he was appointed editor of the main socialist newspaper *Avanti!* He used the paper to rally people against the liberal state and socialists who were prepared to work with it like Turati, as he feared that these reformists were allying too closely with the parliamentary system and Giolitti. He was a successful editor and increased the circulation of the paper considerably.

As the more revolutionary faction of the PSI came to dominate the party after 1912, Mussolini found himself in a powerful position. When the First World War first broke out, Mussolini supported the socialist line of absolute neutrality. However, as the war progressed, Mussolini started to perceive that maybe the war was the answer the socialists needed to destroy the old order of Italy; as he asserted it was 'only blood that makes the wheels of history turn'. On 18 October 1914, he published a crucial article in *Avanti!* where he argued that it was wrong for Italy to stay out of the conflict in which the rest of Europe was involved. He was expelled from the PSI and removed as the editor. Although he still considered himself a socialist, he took an increasingly nationalist line, seeing the war as the great historical event that would change Europe and Italy forever. He began to move further towards the nationalists in asserting that the war might also open up the chance for Italian expansion. In April 1915, he was arrested again, but this time for his part in the riots calling for Italy's intervention in the First World War, a considerable change from his political view in 1911. In September 1915, he was conscripted into the army and it was his experiences in the trenches which would push him further away from the PSI and towards a more right-wing, nationalist ideology.

SOURCE

10

This article, written by Horatio Brown, appeared in *The Times* on 17 June 1915. Brown was a well-known Scottish historian who wrote on Italian history. He lived most of his life in Venice and received many awards from the Italian nation, including a knighthood from the Italian Republic.

Deep down in the mind of the nation, and more especially of the Northerners, gnaws the desire to get at Austria, to avenge the martyrs of Bellfiori and the indignities of the 'bankeraus' at Milan, to cancel the memory of Custozza and of Lissa [these were famous battles in Italy's struggle against Austria during the wars for independence in the 1800s]. Further, there is the lively hope to demonstrate the value of the Italian arms and to win the Trentino and Trieste, not by negotiation, but by the sword. But deeper still, I believe, in the heart of the people – a most potent coefficient in Italy's action – lies a revolt against the arrogance, the inhumanity, the cruelty, the barbarism, in short, of the Germanic Powers in their conduct of this war. It is the Belgian atrocities, confirmed by Lord Bryce's report, the Lusitania, and in a lesser degree, the poisonous gases, that have roused the passion of the Italian populace and made them demand that Rome, the great 'Latin mother' of our Western civilisation, should not stand aside when the achievement is threatened by Prussia... I believe I am not exaggerating the weight of this feeling among the Italians. Since the war broke out I have received many letters from people of the people. It is true these all come from the north-east corner of Italy, but that is just the region most immediately affected by the war.

THINKING HISTORICALLY Evidence (5a)

Context is everything

Carefully read Source 10 on Italy's declaration of war in 1914 and complete the activities that follow.

Work in groups.

Take an A3 piece of paper. In the middle of it draw a circle about 18 cm in diameter. Within the circle is the evidence itself, outside the circle is the context.

1 Think of a question Source 10 could be helpful in answering.

2 Inside the circle, write a set of statements giving information that can be gleaned only from the source itself without any contextual knowledge.

3 Outside the circle, write down statements of contextual knowledge that relate to the source.

4 Draw annotated lines to show links between the contextual statements and the information from the source. Does context change the nature or meaning of the information?

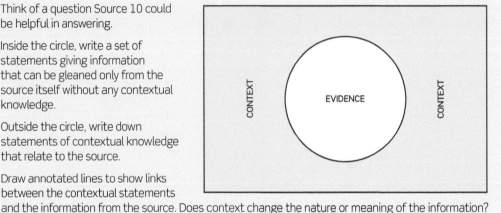

Now answer the following question:

5 Explain why knowledge of context is important when gathering and using historical evidence. Give specific examples to illustrate your point.

SOURCE 11

From the official ANI magazine, *Idea Nazionale*, in an article entitled 'The parliament against Italy' printed on 15 May 1915. Here the magazine argues for Italy to enter the First World War and is angered by the removal of Salandra.

Parliament is Giolitti; Giolitti is parliament: the binomial of our shame. This is the old Italy. The old Italy that is unaware of the new, the true, the holy Italy that is rising again in our history – and the future – ... the struggle is mortal. Either parliament will destroy the nation and over her trembling sacred body resume its profession of procurer, and prostitute her once again to the foreigner, or the nation will overturn parliament, destroy the barrators' benches and purify with iron and ire the boudoirs of the pimps.

SOURCE 12

Gabriele d'Annunzio speaking to the French ambassador in June 1914. D'Annunzio was an extreme nationalist. Here he explains his belief in the power of war to bring about national revival.

We live in a loathsome epoch, under the domination of the multitude and the tyranny of the masses... The genius of the Latin people has never fallen so low. It has completely lost all sense of energy, pride and heroic virtues; it wallows in the mire and revels in humiliation... A war, a great national war, is the last remaining hope of salvation. It is only through war that people who have been turned into brutes can halt their decline, as it offers them a stark choice; either glory or death... Consequently, this next war, that you seem to fear, I invoke with all the passion of my soul.

A Level Exam-Style Question Section A

How far could the historian make use of Sources 11 and 12 together to investigate the motivations for Italy's intervention in the First World War in 1915?

Explain your answer, using both sources, the information given about them and your own knowledge of the historical context. (20 marks)

Tip

These are both from strong nationalists. Consider the influence of the nationalists in Italy at the time. You could consider other factors that influenced Salandra's decision.

Military stalemate, 1915–16

Salandra had hoped for a brief, offensive war that would bring Italy almost immediate territorial gains. This expectation simply demonstrated how misguided his understanding of the conflict was. Instead, the war between Austria and Italy was fought predominately in the mountainous area bordering the two countries and was characterised by mainly static trench warfare in the ice and snow of the difficult alpine terrain. Conditions were horrific and thousands of Italian soldiers were killed by cholera and frostbite. Two years of stalemate followed Italy's declaration of war and thousands of soldiers were often sacrificed in order to move a few hundred metres on the mountainside. In 1915, 62,000 Italians died during four attempted offensives against the Austrians that failed to change the situation at the front. Instead of bringing about the national unity many had hoped for, the war revealed the great problems and divisions within Italian society. Nearly five million men were conscripted into the army, with the majority being peasants or agricultural workers. Southern peasant conscripts were overrepresented and the ideals of the war concerning Italian expansion meant very little to them. It was difficult for these soldiers to comprehend why the frozen wastelands at the front were worth dying for. Crucially, the majority of the peasant conscripts, who spoke a vast range of dialects, could not understand the orders being given to them by those in charge, who were predominantly educated northern Italians and who mainly spoke the official Italian language. Italian conscripts were treated poorly by their commanders and rations were extremely low (around 3,000 calories a day by the end of 1916). Many of the soldiers could not comprehend why the war was being fought or why Italy had joined and around 290,000 Italian soldiers were court-martialled during the war for desertion.

The solution of the Italian supreme commander, Luigi Cadorna, to the lack of discipline and morale was to repress dissent through harsh punishment. Military tribunals passed 4,000 death sentences on Italian soldiers for desertion and indiscipline throughout the course of the war, considerably more per capita than any other Western army. The Italian leaders feared that, given the troops' lack of patriotic feeling towards the war, if soldiers heard that conditions in prisoner of war camps were tolerable they might be inclined to surrender. Thus, the government hampered any attempts to help Italians who had been captured; 600,000 Italian soldiers were captured and had to survive on 1,000 calories a day. Around 100,000 died of hunger-related illnesses, five times the number from France and Britain who were allowed to receive food parcels from home. Those soldiers who survived the prisoner of war camps came out with a strong feeling of abandonment and considerable anger towards a government that had betrayed them.

EXTEND YOUR KNOWLEDGE

Luigi Cadorna (1850–1928)

The commander of the Italian army from July 1914 to October 1917, Luigi Cadorna, was a highly conservative military leader. Like other leaders during the First World War, he found it difficult to adapt to the new conditions of war and insisted on offensive warfare which led to the deaths of thousands of Italian troops. He refused to organise his army for defensive battles and thus the army was unprepared when the Austrian army attacked in 1916. In response to Italy's defeats, he insisted that Italy's military failings could be improved by stricter discipline towards the troops. He insisted on 'decimation' as a means of forcing Italian troops to fight. This meant that if a regiment showed disobedience individual troops would be chosen at random and shot in front of the other soldiers. This, he believed, would make Italian soldiers less inclined to disobey orders or show 'cowardice', but instead it simply lowered morale even further. He blamed poor military performance on domestic forces, such as the defeatism of the PSI for undermining morale, and in 1917 he even went as far as to blame the pope, who had condemned the war as 'useless slaughter'. Cadorna's leadership created a fundamental lack of trust between the commanders and their troops, which reflected the divisions within Italians society. He blamed Italy's massive defeat at the Battle of Caporetto on the cowardice and weakness of his own troops. He was removed by the new prime minister, Vittorio Orlando, and replaced by the more capable Armando Diaz.

Defeat at Caporetto

In 1916, the Austrian army launched the *Strafexpedition*, a major offensive in the Trentine salient, in order to open a path that would allow it to attack Verona and Bologna. Although the Italian army was able to regroup and halt the Austrian attack, it had a severe impact on army and public morale. Salandra was criticised by both military command and parliament and was forced to resign. He was replaced by 78-year-old Paolo Boselli, but Italy's military efforts hardly improved. The situation reached its lowest point with Italy's humiliating defeat by the Austro-Hungarian forces at the Battle of Caporetto in October 1917. The battle took place around the town of Caporetto (today known as Kobarid in Slovenia) on 24 October 1917, when Austrian forces attacked the Italian front line. Poor leadership and low morale saw the Italian army dissolve in the face of the Austrian forces and a humiliating and chaotic retreat took place. What had been an initial victory for the Austrians turned quickly into a rout as Italian soldiers streamed down the mountains, many without weapons, and there were reports of looting, violence between Italian troops and celebrations by some troops who thought the war was now over; 200,000 soldiers lost contact with their regiments, large quantities of military arms were lost, as was the majority of the Veneto region.

The actions of the Italian troops in the face of the Austrian offense was an embarrassment to the Italian leadership, who only months before had been claiming that the war had finally brought about patriotic unity in Italy. One Italian senator, Leopoldo Franchetti, was so overwhelmed by the nature of the defeat at Caporetto that he committed suicide. In total, 10,000 Italians were killed, 30,000 wounded and 300,000 taken prisoner; 400,000 soldiers simply vanished, in most cases using the chaos to head back to their homes in Italy. The defeat revealed the poor state of the army and prompted significant anger and debate within Italy. While the original Austrian victory had been due to tactical reasons, the nature of the retreat afterwards was accentuated by poor morale.

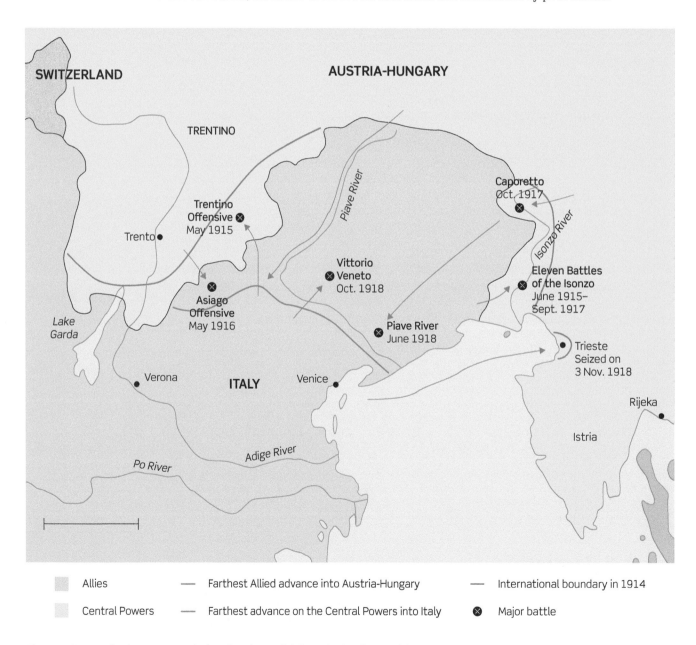

Figure 1.3 Map of Italy's progress during victories and defeats in the First World War.

The defeat at Caporetto was a turning point for the Italian nation. Thoughts of an easy victory that would allow Italy to take Trente and Trieste disappeared; now Italy was fighting for its survival. However, it is important to note that overall the Italian army did not collapse, nor did the defeat precipitate revolution or the collapse of the state. In Italy, Caporetto reignited the divisions that had surfaced during the arguments on intervention in 1914 and 1915. The fact that a majority of Italy's parliament still backed Giolitti and were not completely behind the war was blamed for Italy's poor military performance and there were calls for revolution from many nationalists. Some even went as far as to call for Giolitti and other 'neutralist' politicians to be put on trial for treason. Following Caporetto, Boselli resigned and was replaced by the younger and more dynamic Vittorio Orlando. Cadorna was removed and the Italian army was reorganised under a new commander, General Diaz. Rations for the soldiers were raised and annual leave increased. There was a greater focus on boosting soldier morale through lectures and trench newspapers. Promises of land reform for the peasant conscripts were made and in December 1917, an organisation to look after the welfare of the soldiers and their families was established. General Diaz was also a much more cautious commander, focused on holding the Italian line at Piave and avoiding the needless sacrifice of soldiers in suicidal offensives. Casualty rates fell considerably, from 520,000 in 1917 to 143,000 in 1918.

Socialist responses to the war

Politically, the PSI continued to oppose the war, refusing to vote for war credits in parliament and declaring a policy of 'neither support nor sabotage' to the war effort. Its stance was despised by the nationalists and many liberal supporters who saw it as defeatist, unpatriotic and anti-Italian, blaming it for the poor performance of Italy's military. The hysteria after Caporetto against 'defeatists' who had 'stabbed Italy in the back' led to the arrest and imprisonment of many PSI leaders. Mussolini himself blamed Italian socialists, asserting that they were a more dangerous enemy than the Austrians and calling for a more forceful Italian leader who would help create a united country. The PSI's position on the war meant there was even greater polarisation between left and right in Italian politics.

The war economy and cost of war

The First World War had a significant effect on the Italian economy. At the beginning of the war, Italy was behind Austria in nearly all key economic areas crucial for the war. Steel production was less than one million tonnes, while the Austrians were at 2.6 million tonnes. For every two machine guns per Italian battalion, the Austrians had 12, and Italy was short of artillery and bullets. Over the course of the war, however, Italy made quite significant economic improvements that would overcome its deficits and overall Italy's industry coped effectively with the requirements of the First World War. Fiat established itself as Europe's leading truck and lorry manufacturer, producing 25,000 vehicles in 1918 alone. Italy had created an aeronautical industry that produced 6,500 planes in 1918.

By the end of the war, Italian industry had produced around 20,000 machine guns and 7,000 pieces of heavy artillery, a greater number than the British were able to manufacture. This success was driven by the under-secretariat of arms and munitions, Alfredo Dallolio. He organised the recruitment of women and peasants into the factories and ensured that those men deemed essential to war production were exempted from conscription. Hours of work were increased, strikes made illegal and workers could face military tribunals if their behaviour was deemed unsatisfactory. A quarter of munitions factory employees were women and a third of Italy's 900,000 workers in the war economy were either men exempted from military service or on secondment from the army.

The military industry grew substantially during the war with Fiat increasing its workforce from 6,000 to 30,000. Dallolio's ministry financed industrial expansion by making payments in advance, arranging cheap loans and establishing profitable contracts for big business. There was little government interference in industry and leading industrialists ran the central and regional committees for industrial mobilisation. Italy achieved rapid growth and for the industrialists there was absolutely no risk involved as they were backed up by the state and the banks, which fuelled their expansion. However, worryingly for the long term, this growth was based almost entirely on government investment in war production, which had been paid for by foreign loans and printing more money.

While the war continued these issues could be somewhat ignored, but the conclusion of the war would bring about inevitable inflationary problems and massive cuts to government spending as the country found itself around 23 billion lire in debt (it had been 2.9 billion lire in debt before the war). National debt was at 84.9 billion lire in June 1919 with 15 billion lire owing to Britain and 8.5 billion to the USA.

Italy's economy had become unbalanced with a few war-based sectors such as steel, engineering, vehicles, cement, rubber and chemicals growing at a disproportionate rate compared with other industries. Italy's war economy also accentuated one of Italy's most troubling issues. The majority of war production was based in the north east and the growth of industry in these areas accelerated the division between north and south Italy. While the south remained a predominately impoverished agricultural society, the war saw the north's economy grow by over 20 percent between 1911 and 1921. The bitterness of the south that it was being ignored and left behind as the north progressed would be a major challenge for Italy's politicians after the war. There was also resentment and unrest among the industrial workers in the north.

By 1917, bread and pasta were being rationed and meat and sugar consumption was falling sharply. Long hours and a fall in real wages of around 25 percent at a time when the industrialists were making vast profits fuelled worker anger, particularly as the majority did not support the war. The government increased indirect taxes to pay for the war effort and this in turn led to greater social division, as the poorer in society felt that these affected them more greatly than the rich. In August 1917, 50 workers were killed protesting in Turin against bread shortages and the continuation of the war. The riots shocked politicians who made steps to increase food supplies and pro-war propaganda. Italy's industry had made quite incredible increases during the war, but the long-term economic and social problems would have a profound effect on the country when the war ended in November 1918.

The significance of victory

The shift in military tactics, combined with the disintegration of the Austro-Hungarian Empire due to events elsewhere, saw Italy's prospects in the war improve and by October 1918, the Austro-Hungarian Empire was near collapse. Orlando encouraged Diaz to attack, believing that an Italian victory would help strengthen its position in the negotiations that would come after the war. On 24 October 1918, Italian forces finally launched an offensive across the Piave, entering the town of Vittorio Veneto and splitting the Austrian army in two. Austria signed an armistice on 4 November and the war in Italy came to an end. The Battle of Vittorio Veneto came to symbolise the greatest moment of the Italian nation. The victory was promoted by nationalists as demonstrating the glory of Italy, achieved through patriotism, unity and self-sacrifice. Mussolini would later link the battle to his appointment as prime minister and the success of fascism by claiming they represented the same ideals achieved at Vittorio Veneto. Salandra proclaimed the victory as representing the patriotism and self-sacrifice he had hoped the war would bring about. However, despite its victory, it was difficult to see what Italy had actually won. Italy had suffered 650,000 casualties, its economy was even more greatly distorted between the north and south and suffered from debt and inflation, and the legacy of the war would be a more divided Italy: between those who backed the war and those who had not, and those who fought in the war and those who had stayed at home. After Caporetto, the government had also made promises to the peasants in order to boost morale, but now faced the difficult task of fulfilling these commitments. Returning soldiers wanted compensation for the sacrifices they had made and many Italians believed that the war should bring about major changes in Italian politics. Given the circumstances, the government faced an extremely difficult situation at the beginning of 1919.

ACTIVITY
KNOWLEDGE CHECK

1 What impression does Source 13 give of the Battle of Caporetto?

SOURCE 13 Italian prisoners of war in the city of Udine after the Battle of Caporetto, October 1917.

EXTRACT

5 Paul Corner, writing on the consequences of the First World War, 'State and society, 1901–1922', in *Liberal and Fascist Italy: 1900–1945*, edited by Adrian Lyttelton (2002).

In broad terms, therefore, the consequences of mass mobilisation appear to have been quite the opposite of those envisaged by the authorities at the outbreak of hostilities. Government had seen war as an opportunity for imposing social discipline and reducing internal division. Yet, at both military and civilian levels, popular response was negative and hostile. Instead of the realisation of a patriotic apotheosis [high point], the sufferings and injustices of the war had accentuated feelings of mistrust in respect to the government, whose incompetence, both at the front and at home, was bitterly resented, even by that officer class whose patriotism had been taken for granted. Total war had imposed heavy burdens on the whole population, but there seemed little government recognition of this fact, and little apparent desire on the part of government to compensate for popular sacrifice. For the majority of Italians, the war was something to which they submitted. If it made peasants more aware of belonging to a nation called Italy, something of which many had been largely unaware before the outbreak of the war, it did so on terms which did anything but consolidate patriotic sentiment and reinforce a positive sense of national identity.

ACTIVITY
KNOWLEDGE CHECK

1 Read Extract 5 and summarise in one line what Paul Corner's key argument is regarding Italy and the First World War.

2 What evidence is there to support Corner's argument?

3 To what extent did the First World War simply build on the problems caused by the Libyan War in 1912?

4 The First World War has often been seen as the most important event in helping to create the fascist movement. List the ways in which the war affected Italy. You can also consider the protests and divisions associated with Italy's decision to enter the war in 1915.

A Level Exam-Style Question Section B

To what extent did the social and political tensions that existed within liberal Italy increase during the First World War? (20 marks)

Tip
You need to consider the impact of the war on either adding to or lessening tension in Italy. You may want to consider problems within liberal Italy before the First World War.

ACTIVITY
SUMMARY

1 **Comprehension and summary: Italy in 1918**
You are a foreign diplomat in 1918 who has been asked to write a report on the situation in Italy. Write two paragraphs summarising your views. What are the main issues facing Italy and its parliament that you are most concerned about?

2 **Analysis and argument**
Analyse and discuss how each of the following factors damaged the Italian liberal system. Which of these factors do you consider the most damaging and why? Can you find any links between these factors?

- Refusal of the Catholic Church to recognise the Italian state.
- Industrialisation and the growing gap between the north and south.
- Creation of ANI in 1910.
- Libyan War in 1912.
- Introduction of wider suffrage in 1912.
- Failure of Giolitti's programme and his resignation in 1914.
- Battle of Caporetto in 1917.

WIDER READING

Clark, M. *Modern Italy 1871–1995*, Longman (1996) is very good for understanding the specific problems of liberal Italy and why Giolitti's programme failed

Duggan, C. *The Force of Destiny: A History of Italy since 1796*, Penguin (2008) is an excellent place to start for an overall understanding of Italy, particularly the *Risorgimento* and the problems that arose after unification, which Giolitti and the liberals tried to solve

Lyttelton, A. (ed.) *Liberal and Fascist Italy: 1900–1945*, Oxford University Press (2002) is a collection of essays that also provides an excellent analysis of liberal Italy

2a.2 The rise of Mussolini and the creation of a fascist dictatorship, 1919–26

KEY QUESTIONS

- How effective was the government in dealing with Italy's problems following the First World War?
- What were the key aspects of fascism's development from 1919 to 1922?
- How far was fascism's rise to power due to the leadership of Mussolini between 1920 and 1922?
- To what extent was the creation of a fascist dictatorship between 1922 and 1926 due to the mistakes of Mussolini's political opposition?

INTRODUCTION

'Sire, I bring you the Italy of Vittorio Veneto.' With these words, Mussolini greeted the king at their meeting on 30 October 1922, the day he was appointed prime minister of Italy. As you know, the Battle of Vittorio Veneto was Italy's great victory over Austria-Hungary at the end of the First World War, and Mussolini's choice of words clearly demonstrated his desire to link his fascist movement to Italy's victory. For the fascists, the First World War had been the key event that had prompted their formation and helped propel them to power. The years 1918 to 1922 saw unprecedented turbulence in the Italian state. The failure of the liberal government at the Versailles settlement left a legacy of bitterness. In 1919, the government was further humiliated when the nationalist poet, Gabriele d'Annunzio, along with only 300 ex-soldiers, seized the contested area of Fiume, which Italy had failed to gain at Versailles. Economic problems stemming from the war affected Italians across the country. Politically, many in the middle and upper classes in Italian society feared possible revolution as the Socialist Party made significant gains in both local and national elections. Workers inspired by the Russian Revolution occupied factories and widespread strikes paralysed the nation. Traditional politics appeared to offer no solution and despite two elections and the creation of new parties there was very little political change. Within this context of growing discontent and fear, Benito Mussolini formed the Fasci di Combattimento, a new political movement that promised to save Italy from communist revolution and restore the country to international greatness. Importantly, they represented many in society, particularly ex-soldiers, who were angry that Italy's great victory in the First World War had been squandered by the government. Although they began as a small group on the political extreme, they would take power within three years of forming and fundamentally transform the country.

March 1919 – Fasci di Combattimento founded by Benito Mussolini

June 1919 – Italy fails to achieve territorial gains at the Versailles Treaty. This is dubbed the 'mutilated victory' by the opponents of the liberal government

September 1919 – Gabriele d'Annunzio and his followers seize the port of Fiume

September 1920 – Workers seize control of many northern factories. Strikes end after government compromise with unions and workers

May 1921 – General election in Italy. Fascists make breakthrough, winning seven percent of the vote. Mussolini and 34 other fascists enter parliament

August 1921 – Mussolini signs Pact of Pacification with the socialist trade union and PSI parliamentary leader. Mussolini resigns as leader of the fascist movement

November 1921 – Mussolini reinstated as leader and formalises the fascist movement into an official party known as the Partita Nazionale Fascista (PNF)

1919	1920	1921	1922

November 1919 – National election. Socialist PSI and Catholic PPI win the majority of the votes but can't work together to form a government leaving the liberal politicians still in power

1919–20 – Biennio Rosso ('Two Red Years') take place as socialists and communists encourage considerable unrest across Italy

1920–22 – Considerable fascist violence across Italy as the squads attack socialist and communist politicians and their political offices and newspapers, weakening their political power

October 1922 – Fascists take control of many northern cities through violence and plan a march on Rome to seize power in Italy

30 October 1922 – Mussolini appointed prime minister of Italy by the king. First Mussolini cabinet only has four fascists

November 1922 – Parliament approves year-long emergency powers for Mussolini by 306:116 votes

December 1922 – Mussolini creates the Fascist Grand Council

HOW EFFECTIVE WAS THE GOVERNMENT IN DEALING WITH ITALY'S PROBLEMS FOLLOWING THE FIRST WORLD WAR?

The 'mutilated victory'

The First World War had a profound effect on Italy. The economic and political impact caused fear, resentment and a desire for change among many Italians. Divisions between differing Italian classes were accentuated and violence between political groups rocked the country. The disappointment with the liberal government and what had been achieved following the war created growing anger, particularly in the ex-soldiers who felt betrayed and humiliated and desired a new Italy that would achieve the national greatness they believed they had been fighting for. At the end of the First World War, Italy's government faced several key problems. The campaign against Austria had been sustained through foreign loans and the printing of more money. Now the economy was suffering from debt and inflation. There was rising tension in the south as returning conscripts pushed for the land reform they had been promised during the war. Demobilised soldiers in the south forcibly occupied hundreds of thousands of hectares of farming land. In the industrial north, there was a growing divide between the returning soldiers and the workers who had been exempted from military service in order to maintain the industries needed for the war effort. To many of the soldiers, these workers were simply cowards and shirkers who had stayed behind and got wealthier while the soldiers had risked their lives for Italy on the front line. It was clear that the war had not achieved the unity that those who had originally supported intervention had hoped for.

This disquiet and anger in Italian society was made worse by Italy's treatment at the Paris Peace Conference at Versailles in January 1919. The new prime minister of Italy, Vittorio Orlando, argued that Italy should be given all the territory it had been promised in the 1915 Treaty of London, plus the port of Fiume on the Croatian coast. Fiume had a large community of Italians and Orlando claimed it should be part of Italy based on the 'principle of nationality'. This, however, was a fairly weak argument as the majority of Fiume was not Italian. The key leaders at Versailles were the American president, Woodrow Wilson, and the British and French prime ministers, David Lloyd George and Georges Clemenceau respectively. They had a condescending attitude towards Italy and clearly did not see it as deserving of 'great power' status. To Orlando's horror, they not only rejected Italy's claim on Fiume but also aspects of the Treaty of London, including the Dodecanese Islands and parts of the Balkans. They asserted that Italy's contribution to the war did not justify its territorial claims. Orlando argued that he needed to acquire this territorial expansion to justify the war effort to the Italian people and avoid mass protests, anarchy and possible revolution. Orlando claimed that he faced assassination if he could not secure Dalmatia for Italy and his foreign minister, Sonnino, feared that their failure would lead the country into anarchy. Violent clashes were already taking place in Italy as rumours of a 'mutilated victory' were reported by Italian papers. Orlando pleaded with Lloyd George, 'I must have a solution. Otherwise I will have a crisis in parliament or in the streets of Italy.'

His pleas were, however, ignored and Orlando decided to walk out of the conference in April. Although this improved his popularity in Italy, it simply weakened his position at Versailles. In his absence, Britain and France took Germany's African colonies for themselves with no consideration of Italy's demands. When Orlando tried to return in May, his proposals were ignored and he was forced to accept that he could not achieve the territory he had argued Italy should be given. In June, he was forced to resign as Italy's prime minister. Italy had actually acquired Trent and Trieste as part of the Treaty of London and further occupied

January 1923 – Mussolini creates Fascist Militia which incorporates the fascist squads

February 1923 – ANI amalgamates with the PNF

July 1923 – Acerbo Law, voted through by parliament, guarantees two-thirds of the parliamentary seats to whichever party wins the biggest proportion of votes in an election

January 1925 – Mussolini announces to Italian parliament that he will be enforcing a fascist dictatorship. Arrests and forced closers of antifascist organisations follow

November 1925 – New press censorship introduced

December 1925 – Title of prime minister officially changed to head of government and duce of fascism

1923	1924	1925	1926

April 1924 – General election. Fascists win 66 percent of the vote, gaining 374 of the 535 deputies in parliament

June 1924 – PSI leader Giacomo Matteotti murdered by fascist squad. Opposition MPs leave parliament as a protest

July 1924 – Press censorship introduced and opposition meetings banned

January 1926 – Mussolini granted the right to rule by decree without consultation with parliament

November 1926 – Opposition parties banned

Istria and northern Dalmatia, which would officially become Italian territory in 1920. However, the failure to gain Fiume or any of Germany's colonial territories in Africa undermined the liberal government. According to poet and novelist Gabriele d'Annunzio, it was a 'mutilated victory', a national shame that had disgraced the 600,000 soldiers who had lost their lives in the war. It demonstrated the weakness of the liberal government and Italy's lowly position in relation to the other European powers.

The situation was not helped by the actions of Orlando's replacement, Francesco Nitti. Italy's economy was weak and it needed the coal and money that only the Allies could provide, therefore Nitti chose to play down Italy's claims so as not to jeopardise Italy's relationship with Britain, France and the USA. He thus allowed the newly formed nation of Yugoslavia to take Dalmatia, and Fiume to be deemed a neutral city under the protection of the **League of Nations**. He also reduced military spending and issued an amnesty to those Italian soldiers who had deserted during the First World War. These actions drew considerable anger and disgust from the nationalists and the military, who condemned Nitti as the *Cagoia* (abject coward). The fascists would focus on the 'mutilated victory' as a key aspect of their appeal to the Italian people. Mussolini argued that Italy required a stronger government that would not back down like the weak liberals and would instead fight to regain Italy's former glory and ensure that such humiliation could never happen again. This was a popular message given the widespread anger that existed in Italy towards the Versailles settlement.

SOURCE

From Gaetano Salvemini, *The Fascist Dictatorship in Italy*, 1928. Salvemini, an antifascist academic and member of the PSI, left Italy in 1925, after being arrested for opposing Mussolini. He continued to be a strong antifascist voice outside Italy. Here he describes the power of the 'mutilated victory' myth and the problems it caused for the Italian liberal government.

To all these causes of post-war neurasthenia [fatigue and anxiety] was added another – the worst of all. The war was hardly over when the General Staffs of the army and the navy, and the foreign office, organised a systematic propaganda to convince the people that President Wilson and the Allied Governments of France and England were robbing Italy of the fruits of victory, and that the sacrifices made in the war were in vain, since the Government could not carry out, in its entirety, the programme of territorial expansion that it considered necessary. The authors of this hysterical campaign and the Nationalists and Fascists who were their agents hoped to keep alive the war spirit of the Italian people, and to bring pressure to bear on the Allied Governments and President Wilson, during the interminable peace negotiations. The Allies and Wilson paid no heed to their threats, and the General Staffs and the Foreign Office succeeded only in working up a great part of the Italian middle and intellectual classes into a state of frenzy... Thus the spirit of sedition was fostered in the army and the Government became incapable of suppressing this disorder. Among the working classes this short-sighted policy had a disastrous result. Having been forced against their will into an appalling war lasting three and a half years, and disappointed in all the promise that had been made to them, the Italian people were now told that they had shed their blood in vain.

ACTIVITY
KNOWLEDGE CHECK

1 According to Salvemini (Source 1), who were the main authors of the 'mutilated victory' idea and what were the consequences of this?

2 Why do you think Salvemini argues that the 'mutilated victory' was the most damaging factor in Italy's post-war crisis? What evidence is there to support his argument?

The occupation of Fiume

Against a backdrop of economic problems and political turmoil, nationalist right-wing groups challenged the government in Rome. Predominately made up of returned soldiers and young men angry at the inadequacies of liberal Italy, they spoke of establishing a powerful new government that would assert Italy's greatness. They were particularly furious at the 'mutilated victory', which they believed had betrayed Italy's war dead. The most prominent right-wing leader was Gabriele d'Annunzio, who had led the protests that called for Italy's entry into the war in 1914. D'Annunzio believed that only war could rejuvenate Italy and help it reclaim its glorious past. In post-war Italy he was angered by what he believed was the failure of the weak government to achieve that vision. On 12 September 1919, he took action. With 2,000 men made up of ex-soldiers, **Futurists**, students and patriots, he seized the contested port of Fiume without a fight. For many Italians, Fiume was the greatest example of Italy's humiliating treatment at the Versailles conference. D'Annunzio presented his occupation as redemption for Italy's dead soldiers, the capture of Fiume having overcome some of the shame of the 'mutilated victory'. Scared of d'Annunzio's popularity, the Italian government failed to act for 15 months. Eventually, d'Annunzio and his small army were removed by the Italian navy on Christmas Day 1920.

Despite having little to do with Mussolini, the occupation of Fiume was a crucial episode in the rise of fascism. D'Annunzio's actions were popular across Italy. He had demonstrated the frailties of the Italian government and the success that could be achieved through violent and decisive action. He convinced many Italians

Futurists

Even before the formation of the fascist organisation by Mussolini in 1919, there were groups within Italy that shared similar values and provided the basis for right-wing nationalism's growth as a political idea. The most important of these groups was the Futurists. This was a cultural and artistic movement formed in 1909 by Filippo Tommaso Marinetti, which celebrated violence, patriotism and destruction, believing that war would bring about a new, more militaristic society. They despised the old liberal system, which they saw as corrupt and stale. They were furious at the 'mutilated victory' and called for an end to the weak democratic parties that had allowed Italy's humiliation. Futurists made up some of the founding members of the fascist movement although they would be ultimately disappointed that Mussolini did not take a more radical direction after the establishment of the dictatorship in 1926.

that the liberal government had been weak to accept the Treaty of Versailles and that it could be changed if Italy simply took what was rightfully theirs. The power that assertive nationalism could have over Italians was clearly understood by Benito Mussolini. He was, perhaps, the man who learned the most from the events at Fiume.

ACTIVITY
KNOWLEDGE CHECK

What impression does Source 2 give of the occupation of Fiume by D'Annunzio's army?

Gabriele d'Annunzio (1863–1938)

At the time of the First World War, Gabriele d'Annunzio was Italy's most famous poet. An extreme nationalist, he led the protests calling for Italy's entry into the First World War. He believed that the war would mobilise the Italian nation and bring about a new, unified, more militaristic country. He was a brilliant speaker and understood the popular appeal of nationalism as a means of mobilising the Italian public against the liberal system, which he despised. During the war he became even more famous for his desire to fight for Italy (he lost an eye in battle) and his daring plane flight, where he dropped 400,000 propaganda leaflets over Vienna. At the Paris Peace Conference at Versailles, Italy's prime minister, Orlando warned Lloyd George that unless he was given the territory he sought, he may be replaced by a populist, right-wing government led by d'Annunzio. Disgusted by the 'mutilated victory' and the weakness of liberal Italy, d'Annunzio led the occupation of Fiume in 1919. The occupation was widely popular in Italy and demonstrated to Mussolini the power of direct actions, which appealed to populist national sentiment. Mussolini also appreciated the imagery that d'Annunzio built up around his movement. The fascist anthem *Giovinezza* ('Youth Time'), the wearing of black shirts, the fascist chant *Eia, eia alala!*, the carrying of daggers, the fascist slogan *Me ne frego* (in English 'I don't give a damn') and emotional speeches, which talked of the power of violence to change Italy, were all first used by d'Annunzio. While Mussolini learned from d'Annunzio's popularity, he was also worried about this potential rival for the leadership of Italy. Eventually, however, Mussolini would triumph as the cleverer politician of the two and d'Annunzio was skilfully removed from his prominent position. As prime minister of Italy, Mussolini honoured d'Annunzio with the title of 'Prince', gave him a magnificent villa on Lake Garda and paid him a large state pension every year. D'Annunzio was happy to accept this as payment for avoiding politics and he faded into the background until his death in 1938.

SOURCE
2 Thousands in Fiume celebrate a march of d'Annunzio's forces during their occupation of the town, 1 December 1920.

Post-war economic crisis and social discontent

Italy's economy was also in a difficult situation as the government attempted to adjust to the post-war world. Millions of soldiers were demobilised, flooding the job market, and by November 1919 unemployment reached two million. Inflation was at a high level and the lira collapsed in value. Middle-class Italians saw their savings wiped out and state employees' wages and pensions declined rapidly. Major companies such as Fiat, Ansaldo and Ilva, which had benefited from the war, struggled to stay afloat now the war had ended. The two major munitions companies, Ansaldo and Ilva, collapsed in 1921, causing a banking crisis as one of Italy's major banks, Banca di Sconto, which was closely tied to Ansaldo, was forced to close. This was compounded by considerable labour militancy and strikes which took place between 1919 and 1920, a period known as the **Biennio Rosso**. The conclusion of the war saw the release of anarchist and socialist radicals who had been jailed during the First World War. Inspired by events in Russia, there was a considerable campaign calling for greater worker rights and possible revolution. Italy was rocked by major strikes, factory occupations and violent riots. Membership of the socialist unions had grown from 250,000 in 1918 to two million by 1920. In 1919, rising food prices had caused riots in northern and central Italy where protestors looted shops and granaries. There were railway strikes in January 1920, telegraph worker strikes in April and September of the same year and, most worryingly, an army troops' strike in July. The largest strike took place in September 1920 with over 400,000 workers taking over factories, flying the red flags of communism and the black flags of anarchism over the buildings for nearly four weeks. The government eventually ended the strike and was able to calm the industrial situation but for many Italians, particularly the upper and middle classes, Italy was facing chaos and possible revolution. Their concern about Italy was heightened by recession in late 1920 and the fact that Italy's economy appeared to be close to collapse.

KEY TERM

Biennio Rosso
Roughly translates to 'Two Red Years' and is used to define the period of political turmoil in Italy between 1919 and 1920 when left-wing socialist and communist organisations were at their peak. The Biennio Rosso was crucial for Mussolini's ascension to power. The chaos and fear it created in Italy, particularly in the middle classes, encouraged certain classes to look towards the fascists who were violently confronting the left-wing movement. This contrasted with the liberal government who was trying to find a compromise solution to the workers' grievances.

The countryside mirrored the social and economic discontent. The government had made sweeping promises concerning land reform to the peasants who fought in the First World War. While some land was made available for peasants to purchase, it was not enough to satisfy the numbers demanding land for farming. Many peasants seized land from the owners, who were mostly absent, by simply marching on to barren or uncultivated land, raising flags and setting to work. Land occupations alarmed the wealthy landowners who feared a rural revolution. Rural socialist unions were particularly strong in areas like Ferrara and Bologna where they controlled the employment of rural labourers, excluding farming labourers who were not members of the socialist union, and in many cases carrying out violent attacks on those workers and farm owners who refused to join. Landowners felt threatened by the rising power of rural socialist militancy and were angered by the weak government response.

In both rural and industrial areas, Italy appeared to be in the middle of a social and economic breakdown and the seizure of power by left-wing forces appeared imminent. Many in the upper and middle classes looked towards right-wing organisations that would provide an alternative to the weak liberal government and instead confront and destroy the left-wing organisations that were pushing Italy towards revolution.

Political reforms

The Italian parliamentary elections of 1919 took place against a backdrop of political and economic upheaval. The government hoped that it could ease the public anger through political reforms that would allow more Italians to play a role in the political system. The amount of people able to vote was increased by 11 million. This was achieved by introducing a new law that all Italians who had served at the front and any other male over 21 could now participate in elections. The government also changed the method of voting to **proportional representation** so that the public vote would have greater influence on which parties got elected to parliament.

KEY TERM

Proportional representation
A voting system where the number of representatives elected into parliament is proportional to the percentage of votes a party receives. It is different to the British voting system of 'first past the post' where only one representative is elected for each area. Although it provides a broader representation than 'first past the post', it is extremely difficult for any one party to win a majority in parliament and this can mean a more unstable parliamentary system if parties are not willing to work with each other to pass legislation, as happened in Italy to some extent.

Growth of the socialist and Catholic parties

The problems Italy faced both socially and economically may have been solved by a stronger government but changes to Italian politics weakened parliament and the liberal order even further. The most critical change had been the formation of a Catholic political party, the Partito Popolare Italiano (PPI), in 1919. It was not officially affiliated to the Vatican and did not mention the 'Roman Question' in its manifesto. However, it was led by a priest, Luigi Sturzo, and its policy pushed for Catholic interests and values. It was a major supporter of land reform and campaigned for more farming areas to be made available to Italy's peasants. The strength of Catholic feeling and the popular agitation for land reform made the PPI a strong political force and its hostility to the liberal regime meant that the formation of coalitions in the style of Giolitti was now much more difficult. The political situation was further complicated by the growing power of the PSI. The war and the revolution in Russia had encouraged the PSI in a more radical direction and the party now refused to work with the liberals, instead calling for an Italian revolution. It supported strikes and factory occupations and the days of Giolitti 'absorption' that would encourage the PSI to work with the liberals were clearly over.

Result and impact of elections, 1919

The political reforms introduced had a critical impact on the 1919 election and for the first time the PSI won the greatest share of the vote with 32 percent. This resulted in 156 socialist deputies taking their place in parliament; three times what they won in the previous election of 1913. The next biggest party was the newly formed PPI, supported by the Catholic Church, which won 101 seats. Despite this development neither party had a full majority nor were they willing to work with each other in a coalition. This meant that the old liberals still retained power, putting together several coalition governments that ruled Italy until 1922. This was a dangerous failure for democracy. Despite improvements in the voting system and the growing popularity of the PSI and PPI, the same political groups that had ruled Italy from 1860 remained in power. Nothing appeared to have changed at all. Given the problems in Italy and the anger of the Italian people towards the old political system, the 1919 election was a lost opportunity to show that democracy could help solve Italy's problems.

Now more and more Italians were beginning to question whether a radical political system, either on the right or left of politics, might be a better answer to Italy's post-war struggles. Nitti's government fell in June 1920 and once again parliament turned towards Giolitti to lead the country away from impending social, economic and political meltdown.

ACTIVITY
KNOWLEDGE CHECK

1 Create a spider diagram setting out the key issues affecting Italy from November 1918 to 1920.

2 Historians have called the 1919 election 'democracy's last chance'. What do you think they mean by this? Why was the fact that the old liberals remained in power particularly damaging for democracy?

3 Once you have completed your analysis on Italy's post-war crisis, return to Salvemini's analysis in Source 1. Do you agree with his argument on what was the most damaging factor to the liberal government? Explain why.

WHAT WERE THE KEY ASPECTS OF FASCISM'S DEVELOPMENT FROM 1919 TO 1922?

Foundation of the Fasci di Combattimento and the party programme

On 23 March 1919, Benito Mussolini, former soldier, PSI member and editor of *Avanti!*, called together the representatives of around 20 ex-servicemen's leagues to Milan to form the national organisation of ex-soldiers, the Fasci di Combattimento or **Fasci**. As previously discussed, Mussolini had begun his political life as a strong socialist, but now he was moving towards the right wing, seeking to establish a new movement driven by ex-soldiers who wanted to create the Italy they believed they had been fighting for. His experiences in the trenches had allowed Mussolini to see the power of war to bring Italians together. The extreme nature of the war and the camaraderie felt by those fighting together produced a mutual feeling of belonging that Mussolini had not seen elsewhere. Here, divisions between north and south, upper and lower classes, industrialists and peasants melted away and all that mattered was that they were fighting for Italy and each other. Mussolini described this as '*trincerocrazia*', the rule of the trenches where men were linked by their war consciousness. Mussolini argued that post-war Italy would not be divided geographically or economically, but instead between those who fought and those who stayed at home during the war. It was the *trinceristi*, the returned soldiers, who had the strength and moral right to lead a new Italy that would replicate the patriotic feeling of togetherness they had experienced in the war. Through the formation of the Fasci di Combattimento, Mussolini hoped to destroy the liberal order and create a *trincerocrazia* that would rule Italy.

The party's programme was quite vague at this stage, but it is clear that Mussolini's socialist background had a considerable effect on policy. By June the Fasci di Combattimento had set out a programme that was anticlerical and wanted the confiscation of church property, called for an end to the monarchy and the formation of a republic, suffrage to be extended to women and younger Italians, the establishment of an eight-hour working day and the abolition of the senate. It demanded nationalisation of the armaments industry, progressive taxation and the confiscation of profits from those companies that had made large profits from the war. The major problem with this political programme was that it did not distinguish the fasci from other left-wing parties, particularly the PSI. Although only around 50 attended the original meeting, the party grew quite quickly and had reached around 3,000 members by June. It was predominately made up of *arditi*, crack troop commandos who had been formed in the First World

EXTEND YOUR KNOWLEDGE

Fasci

The word fascio (plural fasci) derives from the Latin word *fasces* and simply refers to the ancient Roman emblem of a bundle of wooden rods bound together with an axe, symbolising strength through unity. The concept is that many sticks bound together are stronger than one stick on its own. From the late 19th century, the word began to be used more in terms of a group, union or league associated with a political movement, the first being the Fasci Siciliani in 1891 who fought for greater political and social rights for Sicilians. There were numerous different fasci formed across Italy over the following years, the Fasci di Combattimento (the league of ex-soldiers) being just one of them. The Fasci di Combattimento under Mussolini was, however, the most prominent and successful group to use the term fasci and over time Mussolini was able to claim exclusive use of the word 'fascism' to define the political programme and beliefs of his political movement. This was cemented when Mussolini formalised the fascist movement into the Partito Nazionale Fascista in October 1921, creating the first Italian political party to use the term 'fascist'.

SOURCE 3

Mussolini speaking at the first meeting of the Fasci di Combattimento in Milan, 23 March 1919, where he set out three declarations. From *Mussolini as Revealed in his Political Speeches*, translated and edited by Barone Bernardo Quaranta di San Severino, 1923.

The first declaration is as follows: The meeting of the 23rd March first salutes with reverence and remembrance the sons of Italy who have fallen for the cause of the greatness of the country and the liberty of the world, the maimed and disabled, and all the fighters and ex-prisoners who fulfilled their duty, and declares itself ready to uphold strongly the vindication of rights, both material and moral, advocated by the 'Association of Fighters.'

Second declaration: The meeting of the 23rd March declares that it will oppose Imperialism in other peoples which would be prejudicial to Italy, and any eventual Imperialism in Italy which would be prejudicial to other nations, and accepts the fundamental principle of the League of Nations, which presupposes the geographical integrity of every nation. This, as far as Italy is concerned, must be realised on the Alps and the Adriatic with the annexation of Fiume and Dalmatia.

Third declaration: The meeting of the 23rd March pledges the Fascisti to prevent by every means in their power the candidature of neutralists of any party. [This refers to those who did not support Italy's intervention in the First World War.]

AS Level Exam-Style Question Section A

Why is Source 3 valuable to the historian for an enquiry into the objectives of the Fasci di Combattimento when it was established in 1919?

Explain your answer using the source, the information given about it and your own knowledge of the historical context. (8 marks)

Tip
Think about Mussolini's priorities at the beginning of his political movement. How does this help to comprehend the goals of the Fasci di Combattimento when it was founded in 1919?

War after the disaster at Caporetto. During the war they had worn a black uniform that defined them as different from other soldiers and their emblem was a black flag with a white skull gripping a dagger in its teeth. Others within the party began to adopt this imagery and soon the black shirts and flag became the identity of the entire fascist movement and members of the Fascist Party were commonly known as the 'blackshirts'.

Squadrismo and the move to the right

The experiences of the war had also created a strong culture of violence among the returning soldiers. They perceived the socialists and the workers participating in strike action as no different from the enemy they had fought in the First World War. The socialists and communists were an internal enemy who were as much a threat to the Italian state as the Austrians had been. The fascists formed themselves into small, military units or squads. This organisation was known as *squadrismo* and the members, or *squadristi*, answered the socialist threat through the only means they believed in: extreme violence. On 15 April 1919, a fascist

squad of around 200 to 300, dressed in black and carrying pistols, attacked a socialist demonstration in Milan and burned down the Milan offices of *Avanti!*. Three socialists and one fascist were killed. Mussolini had not organised or authorised the violence in Milan, but he soon came to realise what a powerful tool it could be.

The fascists had done extremely poorly in the 1919 election, winning less than 5,000 votes and no seats in parliament. Mussolini had seriously considered his political future in Italy and had been humiliated as socialists paraded a coffin symbolising his political career through the streets of Milan. However, the success of *squadristi* violence revealed to Mussolini a different path to power. After the violence in Milan, none of the fascist squad was arrested and the government made no attempt to close down the fascists or condemn their actions. It was clear to Mussolini that the police, army and the government were prepared to tolerate *squadristi* violence because of their fears of a socialist revolution. Mussolini encouraged the formation of more armed squads across Italy. These squads were organised like military units under a commanding officer known as a *ras*. Members wore the uniform of the black shirt and mainly carried a revolver and a *manganello* (club) as their weapons. They attacked socialist councils and supporters across Italy in an attempt to weaken their power. Importantly, many of their weapons were supplied by the local police and army barracks. Key PSI members were targeted specifically. Many were beaten and forced to drink castor oil, although there were many cases of murder. It is estimated that in the first five months of 1921, 200 people were killed and 1,000 wounded in fascist violence against the socialists. The violence not only broke the power of the socialists across Italy but it helped create the myth of fascism – that their 'war' against the socialists had 'saved' Italy from revolution.

The movement was particularly popular in the countryside where wealthy landowners were happy to see the socialist land leagues destroyed and the attempt to bring about land reform for the peasantry ended. The soldiers had saved Italy once from the Austrians; now, within the fascist movement, they had saved Italy from the 'traitors' and 'radicals' who had sought to destroy the country from the inside. This was a powerful idea that would be a key part of fascist propaganda. The fascist failure in the 1919 election and the popularity of the fascist action against the socialists among Italians who feared a revolution, mainly the middle classes, but also powerful elements of the Italian ruling elite such as the military, encouraged Mussolini to take the fascist movement more definitely to the right.

Political legitimacy

Fascism began to achieve a greater political legitimacy. Respectable liberal politicians who feared the socialist threat shared the belief that the squads were restoring law and order to Italy and rescuing the country from radicalism and the fate of Russia in 1917. Police stood by and allowed the fascists to attack the socialists, sometimes evenly actively joining in. The success of the violence against socialism and the shift to the right was shown in the general election held in May 1921. The fascists made use of the squads to attack socialist campaign meetings and intimidate

SOURCE 4

From a speech by Mussolini in Bologna on 3 April 1921. Here, Mussolini explains to his fascist followers why the violence of the squads is necessary and why the socialists are a greater danger to Italy than the liberals. From *Mussolini as Revealed in his Political Speeches*, translated and edited by Barone Bernardo Quaranta di San Severino, 1923.

And, however much violence may be deplored, it is evident that we, in order to make our ideas understood, must beat refractory skulls with resounding blows.

But we do not make a school, a system, or worse still, an aesthetic [sense of beauty] of violence. We are violent when it is necessary to be so. But I tell you at once that this necessary violence on the part of the Fascisti must have a character and style of its own, definitely aristocratic, or, if you prefer, surgical.

Our punitive expeditions, all those acts of violence which figure in the papers, must always have the character of a just retort and legitimate reprisal; because we are the first to recognise that it is sad, after having fought the external enemy, to have to fight the enemy within, who, whether they like it or not, are Italians. But it is necessary, and as long as it is necessary, we shall continue to carry out this hard and thankless task…

The Socialists had formed a State within a State… But this State, and you know it by direct experience, is more tyrannical, illiberal and overbearing than the old one; and for this reason that which we are causing today is a revolution to break up the Bolshevist State, while waiting to settle our accounts with the Liberal State which remains. (Applause).

voters. The police lent vehicles and the army gave weapons to the fascists to help this campaign and the Italian judiciary showed particular leniency to any fascists brought before the courts for attacks against the socialists. Although the PSI still achieved the highest vote, the fascists achieved an electoral breakthrough, winning seven percent of the vote and 35 parliamentary seats. Although not as high as Mussolini had hoped, the election result was crucial in two ways. Firstly, it gave Mussolini a new respectability and authority as a member of parliament, legitimising fascism as a political force. Secondly, as a deputy, Mussolini benefited from immunity to prosecution. A police charge against Mussolini for 'intent to overthrow the government by violence' was now quietly dropped.

The PNF and the 'New Programme'

In May 1920, at the second fascist national congress, a 'New Programme' was adopted. This was much more conservative and right wing, dropping any mentions of removing the monarchy or attacking the power of the pope. References to the nationalisation of businesses were removed, and a more pro-business attitude taken, with the fascists now promising to sell off nationally owned businesses to private investors. The New Programme was also more militaristic in tone, calling for compulsory military service, the goal of complete unification of the Italian *irredente* and an education system that would provide Italy's future soldiers with physical and moral training. Fascism's rise was advanced further in October 1921 when the movement was organised into a formal political party called the Partito Nazionale Fascista (PNF). Through this, Mussolini tried to centralise his control over the fascist movement, as opposed to a wide, disparate conglomeration of radical squads. The PNF founded local branches and attempted to recruit more 'respectable members' who might help advance fascism's appeal beyond the appreciation among certain classes of Italians for the violence used against the socialists.

Nature and extent of fascist support

By the end of 1921, the PNF had grown to around 200,000 members. Support for fascism came from a wide scope within Italian society and it is difficult to define specifically who its supporters were. The PNF's appeal to the urban middle class, professional white-collar workers and small business owners was particularly strong. These Italians feared not only a potential socialist revolution, but also the increase in local taxes the PSI might try to implement. In the countryside, the middle and upper classes of landowners, as well as the wealthier farmers and peasants, saw the fascists as a means of protecting their lifestyle from the socialist agitation for greater land reform. Financial support came from the richer landowners and Italian industrialists who supported fascism's attempts to break union power and socialism throughout Italy. However, fascism also appealed to some workers and peasant farmers who opposed the strength of the socialists and the violence used against those labourers who wanted to continue working during the strikes. Many young Italians who had grown tired of the corruption and lethargy of the old liberal order saw fascism as a new, dynamic alternative that might bring about a revitalised society. Fascism could claim to be the first genuinely national party in Italy in its ability to appeal to both men and women across differing classes, regions and ages. This broad band of support was united by several key aspects: strong patriotism, a hatred of the socialists and the weak liberal government, and a belief in Mussolini as the man who could sweep away the decaying, weak Italy and lead the country to a new, stronger, more nationally united future that reclaimed the glory achieved in the country's military victory during the First World War.

EXTEND YOUR KNOWLEDGE

The problem with fascism as an ideology

As you have read, fascism began as a movement that had quite left-wing policies in 1919, yet by 1921 had formalised into a political party with a conservative, right-wing political agenda. Mussolini understood that a right-wing programme, which focused on the key ideas of nationalism and anticommunism, gave him a greater chance for power than remaining on the left. However, this questions what exactly fascism was. You may decide that fascism was nothing more than a means to power for Mussolini and was never a coherent ideology with a stable base of political beliefs. His policies towards the Vatican and big business, for example, changed numerous times from 1919 to 1945, depending on what gave him the greatest political benefit. One of the key problems is that Mussolini did not really try to define exactly what fascism was until 1932 in an essay entitled 'La dottrina del fascismo' (later published as *The Doctrine of Fascism*) and even this is very confusing and difficult to understand. This question of what exactly defines fascism continues to be a lively debate between historians.

ACTIVITY
KNOWLEDGE CHECK

1 Read through Source 4. In only one sentence, summarise why violence was so critical to the fascist movement.

2 To what extent was fascism a broad movement that appealed to a broad section of the Italian population? Consider differing groups within Italian society and the reasons why fascism appealed to them specifically.

3 Many historians have argued that the Biennio Rosso was the most important factor in fascism's rise to power. What evidence is there to support this argument? Why was the socialists' campaign after the First World War so critical to fascism's popular appeal?

4 Go back and re-examine Source 1, written by Salvemini. Do you still agree with his argument? Why or why not?

AS Level Exam-Style Question Section B

How accurate is it to say that fascist ideology changed considerably in the years 1919 to 1921? (20 marks)

Tip

With a question like this, avoid simply describing those aspects of fascism that changed and those that stayed the same. Instead, think about the key changes over the two years, as well as aspects that remained constant, and argue how far fascism changed.

HOW FAR WAS FASCISM'S RISE TO POWER DUE TO THE LEADERSHIP OF MUSSOLINI BETWEEN 1920 AND 1922?

Taking advantage of political unrest

Mussolini's rise to power was aided by a worsening political situation in Italy. The deteriorating economic situation, the lingering situation in Fiume and the ongoing strikes led to the resignation of Nitti on 9 June 1920. He was replaced by Giovanni Giolitti. While Giolitti's history appeared to make him the ideal politician to deal with the country's worsening crisis, it is important to note that at this stage he was 80 years old and despised by nationalist Italians due to his anti-interventionist policy during the First World War. Giolitti employed his old tactics of compromise and absorption to address the industrial unrest during the Biennio Rosso. His solution to the 1920 strike was to seek compromise for the workers, pressuring Italy's banks to withdraw support for companies that would not negotiate with the striking workers, refusing to use violence against the strikers and encouraging businesses to allow the workers shares in their companies and representatives on management boards. In the short term this was successful; by 25 September 1920, the strikes had ended. However, there was considerable anger from the middle classes, industrialists, nationalists, landowners and Catholics that Giolitti had 'given in' to the workers' demands. This contrasted strongly with the actions of the fascists who used violence to deal with the socialist threat. To their supporters, the fascists were the force that was 'fighting back' in order to stop revolution.

The political and social chaos in Italy helped the fascists. The PNF were further aided by the weakness of fascism's opposition. In January 1921, the more radical members of the PSI split to form the Partito Comunista Italiano (PCI) with support from Russia. The PCI was more radical in its aims for revolution and an end to the capitalist system in Italy. It was also more closely aligned with the Communist Party (Bolsheviks) that had taken power in Russia. The split in the PSI weakened the political strength of the left-wing movement. There was also a growing desire of many Italians for a more stable social and economic situation in Italy. Mussolini, however, claimed that the reason for the Biennio Rosso's failure was due to the actions of the fascists, and the myth that the party had 'saved Italy' from a left-wing revolution was a key part of fascism's appeal. Despite preaching the idea of revolution more vehemently than the PSI, the PCI was too small to provide a political threat via either the ballot box or revolution. However, the appearance of an official communist party that spoke of revolution and was financed by the Bolsheviks in Russia provided excellent propaganda for Mussolini. For the middle classes and industrialists, the formation of the PCI was proof that Italy was on the verge of revolution similar to that which Russia had experienced in 1917.

In July 1922, the PSI and PCI attempted to encourage further pressure on the political system by backing the call for a 24-hour general strike across Italy. Weary of further strike action, most workers did not support the new move and the strike faded out without taking place to any great extent. It was a crucial error by the left-wing parties. Mussolini claimed that the reason for the strike's failure was due to the actions of the fascists, and the myth that it was only the PNF that had spared Italy from revolution became more widely believed.

A further issue was that Giolitti's old tactics of compromise and *trasformismo* were proving inadequate in post-war Italy, where the ideological splits were more defined and deep rooted. Given the strong ideology of the newly formed parties such as the PNF, PPI and PCI, they were less likely to be 'bought off' and support Giolitti in parliament. With the increase in parties, it was more difficult to organise a working coalition that would provide a majority government. The parties despised each other and had no interest in working together in parliament. The PNF and PCI in particular wanted to see the political turmoil continue until parliament collapsed. During the 1921 election, Giolitti tried to 'asborb' the fascists by offering the members running for parliament a place in his 'national bloc' on the ballot paper. Giolitti hoped that fascism would be tamed, as he had done before with other parties, and incorporated within the constitutional parliament of Italy. This proved to be a serious mistake. Immediately after being voted into parliament as a government-backed candidate, Mussolini announced that he would vote with the opposition. The 1921 election was a disaster for Giolitti; parliament was now made up of 123 socialist, 15 communists, 107 PPI and 35 fascist deputies. It was impossible to form a stable government and Giolitti chose instead to resign, his *trasformismo* now obsolete in an era of universal suffrage and formal political parties. Giolitti was followed firstly by Ivanoe Bonomi and then Luigi Facta, both weak liberal politicians, who were unable to deal with the serious problems facing Italy.

Establishing a dual policy

The violence of the squads provided the basis for fascist strength and a possible means to overthrow parliament and seize power through force. However, Mussolini still held out hope that he could manoeuvre himself into the position of prime minister through parliamentary deals and thus take power through more constitutional channels. This dualistic approach was complicated by the difficult balancing act Mussolini had to make between the radical, revolutionary members of the PNF and those who were more conservative and wanted power through parliament. At first, Mussolini appeared to favour the more conservative members of the PNF. In July 1921, he called for an end to *squadristi* violence, concerned that with the fear of communist revolution fading, supporters among the middle classes and industrialists would begin to question why fascist violence was continuing when its aims had been achieved. In August, he made the startling step of signing the Pact of Pacification with the socialist trade union and PSI members in parliament. Mussolini asserted that such a pact was necessary to bring political and social peace to Italy at a time when the nation required it. Despite such lofty goals, the real reason was cynical political manoeuvring; Mussolini was hoping that the liberals and Catholics within parliament would come to a deal to stop him working with the socialists.

One of the key issues for Mussolini was that until October 1921, fascism was a movement, not an organised party. Mussolini was the leader of the movement but the multiple squads had a strong loyalty to their *ras*, who had built up extremely solid power bases in the provinces they had taken from the socialists. The squads were also funded at a local level, not by a centralised body. Mussolini's Pact of Pacification and the call for an end to the violence was also an attempt to assert his dominance over fascism and force the *ras* to follow his political direction. In this sense, Mussolini failed, overestimating his ability to control the *ras*. The three most powerful *ras* bosses, Dino Grandi, Italo Balbo and Roberto Farinacci, condemned the pact and meetings of *squadristi* were held throughout Italy, calling for an end to the deal with the hated socialists. Mussolini, however, showed his political skill by asserting that, as they were not prepared to follow his policy direction, he would resign as leader of the fascists and, on 18 August, he followed through on this threat. However, this was simply another political manoeuvre. Without Mussolini's leadership, the fascists lacked unity or direction. The *ras* were unable to work together to formulate policy and Mussolini's absence as leader consequently strengthened his position by demonstrating how crucial he was to the party.

Mussolini, like Giolitti had been, was also particularly skilful at buying off potential opponents within the party, understanding exactly what could be offered to gain their loyalty. Grandi was offered a prominent role on a new fascist journal and consequently confirmed his support for Mussolini. At the PNF conference in November 1921, fascist delegates overwhelmingly voted to support Mussolini as leader and confirm the organisation of the movement into an official party. This was particularly important. Mussolini's strategic resignation had confirmed the importance of his leadership to the party. Without him, they lacked the vision, charisma and unity that he provided. Grandi and Balbo had taken the step of approaching d'Annunzio, asking him to lead the fascists, but he had refused. With d'Annunzio's refusal, it was clear to the *ras* that there was nobody of the same stature as Mussolini who was willing to lead the party. Crucially, Mussolini had won a significant victory over the *ras*, who were now clearly subordinate to him. The programme of the PNF confirmed that the *squadristi* were ultimately under the control of the party leadership, not the *ras*. The only concession Mussolini was forced to make was to drop the Pact of Pacification. This was hardly a problem as, by October 1921, Mussolini had come to believe that instead of compromise and political deals, the best means to gain power appeared to be through *squadristi* violence. Now, instead of trying to stop it, he actively encouraged an upsurge in fascist violence, hoping he could use this to blackmail the government into giving him power.

At the end of 1921, the squads were more formally organised, being grouped into so-called 'cohorts' under the command of 'consuls'. These 'consuls' were then organised under zone commanders. From spring 1922, fascist violence expanded. Blackshirts attacked areas across Italy where the socialists controlled the local council. Town after town in northern Italy fell to the fascists. Mussolini was helped by the inadequate response of the liberal government. Bonomi's government collapsed in February 1922 and was replaced by Luigi Facta, a weak and complacent prime minister. Fascist violence surged, with the *ras*, Italo Balbo, leading squads through Rimini to Bertinoro on the east coast of Italy, destroying all houses and offices where the socialists and communists held meetings. By September, the squads had taken over areas around Rome and were ready to move on the capital. The government had done nothing to stop this fascist violence that was taking place across the country. The attempted July strike only played into fascism's hands. They kept some public services running with volunteers and asserted that they were saving the nation from the communist threat. With the socialists and communists in a weakened position, the squads launched new attacks in Genoa, Milan, Livorno, Ancona and Bari, murdering socialist leaders and supporters, burning offices and forcing left-wing councils to resign. Between May and October 1922, the fascists had become the *de facto* government in many of Italy's provinces.

The violence had not only strengthened their power but ultimately weakened Facta, who was unable or unwilling to stop it. By 1922, the PNF had grown to around 320,000 members and nearly half a million workers had joined fascist trade unions. The seizure of power appeared to be only a matter of time. Mussolini, however, still favoured his dual policy, pursuing this through September and October 1922. He promised that if the fascists were accepted within a government coalition, he would pursue a moderate conservative policy, backing the monarchy, reducing taxes and balancing the budget. At the same time, he encouraged squads to attack Bolzano and Trent. This was crucial as these towns were not held by socialist councils but by conservative liberals, thus Mussolini was now increasing the pressure by challenging the government itself. The liberal parliamentarians were divided on how to respond. Orlando called for a coalition that included fascism, as did Nitti, who asserted he would now accept an alliance with Mussolini. The problem was that both Orlando and Nitti hoped that an alliance with the fascists would help them become prime minister and refused to enter into any solution where that would not be the case. The key liberal figures, including Giolitti, were more concerned with stopping their rivals becoming prime minister than they were with avoiding a fascist revolution. Giolitti refused to travel to Rome to help Facta's government unless he was offered the prime ministership by the king. Mussolini cleverly encouraged this division, separately promising Nitti, Salandra, Facta and Giolitti that they would be prime minister in a fascist coalition government.

SOURCE

5

From a speech by Mussolini made on 30 October 1923 to party members.

For twenty, perhaps thirty, years, the Italian political class has been growing steadily more corrupt and degenerate. Parliamentarism – with all the stupid and demoralising associations that go with this word – had become a symbol of our life and the hallmark of our shame. There was no government: there were just men continually under the thumb of the so called ministerial majority... When people could read what were referred to as parliamentary proceedings and see what might be described as an exchange of the most banal insults between the so called representatives of the nation, they felt disgusted, and a sense of nausea welled up inside them.

ACTIVITY
KNOWLEDGE CHECK

1 What evidence could be used to back up Mussolini's argument in Source 5?

2 What does this speech demonstrate about Mussolini's skill as a political leader?

3 How do your answers to questions 1 and 2 help explain some of the reasons for Mussolini's rise to power?

THINKING HISTORICALLY Causation (5b)

Relativity

Historical events usually have many causes. Some are crucial, while some are less important. For some historical questions, it is important to understand exactly what role certain factors played in causing historical change.

Significant factors in the rise of fascism in Italy

Italian elites and middle classes feared that Italy was on the verge of a communist revolution similar to what took place in Russia in 1917.	Fascist violence was seen by many Italians as a strong means of confronting left-wing political groups and supporters that the government seemed unable or unwilling to stop.	Mussolini was a strong leader and powerful public speaker. He was able to maintain a clear political direction for the party despite the fact it was made up of many differing political elements.
Following the war, many Italians felt that Italy needed a new direction. The liberal system appeared old and unable to set out a political direction for Italy. Fascism set out a vision of a new, united Italy that would overcome the issues that faced the country.	Many within Italy's military and police leadership opposed the communists and socialists and would not act against fascist violence towards left-wing political parties and supporters.	The liberal parliamentary leaders were indecisive in how to deal with the rise of fascism. They mostly encouraged fascist violence hoping it would destroy their political opponents on the left. They then hoped they could form a parliamentary alliance with Mussolini.

Answer the following question on your own

1 The violence of the fascists.

   a) How important was fascist violence in explaining the movement's growing strength from 1919 to 1922?

   b) In what way did the actions of the socialists and communists contribute to fascism's rise in Italy?

   c) How important was the role of the military and the police?

2 The role of the First World War and the liberal parliamentary leaders.

   a) How far had the First World War undermined the liberal political system in Italy?

   b) What role did the war play in the popularity of fascism's vision for Italy?

   c) How far did liberal political leaders contribute to fascism's growing strength following the First World War?

3 What roles did each of the above causal factors play in the rise of fascism in Italy between 1919 and 1922?

The March on Rome and its significance

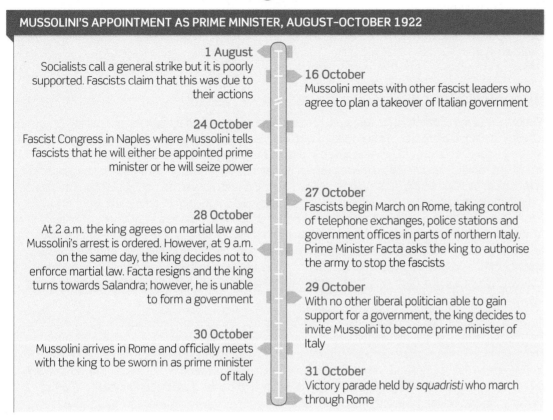

MUSSOLINI'S APPOINTMENT AS PRIME MINISTER, AUGUST–OCTOBER 1922

1 August
Socialists call a general strike but it is poorly supported. Fascists claim that this was due to their actions

16 October
Mussolini meets with other fascist leaders who agree to plan a takeover of Italian government

24 October
Fascist Congress in Naples where Mussolini tells fascists that he will either be appointed prime minister or he will seize power

27 October
Fascists begin March on Rome, taking control of telephone exchanges, police stations and government offices in parts of northern Italy. Prime Minister Facta asks the king to authorise the army to stop the fascists

28 October
At 2 a.m. the king agrees on martial law and Mussolini's arrest is ordered. However, at 9 a.m. on the same day, the king decides not to enforce martial law. Facta resigns and the king turns towards Salandra; however, he is unable to form a government

29 October
With no other liberal politician able to gain support for a government, the king decides to invite Mussolini to become prime minister of Italy

30 October
Mussolini arrives in Rome and officially meets with the king to be sworn in as prime minister of Italy

31 October
Victory parade held by *squadristi* who march through Rome

Despite his political skill, Mussolini was still in a difficult situation. The *ras* were now pushing for a march on Rome and the violent takeover of government. Mussolini, however, still saw an opportunity to be appointed prime minister constitutionally. He felt this was the better option as it would give him a stronger position, not only as leader of Italy, but also over his own party. He was also concerned about the military. He was unsure what their response would be and, despite the growth of fascism, Mussolini knew that the squads would not be able to stand up to an armed response from the army if the king ordered it to crush an armed uprising. On 24 October, Mussolini made a public speech in Naples to *squadristi* who had gathered there, asserting 'either we are allowed to govern or we will seize power by Marching on Rome'. Mussolini continued to hold talks with liberal politicians about the potential to form a coalition government, while at the same time, fascist squads were moving on Rome. On the night of 27 October, *squadrisiti* occupied government offices and telephone exchanges. Facta finally decided to take action, requesting that the king proclaim martial law and use the army to crush the fascist insurrection. On 28 October, the king was informed about the growing takeover by the fascists that had begun in Milan and was now spreading. He agreed with Facta's request for the declaration of a state of emergency and the use of the army to enforce martial law and stop the fascists. The army began to assume control in Milan and an order was drawn up for Mussolini's arrest. It appeared that the attempted fascist revolution would be halted at a very early stage. However, at around 9 a.m. on the same morning, the king suddenly changed his mind, refusing to sign the decree and declare a state of emergency. This was the critical move that would ensure fascist success.

The role of Victor Emmanuel III

King Victor Emmanuel III was a weak and indecisive man whose decision had been influenced by several factors. Primarily, he lacked confidence in Facta to control the situation. He had also been encouraged not to sign the decree by Salandra and his supporters, who believed that Facta's resignation might allow Salandra to become prime minister in a fascist coalition. There is also the possibility that he feared the military would not obey his orders and would instead side with the fascists. The army chiefs had promised the king they would follow his orders, but could not guarantee that the soldiers would stay loyal when asked to shoot at the fascists. It is also possible that Victor Emmanuel III was deterred by the idea of bloodshed across Italy as the military fought the fascists. Crucially, the king's cousin, the Duke of Aosta, was a fascist supporter and Mussolini cleverly hinted that if the fascists took over, Victor Emmanuel III could be replaced by his taller, stronger and 'more manly' cousin.

Mussolini's appointment as prime minister

Without the king's support, Facta resigned. Mussolini was then helped by the disagreements between the liberal politicians who hoped to take over. At first the king turned to Salandra, who asked Mussolini to be part of his new government. At this stage, Mussolini was in a powerful enough position to demand he be made prime minister instead of simply taking a post in a Salandra government. Without Mussolini's support, Salandra turned down the king's offer. Salandra, Orlando and Giolitti all believed they should be made prime minister, but their hatred for each other meant that they recommended to the king that he was better to appoint Mussolini as opposed to one of their other rivals. During this period, Mussolini unhooked his phone and made a show of visiting the theatre in an act of political showmanship, demonstrating his calmness in this time of great political uncertainty. On 29 October, Mussolini received a message from the king with an offer of the prime ministership of Italy in a coalition government. Mussolini had achieved his goal of being made prime minister by constitutional means.

However, Mussolini believed that fascism required a much stronger, more dynamic 'myth' than the political horse trading that had actually taken place. He needed the image of a 'March on Rome', which appeared to have acquired power through the strength of the squads. He arrived in Rome from Milan on 30 October and was sworn in as prime minister. Around 50,000 fascists, organised and led by the **Quadrumvirs**, had made their way to Rome and on the 31 October they were allowed a victory parade, saluting the king who watched from his Rome palace. Mussolini's appointment as prime minister had taken place after a lot of phone calls and political wrangling, but the myth of a 'March on Rome', that power had been taken through armed insurrection, was a powerful idea that Mussolini perpetuated through speeches and anniversary celebrations that would take place during his time in power. State-sponsored history books would later write about civil war and the deaths of 3,000 fascist martyrs who had supposedly died during the march. The truth was much less exciting. He was prime minister at the head of a coalition government in which only the minority of his cabinet were fascists.

KEY TERM

Quadrumvirs
The four main leaders of fascism whom Mussolini tasked with organising the March on Rome. They were Michele Bianchi, Emilio De Bono, Cesare Maria de Vecchi and Italo Balbo. These four leaders were considerably powerful and were often photographed alongside Mussolini in the early stages of fascist rule. One of Mussolini's key political skills was in dealing with these potential rivals for power. De Vecchi and Balbo, for example, were made colonial administrators in Somalia and Libya respectively. While they were prestigious political postings, it meant they were stationed in Africa and were unable to play a leading role in political events in Italy. It is interesting to view fascist propaganda after 1922 and see the gradual removal of the Quadrumvirs' portrayal alongside Mussolini. After 1926, they were rarely depicted with Mussolini as he consolidated his personal dictatorship.

SOURCE 6 Mussolini walking between the Quadrumvirs during the March on Rome, 28 October 1922.

ACTIVITY
KNOWLEDGE CHECK

1 What impression does Source 6 give of Mussolini's relationship with the Quadrumvirs in 1922?

2 What judgement can we make about Mussolini's leadership and the PNF at the time he became prime minister in October 1922?

3 You need to allocate blame points to the key figures in Mussolini's appointment as prime minister. You have ten points. The higher the points' tally, the more responsible the person is. For example, you might allocate four points to the king, so you would then need to divide the other six points among the liberal leaders:

- Salandra

- Facta

- Orlando

- Giolitti

- King Victor Emmanuel III.

Discuss with other students and explain your answer.

4 How far was Mussolini's appointment to prime minister due to his political skill? If this wasn't the key factor, what do you think was and why?

SOURCE 7

From Gaetano Salvemini, *The Fascist Dictatorship in Italy*, 1928. Here Salvemini explains the decision by the king to refuse martial law in October 1922, during the 'March on Rome'.

When, at 10 a.m. on October 28, the Prime Minister, Facta, brought the decree of martial law for the King's signature, the King hesitated. Facta – one of the biggest idiots of all times and all countries, hesitated more than the King. He was then negotiating with the Fascists for an amicable compromise and cherished the confidence that things would mend of themselves. The King clutched at these negotiations as a drowning man clutches at a straw: since there was hope of a peaceable understanding, why should he proclaim martial law? The Cabinet would do well to consider the question. Facta therefore returned to the Cabinet. The Ministers stuck to their first decision. Facta brought back the decree. The King refused to sign it. In the interval, a group of Nationalists and Fascists, and certain Army and Navy Chiefs, had spoken with him, and had assured him that the Army would refuse to fight the Fascists. The news that the Duke of Aosta was among the Fascists, ready to take up his cousin's crown as soon as the King should let it fall, gave the final push... The decree of martial law being recalled, the politicians and Army Chiefs, who had advised the King not to sign it, put forward the name of Signor Salandra as the best man to form the new cabinet. They soon perceived that they had backed the wrong horse. The Fascists, who had been panic stricken at the prospect of martial law, recovered their swagger when the revocation had been announced. The whole country had the impression of a sweeping Fascist triumph. Up till 12:15 p.m. [time when the decree of martial law was refused] Mussolini might have been treated as a subaltern [junior officer]. At 12:15 the subaltern had become the master.

SOURCE 8

From Mussolini's speech to parliament on 16 November 1922. Mussolini describes the role of the king during the March on Rome and argues why he believes the king made the correct decision to appoint him prime minister. From *Mussolini as Revealed in his Political Speeches*, translated and edited by Barone Bernardo Quaranta di San Severino, 1923.

I believe also that I shall be giving expression to the thoughts of a large part of this assembly, and certainly of the majority of the Italian people, if I pay a warm tribute to our Sovereign, who, by refusing to permit the useless reactionary attempts made at the eleventh hour to proclaim martial law, has avoided civil war and allowed fresh and ardent Fascista current, newly arisen out of the war and exalted by victory, to pour itself into the sluggish main stream of the State. (Cries of 'Long live the King!' The Ministers and a great many deputies rise to their feet and applaud.)

> **A Level Exam-Style Question Section A**
>
> How far could the historian make use of Sources 7 and 8 together to investigate the role of the king in Mussolini's appointment as prime minister on 30 October 1922?
>
> Explain your answer, using both sources, the information given about them and your own knowledge of the historical context. (20 marks)
>
> **Tip**
> *Both sources are obviously quite subjective, but this does not mean they are not useful to historians. Think about the limitations of each source as well as areas they both agree on concerning the importance of the king and the reasons for his decisions.*

TO WHAT EXTENT WAS THE CREATION OF A FASCIST DICTATORSHIP BETWEEN 1922 AND 1926 DUE TO THE MISTAKES OF MUSSOLINI'S POLITICAL OPPOSITION?

Parliamentary compromise and coercion

At the age of just 39, Mussolini had achieved his goal of becoming prime minister of Italy. The nature of his appointment was unclear both to Italian politicians and the population in general. Had he been appointed through constitutional means or had it been a violent takeover of the state? Was this the culmination of his work or just the beginning of a more forceful fascist revolution that would overthrow the old order of the liberal state and replace it with the squads? It is difficult to know at this stage if even Mussolini knew the answer to these questions. He had achieved power through his dual strategy, but this in turn made things difficult. Many of the squads were demanding further revolution and greater reward for their part in helping him achieve power. Mussolini, however, was wary; working with the conservative elite and the king may be a better means of consolidating his role as prime minister. It is important to note that, historically, prime ministers in Italy did not tend to last very long, and there was little reason to think at the beginning of November 1922 that Mussolini would be any different. He also faced the serious problem that, despite being prime minister, there were only 35 fascist deputies in parliament with his hated rivals, the PSI, still dominating with 123 seats. His cabinet included four liberals, two members of the PPI, one ANI member and two members of the military. Mussolini appointed himself foreign minister and minister for the interior. At this early stage, his main goal was to placate the old ruling classes. He appointed the orthodox economist, Alberto De'Stefani, minister of finance, a move that helped gain the support of the conservative industrialists who were reassured that the appointment of Mussolini was not going to lead to radical economic changes.

He gained the trust of the powerful Catholic Church by increasing clerical pay and reinstating crucifixes in schools. On 28 October, Mussolini announced that a compromise had been reached between the ANI and the PNF and, in February 1923, the ANI were officially absorbed into the fascist party. This was an important move, taking away a powerful rival and clearly designating the PNF as the only party representing Italian nationalism. He appointed PPI member, Stefano Cavazzoni, as the minister of work and welfare and subsequently Cavazzoni encouraged the party to accept collaboration with Mussolini. This was supported by other Catholic politicians and by July 1923 the leader of PPI, Luigi Sturzo, had resigned over his concern that the party was being too absorbed into the PNF. Mussolini's pro-Catholic policies also encouraged the Vatican to support the PNF at the expense of the PPI. Without this crucial endorsement and the leadership of Sturzo, the once powerful PPI began to decline.

Mussolini's consolidation of power was not simply down to clever political appointments and deal-making. His maiden speech as prime minister, on 16 November 1922, was a brilliant mixture of offers to work with parliament and threats of violence to any who challenged him. The strength of the squads and the violence that had taken place up to 1922 was crucial here. Mussolini told the deputies present that, given the political and economic turmoil, he required a year of emergency powers in order to carry out the reform that Italy required. However, Mussolini warned parliament that he had 300,000 young men ready to take violent action against deputies who would not support him. His carefully worded warning, 'I could have barred up parliament and formed a government only of Fascists. I could have: but I have not wanted to, at least not for the moment', was enough to intimidate those politicians who were antifascist. It was a successful move. Most of parliament felt it necessary to give Italy at least a year of political calm and those that did not may have complied for fear of further civil war and violence from the fascists. Parliament subsequently approved year-long emergency powers by 306 votes to 116 against. This meant that Mussolini could not be removed by parliament and had full power to govern and raise taxes without seeking parliamentary approval for at least a year.

SOURCE

9

Mussolini's speech to parliament on 16 November 1922. Here Mussolini talks about the fascist revolution and the role of the blackshirts. From *Mussolini as Revealed in his Political Speeches*, translated and edited by Barone Bernardo Quaranta di San Severino, 1923.

I maintain that revolution has its rights; and I may add, so that everyone may know, that I am here to defend and give the greatest value to the revolution of the "black shirts," inserting it intrinsically in the history of the nation as an active force in development, progress and restoration of equilibrium. (Loud applause from the Left.) I could have carried our victory much further, and I refused to do so. I imposed limits upon my action and told myself that the truest wisdom is that which does not forsake one after victory. With three hundred thousand young men, fully armed, ready for anything and almost religiously prompt to obey any command of mine, I could have punished all those who have slandered the Fascisti and thrown mud at them. (Approval on the Right.) I could have made a bivouac of this gloomy grey hall; I could have shut up Parliament and formed a Government of Fascisti exclusively; I could have done so, but I did not wish to do so, at any rate at the moment.

EXTRACT

1

From Denis Mack Smith, *Mussolini*, 1981. Here he discusses the significance of Mussolini's speech.

On 16 November he [Mussolini] confronted parliament, where some of his own party now appeared in the uniform of the fascist militia, ominously booted and spurred. Dropping his mask, with studied derision he treated the deputies to what he called 'the most anti-parliamentary speech that history records.' Though he was not going to abolish the constitution – not yet, at least – he taunted them by saying he 'might easily have turned this bleak assembly hall into a bivouac for my platoons.' Threatening that he might still decide to govern without their help, relying instead on the 'fascist revolutionaries,' he asked to be given full powers to carry out any necessary changes in the law. The liberals were not, strangely, much offended by this speech; they liked to think that his contempt was aimed at the extreme left who, in their turn, thought the opposite; and the socialists, though they alone voted against his bold request [for emergency powers] cheered his remarks more than once as they saw liberal institutions disintegrating.

ACTIVITY
KNOWLEDGE CHECK

Read Source 9 and Extract 1 and answer the following questions:

1 Mussolini made the speech in Source 9 to convince parliament to grant him emergency powers for one year. Why do you think he included the section on the blackshirts in his speech?

2 Mussolini was a brilliant speaker who understood the power of language. Why do think he included the repetition of the phrase 'I could have'? What point is he trying to emphasise to the rest of parliament?

3 What factors do Source 9 and Extract 1 demonstrate were crucial to parliament for voting through the Emergency Powers Act for Mussolini?

Controlling the PNF

Mussolini completed his next move in December 1922 when he created a rival organisation to the cabinet, called the Fascist Grand Council, to which he appointed key fascists such as Italo Balbo, Michele Bianchi and Emilio De Bono. The Fascist Grand Council discussed key policy and elevated fascist leadership to the same position as the cabinet. This move was important in two ways. Firstly, it helped Mussolini overcome his weak position in the cabinet and undermined the liberal government institutions by essentially bypassing them. Secondly, as leader of the Fascist Grand Council with the sole ability to appoint its members, Mussolini centralised his power over the party. The Fascist Grand Council thus helped Mussolini consolidate his control over both the PNF and parliament. His next move strengthened his control over the PNF even further. In January 1923, the Fascist Grand Council decided to create the Milizia Volontaria per la Sicurezza Nazionale (MVSN). This absorbed all the *squadristi* and formalised their role as a party-based paramilitary force whose job was to support the army and police in defending the 'fascist revolution'. This was an important decision. The MVSN was an attempt to formalise the role of the *squadristi* within the state. Its 300,000 members pledged allegiance to Italy and their commander-in-chief, Mussolini. This allowed Mussolini to strengthen his control over the blackshirts at the expense of the *ras*. He also hoped to control the *squadristi* and bring an end to continuing fascist violence, which he now felt was detrimental to his support among the liberal elite and the middle classes. Now fascism was in power, it appeared that the chance for socialist revolution had disappeared, continuing fascist violence was now viewed in a much more negative way by those Italians who had once supported it. The king, the army and the liberal elite supported the move believing it was better to have the blackshirts under the control of the government than remaining independent under the leadership of the provincial *ras*. The power of the *ras* and the *squadristi* was also being diluted by the changing nature of the PNF. Since the March on Rome, the party had doubled in size to 783,000 members, with the vast majority being from the middle classes. Thus the older, more revolutionary fascists saw their influence slowly fading away.

The Acerbo Law and the 1924 election

With his power over parliament and the *ras* now tightened, Mussolini looked to hold a general election that would provide the PNF with the parliamentary mandate they currently lacked. The problem for Mussolini was that Italy's system of proportional representation made it extremely difficult for any one party to win a majority in parliament. To overcome this problem, Mussolini introduced a new law, known as the Acerbo Law after Giacomo Acerbo who had drafted it, which proposed that two-thirds of the parliamentary seats would go to the party that won more than 25 percent of the vote. Mussolini claimed that the Acerbo Law would bring stability to Italy by guaranteeing a more coherent parliament that could finally put in place the policies Italy needed. While the PCI and PSI opposed the Acerbo Law, the liberal elites such as Giolitti, the king and the Vatican all supported it, which put pressure on the PPI to abstain from voting. The fascists also applied pressure by staging massive demonstrations in Tuscany and Umbria and threatening violence if the bill did not pass. Mussolini encouraged this, wearing a black shirt in parliament on the day the Acerbo Law was due to be debated. With the Acerbo Law passed, Mussolini called an election for 6 April 1924. The campaign was marred by violence and intimidation as fascist blackshirts destroyed hundreds of opposition clubs and offices and even murdered the PSI candidate Antonio Piccinini. This was despite the fact that Mussolini had tried to suppress the violence, believing that he required a legitimate victory to cement his power.

The PNF's electoral victory was also helped by the choice of several prominent liberals, such as Orlando and Salandra, to have themselves included on the government electoral list alongside the fascists. Crucially, the opposition forces were divided between the PCI, the PSI, the PPI and liberals who refused to work with the fascists such as Giolitti. They were unable to come to an agreement that could have led to a united opposition against the PNF and its allies. Instead, with an electoral turnout of 64 percent, Mussolini won a resounding victory, with the fascist electoral list gaining 66.3 percent of the vote (thus making the Acerbo Law irrelevant). In the greatest electoral victory since unification, the fascists had increased their number of deputies from 35 to 275. Although violence had played a role, the PNF's victory was mainly due to the weakness of the opposition, the electoral support of prominent liberal politicians and a genuine belief that Mussolini could provide the strong leadership Italy needed to overcome its numerous problems.

EXTEND YOUR KNOWLEDGE

Electoral list

Italy's proportional representation voting was based on a system of electoral lists. Instead of voting for a direct candidate, Italians voted for lists of candidates with the seats then allocated to the differing parties in proportion to the number of votes each party received. In the 1924 election, the fascists' list was known as the 'National List' and Mussolini invited liberals and Catholics to join with the fascists. The outcome was that only 150 of the 350 names on the list were not part of the fascists. The inclusion of prominent liberals on the fascist electoral list undoubtedly helped the PNF gain 66.3 percent of the vote for their approved list. Historians have pointed to this as another example of the failure of Italy's liberal political system. Instead of trying to fight against Mussolini and the PNF, many liberals simply tried to get on the fascist electoral list believing it was the best way to maintain their power. This lack of ideology and a willingness to simply work with whoever provided the most effective chance of winning seats in parliament is one of the key reasons for the failure and eventual collapse of liberal Italy and its replacement by a fascist dictatorship.

The Matteotti crisis

It is important to note, however, that despite Mussolini's overwhelming victory, Italy was still a democracy. Although weakened, the PSI, PCI and PPI still held 80 seats between them. The pivotal event that would lead to the end of parliamentary democracy in Italy was the murder of the PCI leader, Giacomo Matteotti. When the new parliament re-opened on 30 May 1924, Matteotti delivered a strong speech denouncing the violence and corruption that had taken place during the electoral campaign. In his speech, Matteotti asserted that the fascists had only won the election due to 'the consequence of obscene violence' and were determined to establish a dictatorship no matter what the electoral results were. While the speech itself was embarrassing for the fascists, Mussolini was more concerned by the rumours that Matteotti had amassed a large file on fascist party corruption and he was about to make it public. On the afternoon of 10 June, Matteotti was kidnapped as he walked towards parliament. His body was eventually found on 16 August in a shallow grave just outside Rome. Although it had taken over two months to find his corpse, what had happened to the PCI leader had become clear only days after his disappearance. A witness had seen the number plate of the car that Matteotti had been dragged into. It belonged to Mussolini's press secretary, Cesare Rossi. The leader of the kidnapping was Amerigo Dumini and he was arrested on 12 June. Dumini was head of a fascist terror squad that had direct links to key fascist figures. Although there was no direct link between Mussolini and Matteotti's kidnapping, the implication of the fascist party and its leader with the murder of a key political leader threatened to topple the PNF government.

Mussolini faced pressure from three sides. Firstly, the old, established elite was concerned about backing a prime minister associated with murder. Secondly, the PSI, PCI and other antifascist parties were calling for the dismissal of Mussolini and the overthrow of the fascist government. Lastly, he also faced considerable pressure from the *ras* who saw Matteotti's murder as the first step in a fascist revolution that would violently establish a dictatorship. From 11 to 13 June, Mussolini was unsure what to do and it did appear that his government may have been in danger of falling. On 13 June, around 100 antifascist deputies left parliament, claiming that the government was unconstitutional, and established their own parliament on the Aventine hill outside Rome, which they called the 'Aventine Secession'. While on the surface this appeared a strong move, it was the decisive break Mussolini needed. It had become clear to Mussolini that he had the backing of the king, the pope, the army and business and political elites, who believed that he and the PNF were the best option for Italy in comparison to any of the other possible alternatives. His strong right-wing, conservative, anticommunist government appealed to these key figures of the Italian political system who had no interest in another change of leader, particularly if it would help the PCI and PSI. Knowing this, Mussolini regained his confidence and there was now little chance he could be removed.

The absence of the 100 antifascist deputies meant that it was easier for Mussolini to pass legislation through parliament. The Aventine Secession was also hampered by considerable ideological differences between its members who spanned a vast range of political ideologies, from liberalism to communism. As it became clear that the king would not dismiss Mussolini as prime minister, the Aventine deputies could not agree on what to do and they offered no threat to Mussolini's rule. To reassure Italy's political elites, Mussolini handed the positions of interior and justice minister to the nationalists, Luigi Federzoni and Alfredo Rocco. Federzoni was well respected and his appointment to such a key position in respect to the Italian constitution and law reassured the old elite. In November, under pressure from the army, Mussolini ordered the PNF to cease all forms of violence and remove any members who were undisciplined and not willing to follow his directives. This move, however, brought him under considerable pressure from the squads. On 31 December, Mussolini met with a delegation of squad leaders who demanded he act to defend the fascist revolution or they would remove him as leader of the PNF. This was only two days after the influential liberal politician Salandra declared his opposition to Mussolini and he was worried that Salandra could influence the king. Under pressure from both sides, Mussolini decided to take the initiative.

EXTEND YOUR KNOWLEDGE

Matteotti's murder and Mussolini

Ever since Matteotti was kidnapped and murdered on 10 June 1924, the involvement of Mussolini has been a considerable area of debate. Some key historians, such as Renzo de Felice, have asserted that there is no evidence Mussolini knew what was being planned or had any direct link to Matteotti's murder. Others, such as Mauro Canali, have argued instead that Matteotti was murdered on Mussolini's direct order. It is difficult to find any concrete evidence implicating Mussolini and it is important to remember that despite Matteotti being a key rival, his murder was poorly planned and almost led to the fall of the fascist government. Mussolini seemed very unsure how to act following the news of Matteotti's kidnapping, which would seem out of place for someone who had planned the murder and knew what was going to take place. However, it is perhaps worth knowing that Dumini, who served only 11 months in jail for the crime, received, in total, around 2.37 million lire in payments from the PNF until 1943. Perhaps what is more interesting is the fact that Mussolini sent financial assistance to Matteotti's widow and children, a surprising act from the fascist dictator who historians are still trying to understand.

SOURCE

10 Caricature of Mussolini during the Matteotti crisis from 1924, printed in the antifascist satirical magazine *Becco Giallo*. *Becco Giallo* was founded in Italy and was the most important antifascist publication in the country. The magazine was shut down by the fascists in 1926.

ACTIVITY
KNOWLEDGE CHECK

1 Consider the cartoon in Source 10 from 1924. What political message is it trying to make?

2 What does Source 10 tell us about Mussolini's rule at this stage in 1924?

3 List the key reasons why Mussolini was able to survive the political crisis caused by Matteotti's murder.

4 What do you believe was the most important factor and why?

The establishment of the dictatorship, 1925

On 3 January 1925, Mussolini made a key speech in parliament where he announced the establishment of the fascist dictatorship. This was not to be dictatorship of the party, however, but a personal rule under Mussolini. On 12 January, Mussolini formed a new cabinet, this time without most of the liberals, where Mussolini himself took on the roles of prime minister and minister to foreign affairs, war, navy and aviation. In February he appointed Farinacci as the PNF secretary, with the task of purging the party of those radicals who would not accept Mussolini's political direction. Farinacci also increased fascist membership from 600,000 to 938,000, diluting the power of the *squadristi* and increasing the numbers within the party who saw membership of the party and loyalty to Mussolini as a career advantage, and were less interested in ideas of fascist revolution and violence. In October, the Fascist Grand Council approved a motion that forced all *ras* to disband any squads still in existence and enlist in the militia. The independence and power of the provincial *ras* and the *squadristi* was now finished. Mussolini gained military support for the dictatorship by increasing officer and generals' pay and appointing the conservative monarchist, Pietro Badoglio, to the role of chief of general staff, as opposed to a radical fascist which the army had feared. More legislation followed. On 2 October 1925, Mussolini announced the Palazzo Vidoni Pact, which established the official fascist unions as the only representatives of Italy's workers, thereby taking power from the socialist and Catholic unions. The fascist unions were also much more subservient to the industrialists, thus gaining their support for the dictatorship.

EXTRACT

From Denis Mack Smith, *Mussolini* (1981). Mack Smith describes Mussolini's political manoeuvring in order to overcome opposition calling for his resignation following the murder of Matteotti.

On 2 January 1925, Amendola [prominent socialist antifascist] told the local correspondent of the *London Times* that Mussolini 'was finished,' but the Duce was in fact already planning his counter attack. He had to act quickly, because the militia might move against him if he faltered, or the opposition might produce further criminal reactions that would make his continuance in office impossible, or else the king might use the occasion to dismiss him as morally and politically unfit to rule. Salandra's group of conservative liberals was on the point of leaving his coalition and that would have had a dramatic effect on opinion at court as well as in the country at large. His first reaction was to recall parliament – there he would have a clear majority because of the continuing boycott by the 'Aventine' deputies of the opposition. Then on 3 January he announced to the deputies that he took personal responsibility for all that happened. [Mack Smith then goes on to describe Mussolini's speech and the announcement that Italy would be a dictatorship.]

EXTRACT

From Richard Bosworth, *Mussolini* (2002). Bosworth describes the growing pressure on Mussolini from his own fascist party who are urging him to act decisively against the PNF's political opposition.

In December Farinacci [leading fascist] was not alone in his mounting impatience to unleash a fascist offensive. The legal process for the Matteotti murder had reached De Bono and Finzi [prominent fascist leaders] and again threatened to inculpate Mussolini himself. There were rumours, too, of open dissidence in the cabinet where De'Stefani had sought permission to resign and where a number of ex-liberal and Nationalist ministers, including Federzoni, were nervous and restive. Among the fascists, discontent grew, focusing on the position of Federzoni as Minister of the Interior and on what seemed Mussolini's own endless prevarications. Although Farinacci could still warn off potential competitors with the advice that 'only one myth' was tenable in Italy – that of the Duce, to his leader he urged the tocsin [alarm] be sounded for the offensive. The Tuscan radical fascist Curzio Suckert, better known under his pen name as Curzio Malaparte, was unrepentant in attacking the Duce himself, warning him that 'it was not Mussolini who had carried the Fascists to… the Prime Ministership, but the fascists who had carried him to power'. Now 'Mussolini must bow to the revolutionary will [of the provincial fascists] or resign, even if only for a short time, the revolutionary mandate entrusted to him.' The pressure had built to breaking point. On 30 December 1924 Mussolini instructed the prefects to convey to deputies at home for the Christmas holidays that they must absolutely attend the parliament on the 3 January, when the Prime Minister would give a major speech.

EXTRACT

4 From Nicholas Farrell, *Mussolini: A New Life*, 2003. Farrell explains Mussolini's actions in 1925 and his decision to establish the fascist dictatorship in Italy following the murder of Matteotti.

Mussolini was an impulsive man who said that he always acted on instinct. Later he would tell Emil Ludwig [German journalist] that he often had 'premonitions' and 'ominous fore shadowings' and that he sensed 'spiritual atmosphere.' These things 'led' and 'troubled' him. 'I have superstitions' he added. 'I fear a jettatore (evil eyed man) more than an anti-fascist!' he told Quinto Navarra (his butler). Mussolini judged people according to whether he felt they were lucky or unlucky – whether they were born under a good or bad star. He was keen on astrology and the reading of palms. He would often sideline highly competent people if he deemed them unlucky. He trusted his instinct, or as he often put it, his blood. The big card, which his blood now told him to play, was dictatorship. This time, unlike in the case of Facta, the King did not stand in his way. The Times of January 2 reported that Mussolini was 'finished' and the next day predicted that he was about to announce his resignation. That afternoon he went to the Chamber for the first session of parliament after the Christmas recess and spoke.

THINKING HISTORICALLY   Evidence (6a)

Arguments and facts

Carefully read Extracts 2–4 explaining why Mussolini decided to make his crucial speech to parliament on 3 January 1925, during which he announced that Italy would become a dictatorship under his rule. Then complete the activities that follow.

Work in groups.

1 Why are facts important in history?

2 Read Extracts 2 and 3.

   a) How do these extracts disagree on the key factors shaping Mussolini's decision-making following the Matteotti murder?

   b) Which one do think is correct? Explain your answer.

3 Read Extract 4.

   a) What does it say was shaping Mussolini's political moves and how does this disagree with 2 and 3?

   b) Extract 4 talks a lot about Mussolini's personality. How important do you think this is to explaining his actions in 1925? Is this more or less important than the evidence used to shape the perspectives of Extracts 2 and 3 and why?

4 None of the historians is 'wrong' in their interpretation. Instead, they have made different conclusions from the facts of what took place in late December 1924. This is shaped by the perspective of their argument. Thinking about this, write down what the key focus for each historian is. For example, the role of the fascist party vs Mussolini's own personality.

5 Now consider how each perspective constructs a very different image of Mussolini. Which extract presents the most positive image of Mussolini and which constructs the most negative? How does it do this?

6 Use one word to describe Mussolini in each extract followed by an explanation using the evidence from the extract. For example, 'In Extract 4, Mussolini is presented as... because... .'

Repression and constitutional amendments, 1925–26

On 4 August 1925, the socialist deputy Tito Zaniboni was arrested for allegedly plotting to assassinate Mussolini. Mussolini immediately announced the banning of Zaniboni's political party, the Partito Socialista Unitario (PSU), and the introduction of a new press law, which meant all journalism had to be supervised and approved by the state. Another law was introduced giving the government the power to sack any public employee whose actions either in or outside of their work was hostile to the PNF. In December 1925, the title of Prime Minister of Italy was changed to Head of Government and Duce of Fascism. The ability of parliament to remove the prime minister through a vote of no confidence was removed and, critically, in January 1926, Mussolini was granted the ability to rule by decree, allowing him to make laws without discussion, consultation or a vote in parliament. Following an assassination attempt against Mussolini on 31 October 1926, the final confirmation of the dictatorship was established, with all political parties apart from the PNF banned. A Special Tribunal for the Defence of the State was set up for the prosecution of antifascists who ultimately would have no right of appeal. The Aventine deputies were permanently excluded from parliament and the communist parliamentarians, who had not joined the Aventine Secession but stayed in parliament to try to fight Mussolini's policies, were banned and their leader, Antonio Gramsci, arrested. By this stage, most opposition leaders had fled into exile in France and elsewhere overseas, their Italian citizenship withdrawn and their property confiscated under new fascist legislation. It is estimated that around 10,000 antifascists left Italy.

Mussolini's final move was to abolish elected local government and replace mayors with a new position called the *podestà*, who would be appointed by local prefects. The prefects themselves were appointed by Mussolini. This finally confirmed that the prefects, accountable to Mussolini, would hold the most powerful positions in the Italian regions, and not the *ras*. It was the dictatorship of Mussolini and the state, not the radical fascists. The new PNF secretary, Augusto Turati, who had replaced Farinacci in March, asserted that in any conflict between the *ras* and the prefects, the prefects would take precedence. The fascist members needed to understand, according to Turati, that Mussolini was dictator both of the party and of Italy. Thus, by the end of 1926, Italy was to all extents and purposes a one party, police state, with opposition banned and persecuted. However, it was not the dictatorship the *ras* had hoped for when they pressured Mussolini to act at the end of 1924. From the time of Matteotti's murder, it had taken Mussolini around 18 months to establish an extremely personalised form of dictatorship, and he would dominate both Italy and the PNF in his role as 'Il Duce', the Leader, in the years to come as he now confronted the task of turning Italians into 'true' fascists.

EXTEND YOUR KNOWLEDGE

The attempted assassinations of Mussolini

There were several attempts to assassinate Mussolini in the early 1920s. The first, as mentioned, involved Tito Zaniboni's failed plan to shoot Mussolini from a hotel room overlooking a balcony where the fascist leader was scheduled to give a speech. The second attempt took place on 7 April 1926, when a mentally unstable Anglo-Irish aristocrat, Violet Gibson, who claimed she had been ordered to kill either Mussolini or the pope, shot at Mussolini as he was giving a speech in Rome, the bullet grazing his nose. The third attempt was made by a 26-year-old anarchist, Gino Lucetti, on 11 September 1926. Lucetti threw a grenade at Mussolini's car. Although it injured eight pedestrians, Mussolini escaped completely unharmed. The final assassination attempt happened on 31 October 1926, when Mussolini's motorcade was shot at as he drove past crowds celebrating the anniversary of the March on Rome. The alleged assassin, a 16-year-old boy called Anteo Zamboni, was attacked by crowds and horribly murdered. Historians are still unsure who shot at Mussolini and what the motive was, but most do not believe Zamboni was involved. The significance of the assassinations was that each was followed by more laws undermining Italian democratic freedoms. The attempts on his life helped Mussolini politically by creating a feeling of fear, particularly in the king, which Mussolini used to justify the laws that transformed Italy into a dictatorship. The Zamboni incident, for example, was immediately used to support the banning of all political parties apart from the PNF. Although Mussolini would probably have tried to establish a dictatorship regardless of these attempts, they clearly helped speed up the process.

SOURCE

From the fascist magazine, *Gerarchia*, in an article entitled 'Forza e consenso', written by Mussolini and printed in March 1923. In this article Mussolini argued no government was ever based on the complete support of the entire population. Force was required, alongside consent, to enable governments to achieve the stability and progress that the majority of the population desired.

I beg the liberal signori to let me know if ever in history there has been a government based exclusively on popular consent. There has never been such a government, there never will be one. Consent is as mutable as the sands of the seashore... mankind is perhaps tired of liberty. It has had an orgy of it. Liberty today is no longer the severe chaste virgin for whom generations in the first half of the last century fought and died. For the intrepid, restless, tough youths who face the twilight dawn of the new history other words exercise a much bigger fascination, and they are: order, hierarchy, discipline... Let it be known, then, once and for all, that Fascism recognises no idols, worships no fetishes. It has already trampled, and if need be will step quietly once again, over the more or less putrid body of the Goddess Liberty.

ACTIVITY
KNOWLEDGE CHECK

One of the most difficult historical questions is whether or not Mussolini planned on setting up a dictatorship before the events concerning the Matteotti murder. Read Source 11 and answer the following questions:

1 What evidence is there that Mussolini was always intent on setting up a dictatorship in Italy?

2 What evidence is there that this was a decision he came to as a result of the pressure he faced after Matteotti's murder?

3 What weight do you give to Source 11 as evidence that Mussolini always planned on establishing a dictatorship in Italy?

A Level Exam-Style Question Section B

To what extent was Mussolini's consolidation of power from 1922 to 1926 due to the mistakes of his political opponents? (20 marks)

Tip
This question requires you to consider a range of factors in Mussolini's consolidation of power and the establishment of the dictatorship. Consider key mistakes his political opponents made in comparison with other reasons for his success. Which is more important? Make sure you focus on the idea of extent, instead of just listing and describing the factors that led to his consolidation of power.

ACTIVITY
SUMMARY

1 Construct a timeline of Mussolini's main actions and legislation and policies he passed between 1922 and 1926 that helped him achieve his consolidation of power and the establishment of his dictatorship. Break it down into two sections: **Consolidation, 1922–24** and **Establishing a dictatorship, 1924–26**.

2 Now categorise the main actions and legislation into:

- compromise with Italian elites

- suppression of opposition

- suppression of the fascist party

- weakening of parliament.

You could include things like Acerbo Law, Fascist Grand Council, etc. It is fine if one of the key events combines two of these categories, and you can add your own categories if you wish.

3 Now look over your completed timeline and answer the following questions:

a) When exactly would you define Mussolini as dictator of Italy and why?

b) What was the key way in which Mussolini established his dictatorship? For example, violence, political legislation, compromise with elites, etc. Write a considered explanation for this question.

c) What are the key differences between the tactics Mussolini used from 1922 to 1924 to consolidate his power and from 1924 to 1926 to set up his dictatorship? What do you believe are the reasons for this difference?

WIDER READING

Hughes-Hallett, L. *The Pike: Gabriele d'Annunzio, Poet, Seducer and Preacher of War*, Fourth Estate (2013) is a useful source on d'Annunzio and provides an excellent understanding of Italian politics in the period before the fascists took power.

Sassoon, D. *Mussolini and the Rise of Fascism,* Harper Collins (2008) is also very informative on the emergence of fascism in Italy and the reasons behind Mussolini's successful rise to power in 1922.

Williamson, D. *Mussolini: From Socialist to Fascist (Personalities & Powers),* Hodder Education (1997) shows the progress of Mussolini's politics from his earlier socialist views to his development of fascism and the formation of the PNF.

The Italian movie *Vincere* (2009) is an accurate portrayal of Mussolini from 1914 to the early years of fascist rule, and covers the foundation of the Fascist Party and how he came to power.

2a.3 The fascist state, 1925–40

KEY QUESTIONS

- How successful were Mussolini's attempts to control the Italian population?
- What was the nature and importance of Mussolini's relationship with Italy's political and economic elite?
- How successfully did Mussolini's economic plans achieve their aims?
- How far did Mussolini's relationship with the Catholic Church impact on his fascist dictatorship?

INTRODUCTION

As Mussolini consolidated his power as leader of Italy, his attention became more focused on the nature of this new state. What would be the nature of a 'fascist state' and how could Italians be transformed into loyal fascists? These were difficult questions that once again demonstrated the tension that lay at the heart of Mussolini's regime. Was his goal simply to keep the Italian people, and more importantly, the powerful elite sections of society, such as the monarchy and the Vatican, content so that he could maintain power? Or was it to actually change Italy into a militaristic culture that believed in fascist ideology and whose people were prepared to die for its cause?

In the period 1925–40, Mussolini grappled with these difficult questions, at times attempting to pursue both policies in equal measure. He would introduce educational policies that would target Italy's youth, incorporate all working social and sporting events within the fascist organisation, create a fascist culture that would permeate Italian society and use oppression and censorship to guarantee that no alternative political ideology could be heard inside of Italy. Through the carefully constructed 'cult of *il Duce*', Italians would worship Mussolini as the greatest Italian leader since Caesar, who was creating a new, powerful

Italy that would take its rightful place as one of the world's leading powers. Through these policies, Mussolini attempted to 'fascistise' Italians, creating a nation where all culture, political thought, education and social activities were incorporated within the ideals of fascism, producing an almost religious faith in Mussolini's unchallenged leadership. However, the extent to which Mussolini was successful is a key debate between historians.

At the same time Mussolini pursued traditional, conservative political policies that aimed at placating the Church, the monarchy and the economic and conservative elites. In this way, his politics was not so far removed from Giolitti and aimed at deal-making with those powerful traditional elites in Italian society that would help keep him in power. His was a unique dictatorship, one in which Mussolini was presented as all powerful, but also had to share power with the pope and the king. There is little doubt that Mussolini was popular during this period. His policies, towards the Church, for example, brought him considerable prestige both within Italy and around the world and by 1935 he was undoubtedly the most popular Italian leader since unification. Yet events after 1935 would question the depth of support for fascism in Italy, as Italy's economy declined and the fascist regime pursued more radical policies that were generally unpopular with the Italian public.

May 1925 – Opera Nazionale Dopolavoro (an after work organisation) founded

October 1925 – Battle for Grain to make Italy self-sufficient in grain production launched

February 1926 – Role of *podestà* replaces elected mayors

April 1926 – Strikes forbidden by Rocco Law. Fascist Youth Organisation (Balilla) founded

July 1926 – Ministry of Corporations established

1928 – 'Empty the cities' campaign announced by Mussolini and internal migration restrictions brought in

May 1928 – Parliamentary deputies to be chosen by the Fascist Grand Council

December 1928 – Constitutional powers of the king limited by the Fascist Grand Council

1925	1926	1927	1928	1929	1930

August 1926 – Battle for Lira launched by Mussolini

November 1926 – Political police divisions established under Arturo Bocchini. Secret police of the fascist state, known as OVRA, created. All other political parties banned

May 1927 – Battle for Births and the policy of 'Ruralisation' launched by Mussolini

December 1927 – Lira artificially fixed at 92.46 against the British pound as part of the Battle for Lira

February 1929 – Concordat with the pope reached

March 1929 – Italians overwhelmingly approve Mussolini's government in national plebiscite

Whether Mussolini's regime would have collapsed without the Second World War is a key area of debate, but there is no doubt that cracks in the fascist state were appearing by 1940. Mussolini's aims, his successes and failures in the years 1925–40 are crucial for understanding the nature of the fascist state: what Mussolini claimed it was, what it was in reality, and the depth and durability of its popular appeal to the Italian people.

HOW SUCCESSFUL WERE MUSSOLINI'S ATTEMPTS TO CONTROL THE ITALIAN POPULATION?

Indoctrination of education and youth

The ideal of focusing on Italy's youth to create a loyal generation of Italian fascists had always been part of Mussolini's political goals. As early as December 1921, the Avanguardia Giovanile Fascista (Fascist Youth Front) had been formed for boys aged between 14 and 17 years. Following Mussolini's appointment as prime minister, the Gruppi Universitari Fascisti (GUF) had been formed in March 1923 and this was followed by the creation of the **Balilla** for children aged between 8 and 14 years. At this stage, however, these youth organisations were not well structured and competed with the youth organisations of the other political parties. By 1924, only 3,000 children were formally involved with fascist youth associations. Once Mussolini established the dictatorship, however, the focus on youth became considerably more formalised. On 3 April 1926, the Opera Nazionale Balilla (ONB) was created by formal decree, with the goal of providing 'for the physical and moral benefit of youth' through the education of boys between the ages of eight and 18 years. In 1934, the *Balilla* was restructured in a more complex fashion into three separate categories: the *Figli della Lupa* (Sons of the She Wolf) from the ages of six to eight years, the *Balilla* from 8 to 14 years and then finally the *Avanguardisti* from 14 to 17 years.

Girls were now included in their own organisations, the *Figlie della Lupa* (Daughters of the She Wolf) from ages 6 to 8 years, *Piccole Italiane* (Little Italians) from eight to 13 years and the *Giovane Italiane* (Young Italian Women) from 14 to 17 years. These organisations were under the control of the Party to the Ministry of National Education, which had been created in 1929 to oversee both the scholarly education and physical training of Italy's youth in a fashion that would create a new loyal and physically strong generation of fascists. Thus the ONB was linked into the formal education system and was compulsory for all boys and girls at elementary school from the age of six to 11 years. The fascist government did not make membership compulsory beyond the age of 11 until 1939, but non-membership made it difficult to enrol in further education, barred employment in the civil service and was seen as reason to suspect families of being antifascist. Membership of the ONB, on the other hand, provided access to jobs and special scholarships.

KEY TERM

Balilla
Balilla was allegedly the nickname of Giovan Battista Perasso, a boy from Genoa who, legend says, started a revolt against Austrian rule in 1746 when he threw a stone at an Austrian official. The name *Balilla* became associated with revolution and independence. The name was chosen for the fascist youth organisation to represent the idea of a militarised youth who were ready to stand up to foreign invaders.

1931 - Tension over Catholic Action leads to criticism from the Church against fascism's youth policies. Compromise reached between the Vatican and Mussolini

1933 - Compulsory for all teachers, clerks, civil servants and white collar workers to belong to the PNF

1935 - Ministry of the Press established

1937 - Compulsory for all young Italians to join fascist youth organisations. Fascists hold large celebrations commemorating the 2,000th anniversary of Augustus Caesar coming to power. Exhibition clearly associates Caesar with Mussolini. Ministry of the Press renamed Ministry of Culture

June 1937 - Leading Italian antifascists Carlo and Nello Rosselli assassinated in Paris

| 1931 | 1932 | 1933 | 1934 | 1935 | 1937 | 1938 | 1939 |

1932 - Exhibition of the Fascist Revolution held in Rome to commemorate ten years of fascist rule. Four million people visit the exhibition

1934 - Balilla restructured and youth organisations for girls established

February 1934 - Mixed corporations of employer and employee groups established. Mussolini's government approved overwhelmingly by the Italian population in another national plebiscite

1938 - Reform of customs brought in to try and change Italian behaviour

March 1938 - Parliament grants the title first marshal of the empire to Mussolini

September 1938 - Racial Laws against Jews initiated

1939 - Pope Pius XI dies before he can publish criticisms of Mussolini's race policy and is replaced by Pope Pius XII

All other youth organisations, apart from those provided by the Catholic Church, were banned. For boys, the youth programme aimed at producing young, fascist soldiers. From 8 to 14 years, they were trained in the moral and spiritual defence of the country and then from 14 they were involved in special gymnastic and sporting programmes to prepare them physically for military life. At 18 years old, all able-bodied males had to undergo military training. For the *Balilla*, sport and military training for the boys involved activities such as marching, wrestling, shooting practice, boxing and bomb throwing. Young boys were taught that the perfect *Balilla* was one who had sworn loyalty to Mussolini and dreamt of fighting and dying for his country. Physical education was also a focus for Italian girls. They did gymnastics, which was meant to ensure they were fit mothers who could bear healthy children and then educate them in the love of Italy and Mussolini. At school, children were taught lessons on patriotic Italians from classical Rome through to the fascist regime and encouraged to make links between Italy's great heroes, particularly Caesar, and Mussolini, who was their modern-day embodiment. School textbooks told students of the poor treatment of Italian soldiers after the First World War and how fascism had saved the country from a communist revolution. Antifascist teachers were removed from their jobs in the 1920s and from 1933 it became compulsory for teachers to belong to the PNF. At university level there was less focus on formal fascist education or military training. The GUF's main goal was to run the *Littoriali*, which were national student games involving cultural and debate competitions centred on fascist themes. These ran from 1934 to 1940. The question of whether these education policies were successful is a very difficult one to answer. By 1937, even before membership became compulsory, the fascist youth organisations had seven million members.

However, for many young people the motivation was not a belief in fascism but due to the enjoyable social occasions it provided, the enjoyment of being outdoors and playing sport instead of studying in a classroom and the employment restrictions non-membership brought. There was also a considerable divide between the success in the north and the south. In the rural south, most did not study beyond the compulsory age of 11 and the nature of agricultural work made participation in youth groups much more difficult. The participation in these youth groups was also quite divided between girls and boys. Not only were girls less likely to continue schooling past the age of 11, there was also a considerable difference between the enjoyment boys found in the focus on physical activities and outdoor games and the more dull activities for girls, which constantly focused on learning how to be good future mothers. A 1937 survey conducted by the PNF in Rome, for instance, found that girls were much more interested in the type of sporting activities provided to the boys than they were about becoming mothers. Thus the success of the fascist youth policy was by no means complete and was hampered by considerable regional and demographic differences. The question of whether these youth groups created 'loyal fascists' is also very difficult to answer. Were these young people truly indoctrinated to believe in the fascist ideals and prepared to die for Mussolini like the ideal *Balilla*, or did they simply enjoy the activities provided? In the Second World War, the most dedicated fascist soldiers who fought to the end were mainly young Italians who were products of fascist youth policy. However, it is also interesting to note that the antifascist forces were predominately made up of young people as well, who had also been brought up in the same fascist educational system.

Young *Balilla* training in Rome, January 1938.

Opera Nazionale Dopolavoro

The Opera Nazionale Dopolavoro (OND) (National Afterwork Organisation) was one of the most popular aspects of the fascist regime. After the implementation of the fascist dictatorship, the socialist organisations for worker recreation and welfare had been closed down. In 1925, the fascist OND replaced them. This provided workers with a considerable variety of social and sporting opportunities including bars, billiard halls, cycling groups, football teams, libraries and radios. Each OND section typically had a clubhouse and a recreation ground where these activities were provided. Plays and concerts were provided for workers, as was the showing of popular films. OND membership entitled workers to rail ticket discounts, as well as other consumer benefits. It also acted as a welfare organisation providing relief for workers in times of need and providing a level of social insurance. The most popular aspect of the OND, however, was the subsidised holidays and excursions it provided where workers could take their families to mountain retreats, sporting events or holidays at the beach, for example, for virtually no cost. This was the first example of popular mass leisure in Italy and was provided and subsidised by the fascists. By 1939, it had over four million members. Around 80 percent of all state and private sector salaried workers were members of the OND as were 40 percent of Italy's industrial workers. However, it is interesting to note that the fascists took particular care to make the OND ideologically free. None of the sporting, social and educational activities that workers were encouraged to go on featured any direct promotion of fascist beliefs and ideology. Again, this questions the depth of the PNF's attempt to create a nation of loyal fascists.

The OND was undoubtedly one of the most popular aspects of the fascist regime and many workers were grateful for the benefits it provided. This reflected on Mussolini's leadership and contributed to his popular appeal. However, the fact is that the workers could benefit from the OND without any real commitment to the ideals of fascism, and it is clear that many simply joined because of the mass range of services it provided. When some within the PNF complained that the OND made no attempt to provide fascist education to the workers, Mussolini replied that the main achievement of the OND was that workers were meeting in places and participating in social activities that were linked to the fascist party. This participation with fascism by the mass of the Italian population was more important, Mussolini believed, as a form of control in comparison to direct ideological indoctrination that might discourage workers from OND membership. Thus, the OND was never used directly to indoctrinate the four million Italians who joined, and the gap between popular policy and creating a nation that actually believed in fascism was difficult to bridge. However, it is questionable whether Mussolini was even interested in pursuing this goal or was simply content that policies such as this brought him popular support.

SOURCE 2

The prominent fascist politician Maurizio Maraviglia on the importance of sport in the fascist regime. From the nationalist, pro-fascist newspaper *La Tribuna*, 5 July 1929.

Sport is not an end in itself. It is no longer a matter of personal choice. Organisations are not built up in accordance with personal tastes, but along military lines. In this transformation of sports, we see one of the most interesting and important phases of Fascism. Fascism avails itself of the various forms of sport, especially those requiring large groups of participants, as a means of military preparation and spiritual development, that is, as a school for the national training of Italian youth. By popularising and militarising sports requiring large groups, Fascism accomplishes perhaps its greatest governmental work. All Italian youths placed under the same discipline will begin to feel themselves soldiers. In this way there is built up in spirit a formidable militant organism which is already a potential army.

ACTIVITY
KNOWLEDGE CHECK

1 What impression does Source 1 give of the *Balilla*'s aims?

2 Using Source 2 and your own studies, explain why the fascist dictatorship was eager for Italians, particularly the youth, to participate in sport.

3 To what extent did ideology play a role in Mussolini's attempts to gain the support of the Italian population? Consider the OND and Mussolini's youth policy to answer this question.

Press control and censorship

One of the key aspects of controlling the Italian population and encouraging a positive image of Mussolini and fascism was through censorship of the press. In 1923 and 1925, the PNF had introduced decrees restricting the freedom of the press in Italy. At the end of 1926, these decrees were formalised into official laws, sanctioned by parliament. Prefects now had the ability to confiscate whole editions of any newspaper, journal or magazine that produced material that could be judged as unfavourable to the fascist regime. They had the power to suspend publication,

replace editors and shut down offending newspaper completely. Left-wing newspapers such as *Avanti!*, *Partito Popolare* and *L'Unita* were all closed. All journalists were incorporated into a fascist union, which controlled access to jobs and promotion within the profession. This enforced a form of self-censorship: journalists had to join up with a fascist organisation and ensure that their work was positive towards Mussolini otherwise they would lose their job. Mussolini's press officer sent out specific instructions on what should be published about the *Duce* and how it should be written. Fascist reports concerning the greatness of Mussolini were written by people working for the PNF press officer and then simply sent to newspapers so they would be printed. Journalists were told not to print stories on crime, suicides or traffic accidents, as this would disturb the fascist image of Italy as a country with no social problems.

Interestingly, apart from the left-wing political newspapers, Mussolini was more interested in controlling the press as opposed to banning newspapers. His fascist newspaper *Popolo d'Italia* only had a circulation of 100,000 compared to 600,000 for the *Corriere della Sera* and the Vatican newspaper, *Osservatore Romano*, remained popular with a circulation of around 250,000. Fascist newspapers only accounted for ten percent of the entire newspaper sales in Italy. Other forms of control were used, such as increased subsidies for those newspapers that printed positive stories about Mussolini. Thus independent newspapers were allowed to exist but under strict guidance that was enforced, in most cases, by the newspaper's own editor who was fearful of the consequences if he did not follow the press office directives. The fascist regime was therefore considerably successful in controlling the image of Italian society, the PNF and particularly Mussolini that they wanted the public to see and it was extremely difficult for the Italian population to view any alternative narrative than the one presented to them by the fascists.

Propaganda

One of the key aspects of the fascist media control was the dissemination of propaganda that celebrated the fascist regime. The goal of Mussolini and the fascists was to manufacture a consensus through propaganda to mobilise support for Mussolini's policies and help to transform the Italian people into 'true' fascists. Fascist propaganda focused on unifying ideals that could draw all Italians together, creating a shared patriotic feeling that celebrated Italy's history and associated the fascists with the rebirth of the Italian nation. In this sense, the symbol of Rome was a very important focus for fascist propaganda. The cult of Ancient Rome was popularised by propaganda that celebrated the greatness of ancient Rome and its leaders, and also the fact that Italians were the heirs to the greatest empire in history and therefore should be proud to be Italian. Medieval buildings were destroyed so that Rome's classical ruins could be better displayed. In 1937, a large celebration to commemorate the 2,000th anniversary of Augustus Caesar was held in Rome, and over one million people visited the exhibition of Roman history that celebrated Rome's historical greatness.

Rome's Ostiense railway station, built in 1938 for Hitler's visit to Italy, featuring this mosaic showing images of ancient Rome alongside fascist symbolism. This type of architecture was a key aspect of fascist propaganda, linking the achievements of fascism with the glories of ancient Rome.

Mussolini was intricately linked to this image of Rome as the heir of Augustus, who, just as Augustus had done, was rebuilding Italy as a great power from the ruins of chaos and war. This propaganda was disseminated through newspapers, radio, cinemas, posters, mass rallies and sport. Sport was particularly important: the Italian football team won the World Cup in 1934 and 1938 and the world boxing champion between 1933 and 1935 was an Italian named Primo Carnera. This success was heralded as demonstrating the re-found greatness of the Italian people, who were demonstrating their supremacy through sporting glory.

Despite the aims of the fascist regime, there was no specific ministry to organise propaganda until the formation of the Ministry of the Press in 1935. In 1937, it was renamed the Ministry of Popular Culture. While the censorship practised by the PNF meant it was difficult for the majority of Italians to hold views that ran against the constant fascist propaganda, there were problems with the mass consensus that the fascists strove to create. The Ministry of Popular Culture was never very sophisticated and had difficulties in fully exploiting modern mediums, such as film, to disseminate propaganda. The lack of mass media in the south made the national integration of all Italians into a consensus for the support of fascism difficult and, despite the popularity of many aspects of the fascist message, the extent to which they actually transformed Italian attitudes is very questionable.

The cult of *il Duce*

The most powerful and successful aspect of fascist propaganda focused on Mussolini's leadership and the creation of what is described by historians as the cult of *il Duce*. This was an image propagated through posters, cinema news reels and radio broadcasts that sought to portray Mussolini as a leader of immense ability who was leading Italy to greatness. This was clearly represented in the fascist slogan 'Mussolini is always right'. An incredible 30 million pictures of *il Duce* in around 2,500 different poses were circulated throughout Italy. The image portrayed Mussolini as a modern, dynamic leader who was a brilliant sportsman as well as an internationally respected statesman. He was described as a superb swimmer and aviator. Unlike other political leaders, Mussolini was frequently photographed shirtless, portraying a leader of physical strength. His image as a man who was attractive to the opposite sex was a key part of the cult, but so too was the portrayal of Mussolini as a traditional family man. These contradictions, as opposed to weakening the cult of *il Duce*, actually helped strengthen it; Mussolini was a leader who appealed to everybody.

As he strengthened his dictatorship, his image as a lone leader, above his party and the nation, become more pronounced; he was without friends who would distract him from his work and was without the normal human emotions that might hinder other men. Mussolini represented, in this image, the hopes and desires of the Italian people: he was the supreme patriot, the first soldier and the heir to Julius Caesar and Augustus, who was leading the Italian nation to greatness. There is no doubting the power of the cult of *il Duce*. In many ways it was the sustaining myth of the regime that united Italians in support for the dictatorship. While the PNF and fascist ideology may not have been popular with the majority of Italians, Mussolini himself stood above the party as a leader whom Italians could believe in.

Official fascist party photos of Mussolini (clockwise from top): with his family in 1933; his portrait, which was the most widely disseminated image of Mussolini as Italians were required to have his portrait displayed in their homes; skiing (undated).

There were, however, key problems associated with this powerful propaganda. Mussolini's image as the focus of the dictatorship was much more popular than the PNF and fascist ideology, and it is questionable how far fascism can be described as simply Mussolinism. If the true goal of fascism was to transform the Italian people into a more militaristic culture, then the cult of *il Duce* did not achieve this. Instead, it focused on the worship of one leader as opposed to an ideology that could sustain itself after Mussolini either died or could no longer carry on. It is therefore difficult to consider fascism being able to survive without Mussolini. There was the added difficulty that as Mussolini aged, the image of a youthful, active and dynamic leader was harder to sustain. Finally, it can be argued that as the 1930s progressed, Mussolini became less inclined to see the cult of *il Duce* as simply a propaganda myth and instead came to believe in it himself, thus explaining his more radical and aggressive policy direction from 1935 onwards.

The influence of fascist culture

For the PNF, producing a cultural revolution that perpetuated the ideals of fascism was a key part in their attempted transformation of the Italian people into loyal fascists. The PNF produced policies for artists and intellectuals in Italy following the establishment of the dictatorship between 1925 and 1926. All art should serve the goals of the fascist state and help to create and sustain the fascist myths and images that were at the heart of their dictatorship. The National Institute of Fascist Culture was created in 1926 and artists and intellectuals organised into particular associations, such as the Fascist syndicate of artists led by Antonio Maraini. The National Institute of Fascist Culture organised cultural events, free concerts and publications that would encourage mass Italian participation in fascist cultural propaganda. The PNF funded the Italian film industry and, in the late 1930s, created a state of the art film production complex known as Film City. In 1932, the Exhibition of the Fascist Revolution was held to celebrate a decade of fascist rule. Artists were commissioned to produce artwork that represented this achievement and over four million people visited the exhibition. Mussolini never attempted to control artistic styles and much of fascist art could be quite modern and experimental; it simply had to correspond to the ideal that through art it was helping to glorify fascism.

Architecture was also an intrinsic part of fascist culture, with new fascist buildings modelled on a neo-classical Roman style that was meant to make the connection between Ancient Rome and the new fascist regime particularly clear. Plays and movies were also crucial mediums of fascist culture. Giuseppe Forzano, for example, produced three plays called *Napolean*, *Camillo Benso di Cavour* and *Julius Caesar* which provided the story of three great patriotic leaders who the audience were encouraged to link to Mussolini, thus reinforcing the cult of *il Duce*. Mussolini was actually listed as the co-author of the plays after suggesting the original idea to Forzano. There were also several popular films that glorified fascism and its achievements, most prominently *Vecchia Guardia*, *Luciano Serra, Pilot* and *The Siege of Alcazar*. Despite this, it is perhaps worth noting that 87 percent of all box-office takings in Italy came from the showings of Hollywood-produced films.

The influence of fascist culture in transforming the Italian people into loyal fascists was not overly successful. While the organisation of artists and intellectuals was efficient in controlling what was produced, and ensuring that it helped boost the image of Mussolini and the PNF, it was never focused in a coherent manner with a key message that would resonate with the Italian people. It lacked an intellectual giant, such as the poet d'Annunzio, who could inspire the population in a popular appeal to the goals of fascism and it is therefore questionable to what extent, if at all, that fascist culture had any transformative effect on the Italian nation.

Repression and terror

While Mussolini undoubtedly tried to sustain fascist power through popular organisations such as the OND, it is clear that repression of political opposition also played a key part in his dictatorship. In November 1926, Mussolini introduced legislation that banned all other political parties and suppressed any Italians who tried to protest against the dictatorship. The death penalty was reintroduced for anybody who tried to assassinate the king or Mussolini or who threatened state security. The Special Tribunals could send political dissidents into exile (usually in the south) for an unspecified amount of time – a process known as *Confino*. This was usually used against those Italians who were judged as potentially dangerous antifascists, despite there not being any concrete evidence of antifascist association or activity. Although exile may not seem a considerable punishment, it is worth noting that *Confino* was financially devastating for many who were sent away and their families faced considerable discrimination from the fascists. It was also seen as particularly dangerous to employ anybody who had returned from *Confino*.

The Political Police division were formed in late 1926 under Arturo Bocchini, and were successful in infiltrating and breaking up antifascist organisations. The Political Police had a considerable network of spies in Italy and among Italian communities abroad. In June 1937, it worked with the Servizi Militari Informativi Italiani (SIM), the military spying organisation, to organise the assassination of prominent Italian antifascist exiles Carlo and Nello Rosselli in Paris by members of a French fascist group. The Italian secret police, known as OVRA, was formed in 1927 by Bocchini, to spy on Italians across Italy and ensure they were able to stamp down on any domestic antifascist sentiment or activities. It is estimated that there were around 5,000 informers operating in Italy and OVRA was successful in stopping the organisation of antifascist groups. OVRA spies infiltrated universities, businesses, fascist unions and could be located anywhere where working men and women were known to meet. Italian mail was examined and phone calls listened to by the Special Reserve Service.

There is no doubt that Bocchini's organisations were successful in suppressing opposition to the PNF. It is estimated that Bocchini held files on over 130,000 Italians. The Special Tribunals prosecuted 13,547 cases and imposed around 27,742 years of jail time. Around 10,000 Italians were sent into *Confino* and hundreds were arrested every week for antifascist activities, which usually meant they had been heard making antifascist or anti-Mussolini remarks. Prominent socialist and communist leaders had all fled the country, mostly to Paris. It should be noted, however, that the regime only carried out nine death sentences before the Second World War. This should not be seen as indicating the lack of repression in the fascist state, but the success of Bocchini and Mussolini in ensuring there was little serious opposition to the fascist regime. In fact, Mussolini's greatest concern with national security did not come from antifascists at all. Instead he was mostly worried about nationalist movements among the Slovenes who lived within Italy's borders. The Slovenes were restricted in their culture and the speaking of their national language and faced considerable oppression from the fascist authorities.

Overall, it is difficult to judge the extent to which fascism relied on repression. Antifascist activities and organisations were suppressed successfully, but the numbers arrested and sent to jail or *Confino* make it difficult to judge the extent of antifascist feeling within Italy. Whether Mussolini relied on repression, popular policy or the cult of *il Duce* to sustain his regime is a key debate between historians and something that you will have to come to a judgement on yourselves. It is entirely possible, that for many Italians, it was a combination of all three.

Anti-Semitic decrees

The cult of *il Duce* and the popularity of Mussolini reached its height in 1936, after which the fascist dictatorship went into

The Rosselli brothers and Justice and Liberty
Carlo and Nello Rosselli were Jewish Italian academics who had been disgusted by the violence of the fascist squads and the rise to power of Mussolini. Carlo was a member of the PSI and various antifascist organisations. In 1926, he was arrested and sentenced to five years imprisonment on Lipari Island for helping opponents to fascism escape overseas. In 1929, he escaped and fled to Paris with Nello where they established the antifascist organisation 'Justice and Liberty'. They wrote about the conditions in Italy and encouraged antifascist activities. During the Spanish Civil War, they organised 30,000 antifascist Italians, known as the Garibaldi Brigade, to join the antifascist forces in Spain. In March 1937, the Italian PNF forces were humiliated when they were defeated in a battle against the Garibaldi Brigade. This was a considerable propaganda success for the Rosselli brothers, which was publicised widely. After this, Mussolini decided to act. His son-in-law, Count Galeazzo Giano, organised a French fascist hit squad and in June 1937, both Nello (who was visiting Carlo) and Carlo Rosselli were murdered. After this, the activities of Justice and Liberty declined substantially.

a slow decline. Economic issues, a growing concern about the relationship with Germany and an inability of Mussolini continually to fulfil the grand promises he had made to the Italian people all contributed to the growing disillusionment with the dictatorship. One of the other key areas of discontent was the introduction of anti-Jewish policy in 1937. There had been little to no anti-Semitic rhetoric from Italian fascism previous to this and, unlike Nazism, Italian fascism had no particular focus on race. There were only around 45,000 Italian Jews in the country, less than one percent of the population. Many Jews had actually joined the fascists and Mussolini had had a Jewish mistress for many years and appointed a Jewish finance minister in 1932. However, in 1938 anti-Jewish legislation was introduced that forbade Italian Jews from marrying 'pure' Italians, holding public office jobs such as teaching, owning more than 50 hectares of land, running any businesses with over 100 employees or employing 'pure' Italians as servants. Foreign Jews were simply to be deported. Over the next three years, 6,000 Jews left the country. Jewish businesses closed down, Jewish students were expelled from Italian schools and Jewish lecturers at university lost their jobs.

While it is true that the anti-Semitic policies came at around the same time as the Nazis were pursuing a harder line on German Jews, there is no evidence that Hitler pressurised the Italian leader to implement anti-Jewish policy. It is possible, however, that the anti-Jewish policy of right-wing dictatorships in Germany, Austria, Hungary and Romania may have influenced his ideas to some degree. More importantly, Mussolini appears to have believed that a harsher policy towards the Jews in Italy would help create a more militaristic, radicalised society that would be united by their hatred for both external and internal enemies (in this case the Jews), thereby mirroring the **totalitarian** state of Germany. Italians needed to develop a 'racial' mentality that gave them a greater sense of their superiority over foreign races and their ability to conquer and rule other nations. Thus Italy would be a harsher, more racially focused society prepared for the war that Mussolini believed was soon to come.

It is worth noting that the anti-Semitic policies came at the same time as the 'reform of customs'. This was an ideological campaign that forced all civil servants to wear uniforms and the army and militia to adopt the *passo romano* or goose step, which Mussolini had witnessed in Germany and believed made the army look more imposing. Italians were forbidden to shake hands, which was seen as foreign and bourgeoisie, and instead had to greet each other with a straight arm salute, known as the 'Roman Salute'. These policies mirrored the anti-Semitic decrees in the idea that it was part of a greater transformation of the Italian people into a radicalised society preparing for war. Instead, the 'reform of customs' was ridiculed by the Italian people as a pointless and ridiculous exercise that was simply copied off the Germans and had no relevancy to their lives. Most chose to ignore it. The anti-Semitic policies were resented by the majority of the Italian people who had little to no history of anti-Semitism. The pope condemned the anti-Semitic policies as an un-Italian attempt to copy German Nazism. Italian people also viewed the policies as a worrying sign of Italy's growing weakness and subordination to German policy. The policy goal of Mussolini to unite the Italian people in a more radical fashion was a considerable failure. Not only did it lose support from the conservative elites of the Church, business and judiciary which Mussolini relied on for power, it caused many Italians to question the direction of fascist policy as the PNF appeared to be pursuing a more radical policy that was pushing Italy in a dangerous and concerning direction.

SOURCE 5

Manifesto of Racial Scientists, *Il Giornale d'Italia*, 14 July 1938. Mussolini was the main author, building upon the ideas of his key adviser on racial theory, the anthropologist Guido Landra, who believed that certain races were inferior to Europeans. Mussolini attempted to give the manifesto a scientific basis by having 42 leading pro-fascist doctors, anthropologists and biologists sign the document in support of racial theory on the grounds of supposed biological and medical 'evidence'.

The population of Italy today is of Aryan origin and its civilisation is Aryan. The Aryan people has inhabited Italy for several thousand years; little remains of the civilisation of the pre-Aryan people. The origin of the Italians today comes essentially from the elements of those same races that constitute and will constitute the permanent living fabric of Europe... There exists today a pure 'Italian Race.' This announcement is not based on the confusion of the biological concept of race with the historic linguistic concept of people and the nation, but on the very pure blood relationship that unites the Italians of today to the generations that for thousands of years have inhabited Italy. This ancient purity of blood is the grandest title of nobility of the Italian nation. The Jews do not belong to the Italian race. Of the Semites that have landed in the course of the centuries on the sacred soil of our Fatherland nothing in general remains. The Jews represent the only population that has never assimilated in Italy because they are composed of non-European racial elements, different in an absolute sense from those elements that gave rise to the Italians. The purely European physical and psychological characteristics of the Italians must not be altered in any way.

AS Level Exam-Style Question Section B

How far did Mussolini achieve his political goals in relation to Italy's youth in the years 1926–39? (20 marks)

Tip

This question is asking you to consider what Mussolini's goals were concerning Italy's youth and then how successful he was in achieving them. To answer it you will need to define exactly what he wanted to achieve, what his actual policies were and whether or not these policies can be said to have been successful.

WHAT WAS THE NATURE AND IMPORTANCE OF MUSSOLINI'S RELATIONSHIP WITH ITALY'S POLITICAL AND ECONOMIC ELITE?

Monarchy and conservative elites

Despite the implementation of Mussolini's dictatorship in the mid-1920s and his image in the cult of *il Duce* as Italy's unchallenged ruler, it is important to note that until September 1943, Italy remained a constitutional monarchy. Fascist propaganda may have proclaimed that 'Mussolini is always right', but in reality Mussolini could not completely ignore the political wishes of the king in order to maintain power. It was therefore a complex dictatorship, one in which Mussolini was both all-powerful ruler of the Italian people, but at the same time shared power with the monarchy in a complicated and sometimes difficult political arrangement. The original 1919 fascist programme had set out the aim of transforming Italy into a republic, but Mussolini had understood that such radical antimonarchy policies were a significant block to his goal of becoming prime minister; the 1920 programme therefore excluded any reference to removing the king. Instead, Mussolini was able to come to a political compromise with the monarchy. The agreement with the king was important for Mussolini's consolidation of power as it helped gain the acceptance of the fascist dictatorship among the armed forces and the state administration, who still retained considerable loyalty and respect towards the king. Mussolini was therefore prepared to work with King Victor Emanuel III in order to ensure he remained in power, but as the dictatorship became stronger, he slowly eroded some of the powers held by the king. In December 1928, the Fascist Grand Council had been granted the constitutional right to limit the king's power to nominate future prime ministers of Italy and to advise the king on any future royal succession. This was a considerable humiliation for the king. He had his power further minimised in March 1938 when the fascist parliament passed a law creating the title of First Marshal of the Empire, the highest rank in the military hierarchy, which was then given to both the king and Mussolini. Previous to this, the king had been supreme military commander. This was taken even further in June 1940 when Italy entered the Second World War and Mussolini deprived the king of his role as supreme military commander and took complete control of the military.

In the terms of the Italian constitution, the king remained head of state with sole power to remove Mussolini. However, throughout the fascist dictatorship, he made little effort to either prevent or minimise the erosion of Italy's constitutional democracy. The king was unwilling to challenge Mussolini and played a subservient role to the dictator as long as he was able to retain his position. King Victor Emanuel III, for instance, made no effort to prevent the implementation of the racist and unpopular anti-Semitic decrees introduced in 1938. By 1938, leading Italian lawyers were calling for a new constitution that reflected the realities of the fascist state. There is evidence that Mussolini was working towards getting rid of the monarchy and was simply waiting for the right time to make this more radical step in the final cementation of his dictatorship. For the most part, however, the relationship between the king and Mussolini was a political balancing act that suited both of them in respect to the positions they held throughout the fascist dictatorship.

Mussolini was also prepared to work with the existing conservative elites in order to cement and retain his power as dictator. Particularly important was the army, judiciary and the civil service. The legal system was largely unchanged and judges retained their independence from the party, although many did join the PNF to ensure they retained their positions. Mussolini also allowed the powerful institution of the military to run independently. Despite holding the position of minister of war, he left the running of the armed forces to the under-secretaries, who were mostly generals or admirals. In government administration there was also little change from the conservative elites who were able to maintain their influential positions in the political system. Some civil servants were removed due to antifascist political ties, but most kept their jobs. The majority of top administrative posts in the fascist ministries were held by career civil servants, for example, in the Ministry of Corporations all the senior staff had been civil servants since 1916. The highest state authority in each Italian province remained the prefect, and in the majority of cases these were career civil servants, not regional fascist leaders. Most critically, the traditional conservative elite was able to retain political influence through the newly created position of the *podestà*. These powerful municipal positions were mostly held by elderly conservatives, particularly in the south. Aristocrats and former generals were also prominent, thus the old ruling class were able to find an accommodation with fascism, retaining positions of power within the political system. For Mussolini, this was a crucial relationship that enabled a greater acceptance of his dictatorship and strengthened his position, albeit at the expense of full fascist control of government.

Central and local government

The laws of December 1925 substantially changed the structure of central government in Italy. Mussolini had taken on a new position as head of government, which meant he was now only accountable to the king, not parliament. The head of government alone could decide what parliament could discuss and only Mussolini could initiate legislation. Although the laws Mussolini implemented had to be ratified by parliament, this was little more than a rubber stamp. A further change took place in May 1928, which set out that parliament was to be made up of 400 deputies chosen by the Fascist Grand Council from a list of 1,000 candidates nominated by fascist confederations and public bodies.

EXTRACT

1   R.J.B. Bosworth, 'Dictators, strong or weak? The Model of Benito Mussolini', in *The Oxford Handbook of Fascism*, edited by R.J.B. Bosworth (2009).

Constitutionally speaking, at least until September 1943, Italy remained a monarchy. Mussolini's own personality cult and charisma therefore had to put up with ongoing competition, open and, more important, implicit, from the king and the numerous, fertile and active royal family... So too this dictator failed fully to conquer the military (not for nothing was Mussolini's replacement after the fall in July 1943 a general, Badoglio, appointed by the king). Big business was scarcely cowed... Despite the totalitarian talk, further down in society patron-client networks flourished and pressure groups remained active, with many Italians being as anxious to see what fascism and its dictator could do for them as they were to offer their service or souls to the regime and the Duce.

In December 1928, the Grand Council's role was formalised in the constitution as the most important legal body in the state. All major matters of government and party policy, as well as ministerial positions, were to be discussed and approved by the Grand Council. On paper this was a significant move that provided a constitutional framework for the PNF to retain power, even after the death of Mussolini. In reality, however, the Grand Council had little influence. Mussolini retained the power to appoint the top PNF leaders and set out the laws to be debated by the Grand Council. Crucially, the Grand Council had no consultation on major policies such as the accommodation with the Catholic Church in 1929 nor Italy's entry into the Second World War in 1940. Central power effectively lay with Mussolini and throughout the 1930s the Grand Council barely met. While this was a considerable change from the previous liberal constitution, Mussolini did chose to leave the Senate, whose members were appointed for life by the king, completely unchanged. In 1932, 148 senators were not members of the PNF. This was another example of Mussolini accommodating the existing political elite in order to cement his dictatorship. Over time, however, Mussolini was able to create a greater fascist presence in the Senate by ensuring all new senators were fascists.

In terms of local government, the traditional position of the Prefect as the highest state authority in each Italian province remained and, as discussed previously, the positions mostly were held by career civil servants. While the *ras* had hoped for considerable reform and the provinces to be placed under their control, Mussolini had no intention of allowing the provincial fascist leaders to hold such powerful positions. The prefect's job was considerably wide-ranging and involved organising the police, ensuring censorship of the local press and implementing the suppression of any antifascist activity. They were also tasked with reporting on the local fascist branches to ensure Mussolini was able to control the actions of the PNF throughout Italy. Although not always fascists, the prefects were appointed by Mussolini (as elections had been abolished) and this ensured loyalty to his political goals. The local councils within each province were run by the *podestà*, who were appointed by the prefect. As previously discussed, these too were usually given to the existing conservative elite rather than fascists. Thus local government was largely out of the control of the fascist party and was instead placed in the hands of conservative elite and career civil servants.

This should not be viewed, however, as lessening the power of Mussolini. It is crucial to note that the prefects and the *podestà* ultimately owed their position to Mussolini, thus ensuring that these local authorities would carry out his political policies and enabling him to strengthen his personal dictatorship at the expense of the PNF.

PNF and nationalists

One of the most crucial aspects of Mussolini's dictatorship was the way in which he was able to minimise the power of his own political party. He did this in various stages. Firstly, in 1925 through the appointment of Roberto Farinacci, who purged the party of those who did not agree with the political direction pursued by Mussolini. Farinacci, however, was an extremist and continued to encourage squad violence in the provinces, not only against the socialists but also towards the Catholics and members of the PPI. In October 1925, fascist squads murdered eight liberals in Florence. Following on from the Matteotti murder (see Chapter 2, page 209), this violence was now becoming considerably unpopular within Italy's population and hindered Mussolini's ability to stay in power. He purged the Florence Fascio and six months later dismissed Farinacci from his position, appointing the much more bureaucratic and reliable Augusto Turati. Turati ensured that the PNF became little more than a means to fulfil Mussolini's personal policies. Mass expulsions of older, more hard line fascists took place, with 50,000–60,000 members thrown out of the party by 1929 and another 110,000 leaving voluntarily, unhappy with the political direction Mussolini was taking. Turati's successor in 1931, Giuriati, oversaw the purge of another 120,000 members. These members were replaced by around 800,000 new fascists. Most of these were clerks, civil servants and white-collar workers, working in public services and local government. They had little interest in fascist revolution or challenging Mussolini and in the most part joined because of the employment opportunities and benefits PNF membership provided. In 1933, PNF membership became compulsory for these workers, thus ensuring that the party was dominated by middle-class members who were prepared to fulfil their roles within the political structure and had no interest in challenging Mussolini's position. Along with the power he held over the Grand Council and the appointment of the prefects, Mussolini ensured that central power lay completely with him and not with the PNF.

In terms of the Nationalist merger with the PNF, it is arguable that their political influence had a greater impact on Mussolini's policies than the more radical aspects of fascist thought. Nationalists such as Luigi Federzoni played an important role in the fascist government. Federzoni was appointed minister of the interior on 17 June 1924, an important move that helped placate the old conservative elites during the Matteotti crisis. As the ANI had accepted their merger with the fascist party, their members tended to follow the directions of Mussolini and posed no challenge to his political direction, unlike prominent members of the PNF. Other former ANI members, Roberto Cantalupo and Emilio Bodrero, would play a role in influencing the direction of fascist educational policy, with Cantalupo asserting that fascism's most important goal should be the creation of a new generation of Italians loyal to fascist ideals. Costanzo Ciano, another ex-Nationalist, played an influential role as minister of communications from 1924 to 1934, making him the longest serving minister in the history of the fascist regime, aside from Mussolini himself. As the direction of Mussolini's policies became more radical in the late 1930s, nationalist ideas took on greater prominence. The nationalist concern that Italy was viewed too much as having a great history but little else, was taken up by Mussolini who said that any real ally of Italy should understand its military power in the present, not focus on past aspects like Rome or the Renaissance. An ex-ANI member, Giotto Dainelli, was key in trying to rid Italy of foreign sounding words, particularly when it came to hotel names, as part of the 'reform of customs' pursued in the late 1930s. Ultimately, Mussolini's aggressive foreign policy, particularly from the mid-1930s, could be said to owe as much to nationalist thought on Italian expansion and imperialism, going back at least as far as the ANI's foundation in 1910, as it did fascist ideology.

Economic interest groups

Mussolini had inherited a difficult but improving economic situation in 1922. His first economic policy had focused on placating the large economic interest groups, such as Fiat and Pirelli. The economic interest of small shop owners was also protected, with a licensing system introduced that protected these retailers against larger supermarkets. However, it was Italian businesses that benefited most from the PNF's economic policies. Trade union policy under the fascists had constantly been adapted to take both the interests of the industrialists and the fascist **syndicalists**, who were in favour of policies that gained the support of the working classes, into account. In October 1925, the industrialists had recognised the fascist syndicates as the only representative body for Italian workers. This was known as the Palazzo Vidoni Pact and ensured the disillusion of the Catholic, socialist and communist trade unions, which were now irrelevant institutions.

KEY TERM

Syndicalism
An ideology that was older than fascism, dating from around 1895. It was presented as an economic system between capitalism and communism. Private businesses would remain but there would be no class conflict between the workers' trade unions and the employers. Instead, employers and employees would form syndicates, cooperative groups combining employee and employer representatives from different aspects of the economy. They would discuss policy on an equal basis and set the economic direction of the country. Many syndicalists joined the fascist movement believing that Mussolini would implement this system in Italy. There was some movement towards syndicalism in the 1920s but ultimately the syndicalists would be disappointed by Mussolinii's economic policies which promised radical changes but never seriously tried to move towards the economic system.

This is not to say that the fascist syndicates were simply subservient to industrial interests. Prominent syndicalists argued that the fascist syndicates should be the basis of the state, whereby corporations of employers and employees would run the economy together in a new order of cooperation. This would both ensure the regulation of big business in the workers' interests and in return

the workers would not engage in industrial unrest, thus heralding an end to the class struggle that had blighted Italy for so long. The conservative industrial elite, however, was gravely concerned about this economic concept and Mussolini had no intention of alienating this powerful group. In April 1926, the Rocco Law was passed, named after the minister of justice, Alfredo Rocco. The law allowed the syndicates some rights of representation and for compulsory arbitration of disputes concerning workers' pay and conditions at special labour tribunals. However, strikes, go-slows and lockouts were banned and the syndicates would have no say in government policy. The absence of strikes and worker ability to disrupt industrial production was, understandably, welcomed by industrial interest groups.

During the international economic slump of the 1930s, the government pursued polices that propped up and supported big business and encouraged further wage cuts for workers, thus favouring the interests of big industry such as the Montecatini (chemicals) and ILVA (steel). Mussolini also pursued a range of policies that pleased Italy's large- and medium-sized landowners. Thus it is clear that the richer industrial and agricultural interest groups were the main benefactors of fascist economic policies. Workers' interests, both in the north and in the south, were subsidiary to concerns of the more powerful economic elites. In the rural areas, there was little benefit for peasants and small landowners and workers across Italy saw their wages reduced below the cost of living from 1927 onwards.

SOURCE 6

From Alfredo Rocco, *The Political Doctrine of Fascism*, 1926. Here Rocco argues why a law is required to restrict the ability of workers to strike.

We must reject, therefore, the socialistic solution but we cannot allow the problem raised by the Socialists to remain unsolved, not only because justice demands a solution but also because the persistence of this problem in liberal and democratic régimes has been a menace to public order and to the authority of the state. Unlimited and unrestrained class self-defense, evinced by strikes and lockouts, by boycotts and sabotage, leads inevitably to anarchy… Class organization is a fact which cannot be ignored but it must be controlled, disciplined, and subordinated by the state.

ACTIVITY
KNOWLEDGE CHECK

1 In Source 6, how does Alfredo Rocco justify the introduction of the Rocco Law?

2 In what way did the Rocco Law fulfil the last sentence of Source 6?

3 Using Extract 1, Source 6 and your own studies, summarise all the ways in which Mussolini compromised with powerful institutions within Italian society.

4 Group discussion: Do you believe that these compromises made Mussolini a weak or a strong dictator? This is a difficult question – if the compromises helped keep him in power for around 23 years, does this mean he was a strong leader? It depends on what you might define as Mussolini's goal: was it to just stay in power or did he truly want to transform Italy?

HOW SUCCESSFULLY DID MUSSOLINI'S ECONOMIC PLANS ACHIEVE THEIR AIMS?

Early policies and the shift towards fascist economics

Mussolini's first goal in economic policy had been to win over the powerful, established industrial elite of Italian society. To this end, he had appointed the conservative economics professor Alberto De'Stefani as minister of finance, a move that had pleased Italy's business groups. De'Stefani favoured an economic policy that had little government interference and focused on reducing government spending in order to balance the budget. De'Stefani privatised the telephone sector and other public-owned industry and reduced state expenditure. He also deregulated the economy and cut protective tariffs. This had some success; from 1921 to 1924, Italy's manufacturing production improved and Italy achieved a budget surplus. However, agricultural groups were unhappy about the reduction in tariffs and De'Stefani grappled with the inflationary problems and pressure on the lira in foreign markets that Italy's rapid economic growth produced.

In July 1925, De'Stefani was replaced by Giuseppe Volpi. This marked a transition in fascist economic policy towards a more regulated, state-run economy that had a greater personal influence from Mussolini. The first example of this was the 'Battle for Lira' launched in August 1926. In 1922, the Italian currency had stood at 90 lira to the British pound sterling, but by 1926 this had sunk to 150 lira. Mussolini was concerned that Italy could face an inflationary crisis that would particularly hurt the middle classes. However, more importantly, Mussolini viewed the strength of the lira as representing the strength of the fascist regime itself. In August 1926, he informed Volpi that 'the fate of the regime is tied to the fate of the lira'. He declared that the revaluation of the lira was a battle that had to be won by the sacrifices of the Italian nation. In December 1927, the lira was artificially fixed at 19 to the American dollar and 92.46 to the British pound sterling. This was meant to demonstrate the will of *il Duce* and his power to uphold Italian economic pride. The economic costs, however, were considerable. Volpi and other economic experts believed that this valuation was too high and the government was forced to introduce a range of deflationary measures, massive price reductions and cuts to workers' wages. Export industries were the main losers, as Mussolini's policy overvalued Italian products in overseas' markets. However, the Battle for the Lira was the first important example of how the economy was shifting towards a greater focus on policies that would represent Mussolini's power and strength as a leader and less on the actual economic needs of the Italian people.

The Corporate State

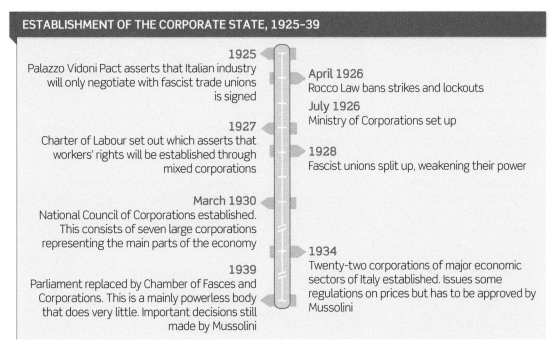

ESTABLISHMENT OF THE CORPORATE STATE, 1925–39

1925
Palazzo Vidoni Pact asserts that Italian industry will only negotiate with fascist trade unions is signed

April 1926
Rocco Law bans strikes and lockouts

July 1926
Ministry of Corporations set up

1927
Charter of Labour set out which asserts that workers' rights will be established through mixed corporations

1928
Fascist unions split up, weakening their power

March 1930
National Council of Corporations established. This consists of seven large corporations representing the main parts of the economy

1934
Twenty-two corporations of major economic sectors of Italy established. Issues some regulations on prices but has to be approved by Mussolini

1939
Parliament replaced by Chamber of Fasces and Corporations. This is a mainly powerless body that does very little. Important decisions still made by Mussolini

One of Mussolini's most prominent policies was the implementation of the Corporate State. The construction of the Corporate State grew out of the Rocco Law of 1926 that had failed completely to balance the interests of the fascist syndicates and Italian industry. Later that year, Mussolini had set up a new ministry entitled the Ministry of Corporations. In theory, the Corporations were meant to be a mixed union of workers and employers who would discuss and implement national economic planning that was conducive to both their interests, thus producing a more productive and harmonious economic order. Under Giuseppe Bottai, the 'Charter of Labour' was drawn up in 1927 which promised that these mixed corporations would organise Italy's economy and guarantee workers' rights in employment, social insurance and welfare. However, the Charter was simply a programme of intent and was never followed through. The Ministry did very little except mediate in labour disputes and reduce the power of the fascist syndicates.

In 1928, the head of the fascist syndicates, Edmondo Rossoni, was dismissed and the syndicates split up into six parts representing the main areas of the economy that were mirrored by six employers' confederations representing the same groups. In 1930, a National Council of Corporations was founded, which was meant to be a consultative body made up of employer and worker organisations representing seven large sectors of the Italian economy. In 1934, another law was passed which implemented mixed corporations representing 22 major economic sectors. These corporations could allegedly fix the prices of goods and rates of service, settle industrial disputes, regulate apprenticeships, advise the government on economic issues and help produce a more productive economic system. On paper, this was a highly complex government system involving the National Council of Corporations and the 22 mixed corporations of major economic sectors. In reality, it was simply propaganda. The corporations were essentially councils where the workers and employers met under the guidance of the PNF. However, only one side was actually represented. While members of the employers' corporations were chosen by employers, the workers were not represented by workers at all, but by fascist officials approved by Mussolini, who was Minister of Corporations. Any plans put forward by the corporations had to be approved by the National Council of Corporations (which became the Central Corporative Committee in 1935) headed by Mussolini, who alone could decide what could become actual law. Real power over the economy was thus held by Mussolini, and major economic decisions were generally made through private discussion with major economic interest groups outside the vast corporate bureaucracy.

You may, therefore, rightly question what was the point of this vast, essentially impractical and useless bureaucratic construction? On a practical level, the Corporate State provided jobs for loyal fascists. It was also excellent propaganda and was used to prove that Mussolini had overcome the problems of class conflict and constructed a 'third way' between capitalism and communism that harmonised industrial relations and meant all Italians, employers and workers, were working in sync towards the national interest. This was essentially nonsense; Salvemini aptly described trying to understand what the corporations actually did as 'looking in a dark room for a black which is not there', but Mussolini's creation

was studied by political scientists and economists from across the world, who acclaimed this new and original economic system. Once again, practical economic policy was subservient to a façade that was more intent on constructing Mussolini as a leader of international renown who could achieve the impossible, rather than actually implementing a workable economic basis for Italy.

SOURCE 7

From speeches made by Mussolini in 1926 and 1927. Here he reflects on the establishment and success of the Corporate State.

We have created the united state of Italy remember that since the Empire Italy had not been a united state. Here I wish to reaffirm solemnly our doctrine of the State. Here I wish to reaffirm with no weaker energy, the formula I expounded at the scala in Milan everything in the state, nothing against the State, nothing outside the state... We have constituted a Corporative and Fascist State, the State of national society, a State which concentrates, controls and harmonises and tempers the interests of all social classes, which are thereby protected in equal measure. Whereas, during the years of demo-liberal regime, labour looked with diffidence upon the State, was, in fact, outside the State and against the State, and considered the State an enemy of every day and every hour, there is not one working Italian today who does not seek a place in his Corporation or federation, who does not wish to be a living atom of that great, immense, living organisation which is the National Corporate State of Fascism.

SOURCE 8

From articles written by Gaetano Salvemini in 1935. Here he argues that the claims about the Corporate State being a fair balance between workers and employers are untrue.

The Fascists claim that the dictatorship has bestowed a legal status upon the organisations of employers, employees, and professional classes. It has given them a place in the public law while in the pre-Fascist period they had merely a de facto existence. But the pre-Fascist organisations operated according to the will of their members. In the Fascist organisations the will of the members is suppressed. The members are passive and inert material. All action is the province of the officials, and they're accountable not to the members, but to the leaders of the party and to the governmental bureaucracy. The organisations are no longer representative and militant organs of masters and workers but devised for the better disciplining of labour and capital... The negotiations of agreements concerning wages, hours, disciplinary sanctions, indemnities etc. is carried out by the official organisations in each economic group, which means in the case of the employers' associations the representatives of the big interests, and in the case of the unions the appointed officials [fascists] who run them... In conclusion, and viewed in the most favourable light, in the Fascist legal organisations the rank and file have no greater authority than do the animals in a society for the prevention of cruelty to animals.

Response to the Depression

Mussolini's economic policies in the early stages of the Great Depression (1930–33) were arguably quite successful in shielding Italy from the full impact of the worldwide economic downturn.

To help businesses survive, the government cut workers' wages by around 12 percent in November 1930 and encouraged price fixing and **cartelisation**. Mergers were common and in some cases were made compulsory. This ensured that employment levels stayed fairly stable as the large mergers meant that fewer businesses were forced to close. Employment was also provided through large public works schemes such as road building, house construction and electrification of railways. Government funding of road building doubled between 1929 and 1933, and 5,000 kilometres of railway was electrified. Welfare was also increased to ease the difficulties of those workers who could not find employment. In banking, the government ensured that major banks that had loaned millions of lire to Italian businesses were protected from possible collapse through the Istituto Mobiliare Italiano (IMI) policy. It provided credit to banks to guarantee they would not collapse. The other major policy was the Istituto di Ricostruzione Industriale (IRI) scheme. Through this policy the government bought up shares in banking, industry and commerce, to help prop up the Italian economy and ensure that these companies did not go bankrupt and collapse. It then provided education on new management techniques and gave financial and technical assistance to support the growth of these Italian industries that were now state owned. Once the companies were in a healthy state, they sold the shares back to private ownership. By 1939, the government owned a majority of companies in the steelworks, shipbuilding, electricity, machine tool construction and telephone industries. Through the IRI and IMI, government intervention guaranteed financial support for both the banks and key employment industries and thus was quite successful in maintaining public confidence in the economy that helped sustain Italy through the Great Depression.

KEY TERM

Cartelisation
Refers to forced mergers whereby the fascist government assisted large businesses to take over smaller companies within certain sections of the economy. This was encouraged during the Great Depression as it meant less competition in the Italian economy and therefore less chance of smaller businesses closing. Cartelisation, made obligatory in 1936, enabled large businesses to avoid competition and fix the prices for their goods within their domestic market. Large companies who dominated Italian industry welcomed the policy, but it also lessened innovation and competition in Italian industry and meant that prices remained high for the Italian public.

Autarky

Another key aspect of Mussolini's economic policy was autarky – the quest for economic self-sufficiency for Italy. This was driven principally by three factors:

- the general decline in Italian overseas trade due to the overvalued lira and the Great Depression

- the sanctions placed on Italy in 1936 in a response to the militaristic actions in Africa

- the preparation for war, which became more prominent in the late 1930s.

Trade was conducted through bilateral agreements, which ensured that the value of imports strictly matched the value of exports. This ensured that Italy could minimise and control imports and would not have to use its foreign currency or gold reserves to pay for them. This was a key part of autarky. Mussolini strengthened the country's control of foreign currency and its import licensing system and boosted Italy's export industry by devaluing the lira in October 1936. Thus it was hoped that Italy would become much more economically self-sufficient and be able to rely less on overseas imports. Through the IRI scheme the government took over private firms if it was justified for the national defence, autarky and imperialist goals of the fascist government. These companies, predominately in the iron and steel sector, were made responsible for improving Italy's economic self-sufficiency by finding sources of energy, metals and raw materials within Italy and its colonies, and where this was not possible developing synthetic substitutes. Agricultural products such as cereals and wool, along with raw materials, were stockpiled in order to boost Italian stocks and guarantee a consistent supply at regular prices. Government spending on autarkic measures and heavy industry doubled from 30 billion lire in 1934 to 60 billion by 1938. Despite this, the government's success in achieving its goals in relation to autarky by 1940 is debatable.

The Battle for Births and the Battle for Grain

The Battle for Births was announced by Mussolini in May 1927, and was aimed at encouraging Italians to increase the size of their families so that by the 1950s, Italy would have a population of at least 60 million. Mussolini believed that Italy's population size of 40 million and its low birth rate was clearly detrimental to the country's goal of becoming a world power. The party declared that 40 million Italians was not a large enough population to compete with the much larger populations of Germany and Russia. Military strength could be boosted by a larger population. Economically, it was believed that a larger population would create more competition for employment and thus keep wages and labour costs low and would also increase the number of consumers. It was also felt that population growth improved the quality of the population.

The policy was closely linked to Mussolini's aims of developing better relations with the Catholic Church. The ideal of Italian women focused on the family with the sole aim of giving birth to and raising as many children as possible fitted very closely with Catholic values. The poorer southern areas, such as Basilicata, where traditional values regarding women and the family still dominated, and which consequently had high birth rates, were now held up as an example to the rest of Italy as the ideal to be followed. Tax reductions and loans were provided for families with large numbers of children and prizes given, sometimes by Mussolini himself in Rome, to the mothers of these families. From 1928, employed men were given tax concessions if they had a family of seven children or more. Alternatively, the bachelor's tax ensured that single men took on more of a financial burden in comparison to married men with families. Fathers of large families were given better career opportunities, with promotions and employment in government jobs favouring married men with families. All forms of birth control were banned and women's employment in industry and service were opposed, as it was believed that this was not compatible with maternal duties. As in his other economic policies, the achievements of the Battle for Births were considerably mixed.

The Battle for Grain was an agricultural policy that was linked to autarky and aimed at making Italy self-sufficient in grain. It was announced in 1925 as a response to a substantial growth both in grain imports and their international price. Wheat tariffs were brought in and then increased in 1928 and 1929. A huge propaganda campaign was launched to free Italy from the 'slavery of foreign bread'. Annual wheat growing competitions were held and farmers were subsidised by government grants to increase wheat and cereal production. The fascists made a considerable effort educating growers on new farming techniques and providing fertilisers, farm machinery and more resistant seeds to boost wheat production. More wheat was therefore able to be grown in previously unsuitable areas and in northern and central Italy grain production rose 50 percent on the levels previous to 1914. However, despite the fact that Italy was largely self-sufficient in wheat production by the mid-1930s, the policy would have serious consequences on Italian agriculture in other areas.

SOURCE

9

From Emil Ludwig, *Talks with Mussolini*, 1932. These were the transcripts of unedited interviews held between 23 March and 4 April 1932. Here, Ludwig asked Mussolini about the role of women in public life.

He [Mussolini] answered more stubbornly than ever: Women must play a passive part. She is analytical, not synthetical. During all the centuries of civilisation has there ever been a woman architect? Ask her to build you a mere hut, not even a temple; she cannot do it. She has no sense for architecture, which is the synthesis of all the arts; that is a symbol of her destiny. My notion of woman's role in the State is utterly opposed to feminism. Of course I do not want women to be slaves, but if in Italy I proposed to give our women votes they would laugh me to scorn. As far as political life is concerned, they do not count here. In England there are three million more women than men, but in Italy the numbers of the two sexes are the same. Do you know where the Anglo-Saxon countries are likely to end? In a matriarchy!

ACTIVITY
WRITING

Read through Source 9 and complete the following exercises.

1 Identify any words that you don't understand and research their meanings.

2 Identify words and phrases that demonstrate Mussolini's attitude to women.

3 Now write a paragraph describing and explaining Mussolini's views towards women using extracts from Source 9 as well as any other research you have conducted on policies such as the Battle for Births to back up your argument.

Agricultural policies

In addition to the Battle for Grain, Mussolini's other major agricultural policy concerned 'ruralisation' and land reclamation and improvement schemes. The policy of 'ruralism' was announced at the same time as the Battle for Births in 1927. The two were somewhat connected; Mussolini believed that the decline in Italy's birth rate was closely tied to industrial urbanisation and modern city life and that in order to maintain its traditional values and boost its population, Italy had to protect and maintain its peasant population and its agricultural industry. Mussolini commonly exalted the traditional values of Italy's rural population in contrast to the decadent and corrupt pleasure-seeking lifestyle found in the modern city, where he still suspected the majority of the working class harboured socialist values. In 1928, Mussolini launched the 'empty the cities' campaign that prevented internal migration from Italy's rural areas to the cities. To encourage peasants to stay in rural areas, a massive land reclamation and improvement scheme was launched, known as the *bonifica integrale*. Marsh draining projects, irrigation, road building, house building and aqueduct construction were all carried out in a project to provide more arable land for Italy's peasantry. The government claimed that this would be carried out on around 475 million hectares and provide land for Italy's peasant farmers. These peasants were to be carefully selected for their working and childbearing qualities, and thus the Italian countryside would be repopulated and agriculture made more productive.

Mussolini with farmers at Littoria, one of the new towns created after the draining of Pontine Marshes in 1932.

ACTIVITY
KNOWLEDGE CHECK

1 Study Source 10. What image was this supposed to give of Mussolini and his relationship with Italy's rural population?

2 How did this official Fascist photo encourage traditional ideals of rural Italy?

Successes and failures

Overall, from a purely economic point of view, it is fairly clear that most of Mussolini's economic policies did not achieve their objectives. As discussed previously, one of the first key fascist policies, the Battle for Lira, caused serious deflation and hampered Italy's export industries. The Corporate State produced a vast, complex and expensive bureaucracy that never achieved its alleged aims. Industrial employers and Mussolini were never entirely serious about developing a representative system where workers and employers would share responsibility for the economy and all the major decisions were made by Mussolini alone in consultation with large industrial interest groups. While it is true that Italy protected employment and its banks during the Great Depression in a more successful way than either Germany or the USA, for example, these policies had more long-term consequences. The IRI was successful in ensuring banking stability and employment by sustaining failing businesses. The public works schemes in roads and hydro-electricity provided jobs and benefits to many Italians. Italy's industrial development by 1939 was considerable in comparison to when the fascists had taken government in 1922.

However, the schemes were expensive; by 1936 the Italian state owned a larger percentage of industry than any other country in Europe apart from the Soviet Union. Italy's budget deficit grew massively and its foreign reserves were depleted. This was accentuated by increased welfare spending during the Depression with the percentage of all state and local tax receipts spent on welfare increasing from 6.9 to 20.6 percent between 1930 and 1940. To try to deal with this problem, taxes were raised and a 'forced loan' of five percent on the value of housing had to be paid. The policy of cartelisation and the IRI maintained jobs but restricted innovation and rationalisation of the economy and kept prices high. Autarky was an almost impossible goal for a country like Italy, which lacked raw materials and had to import coal and oil. Products were being produced that would have been cheaper to buy from overseas companies, thus adding to the national deficit. Italy's economy was becoming seriously distorted in its focus on autarky and war materials and the expense of consumer goods. Wage cuts, the lack of worker representation and four direct taxes on property, capital and shareholdings that were introduced between 1935 and 1939, saw wages fall below the cost of living. There is evidence that the unpopularity of the PNF, although not Mussolini himself, was growing, particularly in the cities, between 1936 and 1939.

Further problems can be seen in relation to the Battle for Grain. Italy was undoubtedly successful in producing more wheat, with production rising from 5.39 million tonnes to 7.27 million between 1925 and 1935 and imports were massively reduced. However, the government incentives meant many farmers in the south removed their olive trees, citrus fruit and vineyards to make more land available for wheat growing. These had been major export industries for Italy that Spain now took over. Cattle and sheep farming were reduced considerably, seriously affecting the Italian diet, and the lack of competition increased the price of grain and bread. It is estimated the families had to pay about 400 lire per year extra in food costs.

Mussolini's other key agricultural policy, ruralisation, was also, overall, a failure. In areas where only marsh draining was required, such as the Pontine Marshes, where, by 1935, marsh lands had been turned into a quite successful farming area, then the land reclamation was quite successful. However, in areas, mainly in the south, where more intense irrigation and complex work was required, it was barely attempted. Only around five percent of the claimed 475 million hectares was actually improved and only 10,000 landless peasants were ever given land through the scheme. The scheme did work in two ways, however. The draining of the marshes reduced malaria by around 50 percent and this huge public work project provided considerable employment during the Great Depression. Most significantly, despite his aims, under Mussolini's dictatorship over half a million people left Italy's rural areas, and for the first time in Italy's history more than 50 percent of the population were not involved in the agricultural industry.

The Battle for Births was also questionable. By the 1930s, Fascist Italy had the highest proportion of married females in employment than any other European country despite their efforts to force women into the home. The government had tried to discourage women from working by lowering their wages in 1927, but this only encouraged employers to hire them. Cuts in men's wages during the Great Depression also meant that many women had to work to provide for their families. Overall, the policy had little success; Italy's birth rate continued to decline and the marriage rate fell.

EXTEND YOUR KNOWLEDGE

The difficulty in assessing the 'successes' of economic policy

It is clear that in most areas, Mussolini's economic policies were either unsuccessful or had negative consequences, as in the Battle for Grain, on other aspects of Italian life. However, what should be noted when assessing whether a policy was successful or not is that in many ways the propaganda of his economic policies was just as important as the reality. The Corporate State, for instance, may have been a confusing failure but the propaganda that Mussolini had developed a truly unique economic system and this was the reason Italy had done better than other nations during the Great Depression was extremely powerful. The Battle for Grain and the Battle for Births were grand campaigns that appeared to show the dynamism of fascism, as did the land reclamation schemes which allegedly demonstrated that Mussolini was actually changing the Italian land itself and providing greater farming opportunities to the Italian people. The announcement of these 'battles' was shown on newsreels at the cinemas and accompanied by dramatic speeches by Mussolini asserting what these policies would achieve. The inauguration of the 'Battle for Grain', for example, showed a bare-chested Mussolini working alongside the peasantry harvesting wheat. Even the fact that the policies were called 'battles' added to the dramatic feeling associated with the economic aims being pursued by the PNF. Mussolini believed that the grand launch of a scheme that people remembered was possibly more important than the success or failure of the policy itself, as long as people believed that fascism was dynamic and making a difference to Italy it did not matter if this was not really the case. Journalism, he claimed, had taught him that people had fairly short memories and tended to remember the drama associated with a story, rather than the outcome. To Mussolini, politics was propaganda; you could not neatly separate the two. There seems clear evidence, however, that by 1939 the growing gap between the propaganda and reality was adding to general disenchantment with the fascist regime.

ACTIVITY
KNOWLEDGE CHECK

1 Summarise the major successes and failures of Mussolini's economic policies.

2 Now try to shorten the list to his top three successes and top three failures. Explain your choices.

3 Finally, shorten your list further to his main success and main failure. Again, explain your answer.

A Level Exam-Style Question Section B

To what extent was Mussolini's economic policy successful in the years 1926–39? (20 marks)

Tip
Make sure you cover the entire period, looking for successes and failures over the 13 years. Don't just focus, for instance, on the Great Depression. You might also want to consider the propaganda value that Mussolini achieved from his policies, as well as their economic outcomes.

SOURCE **11**

From the 1939 revised edition of Benito Mussolini's memoirs entitled *My Autobiography*. Mussolini dictated parts of the text to his brother, Arnaldo Mussolini, who put it together with other material supplied by Margarita Sarfatti, Mussolini's lover. The manuscript was then handed to Richard Washburn Child (the former American ambassador to Italy) who worked with Luigi Barzini, Jr to write the completed 'autobiography' in a form mainly aimed at American readers.

If Mussolini stopped for a few minutes in his work at Palazzo Chigi, at the end of 1928, and surveyed his work over five years, he could have probably felt the pride of a sea captain who sees the ship which he has taken over in a bad state of repair, scraped, painted, repaired, modified, modernized. From all points of view the progress made by Italy under the first five years of Mussolini's rule was astounding. Finances were good, the colonies had been practically reconquered, the Navy and the Air Force were being supplied with new ships, built in Italy by Italian engineers and workmen, the Army was being reorganised. All internal enemies of the regime were either co-operating with it, having discovered the truth that – in times of stress – it is better to do first and to grumble afterwards, or were abroad. There was a steadily increasing influx of foreign tourists into the country, an increase in export trade and increase in gold reserves. Taxes were being reduced, confidence was high. The ship was being equipped for a long trip. What trip? Only the captain knew. But he was too much of a wise man to choose an itinerary which was not in accordance with the history of Italy, with the state of the world at the time.

SOURCE **12**

Benito Mussolini, *My Autobiography*, 1939 (revised edition).

Incidentally, in reading this account of the Fascist state, English speaking readers will find the answer to the famous question which every Italian abroad has been asked hundreds of times: 'What will happen after Mussolini?' The answer, of course, is 'Nothing.' We shall mourn the loss of one of the world's great men, a man who has created a new form of government, a new civilisation, a new conception of law and life. But the machine he created and built will continue to fulfil its functions.

SOURCE **13**

This is the Foreword to Mussolini's autobiography.

Parallel to the meteoric rise of Adolf Hitler is the astonishing career of Benito Mussolini, Italy's great Dictator. This gripping narrative told by himself of his humble beginnings, his activities as a socialist and a soldier in the Great War, his subsequent rapid accession to power, provides a most interesting comparison to his counter part beyond the Brenner Pass [referring to Hitler].

SOURCE **14**

George Seldes, *Sawdust Caesar: The Untold History of Mussolini and Fascism*, 1935. Seldes had been the *Chicago Tribune*'s correspondent in Italy from 1919 to 1925, during which time he documented Mussolini's career and the rise of fascism. In 1925, he was expelled from Italy due to his critical coverage of the Matteotti murder. His negative experiences of fascism were the basis of his 1935 book.

Since the depression Fascism has come to a dead stop. All that it has had in the past four or five years is a record of broken promises, an unbearable debt burden, and the dynamic oratory of the Duce. But one cannot live on oratory alone. We have seen the collapse of every financial and economic factor in Fascist Italy, exports, imports, emigrants' remittances, tourist trade; we have seen the debts grow mountainous, the national debt increase 15,000,000,000 in four years; we know that the international bankers have refused to issue loans, and we know that the tremendous population pressure has increased during the ten years which now mark the Italian depression. Every economist and every intelligent student has been aware of the forces which for a decade have been driving the dictator into either war or collapse... Today the paralysis which has invaded Fascism, its finances, economies, culture, and spirit also demand a blood bath, and to forestall it in civil war and at the same time satisfy imperialism, which historically has advanced from one blood bath to another, Italy must take the road to foreign war. Although black, the Fascist shirts have become very dirty, and must be washed in blood.

How far could the historian make use of Sources 11 and 14 together to investigate the success of Mussolini's economic plans in the years 1925–40?

Explain your answer, using both sources, the information given about them and your own knowledge of the historical context. (20 marks)

Tip

Both these sources are obviously quite subjective, but they are still useful to understanding the goals and realities of Mussolini's economic plans. How accurate are the claims made in Source 11? Consider what Mussolini's motives are and how close Seldes's description is to the historical understanding you have. How can this help us evaluate Mussolini's economic plans?

THINKING HISTORICALLY | Evidence (5b)

The importance of context

Documents (texts) are like small pieces torn from a larger tapestry (context). Historians have to reconstruct the larger pattern into which documents might fit in order to use them to construct accounts of the past. The problem is that texts can have multiple contexts. Historians often debate how best to contextualise the documents that they interpret.

Carefully read Sources 11, 12 and 13 from Mussolini's autobiography and complete the activities that follow.

1 Summarise the overall image of Mussolini that is being presented in Sources 11 and 12. Use quotes to back up your argument.

2 How would Italians have possibly reacted to this source (the autobiography)? Think about how long Mussolini had been in power at this stage.

3 It is crucial to consider Mussolini's audience for his autobiography. It was written primarily for an American audience. How does this information help you understand the purpose of Mussolini's autobiography?

4 How does the context of the source's intended audience change its meaning? Given that the audience was Americans and not Italians, consider the language used in Mussolini's autobiography.

5 The historical context is also critical in interpreting sources. Mussolini's autobiography was originally published in 1929 and then republished with additions ten years later. Consider the very different historical context of Mussolini's rule in 1929 and then in 1939. How would this change the interpretation of the autobiography by American readers?

6 Consider Source 13, the forward to Mussolini's book. What other motivation appears to have driven the publication of his book? How does this provide another understanding of the text?

7 Why is it important for historians to spend time thinking about possible contexts for a document before they start to use it to draw conclusions about the past?

HOW FAR DID MUSSOLINI'S RELATIONSHIP WITH THE CATHOLIC CHURCH IMPACT ON HIS FASCIST DICTATORSHIP?

The move away from anticlerical views

The fascist movement and its original founders, including Mussolini, had been largely anticlerical. Despite the fact that Mussolini's mother was Catholic, he had taken after his father who was atheist and opposed to the influence of the Church. He had published several articles where he contrasted the life of Jesus with the wealth and corruption of the Catholic Church and had even published a book entitled *The Cardinal's Mistress*, which portrayed the Church as a place of hypocrisy, violence and sexual activity. Mussolini's anger towards the Church had been furthered by the events of the First World War. Pope Benedict XV's attempts to end the First World War through the Peace Note of August 1917 had drawn the anger of Mussolini who believed it had helped spread pacifism and defeatism, coming as it did after Italy's defeat at Caporetto (see Chapter 1, page 185). The first programme of the *Fasci di Combattimento* in 1919 had called for the confiscation of all church property (see Chapter 2, page 197). However, as the early fascist movement developed, it was clear to Mussolini that radical anticlericalism was not conducive to taking power in a strongly Catholic country like Italy. As part of fascism's general move to the right, he dropped his anticlerical rhetoric along with his anticapitalism and antimonarchism. At the fascist congress of May 1920, when the new programme was set out, Mussolini declared that Catholicism could be used as a political force that would drive Italian unity and nationalism. While some of the original fascists, particularly the Futurists, were angered by Mussolini's new attitude to the Church, most of the Fasci leadership understood that dropping anticlericalism and finding an understanding with the Catholic Church could help them in their quest for power. During his maiden speech to parliament in May 1921,

Mussolini publicly asserted fascism's positive view of the Catholic Church, saying 'fascism neither preaches nor practises anticlericalism… The only universal values that radiate from Rome are those of the Vatican.'

Pope Pius XI

Mussolini's relations with the Church were helped by the death of Benedict XV in January 1922 and his replacement by Cardinal Achille Ratti, who took on the title Pope Pius XI. This pope's policy towards the fascists differed considerably from his predecessor. Pope Pius XI was predominately concerned with the communist threat in Italy and believed that a government of 'National Concentration' including the fascists was the only means by which Italy could be saved from left-wing revolution. After he became prime minister, Mussolini responded to the pope's positive view of fascism through a range of policies that were favourable to the Church. Religious education was reintroduced into Italian state secondary schools, crucifixes were restored to public buildings and priests had an increase in their pay. The Vatican had a substantial stake in the Bank of Rome that was in danger of collapsing, so in January 1923, Mussolini guaranteed that his government would bail out the bank. Mussolini also banned **Freemasonry** and anticlerical journals and dropped proposed liberal policies on taxing church property. He made the important gesture of having his three children baptised into the Catholic Church and marrying his wife Donna Rachele in a church ceremony (he had married her in 1915 in a civil ceremony). This close relationship with the Church helped to undermine the PPI, as Pius XI put his support behind the PNF at the expense of the traditional Catholic party. In 1923, the pope ordered the PPI leader, Luigi Sturzo, to resign and called on the party to support the PNF. During the Matteotti crisis, he strongly backed Mussolini, believing that the PNF were still the strongest option against the left-wing parties. This strong relationship between Mussolini and Pope Pius XI led to the beginning of negotiations between the Church and the fascist state on a final resolution to the 'Roman Question' (see Chapter 1, page 170), which had troubled Italy since full unification in 1870.

The impact of the Lateran Pacts

After three years of negotiations, on 11 February 1929, Mussolini and the Catholic Church signed the Lateran Pacts, incorporating three sections: a treaty, a financial convention and a **Concordat**. The key aspects of the treaty were:

- a solution to the territorial problems concerning the pope and Rome by providing a sovereign state of 44 hectares of land, with full diplomatic rights, designated in Rome as the state of the Vatican City to be controlled by the pope

- a financial convention that provided the pope with 750 million lire and 1,000 million in Italian State Bonds as compensation for the loss of his territories in 1870

- Catholicism recognised as the sole religion of Italy and granted significant privileges to the Church with religious education established in primary and secondary state schools and church marriages given legal validity (only civil ceremonies had been given this right previously)

- Catholic youth groups (Catholic Action) allowed to continue as long as they did not carry out any political activities. This was a substantial concession to the Church given the fascist dictatorship's focus on youth and the belief that there should be no alternative to fascism within Italy. Catholic Action was the only non-fascist organisation allowed to continue, operating within the fascist state and its various branches together had over one million members, predominately in the north.

For Mussolini, the Lateran Pacts were a great success. He was the man who had finally solved Italy's troubling question that had plagued Church–state relations for over 50 years. He gained not only the admiration of the Italian people but also considerable prestige overseas. It was one of his most popular achievements and cemented his consolidation of power. However, it was also a success for the Catholic Church who could now extend their role and influence throughout Italian life. The end of the Church's separation from the Italian state led to a re-entry into education and ultimately a religious revival in the 1930s as the numbers of Catholic marriages and schools increased. Mussolini's cooperation with the Catholic Church showed the limits of his dictatorship and did question the representation of Mussolini as the ultimate, unchallenged ruler of Italy. Overall, the Lateran Pacts

KEY TERMS

Freemasonry
Freemasonry is a worldwide organisation made up of secretive clubs, known as lodges, which initiate new members through a series of secret rituals. It dates from around the 17th and 18th centuries and developed from workers' organisations known as guilds. Membership within the clubs can be advantageous in providing links between lodge members that can help with employment or social connections.

The secretive rituals allegedly asks new members to assert they believe in a 'Supreme Being,' which the Catholic Church believes is sacrilegious and against the teachings of the Church and in as early as 1738 the Vatican had asserted that no Catholic could belong to a Masonic Lodge. Mussolini's move to ban Freemasonry in Italy was therefore extremely popular with the Catholic Church and helped gain him the strong support of Pope Pius XI.

Concordat
A Concordat refers to any agreement made between the Catholic Church and the government of a sovereign state, setting out the rights of the Catholic Church in that particular country. This usually focuses on the specific taxation requirements of the Church and the right of the country's government to influence the selection of Catholic bishops by the Church.

represented a kind of unsaid power-sharing agreement between the PNF and the Church that suited both institutions' goals at the time.

KEY TERM

Plebiscite
A plebiscite is a direct vote in which the entire population is asked to vote on a particular proposal that may lead to an amendment in the constitution. In Italy's case, the plebiscite of March 1929 asked Italians whether they supported the Lateran Pacts and the list of fascist candidates put forward by the fascist Grand Council. The 1934 plebiscite again asked whether Italians agreed with the new list of fascist deputies approved by the fascist Grand Council and was called the second referendum of fascism by Mussolini. While plebiscites can be a sign of a thriving democracy, in fascist Italy they were contrived exercises used by Mussolini as a means of claiming that he had the consent of the Italian people. Fascist control over Italy meant that the elections were never free and fair and thus historians still debate whether the results can be used as evidence that Mussolini was overwhelmingly popular with the Italian people.

Church support for the regime

The Lateran Pacts helped Mussolini considerably in the support they drew from the Catholic Church. Pope Pius XI called him 'the man sent by providence' and the Church openly endorsed the fascist regime. In 1928, Mussolini had introduced a new electoral law which established that a **plebiscite** would be held no later than April 1929. This was simply a means for Mussolini to claim a broad consensus for his rule as Italian citizens could simply approve or reject a list of candidates from the PNF. As part of the Lateran Pacts, the Catholic Church promised that it would mobilise the Catholic vote for the fascists. The Vatican claimed it was motivated by gratitude to Mussolini and felt that the plebiscite should demonstrate Catholic support for the dictatorship. However, coming as closely as it did after the Lateran Pacts, the Church felt that the pacts would be stronger if they were endorsed by a government with the apparent support of the majority of Italian people. Catholic Action officially appealed to voters to vote 'yes' in the plebiscite, which was held on 12 March 1929. The pope openly asserted in his speeches and the Catholic press that a 'yes' vote would help approve the Concordat. A total of 8.63 million voters participated in the plebiscite, about 90 percent of the electorate, and the fascist list of candidates was approved by around 98 percent of the vote. How much the Catholic support contributed to this result is hard to say but there is no doubt that the Lateran Pacts contributed to Mussolini's popularity as a leader and enhanced the cult of *il Duce*. This Catholic support was repeated again in the 1934 plebiscite and the Church was generally supportive of Mussolini's economic, social and foreign policies.

ACTIVITY
KNOWLEDGE CHECK

1 List the positive and negative aspects of the Lateran Pacts for Mussolini.

2 Discussion: Was the Lateran Pacts more of a success for Mussolini or the Catholic Church and the pope? Explain your answer.

3 Think about the weak or strong dictator question you answered before. Does the terms of the Lateran Pacts strengthen or weaken Mussolini's dictatorship? Again, you will need to debate what you think the goals of his dictatorship were.

Church–state tensions in the 1930s

The Concordat did not mean that relations between the Church and the fascist state were completely peaceful and through the 1930s, there were several areas of considerable tension. The main area of confrontation focused on Catholic Action's youth organisations. Youth movements and the influence they brought were a major aspect for both the Church and the PNF's attempts to ensure the loyalty of the next generation of Italians. Given fascism's totalitarian aims, the fact that a rival youth organisation was allowed to exist with around 250,000 members was always troubling. In 1931, the conflict between fascism and Catholic Action became a serious political issue. This was driven by changes in leadership to the PNF with Giovanni Giurati becoming Party Secretary and Carlo Scorza given responsibility for fascist youth organisations in October 1930. Both men were much more hardline in their attitudes towards Catholic Action than their predecessors. They accused Catholic Action of organising sport (which was prohibited under the Concordat), of being led by former leaders of the PPI, of acting as a sanctuary for antifascist politics and of attempting to form trade unions. Police raids and considerable fascist violence took place on Catholic youth organisations and they were officially shut down by the state. Pope Pius XI responded with an attack on fascism and the PNF, with a strong encyclical entitled *Non abbiamo bisogno* ('We have no need'). In it the pope argued that fascism's ideal that youth belong entirely to the state could not be reconciled with being a Catholic, and he condemned the attempt to steal children from Christ so that they would worship the state alone.

Despite the seriousness of the crisis between fascism and the Church, for both Mussolini and the pope good relations were beneficial and by the summer of 1931, they had come to a deal. Catholic Action youth groups could be reinstated but they were not allowed to organise sporting activities and had to confine themselves to recreational and educational aspects that were strictly religious in character. Any former members of the PPI were not allowed to be youth leaders. In February 1932, Mussolini visited the pope in Rome and both he and Pius XI confirmed their mutual views on societal and gender values and foreign policy towards the Soviet Union and communism. Catholic youth associations grew in popularity through the 1930s and had 388,000 members by 1939.

This was not the only conflict between the state and the Church, however. There were fairly minor disagreements over aspects such as girls' involvement in the physical activities of the fascist youth organisations, which the Church worried was contrary to public decency and did not properly prepare girls for maternity. The fascist attitude to prostitution, in which they viewed visits to brothels as a natural part of young male culture, was also condemned by the Church. However, a more serious tension arose in 1938 as the Church became concerned with Mussolini's growing attack on Italy's Jewish population and the adoption of anti-Semitic legislation. The fascists now defined Judaism in biological terms and prohibited intermarriage with 'pure' Italians. However, this conflicted with the Concordat and the authority of the Catholic Church to assert that Jews could convert to Catholicism through marriage. The pope was gravely concerned about Mussolini's growing nationalism and commissioned a letter against racism. However, the letter was unable to be published before the pope's death on 10 February 1939. His replacement, Pius XII, would subsequently play an extremely controversial role during the Second World War in respect to his dealings with both Fascist Italy and Nazi Germany.

SOURCE
15 1929 image celebrating the Lateran Pacts, showing Mussolini between the king and the pope.

ACTIVITY
KNOWLEDGE CHECK

1 The image in Source 15 was created in 1929. In what ways would Mussolini be happy with the photo? Why might he be concerned about this image?

2 What does the photo demonstrate about the nature of Mussolini's dictatorship?

EXTRACT 2

R.J.B. Bosworth, *Mussolini*, 2002. Here Bosworth describes the massive short-term rewards Mussolini enjoyed from the Concordat with the Vatican.

Pope Pius XI eulogised the Duce as the 'Man whom providence has sent us.' The papal paper, L'Osservatore Romano, applauded a pact, whereby 'Italy has been given back to God and God to Italy.' The Jesuit Journal, Civilta Cattolica, in March 1929 agreed that Fascism incarnated 'the restoration of a Christian Society.' In 1932 Pius XI even for a time favoured something which he called 'Catholic totalitarianism.' Catholic publicists applauded Mussolini and Pius XI as 'the two greatest men in modern Italy.'... Abroad, there was similar approval, especially in circles friendly to the causes of the Church.

EXTRACT 3

John Pollard, *The Vatican and Italian Fascism, 1929–1932*, 1985. Here Pollard argues that not all Catholics and fascists supported the Concordat.

Despite the increasing numbers of leaks of information in official circles as the negotiations neared their end in January and February 1929, the signing of the Lateran Pacts inevitably came as a complete surprise to the overwhelming majority of the Italian population. Whilst the majority of Catholics and Fascists probably approved in a general way of the agreements which their leaders had signed on their behalf, substantial numbers on both sides quickly began to raise doubts and criticisms of the agreements which belied the picture of universal joy and approbation presented by the Italian press: in two or three cases, indeed, neither Fascist press censorship nor ecclesiastical vigilance over the Catholic press managed to prevent some of this dissent appearing in print.

THINKING HISTORICALLY | Causation (6a)

Seeing things differently

Different times and different places have a different set of ideas. Beliefs about how the world works, how human societies should be governed or the best way to achieve economic prosperity, can all be radically different from our own. It is important for the historian to take into account these different attitudes and be aware of the dangers of judging them against modern ideas.

Carefully read Extracts 2 and 3 on the reaction to the signing of the Lateran Pacts in 1929 and complete the activities that follow.

1 Re-read Extract 3 and consider what the Catholic and fascist arguments against the Lateran Pacts would have been in 1929.

2 In Extract 2, where are all the positive reports coming from and what is the historical context that would have shaped this reaction?

3 Current attitudes to Mussolini and Italian fascism are very different today than they were in 1929. What is the historical context that means historians and students today have a different reaction to the Concordat than people in both Italy and around the world in 1929?

4 How does our historical knowledge shape a different perspective of the Concordat then those presented in both Extract 2 and Extract 3?

5 Why is it important for historians to deal with events in the context of the beliefs and values of people in the past and not by the judgements we have today?

ACTIVITIES
SUMMARY

1 Make a summary list of Mussolini's most successful policies and unsuccessful policies. When you compare your summaries, is one list longer than the other? Are there any policies that are both successful and unsuccessful? What might this show?

2 Several historians have argued that Mussolini's economic policies were driven primarily by political gain and propaganda and less so by what Italy required in terms of its economy. How far would you agree with this argument? What evidence can you find that backs this up? Are there any policies that do not support this assertion?

3 Find evidence for each of these statements about Mussolini:

- 'An intelligent ruler who understood how to use Italy's powerful conservative forces to strengthen his dictatorship and stay in power.'

- 'A weak dictator who was forced to share power with Italy's conservative elite and was unable to fully pursue his political goals.'

4 Now consider which statement you agree with and why. Write a detailed argument backed up by evidence to support your analysis.

WIDER READING

The following books give an excellent overview on the fascist state and Mussolini's policies.

Blinkhorn, M. *Mussolini and Fascist Italy*, Routledge (2006)

Bosworth, R.J.B. *Mussolini's Italy: Life under the Fascist Dictatorship 1915–1945*, Penguin (2007)

De Grand, A. *Italian Fascism*, University of Nebraska Press (2000)

Finaldi, G. *Mussolini and Italian Fascism*, Routledge (2008)

Pollard, J. *The Fascist Experience in Italy*, Routledge (2003)

Whittock, M. *Mussolini in Power*, Collins Educational (1998)

2a.4 Challenges to, and the fall of, the fascist state, c1935–46

KEY QUESTIONS

- How successful was Mussolini in achieving his foreign policy aims before 1935?
- How significant were the consequences of Mussolini's more aggressive foreign policy in the years 1935–40?
- What was the impact of Italy's decision to enter the Second World War on the side of Nazi Germany in 1940?
- To what extent did the Italian nation change between 1943 and 1946?

INTRODUCTION

Soon after Mussolini was appointed prime minister in 1922, he asserted that in foreign relations 'Italy wishes to be treated by the great nations of the world like a sister and not like a waitress.' As one of the key reasons for the decline of liberal Italy was the so-called 'mutilated victory' and Italy's perceived weakness at the Paris Peace Conference at Versailles after the First World War (see Chapter 2, page 193), it is perhaps unsurprising that Mussolini saw a strong foreign policy as a key goal. From the very beginning of his rule, Mussolini backed up his strong rhetoric with aggressive action that seemingly contrasted with the weak liberal governments that had preceded him. The idea that Mussolini was standing up for Italy and claiming its rightful place as one the world's 'great powers' was extremely popular with the Italian population, and his foreign policy 'successes' were among his most popular actions as dictator of Italy. The ideal of Mussolini as the supreme nationalist who simply wanted Italy to regain its pride as a nation, and assert its power on a world stage, was a key part of the cult of *il Duce* (see Chapter 3, page 220) and is still a major component of Mussolini's popular image in Italy today. However, behind the rhetoric was the crucial problem of Italy's

weak military position, and Mussolini's grand claims were often tempered by realism.

Mussolini was careful to develop strong relations with Europe's recognised great powers, such as Britain, in order to strengthen Italy's international standing. However, for a variety of reasons, Italy's foreign policy from the mid-1930s pursued a distinctly more aggressive direction, which would ultimately bring it into greater conflict with Britain and France and push Italy towards its fateful alliance with Nazi Germany. Mussolini's relationship with his fascist contemporary, Adolf Hitler, was extremely complex and the relationship between the two men as well as the two countries took several years to develop. In the end, Mussolini's attempts to pursue a middle ground between Britain and Nazi Germany, swaying between the two in order to exact foreign policy concessions from both, would fail and Mussolini would choose to align his country with Germany in 1940 as the Nazis conquered much of Europe. It was a critical decision that would lead to the downfall of fascism and, in the end, cost Mussolini his life.

The end of the Second World War also ushered in an entirely new political system for Italy with the founding of a republic. Foreign policy is therefore crucial to the story of fascist Italy. It

August 1923 – Corfu Incident. Italy threatens war with Greece but backs down under pressure from League of Nations

October 1925 – Mussolini involved in negotiations leading to the Locarno Pact

January 1933 – Adolf Hitler becomes chancellor of Germany

15 July 1933 – Four-power pact between Britain, France, Germany and Italy signed but never ratified by Britain and France

April 1935 – Italy, Britain and France sign the Stresa Front aimed at containing German foreign policy

October 1935 – Mussolini launches Italian invasion of Abyssinia

November 1937 – Anti-Comintern Pact between Germany, Japan and Italy signed

March 1938 – Germany unifies with Austria

1923	1924	1925	1929	1933	1934	1935	1936	1937	1938

January 1924 – Italy gains port of Fiume from Yugoslavia after negotiation between the two countries

1929 – Italy begins brutal crackdown on Libyan rebels seeking independence. Libyan rebellion ends in 1931

July 1934 – Austrian chancellor Englebert Dolfuss assassinated by Austrian Nazis. Mussolini moves troops to the Austrian border in case of possible German invasion of Austria

9 May 1936 – Mussolini announces Italian defeat of Abyssinian army and occupation of the capital Addis Ababa

July 1936 – Italy begins intervention of the Spanish Civil War on the side of General Franco

November 1936 – Informal German-Italian Axis agreement of cooperation announced

contributed, arguably, to Mussolini's most popular and most hated actions and while, at times, it brought him the adulation of the Italian people who proclaimed him Italy's greatest leader since Caesar Augustus, it would also lead to humiliation, death and the destruction of fascist rule in Italy.

HOW SUCCESSFUL WAS MUSSOLINI IN ACHIEVING HIS FOREIGN POLICY AIMS BEFORE 1935?

Mussolini's foreign policy aims

It is clear that foreign policy was one of the key areas of focus for Mussolini and the fascist dictatorship. However, defining long-term goals for Mussolini's foreign policy is difficult, as his actions tended to be rather erratic and opportunistic, often aiming, like a lot of his other policies, to maximise his prestige as opposed to achieving any material gain for Italy. There is a general theme, though, running through all his policies concerning Italy's international position. The key goal was undoubtedly to assert Italy's position as a world power. This meant standing up for Italy's territorial claims and, where possible, revising the Versailles settlements that Italy had disagreed with in 1919 in order to overcome the shame of the 'mutilated victory'. In Africa, Mussolini aimed to consolidate Italy's rule in Libya and, ultimately, to expand Italian imperialism in other parts of Africa. Mussolini's other key aim was to assert greater power for Italy in the Mediterranean Sea, which he believed was unfairly dominated by Britain and thus made Italy a 'prisoner of the sea'. Ultimately, Mussolini hoped Italians would be transformed into a more militant, aggressive race who would claim Italy's position as a dominant European power and achieve the expansion of Italy's *spazio vitale* ('living space'). It was, in many ways, a more aggressive form of irredentism that was as much influenced by the ANI and nationalist thought as it was fascism.

What is important to note is that while the goals did not necessarily change, at least until 1940, the means to achieve them undoubtedly did. While the fascists were consolidating their power in the 1920s, Mussolini was much more cautious in his actions and willing to compromise with Britain and the League of Nations. He was also, at first, quite concerned about Hitler's rise to power and the actions of this much more militant German nation, and looked to Britain and France to join him in an alliance that would restrict Hitler's foreign policy aims. However, as fascism consolidated and became more aggressive, Mussolini's foreign policy aims, particularly in Africa, would bring him into conflict with Britain and the League of Nations and shape his foreign policy in respect to Europe, leading to a growing relationship between Hitler and Mussolini and Italy's intervention in the Spanish Civil War. Italy's aims at revising its borders, asserting its power in the Mediterranean and generally transforming itself and its population into a greater militarised power playing a dominate part in European affairs, would be pursued during the 1930s in a more aggressive manner and ultimately contributed to the onset of the Second World War.

The impact of foreign policy success and failure before 1934

Mussolini's first requirements in relation to foreign affairs was to travel to Switzerland and London within months of becoming prime minister for negotiations on issues still being sorted out from the First World War, such as reparation payments. At this stage, he aimed at demonstrating to Europe's great powers, mainly the British and French, that while Italy may hope for a greater presence in world affairs it was able to work peacefully in trying to achieve its aims. However, with smaller powers, Mussolini was prepared to be more aggressive. This was particularly the case in respect to Greece, which he viewed as a lesser nation to Italy. The key issue rested on the Dodecanese Islands, which Italy had claimed in 1912, leading to long international discussions on the

---

10 June 1940 – Mussolini announces that Italy will join Second World War on the side of Nazi Germany

October 1940 – Italy invades Greece but is pushed back by the Greek army

May 1941 – Italian forces retreat from Abyssinia

5 March 1943 – 100,00 Italian workers go on strike in Turin. Industrial upheaval spreads throughout the north of Italy

13 May 1943 – Axis troops surrender in North Africa marking the end of the war in Africa

9 July 1943 – Allied forces launch invasion of Sicily

25 July 1943 – Mussolini removed from power by Fascist Grand Council and arrested on the orders of the king

8 September 1943 – Italy announces surrender to allied forces. The king and Badoglio flee south establishing the 'Kingdom of the South'

April 1944 – Social Republic of Italy collapses. Mussolini captured by partisan forces on 27 April. Mussolini captured by partisan forces and executed on 28 April

4 June 1944 – Allied forces enter Rome

1939	1940	1941	1942	1943	1944	1945	1946

April 1939 – Italy annexes Albania

May 1939 – Germany and Italy sign the Pact of Steel

September 1939 – Germany invades Poland beginning Second World War. Italy chooses not to join its ally Germany and instead declares itself 'non-belligerent'

8 September 1943 – Germany begins occupation of Italy

12 September 1943 – Mussolini released from prison by German commandoes in a daring, mountain-top raid

23 September 1943 – Social Republic of Italy declared in those areas controlled by Germany under the leadership of Benito Mussolini

13 October 1943 – Italy declares war on Germany

2 June 1946 – Constituent election and referendum on the monarchy held in Italy. Italians vote to remove monarchy and Italy declared a republic

disputed territory. On 27 August 1923, an Italian general, Enrico Tellini, was murdered while leading an inter-allied commission on drawing the border between Greece and Albania. Mussolini used this to attack the Greek government, claiming that they had financed the assassination of Tellini, or possibly carried it out themselves. He demanded that the Greek government attend a funeral service at a Catholic Church in Athens, where they would publicly honour the Italian flag, and that they pay a penalty of 50 million lire to Italy, otherwise the Italian army would invade Corfu. On 31 August, Italy bombarded Corfu without warning and occupied the island. Mussolini's actions were celebrated by Italian nationalists and many within the elite elements of Italian politics, including the head of the navy, Thaon di Revel. However, the League of Nations, with British backing, demanded that Mussolini end the occupation of Corfu and put the issue to international arbitration. The reality of Italy's military position shaped his decisions, with di Revel informing Mussolini that Italy's navy would barely last 48 hours if Britain decided to act. On 27 September, Italy left Corfu and in the subsequent negotiations received the 50 million lire from Greece that they had demanded.

The Corfu Incident was both a success and a failure for Mussolini. His confrontation with Greece had led to opposition from the League of Nations and he had subsequently been forced to accept Italy's position in relation to the greater powers of Britain and France. Despite some angry rhetoric against the League of Nations, he was much more careful through the 1920s and would not repeat this aggressive foreign policy, preferring to achieve his aims through more careful negotiation. However, it was a greater success domestically in that Mussolini had shown that he was a dynamic ruler willing to engage in decisive action to stand up for Italy's national pride. This contrasted greatly with the perceived weakness of the previous liberal governments in respect to foreign policy and helped cement his power in Italy.

His next great success came through negotiation rather than military action when, in January 1924, Yugoslavia recognised Fiume as being part of Italy. Given Fiume's significance in respect to the historical memory of d'Annunzio's occupation of the city (see Chapter 2, page 194), this was a considerably popular achievement by Mussolini. This once again showed him as a leader who could achieve what the liberal government had been unable to. However, Fiume's significance was largely symbolic; Yugoslavia no longer needed Fiume as they had constructed a greater port at Split. They were therefore prepared to give up Fiume to the Italians in return for Italian recognition of Yugoslavian rule at Susak, another disputed area. As with Corfu, the gains for Mussolini were predominately domestic, as opposed to any material achievements for Italy internationally.

This was also the case in 1925 in respect to Mussolini's participation in the negotiations leading to the Locarno Treaty. This was a significant agreement that saw Germany take its place in the League of Nations and accept the pre-First World War borders between itself and Belgium and France, thus, it was thought at the time, finally bringing an end to one of the problems that had continued to threaten European peace. Mussolini had tried and failed to link Locarno to negotiations on Italy and Austria's borders, but the very fact he had been invited to such an important European commission indicated to the Italian people

that he was accepted as equal to the Great Powers. This again contributed to his popularity in Italy. At the same time, Italy was expanding its economic links and political interference in Albania. Mussolini backed Ahmet Zogu's accession to president in January 1925 and, in 1928, supported his self-proclamation as King Zog I. Through the support and bribery of Zogu, Albania became an informal Italian protectorate. This extended Italian influence in south eastern Europe at the expense of Yugoslavia. Mussolini also undermined Yugoslavia, which he saw as a powerful block to Italy's territorial ambitions, by providing support to the Croatian Ustasha and Macedonian nationalist movements that aimed for separation from the newly created Yugoslav state. In 1934, Croatian terrorists, who were financed by the Italian fascists and provided with a training base in Italy, assassinated the Yugoslavian king, Alexander.

In terms of Africa, Mussolini continued the liberal government's brutal war against a Libyan rebellion that had started during the First World War. The Italian garrisons had been driven back towards the coast in the aftermath of the war, but the liberal government had responded with a brutal occupation that aimed to end the rebellion and reassert Italian rule. Mussolini continued the so-called 'Pacification of Libya' through brutal means, such as the use of poison gas, and around a third of Libya's population were either killed or starved to death. Italy finally put down the Libyan rebellion in 1932.

Overall, Mussolini's foreign policy before 1934 was successful in respect to his domestic popularity with his achievements as a decisive, world leader who would fight for Italy's foreign policy aims, supposedly contrasting significantly with the weak liberal governments of the past. In respect to Italy's aims in the Mediterranean, Mussolini was much more cautious at this stage in directly challenging Britain, France and the League of Nations. However, as the fascists consolidated power, the more aggressive foreign policy seen in respect to Libya and Yugoslavia would come to play a decisive part in Mussolini's overall actions in international affairs.

EXTEND YOUR KNOWLEDGE

The 'Pacification of Libya' (1929–32)
Throughout the 1920s, fascist Italy was involved in an ongoing colonial war in Libya. This was mostly kept quiet in the Italian press due to the frustratingly slow progress of the Italian armies. The Libyan forces fighting against Italian colonial rule were small but well organised and it required a large Italian force made up predominately of mercenaries from other African countries to control them. In 1929, Marshal Badoglio took control of the Italian forces and pursued a brutal policy of starvation, mass execution, chemical warfare and the use of concentration camps to bring the Libyan rebellion to an end. The rebel leader, Omar el Mukhtar, was captured and publicly hanged in 1931. Around 100,000 Libyans were forced from their homes and it is estimated that 40,000 people died either in, or while being transported to, Italian concentration camps. The Libyan 'pacification' was one of the first clear examples of the brutality of the fascist regime and an indication of the type of tactics they would later employ during their invasion of Abyssinia.

Relations with Britain, France and Germany

Mussolini's relationship with Britain, France and Germany was highly complex and driven by the contrast between the realities of Italy's military and diplomatic position and the aims of its foreign policy under Mussolini. It would be severely reshaped by the rise to power of Adolf Hitler in 1933. Historically, Italy had a good relationship with Britain. Britain had supported Italy's independence movement and fought alongside it in the First World War. Mussolini himself had good relations with many prominent British politicians including Winston Churchill and British foreign secretary, Austen Chamberlain. Italy and Britain had worked together during the Locarno Treaty negotiations. Britain had helped Italy in its ambitions concerning Albania after Italy helped pressure Turkey into giving up the rich oil town of Mosul to the British colony of Iraq. However, these cordial relations clashed with Mussolini's territorial claims in the Mediterranean that was dominated by the British. Britain and its politicians would not consider any compromise on its naval control of the Mediterranean. The inability of Italy to stand up to the threat of the British navy during the Corfu Incident of 1923 led to a policy of considerable rearmament that it hoped would allow fascist Italy to challenge Britain's power in the Mediterranean. Mussolini also tried to undermine British power by supporting pro-Italian groups in Malta. Complicating Mussolini's relationship with Britain was Italy's economic dependence on the British government and financial markets. The revaluation of the lira in 1927 could only be achieved with funding from the British government and financial institutions and Italy was still intrinsically linked into a world financial system that was dominated by the USA and Britain. Any challenge to British power could not ignore these realties. Mussolini's policy towards Britain, at least up to 1936, was therefore quite ambiguous, as he shared a fairly friendly relationship with Britain while at the same time building Italy's military so as to challenge British power in the Mediterranean.

Italy's relationship with France was affected by the fact that the majority of antifascist exiles from Italy had settled there. Mussolini made complaints to the French concerning Italian antifascist activities in Paris, while the French responded with anger over the fact that OVRA (Italian secret police) and the fascist security police operated agents in France who infiltrated antifascist organisations. Mussolini viewed France as a rival, both to Italian power in the Mediterranean and its imperialist aims in Africa. The French were also worried about Tunisia, a French African colony but one that had a larger Italian population of settlers. The French government believed that the fascists might use this to try to gain control of Tunisia. Again, Mussolini's foreign policy towards France was ambivalent. Mussolini understood French power and influence in Europe and was prepared to work with them in aspects such as the Locarno Treaty. At the same time, he was raising the possibility of anti-French alliances with Germany, Spain and Hungary, all of which came to nothing. His foreign policy desires against the French, as it was with Britain, were tempered by Italy's ability to achieve them.

In relation to Germany, Mussolini's foreign policy, unsurprisingly, differed considerably before and after Hitler's rise to power.

Mussolini was quite contemptuous towards the German Weimar Republic (1919–33), which he believed was run by socialists and pacifists. Mussolini gave support to German nationalist groups which sought to undermine and overthrow the Weimar Republic. However, conversely, he was also greatly concerned that any nationalist German government might seek to unite Austria and Germany (known as **Anschluss**), a move perceived in Italy as a severe danger to the country. Mussolini sought instead to encourage German goals of revising the Treaty of Versailles, but hoped to direct its focus from the Alps to the Rhine. The Nazis had had some contact with the fascists throughout the 1920s and Hitler was open in his praise of Mussolini, whom he proclaimed was a 'brilliant statesman' and an inspiration for the Nazi movement. In 1927, the Italian diplomat in Munich wrote a report that drew attention to Hitler as standing out among the numerous German right-wing politicians who were pushing for the overthrow of the Weimar Republic and the establishment of an authoritarian, nationalist government. Hitler and Mussolini exchanged letters from the early 1930s, with Hitler promising to pursue a German–Italian alliance if he became chancellor and Mussolini providing political advice to the Nazi leader.

KEY TERM

Anschluss
This referred to the concept of a political union between Austria and Germany. At the end of the First World War, Austria had favoured some sort of union with Germany but this was forbidden by the Versailles settlement. Most German political parties within the Weimar Republic believed in eventual unity of the two nations, but Italian foreign policy directly opposed it due to the fact than an independent Austria provided a crucial buffer between Italy and Germany. When Adolf Hitler became dictator, his more aggressive foreign policy and willingness to break the Versailles settlements made the situation much more problematic for Mussolini and the Italian government.

Despite his growing links to Hitler, the Nazi leader's appointment as chancellor of Germany in January 1933 was greeted with some concern by Mussolini. Given that Hitler was both a nationalist and an Austrian, it was felt that he was sure to pursue the issue of *Anschluss*. Mussolini's reaction was to try to bring Britain, France, Germany and Italy together in a 'Four Power Pact'. This Pact would have several benefits for Italy. Through it, Mussolini hoped to both appease and control Germany at the same time. His proposal to Hitler promised parity of arms with Italy and broadly alluded to the possibility of territorial changes to the Versailles settlement. He also hoped to undermine the League of Nations by having key decisions made by the pact and not through the collective security of the League. For example, Mussolini believed that Germany could be given some of its territorial claims within the control of Britain, France and Italy. The 'Four Power Pact' was signed on 15 July 1933 but never ratified by Britain and France. Countries such as Czechoslovakia and Poland, who feared German expansion, protested against the pact, afraid that it could impose territorial changes. Their key alliance with France helped draw the French away from the pact. Hitler's withdrawal from the League of Nations and resumption of rearmament in 1933 also undermined Mussolini's aim of using the 'Four Power Pact' to control revision of the Versailles settlement.

Despite the failure of the 'Four Power Pact', the dangers of growing German nationalism that Mussolini had been trying to control were clearly shown a year later when, in July 1934, Austrian Nazis assassinated the Austrian chancellor and close friend of Mussolini's, Englebert Dolfuss. The Austrian Nazis attempted to take over and pursue *Anschluss* with Germany. Mussolini reacted strongly by proclaiming that he would not allow *Anschluss*, mobilising four divisions and moving some equipment to the Brenner Frontier between Austria and Italy. Hitler refused to back the Austrian Nazis and their attempted coup collapsed. Mussolini's actions were seen in Italy and internationally as key to halting Hitler's attempt at unifying Germany and Austria. However, it was more the case that, at this early stage in Hitler's rule, the German chancellor was more interested in building good relations with Italy and consolidating his power in Germany than pursuing foreign policy adventures. However, the concern that Hitler and the nationalist goals of the Nazi party may not be as easy to control as Mussolini first believed, led to a change in direction for Italian foreign policy.

The Stresa Front 1935

In March 1935, Hitler openly announced Germany's military rearmament that had been going on secretly for two years. This was a direct threat to the Treaty of Versailles and, alongside the attempted Nazi coup in Austria, added to Mussolini's concern at the direction of Hitler's policies. Between 11 and 13 April 1935, Mussolini met with the French and British foreign ministers and prime ministers at Stresa to discuss what to do. Despite much discussion, the so-called Stresa Front did little except issue a resolution stating the three countries' desire for peace and their continuing commitment to the League of Nations. However, what was more crucial was the impact Stresa had on Italy's growing colonial ambitions in Africa. Mussolini had already discussed with the French foreign minister, Pierre Laval, the idea of reaching an anti-German agreement with the French government if they approved Italian plans to colonise Abyssinia. At Stresa, Mussolini claimed that he had reached an implicit agreement with both France and Britain to support Italy's imperialist goals in Africa as a trade-off for Italy's anti-German action in the Stresa Front. In a sentence within the Stresa resolution supporting collective security, Mussolini was allowed to insert the words 'in Europe', which he claimed was a clear understanding from the British and French that it did not apply to Africa. He also firmly believed that the French and British would not break the Stresa Front to prevent Italy from pursuing imperialist goals in Africa that they themselves had already pursued for centuries. For their part, the British government would later claim that they had not understood the significance of Mussolini's insertion of the 'in Europe' phrase and Laval argued he had only approved Italy's economic penetration of Abyssinia. Whatever the case, Mussolini's colonial war against Abyssinia was to be the pivotal point that would turn Italy against France, Britain and the League of Nations, lead to a much more aggressive foreign policy direction in support of fascism and ultimately draw Italy into a dangerous alliance with Adolf Hitler's Nazi Germany.

HOW SIGNIFICANT WERE THE CONSEQUENCES OF MUSSOLINI'S MORE AGGRESSIVE FOREIGN POLICY IN THE YEARS 1935–40?

Invasion of Abyssinia and its consequences

Mussolini's most significant action in relation to foreign policy took place in 1935, with the invasion of **Abyssinia**. Abyssinia, the last African country free of colonial rule, had been the focus for a planned fascist war of conquest as early as 1932. The definite plans to invade and colonise Abyssinia were communicated to Italy's civilian and military leaders in 1934. There were several motivating factors behind Mussolini's decision.

- The planning for war undoubtedly helped the economy. War-related contracts that were commissioned in 1932 helped fuel Italian industry, particularly in those producing the arms, clothing, equipment and transportation required for a colonial war in Africa.

- The invasion linked to the idea of autarky, in the belief that Abyssinia would provide raw materials and areas for agricultural expansion that would advance Mussolini's goal of economic self-sufficiency for Italy. It would also give Italy greater export markets for Italian goods.

- It was hoped that southern Italian peasants would move there and take up farming land, thus easing the growing pressure for land reform in the south. This immigration to an Italian colony would also have a secondary propaganda effect as, instead of land-hungry Italians leaving for foreign countries, it would be the Italian government who would provide them with the better life they were seeking through emigration.

- The establishment of an Italian empire in Africa was also part of the greater radicalisation of policy that took place after Mussolini consolidated his power. Mussolini had often spoken about the militaristic aspects of fascism and how it would bring about a transformation of the Italian people into a more warlike people. The invasion of Abyssinia was thus seen as a means to achieve this and show the dynamism of fascism.

- Within the Fascist Party, there was some concern that Mussolini needed to pursue a more 'fascist' direction and demonstrate that his rule was more than just simply a dictatorship maintaining power through compromise with Italy's conservative elite. Foreign policy appeared to be an easier route for the demonstration of an aggressive fascist policy than that which Mussolini could achieve domestically. A great victory would bring about the unification of the Italian people in the glorification of fascism, which had been a key aim for the fascist party since at least 1922.

- Mussolini also believed that such a victory would add to the prestige of his dictatorship. The shameful defeat at Adwa in 1896 was still remembered by Italians and Mussolini believed that revenging this historical loss would significantly boost the cult of *il Duce* and the belief that he was an Italian leader who was righting Italy's past.

- In respect to the international situation in Europe, Mussolini may have hoped that a successful Italian campaign in Africa would demonstrate to Hitler the power of his fascist rule and dissuade him from seeking *Anschluss* with Austria. The timing was clearly shaped by the Stresa Front and Mussolini's belief that Britain and France would allow this colonial aggression in return for his support against Germany's revision of the Versailles settlement.

KEY TERM

Abyssinia
Abyssinia is today mostly known as the nation of Ethiopia. It is a large, populous country located in the Horn of Africa. By 1935, it was the only fully independent African nation, having seen off an attempted Italian invasion in 1896. It was ruled by the emperor, Haile Selassie I, who fled to Britain in 1936 after the Italian invasion of his country. He returned in 1941 when British forces liberated the country. Ethiopia returned to full independence in 1944.

In October 1935, Mussolini launched the invasion of Abyssinia with a massive force of 400,000 men, hoping for a quick and decisive victory. The Italians quickly seized Adwa and other border towns but after that their progress was slowed and, in November, Mussolini chose to replace the head of the invading army, Emilio De Bono, with Marshal Pietro Badoglio. Badoglio engaged in a brutal war against the Abyssinian army in a similar manner to how he conducted his campaigns in Libya, including mass aerial bombings, the murder of prisoners of war and the illegal use of poisonous chemicals. On 5 May 1936 his victorious army entered the capital of Abyssinia, Addis Ababa. It is estimated that around 20 million Italians listened to Mussolini's public radio broadcast on 9 May, proclaiming that Italy had at last gained its empire – a fascist empire.

The immediate consequences were overwhelmingly positive for Mussolini. During the war, the League of Nations had placed rather limited sanctions on Italy, banning weapons sales to Italy and putting sanctions on rubber and metal imports. Critically, oil was left off the list of goods banned for export to Italy and the Suez Canal was not closed, two actions that may have actually affected Mussolini's actions. Despite the weakness of the League's

response, the sanctions were a propaganda coup for the fascists. Mussolini was portrayed as a leader who was standing up to the whole world and defying attempts to limit Italian power. This had strong parallels with the 'mutilated victory', but this time Italy would not back down. The fascist dream of an Italian nation rallying behind the ideology appeared to become reality when, on 18 December 1935, the royal family launched the 'Gold for the Patria' (country) campaign, where in a solemn ceremony, Queen Elena presented her wedding ring to be melted down in order to help the campaign against the sanctions. Blessed by the Church, thousands of women followed the queen in giving their wedding rings to the fascist cause, many during specially convened church services. In return, they were given steel rings that symbolised their marriage to the nation. The ideal of an Italian people wedded to the nation itself represented one of the key aspects of fascism and appeared to show that the true transformation of the Italian people was now taking place. For Mussolini himself, Abyssinia was the high point of his dictatorship. He had achieved true greatness for Italy and established it as a great power: the equal of Britain and France. The Italian nation, the royal family and the Church (who blessed the invasion as a civilising mission, despite the fact the Abyssinians were Christians) all proclaimed Mussolini's greatness. He had, it appeared, fulfilled the image of a new Caesar who was expanding the Italian empire just as the Romans had done.

However, the overwhelming success of Abyssinia in terms of Mussolini's dictatorship was distinctly short term and, overall, the consequences of Mussolini's actions would be mostly negative. Despite his grand proclamation on 9 May, Abyssinia had not been fully conquered. Two-thirds of the country were still to be occupied and the costs associated with supplying the 250,000 troops that were needed to fight an ongoing guerrilla war were considerable. Only around 130,000 Italians ever settled in Abyssinia and the hope that the colony would provide oil and other raw materials to fuel autarky never materialised. The export markets never developed, with only two percent of Italian trade ever going to Abyssinia. The overall economic consequences of the war were massive, with the lira devalued by 40 percent and the budget deficit rising from 2.5 billion to 16 billion lire. On the international stage, Italy's brutal war, which probably led to the death of up to 500,000 Abyssinians, and the illegal use of chemical weapons, changed the perception of Mussolini and fascism overseas, particularly in Britain. Before this, Mussolini was generally seen as a dictator who had been beneficial to Italy; now, instead, the regime was seen as a danger to European peace. Mussolini's actions had demonstrated the weakness of the League of Nations, a move that encouraged Hitler's own ambitions, disrupting the delicate balance of power that existed in Europe. Although not immediate, Abyssinia was the beginning of a split in Italy's relations with Britain and France and moved Italy towards a stronger relation with Germany. This was enhanced by Italy's economic problems caused by the League of Nation's sanctions that forced a growing trade shift towards Germany.

Perhaps, most worryingly, was the change victory had on Mussolini's own perception of foreign affairs and his understanding of Europe's political direction. Abyssinia, it appeared to him, had shown the weakness of Britain and France and this encouraged in

Mussolini a belief that Italy's aggressive actions would not only enhance his own power domestically but challenge the old balance of power in Europe. It was a dangerous conviction that would see the fascist regime pursue a much more radical direction in both domestic and foreign policy.

SOURCE

Writer and journalist Ugo Ojetti was watching Mussolini announce Italy's victory in Abyssinia at the Piazza Venezia in Rome on 5 May 1936 (Ojetti had a flat that overlooked the square). It is estimated that around 400,000 people were present in the square to hear Mussolini's speech. These are Ojetti's words.

The longer we wait the more we feel charged with a sense of electricity, radiating through us and sharpening our minds, so that not only the present but also the future and the past seem clear and distinct: the past of Rome. I feel a hand on my shoulder: 'Exactly two thousand two hundred years since the first Punic war: 264 BC 1936.' It is the Rector of the university, De Francisci... 'Du-ce, du-ce, du-ce.' The chanting begins each time on the far edge of that sea, as if those furthest away were trying to get close to Palazzo Venezia with their voices, unable to do so in person. Suddenly the rhythm intensifies... Three blasts of a trumpet. Down below they haven't heard and are shouting, crying, calling out. And then there he is, erect and motionless, his face square, his hands on the marble of the balcony. When did he step out? When did he become visible? It seems that he had always been there and that those broad shoulders had forever been in the middle of the huge window, made of marble like the sills and mullions... Every word he utters is like a deliberate step forward, firm and accentuated: 'Finally Italy has its empire.' Then there is a warning: 'Your cry is a sacred oath that binds you before God...' With one statement after another he had filled us with such burning passion and raised our spirits to such heights that his short and infinite words seemed in this way to the people like a natural invocation beyond life. A cry comes back in response as if to say yes, God is already in everyone's heart. At that moment the piazza, under the great canopy of the sky, resembles a temple.

SOURCE

From Carlo Levi, *Christ Stopped at Eboli*, 1944. Levi was an antifascist who was sent to the south as punishment in the 1930s and subsequently wrote about his experiences among the poor southern peasantry. Here he describes the reaction of the town's peasants to the Abyssinian War.

The peasants were not interested in war... War they considered just another inevitable misfortune, like the tax on goats. They were not afraid to go; 'To live like dogs here or to die like dogs there is just the same,' they said. But no one except Donna Caterina's husband enlisted. It soon became clear that not only the purpose of the war, but the way it was being conducted as well, was the business of that other Italy beyond the mountains, and had little to do with the peasants... 'The war is for the benefit of those in the north. We're to stay at home until we starve. And now there's no chance of going to America.'

SOURCE

British cartoon depicting Mussolini, 4 October 1935.

THE MAN WHO TOOK THE LID OFF.

A Level Exam-Style Question Section A

How far could the historian make use of Sources 1 and 2 together to investigate the popularity of the Abyssinian War (1935–36) among the Italian people?

Explain your answer, using both sources, the information given about them and your own knowledge of the historical context. (20 marks)

Tip

Both are eyewitness accounts and both are very different. Think about what the sources demonstrate about the difficulty in assessing the popularity of the Abyssinian War in Italy. In what way is an eyewitness account such as Source 1 valuable for our understanding? What are the strengths and weaknesses of the analysis of just one town in the south in Source 2?

ACTIVITY
KNOWLEDGE CHECK

1 What comment is Source 3, the cartoon from October 1935, trying to make? What do you think is being unleashed?

2 In what ways did Mussolini's invasion of Abyssinia disrupt Europe in the manner depicted by Source 3?

Intervention in the Spanish Civil War and its consequences

In March 1936, Hitler marched German troops into the demilitarised zone of the Rhineland, thus defying one of the key elements of the Treaty of Versailles. Neither the League of Nations nor Britain or France made any real attempt either to stop Hitler's actions or punish Germany after it had taken place. This added to Mussolini's perception that Britain and France were weak and scared of Hitler. While not seeking a complete diplomatic break with Britain and France, Mussolini believed that a move by Italy towards Germany may draw concessions on Africa and the Mediterranean from the British and French governments in order to draw him back. In July 1936, Mussolini committed Italian troops to the Spanish Civil War on the side of General Franco, who was leading the right-wing forces against the Spanish Republican government backed by France and the USSR. Hitler had also committed German forces to helping Franco, and the war therefore marked the first time that Italian fascism and German Nazism fought on the same side. This, Mussolini believed, would put pressure on Britain and France to make the foreign policy concessions he sought. If General Franco was victorious, Italy would gain a strategic ally in the Mediterranean while France would be undermined. Italy could also hopefully gain naval bases in the Balearic Islands. Although Franco was technically not fascist, his rule would help fuel the spread of authoritarian nationalist antisocialist regimes and weaken communism and socialism in Europe. Additionally, the Abyssinian War had shown Mussolini the domestic benefits victorious foreign adventures could have. Another quick victory would keep the momentum of Abyssinia going, adding to the cult of *il Duce* and fuelling the transformation of the Italian population into a more militant fascist society.

Mussolini sent around 50,000 soldiers, thousands of artillery and tanks, 1,400 pilots, 400 fighter planes and 200 bombers into Spain. In 1939, General Franco, with the help of Italy and Germany, was victorious, but the Spanish Civil War had none of the positive consequences Mussolini had gained from Abyssinia. The length of the Civil War had not been anticipated by Mussolini and Italian casualties were relatively high, with 3,266 soldiers killed and 11,000 wounded. The war led to severe disruption in the Italian economy, costing around 14 billion lire and requiring the government to exact special taxes from the population to pay for it. The lira was further devalued and Italy's foreign currency reserves halved. These financial problems pushed Italy further towards economic dependence on Nazi Germany. Despite all this, Mussolini's territorial ambitions came to nothing. Franco was determined not to let Spain become a satellite of fascist Italy and the naval concessions Mussolini had hoped for did not happen. The war also hampered Mussolini's aims in Abyssinia, with the military focus on Spain weakening Italy's attempts to consolidate their position in Africa. Unlike Abyssinia, the intervention in Spain was not popular with the Italian people, who could not understand why Italy had intervened and resented the significant economic costs it had brought. There was growing concern among the population at Italy's gradual move towards Nazi Germany. Militarily, the war had severely weakened the Italian army and by 1939 they were considerably weaker than in 1936. It had also shown up problems within the military when an Italian force was defeated by a republican army made up of antifascist Italian volunteers in the Battle of Guadalajara in March 1937. Overall, the Spanish Civil War, as opposed to the great victory Mussolini had hoped for, was instead a costly and unnecessary endeavour that would lead to the breakdown of his relationship with Britain and France and pushed Italy firmly towards an alliance with Nazi Germany.

EXTEND YOUR KNOWLEDGE

The Battle of Guadalajara (March 1937)

By 1937, around 50,000 Italian troops had been committed to Spain. Against Franco's wishes, Mussolini ordered fascist forces to push towards Madrid in the belief that the capital city would fall to the Italian forces, therefore providing him with prestige as well as bargaining power. Instead, in March 1937, the Italian fascists were defeated in the Battle of Guadalajara, nearly 50 kilometres from Madrid. To add to Mussolini's embarrassment was the fact that the opposing Republican army included Italian antifascist volunteers known as the 'Garibaldi Brigade' that had been organised by the Rosselli brothers in France. The battle had several consequences. Firstly, it was a great propaganda victory for the antifascists and clearly demonstrated the weakness of Italy's army. Secondly, as a result, Mussolini decided to commit further Italian troops to Spain, refusing to leave Spain without an Italian victory to make up for Guadalajara. It was also the involvement of the Garibaldi Brigade that led directly to the assassination of the Rosselli brothers on 9 June 1937 (see Chapter 3, page 222).

SOURCE 4

Report from Berlin by the German Ambassador in Rome, Ulrich von Hassell, to the German Foreign Office, 18 December 1936.

Germany has in my opinion every reason for being gratified if Italy continues to interest herself deeply in the Spanish affair. The role played by the Spanish conflict as regards Italy's relations with France and England could be similar to the Abyssinian conflict, bringing out clearly the actual, opposing interests of the powers and thus preventing Italy from being drawn into the net of the Western powers and used for the machinations. The struggle for dominant political influence in Spain lays bare the natural opposition between Italy and France: at the same time the position of Italy as a power in the Western Mediterranean comes into competition with that of Britain. All the more clearly will Italy recognise the advisability of confronting the Western powers shoulder to shoulder with Germany.

ACTIVITY
KNOWLEDGE CHECK

1 According to Source 4, what were the possible consequences of Italy's intervention in the Spanish Civil War?

2 How far were the hopes set out by von Hassell concerning Italy's intervention achieved?

3 What were the other key consequences of Mussolini's decision to involve Italy in the Spanish Civil War?

Diplomatic breakdown of Stresa Front and the move towards Germany

The gradual breakdown of Italy's relationship with Britain and France and the move towards an alliance with Germany, it is important to note, took place over several years and was never driven simply by ideology. The fact that Italian fascism and German

Nazism shared ideological traits was not the defining feature in their relationship. In fact, when Mussolini met Hitler for the first time in 1934, the Italian dictator had come away with a fairly negative view of Hitler as a fanatical yet boring character. Mussolini had been further alarmed by the murder of Dolfuss and the fear of *Anschluss* had prompted the Stresa Front that was directed against Germany. The turning point had been the Abyssinian War. During Italy's invasion, Britain and France had come to a secret agreement known as the Hoare-Laval Pact (named after the British and French foreign ministers Samuel Hoare and Pierre Laval) that agreed to allocate two-thirds of Abyssinia to Mussolini in return for the maintenance of the Stresa Front. However, when the British press found out about the pact, public opinion was outraged and the plan was dropped. Hoare was forced to resign and was replaced by Anthony Eden, who was much more negative in his opinion of Mussolini. British public and political opinion were both beginning to turn against the Italian dictator. Mussolini, for his part, was convinced that the League of Nation's sanctions had been prompted by Britain and the antagonism between the two countries only grew through Mussolini's actions in the Spanish Civil War. Italy's intervention aimed at undermining France's influence in the Mediterranean. Additionally, during the war, Italian submarines, pretending to be Spanish, attacked and sank neutral shipping in the Mediterranean, thereby angering the British government. This was furthered in the early summer of 1938 when an Italian bombing raid on Spanish ports sunk 11 British ships. Despite this, the British government was still trying to come to some arrangement with Mussolini. In January 1937, the British and Italian governments signed the 'Gentleman's Agreement', which confirmed the status quo in the Mediterranean and limited Italy's intervention in the Spanish Civil War. In April 1938, Britain also took the diplomatic move of recognising Italy's rule over Abyssinia. However, these agreements between Britain and Italy had little real effect. Mussolini simply ignored the 'Gentleman's Agreement' and Britain failed in its attempts to stop Italy's move towards Germany.

In terms of his relationship with Germany, Mussolini had initiated discussions on a Rome-Berlin Axis in October 1936 and this was followed by an announcement in November of the German-Italian Axis, an informal agreement of cooperation between the two nations. The events of the Spanish Civil War had drawn the nations even closer together. Economically, Germany was also happy to take advantage of Italy's economic problems and from 1936 onwards, Italian exports became more and more reliant on German markets. In September 1937, Mussolini visited Germany and 800,000 Germans came out in Berlin to hear Mussolini proclaim that the values of fascist Italy and Nazi Germany were the same. Mussolini was impressed by what he saw in Nazi Germany; a nation, backed by a powerful military that appeared to be fanatically behind the Führer. It was the type of militant society into which he hoped to transform Italy. It was this trip that made him surer that Europe's future was fascist. In November 1937, Italy became part of the Anti-Comintern Pact with Germany and Japan, which claimed to establish mutual support in case of aggression from the Soviet Union. In reality, the pact was aimed at Britain as much as it was the Soviet Union.

Mussolini's direction in foreign affairs was demonstrated further when he withdrew Italy from the League of Nations in December 1937, claiming that the organisation was against Italy and its revolution. This, along with the Anti-Comintern Pact, confirmed Italy's place alongside Germany as a revisionist power that sought to rewrite the Versailles settlement, thus confirming the end of the Stresa Front. Mussolini, however, it should be noted, had not signed any firm alliance with Germany and was still in discussions with Britain. It can be argued that he still had hopes of gaining concessions from Britain, particularly in the Mediterranean, by using the relationship with Germany as a bargaining tool.

The danger of that policy and the weakness of Italy's diplomatic position in Europe was clearly demonstrated in March 1938 when Hitler moved against Austria and crossed the border to begin the process of *Anschluss*. Unlike 1934, this time Mussolini made no attempt to stop the Nazis. The events were unpopular in Italy where the great fear of a powerful Germany on the border of Italy had now come to pass. For Mussolini, it was a personal failure, questioning his image as a leader who would always stand up for Italy's interests in international affairs. Crucially, the *Anschluss* demonstrated that Hitler was now clearly the more powerful leader and it could be argued that from March 1938 Italy began to lose its independence and became more and more a German satellite state. In May 1938, Hitler visited Italy again, this time as a much more celebrated and powerful leader than he had been in 1934. However, Mussolini was still trying to negotiate a path between Britain and Germany. When the Nazis proposed a full-scale military alliance with Italy, it was rejected. When Hitler returned from Italy, he focused on pushing for an invasion of Czechoslovakia. Mussolini was considering Italian options and discussed with his foreign minister, Galeazzo Ciano, the possibility of Italy staying neutral in a possible European war. At the Munich Conference of September 1938 Mussolini played an apparently prominent role helping to broker the deal that gave up the Sudetenland to Germany and supposedly avoided a full blown European war. In reality, he had been subservient to Hitler during the negotiations. On his return to Italy, Mussolini was greeted as the hero of peace, an acclaim that angered him given his goal of turning the Italians into people who desired war and militancy. Instead, for Mussolini, the Munich Conference had confirmed to him the weakness of the democratic powers and the future of a Europe that would be dominated by Germany.

EXTEND YOUR KNOWLEDGE

The Rome–Berlin Axis (1936)

The growing deterioration in the relationship between Britain and Italy after the Abyssinian War led Mussolini to look towards strengthening Italy's ties with Nazi Germany. Mussolini was particularly concerned that Britain and Germany would come to some arrangement that would isolate Italy diplomatically in Europe. In October 1936, Mussolini's foreign minister, Galeazzo Ciano, went to Berlin where he negotiated an informal arrangement with the Nazi government whereby Germany would have freedom of action in eastern Europe and the Baltic while supporting Italian attempts to change the balance of power in the Mediterranean. The two countries also committed themselves to avoiding any conflicts of interest. Despite the rather vague terms of the agreement, Mussolini enthusiastically proclaimed that it was the 'Axis' by which all European countries should rotate. The agreement became known as the Rome–Berlin Axis.

Domestic tensions

In Italy itself, the fascist dictatorship was facing growing opposition. How much this focused on the personality of Mussolini himself and whether the fascists could have been overthrown without the events of the Second World War is debatable, but there is no doubt that disquiet towards the regime was becoming more prominent in the late 1930s. The euphoria of Abyssinia had only been short term and the domestic and foreign policy direction of the Italian fascists was heightening concern among the population. Between 1935 and 1939, military spending accounted for around 80 percent of the massive increase in the state deficit and the squeeze on middle-class incomes and savings to pay for this government expenditure was highly unpopular. The quest for autarky meant many consumer products became more expensive as domestic Italian industry produced goods that would have been cheaper to purchase from international markets. The Battle for Grain (see Chapter 3, page 229) had contributed to a worsening diet among the Italian population and the general living standards of workers in the agricultural, industrial and civil sectors were in decline. Italy's economy was becoming worryingly reliant on Germany, heightened by the fact that in February 1939 a new commercial treaty was signed between the two countries.

This instigated a highly unpopular policy concerning the transfer of Italian workers to Germany, a number that would reach half a million by 1945. These workers were often treated poorly by the Germans, who had a condescending attitude towards Italians. The policy appeared to contradict Mussolini's frequent speeches in which he asserted that Italian workers should remain in Italy and that he would always ensure they were treated with respect and dignity. The transfer of workers was one of Mussolini's most hated policies and for many Italians simply confirmed his weakness in respect to Hitler. This was accentuated by the anger and fear at the *Anschluss* and the growing relationship between Germany and Italy. The 1938 anti-Semitic policy and the 'reform of customs' (see Chapter 3) were unpopular with many Italians and the sight of the Italian military trying to copy the German goose step (*passo romano*) appeared ridiculous. It should also be remembered that Mussolini was 55 and had been in power for 17 years by 1939; the image of the youthful, dynamic dictator as portrayed in the cult of *il Duce* was becoming harder to sustain.

However, the issues facing the fascist dictatorship, although problematic, should not be exaggerated. There is no evidence that antifascist politics was undergoing an upsurge in Italy and the police were still functioning efficiently. Mussolini himself was still popular, even if the fascist party itself was not. Critically, by 1939 there was a whole generation of Italians who had grown up with no other leader except Mussolini and for many of these Italians there was simply no alternative to the fascist regime they had known all their lives.

 THINKING HISTORICALLY   Change (6a)

Separately and together
Below are some different types of history that historians may identify.

Political history	Economic history	Social history
Religious history	Military history	International history

These are thematic histories, where a historian focuses on a particular aspect of change. For example, an economic history of the British Empire would focus on trade and the economic reasons for the expansion of the empire, whereas a political history of the empire would focus on governance of the colonies and strategic reasons for its expansion.

Work in groups.
1 Write a definition for each type of history.
Here are some events in the period covered by this chapter.

1935	1936	1937	1939	1935–39	1935–39
Mussolini orders fascist invasion of Abyssinia	Mussolini commits fascist troops to assist Franco in Spanish Civil War	Mussolini signs Anti-Comintern Pact with Japan and Germany	Commercial treaty signed between Germany and Italy	Military spending in Italy increases 80 percent	Economic issues in Italy force greater reliance on German economy

Answer the following questions.

1 The first two changes can be classified as 'political' events.

   a) Why was it important to Mussolini to commit troops to the Spanish Civil War?

   b) What other area of history does this take it into?

2 What political changes came about because of Mussolini's military actions between 1935 and 1939?

3 Was the growing relationship between Italy and Germany political, military, economic or all three? Explain your answer.

4 What was the social impact of Italy's massive increase in military spending between 1935 and 1939?

5 Did Mussolini sign the Anti-Comintern pact for military or political reasons?

6 Did Mussolini sign the commercial treaty with Germany for economic or political reasons?

Work in pairs.

7 Write a statement attacking 'thematic history'.

8 Write three statements defending 'thematic history'.

9 Explain why 'thematic history' occurs.

Pact of Steel

By 1939, Mussolini was in a difficult situation with regard to Italy's international position. In April of that year he had launched the invasion of Albania, which was already an Italian protectorate. There was an economic motive for the invasion as King Zog had been encouraging investment from other countries, particularly Japan, in order to become less dependent on Italy. However, the major reason was that Ciano had proposed Albania as compensation for letting Hitler take Austria. Italy could show its power to Germany and once again demonstrate Mussolini as a dynamic leader to the Italian people. Ciano also believed that with Italian settlement, Albania could assist the Italian economy. On Good Friday Italy invaded and King Zog, his wife and entourage fled the country.

However, the invasion clearly showed the weakness of the Italian army. Many of the Italian troops were unorganised and using weapons with which they had never trained, and there was poor coordination between the army, navy and air force. Italy eventually overcame the Albanian forces and Victor Emmanuel was crowned emperor of Abyssinia and Albania. However, the invasion had little impact on European affairs or the Italian economy. The real significance was to demonstrate the clear problems with the Italian military in 1939. The invasion also confirmed the aggressive nature of fascist Italy and was another stage in pushing Italy further away from Britain and France.

In May 1939, the growing strength of the relationship between Italy and Germany was fully confirmed by the signing of the 'Pact of Steel' with the Nazi regime. Mussolini had accepted the German proposal for a full alliance in early 1939. Events had led Mussolini to accept that Italian desires in the Mediterranean would bring Italy into greater conflict with Britain and France and this warranted the full support of Germany. The drafting of the pact was, however, crucially left to the Germans. The pact set out military and economic cooperation between the two countries and the permanent political consultation between the fascists and the Nazis. However, the most crucial element was inserted by the Germans; this was article 3, which committed Italy to support Germany if it chose to go to war. This went against diplomatic convention that nearly all military alliances operated only in defensive purposes. Instead, if Germany went to war, Italy had to support it 'with all its military forces on land, on sea and in the air'. Ciano had concerns about signing such an agreement but was reassured by Joachim von Ribbentrop, the German foreign minister. Ciano made it clear that Italy would not be ready for war until at least 1943 and was told by Ribbentrop that Germany had no intention of waging war before that date. With this promise, despite all the risks, Ciano signed the 'Pact of Steel' on 22 May 1939. On 11 August, Ribbentrop and Hitler told Ciano at a meeting in Salzburg that Germany was planning to attack Poland. Ciano returned to Italy horrified and disgusted by what he considered Germany's lies and betrayals. Italy was now trapped in an extremely dangerous situation.

SOURCE
5
Galeazzo Ciano, *Ciano's Diary, 1937–1947*, 2002.

Entry for 15 March 1939.
Events are precipitated during the night. After a meeting between Hitler, Hacha [the Czech president] and Chwalkowsky [the Polish ambassador in Berlin], German troops began their occupation of Bohemia. The thing is serious, especially since Hitler had assured everyone that he did not want to annex one single Czech. This German action does not destroy the Czechoslovakia of Versailles, but the one that was constructed at Munich and Vienna. What weight can be given in the future to those declarations and promises which concern us more directly?

Entry for 16 March 1939.
I had another meeting with the Duce. He now believes that Prussian [German] hegemony in Europe is established. In his opinion a coalition of all other powers, including ourselves, could check German expansion, but could not undo it. He did not count too much on the military help which the small powers could give. I asked whether, as things stand, it would not be more desirable for us to maintain our full freedom of action to redirect ourselves in the future according to our best interests rather than bind ourselves in an alliance. The Duce declared himself decidedly in favour of the alliance.

SOURCE
6
British cartoon from 1939 commenting on the Pact of Steel.

THE AXIS GOES ON A FORMAL BASIS

1 To what extent were domestic tensions impacting upon Mussolini's dictatorship in Italy?

2 Using Source 5 and your own reading on the subject, list the factors that influenced Mussolini's decision to sign the Pact of Steel.

3 What evidence is there that Mussolini made the right decision in signing the Pact of Steel in 1939?

4 What evidence is there that he made the wrong decision in 1939? (Remember you need to consider only those factors that Mussolini himself knew - you cannot include the consequences of the Pact that Mussolini could not have known.)

5 How is the Pact of Steel depicted in Source 6?

6 How far would you say Source 6 is an accurate depiction of the Pact? Provide evidence to justify your answer.

Italian neutrality, 1939–40

Ribbentrop and Hitler's announcement in August 1939 came as a shock to Mussolini. This was followed by the conclusion of the Nazi–Soviet Pact on 23 August about which Hitler had neither consulted Mussolini nor informed him that negotiations were taking place. This agreement was a non-aggression pact between Soviet Russia and Nazi Germany that also incorporated secret protocols concerning the division of eastern Europe into Soviet and Nazi spheres of influence. For Italy, the Nazi-Soviet Pact contravened the Anti-Comintern Pact Mussolini had signed with Hitler. Mussolini had grave concerns about Italy's military position and was urged by Ciano and military advisers to avoid entangling Italy into a costly war when Germany invaded Poland. However, the choice of neutrality was also problematic, given Mussolini's constant rhetoric linking fascism with militarism and aggression. To Mussolini, fascism had been born on the battlefields of the First World War; it was intrinsically linked to war. The ideology would look somewhat hollow if Italy chose to stay neutral in the European war that now appeared inevitable. The fact that Mussolini might be forced to make the same choice as the liberal government had done in 1914 also troubled him greatly, given his anger then at the liberal non-intervention. To stay on the sidelines while Germany waged war appeared a rather shameful choice. Instead, on 26 August, Mussolini presented Hitler with a massive wish list of supplies that he claimed Italy would need before it could wage war with its German ally. This amounted to 170 million tonnes of goods including six million tonnes of coal, two million tonnes of steel and 150 anti-aircraft batteries with ammunition. It would have required around 17,000 trains to transport the goods from Germany to Italy. Hitler clearly understood that Mussolini's demands amounted to Italy's resignation to neutrality and on 27 August Hitler released Mussolini from his obligations to the Pact of Steel, asking instead for psychological support and, if possible, for Italy to engage in military measures that could tie down Britain and France.

On 3 September, Britain and France declared war on Germany. Virtually the entire Fascist Grand Council as well as General Franco in Spain and the Portuguese dictator, Oliveira Salazar, advised Mussolini to avoid intervention in the war. Under pressure, Mussolini agreed but forbade the use of word 'neutrality', instead calling Italy's position 'non-belligerence', but the outcome was the same. For the second time, Italy had chosen to stay out of a major European war instead of supporting their ally. It was a painful choice for Mussolini, who had looked to his alliance with Nazi Germany as a means to put pressure on Britain. Mussolini watched anxiously as the German army swept across Europe in a seemingly unstoppable offensive. The Vatican, Ciano and King Victor Emmanuel all further cautioned Mussolini against intervention and the American President Roosevelt sent his envoy, Sumner Welles, to try to convince Mussolini to stay out of the war.

In March 1940, Mussolini was still unsure what direction he should take. He clearly believed that Italy had to enter the war at some stage, but the possibility of siding with Britain and France still remained. This was unlikely, Mussolini told Ciano and the king, because switching sides would bring a German attack on Italy that they would find difficult to defend. However, the German advance of May 1940 that conquered Holland and Belgium and then moved onto France made his decision-making more limited. During the first part of May, Mussolini grappled with his options. If Germany won the war, which was looking likely, how would they treat an ally who had now betrayed them twice? Italy would be left with an extremely powerful German empire on its borders that could easily invade its smaller neighbour. It was possible that Italy could enter the war, play a decisive part in the conflict and then sit at the victory table without having lost many men or been engaged in a costly, long drawn-out war. This required getting the timing right. Italy needed to enter the war against France in time to play a decisive part, while not allowing itself to be bogged down in any really serious fighting. The decision had to be made soon, as Germany was sweeping through the country towards victory.

On 26 May, Mussolini met his chief of staff, Marshall Badoglio, and informed him that he believed Germany would be victorious by September and that Italy required 'a few thousand dead to be able to attend the peace conference as a belligerent'. He then informed the king of his decision. Despite Badoglio's grave concern at the state of the Italian army and the problems that would arise if Italy had to do any serious fighting, Mussolini had made up his mind. On 10 June 1940, Mussolini announced to the Italian people that Italy had entered the war on the side of Nazi Germany. Ciano wrote in his diary, 'I am sad, very sad. The adventure begins. May God help Italy.'

EXTRACT 1
Martin Clark, *Modern Italy, 1871-1995*, 1996.

The answer was that the Duce would join in. It must have seemed to him as if he had little choice. Since September 1939 he had been chafing at the bit, desperate to play the warlord, yet mindful of the fearful risks. His military and economic advisors kept telling him that Italy was in no position to fight. Suddenly, in May 1940, it looked as if there were no risks, or few to speak of, and no time to lose. Perhaps, too, Italy might be able to restrain the victorious Fuhrer. Furthermore, if she did not join in, Hitler might wreak vengeance: for had not Italy betrayed the German alliance, in 1939 as in 1914? Hitler, having absorbed Austria, might well want Austria's traditional Southern regions of Trentino and the South Tyrol, and Austria's traditional Southern port of Trieste. Fear mingled with greed in Mussolini's frenetic mind. Important too, were his sense of honour, his urge to transform his sheeplike people into wolves, and above all his need to be doing something.

EXTRACT 2
R.J.B. Bosworth, *Mussolini*, 2002.

For all the verbal discomfort Mussolini expressed about continuing peace, he did not actually enter the war until it indeed seemed won by his fearsome German ally. Measured mathematically (to adapt a cherished Mussolini metaphor) Fascist Italy watched the front more carefully than Liberal Italy had done in 1914-1915. Would any Italian leader, it may be asked, who believed in the myth that Italy was or ought to be a Great Power, have waited longer than Mussolini did?

THINKING HISTORICALLY | Causation (6b)

Attitudes and action
Individuals can only make choices based on their context. Prevalent attitudes combine with individual experience and natural temperament to frame the individual's perception of what is going on around them. Nobody can know the future or see into the minds of others.

Carefully read Extracts 1 and 2 concerning the reasons why Mussolini decided to commit Italy to war alongside Nazi Germany in June 1940.

1 Summarise the reasons set out in each extract as to why Mussolini chose to go to war alongside Nazi Germany in 1940.

2 How many of these factors can you link to the First World War and the events affecting both Italy and Mussolini personally? Can you think of specific examples?

3 Are there any other specific events in the years 1922-38 that would have shaped Mussolini's decisions?

4 Using this historical context, discuss in pairs or in small groups whether Mussolini could have possibly come to a different decision.

5 How far should the historian try to understand the context of the beliefs and values of people in the past when explaining why individuals make choices in history?

WHAT WAS THE IMPACT OF ITALY'S DECISION TO ENTER THE SECOND WORLD WAR ON THE SIDE OF NAZI GERMAN IN 1940?

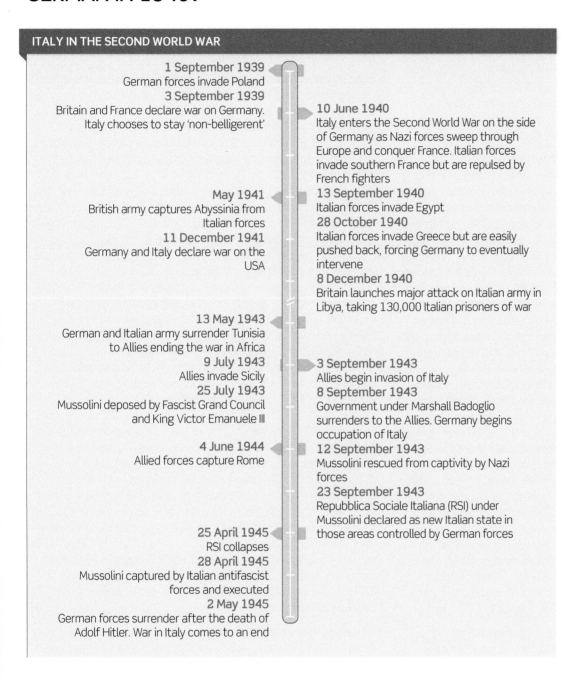

ITALY IN THE SECOND WORLD WAR

1 September 1939
German forces invade Poland
3 September 1939
Britain and France declare war on Germany. Italy chooses to stay 'non-belligerent'

10 June 1940
Italy enters the Second World War on the side of Germany as Nazi forces sweep through Europe and conquer France. Italian forces invade southern France but are repulsed by French fighters

May 1941
British army captures Abyssinia from Italian forces
11 December 1941
Germany and Italy declare war on the USA

13 September 1940
Italian forces invade Egypt
28 October 1940
Italian forces invade Greece but are easily pushed back, forcing Germany to eventually intervene
8 December 1940
Britain launches major attack on Italian army in Libya, taking 130,000 Italian prisoners of war

13 May 1943
German and Italian army surrender Tunisia to Allies ending the war in Africa
9 July 1943
Allies invade Sicily
25 July 1943
Mussolini deposed by Fascist Grand Council and King Victor Emanuele III

3 September 1943
Allies begin invasion of Italy
8 September 1943
Government under Marshall Badoglio surrenders to the Allies. Germany begins occupation of Italy
12 September 1943
Mussolini rescued from captivity by Nazi forces
23 September 1943
Repubblica Sociale Italiana (RSI) under Mussolini declared as new Italian state in those areas controlled by German forces

4 June 1944
Allied forces capture Rome

25 April 1945
RSI collapses
28 April 1945
Mussolini captured by Italian antifascist forces and executed
2 May 1945
German forces surrender after the death of Adolf Hitler. War in Italy comes to an end

Failures in France, North Africa, the Mediterranean

Italy's entry into the war alongside Germany was based on the concept of a 'parallel war'. Italy would concentrate on the Mediterranean basin and hinterland and northern Africa, while the Germans would concentrate on northern, central and eastern Europe. The first part of the campaign went, to an extent, as Mussolini had hoped. On 17 June, France requested an armistice with Germany even before Italian troops had attacked French territory. Mussolini met with Hitler on 18 June and set out Italy's demands for Corsica, Savoy, Nice, Tunisia, the Sudan, Somalia, Cyprus and Crete. However, Hitler explained that Germany did not want to punish France too harshly as he feared that it would drive French troops to defect to Britain, and Mussolini was afraid of pushing Italian claims without the Italians having done any actual fighting.

On 20 June, perhaps to push Mussolini's territorial claims, Italian troops suddenly advanced into the French Alps. However, Italy's first major engagement in the war simply revealed massive problems with the Italian army. The troops lacked the proper clothing for an alpine war, the Italian air force lacked the bombs needed to destroy French fortifications and Mussolini insisted on using tanks that were completely inadequate for the terrain. The advance was slow and the Italians captured only 13 unimportant villages at the cost of 631 men, many from frostbite. On 22 June, the French government under Marshal Pétain, signed an armistice with Germany. Fascist papers claimed that Italy's intervention had been critical to Pétain's decision, but in reality it had saved the Italian army from further embarrassment.

Mussolini had hoped for a short war that would provide Italy with the spoils of war for very little cost. However, when Ciano met with Hitler on 7 July, the Nazi dictator now said that Italy must wait until the defeat of Britain before territorial claims could be discussed. Mussolini ordered the partial demobilisation of Italian troops, mistakenly believing that the war was virtually over and waited for Germany's invasion of Britain to take place. This was a serious miscalculation. In late October, Italian forces in Libya were ordered to attack British positions. They had some early successes crossing into Egypt and towards the Suez Canal, but this was simply a tactical British retreat. When Britain counter-attacked in December, the Italian forces fell into a mass retreat. In the first weeks of 1941, an Italian force of nearly 250,000 were defeated by 30,000 much better equipped British troops. By May 1941, Italy had lost Eritrea, Somalia and, most critically, Abyssinia. In total, around 380,000 Italian troops had surrendered and been taken prisoner, a huge blow to fascist propaganda that proclaimed the transformation of the Italian people into a militant nation willing to die for *il Duce*. The British advance into Libya was only halted by German troops under the command of General Erwin Rommel who had been sent to reinforce the Italian forces in February. This signalled the end of the parallel war concept, as Germany now had to engage in areas where Hitler had hoped the Italian army would do the fighting, thus freeing up German forces elsewhere. Rommel's Italian and German forces had some early victories over the Allies, but by October 1942, they were on the retreat after defeat at El Alamein. In May 1943, the German–Italian Axis surrendered in North Africa, Libya was lost and the Allies were preparing for an invasion of Italy from Tunisia.

In the Mediterranean, which had been a dominant focus for Mussolini all the way through his dictatorship, Italian strategy proved confusing and inadequate. Despite his propaganda, Mussolini had no consistent strategy for attacking key British positions in the Mediterranean. The strategically important British base at Malta faced no sustained attack and nor did British bases at Gibraltar or Alexandria. The Italian navy had been crippled by a British air attack in November 1940. There was poor coordination between the air force and the navy (in July 1940 the air force bombed its own ships) and Italy lacked aircraft carriers without which they could not hope to mount a serious attack on British positions in the Mediterranean. Overall, despite consistent fascist propaganda over the previous 20 years that had proclaimed the greatness of the Italian military under fascism, Italy's army proved completely inadequate for the requirements of the Second World War. By 1943, Italy had failed to achieve any of the aims set out in Mussolini's 'parallel war'.

Disaster in Greece

Running parallel to Italy's failure in France, North Africa and the Mediterranean was the army's humiliating position in its attempted invasion of Greece. Italy had launched its attack on Greece on 28 October 1940 (the 18 year anniversary of the March on Rome) from its base in Albania. Greece had not been a focus for Italian territorial claims and Mussolini's motivations had been shaped by the progression of the Second World War. Italian aims in Yugoslavia had been rebuffed by its German ally and, instead, the Nazis had occupied the Romanian oil fields. This was seen by the Italian dictator as an attempt by Hitler to push German influence into the Balkans, disregarding the agreement they had come to on separate spheres of influence. Moving into Greece would increase Italy's strategic position in the Balkans. It was also part of a power game between Mussolini and Hitler, with the Italian leader deciding not to tell the Nazi leader about the invasion of Greece. The invasion, however, was a disaster. Mussolini assumed that Greece only had 30,000 troops and therefore Italy would attack with only 60,000 men, when in fact the Greek army had 300,000 soldiers. He believed that Bulgaria would join the Italian invasion, although this was completely unfounded. He did not coordinate the attack with the navy or air force despite the fact that this was crucial for the seaborne invasion. The choice of 28 October was also poor, due to the weather conditions in Greece at that time of the year which were extremely wet overall and freezing in the mountainous areas. Italian forces were bogged down in the difficult conditions, they had little mechanical support and their uniforms disintegrated in the heavy rains. Not only did the Greek forces hold up the Italian invasion, but they soon counter-attacked, taking over a quarter of Albania and inflicting painful defeats on the Italian army and navy. Eventually, half a million Italian soldiers would be deployed at the cost of 32,000 killed and over 100,000 wounded. After six months, Mussolini had to call on the help of Germany who humiliated the Italian forces by defeating the Greeks within weeks.

Italy was given administration over Greece but the campaign dealt a serious blow to fascism. Mussolini's dictatorship had been shown to be weaker than Greece, which was not considered a great European power. Fascist propaganda was unable to disguise the truth from the Italian people and the defeat had a major impact in undermining their faith in fascist rule and Mussolini. It also confirmed Italy's subservience to Germany and the end of any belief in a parallel war. The Germans viewed the Italians with contempt and Mussolini was now intrinsically tied to Hitler's war. As Mussolini now told one of his ministers 'given our tragic situation… the only thing left to do is to place everything in Hitler's hand, because we are incapable of doing anything'.

SOURCE
7
Galeazzo Ciano, *Ciano's Diary, 1937–1947*, 2002.

Entry for 12 October 1940.
The Duce returns... he is indignant at the German occupation of Romania. He says that this has impressed Italian public opinion very adversely, because, in view of the decisions taken at Vienna, nobody had expected this to happen. 'Hitler always presents me with a fait accompli. This time I am going to pay him back in his own coin. He will find out from the newspapers that I have occupied Greece; in this way the equilibrium will be re-established.'

ACTIVITY
KNOWLEDGE CHECK

1 Why is Source 7 helpful for understanding why Mussolini chose to invade Greece in October 1940?

2 What other reasons were there for Mussolini's decision?

3 The invasion of Greece has often been cited as one of the biggest disasters for Mussolini and fascist rule in Italy. Explain why it had such an impact on Mussolini's dictatorship.

War economy and military weaknesses

While Mussolini blamed Italy's military defeats on the weakness of the Italian people who had not been transformed into true fascists, the reality was that the poor military performance was due to inadequacies in the economy, military preparation and Mussolini's leadership. Mussolini held the positions of Minister of War, Minister of Navy, Minister of the Air Force and Supreme Commander of the Italian armed forces. He was also head of five separate ministries. This concentration of power hampered Italy's military effectiveness. Mussolini took all the major decisions, often without consultation with military experts. If he left Rome, the government shut down as other fascist ministers were unable to make any decisions without him. Mussolini himself was unable to distinguish between trivial points and major decisions, spending time, for example, in May 1940 on what should be included in the Rome opera season instead of focusing on the war. He was unable to coordinate the navy, army and air force or transform the economy to fulfil the priorities of Italy's war. He was bored by detailed discussion and spent a considerable amount of time working on his German lessons instead. He would often call meetings with his military leaders and gave vague instructions to improve war production without explaining how this was to take place. Despite promising to meet his Chief of General Staff, Ugo Cavallero, every day, he preferred to spend his time with his young mistress, Claretta Petacci.

The military was also in a very poor state at the start of the war and this was never improved upon.

- Italy had 75 divisions but only enough equipment to adequately arm 35 of them. It lacked the tanks and vehicles required for the mechanised fighting taking place in Africa. Around a third of the tanks and a quarter of the artillery being supplied to Africa was destroyed by British attacks in the Mediterranean.

- Many of the rifles and canons supplied to the army dated from the First World War. Italy had very few aircraft carriers and its naval ships had no radar equipment and very little oil. The air force was outdated compared to the British Spitfires and they had no long-range bombers to attack British positions in Egypt or Gibraltar. Rations were low and the state of clothing worse than during the First World War.

- Just as in the First World War, there were language problems between the officer class and the peasant conscripts and many of them did not understand why they were fighting so far from home. Morale was low, as shown in the massive numbers of Italian prisoners taken by the British forces in Africa.

- Tactics were also outdated, with the British reporting that Italians often still employed 19th-century charges against enemy positions, which by the Second World War were virtually suicidal.

Hampering the Italian army further was the fact that the Italian economy was completely inadequate for the requirements of the Second World War. By 1942, for example, the industry in the USA could produce more aircraft in a week than Italy could produce in a year. Italy lacked fuel and raw materials. It imported 1.5 million tonnes of oil from Romania, but this was half of what was required during peacetime. Italy depended on German coal, but was able to receive only around one million tonnes a month. This meant that steel production actually fell during the war to 1.7 million tonnes in 1943, in comparison to Britain, which was producing 14 million tonnes a year. Armoured vehicle production was low, with Fiat and Spa producing only 2,550 vehicles a month in 1941 when they had been able to make 4,883 a month in 1938. Factories lacked the raw materials they required such as oil, steel, iron, rubber and aluminium. Italian military equipment that was produced was often outdated and inadequate.

Germany estimated that the Italian economy was only operating at around 25 percent of its potential and Italy was the only country engaged in the Second World War that did not increase its Gross Domestic Profit (GDP) between 1940 and 1942. Italy still had tens of thousands of unemployed workers, whereas other countries had moved to almost 100 percent employment during the war. Italy did improve its production in 1942, but this was soon set back by Allied bombing of Italy's industrial cities. The coordination of food supplies for the Italian people was poor. Food was rationed at very low levels, with adults only allowed around 1,000 calories a day. Coffee became a luxury item and many poorer Italians found it difficult to get bread or pasta. Heating, shoes and soap were all in short supply. By 1943, the military situation overseas and the domestic difficulties Italians were facing, had brought fascism to a critical point.

Italy's failure in the Second World War

Use the words in the box to complete the following sentences so that they best summarise the reasons for Italy's failures in the Second World War.

inertia obsolete practical prioritise dominance mobile persisted fundamental antiquated

Italy's failings in the Second World War were due to a range of factors. Firstly, Mussolini's _____ of all leadership roles led to _____ at the top of Italy's military. Mussolini was unable to _____ the key aspects of the war that required his attention. Italy's military equipment was mostly _____ and unable to fulfil the requirements of the _____ war in Africa. _____ tactics from the First World War and the problems of language still _____ Economically, Italy's industry was unable to meet the _____ demands of the Second World War. It was never organised to meet the _____ requirements of total war.

Political tensions, 1943

By 1943, the combined effects of economic turmoil, rationing, food and clothing shortages and Allied bombings led to growing unrest among the Italian people, culminating in Italy's first strikes for over 18 years. During the week of 5 March, 100,000 workers went on strike in Turin and this soon spread to Milan and other areas. Communist workers helped organise the strikes, which demanded better pay for people forced to evacuate their homes. The strikes ended when the government agreed to increase the money for evacuees but the industrial action clearly demonstrated the political weakness of the fascist regime by 1943. Not only were these the first strikes in Italy since the 1920s, they were the first mass protest within Axis-controlled Europe. Mussolini himself had been considerably alarmed by these events that appeared to show communism and socialism were still able to influence Italian workers despite 20 years of fascist rule.

Antifascist groups began to resurface in Italy. The still illegal communist newspaper, *L'Unita*, reappeared in 1942 and a new group, including republicans, radicals and left-leaning liberals, called the 'Party of Action' was secretly formed. An antifascist group called the Christian Democrats, made up by members of Catholic Action, was formed with Church backing in the middle of 1942. These groups were still extremely covert and obviously illegal. Mussolini's secret police remained active and 1,400 political arrests took place between March and June of 1943 alone. However, they did represent the re-emergence of political antifascism after 18 years. Strikes were organised and antifascist slogans began to appear on buildings. In April 1943, all groups, except for republicans, agreed to work together against fascism. This was the first time in Italian politics that the communists, socialists and Catholics had agreed to collaborate. None of these groups had the potential to overthrow Mussolini, but antifascist politics was remerging and discussion beginning on the nature of the Italian political system once fascism was removed.

The greater danger for Mussolini, however, came from the conservative elite that he had skilfully worked with since he had become prime minister in 1922. Now that cooperation was in danger, as from the end of 1942, the Vatican, military leaders, industrialists and the police all began to consider how Mussolini might be deposed and Italy removed from the war. Mussolini at this stage was a weakened figure, beset by illness and stress and without any plans for how Italy should progress in the war. The problem for the conservative elites was, however, how to extract Italy from the war and overthrow Mussolini without provoking the Germans who could easily occupy Italy if Hitler believed it was necessary. After six months of general discussions, there was still no course of action. This was to change on 3 September 1943, when the Allies began their invasion of Italy and the question of Mussolini's removal thus took on a much greater urgency.

1 Write down what you believe are the five key problems facing Italy by 1943.

2 Which of these do you think Mussolini should have been most concerned with and why?

Allied invasion of Sicily

On 13 May 1943, Axis troops in North Africa surrendered to Allied forces under General Montgomery. With the occupation of Tunisia, the route was open for the Allies to mount an invasion into Sicily and from there onto mainland Italy. On 9 July, British, American and Commonwealth troops landed on Sicily. They faced little opposition from Italian forces and conquered the western half of Sicily after only a week. Mussolini's Chief of Staff recommended surrendering the island and pulling Italian forces back to defend the mainland. Mussolini met with Hitler on 19 July and asked the Führer to transfer troops and arms from Russia to the Mediterranean to help Italy, but this was refused. On the same day, Allied planes bombed Rome for two hours, killing 1,500 people. Mussolini displayed the clear inadequacies of his leadership when he asked one of his generals if there was any plan in place to defend Sicily, despite supposedly being in charge of Italy's entire military campaign. General Ambrosio's answer to Mussolini was, unsurprisingly, negative. By 17 August, the Allies had control of the island but German and Italian forces had conducted a successful retreat that allowed them to reinforce strategic positions on the Italian mainland. Mussolini, at this stage, was however no longer the Italian dictator as the invasion of Sicily finally prompted his removal from power.

Mussolini deposed

The plan to depose Mussolini had begun in late 1942, as leading fascists Dino Grandi and Galeazzo Ciano raised the idea of Italy seeking peace with the Allies. The Allies made it clear that they would not offer an armistice if Mussolini remained in power. However, only the king could dismiss Mussolini and thus Grandi needed his support. Through the early part of 1943 he discussed with the king his plan for the monarchy to take constitutional and military powers and replace Mussolini with a new government that would open up negotiations with the Allies. Through the Vatican, the king opened up secret talks with the Allies and, on 29 May, President Roosevelt's negotiator let it be known that the USA would negotiate a peace deal with an Italian military government if the king dismissed Mussolini.

The Allied invasion of Sicily forced the fascists to act. On 16 July, a deputation of fascists met Mussolini and convinced him to call a Grand Council meeting for 24 July. Grandi spent the eight days drafting a resolution that called for the removal of Mussolini and the government to be placed in the hands of the king and canvassed support among the other fascist leaders to ensure that the vote for the resolution would be passed. The king's advisors, army generals and the heads of the police were also all informed, as their support was essential if Grandi's plan was to work. The king appears only to have totally accepted the decision to remove Mussolini in the last few days before the Grand Council meeting and even then, Grandi could not be sure he would follow through.

The Grand Council had not met since September 1939 and had always operated as Mussolini's organisation; there was no need for him to accept any vote from the council over which he always had the final say. Mussolini also had the power to order the arrest of any fascists that opposed him. Grandi was extremely nervous about Mussolini's reaction and brought two hidden grenades into the meeting. It is debatable whether Mussolini understood the significance of the meeting. He began with a long, rambling speech on Italy's military situation that lasted for two hours. Then other fascists spoke up and voiced their concern at the situation in Italy and Mussolini's position as dictator. After nearly nine hours of discussion, Grandi's resolution was finally voted on and passed by 19 votes to seven. Mussolini appeared exhausted but calm and did not encourage those supporters in the party that suggested he should act violently against the fascists who wanted to dismiss him. It is possible that, given the nature of the Grand Council, he had little concern for the vote that he did not have to accept.

At five o'clock the next day he met the king for his normal meeting. It is thought that Mussolini believed he could get royal agreement to shuffle his ministries and perhaps give up his military command to the king, but remain head of government. Grandi certainly believed Mussolini left the Grand Council meeting sure that the king would not act on the resolution. It has to be taken into account that Mussolini had effectively dominated Victor Emmanuel III for nearly 20 years. In his audience with the king, Mussolini informed the monarch about the Grand Council resolution and the current military situation. To Mussolini's surprise, the king interrupted him and explained that he had decided to dismiss Mussolini and replace him with Marshal Badoglio. Mussolini attempted to leave the meeting but was met by Admiral Franco Maugeri, who put Mussolini into the back of an ambulance that subsequently took him to prison. Maugeri described Mussolini at the time as looking like a 'wry, sad and even pathetic clown'. The dictatorship that had lasted since 1922 and dominated every aspect of Italian society and politics had come to an anticlimatic end.

SOURCE

8 Grandi's resolution at the Grand Council meeting, 24–25 July 1914.

The Grand Council, meeting at this hour of supreme trial... Having examined the internal and international situation and the political and military conduct of the war... It declares that... it is necessary to revive forthwith the offices of the State and to assign to the Crown, the Grand Council, the Government, Parliament and the Corporations the duties and responsibilities prescribed by our statutory and constitutional laws. It invites the Head of Government to request His Majesty the King – towards whom the heart of the nation turns with loyalty and confidence – to assume, for the honour and the salvation of our fatherland, not only the effective command of the armed forces, on land, sea, and in the air, in accordance with Article 5 of the Statuto of the Realm, but also that supreme power of decision which our laws ascribe to him, and which, throughout the nation's history, has ever been the glorious heritage of our august dynasty of Savoy.

A Level Exam-Style Question Section B

How significant were Italy's wartime economic problems in bringing about the collapse of Mussolini's fascist regime in 1943? (20 marks)

Tip

This is an evaluative question in which you need to consider the key idea of significance. What were the economic problems that Italy faced and how did this shape both the king and Grandi's thinking? Were there other factors that were more important? Think about the evaluative language that will help in answering this question.

ACTIVITY
KNOWLEDGE CHECK

The fall of Mussolini, 1943

1 Grandi's resolution is a difficult and vague text. Historians have argued that Grandi understood that removing Mussolini would mean the end of fascist rule in Italy, but that others voting for the resolution possibly did not. Read through Source 8 and, in pairs or small groups, discuss what part of the resolution appears to accept the end of fascist rule and which part appears to indicate that the fascists will still play a part in ruling Italy.

2 How does this help explain why Grandi's resolution was successful?

TO WHAT EXTENT DID THE ITALIAN NATION CHANGE BETWEEN 1943 AND 1946?

The Allied invasion

After taking Sicily, the Allied command originally lacked any concrete plans to invade Italy. It was acknowledged that invading Italy from the south would be difficult and would divert forces from the main focus on northern France, where a mass invasion was being planned. Winston Churchill, the British prime minister, felt that an attack on Italy would be advantageous for the Allied forces by acquiring more airfields from which to attack German forces, opening up a second front in the Balkans and Aegean, and helping the French invasion by pinning down important parts of the German military in Italy. The Americans were not as enthusiastic but were eventually convinced that they should approve the invasion of Italy after Britain guaranteed that the main focus for the Allies would remain in northern France. The Allied command had hoped that the invasion would be relatively quick with Rome being captured before Christmas. There was little evidence that southern Italy would be defended by the German forces who, it appeared, were being drawn back north of Rome. However, these hopes were quickly shown to be false as the Allied invasion became bogged down in a slow, difficult war of attrition.

One of the key problems for the Allies was what had taken place in the month following Mussolini's removal. While Grandi may have hoped that the fascists could remain in control of the country without Mussolini, this had not happened. Instead, the king had placed the control of Italy and its armed forces under Marshall Badoglio. He, along with the king and other senior military figures, had begun negotiating Italy's surrender to the Allied forces. As part of the surrender signed on 3 September 1943, Badoglio promised to secure all of Italy's airfields and ports and hand over the entire Italian navy and air force. Badoglio also guaranteed the Allies the assistance of 60,000 Italian troops that were based around Rome. Despite this assertion, when the surrender was made public on 8 September, it was clear that neither Badoglio nor the king had actually done anything to put these promises in place. No order was issued to the Italian troops apart from a command that they should retaliate if attacked. Italian soldiers, who up to this moment had been fighting with the Germans, were left in confusion. Some surrendered, with over one million being taken prisoner. Italy's army began to dissolve; Italian soldiers across Europe were unsure what to do. Some surrendered, some tried to get home, others wanted to continue fighting alongside the Germans.

In the Greek islands, fighting took place between the German and Italian forces with around 1,200 Italian soldiers killed and a further 4,800 captured Italian soldiers shot as a punishment for resisting the German army. The month it had taken Badoglio and the king to negotiate Italy's surrender had allowed Hitler time to plan Germany's invasion of Italy. From 9 September, German forces began pouring into Italy. The king, Badoglio and top military leaders fled south towards the Allied forces, leaving Italy in chaos. They refused to issue any orders for the Italian army to fight against the Germans, believing this would incite the Germans to attack Italian civilians, but the lack of direction meant Rome was inadequately defended and taken over by German forces. Only on 13 September (when the king and Badoglio were safely with the Allies) was Italy officially declared to be at war with Germany. By then it was clear that the 60,000 Italian troops promised to the Allies would not materialise and that the Allied soldiers would have do the vast majority of the fighting.

It would take nine months, as opposed to the planned four, to capture Rome. The Germans put up a fierce defence of Italy, with the Allied advance hampered by the weather and Italy's geography. The Apennine Mountains that run down the middle of Italy and in places rise to over 10,000 feet meant much of the fighting took place across mountains, narrow ridges and valleys. This, combined with the weather from October that was predominately wet and freezing, meant the Allies and Germans engaged in a brutal war of attrition, not unlike the First World War, through mud and snow as the German armies destroyed bridges and mountain passes in their retreat. After eight months of fighting, the Allied army was further depleted as troops were transferred for the more important invasion of northern France. The Italian invasion did help the Allies in the fact that it drew in nearly one million German soldiers, thus diverting them from France. On 4 June 1944, Rome finally fell to the Allied forces. However, the battle for the north would drag on until 2 May 1945, exactly 20 months after the Allied invasion of southern Italy. The Allied fighting in the north had taken place parallel to a brutal civil war being waged at the same time between antifascist and fascist Italians that had been accentuated by the return of Benito Mussolini and the establishment of the new Italian Social Republic under his command.

The Republic of Salo and the government in the south

On 28 August, Mussolini had been transferred to a prison on Gran Sasso, the highest mountain in the Abruzzi region south east of Rome, an extremely isolated location where the Italian government believed the Germans would not find him. Despite these hopes, on 12 September he was rescued by German commandoes in a daring aerial raid and brought back to Germany. On 13 September, Mussolini met with Hitler at the Nazi control centre in East Prussia. Here Hitler demanded Mussolini return to Italy at the head of a new fascist government that the Nazis would establish. If Mussolini refused, Hitler would have German forces destroy Milan, Genoa and Turin. Mussolini spent two weeks in Germany, during which time he made radio broadcasts back to Italy announcing the establishment of a new fascist government that would continue to fight alongside Germany and Japan.

On 25 September, Mussolini returned to Italy and established his capital in the small town of Gargano on Lake Garda. It was quite clear that Mussolini's government was to a large degree a puppet of Nazi Germany. At Gargano it was easy for the Germans to control him. The Germans ensured that the government bodies were spread out over 100 miles across northern Italy in order stop it functioning effectively. The Foreign Ministry and the Ministry of Popular Culture were established at a small town at Lake Garda called Salo, which subsequently led to the Repubblica Sociale Italiana (RSI) being known as the Salo Republic. The Germans exercised considerable control, appointing officials in various parts of the RSI without consulting Mussolini and forcing the new republic to sign a deal that required it to pay the Germans seven billion lire a month. Despite these weaknesses, the Salo Republic was not completely useless. Salo controlled the richest and most populated areas of Italy: Piedmont, Liguria, Lombardy, Veneto and Emilia. Mussolini did establish a new cabinet made up of radical fascists, mainly those who had been part of the violent blackshirt militia that had been purged in the 1920s (see Chapter 2, page 197) and had been waiting since then for the chance to take fascism back to its violent origins.

On 14 November, the first congress of the new fascist party was held at Verona. There they drew up the Verona Manifesto that attempted to take fascism back to its original form as proposed in the 1919 programme when it was first founded. Italy was to be an anticlerical republic, industry was to be mostly nationalised and a real cooperative state run by workers and management was to be established. From 12 February 1944, all private companies with more than 100 employees or one million lire in capital, would be managed equally by both workers and employees, as would all state-owned industry.

However, despite Mussolini's grand gestures about returning fascism to its radical roots, he never had the time, support or willingness from the Germans to put any of his policies in place. The Salo Republic was, however, quite brutal. In January, five fascists who had been arrested in the Salo Republic, including Ciano (who was also Mussolini's son-in-law), were sentenced to death for treason due to their involvement in the Grand Council motion that had removed Mussolini from power. Thirteen others, including Grandi, who could not be found, were tried in absentia and given the same sentence. On 11 January 1944, the executions were carried out. Fascists in the Salo Republic were also active in assisting the German plans to send Italian Jews to Nazi death camps. The Verona Manifesto declared that Judaism was a nationality and that all Jews were to be classed as an enemy. The Salo Republic subsequently organised the movement of all Jews into camps. Around 7,500 Jews were taken from Italian camps and sent to Nazi death camps in eastern Europe where nearly 7,000 were executed.

Mussolini was also still able to draw on the support of a large body of radical fascists. A new militia was formed, known as the National Republican Guard (GNR) and was able to recruit 140,000 men. By the start of 1944, the RSI had an army of around 200,000 men. There was also a navy of around 20,000 men, an air force of 28,000 and an anti-aircraft service of around 50,000. In total, about 573,000 men were part of the RSI's armed forces, a number much greater than those Italians who joined antifascist partisan forces. A brutal war raged in the north between Italian antifascists (partisans) and German and RSI forces. The RSI did not usually fight alongside the German army, but was mainly engaged in a civil war with the partisans. The Italian population in the north was terrorised as a means of ensuring they would not shelter partisan soldiers and would report their presence if seen in the area. German policy set out that for every German soldier that died, ten Italians would be executed. Partisan attacks in March 1944 that killed 33 German soldiers, for example, had been answered with the execution of 335 Italians. Of all the cases of civilians being executed during the war in the north, it is estimated that ten percent were carried out by RSI forces operating on their own.

EXTEND YOUR KNOWLEDGE

The Italian antifascist partisans

The Italian partisan forces were irregular rebel fighters that took up arms against the Germans and fascist forces, predominately in northern Italy after the events of September 1943. A large number were ex-soldiers who had returned home after Italy's declaration of war against Germany, but others were simply students or civilians who wanted to fight against the German occupation and Salo Republic. By June 1944, it was estimated that 82,000 partisans were involved in sabotage, political assassination and the destruction of bridges and railways in order to hamper the fascist forces. The largest partisan force was linked to the PCI and included around 60 percent of all active antifascist fighters. The next largest after the communists was the 'Party of Action' who numbered around 28,000. There were also partisan forces linked to the Christian Democrats, the socialists and Italian liberals. In January 1944, a supreme political-military authority, the Committee of National Liberation for Upper Italy (CLNAI) was formed to coordinate the activities of the different partisan forces. It was the CLNAI that would form the provisional government of Italy at the end of the Second World War and these groups (apart from the Party of Action which disbanded in 1945) would dominate Italian politics until 1991. The myths and values of the resistance would form the ideological basis for the Italian republic they founded in 1946. In terms of fighting, the partisans were significant in tying down German soldiers and depriving them of manpower. It is estimated they killed around 5,000 German soldiers and hampered the activities of a further 20,000 to 30,000. They destroyed transport links and disrupted war production. However, the partisans were never able to liberate any areas of Italy on their own and Germany was only defeated by the force of the Allied army.

In the south, the king had established the royal government of the Kingdom of the South. This was effectively a client state, a government with little say in its own affairs and under the control of the Allied occupation that expanded as the Allies pushed north. In this area there was very little change to local leadership. The Allies had spoken about a mass purge of those within government and the police who had worked with the fascists, but overall this was not carried out. The king preferred to leave those conservatives who held the posts of prefects and *podestàs* to remain in place. These conservative elites were strong supporters of the monarchy and helped to control the social unrest that was beginning to take place across the south. Now that fascism was gone, these conservatives feared a re-emergence of communism and socialism, something that the king was extremely determined to resist.

Following the declaration of war on Germany in September 1943, the king and Badoglio had also made little attempt to organise an Italian contribution to the fighting. After the Allied occupation of Rome in June 1944, the king was encouraged by the Allies to broaden his government to include antifascist parties. Badoglio was removed as head of government and replaced by former prime minister and antifascist liberal Ivanoe Bonomi. His government tried to press ahead with the conscription of around 100,000 men to form an Italian army. However, anger at the king and Badoglio's actions in 1943 and the state of the war meant that the conscription order was largely resisted. Although around 50,000 men from the Kingdom of the South did fight alongside the Allies, this resistance to conscription formed a clear separation between the north and south of Italy that would affect the country after the war. The antifascist war of liberation fought by Italians was almost solely confined to the north and the differing wartime experiences between north and south accentuated their divisions in the post-war era.

ACTIVITY
KNOWLEDGE CHECK

1 To what extent was the Repubblica Sociale Italiana (RSI) 'no more than a puppet government of Germany'?

2 How far were King Victor Emmanuel III and Badoglio responsible for the continuation of the war in Italy between 1943 and 1945?

'Blood and honour in the Salo Republic', in *L'Ardimento* (Turin newspaper), 26 September 1944.

Ours is a ruthless battle: against the renunciatory attitudes of the Bonomi and Sforza [leading antifascist politicians] kind, against all who try to destroy the Italian soul, against all coalitions within and without, against the capitalistic plutocracy and destructive Bolshevism, against anyone who tries to oppose us on our painful and bloody road towards resurrection... We know only too well that we have many enemies: powerful and cowardly people, learned and ignorant, rich and poor, humble and arrogant, priests and women. But what does it matter? We believe in the saying: 'The more enemies the greater the honour' and we are determined to live up to it for the sake of Italy.

SOURCE
10

Mussolini's last public speech. Made in Milan at the Lyric Theatre to a large crowd of pro-fascist supporters, 16 December 1944.

Comrades! Dear Comrades of Milan! I shall dispense with any preamble and enter immediately into the heart of the subject matter of my speech... Who is guilty of betrayal? Who has suffered or is suffering the consequences of this treachery?... The unconditional surrender announced on 8 September was desired by the monarchy, by court circles, by the plutocratic currents of the Italian bourgeoisie, by certain clerical forces, combined for the occasion with Masonic ones, and by the General Staff which no longer believed in victory and which were headed by Badoglio... But... to get to 8 September, there first has to be 25 July – viz, the coup and the change of regime. From the social standpoint, the program of Republican Fascism is but the logical continuation of the program of 1919 – of the achievements of the splendid years that took place between the announcement of the Labour Charter and the conquest of the empire... It was necessary to build a foundation of syndical legislation and corporative bodies before we could take the subsequent step towards socialisation... Through socialisation, the best elements drawn from the ranks of the workers will be able to demonstrate their talents. I am determined to continue in this direction.

AS Level Exam-Style Question Section A

1 Why is Source 9 valuable to the historian for an enquiry into the popularity of the Repubblica Sociale Italiana (RSI)?

Explain your answer using the source, the information given about it and your own knowledge of the historical context. (8 marks)

Tip

Consider the claims made in Source 9 concerning the enemies of the RSI. How far could the historian make use of this source in weighing up opposition to the RSI?

2 How much weight do you give the evidence of Source 10 for an enquiry into the objectives of the Repubblica Sociale Italiana (RSI)?

Explain your answer using the source, the information given about it and your own knowledge of the historical context. (12 marks)

Tip

You must go beyond the simplistic idea that this is only one individual's view so therefore can't be given weight. Consider how realistic Mussolini's views may have been at the time, in light of your knowledge concerning how far Hitler controlled the RSI.

German surrender and Mussolini's death

Despite the fact that the Salo Republic was still able to organise quite a large military force, overall the popularity of the RSI was never very high, particularly as the war progressed. By 1944, it was fairly clear that the Germans were losing the war, thus making the RSI's continued existence impossible. The majority of Italians did not join either the RSI or the partisans but simply tried to get on with their lives as best they could as they waited for the Allies to arrive in northern Italy. Mussolini himself was seriously ill; he was having trouble eating and sleeping and was, according to his doctors, on the verge of physical collapse. He was still able to fulfil some of his functions as dictator. On 16 December 1944, he gave his last important speech in Milan where he told a packed theatre that it was the king and Italy's conservative elite who had betrayed the country and led it to defeat. Despite everything that had happened, he was still able to draw enormous cheering crowds as he toured bombed-out areas of Milan.

By April 1945, the Allied forces were beginning to capture major areas of northern Italy. On 18 April, Mussolini left Gargano and established his capital in Milan. There was very little point in this but it appears that Mussolini hoped that the move would bring him into closer contact with those who might be able to guarantee his safety. On 25 April, Mussolini met with partisan leaders to try to negotiate surrender. Mussolini offered to surrender if he was allowed to retreat further north with 3,000 loyal blackshirts. Before a decision could be made, Mussolini ended the talks after he discovered that the Germans were already negotiating surrender with the Allies without informing him. Mussolini now decided to try to escape towards Switzerland with evacuating German soldiers. On 27 April, partisans stopped the convoy Mussolini was travelling in at the town of Dongo and during their inspection discovered the Italian dictator disguised as a German soldier. Mussolini was arrested along with other fascists who were also trying to hide themselves, including his young mistress Claretta Petacci.

After some debate on what to do with Mussolini, the decision was taken to have him executed. On 28 April, Mussolini and his mistress were driven a short distance to a small town near Lake Como where they were both executed by machine gun. A further 12 captured fascists were executed on the same day in the town square of Dongo. Mussolini, Petacci and the 12 fascists' bodies were then driven down to Milan and publicly displayed at Piazzale Loretto, where huge crowds attacked Mussolini's body before hanging it upside down on the girders of the petrol station that was alongside the square.

Despite Mussolini's death, fighting in northern Italy still continued. The Allied forces pushed north as the Germans engaged in a mass retreat. On 29 April, the German command signed the surrender documents and agreed on a ceasefire on 1 May. On the day organised for the surrender in Italy, news came through that Hitler was dead and on 2 May 1944, the war in Italy came to an end.

The outcomes of the referendum and elections 1946

Italy ended the Second World War in a worse situation than it had done in 1918. The country's economy and infrastructure had been wrecked by the war and many Italians lacked food and clean water. In total, nearly half a million Italians, including civilians, had lost their lives during the Second World War. This number included around 17,000 Italian antifascist fighters and 13,000 RSI soldiers, who had died fighting a brutal civil war. Following Germany's surrender, it is also estimated that partisan revenge killings of alleged fascist supporters numbered somewhere around 30,000.

The experience of the war had left Italy severely divided. This was a major problem for the foundation of a new state to replace the fascist dictatorship. The antifascist forces of the Communists, Socialists and Christian Democrats (that would dominate Italian politics up to 1991) established the foundations of the new Italy on the 'values of the resistance' that had fought against the RSI and German forces. This was problematic as those Italians who fought with the RSI or did not support the partisans felt excluded. The fighting had also taken place predominately in the north and thus the foundation of this new state mostly ignored the south, where the experience under the Kingdom of the South had been quite different. This clear division was demonstrated on 2 June 1946, when Italians voted not only for a Constituent Assembly to draw up the new Italian constitution, but also on a referendum to decide on whether Italy should be a republic. The king's support for Mussolini since 1922 and his inadequate action after Mussolini was removed from power in 1943 had made him massively unpopular with the Italian public. He had abdicated in favour of his son, Umberto II, but despite this move, the Italian people still voted for an end to the monarchy and the establishment of an Italian republic by 12.7 million votes to 10.7 million. The vote however, was divided on geographical terms with nearly every area in the north voting for a republic and every province in the south to retain the monarchy.

In the Constituent Assembly vote (which included female voters for the first time), the Christian Democrats were victorious, securing 207 of the 556 seats, the PCI gaining 104 and the PSI 114 seats. The new constitution established a liberal democracy with civil and political freedom guaranteed. The monarchy was replaced by a president as head of state and the rule of law under an independent judiciary system enshrined in the constitution. However, aspects of Mussolini's rule were not forgotten, with the Lateran Pacts included in the new constitution. The unity of Italy's government was not to last. With the onset of the Cold War, pressure from the USA and the USSR saw the Christian Democrats under Alcide De Gaspari announce a new government in 1947 that excluded the PCI under Palmiro Togliatti, thus breaking the antifascist front that that had existed since 1944. Ridding Italy completely of fascism also proved to be incredibly difficult. As late as 1960, most of the country's prefects, police chiefs and deputies were still the same people who had worked for the fascist government. Perhaps more significantly, on 1 September 1957, massive crowds watched on as Mussolini was laid to rest in his family tomb in Predappio and to this day it is still attracts around 80,000 to 100,000 visitors every year.

ACTIVITY
KNOWLEDGE CHECK

1 Examine Source 9. How far was the programme of Republican fascism (RSI) 'the logical continuation of the programme of 1919'? You will need to consider the aims of the 1919 Fascist constitution and actions of the RSI to answer this question.

2 What would you consider the top two concerns for the new Italian republic and why?

3 To what extent had the Second World War left Italy a divided nation?

4 'The death of Mussolini saw the complete end of fascism in Italy.' How far do you agree with this statement?

ACTIVITY
SUMMARY

1 Summarise the reasons why Mussolini chose to enter the Second World War on the side of Germany in 1940.

2 Which do you believe was the most important reason Mussolini chose to enter the Second World War and why?

3 'The period between 1940 and 1945 shows that Mussolini's dictatorship had essentially failed to fulfil its aims.' How far would agree with this statement? What evidence is there to support it? What evidence can you give against this statement?

4 You have been asked to write Mussolini's obituary. You can decide whether you are writing for a fascist or antifascist publication. Think about how you could summarise his rule in either a positive or a negative way, depending on what publication you are writing for. You could then compare it to someone who has written for the opposite publication. What does this tell us about history and the difficulties of perspective?

5 In one sentence, how would you summarise Mussolini's dictatorship?

 WIDER READING

Deakin, F.W. *Brutal Friendship: Mussolini, Hitler and the fall of Italian Fascism*, Weidenfeld & Nicolson (2000)

Holland, J. *Italy's Sorrow*, Harper Press (2008)

Mack Smith, D. *Mussolini's Roman Empire*, Penguin (1977)

Morgan, P. *The Fall of Mussolini*, Oxford University Press (2008)

Moseley, R. *The Last Days of Mussolini*, Sutton Publishing (2006)

Preparing for your AS Level Paper 2 exam

Advance planning

1. Draw up a timetable for your revision and try to keep to it. Spread your timetable over a number of weeks, and aim to cover four or five topics each week.
2. Spend longer on topics which you have found difficult, and revise them several times.
3. Above all, do not try to limit your revision by attempting to 'question spot'. Try to be confident about all aspects of your Paper 2 work, because this will ensure that you have a choice of questions in Section B.

Paper 2 overview

AS Paper 2	Time: 1 hour 30 minutes	
Section A	Answer 1 compulsory two-part sources question	8+12 marks = 20 marks
Section B	Answer 1 question from a choice of 3	20 marks
	Total marks =	40 marks

You should familiarise yourself with the layout of the paper by looking at the examples published by Edexcel. The questions for each section are followed by eight pages of lined paper where you should write your answer.

Section A question

Each of the two parts of the question will focus on one of the two contemporary sources provided. The sources together will total around 300 words. The (a) question, worth 8 marks, will be in the form of 'Why is Source 1 useful for an enquiry into…?' The (b) question, worth 12 marks, will be in the form of 'How much weight do you give the evidence of Source 2 for an enquiry into…?' In both your answers you should address the value of the content of the source, and then its nature, origin and purpose. Finally, you should use your own knowledge of the context of the source to assess its value.

Section B questions

These questions ask you to reach a judgement on an aspect of the topic studied. The questions will have the form, for example, of 'How far…', 'To what extent…' or 'How accurate is it to say …'. The questions can deal with historical concepts such as cause, consequence, change, continuity, similarity, difference and significance. You should consider the issue raised in the question, consider other relevant issues, and then conclude with an overall judgement.

The timescale of the questions could be as short as a single year or even a single event (an example from Option 2C.2 could be, 'To what extent was Russia's involvement in the First World War responsible for the fall of the Provisional Government in 1917?'). The timescale could be longer depending on the historical event or process being examined, but questions are likely to be shorter than the those set for Sections A and B in Paper 1.

Use of time

This is an issue which you should discuss with your teachers and fellow students, but here are some suggestions for you.

1. Do not write solidly for 45 minutes on each question. For Section A it is essential that you have a clear understanding of the content of each source, the points being made, and the nature, origin and purpose of each source. You might decide to spend up to ten minutes reading the sources and drawing up your plan, and 35 minutes writing your answer.
2. For Section B answers you should spend a few minutes working out what the question is asking you to do, and drawing up a plan of your answer before you begin to write your response.

Preparing for your AS Level exams

Section A

Part A requires you to:

- identify key points in the source and explain them
- deploy your own knowledge of the context in which events took place
- make appropriate comments about the author/origin/purpose of the source.

Why is Source 4 (Chapter 2, page 199) valuable to the historian for an enquiry into the importance of violence to the fascist movement before 1922?

Explain your answer, using the source, the information given about it and your own knowledge of the historical context. (8 marks)

Average student answer

This extract focuses on Mussolini's belief that violence is important to the fascist movement. Here he is telling the other fascists that, although it is sad, they must engage in violence against the socialists whom he describes as an enemy within the state. He clearly sees them as a threat and claims that the violence against the socialists is necessary in order to save Italy. The fascists gained popularity by opposing the left-wing parties and therefore looked like they were saving Italy from possible revolution and civil war. This grew their support among the right-wing elites. Mussolini shows this by proclaiming that the socialists and communists are like the Bolshevist state.

Mussolini proclaims that the 'Socialists have formed a state within a state' and that this state is 'tyrannical, illiberal and overbearing'. Thus it is clear that they must be dealt with through violence. This violence is described by Mussolini as 'legitimate' thus showing he believes the violence is justified as the socialists are a threat to the state. Violence was therefore very important to the fascists in building their power. The fascists were able to expand their power through violence against the left-wing parties and build their strength because many within the army and police supported them. Mussolini's speech therefore demonstrates how important violence was to the fascists and their power in Italy.

The source shows that Mussolini believed violence was very important to the fascists coming to power and that the socialists need to be defeated as they were a danger to Italy.

> This is a weak opening paragraph because it does not analyse and define the question.
>
> The student has some good knowledge but the answer lacks focus on the specific question and does not explain why the source would be valuable to the historian.

> This section does make reference to the source and tries to use quotes. However, it is mainly descriptive and never explains exactly how this information would be valuable to the historian. It is vague in its explanations and does not say why many within the army and police supported the fascists or exactly why this was important. There needs to be greater clarity and explanation of the quotes and setting out of their relevance to the specific question.

> The short conclusion describes what the source was saying but does not answer the question or explain how the source might be valuable to a historian studying this area of Italian history.

Verdict

This is an average answer because:

- it quotes from the source but never relates this information to the specific question in a way that demonstrates clear understanding
- there is some knowledge and attempt at explanation but it lacks specific focus on the question

- the answer is mainly descriptive and tends to set out what the source is saying without any clear evaluation of how this might be valuable to a historian.

Use the feedback on this answer to rewrite it, making as many improvements as you can.

Paper 2: AS Level sample answer with comments

Section A

Part B requires you to:

- interrogate the source
- draw reasoned inferences
- deploy your own knowledge to interpret the material in its context
- make judgement about the value (weight) of the source.

How much weight do you give the evidence of Source 2 (Chapter 4, page 246) for an enquiry into the support for the Abyssinian War (1935–36) in Italy?

Explain your answer, using the source, the information given about it and your own knowledge of the historical context. (12 marks)

Average student answer

The source is good in telling us how people felt at the time about the Abyssinian War. The author was there in that town and saw what the people were doing and has then written about the event. In this source it is very clear that 'the peasants were not interested in war', and were angry about what was happening in Italy. This helps us understand that some people did not support the war in Abyssinia.

It is significant that Carlo Levi was sent to the town for opposing Mussolini. He had to live in this town and could not leave. Here he saw the peasant life of Italy and wrote about it later in his book. Thus the source is particularly valuable as he was there. This was the real attitude of the peasants that many people did not see. Mussolini's propaganda proclaimed that the war was a great moment for Italy and all Italians should be proud. Levi's source questions whether this was true and shows that Italy was more divided than Mussolini said. Mussolini did do some things to try and help the southern peasants but did not make much difference to their lives. The source helps to show this clear divide and demonstrates how people in the south maybe thought differently from people in the north. Immigration was a big part of Italy at the time and many Italians wanted to move to the USA. The source says that the peasants were angry because the war meant they couldn't go. This helps us understand why they were perhaps not supporting Mussolini's invasion of Abyssinia.

Although the source is quite short it is still a good account of what people in this area thought at the time. There is a problem in that the source is just from one person and is only their view of what happened, but it is true that most people in the south were very poor and did not care about what was happening in the rest of Italy.

> The answer is weak as it lacks a focused and coherent introduction. There is no clear explanation of how much weight the analysis given by Levi would have or why that would be the case. Most importantly, the introduction never provides an answer to the specific question.

> The student has some good knowledge of Italy and the divisions within it and does relate this to the source. However, the knowledge is vague and not specific and does not relate in clear enough detail to how much weight this provides the source. The comments about Levi are undeveloped. The argument being made is too generalised. The comment about immigration is simply descriptive and asserts what the source is saying. Whether this helps the source's value is not answered and the knowledge used to support the point is vague and undeveloped.

> The conclusion is weak as it does not make a clear judgement concerning how much weight should be given to the source.

Verdict

This is an average answer because:

- it does not interrogate the source in enough detail and the comments about specific points are vague and undeveloped in demonstrating understanding of the source
- the knowledge linked to the source is lacking in detail and tends to only make very generalised comments on how this might contribute to the source's weight

- both the introduction and conclusion do not provide evaluation of the question but are instead descriptive and lacking in direct focus.

Use the feedback on this answer to rewrite it, making as many improvements as you can.

Paper 2: AS Level sample answer with comments

Section A

Part A requires you to:

- identify key points in the source and explain them
- deploy your own knowledge of the context in which events took place
- make appropriate comments about the author/origin/purpose of the source.

Why is Source 4 (Chapter 2, page 199) valuable to the historian for an enquiry into the importance of violence to the fascist movement before 1922?

Explain your answer, using the source, the information given about it and your own knowledge of the historical context. (8 marks)

Strong student answer

This extract is of immense value to the study of the fascist movement before 1922 because it reveals the importance Mussolini placed on violence against the socialists and the way he justified this violence both to his supporters and to the rest of Italy. The source is valuable in demonstrating how Mussolini justified the violence by portraying the socialists as an internal danger to Italy and linking them to the enemies Italy had fought during the First World War. The source is an excellent illustration of the justifications Mussolini made concerning fascist violence and helps us to understand why it had a certain appeal to large sections of the Italian population.

Mussolini clearly depicts the socialists as a grave danger to Italy: 'Socialists have formed a state within a state' and this state is 'tyrannical, illiberal and overbearing'. This is valuable to a historian in understanding the importance of violence in the fascist movement as many Italians, particularly those in the middle classes and elite, believed that this was true. The large socialist- and communist-led workers' strikes that were taking place in Italy during the early 1920s meant there was a genuine fear that something similar to the Russian Revolution could happen in Italy. Therefore the fascists found there was a considerable amount of support for their violence against the socialists and communists, which Mussolini was eager to encourage.

The nature of the source clearly shows how Mussolini justified the violence against the socialists and portrayed his political opposition as a revolutionary danger to Italy that was similar to the Bolsheviks in Russia. This specifically helps to understand why the fascist violence was important as it helped grow Mussolini's support among certain aspects of the Italian population in the early years of the 1920s.

> A very strong opening that is sharply focused on the specific question and indicates a high level of understanding of the question.

> This section develops the analysis of the source and uses excellent own knowledge to explain directly why this source would be valuable to a historian studying the importance of fascist violence.

> The conclusion is strong because it directly answers the question. The way in which the source is valuable to the historian studying this area is explained in specific detail and the importance of this evaluated in response to the overall question.

Verdict

This is a strong answer because:

- it has clear understanding of the specific question
- it deploys appropriate own knowledge accurately and effectively

- it has excellent evaluation that specifically explains the value of the source.

Paper 2: AS Level sample answer with comments

Section A

Part B requires you to:

- interrogate the source
- draw reasoned inferences
- deploy your own knowledge to interpret the material in its context
- make judgement about the value (weight) of the source.

How much weight do you give the evidence of Source 2 (Chapter 4, page 246) for an enquiry into the support for the Abyssinian War (1935–36) in Italy?

Explain your answer, using the source, the information given about it and your own knowledge of the historical context. (12 marks)

Strong student answer

The source would carry some weight and value for any enquiry into the support for the Abyssinia War in Italy during the mid-1930s. The author was present in one of the poorest areas of Italy and relates his experiences of this area during the 1930s. However, there are some clear concerns about the author's background and how representative this area was of the rest of Italy.

It is significant that Carlo Levi was a political dissident who had been sent to this poor southern town as punishment. This banishment of political dissidents to isolated towns in the south was a common form of punishment during the fascist period. Levi would therefore have had some incentive to demonstrate that the fascists were unpopular and that their propaganda was not as effective as Mussolini claimed. This restricts the weight of evidence given in the source. However, despite these issues the fact that Levi has come from the wealthier part of Italy meant he was able to understand the huge contrasts in Italian society much more adequately and this is clearly demonstrated in his portrayal of the peasants' reaction to the Abyssinian War.

His account is valuable in shedding light on the specific ways different parts of the Italian population reacted to the fascist regime. Generally the Abyssinian conflict was massively popular and has been considered one of, if not the most successful action Mussolini ever took as dictator of Italy. However, Levi's source shows that generalisations about the Abyssinian War cannot be made. Levi's source confirms the view that many of the poorer areas of the south were ignored by the fascists despite Mussolini's claims to be working for the greater unity of the country. Overall, the influence of the government and the enthusiasm for fascism was barely felt in these southern areas where the population was mostly illiterate, landless peasants who had lived in poverty for centuries.

Clearly the source only focuses on one isolated town in Italy during this period so there are some questions on how representative it is. However, it does provide a clear illustration that not all of Italy was affected by fascist propaganda or the assertions of Mussolini. There are limits to the value of the source given Levi's background and his antifascist activities, but his account can be linked to the realities of the Italy's north–south divide.

> A focused and well balanced introduction which comments on the value of Carlo Levi as a witness and makes clear judgements about both strengths and weaknesses of the source in direct relation to the specific question.

> Clearly answers the question by first setting out issues in the source that might affect how much weight can be given to it. It then goes on to state why, despite these problems, the source has value in its description of the southern peasantry in Italy.

> A strong conclusion that provides an excellent overall summary of the writer's argument in relation to the source.

Verdict

This is a strong answer because:

- it shows detailed understanding of the question by interrogating the source and selects and comments on specific points

- it brings in some own knowledge and links this source to wider contextual understanding
- it makes an overall evaluation about the value of the source.

269

Paper 2: AS Level sample answer with comments

Section B

These questions assess your understanding of the period in some depth. They will ask you about the content you learned about in the four key themes, but may not ask about more than one theme. For these questions remember to:

- give an analytical, not a descriptive, response
- support your points with evidence
- cover the whole time period specified in the question
- come to a substantiated judgement.

To what extent was the Libyan War in 1911 the main reason for the failure of the Giolitti programme? (20 marks)

Average student answer

It is accurate to say that the Libyan War was a key reason for the failure of the Giolitti programme, but there were also some other reasons as well.

Firstly, one way in which the Libyan War brought about the end of the Giolitti programme was that the socialists stopped supporting his government. In 1911, Giolitti decided to invade Libya and take it from the Ottoman Turks because he was scared France was about to take Libya and this would humiliate Italy. He thought this action would get him support from Italian nationalists and the Church and Italians would support Giolitti because he had got Italy a new colony.

Secondly, another way in which the Libyan War ended the Giolitti programme was that it helped the nationalists instead of him. Giolitti wanted to invade Libya so that Italians would support him. The nationalists were a new, popular political force. Winning the war in Libya could make Giolitti strong with the Italian people and therefore they would not support the nationalists. In 1896, Italy had been defeated by an African force when they tried to colonise Abyssinia. Therefore, lots of Italians felt bad about Italy and wanted a stronger government. Giolitti wanted to achieve something great instead. But with Libya, instead of helping, the nationalists instead said that they were the reason for the Libyan War, not Giolitti. Many Italian soldiers had died during the invasion and the nationalists said this was Giolitti's fault. The nationalists took all the credit for the war and said only their pressure had made it happen. Giolitti lost further support and was accused of not being patriotic. Thus, the Libyan invasion led to the end of the Giolitti programme and was a big problem for his government.

However, although the consequences of the Libyan War helped end the Giolitti programme, there were some other reasons. In 1912, Giolitti's government changed who could vote in Italy. Lots more Italians could now vote in the election, all those over 30 years of age. Giolitti thought this would help achieve national unity and improve the popularity of his party. Instead, he lost lots of seats and the socialists and nationalists did well. This meant he had to rely on the Catholics who were in parliament. He had to make changes to his policies and these made other people in his government angry as well as the PSI. The Giolitti programme was in trouble and when some in the parliament decided to withdraw their support he had to resign. Overall, not everything about the failure of the Giolitti programme related to the Libyan War and there were other factors as well, such as the change in the voting franchise.

This is an example of how not to start an answer. The student has not made any substantial point on the question, nor is there any judgement here.

The paragraph considers the way in which the Libyan War meant the end of the PSI cooperation with Giolitti. It does have accurate points and explains that this cooperation was a major part of the Giolitti programme. However, the points need much more support, with more extensive explanation and detail.

There is lots of information in this paragraph. The details on Abyssinia in 1896 and the problems for Italy in the early part of the 20th century are relevant in some ways to this question, but they need to be explained a lot better so that their relevance is clear. The paragraph requires better focus and clearer argument.

The point is relevant and does make an attempt to answer the question. However, there is not enough direct explanation. Why Giolitti changed the vote and thought this would achieve national unity is not clearly set out.

The final reason why he lost support was that the Catholics and the nationalists had found new forces to gain the support of the Italian people. Giolitti had hoped his programme could make all the parties work with each other. With the socialists he tried to introduce good social policies so that they would support his government. This worked for a while until the party threw out Bissolati and went more radical after the Libyan War. He tried to work with the Catholics and the nationalists as well. The Nationalists would not support him, however. They did not need to work with Giolitti and would not help with *trasformismo*. Even the socialists were now becoming more radical and there were more strikes and violent behaviour by the workers. Therefore, Giolitti's programme failed because it could no longer work. The other political organisations did not want to work with him so his key ideas were failing and he had no other options.

Thus I have shown that the Libyan War did help end the Giolitti programme. It meant that the PSI would no longer support him and made them turn more radical. It also meant that the nationalists gained more support and they refused to work with Giolitti. However, there were other factors. The change in the voting franchise meant that the support in the parliament changed and he had to work with the Catholics, which some people in his own party did not like. Also, there was a change in the politics of Italy with the socialists, Catholics and nationalists which meant his programme could not work anymore. Despite these other reasons I think that the main reason for the failure of the Giolitti programme was the Libyan War.

> The overall idea is good and tries to make the point that Giolitti's programme could no longer work in Italy's changing political situation. However, key aspects like *trasformismo* are not explained, nor is it clearly set out what Giolitti hoped to offer the nationalists nor why exactly they would not work with his government.

> You should not use a phrase such as 'Thus I have shown' in the conclusion: a simple 'To conclude' will suffice. The student attempts to reach a conclusion, but it is not very developed and simply restates the points made in the body of the answer.

Verdict

This is average answer because:

- there is some attempt at explanation, but there are descriptive passages, including some which do not appear directly relevant
- the material included is accurate, but is lacking in depth in several places
- there is an attempt to reach an overall judgement, but is not entirely secure

- the answer is organised on the question, and the general trend of the argument is reasonably clear. However, a couple of paragraphs, though accurate and broadly relevant, are fairly undeveloped and unsupported, and could be improved with sharper links to the question overall.

Use the feedback on this answer to rewrite it, making as many improvements as you can.

Paper 2: AS Level sample answer with comments

Section B

These questions assess your understanding of the period in some depth. They will ask you about the content you learned about in the four key themes, but may not ask about more than one theme. For these questions remember to:

- give an analytical, not a descriptive, response
- support your points with evidence
- cover the whole time period specified in the question
- come to a substantiated judgement.

To what extent was the Libyan War in 1911 the main reason for the failure of the Giolitti programme? (20 marks)

Strong student answer

In September 1911, Giolitti took the fateful decision to invade Libya and capture the colony for Italy from the Ottoman Empire. He believed that this invasion would help build support for his political programme that focused on uniting the socialists, Catholic Church and nationalists behind his liberal government and transforming Italy into a modern, successful country – a policy known as *trasformismo*. The capture of Libya would galvanise the Italian people and bring about a greater unity and national feeling behind the government. However, to a large extent the invasion had the opposite effect.

One key way in which the Libyan War led to the end of the Giolitti programme was the loss of socialist support for his party that the war created. A key aspect of the Giolitti programme concerned cooperation from the socialists. They were an influential political party and Giolitti had gained their cooperation with the liberals through introducing social reform, such as the government non-intervention in labour disputes in 1906. The Libyan War was actually supported by the *Partito Socialista Italiano* (PSI) leader, Bissolati, who believed that acquiring Libya would help provide land for Italy's poor peasantry. However, instead the war brought about the end of the Giolitti programme as the invasion of Libya split the Socialist Party. More radical socialists had been angry with Bissolati's cooperation with Giolitti and the invasion increased their anger. They viewed the war as imperialist militarism and Bissolati as a traitor to the ideals of socialism. Thus the invasion played a large role in the failure of the Giolitti programme as it contributed to the radicalisation of the PSI and the failure of Giolitti's attempts to absorb the socialists into the liberal state.

At the same time Giolitti's belief that the invasion of Libya would lead to greater cooperation with the nationalists was also unsuccessful. The nationalist movement was a new and dynamic political force which believed that a national renewal of the Italian nation would stop the rise of socialism and destroy the corrupt liberal order. They believed war and expansion would help overcome Italy's domestic strife and lead to the end of Giolitti's weak government. The Libyan War, Giolitti believed, would undermine the nationalists by showing that his government could expand Italy and bring about a more powerful and dynamic nation. However, the invasion of Libya failed to achieve Giolitti's aims as the war only increased Italian support for the nationalists. The nationalists also rejected any suggestion of working with Giolitti. The war thus contributed to the failure of the Giolitti programme to some extent. While the war did not actually contribute to a change in direction for the nationalists, who always opposed Giolitti, his belief that the Libyan War would help the liberals and undermine support for the nationalist movement was clearly unsuccessful.

> This is a strong introduction. It gives an explanation of what Giolitti's political programme was and how it linked to the invasion of Libya. The student then carefully explains the key points of their argument concerning both those factors that back up the question premise and those that show that other factors contributed. They end the introduction with a strong and clear argument that uses the key words in the question, namely 'to what extent'.

> The answer maintains focus and looks clearly at one of the ways in which the war contributed to the failure of Giolitti's programme. There is a clear topic sentence and explanation at the end of the paragraph that sets out the argument. The points made are well supported with good information and clear historical context explaining exactly what Giolitti was trying to achieve and why the Libyan War meant this ended in failure.

> An excellent paragraph. It starts with a very clear argument and then sets out good, detailed historical context on exactly what Giolitti was trying to achieve in respect to the nationalist movement in Italy.

However, although the consequences of the Libyan War did help end the Giolitti programme, it is clear that the franchise extension of 1912 also played a considerable role. Before 1912, only literate men over the age of 21 could vote, but in 1912 Giolitti passed a law extending the vote to all men in the armed forces and men over 30 without any literacy considerations. Giolitti believed the extension of voting rights would bring about greater Italian unity and help the liberals as there would be more voters from rural areas who tended to be conservative as opposed to industrial workers who tended to support the PSI. Instead, Giolitti's liberals lost 59 seats and the socialists, nationalists and Catholic parties made gains. To stay in power Giolitti had to work with the Catholic-backed politicians. This made *trasformismo* more difficult to achieve as the socialists opposed Giolitti's concessions to the Catholic Church, as did many liberal members of parliament who feared that the Church was gaining too much influence in politics. Therefore, the political changes brought about by the 1912 franchise changes meant Giolitti had to compromise with the Catholic Church, a move that helped end his political programme to a considerable extent, as it contributed to the loss of support from his own liberal supporters and accentuated the growing anger of the socialists that had been incited earlier by the Libyan War.

> A very clear paragraph that directly explores a different factor that led to the end of Giolitti's government. Again, it has clear historical context that clearly links to the question and shows considerable understanding of the differing reasons for the collapse of Giolitti's programme.

Finally, another key aspect of Giolitti's failure was the overall changes in Italy's political landscape that made *trasformismo* impossible to achieve. The larger involvement of the Italian people in elections after 1912 meant that the socialists, nationalists and Catholic political forces targeted more populist policies to increase their support. There was much less willingness for the other political groups to work with Giolitti and the liberal system and instead, the nationalists and PSI, in particular, proclaimed that only the end of the liberal system could save Italy. Giolitti found that his older ideas of *trasformismo* and compromise were impossible in this new Italian landscape. Therefore, to some extent, changes in the Italian political direction also contributed to the failure of Giolitti's programme.

> A sophisticated paragraph that looks at general changes in the Italian political system that also led to Giolitti's failure.

In conclusion, the Libyan War led to the failure of the Giolitti programme to a large extent. It contributed to the growing strength of the nationalist forces, a factor that directly undermined Giolitti's hope that the war would show that the liberals could achieve Italian greatness and thus undermine support for the nationalist association. However, the changing Italian franchise also contributed in a significant way as it led to major developments in Italian politics such as mass political participation which made Giolitti's older ideas of *trasformismo* more difficult to achieve.

> An excellent conclusion. It sets out both sides of the argument clearly and discusses their relative merits.

Verdict

This is a strong answer because:

- it offers a high level of analysis in putting forward a variety of factors that show the differing aspects of the question, while sustaining a focus on the question set
- it demonstrates in-depth knowledge through wide-ranging evidence that is used to support the points made
- it reaches a secure concluding judgement and the most important point is directly set out
- it is well organised and communication of material is clear and precise

Preparing for your A Level Paper 2 exam

Advance planning

1. Draw up a timetable for your revision and try to keep to it. Spread your timetable over a number of weeks, and aim to cover four or five topics each week.
2. Spend longer on topics which you have found difficult, and revise them several times.
3. Above all, do not try to limit your revision by attempting to 'question spot'. Try to be confident about all aspects of your Paper 2 work, because this will ensure that you have a choice of questions in Section B.

Paper 2 overview

AL Paper 2	Time: 1 hour 30 minutes	
Section A	Answer 1 compulsory source question	20 marks
Section B	Answer 1 question from a choice of 2	20 marks
	Total marks =	40 marks

You should familiarise yourself with the layout of the paper by looking at the examples published by Edexcel. The questions for each section are followed by eight pages of lined paper where you should write your answer.

Section A question

This question asks you to assess two different types of contemporary sources totalling around 400 words, and will be in the form of 'How far could the historian make use of Sources 1 and 2 together to investigate …?' Your answer should evaluate both sources, considering their nature, origin and purpose, and you should use your own knowledge of the context of the sources to consider their value to the specific investigation. Remember, too, that in assessing their value, you must consider the two sources, taken together, as a set.

Section B questions

These questions ask you to reach a judgement on an aspect of the topic studied. The questions will have the form, for example, of 'How far …', 'To what extent …' or 'How accurate is it to say …'. The questions can deal with historical concepts such as cause, consequence, change, continuity, similarity, difference and significance. You should consider the issue raised in the question, then other relevant issues, and conclude with an overall judgement.

The timescale of the questions could be as short as a single year or even a single event (an example from Option 2C.2 could be, 'To what extent was Russia's involvement in the First World War responsible for the fall of the Romanovs in 1917?'). The timescale could be longer depending on the historical event or process being examined, but questions are likely to be shorter than the those set for Sections A and B in Paper 1.

Use of time

This is an issue which you should discuss with your teachers and fellow students, but here are some suggestions for you.

1. Do not write solidly for 45 minutes on each question. For Section A it is essential that you have a clear understanding of the content of each source, the points being made, and the nature, origin and purpose of each source. You might decide to spend up to ten minutes reading the sources and drawing up your plan, and 35 minutes writing your answer.
2. For Section B answers you should spend a few minutes working out what the question is asking you to do, and drawing up a plan of your answer before you begin to write your response.

Preparing for your A Level exams

Paper 2: A Level sample answer with comments

Section A

You will need to read and analyse two sources and use them in tandem to assess how useful they are in investigating an issue. For these questions remember to:

- spend time, up to ten minutes, reading and identifying the arguments and evidence present in the sources; then make a plan to ensure that your response will be rooted in these sources
- use specific references from the sources
- deploy your own knowledge to develop points made in the sources and establish appropriate context
- come to a substantiated judgement.

How far could the historian make use of Sources 7 and 8 (Chapter 3, page 228) together to investigate the success of the Corporate State?

Explain your answer, using the source, the information given about it and your own knowledge of the historical context. (20 marks)

Average student answer

The two sources are very different in their perspective on the success of the Corporate State. Mussolini was leader of Italy and was responsible for the Corporate State. He is therefore going to be very supportive of it as it was a key part of his ideology. Salvemini is against the Corporate State as he was an antifascist. He is therefore not going to be a supporter of anything the fascists do. He was forced to leave Italy by the fascists so he hated Mussolini and it is possible to see this in the source. The historian could therefore use the sources to get a different view on whether the Corporate State was a success or not.

The central aspect of the Corporate State was to bring workers, politicians and industrialists together in a unified organisation that would run the economy. Mussolini sets this out by saying that the Corporate State 'controls and harmonises and tempers the interests of all social classes'. Salvemini disagrees, he says 'the will of the members is suppressed'. The Corporate State was developed in the 1920s and 1930s. One of the big criticisms was that the workers did not get a say and instead the organisation was simply for the fascists and industrialists to make decisions. It did not allow workers to make decisions but was simply an overall trick to make it look like the fascists were actually doing something. Mussolini saw the Corporate State as one of his key policies. He claimed it showed that fascists were coming up with their own economic system that was different to everybody else. He clearly believes that his policy is successful and that everyone wants to be a part of it. In his view, 'there is not one working Italian today who does not seek a place in his Corporation'. Many international visitors to Italy thought that the Corporate State was working and went back to their countries and explained how brilliant Mussolini's economic policy was. The fascists used this to boost the support for Mussolini. On the other hand, Salvemini argues that the workers never really got a say in the Corporate State, which is true. The workers never got to represent themselves and instead had to rely on the fascists. As he says, the corporations 'have no greater authority than do the animals in a society for the prevention of cruelty to animals'. Mussolini and the industrialists simply made the policy they wanted and ignored everyone else. Most

The opening does explain some of the differences between the sources and gives an explanation linked to the question. However, it is a bit general in its points and does not refer to any aspects of the sources that support the argument they are putting forward. The point on Salvemini needs to be more specifically focused on what he is saying in the source instead of making sweeping statements about his antifascism. The attitudes of the differing sources could have been drawn out a bit more through better analysis of the type of language used. Both are quite exaggerated in their claims and this should have been commented on.

There are good ideas and attempts to link own knowledge to the answer, but judgements are based on limited explanation and justification. The details of the Corporate State, for instance, are lacking and it is not clear to the reader what its purpose was.

historians agree with what Salvemini is arguing and say that the Corporate State was really nothing at all. It provided Mussolini with a good idea that made him popular, but was never actually taken seriously. Both sources are very different in their argument on this question.

Both sources are written in quite over-the-top language. This shows how much they disagree with each other on the role of the Corporate State. Mussolini calls the Corporate State a 'great, immense, living organisation', clearly showing how much he believes in the corporations. This is very one sided, which is expected as he created the idea. It is helpful to the historian to understand how Mussolini saw his creation. Salvemini was against the fascists and his language directly shows this, with really strong language such as saying that the workers are simply 'passive and inert material'. Both sources show there was lots of debate on whether the Corporate State worked or not and the differing ideas on it. They help the historian who is studying the issue to understand this. Maybe there are some problems though as both sources are very biased and it is hard to know if either of them is telling the truth exactly as they come from very extreme differences on the issue of the Corporate State.

It is therefore difficult to completely understand the evaluation of the sources being made. The relevance of the foreign visitors who were impressed by the Corporate State is also not explained. The student uses quotes from the sources to support their argument but they needed to be explained. The last part is vague, referring to 'most historians'. This is not untrue but the language could be improved and more specific examples and explanation of the point provided by the student.

The conclusion is long but does not offer a clear evaluation of the question. There is a lot of information on the sources, but not all of it is directly related to the question being answered. There is some assessment of value to the historian but it is somewhat vague and undeveloped. Critically, the answer does not finish with a direct answer to the question, but instead gives some more generalised information without setting out an overall evaluation.

Verdict

This is an average answer because:

- it demonstrates understanding of the source material and shows some analysis from the key points relevant to the question, but these are not developed very far or explained in enough detail
- some contextual own knowledge is used to explain and support points on the sources, but lacks critical detail that would be required for a higher level

- evaluation of the sources is made and related to the usefulness of the source in reference to the position of both the authors. However, these judgements are limited and not developed enough. The language is a little poor and the points could be explained in better detail.

Use the feedback on this answer to rewrite it, making as many improvements as you can.

Paper 2: A Level sample answer with comments

Section A

You will need to read and analyse two sources and use them in tandem to assess how useful they are in investigating an issue. For these questions remember to:

- spend time, up to ten minutes, reading and identifying the arguments and evidence present in the sources; then make a plan to ensure that your response will be rooted in these sources
- use specific references from the sources
- deploy your own knowledge to develop points made in the sources and establish appropriate context
- come to a substantiated judgement.

How far could the historian make use of Sources 7 and 8 (Chapter 3, page 228) together to investigate the success of the Corporate State?

Explain your answer, using the source, the information given about it and your own knowledge of the historical context. (20 marks)

Strong student answer

The two sources certainly provide acutely different perspectives on the Corporate State. Mussolini was the dictator of Italy who created the Corporate State as a key platform of his fascist regime. This was established in 1926 under the Rocco Law and then developed through the 1930s after the establishment of the National Council of Corporations. Mussolini proclaimed that the Corporate State was the greatest economic development that fascism had brought to the world and it is therefore unsurprising that his language is extremely enthusiastic. Mussolini makes it clear that the Corporate State is a considerable change from what he calls the 'demo-liberal regime' and now under fascism the workers have much greater rights and say in the direction of the economy. On the other side, Salvemini questions the fascist claims and asserts that the Corporate State is nothing more than a façade that controls the workers. He directly challenges the idea that it is an improvement on the previous Italian system that the fascists overthrew. Salvemini was an antifascist socialist politician who was forced to leave Italy so his anger at the fascists and Corporate State may question the value of the source. However, despite his quite extreme view, his understanding of the Corporate State is supported by historians.

In theory, the corporations were meant to be a mixed union of workers and employers who would discuss and implement national economic planning that was conducive to both their interests, thus producing a more productive and harmonious economic order. This idea is clearly demonstrated in Mussolini's claims that the Corporate State 'concentrates, controls and harmonises and tempers the interests of all social classes, which are thereby protected in equal measure'. This idea was shown in the 'Charter of Labour' from 1927 that promised that workers' and employers' corporations would organise Italy's economy and guarantee workers' rights. In 1930, this was developed further in the National Council of Corporations and then in 1934 with mixed corporations representing 22 major economic sectors. This was meant to see employers and workers working together in harmony to run Italy's economy in a fair manner. As Mussolini claimed, it was meant to be a new radical idea that was not communist nor capitalist, but somewhere in between. Overseas observers were told that Mussolini had produced an amazing new economic system and that 'there is not one working Italian today who does not seek a place in his corporation or federation'. Support from overseas journalists who were impressed by Mussolini's ideas were then published in Italy in order to boost the idea that the Italian dictator was a world leader who was respected outside of Italy.

A strong opening which explains the background of both sources, emphasing the differing views and explaining the subjective analysis that they put forward. It clearly demonstrates excellent own knowledge and comprehension of the sources' perspective and potential problems a historian may have with using them. The paragraph also explains that despite the strong viewpoint of the second source, it does reflect the view of most historians.

These two paragraphs identify key points made in the sources and illustrate them with specific references and some excellent own knowledge.

However, in reality the Corporate State was simply propaganda. As Salvemini argues, the corporations were simply a façade, one that only really represented the industrialists and the fascists. The workers had no real say and could not represent themselves in the corporations anyway. The key argument of Salvemini that while in the case of the employers they represent themselves, but for the workers they are represented by 'appointed officials [fascists]', is clearly backed up by further analysis of the Corporate State. All economic policy was approved by Mussolini and he rarely consulted with the corporations. As Salvemini argues, 'the rank and file have no greater authority than do the animals in a society for the prevention of cruelty to animals'. Historians analysing the Corporate State have mostly concluded that it played no other role except propaganda in order to support the idea that Mussolini had created a new and dynamic economic system that had never been used previously. However, it was simply a bloated and expensive bureaucracy that interfered with the running of the fascist economy without playing any positive role. Salvemini's assertion that the Corporate State was 'devised for the better disciplining of labour and capital' is clearly supported when looking at the reality of Mussolini's creation.

Both sources are written in a quite subjective style in order to support their viewpoint. Unsurprisingly, Mussolini uses grandiose language to describe the Corporate State and its successes: 'great, immense, living organisation which is the National Corporate State of Fascism'. This reads quite clearly like fascist propaganda and is therefore difficult for the historian to take at face value. However, it is of use in understanding what Mussolini wanted the Corporate State to be perceived as and how he presented it as an organisation. Salvemini is much more critical, analysing the hypocritical elements of the Corporate State. This is influenced by his antifascist views, but there is considerable historical support to back up his claims. The points made in the two sources provide an effective starting point for a debate about the nature of the Corporate State. The value for any historian studying this topic lies in understanding both the nature of fascist propaganda and comparing it with the realities of their policies, an aspect of Mussolini's dictatorship that was not solely isolated to his economic policy.

> This is a strong conclusion that gives a detailed but coherent answer to the question. The student sets out exactly what the strengths and weaknesses of both sources are and explains specifically how they both could be of value to a historian investigating this subject. The analysis of why both sources would be of use to the historian is sophisticated and well evaluated. The final sentence provides a direct summary of their overall answer, showing clear understanding of what the question required.

Verdict

This is a strong answer because:

- it is rooted in the sources and identifies and illustrates their key features

- it deploys excellent and specific own knowledge to support the points and provides historical context
- it sustains focus and develops a clear and balanced argument.

Paper 2: A Level sample answer with comments

Section B

These questions assess your understanding of the period in some depth. They will ask you about the content you learned about in the four key themes, but may not ask about more than one theme. For these questions remember to:

- give an analytical, not a descriptive, response
- support your points with evidence
- cover the whole time period specified in the question
- come to a substantiated judgement.

'Mussolini created a loyal nation of fascists between 1926 and 1939.' How far do you agree with this statement? (20 marks)

Average student answer

In some ways it can be agreed that Mussolini created a loyal nation of fascists between 1926 and 1939, but there were many ways in which Italians were not actually supportive of his policies.

Firstly, one way in which Mussolini created a loyal nation of fascists was through education. When Mussolini was prime minister, the fascists created the *Balilla* which boys were meant to join. This was meant to make them into young soldiers. These young boys between the ages of 14 to 18 would learn gymnastics and have special sporting programmes aiming to make them physically strong and ready for the military. At school they had to learn a lot about why the fascists and Mussolini were so good. Girls had their own youth groups and their activities were meant to make them fit and healthy mothers. The fact that lots of young people had to involve themselves with the fascist youth groups was a key part of fascist indoctrination and helped Mussolini create a loyal nation of fascists.

Secondly, millions of Italian workers joined the after-work organisation known as the OND. The OND was an organisation that gave workers lots of leisure activities. It put on films and plays, organised football games and gave the workers some charity when they needed it. Importantly, it also gave them cheap holidays. It was meant to make Italians love Mussolini because of all the things the organisation gave the workers. The holidays were particularly popular as many Italians were unable to go on holidays before this. The OND had 40 million members and 80 percent of workers joined it. Therefore, because it had such massive membership the OND shows that Mussolini did create a nation of loyal fascists between 1926 and 1939.

The other big way that Mussolini created a loyal nation of fascists was through the cult of *Il Duce*. This was very important and influential to the Italian people. In all the papers, cinemas and radio shows, Mussolini was advertised as an incredible leader. There were millions of photos of Mussolini showing him to be an amazing leader. He was even said to be like Julius Caesar and lots of propaganda said he was a new Roman leader. Mussolini was the man all Italians put their hopes in and believed in and this is why his success shows that he was successful in creating a nation of loyal fascists.

This is an example of how not to start an answer. There are no substantial points nor is there any judgement made.

This paragraph has some good information on the male and female youth groups and what they were meant to do. However, while the points made are accurate it never deals with how far these activities created a loyal nation of fascists.

The argument is set out but is not well supported or analysed. There is good information about the *Opera Nazionale Dopolavoro* (OND), but there is a lot that is not developed. Again, there is some good information but a specific, supported answer to the question is not developed.

Again, there are some good ideas in the paragraph and the point about Mussolini's popularity is somewhat accurate, although it is overly generalised. However, the problem is that the paragraph never deals specifically with the question. The evidence focuses on Mussolini and his popularity.

However, it could be said that Mussolini did not create a loyal nation of fascists because he had to use the police and violence to control the Italian people. Dangerous antifascist Italians were either sent away into exile and some of them were put in prison and even executed. There was a secret police that were very good at knowing what was going on and making sure that anybody who said anything bad about Mussolini was arrested. This shows that some Italians might have been too scared to go against Mussolini and did not really support him. Why would Mussolini need such a big secret police and lots of laws stopping people debating if he had created a loyal nation of fascists?

Also, sometimes Italians would not do what Mussolini wanted them to do which shows that they could not have been that loyal. In 1937 Mussolini introduced anti-Jewish ideas in Italy. He maybe did this so he could be like Hitler. There were not that many Jews in Italy anyway so it is hard to know what he wanted to do. Lots of laws said that Jews could not do certain jobs, like being a teacher. Jewish students had to leave their schools. Lots of Jews left Italy. Mussolini also tried to introduce some other silly policies like not shaking hands and making people wear uniforms while they worked so they could look more like they were in the military. Lots of Italians thought the policies against Jews and the ones on handshakes and others were very silly. Even the pope came out and said Mussolini was wrong, which was a big deal in a place like Italy where the Church is very powerful. The fact that people did not like or follow his policies was a problem for Mussolini and shows that as everybody did not agree with everything he said that he was not creating a loyal nation of fascists.

Thus I have shown that in some ways Mussolini made a nation of loyal fascists. Lots of young people and workers joined fascist associations and all Italians loved him through the cult of *Il Duce*. However, he still needed a secret police and not all Italians liked his policies. The ones on Jews and new customs were seen as really bad. Despite these problems it is still true that Mussolini did create a nation of loyal fascists from 1926 to 1939.

> The idea that Mussolini did not create a loyal nation of fascists but instead relied on fear to rule Italians is a good point. However, the argument is only implicitly made and needs to be more direct.

> The points about the anti-Semitic and 'reform of customs' laws is important and does question how loyal Italians were to Mussolini. However, the detail in the paragraph is a bit poor and the language could be improved.

> Do not start a conclusion with 'Thus I have shown that ...' The paragraph sets out a general overview of the points made in the essay and there is no attempt to develop them further or consider the more complex aspects of the question.

Verdict

This is an average answer because:

- there is an attempt to answer the question, but the passages are quite descriptive without explaining how the points made help answer the question
- the material is accurate, but is lacking in depth in several places
- an overall judgement is reached but it lacks support or developed explanation

- the answer is organised on the question, but the more complex aspects of the argument are never mentioned. There needs to be greater analysis of the specific question and how it could be understood.

Use the feedback on this answer to rewrite it, making as many improvements as you can.

Paper 2: A Level sample answer with comments

Section B

These questions assess your understanding of the period in some depth. They will ask you about the content you learned about in the four key themes, but may not ask about more than one theme. For these questions remember to:

- give an analytical, not a descriptive, response
- support your points with evidence
- cover the whole time period specified in the question
- come to a substantiated judgement.

'Mussolini created a loyal nation of fascists between 1926 and 1939.' How far do you agree with this statement? (20 marks)

Strong student answer

Between 1926 and 1939 Mussolini and his fascist party created a range of policies aimed at creating a loyal nation of fascists. For Mussolini and the fascist ideology, it was important that the fascists do more than simply rule the country. Instead, they wanted to transform the Italians into a new type of people who were militarised, dedicated to fascism and willing to lay down their lives for Mussolini. However, it is very questionable how far Mussolini achieved this aim.

A key aspect of fascist policy was to try to transform Italy's youth into loyal fascists through their involvement with fascist youth organisations, and in some ways this was moderately successful. It is true that millions of Italian boys were involved with the fascist youth organisations known as the *Balilla*. These tried to transform young Italians into fanatic fascists. Boys were taught military skills such as bomb throwing and shooting practice as this would ready them for the fascist wars of the future. This indoctrination of Italian youth did have some success. In the Second World War, the most dedicated fascist soldiers who fought to the end for Mussolini were mainly young men who had been part of the *Balilla*. However, it is questionable whether this created a loyal nation of fascists. Nearly all the successful *Balilla* were in the north as the rural children in the south did not join youth groups as they had to mainly work on the farms with their parents. Also, many young people joined the *Balilla* because they enjoyed the outdoor activities, not because they truly believed in fascism. Therefore, although they had some success, it is clear that they did not truly create a loyal nation of fascists.

The involvement of millions of Italian workers with the *Dopolavoro* (OND), or after-work organisation, could also show that Mussolini was successful in creating a loyal nation of fascists. Millions of workers joined this organisation as it provided a range of benefits. Members were provided with entertainment such as free films and plays and bars where they could relax. The government subsidised holidays and tickets to sporting events so that workers could take their families on social outings for virtually no cost. Eighty percent of all state workers were members and the OND was one of the fascist's most popular creations. However, overall it cannot be said to have created a nation of loyal fascists. The OND was popular, but it never tried to educate workers into the ideals of fascism. In fact, Mussolini believed that any attempt to try and indoctrinate workers would discourage workers from joining the OND. While this made Mussolini and the fascists popular, it cannot be said that it created workers that truly believed in the ideology of fascism.

> An excellent introduction. It sets out exactly what is meant by 'a loyal nation of fascists' and then directly assesses how Mussolini tried to achieve these aims.

> This paragraph is clear and has a very developed argument. The student's own knowledge is excellent, and is always directly linked to the question. The student explains their points coherently, with good detailed evidence.

> This is a clearly argued paragraph that shows considerable depth of analysis. The OND is clearly assessed in respect to the specific question. The complex difference between popular policy and true loyalty to fascism is analysed at a sophisticated level and a well supported argument is set out.

The popularity of Mussolini and the cult of *il Duce* may also point to a nation of loyal fascists. Through fascist propaganda Mussolini was presented as an almost god-like leader, with the fascist slogan being 'Mussolini is always right.' He was depicted in a variety of ways as a modern, dynamic leader who was a brilliant sportsman and an internationally respected statesman. He was seen as heir to Julius Caesar and Augustus as he was leading the Italian nation to greatness. However, again it is questionable whether he created a nation of Italians loyal to fascism. The Italian people appeared to believe in Mussolini, not fascism. Thus, Mussolini might have been loved by the Italian people, but this does not mean he created a nation of loyal fascists.

> Again, this is an excellent paragraph that incorporates some very sophisticated ideas. The student avoids easy generalisations and a complex, but clear argument is made at the end of the paragraph that directly answers the question.

Critically, it is clear that the difficulty in analysing how far he created a loyal nation of fascists lies in understanding the reasons Italians consented to Mussolini's dictatorship. As argued previously, many Italians joined the OND because it provided them with benefits, not because they necessarily believed in fascism. There was also the role of repression and terror that ensured Italians could not speak out against Mussolini's dictatorship. All other political parties were banned in 1926 and political opponents were either sent into exile, forced to leave Italy or faced long years in prison. Some were even executed. Mussolini's secret police had files on over 130,000 Italians and used 5,000 informers to spy on the Italian people. Therefore, it is difficult to judge to what extent Mussolini created a loyal nation of fascists. Repression meant that the true political views of Italians was hard to measure and it was probably a combination of fear as well as the fact that adhering to the fascists would ensure social benefits that meant many Italians went along with the dictatorship, as opposed to any true belief in the values of fascism.

> A coherent and well supported paragraph that makes an excellent argument. The end of the paragraph makes a sophisticated judgement that links ideas developed in the essay and uses this to make a judgement on the question.

The Italian attitude to Mussolini's more radical policies introduced in 1937 also shows his lack of success in creating a loyal nation of fascists. In 1937, Mussolini introduced anti-Jewish laws that forbid Jews from marrying 'pure' Italians, holding public office jobs such as teaching or running businesses with over 100 employees. Mussolini believed that harsher policies towards the Jews would create a more radical, militarised Italian people who would see their superiority over other races such as the Jews. This was a key aspect of trying to create a truly fascist people. Connected to this more radical direction he tried to change Italian customs such as forbidding foreign elements in Italy, such as the handshake, and forcing all civil servants to wear uniforms. Through the anti-Jewish decrees and the reform of customs, Mussolini hoped to radicalise the Italian people. Instead, his policies were highly unpopular and seen as ridiculous. This shows that although Mussolini himself was very popular at times, when he did try and introduce radical policies meant to change the Italian people into militaristic fascists, he failed.

> Good, detailed own knowledge that sets out what Mussolini was trying to do as well as assessing its success. The failure of the policy is then clearly linked to the question with a direct argument.

Overall, it is clear that Mussolini failed to create a loyal nation of fascists between 1929 and 1939. It is true that many of his policies were popular. The OND was popular, but was not aimed at trying to create truly fascist workers and while Mussolini himself was hugely popular, it is hard to argue that this meant the fascist ideology was. Given the repressive nature of the fascist police state it is also hard to judge why Italians may have consented to the fascist dictatorship. When he tried to take a more radical policy direction in 1937 it actually meant many Italians started to question his dictatorship. Therefore, it is clear that Mussolini failed to create a loyal nation of fascists between 1926 and 1939.

> A strong conclusion that summarises their argument and considers the specific aspect of the question again, namely, what does 'loyal nation of fascists' actually mean?

Verdict

This is a strong answer because:

- it puts both sides of the case, analysing the ways it could be argued both for and against the question, and sustains a focus on the question set

- knowledge is strong with a wide range of evidence which is used to support the points made
- it reaches a secure concluding judgement
- it is well organised and communication of material is clear and precise.

Spain, 1930–78: republicanism, Francoism and the re-establishment of democracy

Spain, once one of the major powers of the early modern period, was by the early 20th century in imperial decline. From the beginning of the previous century and the time of the Peninsular War (1808–14), Spain had experienced nationalism; the Spanish people united in the fight against Napoleon's forces; and been inspired by ideas of liberalism and **republicanism** from French occupation. Continual conflict between the forces of progress and the forces of conservatism, however, would subsequently prevail in Spain, with the monarchy, landowners, the military and the Catholic Church resisting change. A pattern of revolution, liberal government and military rule repeated itself over time, and would continue to do so in the years from 1930 to 1978.

> **KEY TERM**
>
> Republicanism
> A system of government that rejects a monarchy and favours democratic rule by elected representatives acting on behalf of the wider population. This concept is often referred to as 'popular sovereignty' and usually features an elected president as head of state, with all elected officials subject to regular electoral accountability.

By 1931, the liberals, radicals and socialists and their desire for change prevailed and republicanism in the form of the Second Republic was declared the preferred political structure to take Spain forward. Opposition from conservative groups, however, remained. Simmering class-based tensions finally erupted in a destructive and ideological civil war (1936–39). This brutal conflict destabilised and ultimately destroyed the Spanish Second Republic, and while it significantly shaped Spain's future ideological direction, it was also the catalyst for a wider European war, which duly occurred in 1939.

SOURCE

1 From George Orwell, *Looking Back on the Spanish War*, 1943.

One has to remember this to see the Spanish war in its true perspective... there is hardly such a thing as a war in which it makes no difference who wins. Nearly always one stands more or less for progress, the other side more or less for reaction. The hatred which the Spanish Republic excited in millionaires, dukes, cardinals, play-boys, Blimps [a type of military officer], and what-not would in itself be enough to show... [that] in essence it was a class war. If it had been won, the cause of the common people everywhere would have been strengthened. It was lost, and the dividend-drawers all over the world rubbed their hands. That was the real issue; all else was froth on its surface.

Spain's capacity to overcome political and social divisions and instability was a formidable challenge for the country's political leaders as the 20th century progressed. Between 1930 and 1978, Spain evolved from a monarchy into a democratic republic, then to a dictatorship, back to a monarchy and finally emerging as a renewed democracy. Despite such volatility, Francisco Franco dominated the country as its dictator for almost 40 years, adopting a version of fascism in the process, no doubt influenced by Hitler in Germany and Mussolini in Italy, who had so willingly assisted him to victory in the civil war.

284

Spain governed by military dictator, Primo de Rivera	1923–30
April: Spanish Second Republic established, with democracy reintroduced	1931
'Years of reaction' under a conservative coalition government	1933–36
March: Victory for Nationalists / April: Francisco Franco declares end of the war and the Second Republic	1939
June: Spain excluded from membership of the United Nations	1945
February: Spain starts receiving financial investment from the USA	1949
December: Spain joins the United Nations	1955
Formation of the European Economic Community (EEC)	1957
Spain's first attempt to join the EEC rejected	1962
March: Press Act	1966
July: Franco names Juan Carlos as his successor	1969
December: Prime Minister Carrero Blanco assassinated by ETA	1973
June: Spain becomes a democracy; Juan Carlos becomes constitutional monarch	1977

1929	October: Wall Street Crash triggers an economic slump across the USA and much of Europe
1931–33	'Years of reform' under a Republican government
1936	July: Attempted military coup leads to the outbreak of the Spanish Civil War
1939–45	Second World War; Spain remains neutral
1947	June: Law of Leadership Succession
1953	August: Spanish concordat with the Vatican
1956–57	Economic problems; Falange ministers demoted and Opus Dei 'technocrats' promoted
1959	June–July: Stabilisation Plan; ETA founded
1964	December: Law of Associations
1967	Religious Freedom Act
1970	April: Falange renamed the National Movement
1975	November: Franco dies
1978	October: New democratic constitution established in Spain

SOURCE

2 Melee in the streets of Madrid during the Spanish Civil War, by the artist Achille Beltrame (1871–1945), published in the Italian weekly newspaper *La Domenica del Corriere*, 22 November 1936.

In 1938, Franco declared 'We do not believe in government through the voting booth. The Spanish national will was never freely expressed through the ballot box. Spain has no foolish dreams.' From this time on to the end of his rule, Spanish citizens enjoyed few individual rights, and Franco's allies in the aristocracy, army and Catholic Church retained most of the political power and influence. As a consequence, the country was conservative and hierarchical in nature, with the lower social classes submitting to an established social order. 'Francoism', as it became known in Spain, therefore encapsulated the core issues of nationalism and **dictatorship** that prevailed during this period of Spanish history, while at the same time determinedly resisting the spread of democracy that was steadily establishing itself throughout the rest of the Western world.

KEY TERM

Dictatorship
A system of government where a single leader has complete and total political power and usually relies on oppressive and undemocratic methods to maintain their position.

Spain's warm climate saw the country becoming an attractive magnet for foreign tourism by the 1960s and 1970s, and the nation became less isolated from the rest of Europe as a result. This created a wider range of economic and social opportunities for Spanish citizens. Developments in international relations also had a transformative impact on the country's political structure in the latter half of the 20th century, creating further challenges for the Spanish government in how it interacted constructively and more openly with the wider world. These developments played an important role in Spain's gradual advancement to a fully fledged democratic state by the end of the 1970s, which marked a major milestone in its modern history.

285

2b.1 Creation and destabilisation of the Second Republic, 1930–36

KEY QUESTIONS

- How significant were political events in Spain in the years 1930–31?
- To what extent can the period 1931–33 be classed as 'years of reform' in Spain?
- What was the significance of events and developments during the 'years of reaction', 1933–36?
- How significant was the 1936 general election in relation to events in Spain between February and July 1936?

INTRODUCTION

By the early 1930s, Spain was entering a period of significant change and development. Having abandoned its **constitutional monarchy** through a bloodless **military coup** in the 1920s, the country's military leadership found itself under growing pressure from reformers to establish a political system that was both liberal and democratic in nature. Such demands had been heightened by the economic problems and hardship that faced the country's citizens in the wake of the global depression triggered by the Wall Street Crash in October 1929.

The government gave way to popular demand and the country became a republic in 1931, with many Republicans fuelled by some of the growing radical ideologies of the time. Military figures were ousted from senior office and democratic elections took place for the first time in almost 60 years. This process was broadly in line with developments across other parts of Western Europe and represented a form of modernisation, although Spain still remained politically, economically and socially underdeveloped in comparison with Britain and France, for example. These apparently 'progressive' reforms were, however, observed with some displeasure by the various conservative groups within Spanish society, notably the wealthy industrialists, key religious figures and senior military personnel. These groups were not able to prevent the changes taking place, but they would continue to watch subsequent developments with some unease.

Such tensions reflected what a divided society Spain had become, with class-based conflict stemming from significant inequalities that existed between the country's rich and poor. The extent of the division was evident during the 1930s when several 'years of reform' pursued by the country's Republican politicians were followed by several 'years of reaction' pursued by their conservative

> **KEY TERMS**
>
> **Constitutional monarchy**
> A political system where an unelected monarch shares power with a democratically elected government.
>
> **Military coup**
> A change in government where the military suddenly takes power, usually involving a degree of force to remove an established politician or figurehead.

1930
January: Primo de Rivera, military dictator of Spain, resigns

1931–33
'Years of reform' under Manuel Azaña

1932
January: Expulsion of the Jesuits
August: Failed military uprising of General Sanjurjo
September: Catalan Statute and Agrarian Reform Law introduced

1930	1931	1932

1931
April: Second Republic proclaimed after Republican groups win a landslide election victory
October: Azaña appointed prime minister (1931–33)
December: Republican constitution introduced, containing radical laws and proposals

opponents. By the middle of the decade, the country's fairly new Second Republic was creaking under the pressure of rival political viewpoints and growing social unrest. Its long-term future was further undermined by Spain's very limited democratic traditions. A series of political crises in the early part of 1936 brought matters to a head, with the result that Spain and its people found themselves on the brink of a destructive and destabilising civil war.

EXTRACT

1 From Paul Preston, *The Spanish Civil War: Reaction, Revolution and Revenge*, 2006. Here, Preston highlights the long-standing divisions within Spanish society that steadily built up in the early 1930s.

The origins of the Spanish Civil War lie far back in the country's history. The notion that political problems could more naturally be solved by violence than by debate was firmly entrenched in a country in which for a thousand years civil war has been if not exactly the norm then certainly no rarity. The war of 1936-9 was the fourth such conflict since the 1830s... Yet the myriad of Spanish conflicts which erupted in 1936, regionalists against centralists, anti-clericals against Catholics, landless labourers against latifundistas [landowners], workers against industrialist, have in common the struggles of a society in the throes of modernization.

HOW SIGNIFICANT WERE POLITICAL EVENTS IN SPAIN IN THE YEARS 1930–31?

The impact of political events, 1930–31

Military dictatorship, 1930

Although the First Republic had briefly prevailed between 1873 and 1874, Spain had traditionally been governed by a monarch. This was linked to people's belief that a monarch's considerable powers were directly awarded from God (known as 'divine right'). Since the country's bloodless coup in 1923, however, Spain had been ruled by the dictatorial General Miguel Primo de Rivera, an unelected military figure who had taken over the formal leadership of the country from King Alfonso XIII in September 1923. This change of governance had occurred primarily because of the corruption and military weaknesses associated with the monarchy, which had led to some notable social unrest. Alfonso XIII, however, remained on the political scene and was broadly supportive of the new regime, because it sought to maintain the existence of the established political and social order centred on what the historian Raymond Carr has described as 'Nation, Church and King'.

Primo de Rivera had initially pledged to hold power for only 90 days, but this supposedly brief interlude developed into several years. Despite some limited attempts to improve the country's

---

1933
January: Casas Viejas massacre
February: CEDA formed
September: Azaña dismissed
October: Nationalist Falange Española (*Falange*) formed
November: Elections to the Cortes held; coalition government led by the leader of the Radical Republicans, Alejandro Lerroux, formed

1936
January: Popular Front established
February: General election in Spain; Popular Front coalition victorious
May: Azaña replaces President Alcalá Zamora as president
July: José Castillo and José Calvo Sotelo assassinated; attempted military coup leads to the outbreak of the Spanish Civil War

1933	1934	1935	1936

1934
June: FNTT land-workers strike
October: The Asturias uprising

1935
September: Various communist groups combine to form Partido Obrero de Unificación Marxista (POUM, Workers' Party)

economic conditions and rather backward infrastructure, the military-led government failed to quell the growing social unrest throughout the latter part of the 1920s and early 1930s. By January 1930, under pressure from the effects of the Great Depression that erupted in the autumn of 1929, the ruling regime had become increasingly weak, unpopular and lacked clear leadership. The government was ultimately unable to deal with the country's various socio-economic problems, lacking any kind of institutional or legal legitimacy, and the army and other conservative elements were unable and unwilling to maintain support for it.

Spain's military-led regime also faced growing pressure and criticism from a range of Republican groups and student protests, as well as the growing influence of socialist ideology and political thought. All were united in their opposition to the lingering influence of the monarchy alongside the dominant power of the military, both of which lacked democratic legitimacy. In January 1930, Primo de Rivera resigned due to pressure from Republican opponents, leaving the country's political structure in an uncertain state with the king asking other military figures to stabilise the government in the short term. However, the military was reluctant to take on the responsibility in such challenging conditions. While the democratic tide was certainly spreading across Europe at this time, it was unclear as to precisely what form or model of government would replace Spain's dictatorship, and Primo de Rivera's departure left something of an uncertain void that needed to be filled.

Republicanism and socialism

Any incoming government faced an uncertain future given that Spain had struggled to establish itself as a stable political system during the late 19th and early 20th centuries. Like most European nations, Spain had been hit hard by the Great Depression. There was a surge in unemployment, financial difficulties and further social unrest. Those in favour of formally establishing a republic argued, therefore, for a fresh start to mark a clean break from the past, overhauling what they viewed as a failing political structure, while advocating some fundamental changes and reforms to the existing capitalist system.

While Spanish republicanism incorporated political figures with liberal viewpoints and even some moderate conservatives, a majority of Republicans were influenced by the ideas of **socialism** that were increasingly in vogue at the time, and which aimed for the redistribution of wealth, public (government) ownership of land and the achievement of a more equal society. This school of thought derived from a range of different left-wing viewpoints, but a major influence was the writings of the German political philosopher Karl Marx, whose key works, such as *The Communist Manifesto* (1848), argued for the need for a revolutionary uprising in the interests of the working classes. Socialism was viewed as a more moderate variant of Marx's communist doctrine, and there were different socialist traditions that offered varying remedies to Spain's ills, which in turn created divisions and friction within the country's increasingly significant left-wing political movements.

Anarchism and **syndicalism** were more extreme and often violent variants of socialist ideology, and both featured an explicit revolutionary message, referred to as anarcho-syndicalism. Anarchism had been a particular phenomenon across Spain and in other European countries in the early part of the 20th century, with its radical revolutionary rhetoric inspiring various groups to generate both instability and political violence in the process. Its activists and supporters had undermined the monarchy in the past, and they continued to cause problems for the Republican government of the 1930s, by inciting strikes and protests. Anarcho-syndicalists were therefore dissatisfied with the various compromises required within the processes of constitutional government. Anarchist views were particularly prominent within the Confederación Nacional del Trabajo (National Confederation of Labour, or CNT), which was founded by anarchist supporters in 1910.

However, mainstream Spanish socialism became aligned with left-wing trends in other European countries that focused on 'reform' rather than revolt, and it generally resisted the influence of communist revolution that erupted in the Soviet Union in 1917. This led to the establishment of particular links between moderate socialist politicians and more moderate trades unions, such as the Union General de Trabajadores (UGT) founded in 1888, whose membership had steadily increased during the early 20th century. Members of these unions focused on improved pay and conditions rather than organising a revolutionary uprising, and the UGT's size and influence grew during the Second Republic due to its influx of agricultural labourers in particular.

The creation of the Second Republic

In the midst of the post-1929 economic slump, the Republicans made political headway, gaining wider public support. In April 1931, they forced the deteriorating government to call national elections. These were to be Spain's first democratic elections for almost 60 years. On 12 April 1931, Republican candidates gained a landslide victory in the Spanish municipal elections. The Republicans garnered most of their political support in the large cities and urban areas and among the working classes, while the rural areas were more inclined to support the political status quo. Such geographical divisions of political support would become more pronounced in the years ahead.

SOURCE

Republican supporters in Madrid celebrate the proclamation of the Spanish Second Republic, 14 April 1931.

The Republicans duly proclaimed the advent of the Second Spanish Republic on 4 April 1931. There were high levels of popular support for the newly installed government, with over 400 elected **deputies** in support of establishing a Republican political structure, and just under 50 classed as official opponents. The new regime was subsequently hailed as *La Nina Bonita* ('The Beautiful Girl'). In the face of such apparent public enthusiasm, the military generals had indicated that they would respect the verdict of the people, having grown disillusioned with monarchical rule and unwilling to defend the previous regime. This development has been described by the historian Stanley Payne as 'a unique event, the only major step towards democracy in Europe during a decade of economic and political crisis'.

The monarchy was formally abolished and the king, and many of his political allies, soon went into exile. They would remain, however, a key element of prominent opposition to the new regime, albeit from a distance. From the outset, the hereditary aristocracy was established as a firm opponent of the democratically elected Republican administration, and such opposition would sow the seeds of conflict and instability in the years to come.

There were 26 different political parties within the Republic's initial parliamentary body (known as the Constituent Cortes), indicating a significant degree of fragmentation within Spanish society and political opinion and suggesting a lack of national unity beneath the surface of government. However, agreement was reached among the various liberals, socialists and intellectuals and a provisional government was duly established in Madrid under the Republic's first premier minister, Niceto Alcalá-Zamora. He was, in fact, a moderate conservative with strong Catholic views but he supported the Republic. This government was therefore a coalition that consisted of a range of different groups and viewpoints, although most accepted the republican model of government in one way or another.

Within the Second Republic, there were four main political parties:

- **Spanish Socialist Party (PSOE):** Of working-class origins and in favour of more radical social change to benefit workers. The key figure was Francisco Largo Caballero, a prominent trade unionist and later minister for labour. This group was on the left of the political spectrum, and the PSOE's tactics and methods became more extreme as the 1930s progressed.

- **Moderate Republicans** in the form of the Republican Action Party, whose leading figure was Manuel Azaña. Middle class in general with **anticlerical** tendencies, it was on the moderate left of the political spectrum.

- **Radical Republican Party:** A fairly middle-class grouping that did not, despite its name, support the more radical social reforms of the socialists during the early years of the Second Republic. The key figure was Alaejandro Lerroux. While being opposed to the monarchy in relation to most other political issues, it was located towards the centre of the political spectrum.

- **Conservatives:** A fairly limited grouping between 1931 and 1933, being weakened by their ongoing support for the monarchy, opposition to the Republic and preference for military rule. Supported by the Church, elements of the army and large landowners, this group was located on the right of the political spectrum. Some supported the Republic, while others opposed it. Their key figure in the early stages of the Second Republic was Niceto Alcalá-Zamora.

EXTEND YOUR KNOWLEDGE

Political spectrum – 'left and right'
The terms 'left' and 'right' derive from the historical period just prior to the French Revolution in the late 18th century, when the commoners sat to the left of the king and the nobility sat to the right.

Left wing: this political viewpoint is usually associated with socialist ideology and reformist politics. It generally tends to represent the views of the working classes and trades unionists, and it favours change and reform of the existing social and economic order by policies that involve significant government intervention.

Right wing: this political viewpoint is usually associated with the propertied members of society, particularly industrialists and landowners from the wealthier middle and upper classes. Such a 'conservative' position favours the general maintenance of the existing social and political order and resists radical change or interventionist policies by the government.

By the end of 1931, the conservatives and radical Republicans had left the government; the former due to growing concerns about anticlerical laws and threats to various landed interests, the latter due to some of the radical social reforms advocated by the socialist members of the government. The moderate Republican regime subsequently consolidated its position with the introduction of a Republican-oriented constitution (in December) that sought to end various social and political restrictions of the past and which prioritised the following values:

- freedom of association (which assisted the growth of trades unions)
- **secular** (non-religious) education
- free speech (favouring political pluralism)
- voting rights for women (from 1933)
- legalising divorce (a threat to traditional family life)
- attacking the traditional rights and privileges of established religion and nobility
- **disestablishment** of the Catholic Church and freedom of religious worship
- preserving regional powers and autonomy.

ACTIVITY
KNOWLEDGE CHECK

1 Draw a spider diagram highlighting the key factors as to why the Spanish Second Republic came into existence in 1931.

2 Write a brief summary explaining why there was public support for the more left-wing and liberal polices of the country's new government in 1931, and provide some judgement as to which Republican policies you believe to be the most popular and significant.

The key forces of conservatism

The introduction of the 1931 constitution was a key turning point in the evolution of the Second Republic. The more radical aims and aspirations evident in aspects of the newly enshrined constitution alarmed the traditional and generally wealthier ruling elite of Spanish society, causing a degree of instability and social tension. There were, therefore, some prominent conservative influences within Spanish society that were hostile to the Second Republic from its inception. In turn, the government of the Second Republic was equally hostile to these 'forces of **conservatism**' and this would be reflected in many of its subsequent policies and reforms. The key conservative influences within Spain in the early 1930s included the aristocracy, landowners, industrialists, the Church and senior military officers.

The aristocracy, landowners and industrialists

The most obvious and notable example of opposition came from the more affluent members of society, in the form of the traditional wealth of the aristocracy and the newer wealth of industrialist landowners. These groups were socially and economically detached from the country's ordinary citizens, and their dominance of land ownership was significant. They faced the prospect of punitive taxation, land seizure and **nationalisation** of property by the new socialist-inclined government.

Long-standing rural poverty caused hardships primarily for ordinary farm labourers whose incomes were often below the level of subsistence. In turn, this impacted on the wealthier farmers who owned the land and whose tenants often struggled to pay rents and generate profit for the landowner. While such problems had been evident before 1931, the government of the Second Republic faced increasing criticisms from the wealthier landowners due to the perception that it had an urban power base and therefore did not do enough to address the rural hardships. Prosperous industrialists also came to be critical of the Second Republic, particularly due to its attacks on 'privilege' and its nationalisation of large private estates and private property.

The Roman Catholic Church

The powerful and wealthy Roman Catholic Church had always been firmly aligned with the monarchy and Primo de Rivera's military dictatorship. Due to its inherent conservative instincts it, too, was alarmed by the socialist and radical influences that surrounded the new government. In the early decades of the 20th century it was estimated that the established Church and its various orders controlled approximately one-third of the country's overall national wealth, as well as having large stakes in key industries such as banking and railways. Hostility between Catholicism and republicanism was mutual. In May 1931, the head of the Spanish Catholic Church, Cardinal Segura, called for Catholics to vote against political groups that supported anticlericalism. He was subsequently expelled from Spain by the new government. In a separate development, various churches and religious buildings were set on fire by anticlerical Republican activists in some of Spain's larger towns and cities, most notably in the capital, Madrid.

The new constitution was certainly hostile to vested religious interests, and the Catholic Church blamed the new government for encouraging obstructive policies in relation to its works and practices within the country. Catholic organisations were subsequently banned from educational roles and the ultra-Catholic Jesuit movement was expelled from Spain by the Republican government in January 1932. Such poor relations with the country's established religion and its personnel of over 100,000 priests, monks and nuns led to allegations of anticlericalism against the Second Republic. This had dangerous long-term implications for the survival of the Republic given the strong influence of Catholicism over ordinary Spanish citizens, as well as its international religious and political connections.

EXTRACT

2 From Hugh Thomas, *The Spanish Civil War*, 1965. Here, Thomas highlights the traditional conservative values of the Spanish military, which as a group was broadly opposed to external influences and ideologies, while also being particularly loyal to 'historical Spain'.

Many Spanish Army officers, saw, in their own traditions, the embodiment of a certain idea of a timeless, supremely **Castilian** Spain, without politics, creating order and banishing all things non-Spanish (by which they understood Separatism, Socialism, Freemasonry, Communism, and Anarchism). They could persuade themselves that their oath, as officers, to 'maintain the independence of the country and defend it from enemies within and without' took precedence over their oath of loyalty to the Republic.

KEY TERM

Castilian
The term 'Castilian' refers to a version of the Spanish language that was traditionally spoken in northern and central Spain. This dialect is also viewed as the historical Spanish language that preceded modern Spanish, and reference to it is often used to present a romantic and idealised vision of the country's past history.

Senior military officers

The military also remained an essential component of the country's forces of conservatism. Its wealthy and aristocratic officer class viewed the new government with suspicion from the beginning, particularly in relation to the socialist and anarchist activities that helped to bring about its creation. The army traditionally had a disproportionately powerful role within Spanish society, and its senior officer class generally came from the upper echelons of Spanish society. These officers numbered approximately 15,000 at the time of the Second Republic's formation, and they presided over a largely conscript army from the lower social classes.

These forces of conservatism comprised some of the most powerful and significant elements of Spanish society. When grouped collectively, they represented a formidable force that had the potential to create some major problems and instability for the government of the Second Republic.

Political unrest

The creation of the Second Republic and the introduction of democratic government did not, however, bring an end to the political unrest that had crippled Spain for some time. While this new and more democratically accountable system of government had appeased the country's more moderate left-wing and liberal-minded reformers, many radical groups such as the anarchists and communists were impatient for change. They quickly became frustrated with the slow political processes that occurred within constitutional government. See the reference to the attempted military coup of 1932 (pages 296-97) and also the Asturias rising (page 301). These were examples of unrest from the political right and left, respectively.

From another political direction, the forces of conservatism at various levels of government and society, including the wealthy landowners and industrialists, sought to limit any proposed radical changes stemming from the new government. The powerful landowners' organisations often managed to successfully avoid the implementation of government decrees relating to land reform, while also managing to manipulate local military and police forces. This created some further levels of political dissent and instability for the new regime.

The ongoing power of the established Catholic Church and the military also needed to be tackled and dealt with by the Republican regime if its political authority was to be maintained in the long term. Both groups had expressed clear concerns about the advent of Republican government in Spain, and both continued to wield significant influence within sections of Spanish society.

Economic and social problems

The Spanish Second Republic came into existence in far from ideal economic and social conditions. As well as emerging from an internal political crisis, it also suffered the unfortunate fate of being formed amid a period of international economic disaster fuelled by the Wall Street Crash. This resulted in a general surge in unemployment and associated poverty, with unemployment rising from 400,000 at the end of 1931 up to 600,000 just two years later. The country's international trade and foreign investment was also adversely affected. By 1935, Spanish stocks and shares were only worth 63 percent of their value in 1929, while industrial output was only 77 percent of the 1929 figure. Although this emerging economic crisis had global origins, it was exacerbated by existing high levels of poverty and hardship in certain parts of Spain (see pages 300–301), as well as a limited infrastructure in terms of a poor national transport network, inadequate public buildings and weak levels of industrial output. The country's predominantly rural economy was therefore in a weak condition in the early 1930s, with many people struggling to make a living due to the small plots of land on which they worked (see pages 294–95). Industrial workers in the cities also faced uncertain employment prospects. How to improve living conditions and address the prevailing poverty in these communities would be a major challenge for the new government.

ACTIVITY
KNOWLEDGE CHECK

1 In what ways did the forces of conservatism challenge the Second Republic and its political values?

2 Identify the three most significant aspects of political, economic and social unrest facing the incoming Republican government in 1931. Provide reasons to justify the aspects that you have chosen.

THINKING HISTORICALLY   Causation (6a)

Seeing things differently
Different times and different places have a different set of ideas. Beliefs about how the world works, how human societies should be governed or the best way to achieve economic prosperity, can all be radically different from our own. It is important for the historian to take into account these different attitudes and be aware of the dangers of judging them against modern ideas.

Divine right of monarchy
In the early years of the 20th century, many countries such as Spain were ruled by monarchs who had absolute and dominant political power. This was linked to the idea that God had awarded such powers to the monarch, and these powers could therefore not be questioned or challenged ('divine right'). However, as the years progressed new ideas and political pressures emerged to undermine the institution of monarchy.

Answer the following questions:

1 Why did the population of countries such as Spain support the institution of monarchy up until the early part of the 20th century?

2 What factors and influences changed people's attitudes towards the institution of monarchy in Spain?

3 Many contemporary attitudes to the monarchy in the early 21st century are different from attitudes to the monarchy in Spain in the early 20th century.

  a) Are there any other ways in which attitudes in Spain approximately 100 years ago differed dramatically from those that are current in Spain and other similar Western democracies today?

  b) Why do you think that they are different?

4 How important is it for historians to deal with events in the context of the beliefs and values of people in the past as well as seeing them as part of a greater pattern?

TO WHAT EXTENT CAN THE PERIOD 1931–33 BE CLASSED AS 'YEARS OF REFORM' IN SPAIN?

The Republican government had exploited growing levels of socio-economic discontent in order to gain political power, but it now found itself faced with addressing those very challenges and dealing with a series of deep-rooted problems. It had to find suitable and appropriate policies to improve people's living standards, and quickly. These policies were at times markedly different from what had gone before, resulting in the period between 1931 and 1933 being referred to as the 'years of reform'.

Provisional government reform of the army and the Church

Manuel Azaña had become prime minister of the Second Republic in October 1931 and had little time for the privileges of many of Spain's established bodies and institutions. From an early stage of its existence, the new Republican administration sought to limit the influence of the army in matters of government, based on the premise that the army had too much political involvement under the previous regime. This saw an estimated 40 percent of senior military figures being forced to retire (approximately 8,000 men). The number of soldiers in general was also reduced, based on the perception that the army had excessive manpower and needed to be streamlined in size, primarily in order to save money given the dire economic situation. Reforms were also introduced that made military figures face civil rather than military law if any of their number committed civil offences. While these initiatives could be argued to be positive developments in line with more advanced liberal democracies, various military figures quickly became dismayed and aggrieved at such political developments. They therefore formed a significant element of underlying and simmering opposition to the Second Republic.

Azaña also opposed the influence of the Catholic Church which he felt was responsible for holding back the country's social and economic progress. For example, the Church's significant influence in education had focused on traditional learning methods which prioritised boys and taught them separately from girls, while also featuring only a limited range of subjects. This resulted in literacy levels of only 50 percent across much of Spain. Such a questionable rate of educational progress suggested the existing system, and its significant levels of Church control, was not delivering the required social results across all parts of Spanish society.

Like the new prime minister, the vast majority of Spanish Republicans were similarly critical of the powers of the Catholic Church, and the established Spanish faith was now dealing with a government that did not view it as an integral component of everyday life. During Azaña's reforming period in office, the established faith of Catholicism was therefore weakened by a series of new laws that went to the root of its traditional authority within Spanish society. As well as targeting the Church's influence within education and its financial interests and investments, the Republican regime also focused on its substantial involvement within ordinary Spanish communities. Within the first two years of Azaña's premiership, the Spanish Jesuit order of priests was dissolved and expelled from the country, religious teaching was banned in schools, priests and religious figures no longer received a salary from the state, while other government subsidies to such religious groups were withdrawn. Much of these developments stemmed from the 1931 constitution, particularly Articles 26 and 27 which focused on this formal separation of the Roman Catholic Church and the Spanish state, a process known as disestablishment.

Although secular educational re-organisation and financial investment in schools was welcomed by many on the Republican left of politics, the combined impact of such policies led to religious figures accusing the Second Republic of adopting anticlerical laws. From the government's perspective, the Catholic Church's traditional control over the ordinary civilian population appeared to be a major threat to its ability to govern the country and to enforce the democratic aims of the 1931 election. Within such a context, its powers were therefore trimmed and reduced in the name of improving democracy and political accountability, although this caused some significant unrest and opposition from religious vested interests. These groups felt that the Azaña-led government was also rather dismissive of the various attacks on Church properties carried out by more militant anticlerical Republicans. As a result, the Catholic Church offered its support to right-wing and conservative political groups who promised to overturn such limitations on its activities.

EXTEND YOUR KNOWLEDGE

Manuel Azaña (1880-1940)

A Madrid-born lawyer by profession and from a middle-class background, Azaña had strong Republican sympathies. He was a member of the more moderate Republican Action Party, and was initially appointed war minister following the declaration of the Second Republic. He became prime minister between 1931 and 1933. During this period, he oversaw some significant social and political reforms, being associated with anticlerical policies and agrarian reform in particular. Such reforming policies had the ultimate aspiration of fundamentally addressing the various challenging economic, social and political issues that the country now faced, but from a more radical perspective. He later served as president between 1936 and 1939, in the midst of Spain's turbulent civil war, after which he fled the country following the fall of the Second Republic. He died soon after while exiled in France.

Tackling agricultural problems

Rural and agricultural areas were hit hard by the impact of the economic depression, and the already poor Spanish farming communities continued to suffer throughout the 1930s. The depression had an adverse impact on crop prices, while agricultural exports fell by 75 percent between 1930 and 1934 and demand for key agricultural resources such as wine and olive oil fell significantly within traditional markets. Large swathes of agricultural land fell into disuse in parts of the country, and while the country's unemployment figures more than doubled between 1931 and 1936, rural unemployment levels rose even higher. In an attempt to counter some of the rural employment problems, the Republican government passed the Law of Municipal Boundaries in April 1931, which sought to promote the use of local labour (as opposed to cheaper, imported workers) on the land.

The plight of impoverished peasantry in many regions of Spain was comparable to some of the worst social conditions in Europe, particularly in Andalusia in the south with its hot Mediterranean climate and its vast estates known as *latifundia*. From the early 1930s onwards, short-term negative developments (linked to the economic slump) ultimately exacerbated the various long-term problems that existed within the Spanish agricultural sector. The Agrarian Reform Law, introduced from September 1932, sought to regenerate agriculture by addressing the country's deep-rooted 'land question' and improve the country's well-documented rural poverty. Various smaller reforms had been experimented with throughout 1931, but this proposal focused on the large and often unworked estates of over 56 acres in size, located mainly in the south. Any farms of over 23 hectares in size had the potential to be nationalised by the government and redistributed in terms of ownership from large landowners to the ordinary peasantry. Those who owned the land, rather than the government, were also required to cover much of the cost of this policy and to maintain the wage costs of the agricultural workforce.

While such radical land reform generated some initial support and enthusiasm among the impoverished peasant class, it ultimately fell victim to the economic conditions of the time and failed to offer the full-blown land nationalisation that many socialist radicals demanded. There was a notable lack of sustained government funding to make the policy practical in the long term and, as a result, relatively few families were actually resettled or received land within the first year of the introduction of the new law. It also ignored many of the smaller farms that were struggling to survive economically in the north. In this context, the policy could be said to have achieved the worst of both worlds and not fully pleased anyone, creating further fear and unrest among conservatives, but frustrating and disappointing those on the political left.

Despite what was a fairly bold initiative by the Republican government to tackle this long-standing land question, agricultural conditions failed to notably improve in the immediate aftermath. Consequently social unrest continued to fester among groups of poorer farmworkers, many of whom were impatient for change and who continued to struggle to make a living due to limited grants and loans from government. These failings, therefore, steadily stirred the working-class elements on the left of the political spectrum as represented by the large numbers of poorer agricultural labourers, who became impatient with cautious, **constitutional politics** and its methods used by the socialist government. This political dissatisfaction created a long-term strategic problem for the Republican regime, as maintaining the support of both the industrial and rural working classes became absolutely crucial to ensuring the long-term political survival of the Second Republic.

KEY TERM

Constitutional politics
An approach to politics that involves working within the existing political system and structures in order to achieve desired policy goals. This approach adopts a reformist approach and rejects the more extremist tactics and direct action of radical, revolutionary groups (e.g. anarchists), who believe that the existing system must be overthrown and replaced in order to secure genuine political change.

Wealthier elements of the farming communities, particularly the influential landlord class and large landowners, were hostile from the outset and became increasingly opposed to the new agricultural policies. Such conservative antagonism and opposition from the political right would form a consistent element of the growing difficulties that the agrarian policies of the Second Republic faced during the remainder of the decade. However, for the first 18 months of Republican government, the conservative interests failed to effectively co-ordinate or articulate their opposition and concerns.

Reforms under Azaña

Industrial modernisation

Although it was a country with a strong emphasis on its agricultural sector, the need to revitalise and invest in Spanish industry was another key challenge faced by Azaña's government. Spain's industrial development was traditionally weak due to its more rural and agrarian infrastructure, a limited amount of foreign financial investment and the weak supply of its own independent mineral resources. Production and exports of iron and steel particularly suffered due to falling demand in other national markets caused by the effects of the depression.

Industrial workers in the larger towns and cities had formed the power base of Republican electoral support and had progressively organised into effective trade union bodies. They expected improvements in their incomes and general quality of life under Azaña's government, with the need for modernisation viewed as a key symbol of progress in this particular sector. Trade union demands were rewarded under the Second Republic by the granting of an eight-hour working day, improved working conditions and enhanced pay and holiday entitlements. However, ongoing economic difficulties throughout the 1930s meant that standards of living struggled to grow at a rate that maintained widespread public support for the Republican administration.

Educational reforms

In pursuing a more secular model of education, a key aim of the new government was to loosen the grip of organised religion and improve both the quality and quantity of educational provision in the country. There was significant financial investment in the state education system with approximately 7,000 new schools built within its first year, and another 2,500 between 1932 and 1933. The wage levels of teachers were improved by reducing state payments to religious orders (although the wages remained fairly low in comparison with other European countries), while co-education was favoured in preference to splitting the girls and boys and teaching them separately. The government also targeted the more remote parts of the country that did not have school facilities with the establishment of travelling schools to such areas. By late 1932, the numbers of Spanish children educated at secondary level had risen from 20,000 in 1929 to 70,000.

Regional reforms and devolution

Although Spain had been a single national entity for the best part of four centuries, regional nationalism remained a powerful source of influence in the country's various provinces. The new government therefore faced long-standing demands for independence from two key parts of the Spanish Republic, namely Catalonia in the north east and the Basque region in the north west. During the 1920s, the Catalonian region had been associated with a high level of political violence and assassinations, as an extreme response to central government's general resistance and opposition to their demands. Variations in income and levels of poverty were also central to this issue, with some poorer areas blaming central government for their economic predicament and lack of resources compared with other regions.

In order to appease regional nationalism, the Republican government considered allowing Catalonia and the Basque region more autonomous political powers. Those of a conservative viewpoint argued that making concessions to regionalism would represent a dangerous development by giving in to violent demands. They also feared creating the conditions for a federal, and more loosely connected, Spain, or even full separatism. From this perspective, by appeasing regional nationalism, the Republican government could be seen to be undermining the fundamental basis of Spanish nationalism. The Spanish military were particularly concerned about this. If these regions subsequently broke away from the rest of the country it would indicate a significant weakening of the government's internal stability and ability to function effectively from the centre. This in turn would damage its reputation both domestically and on an international level, primarily due to the perception that it could not keep the country united.

By a willingness to acknowledge regional diversity, the Second Republic's political leadership believed that it could divert the prospect of breakaway independence for these regions and hold the country together as a single entity. In terms of the practicality of its long-term future, it could not really afford a situation that led to separation when it was still in the early stages of consolidating the credibility of the Republican model of government. In September 1932, in an attempt to maintain national unity, the Cortes granted concessions of enhanced self-government and **devolved** powers to Catalonia and the Basque region. Despite votes among the population of both provinces (plebiscites) which overwhelmingly supported such a proposal, in practical terms the law only came into effect in Catalonia, so this legislation is therefore often referred to as the Catalan Statute.

KEY TERM

Devolution
A model of government where ultimate political power or sovereignty is retained by central government, but where significant powers are passed down or 'devolved' to a regional level.

This policy reflected the Republican respect for long-standing cultural differences and the historic tradition of Spanish 'regionalism'. In turn, the Republican government in Madrid won the loyalty and support of the devolved regions. Despite some notable conservative opposition, this policy has been viewed as one of the most significant and important political achievements of the government of the Second Republic.

Responses from both left and right

There was a varied response to Azaña's reforming policies. A liberal and progressive constitution was established that was highly advanced by European standards and entailed improved political and civil rights for Spanish citizens. Those of a liberal left opinion therefore welcomed this government's arrival in 1931. Azaña's administration was more sympathetic than its immediate predecessor to the values and aspirations of Spanish working-class communities. It sought to deliver improved workers' rights for both industrial and agricultural workers, while there were also enhanced employment conditions and trade union powers. However, many on the radical left grew increasingly impatient with the slow pace of reform and limited improvements in their living standards. This resulted in a steady rise in strike activity and revolutionary agitation among communists and anarchists in particular.

The government also failed to consolidate its already weakened levels of support within Spain's traditional right-wing elements. The negative mood among the conservative groups grew as the government's programme of reforms developed. Senior military officers quickly became disillusioned with this new political settlement due to government-imposed restrictions on their activities, and the wealthy landowners became alienated and antagonised by proposed land reforms. Spain's conservative religious interests were aggrieved by secular reforms to the Church which involved the dilution of their influence on education, alongside the liberalisation and relaxation of marriage and divorce laws, which in practical terms made both easier to be granted. The effects of this growing opposition was an increase in conservative political organisation and activity between 1931 and 1933. This was a reflection of Azaña's failure or unwillingness to sufficiently compromise with the 'forces of conservatism' within Spain. The overall nature of the responses from both left and right ultimately had a destabilising effect on the country's Republican government.

ACTIVITY
KNOWLEDGE CHECK

1 List the key successes of the Second Republic in the years 1931–33.

2 List the key failures of the Second Republic in the years 1931–33.

3 What impact did the years of reform have on Spain between 1931 and 1933? Use your lists to inform your answer to this question.

Unrest and repression

Throughout its time in office, the Republican government had to deal with unrest due to agrarian discontent, demands for regional autonomy, military stirrings or religious agitation, and it often had to resort to repressive measures to deal with them. In July 1931, the **Spanish Civil Guard** brutally suppressed a strike of telephone workers, resulting in 30 strikers being killed. At the end of the year, a socialist-inspired strike broke out in the small village of Castilblanco, situated in the Badajoz province. This episode saw the deaths of four Civil Guards based in the village, who were attacked and killed by locals involved in the uprising. In early 1932, this wave of violence saw the Civil Guard shoot and kill 11 people, including women, in the town of Arnedo in northern Spain; children were among the 30 injured. By 1932, it was evident that the government was dealing with some significant social and political unrest across the country – a clear reflection that various reforms were running into major difficulties and opposition.

KEY TERM

Spanish Civil Guard
A military body under the authority of Spain's government, charged with police duties and keeping public order. The Guard was established in 1844.

The simmering tensions and potential for further violent unrest came to the surface in August 1932 when there was a failed military coup stemming from the political right and led by General Sanjurjo, who had formerly been the director general of the Civil Guard (he was dismissed after being held responsible for the many deaths and injuries inflicted by the Civil Guard). The catalyst for the coup was believed to be the awarding of autonomous rule to Catalonia, although Sanjurjo was said to have taken a dim view of socialist influences within the Spanish government. While the attempted coup achieved some initial success in the southern city of Seville, it failed miserably in Madrid and the military ringleaders were arrested. The coup, however, indicated the fragile and volatile nature of the Second Republic, and how various opponents could emerge with menacing intent at the slightest provocation by government policies.

EXTRACT

From Hugh Thomas, *The Spanish Civil War*, 1965. Here, Thomas outlines the collective grievances against the early policies of the Second Republic in the years 1931–33.

> The Church and many of the respectable middle-classes had been estranged from the Republic by the religious clauses in the Constitution. The landowners had been angered by the Agrarian law. It was the Army who were most offended by the Catalan Statute and the apparent developments in the direction of a federal Spanish state… It was for this reason that Azaña when Minister of War had been determined to reduce the power of the Army… [and] many of the serving officers continued to see the quietly [while] those who had retired continued to plot.

EXTRACT

4

The Spanish journalist Julián Casanova, writing in the popular Spanish newspaper *El Pais*, 12 August 2012. The article recalls the 80th anniversary of the attempted coup of 1932 and assesses Sanjurjo's motives for leading it.

> On August 10, 1932, General José Sanjurjo rose in Seville against the Republic. He declared a state of war and issued a manifesto, written up by the religious-right journalist Juan Pujol, announcing the dissolution of parliament and the army's taking of power. He did this 'for love of Spain,' and to 'save her from ruin, iniquity and dismemberment.' Outside Seville, however, the rising failed. Sanjurjo tried to flee to Portugal, but was arrested on the way.
>
> There had been murmurings in the army since the summer of 1931, when Manuel Azaña announced his plans for army reform, which were hateful to the extreme right. The first attempts at conspiracy were soon thwarted. However a nucleus of top officers, and of civilian monarchists, began to canvass for support in fascist Italy. Sanjurjo was lukewarm at first, but his dismissal as general director of the Civil Guard, after the bloody suppression of a strike-related riot in January 1932, and his relegation to a lesser post, changed his mind. He began to think there were good reasons to substitute the Republic by a dictatorship…
>
> Condemned to death by a court-martial 'as responsible for an act of military rebellion,' the sentence was commuted to life imprisonment, though Interior Minister Santiago Casares Quiroga disagreed, holding that the pardon 'breaks the government's firmness, encourages the conspirators and impedes us from rigorous treatment of extremists.' Sanjurjo was locked up in the prison of El Dueso in Cantabria…

In the initial wave of euphoria that saw the Second Republic established, conservative political interests had generally appeared to be a rather forlorn and demoralised force. However, the Republican government had failed to appease the various conservative interests and grievances stemming from its radical land reforms, restructuring of the army and reduction of the Catholic Church's powers. As a consequence, right-wing opposition to the government's reformist agenda steadily became more organised, significant and effective in holding the Azaña regime to account.

ACTIVITY
KNOWLEDGE CHECK

1 Explain why Azaña's government introduced a series of reforms in the years 1931–33.

2 Why were the various conservative groups opposed to these reforms and what danger did this pose to the Republican regime?

AS Level Exam-Style Question Section B

To what extent was the Second Republic a destabilised regime between 1931 and 1933? (20 marks)

Tip

The question requires you to consider whether the Second Republic was built on stable foundations between the years 1931 and 1933, and it asks you to consider evidence for both stability and instability during this period, before reaching a concluding judgement.

WHAT WAS THE SIGNIFICANCE OF EVENTS AND DEVELOPMENTS DURING THE 'YEARS OF REACTION', 1933–36?

The creation of CEDA

Further unrest occurred in January 1933 with an anarchist uprising in the southern province of Andalusia. This small-scale revolution reflected the growing impatience with the limited improvements that the agrarian reforms were offering the ordinary peasant population. The country's Civil Guard was again duly despatched by central government to bring the situation under control, resulting in a bloody massacre of up to 25 rebel peasants in the village of Casas Viejas, near to the southern city of Cadiz. The brutal manner in which the government sought to regain control of the situation in Casas Viejas significantly damaged and discredited Azaña's administration. By attacking landless peasants in one of the poorest parts of the country, and offering only a remedy of bloody repression in response to clear signs of social unrest, Azaña's government faced growing unpopularity alongside a loss of momentum and political direction. In particular, it faced the withdrawal of support from its working-class and socialist power base.

This would mark the beginning of a turbulent phase of the Second Republic that is often referred to as the 'years of reaction'. During this period, the country would become more polarised and **reactionary**, as conservative political figures sought to overturn many of the social, political and economic changes that had taken place over the previous two years.

KEY TERM

Reactionary
Vigorously opposing adversely to significant political, social or economic change.

EXTRACT

5 From James Joll, *Europe since 1870: An International History*, 1990. Here, Joll explains that the reforming nature of the Second Republic's policies managed to antagonise both the country's conservative and radical left-wing political viewpoints for differing reasons.

Since the foundation of the Spanish Republic in 1931 the situation in Spain had been one of great tension and instability. The inherent problems of the Spanish state – rural underemployment, especially in the vast estates of the south, industrial under-development, separatism in Catalonia and in the Basque provinces – were exacerbated by the bitterness of the conservatives against a regime which they regarded as being in the hands of communists and freemasons, and at the other extreme by the fanaticism of the anarchists determined to wreck the bourgeois republic. The efforts of the first government of the republic to introduce serious reforms, including autonomy for Catalonia, new freedom of action for the trade unions, or the separation of Church and State, only served to irritate the conservatives even more and to spur the anarchists on in their attempts at real, total revolution. Conservative opposition expressed itself in an unsuccessful military coup in 1932. On the other side there were anarchist risings, notably one in 1933, which were suppressed with great ferocity.

The unrest that followed was fuelled by criticism and political attacks from opponents. Radical left-wing groups such as the syndicalists and anarchists were disillusioned with the slow pace of reform and the ongoing failings of capitalism as they saw it. These left-wing groups subsequently became detached from the Republican regime and were instrumental in organising a series of disruptive 'wildcat' strikes across various industries during 1933.

The conservative, landowning and Catholic influences of Spain also opposed the government and its programme of reforms. In February 1933, they united to form a coherent political movement – Confederacion Espanola de Derechas Autonomas (Spanish Confederation of Autonomous Rights, or CEDA). CEDA, led by Jose Maria Gil Robles, was a coalition of right-wing groups that aspired to model itself on Germany's pro-Catholic Centre Party, which had achieved significant political success from the late 19th century onwards. The conservative position within Spain had therefore become far more co-ordinated, effective and vigorous in its political campaigning with the emergence of CEDA, and the fractures appearing in the left-wing coalition of Republican support played directly into their hands. The better organised

forces of conservatism now had a chance to regain the political initiative, and they took it. An effective conservative propaganda campaign was promoted against Republican rule throughout the rest of 1933 with the aim of improving its parliamentary strength. A weakened and pressured Azaña had no option but to call fresh elections, scheduled to take place in November 1933.

SOURCE

2 From a speech by Jose Maria Gil Robles, a lawyer and leader of CEDA, at the party's founding congress in Madrid, February 1933.

When the social order is threatened, Catholics should unite to defend it and safeguard the principles of Christian civilization... We will go united into the struggle, no matter what it costs... We are faced with a social revolution. In the political panorama of Europe I can see only the formation of Marxist and anti-Marxist groups. This is what is happening in Germany and in Spain also. This is the great battle which we must fight this year. We must reconquer Spain.... We must give Spain a true unity, a new spirit, a totalitarian polity... It is necessary now to defeat socialism inexorably... We must proceed to a new state and this imposes duties and sacrifices. What does it matter if we have to shed blood! ... We need full power and that is what we demand... To realize this ideal we are not going to waste time with archaic forms. Democracy is not an end but a means to the conquest of the new state. When the time comes, either parliament submits or we will eliminate it.

The impact of the November 1933 elections

The announcement of elections to the Cortes to be held in November 1933 were a much-anticipated opportunity for the Spanish population to give its verdict on approximately 18 months of Republican government. Although reformist in nature, the incumbent government had struggled to deliver on all fronts. Amid growing unpopularity and developing social unrest, the embattled Azaña resigned in September prior to the elections. By contrast, the rejuvenated and more politically aggressive conservative opposition had steadily gained confidence throughout the year, boosted by the financial support of the Church and large landowners. When the elections eventually took place, the results indicated a significant shift in the public mood, amid a darkening mood of deep-rooted hostility between the competing factions.

SOURCE

3 From an unknown correspondent writing in *The Courier-Mail*, Brisbane, Australia, 31 October 1933 on the 1933 Spanish general election.

VIOLENCE LIKELY. SPANISH ELECTIONS. Madrid, October 31

The Government has taken elaborate precautions to ensure that the forthcoming elections will be fair and peaceful, but violence is threatened from two quarters – from the Socialists, who are continuing their preparations for a dictatorship, and from the newly-formed Fascist party, which is led by Senor Antonio Primo De Rivera, the eldest son of the late Marquis D'Estella de Rivera. The general opinion is that the elections, in which women will vote for the first time, will be the bitterest in Spain's history.

SOURCE

4

Spanish general elections 1931 and 1933, showing number of deputies elected.

	1931	1933
Deputies supporting a Republican/socialist administration	420	119
Conservative and nationalist deputies opposed to the Republican government	48	354*

* This figure included over 100 'radical' Republicans who had become disillusioned with the policies and practices of the government of the Second Republic and could no longer support it.

The electoral figures in Source 4 reflect not only a decline in Republican support but the impact of an 'unholy alliance' of opposition between conservative groups such as CEDA and radical Republicans who could no longer support the Azaña regime. The impact of CEDA and its improved organisation was significant. The party formed the biggest single political grouping after 1933, with 115 seats in the Constituent Cortes. The Socialist Party, which had previously been the largest party, saw its representation halved from 115 to 59 deputies, a scenario created not only by its growing unpopularity and perceived failures, but also by the decision to fight the election as a single party and not in alliance with various Republican and regional parties. Azaña's more moderate Republican Action Party did particularly badly and lost most of its deputies. However, the second biggest elected party was the Radical Republicans led by Alejandro Lerroux. With 102 deputies, Lerroux's party was only narrowly behind CEDA and offered evidence that support for republicanism in Spain had not totally collapsed.

By the end of 1933, the Second Republic had become a deeply divided regime. It was the role of the country's president, Alcalá Zamora, to attempt to bring some order and unity to the delicate political situation that existed following the election results. With broad sympathies that supported the maintenance of the Second Republic, the president did not want to be seen to bring its future stability under threat. He therefore appointed Lerroux as prime minister to lead a government in partnership with CEDA, although CEDA did not take up any cabinet posts to begin with. Following the 1933 general election, the Spanish government remained an administration that stayed broadly Republican and 'centrist' in nature despite the increased conservative presence. However, this curious coalition then embarked on a wave of policies that eroded and repealed most of the reforms of the previous two years, creating further social unrest in the process.

Undoing the reforms of 1931–33

The principal aim of this new government was to undo much of the legislation and reforms that had been passed since April 1931, with many of CEDA's wealthy business benefactors wanting a quick political and economic return on their financial support for the party. While the more radical Republicans differed from the conservatives in their continued hostility to the return of the monarchy, they also had grievances with the previous government. Due to their largely middle-class nature, they were fearful of what they saw as the previous government's radical socialist policies. The radical Republicans subsequently went along with the vigorous attacks on various policy initiatives and supported what was a conservative-driven legislative programme. This left them open to criticism that they were lacking in beliefs and principles and were only concerned with holding political power. As a consequence of the new political agenda, from early 1934 onwards, new policies were instigated.

- The fairly moderate agrarian reforms were scrapped, notably the Law of Muncial Boundaries in 1934, with landowners given enhanced powers to remove peasants who had moved into nationalised land. This resulted in increased evictions and a slump in rural wages, which led to a **general strike** organised by members of the agricultural union, the FNTT.

- Laws that had improved the position of trades unions and the employment rights and wages of industrial workers were repealed. This resulted in substantial cuts in wages.

- The privileges and regional powers of the Catalans were withdrawn.

- The powers of the Catholic Church were restored, with a revival of closer Church–State relations. Government support for clerical salaries was renewed and religious influence over education re-established.

KEY TERM

General strike
A period of co-ordinated industrial action, usually organised by trades unions, involving a number of different industries and covering a broad range of locations. It often has a nationwide element that seeks to involve a high proportion of the overall workforce. It aims to place pressure on the government and achieve political change by utilising direct action and co-ordinating social and economic disruption.

The harsh triumphalism of the landowning classes could best be summed up by their collective lack of sympathy for the landless and hungry rural workers that they subsequently evicted, advising them to seek refuge and support from 'their republic' with the words 'Let the republic feed you.' This was certainly a provocative approach that would stir up an appropriately angry response along class-based lines. Indeed, it served to polarise public opinion.

EXTEND YOUR KNOWLEDGE

Class-based politics
This approach to politics involves the formation of political viewpoints and attitudes that are closely linked to an individual's social class or background. It has the potential to be divisive in its impact on society, as according to theories of Karl Marx and various socialists who developed similar ideas during the 19th century, the interest of the rival classes are ultimately incompatible and only one class can eventually triumph.

In the Marxist model, the class-based conflict stems from the 'proletariat' (working classes) and the 'bourgeoisie' (middle-class landowners), with the former demanding the overthrow of the existing order, and the latter group broadly defending it. In attempting to control the country's political system in its own specific class interests, there is generally little room for compromise between the competing classes, and such conflict was clearly evident within the Spanish Second Republic during the first half of the 1930s.

Having faced largely right-wing opposition for the first two and a half years of its existence and despite its Republican figurehead and ongoing Republican status, the Second Republic now faced protest from the left. This coincided with the new government's political programme. The protest was led by various elements of Spanish society whose interests were increasingly threatened by the new conservative policies. This scenario represented an exact reverse of the situation to how the 'forces of conservatism' had felt during the first phase of the Second Republic. The new wave of government opponents broadly retained socialist and left-wing convictions, although for many it simply boiled down to the practicalities of everyday living and how they would survive under the revival of a conservative political agenda. While many elements of the poorer classes may have been dissatisfied with the previous government, any social progress and economic gains that they had secured under its rule were now under severe threat.

This threat provoked a reaction that was expressed in a more extreme and less constitutional manner, namely by social disorder, chaos, violence and murder. There was a surge of spontaneous strikes led by anarchist activists, whose members would also engage in attacks on isolated Civil Guard posts. In December 1933, political agitators managed to derail the Barcelona-Seville express train, with 19 people killed as a consequence. The bleak socio-economic conditions of the country's poorer workers meant they felt they had little to lose by taking such a radical approach.

In response to the government's moves to reverse the reforms of 1931–33, the Socialist Party executive committee launched a programme of opposition in January 1934. This pledged to reverse and challenge the new government's policy agenda. Its key policy goals included:

* nationalisation of the land

* dissolution of all religious orders, with seizure of their property

* dissolution of the army, to be replaced by a democratic **militia**

* dissolution of the Civil Guard.

This fairly radical policy programme certainly caused alarm to both political moderates as well as conservative opinion within Spain.

ACTIVITY
KNOWLEDGE CHECK

1 What was the significance of the formation of CEDA in 1933, and how did this impact on Spanish politics and society?

2 In Source 2 on page 298, what does Robles mean when he says 'We are faced with a social revolution'? Use examples to support your answer.

The Asturias rising and its consequences

Social divisions and tensions worsened throughout 1934. In early October, another nationwide general strike began, in reaction to the appointment of several CEDA figures to ministerial office as part of a reshuffle within Lerroux's government. Sustained general strikes subsequently broke out in various key cities, most notably in Madrid, Barcelona, Seville, Valencia and Zaragoza, which lasted for weeks. Of greatest significance was the fact that they were located in different parts of the country, which added to the almost permanent state of crisis and socio-political tension across much of Spain. This particular strike was organised by the larger trades unions, such as the UGT, alongside a range of other workers' bodies, who were becoming increasingly concerned at the growing influence of CEDA within the Spanish government. The strikers were a collection of socialists, anarchists and communists, who put their differences aside to form the 'Workers' Alliance'. More militant members of the Workers' Alliance argued for a military uprising, rather than strikes, to stop the right-wing takeover of national government. This fits in with the evolving position of the country's Socialist Party, whose leader, Caballero, was abandoning his traditional moderation for the ideas of Marx, largely due to a growing frustration with the perceived failings of democratic politics. Consequently, from 1934 onwards, Caballero guided his party to steadily embrace the idea of establishing a 'people's democracy' of a similar vein to Marx's 'dictatorship of the **proletariat**', which was to be achieved by a violent uprising as opposed to political and constitutional methods.

KEY TERM

Proletariat
Deriving from mid-19th century Marxist theory, this group were the majority section of society who produced the wealth but did not receive their fair share due to being exploited by the bourgeoisie. Marxist theory argued that this group had to overthrow the bourgeoisie in order to achieve appropriate social and economic rewards.

Industrial action tended to originate in the big, urbanised cities, although in October 1934 more remote and provincial areas also joined the co-ordinated activity. The social unrest in the larger cities lacked co-ordination and planning and was poorly executed on the whole, being effectively suppressed and fairly quickly brought under control by the government. However, it was in the mining communities of the industrialised Asturias region of northern Spain where this particular strike was sustained, mainly due to the presence of influential, politically conscious and resilient miners. This was a location where socialism and trade union influence was strong and despite coal-mining suffering during the economic slump, they were traditionally among the best paid industrial workers in Spain. Their actions were therefore motivated by political ideology rather than economic factors such as seeking better wages and working conditions. There were some notable anticlerical feelings among their members as well.

The miners had planned their revolt and were well organised, with tightly knit revolutionary committees established across various towns and villages and miners organised into military columns in preparation for the fighting. The anarchist-oriented CNT were particularly prominent in this episode, and the determined nature of the miners' actions caught the government by surprise. The uprising began with attacks on Civil Guard positions on 4 October 1934. By 6 October, the regional capital of Oviedo had been seized. Within three days most of the province was under the control of the insurgent miners. Other parts of the region such as the coastal city of Gijon were seized by anarchists. The Asturian miners proved themselves difficult to repress, despite the fact that up to 20,000 government troops under the direct orders of General Franco were sent to the region to quell the uprising, along with support from both the navy and the air force. The Asturias uprising was eventually suppressed and brought under control in a fairly brutal manner. Up to 2,000 insurgents were killed and 7,000 wounded during the bloody rising that lasted for two weeks. Many of the miners who died were executed by the army, with villages within the region indiscriminately bombed and burned to the ground.

SOURCE

5 Spanish government forces with prisoners following the Asturias uprising of October 1934.

Such a forceful backlash against this left-wing resistance certainly allowed the government to maintain social order in the short term, but in the long term it created a bitter legacy of ill feeling which further polarised the country's already fractured rival political factions. Once government control had been restored following the uprising, the bitterness was exacerbated by the mass dismissal of trades unionists from various jobs in the region, with many others imprisoned. It was a clear reflection of how the new regime had eroded much of the trade union rights achieved between 1931 and 1933. Many leading socialists were also jailed. By the end of 1934, the notion of an open and pluralistic Spanish Republic that could appeal to all political viewpoints appeared to be a very distant prospect. The violence experienced during this revolutionary episode was to be a foretaste of things to come for the Spanish nation.

The formation of the Popular Front

The Spanish left had suffered a setback following the crushing of the Asturias rising, and it was forced to re-group and review its options going forward. Some extremists wanted more of the same and felt that the miners' revolt was an example to other left-wing groups; if repeated elsewhere, it was a tactic that could eventually bring the government to its knees. The more moderate socialists felt that violence was irresponsible, unconstitutional and not the way to address what was essentially a political problem. They were also aware of the gradual shift to the conservative right of many people within the moderate Spanish middle classes. Such trends were being fuelled by the often exaggerated media stories about left-wing extremism and violence, frequently involving anticlerical attacks and atrocities. From this perspective, ongoing revolts and direct action would only increase this negative perception and make an electoral recovery for the left-wing parties even more difficult.

This split and diversity in their aims and agendas, with moderate social democrat reformists wanting to adopt a constitutional route, while communists, anarchists and even the Socialist Party embracing more direct and extreme tactics, was a key problem for the various left-wing organisations in Spain. Nevertheless, as 1935 progressed, some evidence began to emerge of Spain's political left adopting a more coherent and co-ordinated approach in its opposition to the increasingly right-wing government. In September 1935, a more united communist grouping was formed, the Partido Obrero de Unificación Marxista (POUM), broadly translated to the 'Workers' Party'. Further to this, in October 1935, the former prime minister, Azaña, re-emerged into the political arena to address a huge public meeting just outside Madrid.

SOURCE

6 Manuel Azaña's speech to Republican supporters in Madrid, 20 October 1935. Here, he warns the people of Spain of the dangers of being ruled by an increasingly right-wing and authoritarian government.

All Europe today is a battlefield between democracy and its enemies, and Spain is not an exception. You must choose between democracy, with all its shortcomings, with all its faults, with all its mistakes and errors, and tyranny with all its horrors... In Spain one hears of frivolous talk of dictatorship. We find it repugnant not only by doctrine, but by experience and through good sense... Dictatorship is a consequence or political manifestation of intolerance; its propellant is fanaticism; and its means of action, physical violence. Dictatorship leads to war... it stupefies people and drives them mad.

Azaña's intervention was a significant one. The core message of his powerful speech was that the forces of the Spanish left needed to rally together in order to salvage both democracy and the existence of the Second Republic itself. Given his stark warning that the conservative ascendancy was becoming more extreme in its policies and gaining too much power and momentum, the left promptly re-aligned and re-organised itself to form the **Popular Front** in January 1936. This group featured a broad alliance of socialists, communists and anarchists and became primarily focused on preventing the further spread of fascism across Europe, with the communists receiving external guidance from the Soviet Union.

This amalgamation of left-wing forces subsequently developed into a coalition or formal pact that would fight the forthcoming national elections of February 1936, although how it would co-operate in practical terms if returned to government office was open to question. While the Popular Front was a natural left-wing reaction to the organised growth of CEDA, it had also been prompted by growing fears about the spread of fascist influence across Europe, including Spain. This concern had been heightened by the formation of the **Falange Española** in late 1933, which represented a more extreme form of conservatism and which had been steadily growing ever since. The Falange Española embraced a dictatorial, expansionist and nationalist brand of right-wing politics that had similarities with the fascist agenda of Adolf Hitler's Nazi Party in Germany and Benito Mussolini in Italy. Even the CEDA grouping began to express more explicit right-wing viewpoints, a factor that can be linked to increased political competition on the right from the Falange. Falange-Española members began to operate as militias, wearing uniforms and military regalia similar to the type worn by fascist regimes in other countries, while its leadership began to consider the restoration of dictatorial government as a means of offering the strong leadership it felt Spain deserved.

KEY TERMS

Popular Front
Formed in early 1936, this was an electoral pact signed by a range of left-wing political organisations in Spain. It was headed and organised by Manuel Azaña, with the key aim of fighting that year's general election in a co-ordinated rather than a fragmented manner.

Falange Española
A Spanish political organisation that was founded by José Antonio Primo de Rivera in 1933. It represented a more extreme form of conservatism, and was broadly fascist in nature.

ACTIVITY
KNOWLEDGE CHECK

1   Draw two flow diagrams to show the development of the political left and right in Spain in the years 1933–36.

2   What was the impact of the 'years of reaction' on different areas of Spanish society? Provide some examples to illustrate your answer.

3   What was the significance of the formation of Falange Española and the Popular Front for Spanish politics and society?

A Level Exam-Style Question Section B

'The 1933 Spanish general election signalled the beginning of the end of the Spanish Second Republic.'

How far do you agree with this statement? (20 marks)

Tip

This question makes the assertion that the 1933 general election was a notable turning point in terms of weakening the Spanish Second Republic. The response must ultimately seek to address such a claim. Evidence is therefore required on both sides of the argument to assess whether this election was a major turning point that undermined the Republic, or whether there were more significant factors and events before and after this event that hastened its demise.

HOW SIGNIFICANT WAS THE 1936 GENERAL ELECTION IN RELATION TO EVENTS IN SPAIN BETWEEN FEBRUARY AND JULY 1936?

The election of February 1936

It was within this atmosphere of sharp social divisions and increasing political polarisation between left and right that the Spanish elections of 16 February 1936 took place. The need for an election had come about due to the dismissal of the government at the end of 1935 as a result of a gambling scandal. CEDA had subsequently hoped to inherit the government's key political positions, but President Alcalá Zamora opted for fresh national elections instead.

The election results clearly illustrated the class-based division of the country. From an electorate of over 13 million voters, the parties of the right gained approximately 3.8 million votes, which equated to 46 percent of the popular vote, while the parties of the left (the Popular Front) achieved 4.2 million or 48 percent of the national vote. By contrast, the more moderate, centrist parties trailed in their wake, achieving a dismal 680,000 votes by comparison. The clear spilt in public opinion indicated an obvious lack of agreement about what was the most appropriate political

SOURCE

7   Poster of the Communist Party for the 1936 general election. The image shows a woman who is seeking to vote for communism (as part of the Popular Front) being pulled back by figures from the Church and business (who appear to have trampled on other citizens).

remedy for the country's various problems. Although CEDA was the largest single party with 101 deputies, beating the Socialist Party into second place with 88, the combined forces of the Popular Front were able to form a clear parliamentary majority (see Source 8 on page 304).

To the left, their electoral triumph marked a return to power and an end to the reactionary policies of the previous two years; a period of fairly unstable conservative government that they had scornfully referred to as *Bienio Negro* or 'Two Black Years'. For their part, the conservatives sought to cling on to power by imprisonment and other coercive threats to political opponents, with underhand and fraudulent electoral tactics such as employers threatening their workers to vote a certain way, or the police in

SOURCE

8
Spanish election results for 1936, showing the number of deputies elected to the Cortes (government).

Political grouping	Number of deputies (in Cortes)
Popular Front (Republicans)	263
Right-wing (conservative) parties	156
Centre parties	54

some areas stopping anyone from voting who did not wear a collar. Nevertheless, the democratic will of the Spanish people prevailed, and the new left-wing coalition government under Azaña now had to be maintained in the face of the ongoing opposition from conservative political opponents. However, the diverse, disjointed and often extreme range of policy priorities of the incoming government would indicate that there was trouble ahead on this front.

Political instability and social unrest

There was a renewal of public enthusiasm for the new government among many poorer Spanish citizens, with crowds gathering to celebrate in various large cities. However, the composition of the new government caused major concerns to the country's conservative forces and, in particular, elements of the military. The increasingly prominent General Franco, now chief of the general staff, voiced concerns to right-wing politicians and suggested that a 'state of war' be declared in order to prevent this new administration from taking office, with some form of martial law being imposed by the army in the process. This appeared to indicate that, unlike 1931, the country's senior army officers were reluctant to sit back and allow the liberals, socialists and Republicans to take the power that a democratic election result had awarded them. In the short term, however, they were not encouraged to take any immediate action by the country's conservative politicians and instead bided their time. This concern about the direction of a more left-wing, Republican Spain was particularly felt among a younger generation of officers such as Franco, who saw the new government's agenda as being incompatible with their military oath to protect the country's interests and a major threat to the traditional image of 'Holy Spain'. While there were no explicit communists or Marxists wielding any significant power within the new administration, right-wing interests spoke of their fears of the gradual '**Bolshevisation**' of the Spanish left, particularly given the extremist drift of the country's Socialist Party.

In seeking to impose the policy agenda of the Popular Front, the incoming administration significantly threatened various conservative interests. It swiftly became clear that the policy agenda of the incoming Azaña administration would be both more interventionist and more radical than the government of 1931–33. The more liberal and socialist government would therefore seek to undo the more conservative policies that had prevailed between 1933 and early 1936. This development seemed to symbolise something of a cyclical and destructive political process whereby each ideological viewpoint sought to undo and overturn the laws passed by its predecessor.

As the prime minister of the new government, Azaña immediately sought to bring some degree of calm and stability to what was a tense situation. Press censorship was one method used to ensure political control. Another was known as a 'State of Alarm', which gave the government enhanced repressive powers to be imposed in extreme circumstances in order to maintain social order. However, conservative interests were critical of this approach and felt that Azaña only focused on right-wing unrest and protest and appeared to overlook left-wing agitation. Despite this focus on controlling power from the centre, regional government was again quickly restored to Catalonia in order to quell any further unrest developing there. This won the Republican Popular Front administration the long-standing loyalty of this region. However, military interests were further offended when the two key generals involved in the Asturias uprising, Franco and Goded, were removed from their positions at central-government level and relocated to the Canary and Balearic islands respectively. Their presence had become untenable under the new government given their previous role in the repression of the working-class unrest. Some left-wing figures even claimed that they were guilty of treason against the Republic. They were also viewed as potential figureheads if there was any further attempt at a military coup, which seemed a genuine possibility in the circumstances.

In March 1936, right-wing opinion was further antagonised when the Falange group was banned and its leaders jailed. This was in response to unrest, shootings and other violence stemming from clashes between the Falange and left-wing trade union activists. These government actions heightened the existing anger that prevailed within the more extreme sections of Spanish conservatism and its growing links to other European fascist regimes. There was a notable escalation of unrest as a result of Azaña's clampdown on the extreme right. By the middle of 1936, the Falange's membership had grown to 40,000. To round off the development of conservative unease at the new government's political agenda, in May 1936 the long-standing and moderate President Alcalá Zamora was dismissed from office, being replaced by Azaña, with Santiago Casares Quiroga of the Republican Left becoming prime minister. The new government also appointed civil governors from the main parties of the Popular Front to control and run key provinces to further consolidate its renewed grip on power.

The unfinished business of agrarian reform was also revisited by the Popular Front. This caused further divisive controversy, with the ongoing and unfulfilled demands of the peasantry prompting many of their number to seize land from the aristocratic landowners. At the end of March, the western region of Extremadura saw 60,000 peasants take over approximately 3,000 farms. Such actions were tantamount to nationalisation, and were encouraged and legalised by the new government which assumed overall ownership in many cases. Only 12,500 peasants had been given additional land over the previous four years. In the first half of 1936, under the auspices of Azaña's government, almost 72,000 new farm workers (or *yunteros*) had been allocated new plots of agricultural land. This provoked anger from the conservative landowners whose land was being attacked and it hardened their opposition to the government of the Popular Front. The incoming government had also imposed and maintained high levels of taxation on the rich, and this led to wealthy individuals withdrawing money from the country, which impacted on levels of investment in industry and workers' wages. From a conservative political perspective, such confiscatory land and taxation policies were a further example of why the Popular Front administration could not be tolerated and why powerful right-wing groups began to demand its removal from office.

EXTEND YOUR KNOWLEDGE

General Francisco Franco (1892–1975)

A conservative general who became the dictator of Spain between 1939 and 1975. He was born in Ferrol in the region of Galicia in north western Spain, and his father was a naval postmaster. He opposed the establishment of the Second Republic in 1931 and had been a firm supporter of Primo de Rivera's military dictatorship. He made swift progress through the military ranks and rose to prominence in dealing with the Asturias uprising of 1934. After being despatched to the Canary Islands in early 1936, he returned to the mainland later that year to become involved in the military coup that triggered the Spanish Civil War.

One of the most controversial and somewhat impulsive actions of the government of the Popular Front was the release of all those detained following the 1934 'revolutions', which had primarily stemmed from the Asturias region, with the government declaring an amnesty for these political prisoners. Prisons were subsequently opened in Oviedo, Valencia and Catalonia, although not all of those released were released with government authority, and there was a developing sense that Azaña and his ministers were not fully in control of the situation and the accompanying disorder. This somewhat chaotic situation horrified conservatives and coincided with a further wave of social unrest and ongoing clashes between left-wing and right-wing factions across the country. The full depth of this unrest is illustrated in a speech made by the CEDA leader, Gil Robles, in the Cortes. He highlighted the fact that between February and June 1936 there were almost 1,300 serious civilian injuries, an estimated 270 deaths, 300 significant strikes and almost 400 attacks on key political buildings, including 250 churches. This final dimension raised renewed fears among conservatives of a revival of anticlericalism, which had created such ill feeling between the left-wing government and the Catholic Church between 1931 and 1933.

SOURCE

9

Part of a speech by the Spanish conservative politician Jose Maria Gil Robles in the Cortes, April 1936, about the social unrest in Spain.

A considerable mass of the Spanish people which is at least half the nation will not resign itself implacably to die, I assure you. If it cannot defend itself one way, it will in another. Against the violence there will arise violence from the other side, and public power will have the sad role of being merely spectators in a civic conformation that will ruin the nation materially and spiritually... if the way is not rapidly rectified, no other solution will remain in Spain save that of violence; either the red dictatorship advocated by those gentlemen, or an energetic defence of the citizens who will not allow themselves to be run down. I think that you [Azaña] will suffer a sadder fate, which is to preside over the liquidation of the democratic Republic... when civil war breaks out in Spain, let it be known that the weapons have been loaded by the irresponsibility of a government that failed to fulfil its duty toward groups that have kept within the strictest legality.

ACTIVITY
KNOWLEDGE CHECK

1 List the key policies of the Popular Front government in the months February to June 1936.

2 Which of these policies were most significant and controversial? Explain your answer.

3 What were the major causes of political instability and social unrest facing the government of the Popular Front?

The significance of Sotelo's assassination

On 13 July 1936, the growing tensions crippling Spain took a dramatic new turn when the outspoken conservative politician Jose Calvo Sotelo was assassinated in Madrid at the hands of a detachment of police officers. Sotelo was a prominent monarchist and had previously been in exile after the demise of Primo de Rivera, only to return in 1934 after the conservatives became part of the Spanish government. He became the successor to Gil Robles as leader of CEDA, and subsequently adopted a combative style at the head of the country's official opposition group in the Cortes, making frequent attacks on the policies of the government and the violence erupting across various parts of the country. Both Sotelo and other right-wing figures such as Robles were becoming increasingly attracted to the idea of some kind of coup to seize political power and restore social order, even if this was at the expense of democratic and constitutional government.

Sotelo's shocking and high-profile death was perhaps a reflection of him being perceived as a dangerous figure by his more extreme political opponents. It also marked a dangerous escalation in the country's growing level of political violence and anarchy, and it brought the Second Republic to a heightened level of crisis and instability. This violent political act was claimed to be a direct response to the assassination of Jose Castillo a day earlier by members of the right-wing Falange militia. Castillo was a senior left-wing member of the country's Assault Guard, and although the government of the Popular Front had not organised or been directly responsible for what was clearly a revenge attack on Sotelo, it was heavily criticised and implicated due to the involvement of government forces in it. This sequence of developments appeared to signal the breaking point for many figures on the conservative right of Spanish politics. Groups that had been observing political developments with a growing sense of despair, now felt inclined to actively intervene in order to address what appeared to be the country's spiral into turmoil and chaotic disorder.

The attempted military coup, 1936

The military had been closely watching the political situation with some unease following the election results of February 1936. Given the increasingly chaotic disorder that was evident across Spanish society, this sequence of assassinations was the catalyst that convinced various generals that they had to make a move against the Popular Front government. In conjunction with the leading conservative politician Gil Robles, the initial activities that triggered what became known as the 'Generals Rising' were orchestrated by General Emilio Mola. Mola had cultivated links with various conservative political figures and felt he could be sure of their support if the army felt the need to intervene to restore the rapidly deteriorating social order and from their perspective, to 'save Spain' from its own destructive tendencies. As a back-up to his more formal political connections, he believed that he could also rely on the militias of the Falange, as well as the conservative monarchists (also known as Carlists), in dealing with any left-wing resistance that would likely emerge in response to any coup attempt.

The rising was no great surprise, having being shaped by monarchist and military influences, as well as lingering conservative resentment that had existed since the formation of the Second Republic in 1931. This would indicate a long-term build-up to this military coup. Its primary motives appear to be that various right-wing bodies, including senior levels of the Spanish military, had become convinced that a social revolution was imminent. If this occurred, it would lead to the further spread of communist influence across the country and within Spain's senior political circles. Whether communism was likely to significantly develop in Spain is open to some conjecture, although conservative figures were said to be particularly fearful of the influences of Caballero's Socialist Party and its increased links to Moscow.

The coup began on 17 July 1936, when the army overthrew the civilian government in Spanish northern Morocco, Africa, that was under the control of the Spanish Empire and which was the base of the country's elite troops, the Army of Africa. The next day, General Franco arrived from his outpost in the Canary Islands, having been initially cautious about a military revolt, but having been eventually convinced by the Madrid-based Mola to instigate the military uprising at this specific location. Franco was feared by left-wing members of the Popular Front, being viewed as a strong character whom the army could rally around as a revived military dictator. He had certainly proved his military capabilities and leadership qualities and had warned Azaña about the dangers of communism before his exile to the Canaries earlier in the year. He had now returned as the great hope of Spanish conservatism with the determined aim of preventing such an extreme left-wing ideology gaining a significant political foothold in Spain.

SOURCE

10 Speech made by General Franco to Spanish troops on his arrival in Morocco, 17 July 1936. Here, Franco is seeking to motivate his forces as part of the attempt to seize back control of Spain's government.

Spaniards! The nation calls to her defense all those of you who hear the holy name of Spain, those in the ranks of the Army and Navy who have made a profession of faith in the service of the Motherland, all those who swore to defend her to the death against her enemies. The situation in Spain grows more critical every day; anarchy reigns in most of the countryside and towns; government-appointed authorities encourage revolts, when they do not actually lead them; murderers use pistols and machine guns to settle their differences and to treacherously assassinate innocent people, while the public authorities fail to impose law and order. Revolutionary strikes of all kinds paralyze the life of the nation, destroying its sources of wealth and creating hunger, forcing working men to the point of desperation. The most savage attacks are made upon national monuments and artistic treasures by revolutionary hordes who obey the orders of foreign governments, with the complicity and negligence of local authorities. The most serious crimes are committed in the cities and countryside, while the forces that should defend public order remain in their barracks, bound by blind obedience to those governing authorities that are intent on dishonoring them. The Army, Navy, and other armed forces are the target of the most obscene and slanderous attacks, which are carried out by the very people who should be protecting their prestige. Meanwhile, martial law is imposed to gag the nation... and to imprison alleged political opponents.

Franco was motivated by a desire to restore order and stability and to conserve the key Spanish cultural traditions of 'Old Spain', which he and his military allies felt were now in serious jeopardy due to the continued existence and activities of the Popular Front government. By the early hours of 18 July, the coup had rapidly spread from northern Africa to the Spanish mainland, with Franco launching an invasion of the country from the south. The overlapping hours of 17 and 18 July 1936 are generally seen as the formal starting point of the Spanish Civil War, a cataclysmic episode that would last for almost three years. The initial developments of the conflict saw geographically separated areas such as Seville and other parts of Andalusia in the south, along with Valladolid in the north quickly fall to the military forces that made their moves from the country's various barracks. However, Mola and his 'Generals Rising' underestimated the resilience of the Republican forces, and while parts of the countryside were swiftly taken over, the major urban areas were much more difficult to seize control of, with five of Spain's seven largest cities including Madrid, Barcelona and

Valencia remaining under government authority. Support for republicanism and the Popular Front was much stronger in urban Spain, and the governing regime was further boosted by the emergence of local left-wing militias that were provoked into action by the prospect of a right-wing political group seizing control of the country in such an undemocratic manner. Many of these groups were explicitly antifascist in nature, and evidence of their effectiveness occurred when the Montaña Barracks in Madrid was overrun by Republican militia forces and Spanish civilians on 20 July. As a consequence, an estimated 2,500 soldiers who had initially supported the uprising were massacred at this location within the first few days of the civil war erupting, with numerous other violent deaths occurring across other parts of Spain.

A Level Exam-Style Question Section B

To what extent were the policies of the Popular Front government the cause of the Spanish Civil War? (20 marks)

Tip

This question implies that the policies of the Popular Front government were an immediate short-term cause of the Spanish Civil War. The response therefore needs to compare short-term factors with other more long-term developments, and some judgement needs to be reached as to whether long- or short-term factors were the most significant reasons for the coup that led to the outbreak of war.

SOURCE

11 Men and women volunteers (militia) of the Popular Front leaving for the Guadarrama front on 30 July 1936, to defend the Second Republic against the military coup.

The attempted coup had ultimately not fulfilled its aim of a quick and efficient seizure of power for the Spanish military. However it had not failed completely, as the Republican government had lost control of much of its army and police force to the instigators of the military uprising and a civil war had erupted as a result.

ACTIVITY
KNOWLEDGE CHECK

1 What was the significance of Sotelo's assassination for the long-term future of the Second Republic?

2 To what extent did Franco's claims in Source 10 on page 307 justify the military coup in July 1936? Explain your answer, using examples.

ACTIVITY
SUMMARY

1 Draw a spider diagram to summarise how the Second Republic became destabilised between 1931 and 1936. Highlight the key events and developments. Which events were more significant and why?

2 Identify the key government policies passed by both left-wing and right-wing Spanish governments between 1931 and 1936.

   a) Which policies had the most impact on working-class citizens in either a positive or a negative sense? Explain your choices.

   b) Which policies had the most impact on the wealthier sections of society in either a positive or a negative sense? Explain your choices.

3 Write a newspaper article of about 500 words which reports on the atmosphere and outcome of the 1936 Spanish general election. Use sources and other information available to help you with this task.

 WIDER READING

Beevor, A. *The Battle for Spain: The Spanish Civil War 1936-39,* Phoenix (2006) provides some background information to the Spanish Civil War

Carr, R. *Spain: 1808-1939,* Clarendon Press (1966) covers the development of the Spanish nation from the start of the 19th century until the end of the Spanish Civil War

Joll, J. *Europe since 1870: An International History,* Penguin (1990) provides some informative and interesting coverage of events in Spain

Payne, S. G. *Spain's First Democracy: The Second Republic, 1931-1936,* University of Wisconsin Press (2003) provides some detailed and informative coverage of how Spain adjusted to democratic rule under the Second Republic

Payne, S. G. *The Collapse of the Spanish Republic: 1933-1936: Origins of the Civil War,* Yale University Press (2006) focuses on the gradual collapse of the Spanish Republic and the outbreak of civil war in Spain

Quiroga, A. *Right-Wing Spain in the Civil War Era, Soldiers of God and Apostles of the Fatherland, 1914-45,* Bloomsbury (2012) provides an analysis and historical overview of the nature of the right-wing and conservative political activities that occurred in Spain either side of the country's civil war

Thomas, H. *The Spanish Civil War,* Penguin (1965) provides some informative contextual background as to the reasons why the civil war broke out

2b.2 The Spanish Civil War, 1936–39

KEY QUESTIONS

- What were the key factors in July and August 1936 that led to the outbreak of war in Spain?
- What was the nature and impact of the course of the war in Spain in the years 1936–39?
- How significant was the impact of the civil war on the lives of ordinary Spanish citizens?
- What factors had the most influence in determining the outcome of the war?

KEY TERMS

Republicans
A term to describe those who supported the government of the Popular Front and who were opposed to the military uprising. They were stronger in number in Spain's urban areas and usually came from a working-class or liberal middle-class background.

Nationalists
A term to describe those who supported the army rebellion against the government of the Popular Front, primarily consisting of wealthier, conservative-minded citizens, with greater strength in number in the more rural parts of Spain.

INTRODUCTION

The economic hardships and political failings experienced under the rule of the Second Republic since 1931 had caused many Spanish citizens to reject a democratic solution to Spain's deep-rooted problems and lingering social and political divisions. Years of simmering unrest and recurring outbreaks of political agitation and violence finally resulted in the eruption of internal conflict. By July 1936, Spain had become engulfed in an escalating civil war between two committed opponents – **Republicans** and **Nationalists** – whose views and attitudes were shaped by bitterly contrasting ideological positions. The forces on each side appeared to be sufficiently organised and willing to endure a drawn-out conflict in order to achieve political control of the entire country.

As the civil war progressed, the mainly urban areas largely remained under the control of the forces of the Republican government, while more rural areas were seized by army-led Nationalists. With both sides of the conflict quickly establishing zones of influence, life for civilians became extremely difficult for the duration of the civil war. What had previously been considered a 'normal' lifestyle quickly became a thing of the past for many people. In addition to the dangers to life, regular military bombardment of civilian areas meant that previous types of stable employment were difficult to maintain, farming and agriculture were disrupted and many factories operated in a state of 'war production'.

As the war entered its final stages during 1938 and 1939, the Nationalists steadily gained the upper hand and made further inroads into Republican-controlled zones. Their progress was bolstered by the military prowess and leadership skills of General Franco, along with notable foreign support from Germany and Italy. This pushed the Republicans back into a limited number of strongholds, gradually reducing the geographical area they controlled by the end of 1938. Foreign troops and other national governments played a significant role in the evolution and outcome of the war. This ultimately worked in the Nationalists' favour and was a key factor in their eventual victory in the spring of 1939.

1936
July–August: Support for Nationalists from Hitler and Mussolini

August: Non-Intervention Pact signed by France, Britain and others

September: Francisco Largo Caballero appointed prime minister of the Second Republic
Franco assumes the role of *Generalissimo* of the Nationalist forces

1937
February/March: Republicans defeat Nationalist forces at Jarama and Guadalajara

March: Nationalist advance on northern Spain

April: The Basque town of Guernica is destroyed by the German *Luftwaffe*
Right-wing Falange and Carlist movements merge

July: Republican offensive at Brunete

August: Republican Aragon offensive launched

October: Asturias falls to Nationalists

1936	1937	1937
July–December	January–June	July–December

October: First military aid from Soviet Union arrives for Republicans

November: Franco's forces come within sight of Madrid
Republican government relocates to Valencia

May: Juan Negrín Lopez replaces Francisco Largo Caballero as prime minister

June: Nationalist General Mola dies in a plane crash

November: Republican government again relocates, to Barcelona in the Catalan region

December: Battle of Teruel begins

WHAT WERE THE KEY FACTORS IN THE MONTHS JULY–AUGUST 1936 THAT LED TO THE OUTBREAK OF WAR IN SPAIN?

Nationalist and Republican leadership, support and relative military strength

Nationalists

The Nationalists were initially led by a military **junta**, namely a committee of generals that was formally established within a week of the military uprising, on 24 July 1936. The junta was based in the northern city of Burgos, within the Nationalist zone of Spain. Prominent individuals in the junta included Generals Cabanellas, Mola and Franco. However, the key figure of General Sanjurjo, whom many had viewed as potentially the most powerful military figure on the Nationalist side, was killed in a plane crash within days of the start of the conflict. While not all military figures had sided with the Nationalists in the July uprising (17 out of 21 senior generals had initially remained loyal to the Republican administration), many of the most prominent, skilled and experienced ones had done. Their leadership, logistical and strategic qualities would become apparent as the conflict developed. While Franco was still making slow but steady progress in moving his forces from North Africa, Mola was initially the most visible and prominent Nationalist leadership figure on the mainland. On the junta's formation, Mola publicly and dramatically announced to the people of Burgos that civil war was under way (see Source 1). In combining the themes of religion and Spanish patriotism in his speech, Mola sought to strike an instant chord with the various forces of conservatism that formed the Nationalist powerbase throughout the civil war. Initially, they were not evenly matched, with the Republicans mustering a force of some 450,000 infantry and 350 aircraft and the Nationalists some 600,000 infantry and 600 aircraft.

KEY TERM

Junta
A specific government or type of political leadership that consists of a group of military figures.

SOURCE

1 General Mola's speech to the citizens of Burgos, 24 July 1936. Here, he explains the reasons for civil war and announces his intentions of leading the Nationalist army.

Spaniards! Citizens of Burgos! The government which was the wretched bastard of liberal and Socialist concubinage is dead, killed by our valiant army. Spain, the true Spain, has laid the dragon low, and now it lies, writhing on its belly and biting the dust. I am now going to take up my position at the head of the troops and it will not be long before two banners – the sacred emblem of the Cross and our own glorious flag – are waving together in Madrid.

1938
February: Nationalists win Battle of Teruel

March: Italian planes bomb Republican-held Barcelona

April: Nationalist advance to the west sees its troops reach the Mediterranean coast

July: Republican offensive along the River Ebro launched

September: Munich Conference indicates that further foreign intervention on behalf of Spanish Republicans is unlikely

1939
January: Fall of Barcelona to Nationalist troops

February: Final meeting of the Constituent Cortes presided over by Negrín

1938 January–June	1938 July–December	1939 January–April

May: Negrín publishes his 13-point manifesto to settle the conflict Franco rejects its terms

November: Nationalists win Battle of Ebro
International Brigades start to leave Spain

December: Nationalist Catalan offensive launched

March: Valencia and Madrid both fall to the Nationalist forces

April: Franco announces Nationalist victory in the Spanish Civil War

Civilians were considered as potential members of the Nationalist leadership, but there was some difficulty on reaching agreement on appropriate figures to include from the various conservative political groupings. This was largely because these civilian-led groups differed in their aims for the future of Spain, with **Carlist** and monarchist sympathisers openly supporting the return of the monarchy and the end of Republican government, while the Falange wanted the opposite outcome of a social revolution against the aristocracy and middle classes. In another set of priorities, supporters of CEDA, such as the prominent conservative politician Jose Maria Gil Robles, primarily wanted the restoration of social order, the reassertion of Church and military power and the repression of communist activities and trade union powers (see Chapter 1).

These differences had the potential to destabilise the important Spanish right-wing interests that were at stake in the emerging conflict. The military's control and dominance of the Nationalist leadership, therefore, was crucial from the outset in suppressing differences and preventing them from undermining the uprising's initial momentum. The military leaders subsequently instilled a more focused vision that prioritised broad and popular conservative themes, such as the removal of extreme left-wing influence from Spanish government, and the restoration of law and order, while also preserving some of the country's most important cultural traditions. The army's unerring influence culminated in the emergence of the personal dominance of Franco as *Generalissimo* from 29 September 1936, largely due to his military successes, his political networking skills and the demise of potential rivals. This role would instil further focus and unity that the Republicans often lacked during the sustained period of conflict.

KEY TERMS

Carlist
A conservative and traditionalist political movement that sought the restoration of a Spanish monarch from a separate line of the Bourbon dynasty.

Generalissimo
A supreme military leader, which was the specific title given to Franco both during and after the Spanish Civil War.

Guerrilla warfare
An irregular form of warfare or military combat involving small-scale battles and ambushes, often utilised by unofficial and civilian-based armies against a larger and superior army.

Collectivised
An economic model where key industries and the means of production are owned and run by the people (often in the form of the state), as opposed to private industry or businesses.

Republicans

Republican forces were a more varied and disparate collection of groupings than the Nationalists. They primarily consisted of socialists, communists, trades unionists, syndicalists, anarchists, republicans and moderate liberals. In comparison with the Nationalists, who had a greater conventional army influence, a significant number of the Republican forces were ordinary civilians

motivated by strong ideological reasons. Their lack of military training meant they were therefore more likely to engage in **guerrilla warfare** as opposed to traditional military battles. In the army-led uprising of July 1936, however, the navy and air force had remained loyal to the Republican administration. The navy, for example, took control of the Strait of Gibraltar, preventing Franco's Army of Africa from accessing the mainland from Morocco. Although the Republican forces were broadly united in their opposition to the right-wing Nationalist uprising, there were some significant divisions between the factions about what kind of Spain they would like to see in the event of them emerging victorious from the civil war. While moderate socialists and liberal republicans had dominated the left-wing governments of the Second Republic, one single grouping failed to control and direct the Republican forces during the civil war in the same way that Franco and his army allies did on the Nationalist side. This created a more fragmented and weaker Republican leadership.

Various groups within Spanish republicanism did have specific and important functions. The communists, for example, were notably skilled in their political organisation and use of propaganda, alongside vital links to securing aid from the Soviet Union. Consequently, the Spanish communists came to wield a dominant influence in the Republican government during the civil war. Leading communist activists would subsequently play a significant role in organising the government of the Second Republic amid an atmosphere of crisis in responding to the Nationalist uprising, particularly in terms of defending Madrid in the autumn of 1936. The trades unions played an equally important role, functioning as the executive organ of Madrid and ensuring the efficient flow of food supplies and essential public services. For example, the large unions, including the UGT, played a prominent role in ensuring the regular supply of goods and produce to the population of Madrid, as well as to some outlying Republican-controlled regions. This was an impressive achievement given that in Madrid only 30 percent of industries were **collectivised**, making the co-ordination of different businesses and industries more challenging as a result.

The co-ordinating role of government and trades unions was particularly important in larger cities like Madrid, where there were problems with some prominent civil servants not always being willing to co-operate and support the Republican war effort. This was due to the more socially conservative and affluent background of many senior civil servants, which made them broadly unsympathetic to the Republicans' cause. In other towns and cities within Republican-controlled zones, communist-inspired collective organisations and bodies that focused on sharing produce and resources were a common feature of civic life. These groups provided an alternative means of maintaining some degree of stable political leadership for ordinary people amid the disruption to normal systems of government caused by the conflict.

In early September 1936, the increasingly left-wing Socialist Party leader Francisco Largo Caballero emerged as the country's new prime minister. His experience of holding political office had been a key factor in him taking on this role. The more liberal-inclined President Azaña was opposed to communists and extremists holding office, but the new prime minister ignored this and appointed two communist ministers who only accepted their posts after making contact with Moscow. Significantly, Caballero had also invited his former rivals, the anarchists, to join his government in order to widen the coalition and broaden the range of anti-Nationalist groups that were involved. However, despite these appointments and his left-wing pronunciations, Caballero did not enjoy the clear and undivided loyalty of the various extremist elements of republicanism.

EXTEND YOUR KNOWLEDGE

Francisco Largo Caballero (1869–1946)

Caballero, Socialist Party leader since the mid-1920s, had a background within the trade union movement, particularly the powerful UGT. He was a key supporter of the establishment of the Second Republic in 1931, but following its political difficulties his views shifted towards a more radical left-wing position. This saw him gradually abandoning support for constitutional politics in favour of a more revolutionary and violent approach. The growing extremism of Caballero and his supporters caused divisions in the government of the Popular Front during the civil war, particularly when he served as prime minister between September 1936 and May 1937. He was eventually replaced by the more moderate figure of Juan Negrín y López.

While the more traditional and moderate left-wing factions saw the need to maintain constitutional government and to organise their troops in a similarly disciplined way to the Nationalist military forces, more radical groups such as the anarchists progressively came to reject this approach. They favoured instead the use of decentralised militia bodies and revolutionary volunteers that were not always directly controlled from the central government. Although the Republican regime did formally create a **Popular Army** on 30 September 1936, the absence of a clear and united leadership structure, alongside a lack of clarity and co-ordination when it came to overall military strategy, clearly weakened and undermined the efforts of its armed forces.

KEY TERM

Popular Army
The name of the official army of the Popular Front government, which was the main fighting force of the Republicans during the Spanish Civil War.

ACTIVITY
KNOWLEDGE CHECK

1 Create a table to compare the Nationalists and Republicans in terms of their leadership, support and military strengths at the start of the civil war in Spain.

2 Use your table to reach a judgement as to which side seemed to be stronger at the outbreak of the war. Explain your answer.

The geographical division of Spain in 1936

Within a week of the civil war starting, the country had the appearance of a patchwork quilt of divided political authority (see Figure 2.1). This reflected the fragmented and fractured nature of Spain at this time. The Republicans initially controlled most major towns and urban areas where industries were based. The Basque and Catalonian regions in the north and north east also remained firmly loyal to the Republicans, who had granted them regional autonomy (see page 295). The Nationalists, however, controlled extensive rural areas that produced the agricultural goods and raw materials that the cities required for food and industry. The bulk of Andalusia in the south was also aligned with the Nationalists and close to Morocco, in Africa, from where the Nationalist Army of Africa invaded (see page 307).

The regional divisions of Spain generally worked to strengthen the existing class disunity between socialists and conservatives. The Republicans were supported by urban-based industrial workers, trades unionists and middle-class educated liberals, while the Nationalists were supported by wealthy landowners, religious groups and the more prosperous suburban middle classes. In geographical terms, from the earliest stages of the war much of the centre and north east of Spain was firmly held by the Republicans, while the Nationalists swiftly made inroads into the south east and north west of the country.

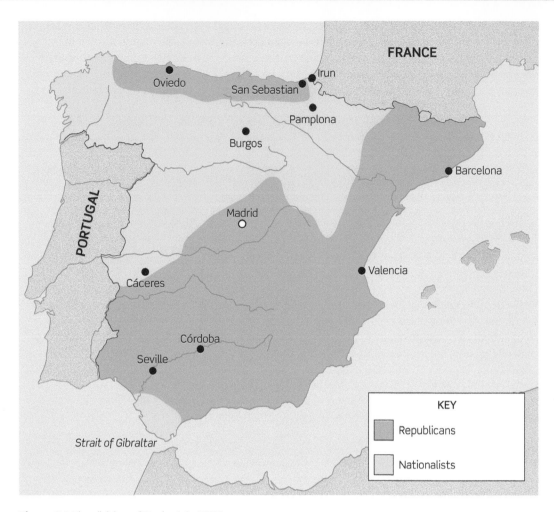

Figure 2.1 The division of Spain, July 1936.

The significance of the international response

The initial failure of the Nationalists to seize the levers of power gave the Republican government some confidence in its ability to suppress and defeat this military-led uprising in the long term. However, various international developments were to undermine that belief.

EXTRACT

1 From James Joll, *Europe since 1870: An International History*, 1990. Here, Joll summarises the scale and impact of international developments, suggesting that the conflict in Spain was something of an inevitable prelude to a much wider European war.

At the outset… the Spanish government believed that they could crush the rising providing Franco did not receive assistance from outside… Within weeks, however, it was plain that both Italy and Germany were giving substantial help to Franco, while the Soviet Union responded by sending supplies and advisers to the Republicans… The intensification of the civil war in Spain by foreign intervention had political and emotional repercussions which affected Europe. It was widely believed that the confrontation in Spain between Germany and Italy on the one hand and the Soviet Union on the other was the first round of a worldwide struggle between communism and fascism. Both Hitler and Stalin gave encouragement to this view by publicly basing their foreign policy on ideological principles.

Republican hopes for a quick victory were frustrated by the fact that the Nationalist rebels were aided from an early stage of the conflict by military and financial support from sympathetic European leaders, namely Hitler in Germany and Mussolini in Italy. Both men presided over right-wing, nationalistic regimes and had been contacted via Franco's network of political connections. Hitler in particular placed great initial faith in Franco and provided him with transport planes to airlift the marooned Nationalist forces in northern Africa to the mainland throughout late July and early August. Meanwhile, Italy provided air cover for ships transporting nationalist troops from Morocco to Spain. This development ultimately provided the Nationalists with some significant military impetus, however it represented a major setback to the Republicans.

In August 1936, a formal Non-Intervention Pact was signed by 24 European nations (27 nations in total, including the USA) due to fears that the conflict in Spain could escalate and drag other countries into it. However, while some nations adhered to this pact, such as Britain and France, others clearly did not, and it effectively created conditions for a **proxy war** with rival countries funding and supporting different sides in Spain. Germany and Italy had both signed the pact, but each ignored it from the earliest stages of the conflict. That both these nations had political sympathies with the Spanish Nationalists and their own regimes were increasingly viewed by many contemporary observers as being fascist in nature was a significant factor in other international involvements, such as that of the Soviet Union, in the Spanish Civil War.

The involvement of the Soviet Union was a consistent element throughout the civil war. Its role was often crucial in providing aid to Republican forces while spreading fear among Nationalists about the further encroachment of communism into Spain. The Soviet leader Joseph Stalin argued that in extreme situations such as Spain in the mid-1930s, communist parties should work alongside left-wing parliamentary parties in a bid to prevent the spread of fascism. In October 1936, therefore, the first substantial military aid from the Soviet Union arrived to support the Republican government (the Soviet Union had previously provided humanitarian aid), notably in the form of aircraft and tanks. This, along with the determined resistance of Madrid in the face of Nationalist forces in the autumn of 1936, provided a major boost to Republican morale, while ensuring that vital routes into the city remained open and that key supplies could continue to be provided to Republican forces and the city's besieged citizens.

Further foreign intervention, in the form of the International Brigades (volunteers from different countries), arrived to support the government of the Second Republic and the Madrid-based **People's Defence** from autumn 1936 onwards. The International Brigades significantly enhanced the military capacity of the Popular Front to defend Madrid and confirmed that the Republicans could also access foreign backing and intervention in support of their cause. The Republicans could now count on 23,000 troops in and around Madrid compared with the Nationalists' 8,000, a factor significantly in their favour. Their greater numbers of civilian and irregular soldiers enhanced their ability to fight guerrilla-style urban warfare.

EXTEND YOUR KNOWLEDGE

International Brigades
The International Brigades emerged in response to the assistance given to Franco from fascist leaders (Hitler and Mussolini), confirming the suspicions of many on the political left across Europe that Franco himself had fascist tendencies. These brigades were therefore left wing in their politics and were organised by the Comintern, the Soviet-based body that co-ordinated and promoted international communism. They began to arrive in the autumn of 1936 and subsequently provided vital manpower to the Republicans from an early stage of the war and boosted their military capacity considerably.

Most members of the brigades were left-wing idealists who were volunteers prepared to sacrifice their lives if necessary to save the Spanish Republic and prevent the spread of fascism. The vast majority held strong socialist or communist views. One of the most well-known figures involved in this movement was the writer George Orwell, who used his experiences in reporting on the war when writing *Homage to Catalonia* (1938).

It has been estimated that during the course of the war between 35,000 and 40,000 people joined the International Brigades, although there were never more than 16,000 at any one time. Of their number, almost 3,000 came from the USA, 2,000 from Great Britain and 9,000 from France, with a range of other European nations providing the bulk of the remainder (of an estimated 53 national groupings in total). The major problem faced by such groups was that while the volunteer recruits were brave, idealistic and ideologically motivated, they were not all professional soldiers, were often under-equipped and were therefore at a disadvantage when facing the more experienced armies of Franco in military battle. In this context, their impact on the outcome of the war was fairly limited, although it did raise Republican morale and boosted their levels of resistance.

KEY TERMS

Proxy war
A war fought by combatants that are supported by other external agents (often more powerful), and who are fighting on behalf of such outside interests.

People's Defence
A civilian-based army whose principal aim was to defend Madrid and the Second Republic from the Nationalist insurgency.

The situation by the end of August 1936

By early August 1936, Franco's Army of Africa had reached the Spanish mainland and was steadily advancing from the south (see Figure 2.2). By 14 August, the Nationalists had taken control of Badajoz, triggering a wave of terror and counter-terror following the so-called 'Massacre of Reds', where between 650 and 1,300 Republican soldiers and civilians were killed by Franco's troops.

Mola's forces, meanwhile, were making some initial inroads into Republican areas from their location in the north. The Nationalists' immediate priority was to maintain the momentum of the military-led uprising of July 1936. To this end, they had quickly organised conscription to boost their numbers. In international terms, France had closed its borders and Britain had banned the export of arms as part of the Non-Intervention Pact. However, this was of little concern to the Nationalists as they had already cultivated alternative supply lines with Italy and Germany, who would continue to support them in a variety of ways as the war developed.

In contrast, the Republicans found themselves in a more defensive position by the end of August 1936. Given that most of the larger towns and cities were under Republican control, the government's immediate aim was to maintain control of these urban areas and prevent the insurgency spreading further across the country. These Republican-controlled zones would swiftly come under intense pressure from the advancing Nationalist forces.

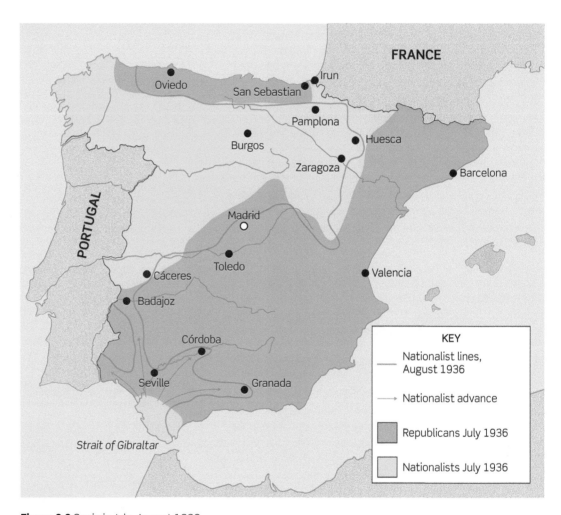

Figure 2.2 Spain in July–August 1936.

ACTIVITY
KNOWLEDGE CHECK

1   To what extent did foreign intervention influence the strength of the Nationalist and Republican forces at the start of the Spanish Civil War?

2   Explain the difficulties faced by both sides of the war in dealing with how Spain was geographically divided by August 1936.

WHAT WAS THE NATURE AND IMPACT OF THE COURSE OF THE WAR IN SPAIN IN THE YEARS 1936–39?

The main campaigns and the stages of the Nationalist advance

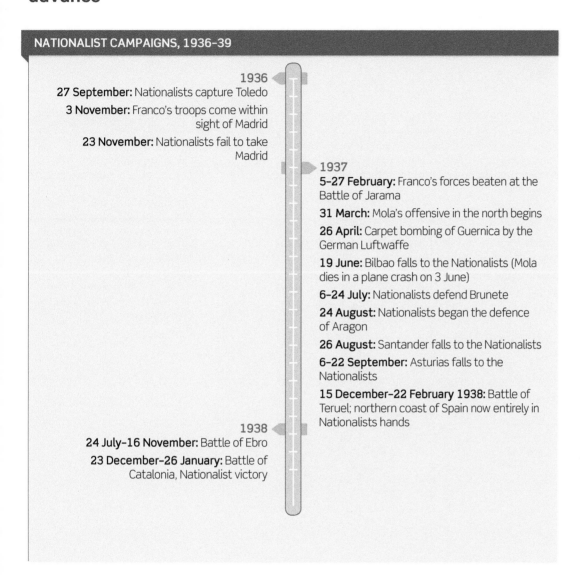

NATIONALIST CAMPAIGNS, 1936–39

1936
27 September: Nationalists capture Toledo
3 November: Franco's troops come within sight of Madrid
23 November: Nationalists fail to take Madrid

1937
5–27 February: Franco's forces beaten at the Battle of Jarama
31 March: Mola's offensive in the north begins
26 April: Carpet bombing of Guernica by the German Luftwaffe
19 June: Bilbao falls to the Nationalists (Mola dies in a plane crash on 3 June)
6–24 July: Nationalists defend Brunete
24 August: Nationalists began the defence of Aragon
26 August: Santander falls to the Nationalists
6–22 September: Asturias falls to the Nationalists
15 December–22 February 1938: Battle of Teruel; northern coast of Spain now entirely in Nationalists hands

1938
24 July–16 November: Battle of Ebro
23 December–26 January: Battle of Catalonia, Nationalist victory

Stage one: September 1936–March 1937

By the end of September, the Nationalists had taken Toledo in the south west of Madrid and Irun in the Basque region, while also linking up with Mola's northern-based troops. Nationalist forces now formed an arc of influence to the north, west and south of Madrid. They had also taken control of access to the French border close to the Pyrenees, isolating the pro-Republican Basque region from any prospect of aid arriving from France (see Figure 2.3 on page 318). This rapid absorption of territory led many to believe that the capture of Madrid would quickly follow, particularly as Mola's forces were also advancing on the capital from the north. Madrid eventually came into range of Nationalist forces by early November. However, due to logistical problems and internal strategic disagreements, the Nationalists failed to build on their momentum and the capital stood firm under Republican control. Madrid's position remained highly vulnerable and under pressure, leading to the Republican government moving from Madrid to Valencia in early November 1936. Valencia was a more secure stronghold at this stage, as the seizure of Madrid was now the main symbolic focus of the war; whoever held the traditional seat of government could claim a stronger sense of authority over the divided nation.

The successful Republican defence of Madrid during 1936 created a tense stalemate in the surrounding areas. As the main Nationalist forces were diverted to other areas, such as Toledo, to relieve the forces under siege there, Mola was left to co-ordinate the continued assault on the capital and the disruption of its supply routes. Mola's tactics appeared to be ineffective in the face of the entrenched opposition, and some historians have suggested that Franco was happy for Mola to lead the Madrid campaign at this point, as he realised the major difficulties involved in taking the city. By early 1937, realising that the capture of the Spanish capital was still beyond the reach of their armies, Nationalist military strategists decided that they would try to place the city under a sustained siege.

EXTRACT

2   From Paul Preston, *Franco*, 1995.

> He [Franco] seems to have taken less direct interest in the campaign for Madrid. It was not until 20th October [1936] that he seemed to wake up to the extent to which the capital was being strengthened and issued the order to 'concentrate maximum attention and available combat forces on the fronts around Madrid'. Indeed, his absence from the operations to take Madrid, and from the subsequent Nationalist chronicles thereof, was quite remarkable. Perhaps Franco suspected that there was little easy glory to be won and thus slyly left Mola to take responsibility.

In February 1937, Franco's forces were beaten at Jarama. There was better news from the south, where pro-Nationalist Italian **blackshirts** took the city of Malaga. In March, however, the Italian blackshirts were comprehensively defeated at Guadalajara. These 'unofficial' Italian militia forces had arrived in the southern port of Cadiz at the end of 1936 and were quickly absorbed into the military fray, with the vast majority being voluntary soldiers who were guided and led by a small number of regular officers from the Italian army. This led to some questions being raised about their

KEY TERM

Blackshirts
The name given to a body of fascist militia or paramilitaries who originated from Italy in the years after the First World War. The Italian leader Benito Mussolini was involved in the group's establishment, and its brigades fought in both Italy and abroad. The name of the group derived from the colour of the military-style outfits that members wore.

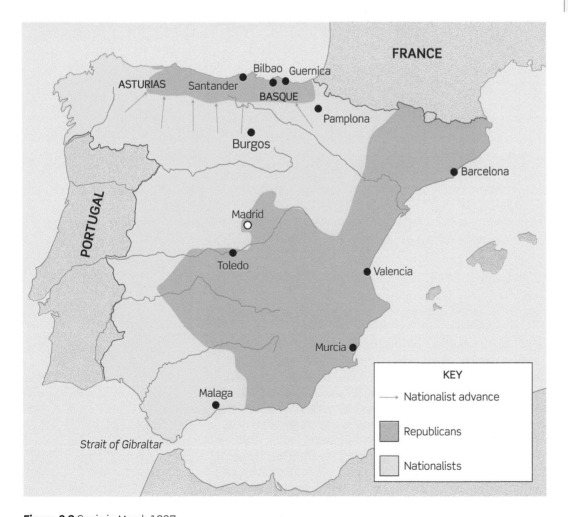

Figure 2.3 Spain in March 1937.

effectiveness and military skills, particularly in comparison with the largely professional Spanish army under Franco. However, their numbers were of use to the Nationalist forces in assisting with the military progress and territorial gains they made throughout 1937. The Italian blackshirts were often referred to as the 'Italian Corps' or the *Corpo Truppe Volontarie*. During the civil war, an estimated 75,000 Italian volunteers served alongside the Spanish Nationalist forces.

Stage two: April–June 1937

The Nationalist encroachment into northern Spain resulted in one of the worst atrocities of the entire war, when the town of Guernica in the Basque region was **carpet bombed** by the German air force (known as the *Luftwaffe*). On 26 April 1937, the well-equipped and sizeable Condor Legion of the *Luftwaffe* targeted the town in a bid to break resistance to the Nationalist military advances. Although Guernica was some 30 km behind the front line, it did have some strategic value and was a communications centre for Republican forces. Some German commanders later claimed that the bombing was an error due to inexperienced pilots and inaccurate targeting, but various historians and contemporary observers have concluded that the attack was a deliberate attempt to bomb the town into submission. Whatever the motives, the outcome was devastating. Over 40 tonnes of high explosive bombs were dropped in just three hours, while those who tried to escape were shot by a further aerial bombardment.

The bombing seemed to be aimed at destroying the morale of the local civilians, with the most populated parts of the town deliberately targeted. With a population of just 7,000, hundreds were injured while estimates of those killed have ranged between 126 and almost 1,700 (depending on which side of the conflict was responsible for the figures). Nationalists initially denied any responsibility and claimed that retreating Republicans had caused the carnage. This was ultimately untrue. What is without doubt, however, is that the town was virtually annihilated and images of Guernica have subsequently been viewed as an iconic symbol of this destructive conflict (see Source 2). The community was devastated and it left a lasting legacy of bitterness among the surviving inhabitants of this city towards the Nationalist forces, with many accusing the Franco regime of 'covering up' this notorious event in later years.

SOURCE

Following the carpet bombing of Guernica on 26 April 1937 by the Condor Legion of the German *Luftwaffe*, the town was left in ruins. Most of the victims were innocent farmworkers and their families. Here, Nationalist troops are clearing rubble from the destroyed buildings.

KEY TERM

Carpet bombing
This term refers to heavy and steady saturation bombing of a location from the air, with the aim of causing maximum destruction to an entire area (town or city) over a short period of time. It usually involves targeting a broad and imprecise geographical area and tends to result in heavy civilian casualties.

EXTRACT 3

From Antony Beevor, *The Battle for Spain: The Spanish Civil War, 1936–1939*, 2006. Here, Beevor highlights the overall significance for the war of the Nationalists' attack on Guernica.

The most emotive issue in warfare is that of atrocities. It is nearly always the most visually horrific of them which become fixed in the imagination. Spain witnessed many during its civil war… [but] not until the bombing of Guernica in April 1937 did the battle for world opinion really change in the Republic's favour, but by then the republicans were already losing the war.

There was widespread international condemnation of this atrocity. Republicans subsequently gained a great deal of global sympathy as a result and this accelerated demands for international intervention on their behalf. In this sense, it was an ill-judged tactical move by the Nationalists. However, the Republicans were by this stage in retreat and under severe pressure from the superior Nationalist forces with their more advanced military capabilities.

Mola's troops began a military offensive against the Basque province, and the key Basque city of Bilbao, to the west of Guernica, fell in June 1937. The Nationalists' aim was to gain control of key industrial northern areas, which would provide them with the capacity to control north west Spain's valuable iron and coal resources as part of the long-term strategy of disrupting the flow of supplies to Madrid. However, Mola died in a plane crash that same month, leaving Franco as the pre-eminent leader of the Nationalist cause.

Stage three: July–December 1937

Given the series of setbacks in the north, forces from Republican-controlled territory in the south attempted to launch a military counter-attack to restrict further Nationalist progress and to ease some of the pressures being inflicted on their comrades' positions around Madrid. On 6 July 1937, a Republican army of 80,000 men attacked Brunete to the south east of Madrid. In a battle that lasted almost three weeks (until 25 July), the Republican Popular Army made limited progress in the face of the embedded Nationalist troops, taking only about 5 km of additional territory while losing approximately 25,000 soldiers (many from the International Brigades), as well as a significant amount of vital military equipment. By comparison, the Nationalists suffered about 10,000 deaths over the course of the battle, but managed to retain most of the territory that their opponents were trying to gain.

As 1937 progressed, the northern city of Santander (in August) along with the Asturias province (September) were seized during the renewed advance of Franco's forces. By the end of 1937, the Battle of Teruel, in the north eastern province of Aragon, was underway. By mid-December, the scale of the Nationalist gains in the north indicated the direction that the conflict was steadily heading in, with 62 percent of Spanish territory and over half of the population now under the control of Franco's forces. However, the advance to this stage had not been as rapid as Franco and other generals would have liked, with the capital city still under siege but in Republican hands, and Nationalist troops bogged down in a variety of small-scale battles across the country.

Stage four: January–March 1938

The year 1938 began in a similar vein to how 1937 ended for the Republicans, with a Nationalist resurgence driving their forces back towards its southern coastal strongholds. The Battle of Teruel had by February been won by the Nationalists. Having taken control of this strategically important north eastern town, Franco's forces now controlled the country's entire north coast, which was a damaging blow to their Republican opponents. By this stage of the conflict, it was becoming clear that the Republicans could not win the civil war, as it would be impossible to reclaim the large swathes of Spain now in the firm grip of the Nationalists and their European allies. They were also significantly outnumbered in terms of military forces and equipment, with the Nationalists having 600,000 soldiers to the Republicans 400,000, and Franco's forces were generally also in better condition. The main challenge for the Republican Popular Front government would therefore be to hold on to its diminishing areas of geographical authority, which now largely covered just a western strip of the country.

However, the Republicans continued to display resilience against the increasingly dominant Nationalist position. In March 1938, they launched a further offensive in the fiercely contested Aragon region in the north east. In a pattern similar to previous initiatives, this was met with some initial Republican success, as they moved towards their existing stronghold of Valencia on the Mediterranean coast by forcing back Nationalist positions and cutting part of the Nationalist zone in two in the process. However, they found themselves under immense pressure to the north as Italian planes launched an intensive bombardment of Republican-held Barcelona between 16 and 18 March, flying in from bases in Majorca. This stretched Republican resources and placed them back on the defensive in terms of keeping control of land that they currently held, with the Nationalists now embarking on a full-scale counter-attack towards the Mediterranean coast (see Figure 2.4).

Stage five: April–November 1938

By mid-April 1938, Nationalist troops had turned the tide in this campaign, with the first of their number reaching the Mediterranean shoreline between the Republican bastions of Barcelona and Valencia. Valencia was also subject to regular bombardment from Italian planes based on the island of Majorca.

Given this ongoing Nationalist encroachment into Republican-held territory, the Republicans had little option but to try to divert the Nationalist armies away from besieged Valencia. With this aim, on 24 July a large Popular Army of up to 100,000 soldiers crossed the River Ebro into Nationalist-held territory. The Battle of Ebro initially began well for the Republicans, with the opening attack effectively co-ordinated and organised by their commanders. Nationalist forces were taken by surprise and the Republicans were boosted by this initial military success. For a brief period in mid-1938, the Republican leadership believed they could reclaim significant territory, while hoping that an improved military showing would encourage other European nations such as France and Britain to explicitly support them. Republican hopes for further intervention at this time were high, as Hitler's attempts to invade Czechoslovakia at the same time had heightened tensions across the Continent and re-ignited fears among the European

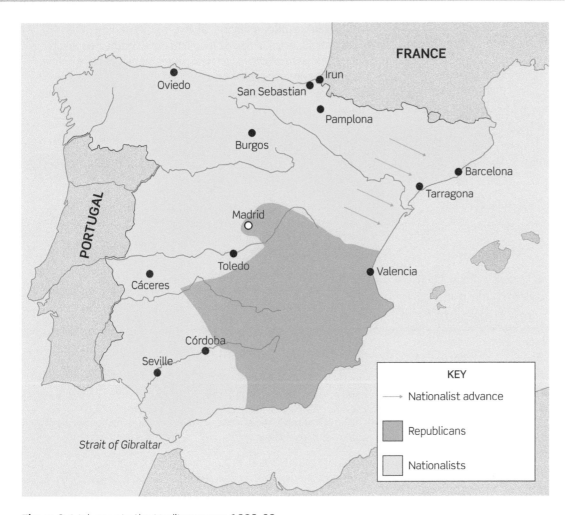

Figure 2.4 Advance to the Mediterranean, 1938–39,

left about the need to proactively address the further spread of fascism and the potential for a wider Europe-wide war erupting.

However, at Ebro, Franco swiftly reorganised his forces and displayed his superior military skills with an effective counter-attack. Franco needed to ensure a Nationalist victory so that Republican morale would be irrevocably broken. In a protracted battle, Republican troops gradually ran out of resources and supplies and succumbed to Franco's new tactics of sending aircraft in advance to bomb enemy positions, while also covering Nationalist tank and infantry forces. His ground troops would then engage with what was left of the Republican army units. This effective tactic forced the Republicans back to their original position. By 15 November, they were in full retreat with the Battle of Ebro definitively won by Franco's army.

Stage six: December 1938–January 1939

As 1938 neared an end, the Republicans had been pushed back even further and found their western zone now spilt in two, with Barcelona and the Catalan region in the north east being cut off from the rest of Republican-held territory. The departure of the International Brigades in November had been an ominous sign as far as the Republicans' prospects were concerned, although the casualty and desertion rates of these forces had steadily grown throughout the war. They officially left as a consequence of Prime Minister Negrín's attempts to achieve the full support of Britain and France in the conflict, as it was felt that the International Brigades were preventing larger European nations potentially getting involved on the Republicans' side. The legitimacy of such unofficial armies had raised concerns from other European nations, particularly when they resulted in injury and death to their citizens within the brigades. Despite ongoing efforts to bolster the Republican position with international support, by 15 January 1939 the city of Tarragona had been overpowered and brought under Nationalist authority. This opened a direct path towards the big prize of Barcelona, the provincial capital of Catalonia and a hotbed of Republican strength and activity.

ACTIVITY
KNOWLEDGE CHECK

1 Refer to the timeline showing the Nationalist campaigns, 1936–39. Choose three campaigns that you feel were key turning points for the Nationalists. Explain your choices.

2 Compare Figures 2.2 (page 316) and 2.4 (page 321). Explain why the Nationalist advance across Spain was so successful between August 1936 and January 1939.

The impact of Republican political divisions

Internal tensions within the Popular Front government undermined Republican co-operation throughout the civil war and on occasion even exploded into street battles between different left-wing factions. In particular, the **Trotskyite** Workers' Party (POUM) became increasingly disenchanted with the policies and strategy of the government (regardless of war conditions), and demanded greater revolutionary activity originating from the working classes. Radical elements of the Popular Front would continue to be disappointed by its political agenda, particularly when in May 1937 the left-wing socialist Largo Caballero was replaced by the more moderate socialist Juan Negrín López as prime minister of the Second Republic, although he did secure some notable communist support in order to gain this position. The change in leadership was a direct consequence of disagreements over military strategy. Caballero had opposed the communists' plans for the Republican offensive at Brunete. He was also accused of allowing too much independent activity by extreme communist and anarchist groups, particularly within the city of Barcelona, which was crippled by social tensions. He therefore lost his job.

EXTEND YOUR KNOWLEDGE

Juan Negrín López (1894–1956)

Juan Negrín López succeeded Largo Caballero as prime minister of the Spanish Second Republic in May 1937, at the height of the civil war. He assumed the role with a reputation as someone who would bring a greater amount of centralised control to the Republican war strategy, particularly given the growing splits and divisions between the different factions of the Popular Front. Viewed as having more moderate politics than his immediate predecessor, he nevertheless relied on support from the communists and they formed a key part of his government. However, his period in office was a difficult one and he failed to stem the tide of Nationalist progress across Spain. His attempts to negotiate a settlement with Franco also resulted in failure. He fled the country during the final weeks of the war in March 1939, having been faced with growing opposition from some Republican elements. He died in exile in France.

Negrín sought to assert greater centralised control over all Republican activity. Within a month of his accession to office, his new leadership regime outlawed POUM. POUM's leader, Andreu Nin, was viewed by some Republican supporters as a destabilising force on the political left. On 21 June, Nin was murdered by Soviet agents who were acting on Moscow's instructions to support the Negrín administration as the best chance to prevent a Nationalist

victory. Nin's murder reflected the evolving political agenda of the international body of communism, the **Comintern**, which in the past had advocated purely revolutionary means of action, but which now supported constitutional politics. Nin's death also highlighted the growing state of disunity and division within Spanish left-wing groups and senior Republican ranks, which wartime losses were exacerbating.

KEY TERMS

Trotskyite
A faction of communist ideology influenced by the Russian revolutionary Leon Trotsky (1879–1940) who argued for a 'worldwide revolution' that should be exported from country to country. However, Trotsky's specific interpretation of this ideology was viewed negatively by the communist establishment based in Moscow, and the Trotskyite viewpoint was generally seen as one of the more radical versions of communism. It certainly influenced some prominent left-wing and Marxist groups in Spain during the 1930s, notably POUM (Workers' Party).

Comintern
Also known as the 'Communist International', this group was established by the Soviet Union in 1919 after the country's successful revolution. Its aim was to promote the spread of communist revolutionary activity on an international basis, but during the Spanish Civil War it modified its position and supported left-wing parliamentary parties against fascism. It was influential in organising the International Brigades.

The Soviet influence aimed to steer the Republican forces in a more co-ordinated direction. They, along with the middle-class liberals and socialists, called for the use of a disciplined, centralised and traditional army as the way to defeat the Nationalist forces, while the anarchists and POUM favoured militias and irregular armies. Both kinds of armies fought against the Nationalists, but they also fought against each other. In May 1937, for example, communist and government forces clashed against anarchist CNT and the Trotskyite POUM at the Barcelona telephone exchange. Government forces ultimately prevailed, with POUM leaders executed by communists in June 1937. In August, the Popular Army moved into Aragon and crushed another rival left-wing grouping known as the Peasants' Council. In his book *Homage to Catalonia*, the novelist George Orwell claims that this repression of various workers' groups was a key factor in the eventual defeat of the Republicans during the civil war, and was particularly significant in the fall of Barcelona in early 1939. Orwell argued that many of these left-wing groups wanted to fight for the values of revolution and in opposition to the 1936 uprising, but not in the name of a repressive Republican government. This tension within republicanism went to the heart of the divisions endured by its various supporters and groupings during the civil war.

As Spain's bitter conflict drew to its conclusion, further Republican divisions erupted in the besieged capital city of Madrid, where elements of the left-wing Popular Army were dismayed by the ongoing communist influence over Negrín. Some Republican commanders felt that this rather hardline ideological influence was preventing a negotiated settlement to the conflict. At the beginning of March 1939, the leader of the Popular Army, General Casado, launched an attempted coup to overthrow

Negrín. Casado was officially dismissed from his military position, but the coup continued. Casado's ultimate aim was to weaken the communist grip on the Popular Front government. To this end, Casado and his supporters arrested various communist figures within Negrín's administration. During the course of the Spanish Civil War, therefore, the Republican government was not only fighting the Nationalists, but also the radicals in its own territory.

The impact of atrocities by both sides

From the earliest stages of the war there were many atrocities committed against ordinary Spanish citizens by both Nationalists and Republicans. The majority of the victims were not directly involved as combatants but were merely caught in the crossfire of this ideological conflict. The innocent farm workers and their families at Guernica (see page 319) represent just one example. Militant Republican militias pursued a class-based agenda by inflicting various atrocities on middle-class Nationalist supporters and religious figures and buildings, driven by what they felt were in the best interests of the proletariat. Likewise, the right-wing conservative Nationalists viewed the working-class and trade union activists as revolutionary extremists. They were rounded up and imprisoned or executed by the more extremist Nationalists in a similarly ruthless fashion. The atrocities and extreme methods of dealing with perceived opponents left many of the Spanish civilians living in a constant state of fear (see, for example, the massacre at Badajoz). No one and nowhere was safe from potential persecution. In fact, within areas won by the Nationalists, former Republicans and trades unionists joined the Falange as a way of showing their loyalty to the new regime and avoiding execution.

The countless atrocities had devastating social, economic, human and political repercussions, impacting not only on those directly involved in the war, but also scarring the collective conscience of Spanish civilians that would remain for many years. The extreme nature of Republican and Nationalist activities deepened the divisions and ill feeling between both sides, and would leave a lasting legacy of bitterness across Spain, undermining attempts to create a more unified nation once the civil war was over. The impact was felt internationally, too. The persecution of priests and burning of religious buildings persuaded the Vatican and the wider Catholic community to side with the Nationalists, and gave the British a reason to refuse the Republicans their support.

The atrocities significantly inflated the casualty rate for the civil war. This figure was originally estimated as approximately one million deaths during the conflict, including a large number of civilians not directly involved in the fighting. The total figure has since been revised to nearer the half million mark, to include those killed by starvation, malnutrition and disease caused by conditions brought on by the war. The final total of all casualties is probably more realistically somewhere between the two.

A cartoon by Bernard Partridge, published in the British satirical magazine *Punch* in March 1937. The caption reads 'To Lovers of Spain. Wherever the guilt may lie, *these* at least have done no wrong.' Distraught women and children are huddling together in the ruins of a bombed-out house.

TO LOVERS OF SPAIN
WHEREVER THE GUILT MAY LIE, *THESE* AT LEAST HAVE DONE NO WRONG.

The fall of Barcelona and Madrid in 1939

By early 1938, Madrid remained under siege, facing potential famine in places and with frequent aerial bombardments. The novelist Ernest Hemingway wrote *For Whom the Bells Tolls* (1940) about a young American attached to the Republican International Brigades. As a resident of Madrid at this time, he recalls his hotel being hit over 30 times by Nationalist shells and missiles. Literary works by the likes of Hemingway and Orwell, and the artist Pablo Picasso's famous painting *Guernica* (1937), are all examples of artistic expression that gained creative inspiration from personal experiences of the Spanish Civil War. They have each contributed to a lasting impression of the broader understanding of this conflict.

On 23 December 1938, the Nationalist advance into Catalonia commenced, Franco's goal being the Mediterranean coast and the city of Barcelona (see Figure 2.4 on page 321). Unlike many previous battles, the Republicans offered very little resistance as Franco sought to secure the final part of northern Spain that had so far eluded him. Up to 200,000 Republicans were subsequently taken prisoner (a testimony to this lack of opposition) and large amounts of military equipment were abandoned, suggesting a rapid loss of Republican morale and a quick surrender in various locations. Barcelona eventually fell on 26 January 1939, after further heavy bombardment from Nationalist positions.

SOURCE

4 From George Orwell, *Homage to Catalonia*, 1938. Orwell was a British writer who volunteered to serve in the International Brigades in support of the Republicans. Here, he highlights the growing fears of the Republican forces in Catalonia towards the end of 1938.

In Barcelona, during all those last weeks I spent there, there was peculiar evil feeling in the air – an atmosphere of suspicion, fear, uncertainty and veiled hatred... [with fears that] a certain party [the communists] were plotting a coup d'etat [seizure of power]. There was also a widespread fear that Catalonia was going to be invaded. Earlier, when we went back to the front, I had seen the powerful defences that were being constructed scores of miles behind the front line, and fresh bomb-proof shelters were being dug all over Barcelona. There were frequent scares of air-raids and sea-raids; more often than not those were false alarms, but every time the sirens blew, the lights all over the town blacked out for hours on end and timid people dived for the cellars. Police spies were everywhere.

Many Republican figures and supporters swiftly fled in panic towards the French border and into exile, knowing that Nationalist troops displayed little mercy to those whom they encountered in battles or subsequently captured. President Azaña fled to France after escaping through the Pyrenees. His departure left little doubt that the end was close for the Republicans and the government of the Popular Front. On 1 February, Negrín held a symbolic final meeting of the Constituent Cortes to indicate defiantly to his opponents that normal political proceedings were continuing, yet it had a much depleted attendance due to the ongoing collapse of the governing regime. The spoils of military success were enjoyed with enthusiasm by the Nationalists, and they were swift to assert their newly found authority on the captured Republican zones. Barcelona faced inevitable reprisals, with Catalan autonomy immediately rescinded, and the Catalan tongue swiftly banned as the province's official language.

The Nationalists then moved south, turning their attention to the remaining areas of resistance. Valencia finally succumbed to a sustained period of heavy bombardment at the end of March 1939, with thousands of its citizens killed or injured by the frenzied Nationalist onslaught. At the same time as Valencia's defences were crumbling in the west, so too was the symbolic capital of Madrid, which saw Nationalist soldiers breaching its territory. They were aided by ongoing Republican in-fighting, provoked by Negrín's increasingly dictatorial powers that he justified as a desperate means of retaining some kind of grip on political power, but which angered others within the government. By the time Franco's forces launched their final push on Madrid on 26 March, many of the Republican troops had either fled or surrendered, including Negrín, his various Soviet military advisors and General Casado (leader of the Popular Army). The levels of resistance were minimal by comparison with previous

occasions when Nationalist forces had attacked Madrid. By 27 March, Franco's troops had entered and secured much of Spain's capital city. This was a symbolic and decisive moment in the war's duration.

There were last-ditch attempts by the remaining Republican leaders to strike a deal to resolve the conflict peacefully. The Nationalist leadership, however, rejected such a proposal. On 1 April 1939, Franco declared outright victory proclaiming 'Today, the Red Army captured and disarmed, the national troops have achieved their final military objectives. The war is over.' Although the war officially came to an end, pockets of die-hard Republican resistance continued.

ACTIVITY
KNOWLEDGE CHECK

1 Draw a spider diagram detailing the social, economic, human and political impacts of the atrocities committed during the civil war on the ordinary people of Spain.

2 Summarise the main reasons why the Spanish Civil War lasted for as long as it did.

AS Level Exam-Style Question Section B

To what extent was Franco's superior leadership the main reason for the Nationalists' eventual success in the Spanish Civil War? (20 marks)

Tip
The question requires you to consider a range of factors and weigh up their relevant importance. What were the key reasons that determined why the Nationalists were ultimately victorious in 1939? Was Franco's leadership the most important factor?

HOW SIGNIFICANT WAS THE IMPACT OF THE CIVIL WAR ON ORDINARY SPANISH CITIZENS?

The variety of experiences in the Republican zones

There was arguably a greater variety of social and economic conditions within Republican-controlled zones given the differing political groups (socialists, communists or anarchists) that controlled different areas. The Republicans in Madrid, for example, organised a war economy with key industries and factories brought under direct government control, with the aim of improving the co-ordination of the Republican war effort. Certain types of employment were also run collectively by the state, including factory work, industrial production and public/government services. Under this state direction, their focus was now primarily on maintaining the war effort and the production of key wartime supplies.

In the more radical Republican region of Catalonia, an estimated 70 percent of Barcelona's industry was collectivised (owned and run by the people). These collectivised bodies represented something of an economic revolution, offering a radical alternative to the more explicit profit motives of capitalist big businesses. This type of system encouraged the greater involvement of ordinary citizens in the key decisions of the workplace, specifically in relation to determining their wages and working conditions, with vouchers used instead of conventional money in some locations. Workers' committees therefore became powerful bodies in these collectivised working environments. Former owners and employers who refused to co-operate were known to have been executed by anarchists. As well as benefiting the workers, the system ensured a regular flow of vital wartime resources and materials, such as bullets.

In terms of experiencing a stable domestic life, Nationalist air raids starting from late August 1936 made this very difficult for ordinary citizens living in the large Republican-controlled cities such as Madrid and Barcelona. In Madrid, for example, barricades, trenches and air-raid shelters were constructed by various residents' committees in order to combat the bombardment of shells falling from the skies. Blackouts were also a regular occurrence during these raids, leaving ordinary families scared and demoralised by the siege conditions within Republican zones. In *Homage to Catalonia,* Orwell describes the fear, disruption and destruction caused by Nationalist bombing raids on Barcelona (see Source 4 on page 324). The bombing disrupted trade and food supplies within the cities and towns, leading to long queues for food and shortages of basic provisions.

Republican militia became a common sight on the city's streets, their members recognised by their blue boiler suits or 'monos', which effectively represented a military uniform. This encouraged Republican 'volunteer citizens' in general to become more disciplined in their civic commitment to defending their city, and explicit revolutionary activity was curtailed in the name of securing the long-term future of the Second Republic. Various left-wing and trade union militias came to view themselves as a combination of soldiers, streetfighters and revolutionaries. They were known to take extreme vengeance on any civilians they suspected or knew of having sympathies with the Nationalist uprising, in particular members of conservative and **bourgeoisie**

political groupings such as CEDA and the Falange, along with known religious figures. The founder of the Falange, José Antonio Primo de Rivera, for example, was arrested in Madrid and later executed by a Republican firing squad in November 1936.

Life in the Nationalist zone

As the Nationalist forces advanced and towns and cities came under their control, Nationalist leaders were tasked with establishing a sense of order in these urban areas. **Martial law** was swiftly imposed in all Nationalist zones from 18 July 1936 onwards. The power of the secret police was enhanced, leading to further violence and executions, tough curfews were set and harsh criminal sanctions were put in place to keep order. As the war progressed and the Nationalist forces swallowed up more territory, the ability to keep control became more difficult. However, the Nationalists generally managed to maintain social stability more successfully than the fragmented Republicans, largely through the use of terror and military repression, as well as through more experienced military leadership.

Within the Nationalist zone, Franco banned all the political parties that had not supported the coup. At the same time, he set up a new political party, the Falange Española Tradicionalista y de law – Junta de Ofensiva Nacional Sindicalista (FET-JONS), which amalgamated all the different Nationalist political groups. On 19 April 1937, the Decree of Unification outlawed all other political parties, making Nationalist-controlled Spain a **one-party state** – the party being FET-JONS – under Franco's control. This erosion of democracy within Nationalist areas was a sign of things to come for the whole of Spain after 1939.

Under this one-party rule, strikes were banned and trade unions abolished. Franco's Labour Charter of 1938 established state-run alternatives to trades unions, with far less freedom to operate and take industrial action. This gave increased powers to factory owners. In more rural areas, the Republican land reforms were abolished, and power and control was returned to the landowners at the expense of the poorer peasants. These changes often made working life in the Nationalist zones harsh and unrelenting.

KEY TERM

Bourgeoisie
Stemming from the writings of the communist founding father, Karl Marx, this term refers to the property owners and middle-class industrialists. Marx and his followers argued that this group possessed an unfair allocation of most of a country's resources, and this subsequently allowed them to exploit the workers (the proletariat) by paying them less than they were entitled to for their labour.

KEY TERMS

Martial law
Rule by the military involving the army taking on the role of the police force, but with enhanced powers in order to keep public order in often extreme social conditions.

One-party state
A political system where only one party is allowed to exist, and there are no competitive democratic elections where citizens have a genuine choice as to who governs them.

As in the Republican zones, civilian work such as in local government and industry was severely disrupted by the conflict. Agricultural work was also adversely affected, with traditional trade and supply links disrupted. This made some food resources more difficult and expensive to obtain, although shortages were very limited in comparison with the besieged Republican towns and cities. According to the historian Michael Seidman, Franco's tightly controlled and highly disciplined wartime regime was largely successful in ensuring a fairly regular supply of food and resources for both troops and civilians, while also ensuring fairly stable economic conditions alongside regular pay for soldiers, farmers and factory workers. This made keeping social order easier and ensured the survival of a successful counter-revolution against more radical left-wing forces. While there was greater stability and more limited enemy bombing within Nationalist zones (due to weak Republican air power), it came at the expense of basic civil liberties and freedoms.

SOURCE

5 A Republican propaganda poster distributed during the civil war, highlighting the role women had to play. The message is translated as 'Women can contribute to the victory'.

Attitudes towards women

Amid the general disruption and upheaval that it caused, the Spanish Civil War also created something of a social revolution across Spain, with the role of women particularly affected by its impact. Social and political freedoms for women increased significantly and to unprecedented levels. In support of the war effort, many women took on jobs in factories and industries traditionally considered to be only suited for men. This was most notable on the Republican side, due to the more progressive and liberal attitudes that prevailed among its supporters and activists. There was generally, therefore, a more egalitarian attitude towards gender roles, especially in some of the more radical communities such as Aragon and Barcelona. Here, pay was equalised regardless of employment role and gender. This created some difficulties for employers who traditionally paid women less, but the power of trades unions and collective working practices made this policy easier to implement.

Many women took their involvement in the war to a much more significant level and joined the various communist and anarchist militia groups, with an estimated 1,000 fighting on the military front line and sharing duties with men. Many of these social trends went against the conventional role of women as domestic figures, whose primary role was to raise a family and who had only recently won the right to vote. However, it was mainly younger and unmarried women that fulfilled these roles, with many of those with families continuing to live in a fairly traditional manner.

There were some key female figures who emerged from the war, most notably Dolores Ibárruri, a communist daughter of a mineworker from the Basque region. Her powerful public speeches and radio broadcasts during the civil war were said to have inspired and maintained Republican morale. She became known as *La Pasionaria* ('The Passion Flower'). Her saying of '¡No pasarán' ('They shall not pass') became one of the most memorable mottos of the Spanish Civil War. It ultimately came to symbolise the defiance of Republicans in Madrid against the Nationalist siege of the city. Such a prominent role was unusual for a woman of this historical period within Spanish society, but the wartime situation saw the abandonment of many of Spain's social conventions, and this created opportunities for motivated and ideologically driven women such as *La Pasionaria*. Other notable female figures included Federica Montseny, an anarchist who was appointed minister of health in Caballero's government. Women in high-profile roles had the opportunity to take up women's issues, for example the legalisation of abortion within Republican-controlled areas, along with greater controls affecting brothels and prostitution, which were viewed by many as being exploitative in nature. Many brothels were subsequently closed down completely in some locations such as Barcelona, while others were collectivised to allow the prostitutes greater control of how they worked and to reduce levels of female exploitation.

SOURCE

6

La Pasionaria, pictured with Republican officers, addresses members of the International Brigades during the Spanish Civil War. Here, she is encouraging them in their efforts against the Nationalist forces.

SOURCE

7

Part of a radio broadcast, 'Danger! To Arms!', given by Dolores Ibárruri (*La Pasionaria*) in Madrid, 19 July 1936. Here, Ibárruri is warning Spanish citizens about what she believes to be the dangers of fascism spreading across Spain as a consequence of the Nationalist uprising in the summer of 1936.

Workers, anti-fascists, and labouring people!

Rise as one man! Prepare to defend the Republic, national freedom and the democratic liberties won by the people! Under the slogan, 'Fascism shall not pass!'… communists, socialists, anarchists and republicans, soldiers and all the forces loyal to the will of the people, are routing the traitorous rebels, who have trampled in the mud and betrayed their vaunted military honour.

The whole country is shocked by the actions of these villains. They want with fire and sword to turn democratic Spain, the Spain of the people, into a hell of terrorism and torture. But they shall not pass! All Spain has risen to the struggle. In Madrid the people have come out into the streets, lending strength to the government by their determination and fighting spirit, so that it may utterly exterminate the reactionary fascist rebels.

Young men and women, sound the alarm! Rise and join the battle! Women, heroic women of the people! Remember the heroism of the Asturian women! And you, too, fight side by side with your menfolk; together with them defend the bread and tranquility of your children whose lives are in danger! Soldiers, sons of the people! Stand steadfastly as one man on the side of the government, on the side of the working people, on the side of the People's Front, on the side of your fathers, brothers and comrades!

ACTIVITY
WRITING

Read through Source 7 and complete the following exercises:

1 Identify any words or phrases you don't understand and research their meanings.

2 Identify words and phrases that show the writer's feelings towards those involved in the Nationalist uprising.

3 Now write a paragraph describing and explaining *La Pasionaria*'s views on fascism using extracts from Source 7 as well as any other information you have to back up your argument.

By contrast, women in the Nationalist zones generally maintained the more traditional role that they had always fulfilled within Spanish society. The revived role of the Catholic Church within this sector of Spain meant that strict views on marriage and divorce were swiftly reimposed, and women were expected to support the prevailing political values of conservative Spanish Catholicism. They were viewed as inferior to men and were expected to run the home, while also being expected to dress plainly and in a conservative manner. They were therefore forbidden from dressing in trousers and were expected to refrain from 'modern' fashions and activities such as wearing make-up. The very military culture within these zones placed men on a higher level of significance, although some women did provide support as volunteer nurses and social workers, while others distributed food to the poor. The kind of political, social and economic freedoms enjoyed by women in the Republican zones were, however, completely out of the question within the Nationalist-controlled areas.

Many conservatives viewed this maintenance of traditional family values as a positive thing at a time of social unrest and instability, although the more egalitarian socialist perspective viewed it as a backward development. However, attempts to maintain normal family life were undermined by the need to evacuate children from zones under both sides' control. Somewhat ironically, given the moralistic agenda and conventional attitude towards women in Nationalist areas, a growing concern within such areas and across Spanish society as a whole between 1936 and 1939 was the growth in prostitution. Many women widowed by the conflict had little other means of making an income, while soldiers would often be tempted to use brothels while separated from their families for long periods of time. This meant that Nationalist soldiers were reluctant to follow orders to close these establishments down.

A Level Exam-Style Question Section A

How far could the historian make use of Sources 5 and 7 together to investigate changing attitudes towards women during the Spanish Civil War?

Explain your answer, using both sources, the information given about them and your own knowledge of the historical context. (20 marks)

Tip
Both sources reflect the role of women from a Republican perspective during the civil war. Consider the influence of Nationalist attitudes towards women and make comparisons. How did the role of women differ within the Republican and Nationalist zones?

The use of political terror

In addition to direct military casualties, there were also thousands of civilian deaths between 1936 and 1939 as a consequence of the political 'terror' that the war inflicted on the ordinary citizens of Spain. This was a more deliberate and specific policy authorised by military commanders, as opposed to the more arbitrary and random atrocities carried out lower down the chain of military and political command.

The Red Terror

The 'Red Terror' is used to describe how left-wing and pro-Republican armies and militias dealt with their political opponents in an often brutal manner, featuring violence and torture. The killings of priests, landowners, factory owners, *Falangists* and members of CEDA formed the basis of the Red Terror. Priests were often humiliated during their execution. In Ciudad Real, for example, the priest was castrated and his genitals stuffed in his mouth. In Aragon, landowners were killed, while in Catalonia the terror concentrated on factory owners. Nightly raids in Republican cities resulted in local militia arresting suspected Nationalist sympathisers, transporting them out of town and executing them. The Red Terror 'execution' of the Sacred Heart of Jesus involved the destruction of a well-known religious icon close to Madrid in early August 1936. In addition, an estimated 6,800 priests were murdered by Republican supporters throughout the course of the conflict due to suspicions that they were enemy agents or spies. Republican government officials quickly put an end to the Red Terror; it lasted only until the end of 1936. Despite its short term, attacks on religious buildings and symbols continued as part of an ongoing wave of anticlericalism by left-wing forces, with many churches destroyed and closed in Republican areas. It was in part these terror attacks on Catholic priests and churches that persuaded senior Church leaders to back the Nationalists.

The White Terror

The 'White Terror', carried out as part of party policy by Nationalist military forces, was an attempt to remove political opponents. It was also a moral crusade against supposed enemies of Catholic Spain. People in positions of power, such as left-wing radicals and trades unionists, were most at risk from the White Terror. For example, anarchists were targeted in Andalusia. In other areas, the implementation of Nationalist policies led to mass killings. In rural Extremadura, for example, an estimated 1,800 peasants were slaughtered by Nationalist troops when the land was returned to the landowners. Their bodies were left unburied in the fields, as an example to frighten others. Following the fall of Badajoz to Nationalist troops on 14 August 1936, Franco's troops carried out the 'Massacre of Reds', killing between 650 and 1,300 Republican soldiers and civilians. Nationalist forces also killed 4,000 residents of Malaga when they took the southern city in February 1937. In moral terms, the White Terror was described as a 'clean-up operation', cleansing Spanish society of moral 'evils' such as independent women and homosexuals. The mass execution of citizens of Pamplona following the annual celebration of the Virgin Mary was described as a 'bloody sacrifice' necessary to win God's favour.

Regardless of the actual military fighting, it has been estimated that the Red Terror inflicted by Republican forces claimed between 38,000 and 55,000 lives, while Franco's White Terror during and after the civil war would go on to exceed 200,000 lives.

SOURCE
8
From Antony Beevor, *The Battle for Spain: The Spanish Civil War 1936–1939* (2006).

The nationalists justified the brutality of their repression as reprisals for the red terror, but as had been the case in Seville, Cordoba and Badajoz, and as would be the case in Malaga... the subsequent nationalist killings exceeded those of the left several, if not many, times over. In Malaga the nationalist executions took place after the militia, and undoubtedly almost all of those responsible for killing right-wingers, had escaped up the coast. This shows there was little attempt to identify the guilty. But above all, the contrast in the numbers killed by each side could not be starker.

ACTIVITY
KNOWLEDGE CHECK

1 Create a table comparing the ways in which everyday life in the Republican and Nationalist zones was both different and similar during the Spanish Civil War.

2 Study Sources 5 (page 326) and 6 (page 327) and read Source 7 (see page 327), all featuring women in the Spanish Civil War. To what extent do they challenge the traditional role of women in Spanish society?

3 Create two spider diagrams to compare the Republican (Red) Terror and the Nationalist (White) Terror. Use the headings 'Atrocities', 'Impact' and 'Victims'.

A Level Exam-Style Question Section B

'Nationalist forces were more effective in their use of political terror during the Spanish Civil War.' How far do you agree with this statement? (20 marks)

Tip
You need to consider the impact of the use of political terror during the civil war. You may want to consider and compare how such tactics were used by both sides of the conflict, and whether one side employed such tactics with greater regularity and effectiveness than the other. Use evidence to support your discussion.

WHAT FACTORS HAD THE MOST INFLUENCE IN DETERMINING THE OUTCOME OF THE WAR?

Republican weaknesses and Nationalist strengths

As the civil war had progressed, the Republicans had been steadily weakened by a number of key factors, most notably a weak and fragmented political leadership that lacked a clear focus, divided ideologies among its various left-wing components and a limited amount of foreign support in comparison with their Nationalist adversaries. Following a series of Nationalist territorial gains throughout 1937, by 1 May 1938, the Republican Prime Minister Negrín was in an increasingly vulnerable position and subsequently launched a political initiative entailing a 13-point

'manifesto'. This contained a series of proposals and ultimately sought a negotiated diplomatic settlement of the war. It demanded a national referendum of the Spanish population in order to settle some of the war's outstanding and most contentious issues, in particular relating to the scale of government powers, the extent of religious freedoms and the nature of civil liberties. However, from a position of strength, Franco rejected this proposed solution and instead wanted the Republicans to surrender without conditions.

By contrast, the Nationalists had grown increasingly strong and more confident as the war had progressed. Key reasons for this were the superior levels of foreign support from prominent countries such as Germany and Italy, the superior experience and quality of their troops, and a more stable flow of financial support as well as access to more advanced technological military equipment. Of particular significance was the much better leadership evident within the senior ranks of the Nationalist military, for example General Franco. By the time the Republicans were in retreat by mid-1938, Franco had generated momentum and confidence in his forces, and he had no desire to compromise his pursuit of an outright military victory.

Overall, there were a number of key reasons why the Nationalist offensive succeeded and Republican counter-attacks failed.

- The Nationalists were far more united than the Republicans, and they had a clear and centralised command structure under Franco's leadership, as opposed to the rivalry, lack of co-ordination and often hostile ideological factions within Republican ranks.

- Any conflict involving conventional military battles favoured the professional soldiers of the Nationalist armies.

- Nationalist forces were ultimately better equipped, had greater numbers, better quality foreign support and had more training to deal with the prolonged nature of the warfare. They therefore emerged victorious from the majority of battles.

- The Republican Popular Army should have made greater use of Republican militias and drawn its opponents into more guerrilla warfare and street fighting, which better suited its mainly irregular citizen soldiers. While there was some guerrilla activity, failure to widen its usage represented a tactical failure on the part of the Republicans' military strategy.

The role of Franco

Franco's role was a highly significant one in determining the outcome of the conflict. He quickly established himself as a shrewd politician and was careful not to make explicit comments that would alienate any particular factions of his conservative base of support. His reputation was boosted not only by his association with the elite Army of Africa, but also by his success in obtaining foreign financial aid in the crucial first days and weeks of the conflict. His position as the unrivalled leader or *Generalissimo* of the Nationalists was further strengthened in November 1936 when the Republicans executed the imprisoned Falange leader and son of the former Spanish dictator, Antonio Primo de Rivera. This act further inflamed the bitter and internecine nature of the conflict, but Franco took advantage of it by instigating the merger of the

Carlist and Falange parties into one single entity in April 1937, which from then on was known as the Movimiento Nacional. This move further unified Spain's right-wing forces and enhanced the loyalty of these groups towards his leadership.

Franco's military skills and experience were a key element in the Nationalists' eventual success. He took credit for a series of military victories as the Nationalist forces moved swiftly through northern Spain during 1937. His strong leadership and more united base of support contrasted sharply with the various divisions evident within Republican ranks. He also ruthlessly tightened his grip on his opponents as the war progressed, refusing to compromise or negotiate with the Republicans from a position of increasing strength.

Despite Franco's influence and strength, it was not sufficient to bring the war to a swift conclusion. The conflict featured great resilience on both sides and at times became a war of attrition. It was therefore a prolonged and destructive civil war that divided and devastated Spain and its people. The military elements of the conflict certainly suited Franco's years of strategic army experience, but this also led to a high number of casualties, particularly due to the guerrilla methods often employed by more irregular forces. The bad feeling and animosity between the two warring sides was evident in Franco's victory speech (see Source 9).

SOURCE
9

Franco's victory speech, broadcast over the radio from Madrid to the Spanish population on the 20 May 1939 and reported in *The Tablet*, a Catholic newspaper, on 27 May 1939.

Madrilenos and Spaniards! In Madrid, the martyr city now freed from the tyranny of the Barbarians, you have witnessed the Victory Parade in which 120,000 warriors, provided with the most modern and efficient armament, marched past in perfect formation, representing the million men constituting the National Army. What our victory means, you know better than anyone else. The very existence of our country was at stake. You are the best witnesses, you who suffered under that tyranny and saw Spain a captive, subjected to a barbarous foreign yoke and sullied with Marxist crime. The martyrdom of Madrid is the gravest charge that can be brought against the Red leaders who, after being beaten in all the battles and hopelessly defeated, sacrificed the capital in vain by shielding themselves behind the non-combatant population, and delivered her over to the perverse methods of Russian Communism. Not for a moment did the eager activity of our troops cease. To achieve its deliverance the capital had to be taken without destroying and without burying beneath its ruins so many of our brave crusaders. Methodically we prepared the way for the victory that has given the lie to the hysterical boast of 'No Pasaran' ['They shall not pass'].

The role of foreign intervention and the impact of non-intervention

The role of the International Brigades, the Italian blackshirts and the bombing of Guernica by German Luftwaffe are all high-profile examples that indicate significant foreign involvement within an apparently internalised conflict. This was despite there being an official international agreement of non-intervention signed in the summer of 1936 by the majority of European nations and endorsed by the League of Nations, with the primary aim of

containing the war within Spain. However, while the League of Nations did not intervene in the conflict, it did not actively prevent other nations from doing so. As a consequence, Italy and Germany ignored the non-intervention agreement, while irregular forces from other European nations also participated in the conflict.

SOURCE
10

From George Orwell, *Looking Back on the Spanish War*, 1943. Here, Orwell highlights what he believes to be the foreign influence in determining the eventual outcome of the Spanish Civil War.

The outcome of the Spanish war was settled in London, Paris, Rome, Berlin — at any rate not in Spain. After the summer of 1937 those with eyes in their heads realized that the Government could not win the war unless there were some profound change in the international set-up, and in deciding to fight on Negrin and the others may have been partly influenced by the expectation that the world war which actually broke out in 1939 was coming in 1938. The much-publicized disunity on the Government side was not a main cause of defeat. The Government militias were hurriedly raised, ill-armed and unimaginative in their military outlook, but they would have been the same if complete political agreement had existed from the start. At the outbreak of war the average Spanish factory-worker did not even know how to fire a rifle (there had never been universal conscription in Spain), and the traditional pacifism of the Left was a great handicap. The thousands of foreigners who served in Spain made good infantry, but there were very few experts of any kind among them. The Trotskyist thesis that the war could have been won if the revolution had not been sabotaged was probably false. To nationalize factories, demolish churches, and issue revolutionary manifestoes would not have made the armies more efficient. The Fascists won because they were the stronger; they had modern arms and the others hadn't. No political strategy could offset that.

AS Level Exam-Style Question Section A

Why is Source 10 valuable to the historian for an enquiry into the significance of foreign intervention on the outcome of the Spanish Civil War?

Explain your answer, using the source, the information given about it and your own knowledge of the historical context. (8 marks)

Tip

The source offers a British perspective during the civil war. Consider the influence of the author's observations and assess how typical his views were. Broaden out the question to consider the attitudes of various international governments towards the conflict, and how foreign intervention affected its outcome.

From the outset of the civil war, the left-wing French prime minister, Leon Blum, had been keen to support the Republicans for primarily ideological reasons. He quickly concluded that his own left-wing Popular Front government in France must supply the Spanish Popular Front with the necessary arms and equipment for it to remain in power and prevent the spread of fascism. However, he was subsequently pressured to sign the non-intervention agreement of August 1936 by the combined forces of British politicians such as Neville Chamberlain and Stanley Baldwin, along with his own anti-war radicals in France. Both the French and British governments comprised prominent figures with painful memories of the First World War. British politicians in particular were anxious to prevent a further Europe-wide war, and the French government came round to support Britain's position due to fears that it could not take on the combined might of Germany and Italy alone. As a consequence, the Western liberal democracies of Britain and France gave little official support or aid to either side of the conflict and sought to stay neutral throughout its lengthy duration. This stance ultimately worked to favour the better-resourced Nationalist forces. There was, however, sympathy for the Republicans from left-wing politicians and activists, and many citizens of France and Britain took up the cudgels and joined the International Brigades.

The ideological and class-based nature of the conflict was ultimately sharpened by the fact that while the Nationalists were heavily bolstered by the military and financial support of the fascist-inclined **totalitarian** dictatorships of Italy and Germany, the Republicans became increasingly reliant on significant levels of equipment and aid received from the communist bastion of the Soviet Union. The fact that the involvement of Italy and Germany was more explicit and wholehearted certainly angered and alarmed the Spanish Republicans, who were increasingly aware of the steady flow of foreign support provided to Franco between 1936 and 1939. The Republican position was further comparatively weakened by the fact that the Soviet Union had more logistical problems in supplying resources from its greater geographical distance. Stalin also operated more discretely than the Germans and Italians, and his initial support for the Republicans was humanitarian, with military support more covertly and secretly provided. Over the course of the war, while the Nationalists benefited from much greater manpower and significant varieties of military equipment provided by their European allies, the Republicans benefited from humanitarian support, military and technical advice and financial loans from the Soviet Union (see Figure 2.5). In addition to this, the more rigid non-intervention of Britain and France gave a clear advantage to Franco's Nationalists. This indicated that non-intervention in the war had as much of an impact on its outcome as intervention did.

> **KEY TERM**
>
> Totalitarian
> A system of government where there are few if any individual liberties, and where the state controls every aspect of citizens' lives.

The involvement of German and Italian forces throughout the civil war clearly breached the 1936 Non-Intervention Pact, which undoubtedly boosted Franco's Nationalist forces. As Spain's prolonged internal conflict turned against the Republicans throughout 1937 and 1938, the Spanish Popular Front government forcibly argued for the direct intervention of Britain and France on their behalf in order to counteract the German and Italian activity. The French and British were targeted due to their historic suspicions of Germany, their relatively powerful status and their geographical proximity to the conflict. These Republican demands were heightened after incidents such as the Guernica bombing in April 1937. While this event certainly had an impact in advancing international opinion in favour of the Republicans, it was not to the extent they wanted as it failed to instigate direct intervention from more sympathetic nations.

Nationalists	Republicans
600 aeroplanes (including 6,000 men within the Condor Legion) and 200 tanks from Germany.	Approximately 1,500 aeroplanes from the Soviet Union.
An estimated 16,000 German troops, although never more than 10,000 at one time.	An estimated 2,000–3,000 key individuals from the Soviet Union, including military advisors, technicians, doctors and pilots.
German financial support has been rounded up to the value of 500 million Reichsmarks (equivalent to £43 million in 1939 prices).	Soviet financial support has been rounded up to a value (equivalent to £81 million in 1939 prices).
Approximately 75,000 Italian forces in total, which stood at 50,000 at their maximum in mid-1937. Italy also sent key military equipment including 950 tanks and almost 800 aircraft and 1930 cannons.	Between 35,000 and 40,000 volunteers from the International Brigades whose members came from over 50 different nations.

Figure 2.5 Summary of key Nationalist and Republican foreign support during the Spanish Civil War.

More widespread foreign intervention occurring was ultimately prevented by a deep-rooted fear of a full-scale European war. This Anglo-French approach towards European foreign policy came to fruition in the policy of **appeasement** that was formalised at the Munich Conference of September 1938, where Hitler's conquest of the German-speaking part of Czechoslovakia was confirmed (albeit reluctantly) by the key European powers. In a similar vein, when this policy was applied to Spain, Britain and France were equally willing to appease Franco's expansionist activities. By the end of 1938, this made any lingering Republican hopes of more significant foreign intervention on their behalf highly unlikely to materialise.

> **KEY TERM**
>
> Appeasement
> A policy relating to diplomacy or foreign affairs where significant concessions are made to a particular nation in order to prevent a military conflict from taking place. It is often linked to how other European powers dealt with the rise of Germany's Adolf Hitler and his expansionist foreign policy during the mid to late 1930s.

Foreign intervention ultimately prolonged the duration and escalated the scale of the Spanish Civil War, with different European nations exploiting the conflict for their own national and ideological interests. The issue of non-intervention was equally significant in that the lack of involvement of certain nations resulted in the policy of appeasement emerging. Despite the fears of various European statesmen, the Spanish conflict did not spread but was merely a prelude to the major European war that broke out five months after military affairs had been officially concluded in Spain. However, whether earlier intervention by Britain and France in the Spanish Civil War would have deterred and prevented German expansion into Poland in September 1939 (which triggered the outbreak of the Second World War), remains a matter of significant historical speculation and debate.

ACTIVITY
KNOWLEDGE CHECK

1 Study Source 9 on page 330. Note down and explain some phrases from Franco's speech that indicate his feelings about his Republican opponents.

2 How far were Republican weaknesses rather than Nationalist strengths to blame for the fall of the Republican regime in 1939?

3 To what extent did non-intervention influence the outcome of the Spanish Civil War?

THINKING HISTORICALLY   Change (6a)

Separately and together

Below are some different types of history that historians may identify.

Political history	Economic history	Social history
Religious history	Military history	International history

These are thematic histories, where a historian focuses on a particular aspect of change. For example, an economic history of the British Empire would focus on trade and the economic reasons for the expansion of the Empire, whereas a political history of the Empire would focus on governance of the colonies and strategic reasons for its expansion.

Work in groups.

1 Write a definition for each type of history.

Here are some events in Spain in the period 1931–39.

1931–36	1936	1936–37	1937	1938	1939
Consolidation of the Spanish Second Republic. A government crisis erupts in 1936 following an attempted military coup.	Outbreak of the Spanish Civil War. Republicans maintain control of Madrid and most large cities.	Foreign intervention appears in the form of Italian blackshirts, International Brigades and the German air force.	A major atrocity sees the town of Guernica carpet-bombed by German warplanes.	The Nationalists make progress and seize further Spanish territory, with Republicans in retreat.	Franco's Nationalists win the Spanish Civil War.

Answer the following questions:

2 The first event highlighted can be classified primarily as a 'political' event, and the second one a 'military' event.

   a) What connection can be made between the attempted military coup and the outbreak of the Spanish Civil War in 1936?

   b) What other areas of history do these events cover?

3 What major political changes occurred in Spain between the years 1936 and 1939?

4 In terms of historical change, what was the social, economic and political impact of the war on Spanish citizens? Explain your answer.

5 What was the international impact of the Spanish Civil War?

6 What particular aspects of religious and military history can be identified from the study of Spain between 1936 and 1939?

Work in pairs.

7 Write a statement criticising 'thematic history'.

8 Write three statements defending 'thematic history'.

9 Explain why 'thematic history' occurs.

ACTIVITY
SUMMARY

1 Identify the factors that explain why the Nationalists won the Spanish Civil War. List these in order of priority, with the most important first.

2 Explain why you have come to this judgement, using evidence to support your explanation.

3 To what extent was Franco the reason for the outcome of the Spanish Civil War?

 WIDER READING

Beevor, A. *The Battle for Spain: The Spanish Civil War, 1936-1939*, Weidenfeld & Nicolson (2006) is a detailed summary of the key events and developments of the Spanish Civil War by a high-profile military historian

Beevor, A. 'The Spanish civil war: men of la Mancha', in *The Economist*, 22 June 2006 – in this article, Beevor focuses specifically on the various atrocities and 'terror' inflicted by both sides of this brutal civil war

Hemingway, E. *For Whom the Bells Tolls*, Charles Scribner's Sons (1940) is a fictional account of a Republican fighter in the Spanish Civil War, written by an American author who reported on and made documentary films about the conflict

Joll, J. *Europe since 1870: An International History*, Penguin (1990) is a wide-ranging and comprehensive historical coverage of Europe by a well-known historian

Orwell, G. *Homage to Catalonia*, Martin Secker & Warberg (1938) – an early account of the Spanish Civil War by Orwell, who participated as part of the International Brigades, and which was published while the war was still taking place

Orwell, G. *Looking Back on the Spanish War*, Lawrence & Wishart (1943) is a further personal account of the Spanish Civil War

Preston, P. *Franco: A Biography*, Fontana (1995) is a comprehensive biography of this iconic and dominant Spanish leader by a specialist historian of this period

Seidman, M. *The Victorious Counterrevolution: The Nationalist Effort in the Spanish Civil War*, University of Wisconsin Press (2011) is a study of the tactics and methods used by Nationalist forces to sustain their efforts during the Spanish Civil War

Thomas, H. *The Spanish Civil War*, Penguin (revised edn, 1965) is one of the most established and detailed summaries of the Spanish Civil War

2b.3 Establishing Franco's dictatorship, 1938–56

KEY QUESTIONS

- How effectively did Franco establish a 'new state'?
- To what extent did Franco's government control the Spanish people after the civil war?
- How well did the Spanish economy perform in the years following the civil war?
- To what extent did the dictatorship and Spain's international relations change in the years 1939–56?

INTRODUCTION

Having secured victory in the civil war by the spring of 1939, Franco was faced with the major challenge of constructing and stabilising a new state that could survive and be sustained in the long term. Spain had been torn apart by the conflict and some major social and political divisions remained. Franco's new government was therefore required to bring order to the fragmented nation, and it soon became apparent that he sought to establish a fascist dictatorship as the means of delivering a stable model of governance.

The type of Spanish society that developed would be a very controlled one, with many of the repressive policies of the civil war era carried over into peacetime. Key Franco allies such as the Church, the army and the industrial business classes all provided him with important and ongoing support on various levels, but his own dominance was such that a '**cult of personality**' would soon develop that centred on his strong and dominant leadership style. As with social recovery, economic development would also prove difficult after 1939, particularly in terms of improving the lifestyles and living standards of ordinary Spanish citizens. In operating as a fairly isolated nation detached from most of Europe and the outside world, Franco's key economic policies would be hard to implement and to make work effectively. If Franco's proposed social and economic remedies did not work, then his own long-term position at the helm of Spain's political system would be in jeopardy.

On an international dimension, Franco faced relative political isolation after 1939, having endured criticism from much of western Europe during the civil war, with only the fascist dictatorships of Germany and Italy offering him any significant support. This situation worsened with the development and eventual outcome of the Second World War, as both Hitler and Mussolini were defeated and fell from power, and Franco tried to steer a difficult path of wartime **neutrality**.

1945
July–August: Second World War ends
Spain declared a fascist regime at the Potsdam Conference and denied membership of the United Nations

1938
March–April: Clerical Laws
Press Law
Reintroduction of 1889 Civil Code in Nationalist zones

1940
October: Franco meets Hitler to discuss Spain's entry into the Second World War

1938	1939	1940	1941	1942	1943	1944	1945	1946

1939
February: Law of Political Responsibilities
March: Treaty of Friendship signed between Franco and Hitler
April: Franco declares end of civil war; repression of opponents commences
September: Second World War begins

Once the Second World War was over, Spain's fascist political agenda faced further criticism and hostility from the newly formed **United Nations (UN)**. This led to considerable difficulties in securing both political and economic support from outside the country. It would therefore be a major challenge for Franco's government to bring the country back into the international arena during the 1940s and 1950s, and this added to the vulnerability of Spain's 'new state'.

HOW EFFECTIVELY DID FRANCO ESTABLISH A 'NEW STATE'?

Following the end of the Spanish Civil War in April 1939, the jubilant General Francisco Franco found himself in an unparalleled position of political power. After years of struggle between the political left and right, and following a series of weak national leaders and fragile coalitions, the country's internal conflict had eventually resulted in a convincing victory for the conservative Nationalists led by Franco. This meant that Spain now had a dominant figure at the helm of government; a leader boosted by wartime success, who had fewer limits on his power than his immediate predecessors, although he had to deal with the challenges of presiding over a bitterly split nation. Having developed dictatorial powers while leader of the Nationalist forces during the civil war, Franco quickly made it apparent that he planned to consolidate his position of strength and continue this leadership style into a period of relative peace.

Franco was now in a position to reject the country's democratic experiment of the early 1930s and, instead, establish a dictatorship featuring himself at the centre of power and influence. While many on the liberal left across Europe and within Spain viewed such a development as a backward step in the country's development as a nation, such a move was justified by Franco and his allies in their belief that following a period of violent division and bloodshed, a sustained spell of strong, decisive and **authoritarian** leadership was required to restore order to the shattered country. The ultimate legacy of the civil war was therefore an unsettled state of affairs that Franco exploited for his own political benefit and to further secure his own interests.

Establishing control in the Nationalist zone, 1938

During the course of the civil war, Franco had progressively strengthened his authority across the Nationalist zones. As a result, the degree of social order in these areas was far more stable and disciplined in comparison with the Republican-controlled regions and provinces. As the Nationalists advanced in 1938, Franco was successful in instilling effective government authority and order over newly acquired territories. He achieved this through ruthlessly using his secret police to monitor and arrest suspected opponents, imposing martial law to control the broader civilian population

KEY TERMS

United Nations (UN)
An international organisation established in October 1945 in the aftermath of the Second World War, originally consisting of 51 member nations. The UN's principal aim was ensuring international peace and co-operation after two world wars in less than 30 years. It replaced the League of Nations.

Authoritarian
A system of government where citizens are expected to display complete obedience to a dominant figure or structure of absolute political authority at the expense of personal freedoms and liberties.

1947
June: Law of Leadership Succession

1949
February: USA begins a series of financial loans to Spain

1953
August: Concordat signed between Spain and the Vatican
September: Treaty of Madrid

1955
December: Spain joins the United Nations

1947	1948	1949	1950	1951	1952	1953	1954	1955

1948
April: Spain excluded from the Marshall Plan

1954
July: Homosexuality declared illegal

and banning all other political parties and organisations apart from the FET-JONS (see page 325). Franco's forces regularly resorted to terror in dealing with opposition. This would involve the use of both the army and his Falangist militia in arresting, torturing and imprisoning political opponents, with left-wing agitators and trades unionists particularly targeted. From the perspective of mainstream conservative opinion, this approach was seen as justified in order to restore social order to Spain.

Initial policies

In 1938, Franco reintroduced the 1889 Civil Code, a collection of key laws and regulations designed to provide a framework of stability and normality to everyday civilian life. For example, how everyday business and trade transactions should be conducted, as well as regulations relating to non-criminal legal matters. Many of these customs had been disrupted by the civil war, resulting in a significant reduction in the observation of civic rules in general. Their reintroduction meant, however, that some of the previous freedoms and social equality enjoyed by citizens, particularly in the Republican zones, were now threatened by the imposition of more centralised and authoritarian rule. The code subsequently emphasised a more traditional structure for Spanish society, with a focus on law and order, and traditional gender roles re-emphasised. This meant that after some had experienced more independence and equality during the war, women once again became primarily dependent on their fathers before marriage and their husbands afterwards (the latter known as *permiso marital*).

The Clerical Laws introduced in 1938 reversed much of the anticlerical legislation of the Second Republic. They were initially passed within Nationalist areas, and their focus was to give the Roman Catholic religion a much greater influence and independence. Catholic control, for example, was once again established over the education system and crucifixes were reintroduced into schools. With the Nationalist advance, the Church's powers extended across captured Republican zones and then all of Spain once the war was over. A Press Law was also passed in 1938, limiting what newspapers could publish and giving the government the power to appoint and dismiss editors and journalists. The government could even shut down a publication, and publishers had no right to appeal such decisions.

Consequently, conservative policies affecting family life, education, law and order and the media established in Nationalist zones during the civil war extended across the whole of Spain after 1939. These included policies such as single-sex education, capital punishment, press censorship and harsher prison sentences. Many of these social policies came as a shock to those Spanish citizens with more liberal political viewpoints who had enjoyed greater social freedoms and political liberties while under the governance of the Second Republic.

The influence of the Falange

While the war was ongoing, Franco had established an effective one-party state within the Nationalist zones. This was centred on his revitalised Falange political party, which was essentially anticommunist, antidemocratic and antiliberal in nature. When the war was over, the principles and practices of this emerging one-party state were extended across the whole country, with alternative political viewpoints no longer permitted to compete for government office. These measures clearly marked a rejection of the principles of liberal democracy and competitive pluralistic politics that were becoming standardised across much of the Western world. Instead, it indicated the general political direction in which Franco wished to take Spain, and this revived fears among his political opponents that he would develop and consolidate a state based on fascist principles – something many of his most ardent supporters desired.

Franco's style of political rule ultimately revolved around the primary importance of his own position as Spain's *Caudillo*. He did, however, acknowledge the important supporting role provided by the Falange by appointing various senior figures in the party to influential positions in the new government. The Falange president (and Franco's brother-in-law) Ramón Serrano Suñer, for example, was made minister of the interior (1938–40) and foreign minister (1940–42), and Alfonso Peña Boeuf became the minister of public works (1938–45). Other Falange ministers would have influence in shaping policies concerned with the economy, domestic and foreign affairs and media management during the formative years of the new state: for example, imposing censorship laws and the reversal of the radical land reforms of the Second Republic. The Falange would continue to wield considerable political power for the first two decades of Franco's rule.

The Falange sought to wield political control at all levels of society, not just within government. The Falange youth movement, for example, was established with the purpose of converting supporters to its cause from a young age. Young members of the Falange were taught military rules and discipline, as well as the ideological principles of the party. The Falange also organised educational activities, social gatherings and political rallies in support of Franco's leadership across many parts of Spain.

SOURCE 1   Young boys in Irun, northern Spain, forming part of the Falange guard during the civil war.

Managing Nationalist rivalries

With victory in the civil war, Franco and his allies had resoundingly settled a long-running debate about the type of country Spain should be in favour of their own ideological and political viewpoint. Theirs was essentially a conservative and traditionalist political agenda, one that was suspicious of external ideologies and which favoured strong individual leadership. Following the considerable disorder of the final years of the Second Republic as well as the turbulence of the civil war era, the victorious Nationalists also sought to justify the establishment of an undemocratic political system in order to maintain social order. However, Franco continued to face post-war difficulties in balancing the interests and priorities of the various conservative groups that supported him. By the end of the war, for example, some conservative groups, particularly the Carlists, felt the time was right for the return of the Spanish monarchy in order to further secure the Nationalist ascendancy. Franco, however, was reluctant to relegate his personal achievements in favour of an exiled and distant monarch.

In dealing with monarchist demands, Franco cleverly adopted an ambiguous position on the issue that managed to maintain his own dominance while also ensuring the continuation of his broad coalition of support that bound together rival Nationalist traditions. He stressed how important his own position was to ensure the country's stability, while never fully ruling out the restoration of monarchy as a likely future prospect. He even made contact with the Spanish heir to the throne, Don Juan, who had been residing in exile since the advent to the Second Republic in 1931. Franco offered assurances to monarchist figures and sympathisers that this institution would one day return to Spain, but at a time that he would choose. He subsequently passed a Law of Leadership Succession in 1947 that established the country as a monarchy or kingdom on a formal level. However, in practical terms, the longer Spain existed without a monarchy, the less likely that such a figurehead would be restored. Franco declared himself as 'regent' for the foreseeable future and ultimately was unwilling to sacrifice the considerable powers and status that he had accumulated to a rival figure.

If a returning monarch was unlikely in the short term, then the pro-monarchist Carlist movement were generally willing to support Franco as a more appealing alternative than Republican socialism. The Carlists were further restricted in their options by being effectively absorbed into the broader Falangist movement during the civil war, which ultimately reduced their ability to act more independently. The Carlists, the Falange and Franco's military allies all favoured strong individual leadership. The Spanish *Caudillo* could also continue to rely on the general goodwill of wealthy industrialists, landowners and businessmen from the capitalist classes, who were long-term conservative pillars of support. Franco achieved loyalty by offering appropriate policy concessions that favoured the interests of his wealthy and conservative supporters, particularly in relation to halting any further land reforms and adopting economic policies that favoured Spanish big-business interests, such as banning strikes and abolishing trades unions. As with the Falange, many members of these more affluent and conservative groups, notably the military, subsequently served as ministers within Franco's government. In 1939, for example, José Enrique Varela, a military commander in the civil war, was appointed minister of war, and Juan Yagüe, an army officer (known as 'The Butcher of Badajoz' due to the thousands he ordered killed after his forces took the city) as minister of the air force. By 1945, approximately 50 percent of Franco's ministers were ex-army personnel. Franco was ultimately far more successful in uniting the broad forces of the conservative right than the Republicans had previously been in trying to keep together the different components of the Spanish left.

EXTRACT
1 | From Hugh Thomas, *The Spanish Civil War*, 1965.

Caudillo and head of state... [and ruling] according to no theory of government save his own brand of compromise developed during the Civil War, between Falange, Church and Monarchists. At one time or another, each of these groups has been in the ascendant or in decline... [but] Franco treat[ed] them as cavalierly as he did the Moroccan chiefs of his youth... Most of the political leaders since the Civil War were new men, to whom the war and the peace brought the opportunity for advancement. Some of the leading Generals of the Civil War were used by Franco as Ministers or in other posts.

The establishment and survival of a fascist dictatorship under Franco

While in the immediate aftermath of the civil war there remained some uncertainty about the precise nature of Franco's long-term policy agenda, it soon became apparent that he intended to extend his undemocratic and repressive one-party state structure across the entire country. Any signs of lingering civil war dissent were ruthlessly and often brutally dealt with, repressive laws that outlawed political opposition were imposed, the media was controlled, government propaganda was used to promote Franco's achievements and Falangist activities sought to indoctrinate Spanish citizens to the fascist cause. From an early stage, therefore, his government bore many of the hallmarks of fascist dictatorial regimes of the type established in previous years by Franco's civil war allies, Germany and Italy.

Franco's desire for this particular political model to flourish and survive was evident in a series of speeches he delivered to supporters from 1938 onwards, where he regularly expressed nationalistic, antidemocratic and anticommunist sentiments (see, for example, Sources 2–4 below). These three elements were key features of Hitler and Mussolini's fascist regimes. The events featured Franco speaking to large crowds of people, who listened intently (often under duress) and who were encouraged by the ruling regime to display the fascist 'power-fist' salute as a sign of visible public support. His speeches and observations would regularly involve a powerful and dramatic style of oratory, which Franco would use in order to further strengthen his political position. He demonised his political opponents with dramatic language and imagery, calling for national unity and endeavour for the country to advance further in the future, while also invoking the country's deeply held Christian values.

SOURCE

2 | Franco's comments to Nationalist colleagues during the civil war, 1938.

We do not believe in government through the voting booth. The Spanish national will was never freely expressed through the ballot box. Spain has no foolish dreams.

SOURCE

3 | Franco's victory speech, broadcast over the radio from Madrid to the Spanish population on the 20 May 1939 and reported in *The Tablet,* a Catholic newspaper, on 27 May 1939.

Let us have no illusions. The internationalist spirit which allowed capitalism to ally itself with Marxism and inspired so many a pact with the anti-Spanish revolution, that spirit is not extirpated in one day, and still breathes in many a breast. Too much blood has been spilt and the crusade has cost Spanish mothers too heavy a price for us to allow our victory to be frustrated by foreign agents who have filtered into our great companies, or by the base muttering of mean tongues. The Spain we are making is for all. We welcome to our camp all who have repented and wish to collaborate in the greatness of Spain; but if they sinned yesterday they must not expect applause until they redeem themselves by deeds.

SOURCE
4

Franco's speech to supporters in the Falange women's section, Madrid, 11 September 1945, where he celebrates the defeat of left-wing ideology during the Spanish Civil War.

We have torn up Marxist materialism and we have disorientated Masonry [**Freemasonry**]. We have thwarted the Satanic machinations of the clandestine Masonic superstate, despite its control of the world's press and numerous international politicians. Spain's struggle is a Crusade; as soldiers of God we carry with us the evangelism of the world!

KEY TERM

Freemasonry
A non-religious global organisation that can be traced back to the 14th century. It originated from co-operation by various craftsmen and professionals, and it is fraternal and charitable in its outlook. It claims to be non-political, yet critics across various countries have regularly accused its members of seeking to influence public policy in a secretive manner. Freemasonry emphasises ceremonial procedure and personal morality and seeks to extend the movement's values and influence within civic life.

The foundations of this emerging totalitarian state had been considerably strengthened by Franco's ideological affinity with Hitler and Mussolini during the civil war. Citizens of both Germany and Italy were controlled by the state and any dissent was crushed. Each dictatorship also expected its citizens to demonstrate enthusiastic commitment towards the regime. On a domestic level, Franco managed to develop a similar political system by applying a strong, authoritarian model of leadership, which was a key component of fascist political models elsewhere. This allowed him to manage and exploit divisions within both his opponents on the political left and his own support base among the various factions of the conservative right. He achieved this through a combination of effective diplomacy and repressive control. For example, in the early years of his rule, Franco's regime established key nationalistic economic policies that were consistent with the fascist ideology and imposed traditional social structures.

His capacity to manage and manipulate the different dynamics within a fragmented Spanish society won him sufficient public support and allowed his regime to establish itself and then consolidate its position in the years ahead. In subsequent years, Franco would have to continue to pay close attention to the various groups that had the potential to disrupt this personalised and repressive model of government, in particular the nostalgic monarchists and the vanquished yet still radicalised Republicans. From the earliest stages of his rule, Franco's regime was therefore

focused on establishing a fascist dictatorship in his name, and then maintaining the appropriate political conditions for it to survive and prosper in the long term.

ACTIVITY
KNOWLEDGE CHECK

1 Summarise the challenges that Franco faced in creating a new state after 1938. Which was the most significant challenge? Explain your answer.

2 How effectively and by what means did Franco overcome the challenges you have identified in question 1?

3 With reference to Sources 2–4 on pages 338–39, explain how Franco's oratory and use of language effectively attacked his opponents while also promoting his own viewpoint.

TO WHAT EXTENT DID FRANCO'S GOVERNMENT CONTROL THE SPANISH PEOPLE AFTER THE CIVIL WAR?

The legacy of the civil war

Franco had developed a firm and authoritative style of political rule during the civil war, and this manner of leadership would continue into the post-civil war era. A controlling approach had seemed well suited to the conditions of war, leading to order in the Nationalist zones, although usually at the expense of people's individual liberties. Given the ongoing instability in many parts of the country when the war had ended, Franco appeared determined to extend this system of government beyond its conclusion, on the basis that the country's crisis was not yet fully stabilised. A dominant and centralised style of leadership was arguably what was required now that many of the country's established political structures were shattered and various opposition groups were either in exile, hiding or imprisoned. Spain's very limited democratic tradition had proved itself unable to survive the strains of governance after less than a decade of existence. By 1939, therefore, the focus was very much on Franco emerging as the overwhelming and dominant political figure that no one else could rival. Given the perceived failings of the country's experiment with liberal democracy, Franco embraced an alternative approach to governance, one that endorsed a repressive political structure as a means of controlling society and maintaining public order. Once in place, this would have some significant consequences for the wider Spanish population in terms of how Franco's government sought to control their everyday domestic activities.

Political terror and repression

Franco sought to maintain many of the structures and methods of repression that were brought about by the crisis of war in order to consolidate and ensure the security of his own post-war position and that of his new regime. He was therefore willing to use the ruthless and brutal practices that his regime's so-called White Terror had employed during the civil war (see Chapter 2) to deal with those who did not share his own political outlook or opinions and threatened his new state. This approach continued well into the 1940s and involved arbitrary arrests and imprisonment, active prevention of non-approved political meetings or activity, and also state-instigated violence against strikers, protestors and political agitators. An example includes the Franco regime's purge of teachers, the military and the civil service, with those perceived to have Republican sympathies removed from their jobs and replaced with others considered more loyal to the Nationalist cause.

Once his own position was relatively secure, one of the most pressing challenges for Franco was how to restore order and effective political control to the Republican hotbeds of resistance, namely the formerly autonomous parts of Catalonia, such as Barcelona, and other key urban locations, including Valencia and Madrid. These were the areas that had held out the longest during the civil war and where the doctrine of anarchism had remained a strong political presence. While many Republicans had fled abroad into exile (with an estimated 350,000 in France alone by early 1940), there remained significant elements of political opposition and lingering military resistance in these former Republican strongholds. Many of those in exile were afraid to return to Spain out of fear for their own safety if they did so. In February 1939, Franco passed legislation known as the Law of Political Responsibilities, which in its simplest sense made involvement in radical political activities a criminal offence. It was essentially aimed at left-wing activists who had opposed the Nationalists both during and after the civil war. He also backdated it to 1934, allowing his government agencies – the police, Falange militia and military courts – the opportunity to deal with issues and alleged offences that took place before the 'official' military conflict began. Once the police arrested suspected radicals, the courts had the power to sentence them to long-term imprisonment, house arrest, exile and even death. The Falange militia carried out the executions.

These acts of terror have been deemed to be a result of Franco's desire to 'purify' Spanish society of what he considered to be its undesirable elements. Franco's secret police specifically targeted those who remained loyal to the former Republican regime, along with working-class activists and those that had been prominent in support of regional autonomy for areas such as Catalonia. In the four years after the civil war (1939–43), between 100,000 and 200,000 Spanish citizens were executed by a wave of further 'Red' repression, so-called because it targeted those with alleged left-wing and communist sympathies. This approach was driven by the Falange Party's fervent anticommunist feelings. Between February 1937 and August 1944, an estimated 20,500 suspected Republican sympathisers and political **dissidents** were killed in the southern city of Malaga alone.

Spanish citizens who shared the values of communism, liberalism and republicanism were viewed by Franco and his allies as having 'foreign' and 'alien' traits that were somehow not compatible with traditional Spanish values and culture. The law targeted these citizens and many of the victims were kept in concentration camps and made to carry out forced labour. The use of these tactics became increasingly widely known across Spain, but many were too scared to oppose and object. The silence of Catholic religious leaders in particular indicated an implicit approval for the practices, a stance for which they have received notable criticism, both at the time and in the years since. The historian Paul Preston has described this era of repression by the Nationalist force as 'the Spanish Holocaust'. The terror and repression continued in this vein for many years after Franco came to power, lasting until approximately the end of the Second World War in 1945.

SOURCE

5 From an article in *The Telegraph* by journalist Fiona Govan, dated 1 February 2012. The article is about a Spanish judicial investigation into the 'terror' inflicted by the Franco regime, and the impact it had on the lives of ordinary citizens.

In a barely audible voice choked with emotion, a bowed old lady, dressed in black and supported by a Zimmer-frame, called for the justice her family had been waiting for since 1936. 'They took her out and they took her away,' wheezed Maria Martin, 81, from the witness box. 'I never saw my mother again.' She was the first of a string of witnesses called to defend Spain's crusading judge Baltasar Garzon, 56, who stands accused of overstretching his judicial powers with an attempt to investigate Spain's darkest era. The investigating magistrate is accused of breaching a 1977 amnesty law to explore the fate of the more than 114,000 victims who disappeared during the 1936–39 civil war and ensuing 36-year dictatorship and whose bodies lie in unmarked graves across Spain.

She recalled how when she was a mere six years-old, her mother, Agustina, was one of three women and 27 men, shot dead and their corpses dumped into a mass grave on the side of a road. The desire to recover the remains of her mother for a proper burial had haunted her family life ever since. 'Until the day he died in 1977 my father wrote to the local authorities to try to recover the body. They told him: "Go away, leave us in peace or we will do to you what we did to her",' she told the Supreme Court. Another told how her father had been taken from their home in the Canary Islands in the middle of the night by Franco's guards and never seen again. 'They beat them. They kept them as prisoners and did a lot of things to them,' Pino Sosa Sosa, 75, told the court.

AS Level Exam-Style Question Section A

Why is Source 5 valuable to the historian for an inquiry into the nature of Franco's 'White Terror' from 1936 onwards?

Explain your answer, using the source, the information given about it and your own knowledge of the historical context. (8 marks)

Tip

Think about the comments of the witnesses involved, and compare them with your own knowledge of the reasons the government pursued such a policy. How can this further our understanding of why terror was so crucial to Franco's regime? What are the issues relating to this information that might weaken it as a source?

Censorship and propaganda

The Franco regime made effective use of censorship, propaganda and the widespread circulation of pro-government literature to assert its authority (for example, *No-Do*, a state-controlled series of cinema newsreels). The passing of the Press Law in April 1938 meant the government could regulate and restrict the Spanish press and media (see page 336). This gave Franco's administration the means by which to control and manipulate, in other words, to censor what kind of news was delivered to the Spanish people. The Press Law was criticised by political opponents for being illiberal and repressive, but was justified at the time as a vital means of controlling information and securing victory. Even after 1939, the civil war appeared in government propaganda.

From 1942, government propaganda films were broadcast before the showing of ordinary feature films at the cinema. These short films were used to highlight Franco's personal achievements and to remind the Spanish population of the horrors of the 'Red Terror'. Propaganda messages of this kind were particularly aimed at maintaining a significant amount of hostile public opinion towards socialist and left-wing ideologies, while also cementing the support and loyalty of the more conservative middle classes, religious orders and those loyal to the established Catholic faith to Franco's regime.

The role of the Church

From the very beginning of the new regime, Franco encouraged a revived and more prominent role for the Roman Catholic Church. The Church had been a strong supporter of Franco and the Nationalists from the early stages of the civil war, seeing them as an effective part of Spanish Catholicism's campaign against the 'godless communism' of the Second Republic. Franco could therefore afford to give them a degree of autonomy because he could rely on their support. The Clerical Laws, introduced in 1938, could now take effect across the whole of the country, giving the Church much greater influence and independence within Spain. Franco allowed the Church, for example, to once again be in control of primary education and to run youth groups independent of the Falange youth movement. Other religions were either outlawed (non-Christian types) or restricted (in the case of other Christian sects such as Protestantism).

SOURCE 6

Cardinal Isidro Goma decorating Franco during the celebration of the third anniversary of the liberation of Toledo, 1939. General José Enrique Varela stands behind them.

SOURCE 7

A radio message from the newly ordained Pope Pius XII to the Spanish people to commemorate the end of the country's civil war, 14 April 1939.

With great joy we address you, most dear children of Catholic Spain, to express to you our fatherly congratulations for the gift of peace and of victory, with which God has deemed worthy to crown the Christian heroism of your faith and charity, tried in so many and so generous sufferings.

We thus exhort the Authorities and Shepherds of Catholic Spain to enlighten the mind of those who were deceived... Propose to them the principles of individual and social justice, without which the peace and prosperity of nations, as mighty as they may be, cannot subsist, and which are those contained in the Holy Gospel and in the doctrine of the Church.

We do not doubt that it will happen thus, and the bases for Our firm hope are the most noble and Christian sentiments, of which the Chief of State and so many gentlemen, his faithful collaborators, have given unequivocal evidence with the legal protection which they have granted to the supreme religious and social interests, according to the teachings of the Apostolic See. The same hope is also founded upon the enlightened zeal and abnegation of your Bishops and Priests, tempered by pain, and also in the faith, piety, and spirit of sacrifice of which, in terrible hours, all classes of Spanish society gave heroic proof.

It falls upon You, Venerable Brothers in the Episcopate, to advise all, so that in their policy of pacification all will follow the principles taught by the Church, and proclaimed with such nobility by the Generalísimo: of justice for crime, and of lenient generosity for the mistaken.

Following the reintroduction of the Civil Code (see page 336) alongside the Clerical Laws, Franco and the Church were united further by their traditional and conservative vision of society and family life. Franco saw in the Church a link to the 'purer' culture and traditions of a bygone era of Spain. He therefore wanted to re-establish and consolidate the influence that the Church had formerly had over Spanish society prior to the Second Republic.

Under the influence of his Catholic allies, therefore, Franco's conservative administration took a moralistic line when dealing with people's personal behaviours. This resulted in gays, lesbians and bisexuals being persecuted by the state, and divorce being virtually outlawed. Such lifestyles were viewed as being contrary to Christian morality and traditional family life, and homosexuality was eventually declared illegal by the government in 1954. The Church also frowned on overt types of public behaviour or expression.

SOURCE

8

Directive issued to Spanish Roman Catholics by Cardinal Pia y Deniel, Archbishop of Toledo, Spain, 1959.

Public bathing on beaches, in swimming pools or from river banks constitutes a special danger for morality. Mixed bathing must be avoided because it always gives rise to sin and scandal. As for engaged couples, they must shun solitude and obscurity. Walking arm in arm is unacceptable. It is scandalous and indecent to walk about linked in any way whatsoever.

In 1953, the relationship between the regime and the Church gained further strength when a **Concordat** was signed between Franco's government and the Vatican. This formally recognised the special status of Catholicism as the established religion within Spanish society. It also suggested a degree of approval and acceptance of the pope and the Vatican for the Spanish government. Franco had previously tried to develop a formal Concordat between Madrid and the Vatican in 1948, but at this point in time the effort appeared to be more for Franco's own gratification than for the benefit of the Church.

KEY TERM

Concordat
An agreement signed between a sovereign nation state and the senior representatives of the Roman Catholic Church. It deals with establishing rights and privileges of Catholicism within that country, often above those of other religious groups. It also addresses the impact of government policy on the Church's interests, as well as clarifying issues such as the state's influence over religious appointments.

EXTRACT

2

From Paul Preston, *Franco*, 1995. Here Preston illustrates the attention that Franco gave to maintaining good relations with the Roman Catholic Church, for both domestic and international reasons.

[Franco] concentrated his diplomatic efforts on the United States and the Vatican. The piously Catholic Joaquin Ruiz Gimenez was despatched as Ambassador to the Holy See at the end of November 1948. His mission was to pave the way for a Concordat which Franco wanted as a public seal of divine approval for his regime. Privately, he already assumed himself to have that approval. In his broadcast to the nation on 31 December 1948, he thanked God for giving a 'pleasant wind a calm sea to the ship of the Patria [homeland]'. In the main however, his speech was a complacent anthology of self-congratulation.

When it was finally agreed, the Concordat gave Franco the right to appoint Spanish bishops, while giving the Church a degree of consultation and input before specific policies were adopted. The Catholic Church was therefore an important mechanism for maintaining long-term public support for Franco's government and its various policies, and in turn strengthening Franco's own political position by giving his regime a degree of international credibility at a time when it was fairly isolated in relation to other nations. This relationship between Franco and the Catholic Church would go on to develop into one of the most durable and formidable structures of mutual support during his long period in power. However, the closeness of the link between the Spanish state and established Church provoked criticism from more liberal and democratic nations, with the Catholic Church often being accused of ignoring or overlooking some of the more repressive and brutal elements of Franco's regime.

THINKING HISTORICALLY | Evidence (5a)

Context is everything

Study Sources 5, 6, 7 and 8 on pages 340–42.

Work in groups.

Take an A3 piece of paper. In the middle of it draw a circle about 18 cm in diameter. Within the circle is the evidence itself, outside the circle is the context.

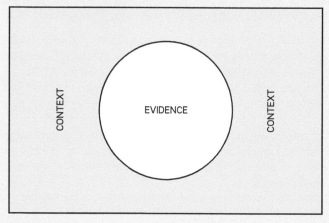

For each source:

Think of a question that the source could be helpful in answering.

Inside the circle, write a set of statements giving information that can be gleaned only from the source itself without any contextual knowledge.

Outside the circle, write down statements of contextual knowledge that relate to the source.

Draw annotated lines to show links between the contextual statements and the information from the source. Does context change the nature or meaning of the information?

Now answer the following question:

Explain why knowledge of context is important when gathering and using historical evidence. Give specific examples to illustrate your point.

Cult of personality

Franco's style of individualised and ruthless leadership would become a key feature of Spain's emerging fascist state, based on the core premise within the ideology of fascism that desired an all-powerful and charismatic single leader. As with other political dictators of the 20th century, there subsequently developed a 'cult of personality' that revolved around the powerful status and personality of Franco. This involved the use of propaganda (see page 341), and high-profile imagery and icons of the dominant leader became increasingly evident across Spanish society. These images usually depicted Franco in military uniform, often making speeches to large crowds of people or inspecting troops. Pamphlets promoting the significance of Franco's position within the new state were also circulated around Spain. They specifically emphasised the importance of unifying the formerly fragmented country under his leadership. These propaganda-based measures further elevated Franco's role and presented him as a national 'messiah', whose role was essential for the salvation and 'unification' of the nation, a notion that was broadly consistent with fascist beliefs and principles.

As a strategy for political rule, this 'cult of personality' aimed to encourage a sense of worship and reverence among ordinary citizens towards Franco's personal importance and indispensable value in securing a more positive and stable future for Spain. At public meetings and in his broadcast speeches, the focus would always be on Franco as an individual as opposed to his collective government of ministers. The cult of personality was ultimately another method by which he sought to further consolidate long-term public support for himself and his political regime.

SOURCE

9 Francisco Franco pictured speaking at a Falangist celebration in the Metropolitan Stadium in Madrid, following the end of the civil war in 1939.

ACTIVITY
KNOWLEDGE CHECK

1 What were the key methods by which Franco strengthened and consolidated his power in the years following the civil war?

2 To what extent were these methods a legacy of civil war practices? Provide examples to support your answer.

3 To what extent did the alliance between Franco and the Catholic Church support each other's goals for the 'new state'?

Education policies

As a consequence of the close relations between Franco and the Church, from the late 1930s onwards Catholicism once again played a significant part in the provision of education in Spain. Priests and nuns re-emerged from the anticlerical atmosphere of the Second Republic to teach the principles and values of Catholicism to the Spanish masses. In 1938, Franco had abolished co-education in schools within the Nationalist zones, ordering that male and female students were to be educated separately. Furthermore, female students were to be taught only by female teachers and male students by male teachers, as a means of further reinforcing traditional cultural and social values. In addition to Catholic studies, girls were taught skills to enable them to pursue a more traditional domestic role of raising a family and running a home, while boys enjoyed sports and were taught vocational skills. Once the civil war was over, these educational practices were extended across the whole country. The Catholic Church therefore worked closely with Franco's regime to restore traditional gender roles within Spanish society which had been blurred and disrupted by the civil war.

Children were also taught about the merits of the new state and of the perils of Marxism; these were topics and messages that both Franco and the Church fully endorsed. Foreign languages were forbidden in Spanish schools during the Franco era. This caused particular controversy within the autonomous regions of the Basque province and Catalonia, which each had distinct languages of their own. Government propaganda slogans of the time would declare 'If you are Spanish, speak in Spanish.' The visible display of the national flag and crucifixes clearly emphasised that the focus of Francoist education was on Spanish patriotism, nationalism and the Catholic faith. In 1945, the Law of Primary Education formally applied Catholic values to all primary education in Spain. Following the 1953 Concordat, Catholicism was able to more explicitly shape all aspects of educational policy within Spain. The role of minister for education was usually reserved for an ultra-Catholic figure, for example, José Ibáñez Martín, who held the post from 1939 to 1951. As well as maintaining a firm grip on broader Spanish society and culture within the new state, such developments ensured that Catholicism reasserted its influence to play a large part in the learning curriculum of Spanish children for the foreseeable future.

Attitudes towards women

Hundreds of thousands of women had played active and prominent roles within the Spanish Civil War, particularly on the Republican side, with a small number involved in military fighting and a more substantial group engaged in support roles in hospitals and canteens (see page 325). During the conflict and for a period beforehand under the Second Republic, women had enjoyed an unprecedented degree of social, political and economic independence by Spain's historic standards. The Nationalists, however, generally continued to view the female role within Spanish society as being of a more traditional domestic type. This was despite the fact that the Falange had its own women's section (*Sección Femenina*) that numbered almost 600,000 by the end of the civil war, and which provided thousands of women with active nursing and support roles for the Nationalist forces.

Under the new regime, many of the progressive and liberating social policy achievements that were secured for women, various minority groups and liberal-minded citizens during the Second Republic became a thing of the past. This post-civil war environment was defined by the 1889 Civil Code reintroduced by Franco in 1938 (see page 336), and for women entailed a largely home-based role, which primarily focused on raising families within a stable domestic setting and having little or no economic independence due to the return to civilian life of the men who had fought in the war. Women were once again legally reliant on their fathers or, if married, their husbands, reinforcing the traditional social values at the heart of Franco's political regime. Any prior notions of **feminist** expression were swiftly suppressed and stricter and more conventional community structures were re-established. This frustrated the more liberated and egalitarian-minded women of Spain, particularly those who had witnessed the roles of figures such as *La Pasionaria* during the civil war (see page 326). Dissent from left-wing and liberal feminists would grow steadily stronger throughout the Franco era, particularly as the country became more exposed to influences from other more liberal Western nations.

Traditional attitudes towards women and marriage were further endorsed by government propaganda films that sought to emphasise and reassert an idealised view of the conventional family and which censored any suggestions of extra-marital relations, unmarried mothers or alternative lifestyles to the one favoured by Franco and his conservative, religious support base. With Franco's government re-establishing elements of the 1870 Criminal Code from 1938 onwards, women found guilty of extra-marital affairs were now also liable for criminal prosecution. The government also sought to strengthen the institution of marriage, made divorce virtually impossible and prohibited abortion along with the emerging use of contraception. In reality, only marriages carried out by the Catholic Church were valid, and the idea of civil marriages with no religious element was unheard of.

> **KEY TERM**
>
> Feminism
> A social and political movement that advocates complete gender equality between women and men on all levels.

AS Level Exam-Style Question Section B

To what extent did Franco's government control Spanish society in the years 1938–56? (20 marks)

Tip
With a question like this, avoid simply describing government policies of the period in question. Instead, assess and analyse the evidence that Franco's government was in control of Spanish society between the years in question. Was there are any evidence of opposition activity, and what concluding judgement can therefore be reached?

HOW WELL DID THE SPANISH ECONOMY PERFORM IN THE YEARS FOLLOWING THE CIVIL WAR?

Economic problems and the impact of the civil war

From 1939 onwards, Franco's government had to deal with major debts. In the first instance, those accumulated during the civil war, and in the second, those arising from the wider European disruption caused by the Second World War up to 1945. As a result, Spain experienced significant economic hardship and bleak social conditions in many areas. In addition to restoring social order, therefore, Franco's other major domestic priority after 1939 was to generate a significant economic recovery for Spain and its beleaguered and war-weary population. Much of the country's infrastructure, industry and trade had been badly damaged and destabilised by the civil war, and the Spanish people generally wanted to be able to lead ordinary civilian lives and have the capacity to earn a basic living once again.

What further weakened the country's economic performance were the relatively high levels of military expenditure during the early years of the Franco regime. Between 1939 and 1945, an estimated half of all government spending was on the military; it was the single biggest area of public spending in Spain at this time. This was not only a legacy of the civil war, but also a reflection of Franco's own militaristic background and the importance he placed on the army's vital role within his new state. Spanish industrialists with business interests directly linked to the military sector (for example, armaments) therefore benefited from government investments. Although expenditure on the military did fall slightly as the 1940s progressed, it remained relatively high, resulting in low levels of government expenditure in other key policy areas such as industrial reconstruction, public works, agricultural investment and social policies, including education. By neglecting these policy areas, the new regime's economic approach was failing to address issues that directly affected ordinary Spanish citizens' everyday lives such as employment and their standard of living, as well as opportunities offered by setting up strong trading links with other nations.

SOURCE
10
Spanish government's budget expenditure in selected key policy areas, 1940–45, as a percentage of total government annual spend.

Area	1940 (%)	1945 (%)
Army	40.6	34.0
Police services	10.5	6.4
Education	6.4	5.4

KEY TERMS

Inflation
The average price increase for everyday goods, which can have an adverse economic effect if wage levels are not increased at a similar rate.

Underemployment
An employment situation that does not utilise the worker to their maximum potential, and where the numbers of workers employed is insufficient for the amount of work needing to be done. Such a situation often occurs as a consequence of employers trying to keep down wage levels for economic reasons, and can also be linked to seasonal work.

Balance of trade
The difference between a country's imports and exports, which indicates how strongly it is trading with other nations.

Corporatism
An economic policy where outside bodies are given some input into government policy-making, particularly in relation to economic and industrial management. Businesses, employers and trades unions are typically the kinds of groups 'incorporated' into this style of government.

For much of the period between 1938 and 1956, wages remained low and failed to keep up with rising prices. In addition, the country experienced the worst **inflation** in its history. As a result, average income levels in 1951 had only just reached the levels of the mid-1930s. The general standard of living did not reach the levels of 1936 until 1952. Unemployment figures did steadily fall, from approximately 750,000 just before the civil war erupted, to 500,000 by 1940, and to just over 150,000 by the end of 1944. However, these figures disguised the high levels of **underemployment** within rural parts of Spain. The figures were also artificially lowered by the civil war casualty figures. Further negative economic indicators were reflected in the fact that by 1939 the country's industrial output was 31 percent lower than it had been prior to the civil war and agricultural production had fallen by 21 percent. In a similar vein, the country's **balance of trade** figures remained negative for much of the 1940s, and Spain's pre-civil war levels of exports were not achieved again until 1950. The official currency of Spain, the peseta, was also struggling to compete with other currencies and having a negative effect on currency exchange and export costs. These bleak economic conditions created significant hardships for the Spanish population and had the potential to jeopardise Franco's political position. The Franco-led regime, when it came to power, therefore needed to establish an improving and developing economy, one which would ensure that social and political stability was more likely to be maintained in the long term.

The development of corporatism

In order to improve Spain's economic performance, Franco adopted a measure known as **corporatism**. This involved the government bringing employers and workers (primarily trades unions) into the decision-making process, particularly regarding the practical implementation of economic policy. Together they formed a government-run corporation or syndicate with the aim of improving industrial relations between businesses and their employees. Under a corporatist system, capitalism and labour came to work together. On a practical level, boards were established as part of the syndicates, primarily consisting of employers' representatives and trades unionists. The employers would negotiate employment conditions with the trade union representatives, who acted on behalf of the wider workforce. The syndicates were, however, ultimately responsible and accountable to the government rather than the workers. In practice, therefore, the government used the syndicates to impose wage rates, production targets and the price of goods. There were further criticisms that the focus was on large employers to the exclusion of small businesses, who did not form part of these syndicates. After a period of consultation, if a broad agreement over employment conditions, rates of pay and prices could be reached, then workers would in turn promise not to take disruptive strike action and to sacrifice some of their traditional industrial powers. These boards operated on a regional level in order to take into account economic variations across the country when setting wage levels.

Corporatism was seen as an attempt to reach a stable compromise between the two ideological extremes of capitalism, which favoured big business, and communism, which favoured the workers, and to move on from some of the class-based tensions of the civil war era. The policy ultimately aimed to prevent recurring industrial unrest. Through corporatism, strikes were effectively outlawed, thereby providing Franco's regime with a means of controlling the working class and its potentially disruptive activities. However, negotiations were not always successful, and some regional syndicates reached agreements while others did not. Many employers also gradually came to resent the regulations and costs created by this corporatist approach. Likewise, workers were unhappy with the policy, believing that it favoured the employers, which led to some workers' groups establishing illegal syndicates and organising strikes, which in turn were then brutally crushed by both the *Falanagist* militia and the Civil Guard. Industrial tensions and unrest subsequently worsened, especially during the economic difficulties of the mid- to late 1950s.

The implementation of autarky

Given the country's relative isolation from much of Europe in both political and economic terms during the civil-war era and throughout the Second World War, Franco was also attracted to an economic policy that was based on the general principles of self-reliance and **autarky.** Autarky was endorsed by the Falangists due to its focus on economic nationalism, and was adopted in conjunction with corporatism. In practice, autarky encouraged the Spanish people to focus on producing only what they as a nation needed to live on. The policy's advocates argued that it would be the most appropriate means of regenerating the country's post-war economy, while also reducing reliance on other nations in terms of trade and credit deals. A small amount of foreign trade did continue to take place while autarky was being pursued from the late 1930s onwards, but it only contributed to a meagre five percent of the country's **Gross Domestic Product (GDP)**. In other European countries, high levels of foreign trade were driving post-war economic recovery, but in adopting autarky, Spain was essentially using a process of **protectionism**, where foreign imports were expensive and therefore unaffordable to most Spanish citizens. Protectionism was established in October 1939 in Spain with the passing of the Law for the Protection and Development of National Industry.

Autarky enabled Franco's regime to maintain a tight control on industrial production and output by the use of various regulatory legislation. The policy was therefore compatible with the kind of totalitarian state that was being developed in Franco's Spain, where the government kept a tight rein on all economic, social and political activities. In reality, however, autarky resulted in a lack of large-scale foreign investment in Spain. This acted as a major restriction on the development of Spain's stuttering economy and living standards suffered as a consequence. By the early 1950s, both bread and meat consumption were half of the 1936 and 1926 levels respectively, an indication of an increasingly impoverished population in many parts of Spain. Corruption and food shortages meant that many hard-pressed families were forced to turn to the **black market** for basic products, paying excessive prices to further undermine and weaken the mainstream Spanish economy.

As a consequence of the implementation of autarky, unemployment-related problems steadily became more evident in the traditionally poorer south, where entire villages were known to have abandoned their destitute properties in order to seek improved living conditions and employment opportunities in the north. When large influxes of people arrived at locations in the north, there were no housing facilities for them to live in, so they would construct ramshackle shelters (sometimes referred to as *barracas),* using whatever materials they could find. Consequently from the early 1940s onwards, shanty towns (known as *chabolas*) had begun to appear on the outskirts of large towns and cities in northern Spain. They lacked basic amenities, including electricity, sewers or clean running water of any kind.

Franco formed the opinion that this bleak socio-economic scenario was a God-given punishment for the country's previous excesses, in particular during the period of the Second Republic. At a speech in Jaén in March 1940, he stated that 'The suffering of a nation at a certain point in its history is no chance; it is the spiritual judgement which God imposes for a corrupt life, for an unclean history.' The lack of government funding and investment for social policies relating to everyday life in Spain merely exacerbated existing levels of poverty and exposed the economic stagnation that haunted much of Spain. A major drought during 1944–45 along with ongoing underinvestment in agriculture and the country's limited supplies of fuel and raw materials, made matters worse.

KEY TERMS

Autarky
This term describes when a nation is economically self-sufficient and is not reliant on the resources of other countries.

Gross Domestic Product (GDP)
This term refers to the estimated value of the total worth of a country's production and services located within its national boundaries and produced by both nationals and foreigners, over the course of one year.

Protectionism
This policy makes imports from other countries more expensive due to additional taxation and tariffs.

Black market
An economic system that operates beneath the surface of the normal economy, usually on an illegal basis. The state therefore has no formal role in such an economy and is unable to control the supply and purchase of goods within it, while government taxation of such activities is bypassed and avoided.

EXTRACT

3   From Paul Preston, *Franco*, 1995. Here, Preston is commenting on Franco's broadcast speech to the Spanish nation on 31 December 1948.

He declared that 'we have come through the worst years' and then went on a hymn of self-praise in an entirely surrealistic account of the great economic progress of Spain under his present guidance... Franco's self-congratulation suggested that he was oblivious to the fact that, in working class districts of major towns, people in rags could be seen hunting for scraps. Outside Barcelona and Malaga, many lived in caves. Most major cities had shanty towns on their outskirts made of cardboard and corrugated iron huts where people lived in appallingly primitive conditions. The streets were thronged with beggars. State medical and welfare services were virtually non-existent other than the soup kitchens provide by the Falange. Hardship, malnutrition, epidemics, the growth of prostitution, the black market, corruption were consequences of his regime's policies which inevitably did not figure in the Caudillo's optimistic survey. He was concerned only with 'his' Spain, not that of the left-wing workers who belonged to the 'other' anti-Spain.

Successes and failures

There were both successes and failures stemming from the key economic policies implemented by Franco in the aftermath of the civil war.

Successes of Franco's economic policies

- Corporatism gave workers and trades unions a stake in government and an apparent ability to influence its economic management. As a consequence, this limited the likelihood of strikes and industrial unrest and provided Franco's government with some degree of control and influence over the working classes. The policy therefore provided relative economic and social stability in Spain for a time.

- Autarky appeared to prioritise and promote Spanish interests and living standards over those of other nations. This form of economic nationalism appealed to many of Franco's key conservative supporters and therefore limited the likelihood of any challenges to his position. For a while, it resulted in steadily falling levels of unemployment and a stabilisation and steady improvement of the country's economic status in terms of **Gross National Product (GNP)** per capita.

- Falange Party supporters were the most enthusiastic advocates of autarky and corporatism, believing that both policies were key steps to achieving a full-blown fascist state, as both policies were tightly controlled by the government. The fact that both policies had been developed and implemented in such a short space of time was seen as a major achievement of Franco's regime.

Failures of Franco's economic policies

- Corporatism was something of an illusion. External stakeholders (employers and trades unionists) had limited input into policy-making as the government remained firmly in control of them, their wages and the price of goods. Prices were at times set too low, for example creating shortages of staple food types such as bread. Corporatism therefore failed to generate innovative or creative economic policies and struggled to inspire the long-term enthusiasm of the wider Spanish public. It also favoured larger, more established businesses at the expense of smaller ones, experienced significant regional variations in terms of how effective it was and illegal strikes continued to take place.

- The corporatist approach ultimately resulted in falling living standards for most of the Spanish workforce, with high levels of government intervention creating artificial conditions and suppressing the necessary dynamism for a **free market economy** to flourish effectively. Average wages subsequently failed to keep pace with price rises and during the 1940s, for example wage increases averaged 30 percent compared with a 600 percent average surge in prices. Vital industries such as agriculture also continued to stagnate, with underemployment, unemployment and inefficiency hampering its capacity to function at its full potential, despite growing employment levels in other sectors.

- The policy of autarky stifled vital foreign investment and trade. As a result, low quality synthetic materials were produced in Spain as alternatives to traditionally imported resources. For example, oil was made from coal, and cotton was replaced with synthetic fibres made from chemicals.

KEY TERM

Gross National Product (GNP)
This term refers to the estimated value of the total worth of production and services by a country or its citizens, on both its own land and foreign territories, over the course of one year.

KEY TERM

Free market economy
An economic theory that advocates limited intervention in the economy by governments and politicians, and which prefers market forces to drive economic policy. In practical terms, such an approach places greater focus on individual economic freedom and the market choices made by consumers within a competitive trade environment.

Synthetic materials were expensive to produce; it would have been cheaper and more efficient to import them from other countries using regular trading channels.

- There was also a shortage of vital products such as fertilisers, which could not be synthesised (artificially created) and were no longer imported. This had a negative impact on Spain's agricultural production levels, resulting in shortages of key cereals such as wheat, which led to hunger and malnutrition in many rural communities. Production of agricultural cereals during the 1940s averaged only a quarter of what had been produced in 1935. Consequently, an estimated 200,000 people died during the so-called 'years of hunger' (1939–44), due to shortages of crops and vital food resources. This situation coincided with the agricultural and trading disruption caused by the Second World War, and this European-wide conflict made a difficult economic situation for Spain even worse.

By the late 1940s, it was becoming apparent that neither corporatism nor autarky were capable of delivering a sustainable level of economic growth for Spain and its population, with limited progress and extreme regional variations a consequence of both policies. While each policy initially appeared to be an appealing method for achieving Spanish economic recovery while also being aligned with fascist principles, their practical features proved to be rigid and bureaucratic in nature. The associated growth in poor living conditions symbolised the grim social repercussions that were emerging due to the failures of such policies, and the country's economy was performing weakly in comparison with similar nations. Franco therefore began gradually to abandon these policies as potential economic solutions for Spain. In hindsight, they increasingly appear to have been pursued for ideological rather than practical reasons. Instead, as the 1950s progressed, Franco was more willing to accept the views of a new generation of officials who advocated economic modernisation and liberalisation of trade links as part of a more outward-looking focus.

EXTRACT

4 From Stanley Payne, *The Franco Regime, 1936–1975*, 1987. Here, Payne provides an overview of the economic record of Franco's government during the 1940s.

For Spain as a whole, the 1940s were a decade of prolonged hardship. Actual conditions varied somewhat from region to region, for the more advanced areas normally did better, and energetic civil governors sometimes managed to expand the food supplies for individual provinces. To some extent the black market created a new middle class and was actually necessary for survival; the civil governor of Valencia pointed out in 1947 that the daily food consumption guaranteed by rationing in his province amounted to only 953 calories. Rationing, of course, was common to most of Europe throughout the decade, but the Spanish system could not guarantee the same minimum as those of the more advanced countries. Nonetheless the overall rhythm of Spanish economic suffering was about the same as that for Europe as a whole. Sustained development began in 1948–49, just as it did for most of Europe.

ACTIVITY
KNOWLEDGE CHECK

1 List the key economic problems facing Spain at the end of the civil war.

2 To what extent were Franco's economic policies in the years 1939–45 successful in addressing each of the problems you have listed in question 1?

3 How far did Franco's desire to establish a totalitarian state hinder the economic recovery of Spain in the years 1939–45?

A Level Exam-Style Question Section B

To what extent did Spain recover from the economic effects of the civil war by 1945? (20 marks)

Tip

You need to consider the impact of the civil war on the Spanish economy, and how Franco's policies such as corporatism and autarky influenced recovery. You may want to compare and assess the situation by 1945 with the situation in the mid-1930s before the civil war broke out, using appropriate supporting data where possible.

TO WHAT EXTENT DID THE DICTATORSHIP AND SPAIN'S INTERNATIONAL RELATIONS CHANGE IN THE YEARS 1939–56?

Maintaining neutrality, 1939–45

In September 1939, the Second World War erupted. From a Spanish perspective, this development created the potential for further instability so soon after the country's own civil war had come to an end. European tensions had been simmering for years, and Spain's internal conflict did indeed appear to have been a dress rehearsal for what was now a much wider conflict between the forces of fascism and liberal democracy. Given the vital and sustained support that Europe's two foremost fascist regimes, Germany and Italy, had provided the Nationalists during the Spanish Civil War, it was now widely expected that Franco would return the favour and formally support Hitler and Mussolini. This was strengthened by the fact that in March 1939, Spain and Germany had signed a secret pact or 'Treaty of Friendship'. This had followed on from the Spanish Nationalists signing the Anti-Comintern Pact at the end of 1936 (see page 321), which moved Franco closer to Germany during the civil war and strengthened his anticommunist credentials.

However, a formal alliance between the two nations did not materialise at the outbreak of the Second World War. Spain's desire for a period of stability and economic recovery was at the heart of this failed diplomatic connection. When discussions took place between Hitler and Franco on 23 October 1940, they were notable for Hitler's attempts to formally establish Spain's wartime support for Germany. During the talks, Hitler proposed that the Spanish enter the war in January 1941, primarily to deal with British activity in Gibraltar and to support German military excursions in northern Africa. However, Franco emphasised and prioritised his own country's economic needs, specifically its shortage of basic food products such as wheat, and its limited military equipment to sustain a significant war effort. He also stressed his desire for territorial expansion, specifically French territory in Morocco, and questioned the viability of his forces holding on to Gibraltar in the long term.

EXTRACT

 From Stanley Payne, *The Franco Regime, 1936–1975*, 1987. Here, Payne summarises what Franco demanded of Hitler at Hendaye, South West France, in October 1940.

> Franco presented what had now become the standard Spanish shopping list, territorial and economic, and was evidently prepared to enter the war at that point if Hitler would grant Spain control of most of northwest Africa. This had been the dream of Spanish expansionists, such as they were, for forty years, and few ambitions were dearer to the heart of the Caudillo than domination of all Morocco and the Oran district. To the end of his days, Morocco would represent for Franco the golden illusions and fulfilment of his youth, and at one point he silenced the talkative Fuehrer with an hour-long monologue on the history of Spain's role in Morocco that reduced Hitler to yawns and probably also to the conclusion that Franco was no more than a provincial African colonist... At Hendaye he [Hitler] told Franco that, given the need to conciliate France, he could offer Spain no guarantee at that time. After enduring some seven hours of the polite, fawning, and evasive but obdurate conversation of the 'Latin charlatan', as he called Franco, Hitler later declared that he would prefer 'having three or four teeth pulled' to enduring such an experience again.

KEY TERM

Realpolitik
A term to describe a country's foreign policy and diplomacy which is primarily shaped by its national self-interest, personal power and practical factors as opposed to ideological pressures or influence.

In response to Franco's request for territory and financial and food aid from Germany, Hitler prevaricated and was ultimately unwilling to meet the demands due to Germany's own extensive wartime commitments. The German leader was particularly concerned at further requests for financial support as a condition for Spanish entry, as he believed that Franco's government still owed the Germans a considerable amount of loyalty and reciprocal support stemming from the various levels of support that his regime had provided during the Spanish Civil War. Hitler was therefore said to be somewhat offended by Franco's perceived reluctance to commit himself to supporting Germany's war efforts. This apparent breakdown in previously constructive relations was an example of **realpolitik** in action, where Franco pragmatically placed Spanish needs above those of his erstwhile allies, and national self-interest appeared to take priority over any desire for a firm ideological alliance. The efforts to bring Spain into the war as an official wartime partner of Germany therefore ended in failure, with Franco displaying limited gratitude for the help that Hitler and Mussolini had given him in the civil war, insisting that his support would be based on levels of aid that Germany did not have the capacity to provide. Correspondence between the two leaders did continue, however, with Hitler persisting in his efforts to persuade Franco to align with his **Axis Powers**, but it was ultimately to no avail.

KEY TERM

Axis Powers
The countries that fought against the Allied forces during the Second World War, namely Germany, Italy and Japan.

SOURCE 11

Hitler's letter to Franco, dated 6 February 1941, concerning the Spanish government joining the Axis.

Dear Caudillo!

When we had our meeting, it was my aim to convince you, Caudillo, of the necessity of common action of those states whose interests in the final analysis are certainly tied up indissolubly with each other. For centuries, Spain has been persecuted by the same enemies against whom today Germany and Italy are forced to fight. In addition to the earlier imperial strivings inimical to our three nations there now arose, moreover, antitheses conditioned by world-outlook: The Jewish-international democracy, which reigns in these states, will not excuse any of us for having followed a course which seeks to secure the future of our peoples in accordance with fundamental principles determined by the people and not those imposed by capital.

It is my most heartfelt conviction that the battle which Germany and Italy are now fighting out is thus determining the future destiny of Spain as well. Only in the case of our victory will the present regime continue to exist. Should Germany and Italy lose this war, however, then any future for a really national and independent Spain would be impossible.

I have thus been striving to convince you, Caudillo, of the necessity in the interests of your own country and the future of the Spanish people, of uniting yourself with those countries who formerly sent soldiers to support you, and who today of necessity, are also battling not only for their own existence, but indirectly for the national future of Spain as well.

SOURCE 12

Franco's reply to Hitler, dated 26 February 1941.

Dear Fuehrer:

Your letter of the 6th makes me wish to send you my reply promptly, since I consider it necessary to make certain clarifications and confirmation of my loyalty.

You speak of our demands and you compare them with yours and those of Italy. I do not believe that one could describe the Spanish demands as excessive, still less, when one considers the tremendous sacrifice of the Spanish people in a battle which was a worthy forerunner of the present one. Concerning this point the necessary preciseness does not exist in our agreement as well. The protocol of Hendaye… is in this respect extremely vague and Your Excellency remembers the conditions (today so changed) of this vagueness and lack of preciseness. The facts in their logical development have today left far behind the circumstances which in the month of October had to be taken into consideration with respect to the prevailing situation, and the protocol then existing must at the present be considered outmoded.

These are my answers, dear Fuehrer, to your observations. I want to dispel with them all shadow of doubt and declare that I stand ready at your side, entirely and decidedly at your disposal, united in a common historical destiny, desertion from which would mean my suicide and that of the Cause which I have led and represent in Spain. I need no confirmation of my faith in the triumph of your Cause and I repeat that I shall always be a loyal follower of it.

Believe me your sincere friend…

> ### A Level Exam-Style Question Section A
>
> How far could the historian make use of Sources 11 and 12 together to investigate the reasons for Spanish neutrality during the Second World War?
>
> Explain your answer, using both sources, the information given about them and your own knowledge of the historical context. (20 marks)
>
> **Tip**
> *The sources provide an insight into the mindsets of both Franco and Hitler during the Second World War, as well as highlighting the nature of their relationship at this time. You need to provide some valid assessment of this relationship and offer some judgement as to why Spain remained neutral.*

These ultimately unsuccessful negotiations pushed Franco's Spain towards an official position of wartime neutrality, which came as a surprise to many observers, although Spanish attitudes to the conflict evolved as the war dragged on. Given the diplomatic and political pressures inflicted upon Franco to throw the full weight of his regime behind Hitler, historians have commented that his achievement of such a neutral position was 'remarkable'. In the first phase of the prolonged conflict there was nevertheless some obvious Spanish support for the Axis forces of Germany and Italy. In 1942, for example, a large contingent of Falangist volunteers formed the 18,000 strong 'Blue Division' and went to fight on the Russian front in support of German troops. Spain also sent raw materials, permitted German submarines to be docked in Spanish waters and some Spanish workers were even employed in German factories to bolster the country's war production. These activities were a reflection of a notable enthusiasm among some of Franco's Falange Party to actively assist Hitler's fascist agenda. There was not, however, a unified position on wartime involvement among Franco's broader coalition of conservative support. Monarchists within Spain were more inclined to support Britain due to the historic links between the respective nations' royal families. This in part influenced Franco's decision to steer a neutral line during the Second World War.

In the wake of the entry of the USA into the war at the end of 1941, coupled with Hitler's difficulties in breaking down Soviet resistance on the Eastern Front, by 1942–43 Franco revised his position further and came to the conclusion that Germany was likely to be defeated. Franco proceeded to detach himself from his formerly close association with Hitler's Nazi regime, and the 'Blue Division' was withdrawn from operational activity in the autumn of 1943. In doing so, the Spanish leader was showing some political awareness of the likely post-war settlement, and therefore aimed to manoeuvre Spain into a more favourable position with the Western international community that was dominated by liberal democracies. He subsequently limited the extent of his support for Germany and avoided direct military engagement with Western Allied troops due to an unwillingness to further antagonise the likely victors of the war, namely Britain and the USA.

By staying out of the war, Franco also managed to restrict any significant military expenditure for the weakened Spanish economy. He also secured vital oil supplies and loans from both the American and British governments as a reward for not formally siding with Hitler. Franco's neutral position, however, appeared ultimately to backfire in political terms when at the post-war Potsdam Conference during the summer of 1945, Spain was branded a fascist regime. Spain was therefore not permitted to join the newly established United Nations due to the country's apparent incompatibility with the UN's liberal principles and human rights agenda.

ACTIVITY
KNOWLEDGE CHECK

1 Make a table with two columns and write down the key arguments for and against Franco adopting a formal alliance with Hitler during the Second World War.

2 What do you think was the most significant reason why Franco was ultimately unwilling formally to support Hitler during the Second World War? Explain your answer.

Creating international relations in the Cold War environment, 1945–56

The international scene after 1945 remained a dangerous and demanding one for Spain to have to deal with, principally because it faced diplomatic isolation for primarily ideological reasons. In a developing Cold War environment, the post-war superpowers of the USA and the Soviet Union both had strong reasons to find Franco's regime objectionable: the Americans for its fascist tendencies and lack of democratic liberties, while the Soviets also adopted an antifascist stance in response to the Franco regime's fierce hostility to communism. This diplomatic situation had adverse implications for the Spanish government, creating potential conditions for domestic disquiet amid fears that Spain's 'new state' would struggle to survive and sustain itself in such a hostile international environment.

By 1945, Franco had not only lost his two key allies from the civil war era, but his attempts at rapprochement and reconciliation with the rest of Europe had been rejected. If Spain continued to have limited interaction and dealings with the outside world, then there were dangerous implications for the Spanish government. An isolated position ultimately had the potential to cause some major economic difficulties due to the lack of foreign investment, which in turn could generate social and civil unrest, and eventually expose political weaknesses in Franco's ultra-conservative and authoritarian administration. The urgent requirement to address the country's economic revival was heightened by the failings of the policy of autarky and the vital need to cultivate improved trade links with other nations after 1945. This challenging state of affairs was something that Franco had to address as a matter of priority in the aftermath of the Second World War.

Spain's position of neutrality had failed to sufficiently convince various countries of its commitment to being a co-operative member of the post-war international community. Several critical United Nations resolutions reinforced international perceptions of Spain. Each contained distinctly negative views of Franco's regime, resulting in formal international condemnation of the Spanish government. They also highlighted concerns about Spain's potential threat to the achievement of long-term international peace and called for the continued political and economic isolation of Spain.

Spain was also initially excluded from the Marshall Plan, an American initiative set up in April 1948 offering financial support to various European nations. The worsening tensions of the Cold War prompted the USA to reconsider Spain's position. Given the ongoing expansion of Soviet control across Eastern Europe and a crisis over the future of the German capital city of Berlin erupting in mid-1948, American political leaders concluded that it was vital to their national interest to bring as much of Western Europe as possible under its pro-capitalist influence. The Americans therefore acknowledged that Spain would be a useful ally and approached Franco's regime accordingly, courting Spain with American diplomatic initiatives. This led to the first of a series of American financial loans being offered to Spain from early 1949 onwards (the first totalling US$25 million), with both

EXTEND YOUR KNOWLEDGE

The Cold War

A period of sustained political, diplomatic and military tension primarily between the USA and the Soviet Union, that lasted from approximately 1945 to 1990. While never developing into a full-scale war between these two superpowers, it did involve various small-scale conflicts and proxy wars over the course of almost five decades. Many other nations offered various levels of support to either superpower, and this was often linked to ideological sympathies with the capitalist Americans or the communist Soviets. This created significant geo-political divisions, particularly between Eastern Europe, which was broadly aligned with the Soviet Union, and Western Europe, which was broadly under the influence of the USA. Such an international situation created a bipolar world order, where two large power blocs competed for absolute dominance, supported by a range of smaller allies. This international situation ultimately heightened the continued threat of a third major world war in the latter part of the 20th century.

 SOURCE

13 United Nations General Assembly Resolution 39 (1), 12 December 1946, concerning Spain's position in the international community.

The peoples of the United Nations [have] condemned the Franco regime in Spain and decided that, as long as that regime remains, Spain may not be admitted to the United Nations.

The... Security Council conducted an investigation [and] found unanimously:

'(a) In origin, nature, structure and general conduct, the Franco regime is a fascist regime patterned on, and established largely as a result of aid received from, Hitler's Nazi Germany and Mussolini's Fascist Italy.'

'(b) During the long struggle of the United Nations against Hitler and Mussolini, Franco, despite continued Allied protests, gave very substantial aid to the enemy Powers. For example, from 1941 to 1945, the Blue Infantry Division, the Spanish Legion of Volunteers and the Salvador Air Squadron fought against Soviet Russia on the Eastern front.'

'(c) Incontrovertible documentary evidence establishes that Franco was a guilty party with Hitler and Mussolini in the conspiracy to wage war against those countries which eventually in the course of the world war became banded together as the United Nations. It was part of the conspiracy that Franco's full belligerency should be postponed until a time to be mutually agreed upon.'

The General Assembly,

Convinced that the Franco Fascist Government of Spain, which was imposed by force upon the Spanish people with the aid of the Axis Powers and which gave material assistance to the Axis Powers in the war, does not represent the Spanish people, and by its continued control of Spain is making impossible the participation of the Spanish people with the peoples of the United Nations in international affairs;

Recommends that the Franco Government of Spain be debarred from membership in international agencies established by or brought into relationship with the United Nations.

countries united by their explicit desire to prevent the further spread of communism. In September 1953, the Treaty of Madrid was signed by Franco and US President Eisenhower, which represented a 20-year defence agreement featuring further American financial aid that would eventually total US$625 million, alongside significant military grants. In return, Franco granted NATO the right to set up military bases within Spanish territory; by 1959, the Americans had four bases in Spain. This represented a notable warming of relations and a clear American commitment to support improvements in Spain's military capacity.

EXTEND YOUR KNOWLEDGE

The Marshall Plan (1948–52)

The Marshall Plan was primarily aimed at supporting the reconstruction of Europe after the Second World War with significant economic funds. This policy was spearheaded by the USA under President Harry Truman and was motivated by American fears about the post-war intentions of the Soviet leader Joseph Stalin. It was named after the US secretary of state George Marshall, whose responsibility was to develop and promote this plan within as many parts of Europe as was financially and politically possible. The policy came into practical effect from April 1948, and its underlying priority was to prevent the further spread of communism across Europe, particularly in the centre and west of the Continent.

NATO

NATO's formation was a consequence of the emerging Cold War, and it originally consisted of 12 members, mainly from Western Europe but including the USA and Canada. Its principal goal was to protect Western Europe from communist expansion, using primarily military means if required. This body's establishment added a more dangerous element to the emerging Cold War, as NATO posed a clear military threat to the Soviet Union and its membership grew in size in later years. In response, the Soviets formed a similar military body in 1955, The Warsaw Pact, which was based in Eastern Europe. In subsequent years, both bodies sought to counterbalance the potential power and influence of the other.

AS Level Exam-Style Question Section A

Why is Source 13 valuable to the historian for an inquiry into Spain's international status during the 1940s?

Explain your answer, using the source, the information given about it and your own knowledge of the historical context. (8 marks)

Tip

Think about the context of the source, namely where it originates from and what kind of document it is. Assess the reasons why the United Nations adopted this position, and also consider the attitudes of other key nations, specifically what their view of the Franco regime was at this point in time.

These developments had the notable impact of bringing Spain out of political and economic isolation. The Franco regime's steady reintegration into the international community came to a constructive conclusion when the country was admitted into the United Nations in 1955, ten years after its initial rejection. The event marked a significant achievement for Franco's government, and it had the dual benefit of securing substantial economic investment into the country, while further improving Spain's international prestige in the process.

Franco had ultimately proved himself to be extremely durable. With both Hitler and Mussolini and their tyrannical regimes removed from the political and diplomatic stage, the Spanish *Caudillo* was now the most prominent fascist leader in the Western world. Franco's Spain was therefore nestled between a host of emerging and established European liberal democracies with distinctly different political values and cultures to those of his Falangist power base. However, by the mid-1950s his government appeared to have been stabilised, notably by improved foreign relations and burgeoning trade links with the outside world. Franco's various critics and exiled opponents were reluctantly forced to accept that there appeared to be no likelihood of his political downfall occurring in the foreseeable future. However, the economic difficulties that had prevailed on the domestic front since the end of the civil war would continue to present worrying undercurrents for Franco and his government, as well as having an adverse impact on the living standards of ordinary Spanish citizens.

SOURCE 14
A cartoon depicting the USA ('Uncle Sam') tempting Spain (Franco) with admission to the United Nations (UN) in the 1950s, while Hitler and Mussolini are forgotten (both dead and buried by this point in time).

ACTIVITY
KNOWLEDGE CHECK

1 Was Franco right to maintain neutrality during the Second World War? Consider the consequences of his decision as you explain your answer.

2 To what extent did Franco establish and maintain international relationships within the Cold War environment in the years 1945–56?

A Level Exam-Style Question Section B

'Spain's foreign relations between 1938 and 1956 resulted in political isolation from the rest of Europe.'

How far do you agree with this statement? (20 marks)

Tip
You need to consider the overall impact of Spain's foreign relations during the period in question, while assessing to what extent the country remained isolated by the mid-1950s. Avoid a narrative list of events, and arguments both for and against the statement need to be provided, with some clear judgement offered as part of a conclusion.

THINKING HISTORICALLY Evidence (6a)

Arguments and facts

Study Sources 11, 12, 13 and 14 on pages 351–55.

Work in groups.

1 Why are facts important in history?

2 Read Sources 11 and 12.

   a) How do these sources disagree about why Spain should have formally supported Germany during the Second World War?

   b) What do you think is the significance of Franco's attitude towards Germany after 1939? What do you think were the key reasons why Franco's actions did not match his words of support for Hitler? Explain your answer based on Source 12 and your own knowledge.

3 Read Source 13 and study Source 14.

   c) How do these sources appear to disagree about the international reputation of Franco's regime after 1945?

   d) Which one do you think is more significant in terms of explaining how the international community viewed Spain after 1945? Explain your answer.

4 All these sources provide evidence and information about the significance of Franco's relations with the international community after 1939. Which source do you think most accurately reflects Spain's position within international relations between 1938 and 1956? Provide reasons for your answer.

5 If we accept that Source 14 is satirical (mocking) in its tone and not a completely accurate factual reflection of Spain's international position in 1955, do we discount it as being useful? Explain your answer.

ACTIVITY
SUMMARY

Key pillars of Franco's support

| Roman Catholic Church | — | Falange Party, militia and youth movement | — | Conservatives: monarchists, military officers, landowners, industrialists |

1 Write a brief summary explaining why Franco needed the support of each of these three groups as he established himself in power.

2 Which of the three pillars of Franco's support do you consider to have been the most significant to him during the years 1938–56? Provide reasons for your answer.

3 Study the timeline in the Introduction to this chapter.

   a) Explain which event or development had the biggest impact on Franco's leadership, either positive or negative.

   b) Explain which methods were the most effective in consolidating Franco's grip on power. For example, legislation, terror and repression, economic development or his own style of leadership. Provide evidence in support of your judgement.

   c) Summarise the three most difficult challenges that Franco's government faced between 1938 and 1956, and how they were overcome or not. Provide reasons for your answer.

WIDER READING

Beevor, A. 'The Spanish civil war: men of la Mancha', in *The Economist*, 22 June 2006

Payne, S. *The Franco Regime 1936-1975*, University of Wisconsin Press (1987) is a comprehensive and detailed account of the system of political rule and policies adopted by the Franco regime in Spain for over 30 years

Payne, S and Palacios, J. *Franco: A Personal and Political Biography*, University of Wisconsin Press (2014) is an account of the life of Franco and his impact on Spain, based on both traditional historical sources and investigative journalism

Preston, P. *Franco: A Biography*, Fontana (1995)

Preston, P. *Franco and Hitler: The Myths of Hendaye 1940*, London School of Economics (1992)

Preston, P. *The Spanish Holocaust*, Harper Press (2012) is a recent summary offering a more shocking and dramatic angle to Franco's period of terror

Thomas, H. *The Spanish Civil War*, Penguin (revised edn, 1965)

2b.4 Dictatorship remodelled and the transition to democracy, 1956–78

KEY QUESTIONS

- How far-reaching was economic and social change in Spain in the years 1956–75?
- To what extent did political developments affect Spain in the years 1956–75?
- How successfully was succession planning managed for a post-Franco head of state?
- How successfully did Spain make the transition to democracy and establish a democratic constitution in 1978?

INTRODUCTION

Between 1956 and 1978, Spain went through a significant transformation on a number of different levels as part of a broader process of modernisation. These changes affected all aspects of Spanish life, particularly the economic, political and social dimensions. The country's cautious emergence from political isolation in the early 1950s had highlighted how burgeoning international links could be the key means of regenerating Spain's long-term prospects. This had the potential to not only have an impact on its role as a European nation, but also to influence its status across the wider world and shape its domestic fortunes. Spain's steadily increasing involvement with other nations could therefore be seen as the catalyst for the domestic reforms that followed.

Franco's acknowledgement that he had urgently to address Spain's escalating economic problems with radically different policy initiatives proved to be the turning point in the country's quest for modernisation. A new economic approach and the rapid growth that followed paved the way for further significant changes for Spanish society. This was evident in a series of political developments that emerged from the mid-1950s onwards, including a more independent and critical voice for the Catholic Church and the growth in levels of regional nationalism, as well as a steady rise in active opposition to the Franco regime. A surge of dissent provoked a strong reaction from the government. The extent of the repression, however, did not seem to suppress ongoing demands for further political reforms.

1956
April: Morocco gains independence from Spain

October: Spanish state television, Televisión Española (TVE), established

1957
February: Cabinet reshuffle demotes Falangist minsters and promotes Opus Dei technocrats

1959
June–July: Stabilisation Plan; ETA founded

December: US President Eisenhower visits Spain

1962
Spain's application to join the EEC is rejected; strikes in Asturias

1964
December: Law of Associations

1966
March: Press Act

| 1956 | 1957 | 1958 | 1959 | 1960 | 1961 | 1962 | 1963 | 1964 | 1965 | 1966 |

The government faced some significant challenges, particularly during the 1960s and 1970s, in order to make the regime more secure and the country more stable. The nature of Franco's dictatorial leadership and its functional effectiveness, alongside the planning of a long-term succession to his role, were central features of this critical phase of Spain's modern history, and the eventual democratic outcome was far from certain.

HOW FAR-REACHING WAS ECONOMIC AND SOCIAL CHANGE IN SPAIN IN THE YEARS 1956–75?

Economic problems in the 1950s

Under Franco's stewardship, the Spanish economy had on the whole performed sluggishly since the end of the civil war in 1939. Although international trade had slowly improved after the Second World War and American loans had provided a further boost, by the middle of the 1950s the country's economic problems had mounted to a seriously destabilising extent. The American loans that had filtered through since the 1953 Treaty of Madrid (see page 354) were limited in their impact by the fact that the government decreed that the money could only be spent within Spain. This ultimately created a situation where too much currency was in circulation within Spain's domestic economy. There were not sufficient goods or produce on which to spend it, thus creating a surge of price inflation on a whole range of consumer goods.

Of major concern was the fact that this rise in inflation appeared to be a long-term problem. Between 1956 and 1959, the price of goods grew at an average rate of 20 percent per year, and wages could not keep up with these rapid increases. By the end of the decade, Spain was virtually bankrupt and unemployment had reached 35 percent, which subsequently had an adverse effect on the living standards of ordinary people. As with earlier years, this created a dangerous situation for the Spanish government, with the potential for significant social agitation and political unrest to arise if the situation was not addressed. By 1957, some initial stirrings of discontent began to appear in the form of working-class and student protests, demanding economic reforms that featured fewer government restrictions, while also generating improved social conditions. While repression and censorship remained in place, this alone was not enough to keep the government in power if an economic recession was to be long term and entrenched.

There was also a different set of political demands for urgent remedial action from younger and more radical members of Franco's Falange Party, such as Jose Luis de Arrese, a leading Falangist, who argued that full-blown fascism and a re-emphasis of Nationalist policies, such as autarky (see page 347) and more controlled economic regulation, were the solution to this state of affairs. Within

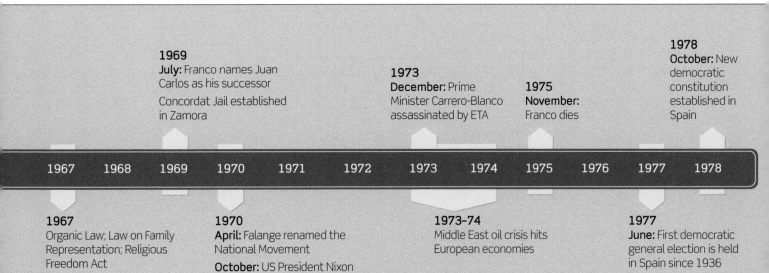

1969
July: Franco names Juan Carlos as his successor

Concordat Jail established in Zamora

1973
December: Prime Minister Carrero-Blanco assassinated by ETA

1975
November: Franco dies

1978
October: New democratic constitution established in Spain

| 1967 | 1968 | 1969 | 1970 | 1971 | 1972 | 1973 | 1974 | 1975 | 1976 | 1977 | 1978 |

1967
Organic Law; Law on Family Representation; Religious Freedom Act

1970
April: Falange renamed the National Movement

October: US President Nixon visits Spain

1973–74
Middle East oil crisis hits European economies

1977
June: First democratic general election is held in Spain since 1936

this gloomy picture, a particular source of embarrassment and humiliation to Franco's Nationalist political supporters was the granting of independence to Morocco in 1956. A policy decision fuelled by economic factors, it destroyed any hopes Spain had of developing a successful overseas empire.

This dire situation represented the bleakest economic scenario since the civil war era, and certainly posed a significant threat to the long-term viability of Franco's political position. From the late 1950s onwards, therefore, Franco's regime chose to follow a revised economic agenda. This departure from an economic model that was heavily influenced by his Falangist power base would eventually culminate in a so-called 'economic miracle', and such a development would have major domestic and international implications for the future of Franco's Spanish state.

The decline of the Falange and the rise of the technocrats in the late 1950s

It was clear that by the late 1950s Franco needed to take some drastic action in order to resolve the economic crisis in Spain. In a bid to turn the country's fortunes around, therefore, he detached himself from the Falange Party that had for so long formed the bedrock of his political power base, but which by now appeared to be holding both Spain and Franco back. Franco's desire to make further links with Western European countries had previously been thwarted by the fascist tendencies of various Falangist figures who were unwilling to compromise and cultivate further links with other liberal democratic regimes. However, with a falling membership and their rigid and extreme political views, the Falange Party appeared to be increasingly out of touch and outdated with regard to the contemporary needs of the Spanish nation, particularly in relation to economic policy. As far as the Spanish dictator was concerned, Falangism had served its purpose, and Franco saw an opportunity within this mood of crisis to move against his long-term supporters.

Franco's changing political loyalties first became evident when he reshuffled his cabinet in February 1957, a development that saw Falange ministers either removed from their posts or demoted to junior positions in less prominent policy areas such as education and housing. In their place, Franco promoted figures with more open-minded and reformist economic views, although a significant number were linked to the secretive Catholic organisation Opus Dei. Once again the unerring power and influence of the Roman Catholic faith could be seen within senior levels of the Spanish government, and this caused concern among Franco's liberal and republican critics. New ministers given important departments to run included Alberto Ullastres Calvo (Trade) and Mariano Navarro Rubio (Finance), both of whom were more **technocratic** in nature

KEY TERM

Technocrat
An individual whose actions are primarily based on technical skills, knowledge and expertise as opposed to ideological influences.

EXTEND YOUR KNOWLEDGE

Opus Dei
Established in 1928 by the Spanish Catholic priest, Josemaría Escrivá, this secretive organisation ultimately aimed to protect and promote the interests of the Roman Catholic Church within contemporary political life. It tended to attract highly educated people to its ranks, and many of its members took up key positions within professions such as education, government administration and business. As a body, it developed a clear and focused vision of the kind of society Spain should be in the 20th century, adopting the view that modernisation threatened to undermine cherished Catholic traditions due to liberal and secular policy developments. This had been evident in the anticlerical policies of the 1930s. Within this context, Opus Dei advocated that Catholics had an active role to play in maintaining a political influence so as to protect the values of Catholicism in the long term. Members of this group were broadly sceptical of democracy, were well organised and they took a moralistic position regarding how people should live their lives.

and less wedded to ideological dogma. However, the avowed Catholicism of these emerging political figures was a major influence in shaping their political actions. The Catholic and free-market elements of Franco's conservative coalition were now asserting themselves over the economic nationalists, monarchists and fascist sympathisers.

These new ministers were, however, experts in their field and were far more flexible and open-minded regarding enhanced international trade links and more foreign investment. They were particularly willing to embrace the ideas of the free market as opposed to the state intervention and corporatism that had previously been adopted by the Spanish government (see page 346). Indeed, these technocrats had identified that excessive state intervention and regulation had been one of the key factors that had held back the growth and development of the Spanish economy over previous years. Free trade was also preferred over the increasingly discredited policy of autarky. This new economic approach appealed to powerful capitalist nations such as the USA whom Franco remained keen to cultivate further links with. In policy terms, it culminated in the Stabilisation Plan that was introduced in the summer of 1959. As a practical proposal, the plan sought to open up the Spanish economy to much wider external influences and global connections. This period also saw Spain abandon the previous description of itself as a 'National Syndicalist State', a title which was another legacy of Falangist influence and which appeared increasingly anachronistic in relation to the modern era. In 1958, new and revised principles of Franco's one-party political structure were published to reflect this.

The demise of the Falange Party's influence over Franco's political reign would continue in the years that followed. Its declining status came to a head in 1970 when the party's name was changed to the National Movement. This development symbolised the way that Spain had sought to change and modernise itself in the intervening years, and how Franco had ruthlessly discarded a formerly crucial pillar of support that had helped him seize power in the first place.

The reality was, however, that by the late 1950s, Franco had to look outwards in order to further secure both his and Spain's future prospects, and in doing so he was required to abandon the inward-looking policies of the ultra-nationalists within the Falangist political grouping.

The 'economic miracle', 1960–75

The initial impact of the technocrats and their new approach to economic management was evident in the liberalisation of price levels, as increased competition and reduced state controls saw the cost of consumer goods determined by market forces rather than the actions of government ministers. Everyday items such as tobacco, petrol and food were particularly affected by this development, with prices falling in general terms due to the fact that they had previously been artificially inflated by government duties and state intervention. This in turn had a positive impact on the living standards and lifestyles of the average Spanish citizen. The government and various corporations subsequently saw their economic influences weakened, while there was a more constructive attitude from Franco's administration in relation to foreign countries and international businesses.

SOURCE 1

Spanish balance of trade figures, 1959–73. Based on economic data from the Banco de Bilbao. These figures indicate how much profit Spain was making (converted into US dollars) in foreign trade.

Year	Balance of trade (million dollars US)
1959	253
1961	279
1963	1,004
1965	1,737
1967	1,745
1969	2,333
1971	2,025
1973	4,405
1975	8,516

The rapid improvement in Spain's international trade position from the late 1950s (see Source 1 above) was fuelled by a more outward-looking economic policy that triggered a notable surge of foreign finance. Between 1959 and 1973, the rate of foreign investment into Spain grew from 3,895 million pesetas a year to 105,430 million pesetas. Of this, over 40 percent came from the USA, almost 17 percent from Switzerland, just over 10 percent from both Germany and Britain, and the remainder from other European countries. This increased willingness to engage with foreign investors (the USA in particular) was symbolised by the prestigious visit to Spain of US President Eisenhower at the end of 1959. Such a high-profile diplomatic encounter on Spanish soil was a boost for Spain's image and appeared to indicate a further endorsement and acceptance by the Americans of the regime of the *Generalissimo*.

SOURCE 2

US President Dwight Eisenhower's speech on arrival at Torrejón Air Force Base, Madrid, 21 December 1959. Eisenhower spoke of his desire to consolidate and build on the relations between Spain and the USA.

I say to Spain and the Spaniards: let us work together so that in our own day we may see a long advance toward a world free from aggression, from hunger and disease – free from war and free of the threat of war. Let us work together so that we may pass on to our children a golden promise that mankind will achieve. By this visit I hope to bring to all of you the personal assurance of America's determination to work toward the attainment of that goal, striving always for stronger bonds of understanding and high purpose between Spain and the United States.

While Franco believed that his domestic policy reforms known as *desarrollismo* 'developmentism' were at the heart of the country's economic progress, more objective historians have prioritised the impact of foreign financial investment as the most significant factor. Between 1960 and 1974, US\$7.6 billion of foreign capital was invested in the Spanish economy, alongside a further US\$1 billion in loans to Franco's government. However, it must also be acknowledged that Spain's economic growth in this period coincided with a broader post-war boom across Europe. As the 1960s commenced, there was a surge of foreign investment that led to the creation of more jobs, with international companies establishing bases in Spain and investing in both existing Spanish industries and modern high-tech production. As a consequence, by 1970 overseas investment accounted for:

- 42 percent of investment in the Spanish electronics industry

- 50 percent of investment in Spain's car manufacturing industry

- 37 percent of investment in the country's chemical industry.

One of the key attractions to external investors was the cheap labour costs and limited civil and employment rights of the Spanish population, which meant that Spanish business operations were cheaper in comparison with most other European countries.

Ordinary Spaniards subsequently experienced falling prices that were caused by enhanced levels of competition within a more liberal and globalised economic model. This exposure to free market forces saw the country's average income almost triple during the course of the 1960s, although not all citizens shared the benefits equally. A flourishing consumer economy was, however, evolving. These improving levels of economic prosperity and falling rates of unemployment also resulted in better diets and more leisure time for the ordinary people of Spain, and average calories per citizen rose from just under 2,200 per day in 1960 to almost 3,000 in 1975. Consumer durables and technological products imported from abroad were also being purchased in increasing numbers by the Spanish population.

SOURCE 3

Spanish increase in consumer goods, 1960–75, by percentages of families owning items. Based on data from a compilation of various national surveys.

Goods owned (% of households)	April 1960	July 1975
Refrigerator	4	87
Washing machine	19	55
Television set	1	89
Phonograph (record player)	3	41
Car	4	48

As a consequence of the regime's revised approach to economic management, the Spanish economy was transformed from its stuttering past into one of the fastest growing in the world between 1960 and 1975, albeit from a fairly low starting point. Broader implications of this were that the country became less reliant on agriculture and became a more industrialised society, with growing urban settlements in and around the tourist resorts. Overall, the more technocratic and less dogmatic approach to economic policy making had generated a level of economic wealth, a rate of social change and general lifestyle improvements that the Spanish nation had not previously experienced. Although such benefits were unevenly spread across society, progress was undeniable and Spain's industrial size was even considered to have risen as high as the ninth biggest in the world by the time the *desarrollos* (development) of the country's economy had started to slow down slightly by the mid-1970s. By this time, however, Spanish people were more educated, enjoyed better health and had become increasingly westernised in their outlook and attitudes. These dramatic and significant developments were generally viewed as having more positive than negative implications, and this appeared to vindicate Franco's bold decision to steer a new economic and political direction for the country from the late 1950s onwards.

EXTRACT 1

From Stanley Payne, *The Franco Regime 1936–1975*, 1987. Here, Payne highlights the extent and scale of Spanish economic growth between 1950 and 1975.

The last twenty-five years of the Franco regime, from 1950–1975, were the time of the greatest sustained economic development and general improvement in living standards in all Spanish history. In one sense this was not so remarkable, because it coincided with the greatest period of sustained prosperity and development in all world history as well. Nonetheless, the proportionate rise in living standards and general productivity and well-being was greater than in other right-authoritarian regimes such as that of Portugal or those in the Middle East, Africa and Latin America, and it was also greater than in the totalitarian regimes in eastern Europe, Asia, or Cuba. Only Japan made greater proportionate progress than Spain during this period.

However, the rate of economic growth did not last indefinitely, and a worsening economic situation during the 1970s placed increased pressure on Franco's government. Major unrest in the Middle East led to OPEC (Organization of Petroleum Exporting Countries)

increasing the price of oil to Western nations by 70 percent, and by January 1974 the price of a barrel of oil had quadrupled. There was a significant negative impact across Europe following these events, and Spain was no exception, with both foreign investment and tourism entering a steep decline as a consequence. By 1974, inflation peaked at a damaging 24 percent and the country's 'economic miracle' drew to a shuddering halt, with a recession emerging in its place.

ACTIVITY
KNOWLEDGE CHECK

1 What factors explain the decline of the Falange's political influence and the rise of the technocrats in Franco's Spain during the late 1950s?

2 What do the figures in Sources 1 (page 361) and 3 tell us about the nature of Spain's economic progress after 1959?

3 How important was Spain's improving international position to the country's domestic economic progress in the years 1956–75?

The impact and growth of tourism, 1960–75

Franco's new economic approach from the late 1950s onwards had effectively sent a signal to the outside world that Spain's borders were to be opened up and made more accessible. This initially applied to international business investors and foreign governments, but it also sought to tap into the increased leisure time and growing post-war wealth of many ordinary European citizens. The country's warm climate and idyllic beaches had obvious potential as a holiday destination and provided Spain with the opportunity to tap into the lucrative market of tourism by promoting a range of appealing resorts to holiday-making families. A significant starting point was the decision by Franco's government to abolish visas in 1959, making it far easier to travel to and from the country. Along with the growth in air travel and Spain's attractive geographical location, such conditions resulted in a major boom in the country's tourism industry, with four million foreign visitors holidaying in Spain in 1959. This figure rose rapidly to 14 million by 1965.

By the mid-1970s, approximately 30 million tourists a year were flocking to Spain, most of whom purchased 'package holidays' that covered both travel costs and accommodation. As a consequence, there was a rapid growth of hotels, bars and restaurants (the service sector) within the various tourist hotspots. There were few government restrictions imposed on the rapidly developing 'Costa' resorts and the newly constructed high-rise apartment blocks that gradually emerged to dominate Spain's coastal skylines. These dynamic socio-economic trends established tourism as a major industry in Spain that brought an estimated US$3.5 billion into the country's economy every year.

Tourists also brought Western European values into Spain. This had a broader impact in how it changed Spanish culture and social attitudes, having a liberalising effect in general. However, such

SOURCE 4

Spanish tourist figures, 1959–75. Based on data from the Ministry of Information and Tourism, Spain.

Year	Tourists visiting Spain (in millions)
1959	4.2
1961	7.4
1963	10.9
1965	14.3
1967	17.9
1969	21.7
1971	26.8
1973	34.6
1975	30.1

westernised values and attitudes did not go down well with Spain's more traditional and conservative institutions such as the Catholic Church. Scantily-clad female tourists caused particular concern among this traditional sector of Spanish society, who favoured a more modest approach to fashion and dress sense. The 'sun, sand and sex' culture of package holidays, particularly the more hedonistic 'Club 18–30' varieties, aimed at young people, were a further cause of moralistic anxiety and opposition. Consequently, 'dressing houses' were built close to various beaches for women to get changed, while bikini wear was initially banned in locations other than the beach.

Even as early as the 1960s, however, such restrictions were not fully enforced, largely due to a fear among the Spanish authorities that it would drive the valuable tourist income away. It was for this reason that Spain was forced to adapt to foreign cultures and fashions. These trends eventually resulted in Spanish men and women gradually abandoning their own more conservative dress sense and increasingly wearing shorts and bikinis themselves. Women were particularly liberalised and liberated by the tourist industry, with the creation of significant employment opportunities for Spanish females as hotel staff or tour guides. By 1974, the number of women in the country's workforce had almost doubled since 1950, standing at approximately 30 percent and rising exponentially.

This more 'open' image also created opportunities for the traditionally low-paid Spanish workers. Not only did tourism create thousands of new jobs in various blossoming holiday resorts, but the country's less isolated position and improved European links led to thousands of the country's citizens emigrating to seek enhanced employment opportunities and higher levels of pay in other parts of the Continent. Consequently, Spanish emigration rose steadily in the years 1959–75, and this created positive implications for further economic growth. The resulting reduction in competition for jobs within Spain lowered domestic unemployment levels, while many workers who went abroad sent a portion of their wages back to their families in Spain.

For example, in 1959 alone, an estimated US$126 million was sent back to Spain from Spanish workers abroad, which provided a further major boost to the national economy.

SOURCE 5

Spanish emigration figures, 1959–75. Based on data from the Spanish Institute of Emigration.

Year	Numbers emigrating	Numbers returning	Net emigration
1959	55,130	41,309	13,821
1960	73,431	35,308	38,123
1961	115,372	7,815	107,557
1962	142,505	45,844	96,661
1963	134,541	52,230	82,311
1964	192,999	112,871	80,128
1965	181,278	120,678	60,600
1966	141,997	143,082	-1,085
1967	60,000	85,000	-25,000
1968	85,662	67,622	18,000
1969	112,205	43,336	68,869
1970	105,538	40,000	65,538
1971	120,984	60,000	60,984
1972	110,369	70,000	40,369
1973	100,992	110,000	-9,008
1974	55,347	140,000	-84,473
1975	24,477	70,000	-45,485

Spain's rate of economic growth (boosted by increased tourism and emigration) only began to slow down in the wake of a major global slump following the 1973 Yom Kippur War in the Middle East, which had an adverse effect on oil supplies that were crucial to the strength of various national economies. The downturn affected most of Europe. It subsequently resulted in the flow of Spanish emigrants slackening off with many returning home, as well as causing a temporary blip to the rapidly rising levels of tourism. Nevertheless, there remained a solid core of Spanish emigrants inhabiting various parts of North West Europe. By 1973, there were approximately three-quarters of a million Spaniards working in France and Germany alone.

AS Level Exam-Style Question Section B

To what extent did tourism drive Spain's economic recovery between 1956 and 1975? (20 marks)

Tip

The wording of this type of question provides you with a suggested factor, and there is often a temptation among some students to merely agree with the proposition that tourism did drive the Spanish economic recovery. For a more balanced and well-rounded answer, other factors should also be introduced and considered, so that a more rigorous judgement can be offered.

Social developments and tensions

Spain's newly found levels of prosperity were not experienced by all of its citizens, and significant economic and social problems continued to exist during this period of general growth and expansion. House-building, for example, was not meeting social demand, and there was a severe lack of affordable houses in many of the country's large cities. Shanty towns (known as *chabolas*) continued to build up in close proximity to Spain's large urban locations. For example, 70,000 people settled in ramshackle homes and tents on Montjuic, a hill located close to the centre of Barcelona. Where the government did invest in housing, it was often of a poor standard.

SOURCE

6 An inspection report on new Spanish housing built during the 1950s, listing the difficulties found in them.

A group of 'economic houses' built at Hernán Cortés, a development in Castro Del Rio – 'unacceptable foundations', 'bad roofs which cause leaks', 'roofs collapsing leaving rooms completely exposed', 'useless kitchens', 'lamentable carpentry'; the Padre Jesus Nazareno development in Priego de Cordoba – 'bad foundations', 'collapsing walls', 'deficient roofs', 'cracking floors', 'leaking w.c.'. The local teacher in Montilla denounced the low quality of the Gran Cápitan project stating that the 'foundations were made with no cement'. There were also 'blocked sewers', 'unusable kitchens', and 'completely unusable' sanitation systems while the streets of the development were 'true rivers of pestilence'.

The poor quality conditions caused by limited investment in public housing was symptomatic of the poverty that stubbornly refused to be removed from elements of Spanish society. It was also not just an urban phenomenon as areas with significant poverty and low wages remained within the Spanish countryside too. This was particularly the case for the farming communities that continued to be reliant on agriculture, as well as other associated rural industries that were unaffected by the developing tourist boom. Farmers in rural Andalusia in the south, for example, had a typical income level that was only 40 percent of the European average. In contrast, the tourist islands of the Balearics and the Canaries had over double the income of the poorer parts of Spain. There was therefore clearly something of a geographical divide, with the more prosperous north generally faring better in economic terms than the less developed south. This resulted in widely varying levels of expenditure on the increasingly available consumer goods. There were also divisions evident between the larger towns and cities that had received significant investment and been modernised, and some of the more remote parts of Spain still wedded to traditional cultures and industries. Ongoing inequality and disparity in living conditions resulted in social unrest, with strikes erupting in the less developed northern region of Asturias in 1962.

Tourist locations such as the Costa Brava and Costa Blanca on the Mediterranean coast benefited heavily and disproportionately from various road-building projects and improvements to the country's infrastructure. In 1965, more than half of government investment in roads was allocated to these areas, despite the fact that just less than a third of the overall Spanish population lived there. The county's inland areas where almost half of the population lived received just 12 percent of road investment by comparison. This suggested that tourists were gaining more benefit from public expenditure than most of the indigenous Spanish population.

The country's recently acquired financial riches ultimately did not appear to be shared equally, with only 30 percent of Spain's population living in the more lucrative and heavily invested tourist areas, with the richest one percent owning just over a fifth of the country's wealth (22 percent). In the capital city of Madrid, for example, approximately 50,000 luxury flats lay empty during this period, built by private property speculators for the growing tourist and foreign business market, but beyond the financial reach of the average Spanish worker. This unequal distribution of economic resources compared poorly with other European nations that had a more **social democratic** nature or culture. For example, in Britain the richest one percent of the population owned only 11 percent of the country's overall wealth.

KEY TERM

Social democracy
A political system where there is a fairly generous welfare state operating within a capitalist economic model. Such systems aim to establish a more equal society by balancing the workings of capitalist economics with some degree of state intervention. By virtue of its name, such a system usually involves offering a democratic choice to a country's population as to who governs them.

The growth in skilled industrial workers alongside the employment surge in the tourism industry significantly altered the traditional class structure in Spain, with new social groupings emerging mainly in urban areas at the expense of the declining agricultural workforce. Many rural-based Spanish citizens moved to the cities and tourist resorts for better employment opportunities and higher salaries. The growing number of industrial jobs generally paid better and guaranteed a more steady income and, like other European citizens who now holidayed in Spain, the average Spaniard also had increased leisure time and more disposable income due to their generally improved employment prospects.

- By 1975, about 40 percent of the Spanish population were employed in tourism, 38 percent worked in industry and only 22 percent worked in agriculture.

- In the late 1960s, the average Spanish employee worked 49 hours per week; by 1975, this had fallen to 44 hours.

- By 1975, average life expectancy in Spain was 73 years, compared to just 62 in 1950.

- Infant mortality had fallen from 43 per 1,000 births in 1960 to approximately 28 in 1970.

- By 1975, an estimated 80 percent of working people were covered by the government's social welfare programme, in comparison to just 29 percent in 1950.

- In 1950, there was just one doctor for every 650 Spanish citizens; by 1975, there was one doctor for every 106 people.

Another element of the country's steady social transformation was the growth in the country's educational sector, which in the 1960s saw expenditure on it overtake military spending for the first time under Franco's rule. Not only did this reflect the reduced influence of both the *Falangists* and the ageing civil war generals, it also indicated the desire of the Spanish government to improve the educational prospects and employment skills of its population within an increasingly globalised employment market. All sectors of Spanish education saw improvements, with illiteracy being more than halved within ten years, falling from 11 percent in 1960 to only six percent in 1970. The number of universities also almost doubled (from 12 to 22) between 1959 and 1974, resulting in a 500 percent increase in university student numbers. Women in particular benefited from this transformative educational environment, which helped many of them to move away from the traditional domestic image that had prevailed during the early period of the Franco era. By 1970, approximately a third of all university students were female. It was only in the most remote rural areas that education standards remained low. However, a more educated population had potential dangers for authoritarian regimes such as Franco's, as it generated the risk of people being more questioning of their government and more demanding of their social and political rights as Spanish citizens.

A further source of 'modernising' social influence was the thriving cinema industry, which brought external cultural and social forces into conventional Spanish life. During the 1950s, Spain had more cinema seats per person than anywhere else in Europe, along with the second highest levels of cinema attendance in the world. This trend was a reflection of both growing literacy levels and a steady rise in leisure time linked to growing levels of prosperity among significant swathes of the country's population. While Spain's own state cinema industry was booming and produced many of the films shown, the country's citizens sought some escapism and wider experiences of other cultures that were often depicted in foreign films. However, centralised government censorship remained. Anything considered as being too controversial or subversive by the official censors would be blocked from wider public viewing.

This affected both domestic independently made films with left-wing themes, as well as foreign films which often had sexualised content, nudity or were considered blasphemous by the country's underlying Catholic culture which sought to exert its influence within the media as well. Many foreign films were dubbed by the censors so as to control the language content within them, and a similar policy of censorship was applied to Televisión Española (TVE), the Spanish state television service that was established in 1956 and which grew in significance due to the surge in television usage by the general public. Spanish television output was at this stage a state monopoly with no alternative channels, and it featured significant government control and influence on a similar scale to the authoritarian communist regimes of Eastern Europe.

Exposure to foreign advertisements and popular international cultural forces saw a rapidly growing interest in areas such as fashion, pop music, consumption of alcoholic drinks and smoking cigarettes, particularly in the younger generation. By 1971, almost three-quarters of Spanish men and just under half of Spanish women smoked. The desire to absorb popular music saw radio sales surge, with 82 percent of Spanish teenagers owning a radio by 1971, while just over half possessed a record player. Further evidence of the growing influence of popular music could be seen when Spain won the 1968 Eurovision Song Contest, to much national acclaim. Spain's Catholic religious influence and its social conservatism was alarmed at such emerging social trends and generally viewed them as a negative development. It voiced its concerns to the government and sought to impose restrictions and further aspects of censorship. However, this proved increasingly difficult to achieve within a rapidly changing Spanish society that was daily becoming more connected to the outside world.

ACTIVITY
KNOWLEDGE CHECK

1 Based on the information in Sources 4 and 5 on page 363, what were the advantages and disadvantages to Spain of both rising levels of tourism and increased emigration in the years 1956–75?

2 Draw a spider diagram of the key social changes experienced by the Spanish population between 1956 and 1975. Highlight which one you feel was the most significant, and provide reasons for your answer.

3 How was the country's growing wealth and resources distributed in the years 1956–75, and what tensions did this create?

AS Level Exam-Style Question Section B

To what extent did economic and social changes benefit Spanish society in the years 1956–75? (20 marks)

Tip

With a question like this, try to analyse and assess the impact of economic and social changes in Spain during the period in question, providing examples where possible. Focus on how much change they delivered, and whether their impact was felt across all parts of Spanish society. Was there any counter-evidence to suggest that economic and social change was not sufficiently beneficial to all and can a clear judgement be reached on this matter?

TO WHAT EXTENT DID POLITICAL DEVELOPMENTS AFFECT SPAIN IN THE YEARS 1956-75?

The reasons for, and nature of, political change, 1956-70

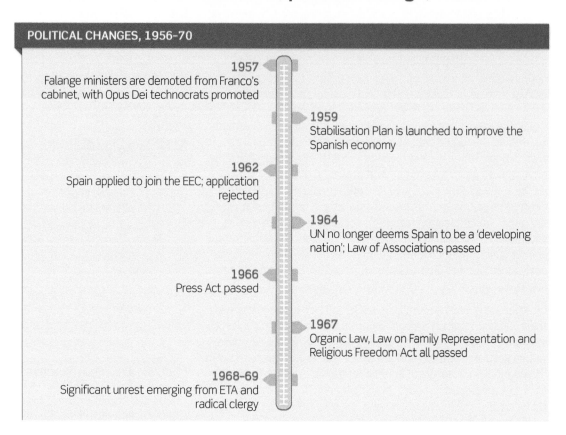

POLITICAL CHANGES, 1956-70

1957
Falange ministers are demoted from Franco's cabinet, with Opus Dei technocrats promoted

1959
Stabilisation Plan is launched to improve the Spanish economy

1962
Spain applied to join the EEC; application rejected

1964
UN no longer deems Spain to be a 'developing nation'; Law of Associations passed

1966
Press Act passed

1967
Organic Law, Law on Family Representation and Religious Freedom Act all passed

1968-69
Significant unrest emerging from ETA and radical clergy

KEY TERM

European Economic Community (EEC)
A trading bloc of six European nations formed in 1957 in the aftermath of the Second World War. Its primary aim was to prevent continental food shortages by the promotion of improved cross-border trade and economic links. It also aspired to prevent further European conflict following two major wars on the Continent in the first part of the 20th century. Its six original members were West Germany, France, Italy, Belgium, the Netherlands and Luxembourg, but it would grow in size and absorb new members in subsequent years. Spain was unsuccessful in its initial bid to join in the 1960s, but it would eventually become a full member in 1986. The EEC later became known as the European Union (EU) in the early 1990s.

A combination of economic pressures, an evolving and more educated Spanish society, as well as an instinctive desire from within the regime to ensure its own survival ultimately fuelled demands for significant political change and reform from the mid-1950s onwards. There were both internal and external demands for the country to embrace liberal democratic political reforms. However, in responding to such demands, a balance needed to be struck between securing the long-term maintenance of the authoritarian structure of Franco's government, while at the same time managing the social aspirations and renewed economic freedoms of Spanish citizens.

As part of the ongoing political change, in 1962 Spain formally applied to join the **European Economic Community (EEC)**. The EEC rejected Spain's application, with the country's undemocratic status being a potential reason for this decision. However, Spain's application for membership was an indication of both the growing ambition of the Spanish government and its changing view of relations with its influential European neighbours.

Further political ramifications saw the country's rapidly improving economic health lead to it being removed from the United Nations' list of 'developing nations' in 1964. However, the failure to be accepted by the EEC caused concern among some of Spain's senior political figures that the country continued to be viewed as a priest-ridden, undemocratic and rather backward society. They feared that this would harm the country's bourgeoning appeal to foreign tourists in the long term. Manuel Fraga, Spain's minister for information and tourism, sought to promote some key political reforms to challenge this lingering negative perception of Spain and its political and social structure. In 1964, and with Franco's approval, he was therefore involved in passing the Law of Associations, which permitted the formation of small social groups or organisations that were primarily community focused and were not explicitly 'political' in their activities. Prior to the passing of this law, the only group that had been allowed to exist was the Falange Party. There now followed a significant growth in local and community group activities, with family-based associations, women's groups and neighbourhood bodies becoming increasingly prominent across Spanish society. Their activities would provide the framework for a stronger **civil society**, which would steadily improve levels of social pluralism across Spain. Many of these groups, however, would go on to form the basis of the political opposition that would emerge against Franco's rule in later years – something that his conservative supporters always feared may occur as a result of the reforms.

As a reaction to the issue of censorship came greater freedoms for the press in the form of the 1966 Press Act. It allowed individual newspaper owners and proprietors greater independence from state influence in appointing their editorial boards, and stories were no longer censored before they were published. Journalists were given greater freedom in what they reported, although the Act required that their writing 'showed respect for truth and morality and obedience to the principle of the National Movement'. While fines could still be imposed on newspapers that breached these principles, as well as journalists being sacked or suspended for such actions, this was a process that was now effectively self-censorship and not under the rigid control of the state.

In another act of political reform, Franco introduced the Organic Law in January 1967, creating a new office 'chief of government' that was independent of the head of state. This was an important piece of legislation that appeared to offer some initial prospects of democracy for Spain, particularly in the way that it divided the two roles. This law therefore provided some limited evidence of a developing **separation of powers** within Spanish government, although it appeared to be something that was more likely to come to fruition in the future than in the immediate present, as while he was alive Franco continued to hold both roles. Such new legislation also increased the country's parliament (Cortes) by 20 percent, which expanded the numbers of Spanish citizens directly involved within the political process, although different political parties (other than the Falange) remained outlawed. In the same year, the Law on Family Representation was also passed which permitted the heads of families to vote. In practical terms, this applied to both married men and women and therefore extended female voting rights.

The changing influence of the Church

During this period of dynamic change, the forces of Spanish conservatism sought to resist many of the reforms and maintain some influence across the wider population. Spain's political hierarchy continued to be dominated by predominantly conservative and religious figures, although in some cases they proved to be increasingly pragmatic in the face of international modernising influences. In July 1967, the Religious Freedom Act was introduced. This law significantly weakened the overwhelming dominance of the Catholic religion in Spain by accepting other religious practices within the country. As a consequence of this Act, a new synagogue (Beth Yaacov) was opened in Madrid in 1968, civil marriages that did not involve church services were legalised and non-Christian religions were also made legal. Although restrictions remained with regard to other religions being publicly practised, and Catholicism remained the state religion, the Catholic Church and its dominant position within Spanish society was being challenged.

The moral pressures of the Catholic Church did, however, have some influence on the government and various social policy issues. For example, following on from the Church's conservative attitudes towards sexual matters, the practices of abortion, homosexuality and pornography all remained illegal throughout the duration of Franco's rule. However, the Catholic moral code was slowly being eroded and a black market in pornography and contraception prospered, with an estimated 300,000 illegal back-street abortions being carried out in 1974 alone. This resulted in the deaths of 3,000 women who often had to endure grim conditions and poor sanitation when undergoing these procedures and complications often arose as a result. This primarily affected the poorer members of Spanish society, as many wealthier citizens who sought an abortion simply travelled to other European countries where the operation could be carried out legally.

Catholicism continued to wield a significant influence over the country's education system, with social values in relation to issues of abortion, contraception and sex before marriage prevailing within the broader curriculum and specifically the kind of sex education taught to Spanish pupils. These attitudes were so resilient that even by 1973 a large number of Spanish Catholic women (86 percent) said that they would not use contraception. This was a trend that did not align itself with more liberal and progressive feminist attitudes in other parts of the Western world. Although some small improvements in their social and economic lifestyles were evident, this religious influence saw women continue to be treated as second-class citizens in Franco's Spain. Despite there being evidence of Catholicism's weakening political influence, alongside an acceptance of some changes and the increased radicalism of some of its younger clergy, the Franco regime continued to have close links to the Catholic Church throughout his rule.

KEY TERM

Workers' Commissions
Working-class trade union bodies that emerged in Spain during the 1960s, and actively opposed the policies of Franco's government, usually via strike activity and direct action.

ACTIVITY
KNOWLEDGE CHECK

1 Draw a flow chart to show how economic change can lead to social change, which in turn can lead to demands for political change, as was the case in Spain between 1956 and 1970.

2 Use your flow chart and the timeline on pages 358-59 to write a brief summary of the key political changes that occurred in Spain in the years 1956–70, and the reasons for them.

The reasons for, and nature of, increased opposition to Franco's rule

By the late 1960s, Franco's iron grip on political power was coming under increasing scrutiny, with levels of hostility to his rule emerging on an unprecedented scale. Regardless of his cautious reforms, his regime faced fierce opposition from a range of groups who had differing grievances, the most prominent being:

- factory workers from working-class backgrounds who demanded improved pay and conditions

- university students who were increasingly well educated and who desired democratic reform

- radical Catholic priests who began to question government policies

- regional nationalists who revived demands for increased political autonomy.

The unrest stemming from factory workers took the form of a wave of strikes and industrial protests that escalated during the late 1960s and the early part of the next decade. The total number of working hours lost steadily rose and peaked in 1974, and the largest-scale strikes (in terms of numbers of workers involved) took place in 1968 when over a million workers withdrew their labour (see Source 7). These strikes were motivated by a desire for improved pay and economic conditions as opposed to political reforms. They stemmed from some of the poorer areas such as the Asturias and Basque regions in the north of the country, with low wages affecting both industrial and rural areas. The strikes were both unofficial and illegal and were organised by so-called '**Workers' Commissions**', bodies that were heavily influenced by left-wing Marxist ideology. Although disruptive, the strikes were largely unsuccessful in achieving their aims. They did, however, highlight the extent of the country's ongoing class tensions, as did the failed attempts to reach any compromise by the Trade Union Organisation (the Syndical Organisation), the body that oversaw the country's corporatist relations between trades unions and the government.

These disruptive actions, fuelled by radical political viewpoints, were a major challenge and source of concern to Franco's government. That they took place at all, and in such volume, was indicative of a growing sense of defiance and reduced fear of the authorities among the wider Spanish population. The strike activities provoked a wave of repression and violent clashes with the Spanish authorities. Three strikers were killed by police at a demonstration in Granada in June 1969, while in 1974, almost 4,500 strikers were sacked from their jobs for their militant actions. This hard-line government response merely heightened the ill feeling and failed to quell the unrest, which became a regular feature of everyday Spanish life by the early 1970s.

SOURCE

7 Hours lost in strikes in Spain, 1967–76. Based on data from the Spanish Trade Union Organisation.

Year	Strikes	Workers on strike	Lost hours
1967	402	272,964	2,456,100
1968	236	1,114,355	2,224,100
1969	459	174,719	5,549,200
1970	817	366,146	6,950,900
1971	601	266,453	8,186,500
1972	688	304,725	7,469,400
1973	811	441,042	11,120,251
1974	1193	625,971	18,188,895
1975	855	556,371	11,120,251
1976	1568	3,638,952	18,188,895

Student protests were fuelled initially by the desire for democratic reform within Spain. Strikes and protests at universities reached a crescendo in the mid- to late 1960s, with campuses regularly disrupted and buildings occupied. As a result, the country's official Student Union (SEU) was banned by the government in 1965, although in general the authorities dealt cautiously with this unrest and its more intellectual basis. By the 1970s, student activists took encouragement from the government's fairly restrained approach in dealing with their protests, and agitation took on a new dimension, with demands for democracy being transcended by growing support for anarchist and Marxist radicalism. Student supporters of these political viewpoints now wanted to overthrow rather than reform the capitalist system, which along with socially conservative Catholic teachings was increasingly unappealing to the country's younger generations. By the winter of 1971, the government was forced to take a tougher line by temporarily imposing martial law in Granada. Universities were becoming established as hotbeds of radical agitation, and a number of university lecturers were sacked because of their left-wing political views and activities. Government repression did not stop such protests from reoccurring, however, leading to prolonged unrest within the country's expanding educational sector.

Trade union and student unrest was surprisingly boosted by the growing amount of co-ordinated support and dissent arising from the Catholic clergy, with various younger priests becoming politically radicalised in pursuit of greater social justice within Spain. Catholicism had always been one of Franco's most staunch institutions of support, but by the late 1960s, the poor social conditions and poverty experienced by the priesthood across various communities indicated that the government's free-market agenda did not benefit everyone. Indeed, many priests were exposed to ongoing inequalities and hardships within Spain, despite the country's so-called 'economic miracle'. This led them to co-operate with both student and trade union unrest, while in the Basque region they gave support to its growing demands for separatism and regional nationalism. Where the radical Catholic priests were concerned, Franco's 1953 Concordat (agreement) with the Vatican (see page 342) gave the growing number of dissenting priests legal protection. In 1969, however, the government decided to take action and established a 'Concordat Jail' in Zamora, close to the northern border with Portugal. This was where the so-called '**red clergy**' and the radical priests were detained in subsequent years.

EXTRACT

2 From Stanley Payne, *The Franco Regime 1936–1975*, 1987. Here, Payne describes the radical activities of some members of the Spanish clergy in the 1960s.

Many of the clergy had become the de facto leaders of the visible (as distinct from the clandestine) domestic political opposition. From petitions in the early 1960s they had moved to protest marches in Barcelona in 1966 and then to occupations of buildings and to independent politicized assembles, all of this accompanied in the larger cities by inflammatory sermons and agitation by individual priests. A few of the most radical proclaimed the aim to put an end to capitalism... Hundreds of clergy were involved in political activities that a quarter-century earlier would have brought immediate imprisonment, beatings, and long prison terms to laymen. Since the clergy had special judicial privileges under the Concordat, they were treated with kid gloves, however.

Franco wrote to the pope in the early 1970s to express his concerns about the so-called 'Marxistisation' of the Spanish Catholic Church and launched a propaganda campaign to try to suppress such developments. He was ultimately reluctant to come down too hard on a movement that had formed a key element of his traditional support base. However, it appeared that the Spanish dictator was standing against an irresistible social tide.

In early 1973, the Spanish Church published *The Church and the Political Community*, which highlighted the spread of liberal political thought by its public expression of support for a democratic Spain. This document also declared that the lack of democratic and civil rights experienced by Spanish citizens was incompatible with the principles of Catholicism, and it signalled a distinct cooling of relations between Franco and his minsters and the Spanish Catholic hierarchy.

The growth of regional nationalism

The other significant dimension of growing opposition to Franco's rule came from the aggressive re-emergence of regional nationalism, specifically within the Basque region of northern Spain. This region had a long tradition of political autonomy, which had been granted and withdrawn over different stages of modern Spanish history. A key development in relation to this political issue occurred in 1959 when a group known as **Basque Homeland and Freedom (ETA)** was formed. Having initially been involved in a wave of bank robberies that its sympathisers were dismissed as merely the poor stealing from the rich, by the late 1960s ETA's activities had evolved into a concerted terrorist campaign against Franco's government. In 1968, ETA assassinated the head of the police's political section, and two further assassinations were carried out during 1968 and 1969; senior government officials and politicians were the prime targets. Other assassinations were planned and thwarted by the authorities, notably one targeted at Franco himself. The government's response was a tough one and an estimated 3,000 members of ETA were arrested between 1968 and 1970 alone, with military trials then conducted in the northern city of Burgos.

SOURCE

 ETA killings and arrests, 1968–75. Based on data from Luis C. Nuñez Astrain, *La sociedad vasca actual*, 1977.

Year	Victims of ETA	ETA activists arrested
1968	2	434
1969	1	1,953
1970	0	831
1971	0	N/A
1972	1	616
1973	6	572
1974	19	1,116
1975	15	518

However, this judicial process appeared to backfire when ETA activists used their trials as opportunities to publicly attack and criticise Franco's regime. Far from exposing ETA as a vicious terrorist organisation, the high-profile trials actually won the group some significant public support, notably from radical student activists. Under international pressure, prominent ETA ringleaders were sentenced to life imprisonment as opposed to receiving the death penalty, as had been the Spanish government's original intention. In December 1973, ETA achieved their most high-profile assassination when their activists planted a bomb in Madrid, killing Franco's ultra-conservative prime minister and powerful political ally, Luis Carrero-Blanco. ETA's aim had been to disrupt the government's reactionary conservative elements. The episode shook Franco, who was said to have remarked that it undermined the very foundations of his long-established political regime. This would suggest that ETA was achieving some degree of success in the nature of its attacks on Franco's conservative framework of government. It also indicated that government repression had not stopped ETA's activities.

Government reaction, 1970-75

Franco's regime embarked on a wave of repression following the assassination of Carrero-Blanco. Under the orders of the newly appointed conservative prime minister, Carlos Arias Navarro, the police, along with new fascist groups such as Fuerza Nueva ('The New Force') and Guerrilleros de Cristo ('Warriors of Christ the King'), mounted a crackdown on the various workers' groups and ETA. The government used ruthless and brutal tactics in dealing with these opponents. In extreme cases it resorted to execution, including the particularly brutal method known as *garrote vil* used until 1974. The widespread political violence and subsequent escalation of killings during 1974 and 1975 had a demoralising impact on the morale of Franco's government. Despite this, Franco remained defiant to the bitter end in the face of ETA's activities. One of his final major decisions was to endorse the death sentences for five ETA members, including Salvador Puig Antich, an anarchist who had killed a policeman. Despite a wave of global opposition led by Pope Paul VI, their executions were nevertheless carried out just before Franco's own death in 1975.

Regardless of the fact that Spain's long-standing dictatorial regime became gradually more pragmatic and willing to offer some moderate reforms, Franco continued to maintain a firm and repressive hold on Spanish society in the years 1970–75. As a consequence, various political activists from ETA, the trades unions and the Church continued to be arrested, exiled, imprisoned or brutally injured by police, especially during the peak of strike activity and ETA violence that coincided in 1974. This highlighted the fact that civic and political freedoms within Spain compared poorly to the rights and liberties enjoyed by the populations of other Western European nations.

Developments in international relations

President Eisenhower's prestigious and morale-boosting visit to Spain in 1959 was followed by ongoing attempts by Franco's government to move closer to its European neighbours throughout the 1960s, via both trading and political means. Spain's economic growth of the 1960s dovetailed with improving political links and diplomatic connections with the outside world, and such external aspects continued to be pivotal to the resurgence of the country's economy.

Having sought to make closer links with Europe during the 1960s, Spain's initial application to join the EEC had been rejected in 1962. However, Franco continued to cultivate links with both Europe and the key Western superpower, the USA, fuelled by a growing awareness of Spain's value to the Americans within an ongoing Cold War environment. In the autumn of 1970, US President Richard Nixon paid an official diplomatic visit to Franco in Madrid, at a time when Spain's thriving economy was approaching its peak. From the Spanish *Caudillo*'s perspective,

Franco (left) meets US President Richard Nixon (right) in Madrid in October 1970. The main purpose of Nixon's visit was to discuss ongoing economic, trade and political links between the two countries.

this event provided further international endorsement of himself as a political leader and his political regime. American financial investment remained a vital component of Spain's ongoing economic and social development. In turn, Spain and its provision of military bases played an important role in the USA's ongoing Cold War strategy (see page 353). Franco's regime was, however, now in a far more buoyant position in its own right, although the USA also retained some significant political influence and sought to convince the Spanish government of the merits of more widespread reforms to its political structure. This, it was argued, would assist Spain in making further progress in its dealings with various Western liberal democracies. This persuasive diplomacy by the Nixon administration reflected a degree of American unease about the nature of its relations with a regime as authoritarian and undemocratic as Franco's. Its improving relations with Spain also left the Americans open to accusations of double standards, particularly within an ideological Cold War environment whereby the USA was supposedly advocating the extension of liberal democratic values in contrast to the repressive and illiberal image of the Soviet Union.

Despite apparent inconsistency in how it dealt with authoritarian and undemocratic nations, successive US governments of the 1950s, 1960s and 1970s ultimately adopted a pragmatic and patient diplomatic approach in their relationship with Spain, hoping to consolidate a primarily economic association into a more fulfilling and liberating political one. The Americans therefore offered constructive advice and guidance about how the Spanish state could embrace the competitive principles of capitalism, while simultaneously evolving in a more democratic and liberal direction in the future. This was justification for the visits of Eisenhower and Nixon in particular, both of whom shared some of Franco's conservative social principles and who valued his staunch anticommunism. Various American presidents of this period therefore viewed Franco as an important figure on the European political scene, and it was a matter of self-interest that the USA sought to integrate Spain further into the mainstream group of Western European nations that were already under its influence. This significant 'superpower' input into Spain's development offered the potential for the remodelling and adapting of Franco's dictatorship so that it could operate and function within a more modern and contemporary political framework; namely one that was more aligned and synchronised with its European neighbours. The exchange between each country's leaders indicates the cordial and friendly nature of Spanish-American relations by this point in time.

SOURCE 10

Toast made by US President Richard Nixon to General Francisco Franco of Spain at a state dinner in Madrid, 2 October 1970.

We think of the words of welcome which you have so generously spoken. We think also, of the tremendous crowds in the streets of Madrid as we drove together to the Palace where we are staying. And as we heard and saw those crowds, they were saying many things. Among them were these: First, General Franco, they were expressing their respect and their affection for you. Second, they were expressing their friendship for the people of the United States. Third, as I saw those crowds, I saw the past of Spain and the future of Spain, and it is truly a great future, because I saw a vigorous people – a proud people, a young people, a dynamic people – the people that have been responsible for Spain having the fastest growth rate of any country in Europe over these past years; the people who will be responsible for Spain, in the last 30 years of this century, moving into a new period of economic progress.

SOURCE 11

General Franco's reply to President Nixon at the state dinner in Madrid, 2 October 1970.

In the short hours that his tight schedule has allowed the President to dedicate to our country, we have had the opportunity for a broad exchange of views which, in my opinion, has been of great interest.

The problems which, at this time, are of common concern for the United States and Spain, and which are also, most of them, of common concern for the West as a whole, are beyond doubt grave and urgent. I am glad, therefore, to be able to state that in this moment, in the presence of the dangers that confront us, our views have been basically coincident. This is all the more significant if we take into account the fact that the international position of Spain has very special and characteristic features. Our kinship and our historical and cultural ties with Latin America; the fact that we are, at the same time, a part of Europe; the traditional friendship with the Arab countries; our geographic position at the crossroads of two seas and two continents – all those are factors which determine and shape the international policy of our country.

In this connection I cannot fail to recall the visit in 1959 of your predecessor, President Eisenhower, a perennial example of civic and military virtues. His stay among us was a cause of the deepest personal satisfaction for myself and of sincere joy for every Spaniard.

ACTIVITY
KNOWLEDGE CHECK

1 What was the significance of the USA in improving Spain's economic and political position between 1956 and 1975? Explain your answer.

2 In what ways did Spain's relations with neighbouring European states change from 1956 onwards?

THINKING HISTORICALLY Causation (6b)

Attitudes and actions

Individuals can only make choices based on their context. Prevalent attitudes combine with individual experience and natural temperament to frame the individual's perception of what is going on around them. Nobody can know the future or see into the minds of others.

Based on the diplomatic visit of President Nixon to Franco's Spain in October 1970 as outlined in Sources 10 and 11, read the summary points below and answer the questions that follow.

Context	Action
• Although Spain was neutral during the Second World War, the country sought to improve relations with the USA and other Western European nations (including the EEC) after 1945. • Franco was extremely keen to continue the process of bringing Spain out of its former position of international isolation. • Key members of successive US administrations viewed Spain as being a vital element to its ongoing Cold War dispute with the Soviet Union. • Nixon also believed that Franco was an important individual figure within European politics, who could consolidate improved relations between the two countries. Franco's anticommunism also meant he would remain loyal to American interests during the Cold War. • From an American perspective, the negative aspect of this relationship was Spain's status as an autocratic dictatorship whose citizens had few civil liberties and lacked democratic freedoms.	• On 2 October 1970, US President Richard Nixon flew into Madrid on a formal state visit to meet Spanish *Caudillo* Francisco Franco. The main purpose was to discuss ongoing economic, trade and political links between the two countries. Such a visit signified a further stage in Spain's development and modernisation.

Answer the following questions individually and discuss your answers in a group:

1 Why might Franco have believed that Nixon broadly supported his regime?

2 Why could Franco have thought that the American government might be willing to develop further links and improved relations with his administration?

3 What other information and factors would Nixon have considered in helping him decide on his course of action with regards to the development of American relations with Spain?

4 How reasonable was Nixon's course of action in 1970 given what he understood about the nature of Franco's regime at the time, and how did such actions influence change?

5 On the basis of the diplomatic actions of Franco and Nixon in 1970, how far should the historian try to understand the context of the beliefs and values of people in the past when explaining why individuals make choices in history?

HOW SUCCESSFULLY WAS SUCCESSION PLANNING MANAGED FOR A POST-FRANCO HEAD OF STATE?

The Law of Leadership Succession, 1947

The issue of Franco's succession had grown in significance as he grew older and more entrenched into the role of Spanish *Caudillo*, with all of the dictatorial powers associated with it. Legitimate questions therefore gradually emerged about who was to succeed him and what kind of political regime Spain would become in the long term after his death. He had initially dealt with this issue in the short term by passing the Law of Leadership Succession in 1947. This had secured his own role at the helm of Spanish politics but did not rule out an eventual return of the monarchy. This law had been an attempt to deal with the demands of the Carlists and other royalist sympathisers for the resurrection of the Spanish monarchy after the civil war, primarily in an attempt to maintain their support for Franco's government (see page 337). However, it quickly became clear that Franco was not prepared to sacrifice his own position for a returning king. In practical terms, therefore, this law merely appeared to be paying lip service to the likely return of the Spanish monarchy. By the 1960s and the 25th anniversary of the end of the civil war (1964), Franco remained as prominent and as dominant as ever. The Law of Leadership Succession therefore did not really resolve the key issue that it was established to address. This became quite evident in the years that followed as Franco's powers and status grew considerably at the head of a one-party state, with no indication that he was planning to relinquish the position for the foreseeable future.

The decision to return to monarchy, 1969

A significant development regarding Franco's succession took place in July 1969, when Prince Juan Carlos was named by the *Caudilllo* as his chosen successor. Juan Carlos was a member of the once-exiled Spanish royal family who had returned to Spain in the late 1940s. He had gone on to loyally serve both Franco and his country as an officer in the Spanish army. His military connections and conservative-orientated royal pedigree appeared to make him a credible candidate as a successor, as far as Franco was concerned, although Spain's ordinary citizens would have no say in the matter. This was the first major indication of any long-term, specific planning for what would happen to the Spanish political system beyond Franco's rule. It appeared finally to indicate that Spain would indeed seek to return to a monarchical model of government once Franco's period of rule had come to an end. Although the timescale for such a development continued to remain hazy and uncertain, the catalyst for this development appeared to be Franco's worsening health. His awareness of his physical decline prompted him to address the issue of his succession. From this point onwards, Juan Carlos began to work more closely with Franco and would often be seen accompanying him to various events.

EXTEND YOUR KNOWLEDGE

Juan Carlos (1938–)

Born in 1938, Juan Carlos was the grandson of the last king of Spain, Alfonso XIII, who was on the throne until the formation of the Second Republic in 1931. His family went into exile in Italy, which was the place of his birth, and he did not move back to Spain until 1948, a year after Franco had declared that the country was once again a monarchy in his Law of Leadership Succession. Although Franco remained in power, Juan Carlos became integrated into Spanish life and served in the country's army during the 1950s. It soon became clear that he was Franco's preferred successor, with this decision being formally announced in July 1969. Some believe that he was manipulated by Franco when named as his successor, but after Franco's death in 1975, Juan Carlos presided over the country's transition into a full-blown democracy, and he subsequently reigned as a constitutional monarch with limited political powers.

SOURCE
12 Franco (right) with his designated successor, the 'Prince of Spain', Juan Carlos, c1973.

These developments frustrated some of Spain's liberal reformers and a growing number of opposition forces who wanted the establishment of a liberal democratic government with civic rights and liberties as enjoyed by much of the rest of Western Europe. However, when Franco made this announcement in the late 1960s, no one knew how long the *Caudillo* would remain in power or whether his successor would serve as a conservative dictator or as the head of a more liberal political regime. Franco had ultimately hoped that the series of cautious political reforms that had proceeded from the 1960s would be sufficient to secure both his own position and that of Juan Carlos at the helm of Spain's political system, with most of his dictatorial political powers intact. Nevertheless, there was some uncertainty as to whether Franco's choice of successor marked the beginnings of a return to a full-blown monarchical system, and also whether the country would continue to reject the option of democracy when Franco's death did eventually occur.

Reaction to the decision from reformers and conservatives

Franco's choice of successor split his government. There were some conservative figures within Franco's government who felt that even moderate political reforms were a threat to the long-term future of Spain's authoritarian regime, and that the country's 'economic miracle' was proof of the success of this type of political system where strong individual leadership was a key strength. Luis Carrero-Blanco, prime minister in 1973, was one such conservative. His uncompromising views and repressive approach to dealing with political opposition were a factor in his assassination by ETA later that year (see page 370). However, there were also more moderate influences such as Adolfo Suarez, head of Spanish television and future prime minister, who argued that Franco's government had to 'reform or die' in the face of globalised liberal pressures and external demands to embrace democratic reform. These two rival factions within Franco's administration materialised in the form of the 'immobilists' (sometimes referred to as the 'bunker' faction), whose deep-rooted conservatism fiercely resisted change, and the reformers who demanded political change.

The members of the conservative immobilists were generally obstructive in response to plans for Franco's desired succession, as well as to any other proposals that suggested broader political reform or radical overhaul of the country's political structure. In 1972, they went so far as to find an alternative successor – Alfonso de Borbón-Dampierre, the husband of Franco's eldest granddaughter, Doña Carmen. Borbón-Dampierre was descended from Alfonso XIII, the last king of Spain. While Juan Carlos was also a direct descendent, the conservatives argued that Borbón-Dampierre had a greater claim to the throne as he was descended from Alfonso XIII's second son, while Juan Carlos was descended from the third son. The conservatives also favoured Borbón-Dampierre because he had never expressed a wish for a democratic Spain and was therefore unlikely to call for destabilising reforms if he succeeded Franco.

By contrast, the reformers or *Juancarlistas* felt further significant political reforms were the right path to follow. They believed that Juan Carlos, who had spoken about the need to modernise Spain, could lead the country to a more democratic future. They sought to cultivate allies within the media and outside of Spain, particularly in the USA, with the aim of generating further political reforms that would bring Spain closer in line with the rest of Western Europe. This power struggle between the conservatives and the reformers went to the heart of the controversial and contentious issue of Franco's succession. There were distinctly different visions regarding the type of political system that should prevail when his prolonged reign came to an end.

The role of Juan Carlos, 1969–74

Following the announcement that he was to be Franco's chosen successor, Juan Carlos moved away from his former military role and became more active in ceremonial and diplomatic events on behalf of Franco's ruling administration. It appeared that he was effectively being 'groomed' or trained to hold high office. This period could therefore be seen as preparing him for the momentous political position he had been chosen by Franco to fill. However, in the short term, his position lacked some clear purpose and he initially fulfilled a symbolic role as a representative of the Spanish government at both domestic and international events. Between 1969 and 1974, as part of his preparations for eventually succeeding Franco, Juan Carlos became more active in political circles and made important diplomatic connections with various foreign statesmen.

Juan Carlos' appearances in the media were not always successfully portrayed, however, and critics questioned his credentials to lead the nation due to his foreign birth. He subsequently had to work on improving this particular aspect of his image, and ultimately convince the sceptics that he was ready and willing to prove himself as a capable successor to Franco when the appropriate time came, by developing the required political skills and experience. He was also part of a new Spanish generation compared with Franco, being just over 45 years younger than the *Caudillo*. This provided him with the capacity to be more in tune with the growing numbers of citizens that had limited and less direct involvement with the country's landmark civil war, and as a consequence he developed a different and broadly more 'progressive' outlook compared with Franco and the majority of his ministers in how to address the country's ongoing challenges and problems. This created the potential for him to be able to govern Spain in a distinctly different style and manner as a result, with further reformist implications.

The death of Franco, 1975

Spain's political uncertainties and festering unrest came to a head when General Franco died at the age of 82, on 20 November 1975. His death followed a long period of illness that had distracted his attention from the country's various problems. For periods throughout 1975, Juan Carlos had effectively been temporary head of state. Franco's death marked the end of a remarkable and durable period of political rule that lasted for over 36 years. He had outlasted all other prominent European dictators of his time. Tributes flowed in from across the world, and the former US president, Richard Nixon, referred to him as the USA's friend. However, due to Spain's questionable and undemocratic political system, few heads of state attended his funeral. Despite this, Franco had certainly manoeuvred himself and Spain closer to various prominent Western leaders, establishing himself as an important player in the European and Cold War political environments at least. He had raised Spain's international profile and significance, although at the same time he had proved to be a formidable obstacle to the country fully embracing a democratic structure. What type of political structure would follow his rule was now the main focus of attention. While there had been some cautious political reforms during the 1960s and 1970s, Franco's death now paved the way for a potentially more significant phase of change that would bring Spain broadly into line with the other liberal democracies of Europe.

SOURCE

13 An article by the journalist Peter Niesewand, from the *Guardian*, 7 November 1975. Here, Niesewand provides a liberal British perspective on the accession of Juan Carlos to the Spanish throne, and offers some assessment of the new monarch's chances of success.

As General Franco lingers on his deathbed, Prince Juan Carlos is preparing to put his political future at risk.

Recent soundings in Madrid have convinced Britain and other EEC countries that – in spite of opposition from the military – the Prince is going to attempt the creation of a liberal, democratic Spain.

The Spanish armed forces are Juan Carlos's only power base, and if they feel he is moving too quickly, he will risk a coup d'état [seizure of power]. His attempt will be a delicate balancing act by an untried politician, and Western nations are prepared to move in quickly with moral encouragement and financial support. Privately, diplomatic sources give the Prince no more than a 50/50 chance of success. Juan Carlos has used the last few days to put the final touches to the speech he will deliver after Franco's death. It will indicate that he plans a liberalisation, but probably without detailing what he has in mind. A further indication that a new day may be dawning for Spain is expected to be an amnesty for political prisoners – outright release for some and the commutation of the death penalty or a reduction in sentences for others.

The Prince believes that he has a year in which to convince the embryo political groupings in the country of his good faith – a 12-month honeymoon for the new leader to set Spain on the road to a constitutional monarchy.

ACTIVITY
KNOWLEDGE CHECK

1 List the reasons for and against Juan Carlos succeeding Franco.

2 Explain why there were divisions within Franco's government about his succession, and how they were overcome.

ACTIVITY
WRITING

Planning and managing Franco's succession

Use the words in the box to complete the sentences below so that they best summarise the issues facing Spain in relation to who should succeed Franco following his death in 1975.

repressive	reformers	progressive	inexperience	generation	democracy
conservatives	direction	authoritarian	dictator	liberal	

Franco had ruled Spain in the manner of a _____ for almost four decades, and his death in 1975 left the country at a crossroads about its future political _____. The governing regime was divided between _____, who favoured a continuation of _____ rule, and _____, who wanted the country to follow the path of most other Western European nations and become a _____. In 1969, Prince Juan Carlos had emerged as Franco's chosen successor, but his relative _____ in political affairs created some doubt about his suitability for this role. Juan Carlos was from a younger _____ than Franco and most of his ministers, and his views seemed to be more _____ by comparison. As the 1970s progressed, his active diplomacy and less _____ approach won him increased support from both the Spanish public and the wider international community.

HOW SUCCESSFULLY DID SPAIN MAKE THE TRANSITION TO DEMOCRACY AND ESTABLISH A DEMOCRATIC CONSTITUTION IN 1978?

The role of Juan Carlos

Just as Franco had planned, 37-year-old Juan Carlos formally succeeded him two days after his death and for a short period the country's dictatorship continued as Franco had desired. Unlike Franco's funeral, Juan Carlos' inauguration ceremony was well attended by Western political leaders. The new government went through something of a transitional and uncertain phase in the first months of the post-Franco era. By 1976, and within a year of becoming the country's leader, Juan Carlos made the major decision that he intended to preside over Spain's swift transition to a full-blown democracy. He had pledged to deliver this as quickly as was practically possible and he pragmatically allied himself with the country's political modernisers to help him do this. One of the most influential modernisers was Adolfo Suarez, who became the country's youngest ever prime minister in July 1976, at the age of 43. Suarez was primarily a conservative figure, yet he had steadily gained the reputation as a reformer who felt that democracy was inevitable in Spain, and had advised Franco as such when the *Caudillo* was close to his death. He became a key figure in the country's bloodless transition to democracy (*La Transición*). He sought to promote the image of Juan Carlos in a positive manner, with the support of America.

In the summer of 1976, Juan Carlos paid a diplomatic visit to meet key American politicians in Washington DC. The visit attracted both public and media interest, as people clamoured to hear what a post-Franco Spain would be like and what policies it proposed. Juan Carlos' speech to the US Congress on 2 June 1976 (see Source 14) indicated that the restored monarchy would act swiftly to ensure that Spain became a democratic regime. This positive diplomatic initiative had the additional effect of boosting Juan Carlos' previously unconvincing media image, and reflected the fact that Spain's reformers had successfully managed to align the new king with their ambitious plans for the country's political transformation, which was to be achieved with impressive speed.

SOURCE

14 From the address of King Juan Carlos to the US Joint Houses of Congress, 2 June 1976. Here, Juan Carlos pledges his commitment to a democratic future for Spain.

The monarchy is an open institution, one in which every citizen has full scope for political participation. The crown protects the whole people and each and every one of its citizens, guaranteeing through laws and by the exercise of civil liberties the rule of justice. The monarchy will ensure under the principles of democracy, that social peace and political stability are maintained in Spain. At the same time, the monarchy will ensure the orderly access of power of distinct political alternatives in accordance with the freely expressed will of the people.

Initial reforms established under Juan Carlos included developing the framework for a functioning parliamentary democracy, the legalisation of political parties and trades unions, as well as the granting of amnesties to various prisoners and former opponents of the Franco regime. Many of these measures were contained within the Political Reform Law of 1976. This reformist agenda represented a clear gesture of reconciliation towards the Spanish left and liberals, granting them greater freedoms to participate within a genuinely competitive political system. Juan Carlos met with a number of prominent left-wing politicians in 1977 as part of his efforts to win their support for the democratic and more inclusive political system he was proposing to construct. This was significant in that it improved relations with groups that had traditionally held Republican political views and were therefore hostile to the monarchy, and who had also been broadly opposed to Franco's dictatorial system of government.

EXTRACT

3 From James Joll, *Europe since 1870: An International History*, 1990. Here, Joll describes the reformist approach adopted by Juan Carlos.

Within a few days of Franco's death, Juan Carlos was crowned King; and within a year the political system of Spain as transformed... there was [then] a new constitution based on universal suffrage, measures of decentralisation were started, the Communist Party became legal. Considering the bitter memories of the previous forty years, the transition was surprisingly smooth [and] was helped by the sympathy of the West European governments.

A Level Exam-Style Question Section A

How far could the historian make use of Sources 13 and 14 together to investigate Spain's transition to democracy by 1978?

Explain your answer, using both sources, the information given about them and your own knowledge of the historical context. (20 marks)

Tip
Both sources provide contemporary information about the role of Juan Carlos in Spain's transition to democracy after the death of Franco in 1975. Think about the strengths and limitations of each source as well as areas they both agree on concerning the relative significance of Juan Carlos, and then compare with other factors in explaining why Spain embraced democracy during the late 1970s.

Immediate steps towards democracy

As a vivid illustration of the impact of Juan Carlos' reformist political agenda, in May 1977, one of the Republican heroines of the Spanish Civil War, *La Pasionaria*, more conventionally known as Dolores Ibárruri (see page 326), returned to the country after 38 years of living in exile in Moscow. This symbolic and conciliatory event indicated a relaxation of previous political tensions and hostilities, and suggested that the Spanish nation's old wounds were slowly healing. The re-appearance of this colourful political figure was the prelude to an even more significant event on 15 June 1977. On this day, 18 million voters participated in Spain's first democratic general election for over 40 years; the previous one had occurred in February 1936 (see page 303).

When election day finally arrived, the country's much-awaited democratic moment was greeted with great public enthusiasm. More than 200 political parties were registered, and the turnout reached almost 80 percent. It also featured *La Pasionaria* being elected to the Cortes. The election of the new parliament was ultimately a landmark episode that heralded a new phase in the country's modernization and democratisation. The outcome of the 1977 Spanish general election (see Source 15) again re-enforced how divided the country was in purely political terms, with the left-wing socialist parties dominant in the cities and the more conservative Union of the Democratic Centre (UCD) doing better in rural areas. The UCD was a coalition of right-wing conservative parties co-ordinated by Suarez to ensure that there was an organised presence of conservatives within Spain's new democratic era.

SOURCE

15 Spanish general election result for the main parties, 1977. Based on data from the Spanish Ministry of Interior and Inter-Parliamentary Union, using the official government records of the election result.

Party	Votes (%)	Seats in Cortes (parliament)
Union of the Democratic Centre (UCD)	6,310,391 (34.4%)	165
Spanish Socialist Workers' Party (PSOE)	5,371,866 (29.3%)	118
Spanish Communist Party (PCE)	1,709,890 (9.3%)	20
Popular Alliance (AP)	1,504,771 (8.2%)	16
Popular Socialist Party-Socialist Unity (PSP-US)	816,582 (4.5%)	6
Basque and Catalonian Nationalist parties	810,840 (4.4%)	19

There remained some small-scale incidents of violence that marred this turning point in Spanish politics, most notably in Barcelona, Seville, Pamplona and Cordoba. Yet despite this, Suarez was returned as the first democratically elected prime minister of the new Spain. He subsequently adopted a moderate and centrist political agenda, based on the mood of consensus and conciliation as well as the fact that no party had gained an absolute majority within the 350-seat Cortes. Of great significance was the fact that the new leader of the opposition was Felipe González, who headed the country's revived Socialist Party (PSOE) that offered an alternative left-wing solution to the country's various challenges. This was a state of affairs that would not have existed under Franco. This landmark electoral event clearly indicated that a pluralistic and democratic approach was now the more civilized and accepted means of resolving Spain's political differences. A stark contrast to the Francoist methods of repression, authoritarianism and permanent one-party rule.

Conservative obstacles

Some of the hardline conservative figures from Franco's regime proved to be obstructive and unco-operative in the period before and after Juan Carlos' succession, as well as up to and beyond the 1977 general election. (See also page 376 and the initial negative reaction to Franco's choice of successor from key conservative figures.) Alternative and less reformist leadership candidates were considered by the 'bunker' faction (see page 376). However, although threats of a military *coup d'état* and extremist right- and left-wing opposition remained, such reactionary political options never materialised, allowing Juan Carlos' modernising reforms to gain momentum. There continued to be, however, flashpoints of violence and lingering class-based tensions in some locations, including the separatist-inclined regions of Catalonia and the Basque province. This reflected the fact that the country was struggling to readjust to its impending democratic status after decades of authoritarian government. However, the suspicions and mistrust of the new regime among conservative politicians and elements of the army would not completely fade away, and this mood would resurrect itself in the form of a failed *coup* attempt in 1981.

Agreeing a democratic constitution in 1978

These tumultuous developments culminated in the creation of a new Spanish Constitution which formally established the country's democratic political structure. The constitution was ratified by the Cortes on 31 October 1978, and was endorsed by a national referendum on 6 December, which featured a high level of public support (approximately 90 percent). This date, 31 October, has subsequently been known as 'Constitution Day' and has become a national holiday in Spain. On a positive level, the new constitutional document established key social rights for Spanish citizens, autonomous political rights for Spanish provinces, full electoral voting rights and the abolition of the death penalty. It also reduced the power and influence of the key institutions of the Roman Catholic Church and the Spanish army, although it did not isolate them to the extent of the 1931 Republican Constitution (see page 292). Religious freedom was guaranteed and, significantly, Roman Catholicism was not granted the status of 'state religion', although it retained some notable educational influence. This would however create rumblings of conservative discontent among both religious and military figures which would re-emerge in future years.

Support for this new political structure was also significantly lower in the troubled Basque region, with the specific type of autonomy on offer failing to meet ETA's demands. The political violence stemming from this issue of regional separatism would soon increase once again, threatening the stability of Spain's new social democracy in the process. Despite such negative undercurrents, Spain had clearly made some major progress in a short space of time. These developments had the broad support of the international community. The unerring shadow of Franco had ultimately not prevented the country from moving on to the next major stage in its political, social and economic evolution, although the legacy of his rule would continue to be felt well into the future.

ACTIVITY
KNOWLEDGE CHECK

To what extent did Spain make a successful transition to democracy between 1975 and 1978? Consider the obstacles and the legacy of Franco before reaching a judgement.

ACTIVITY
SUMMARY

1 Write an obituary for Franco looking back on his life and highlighting his key political achievements and failures since 1936 (about 500 words).

2 Draw a spider diagram charting the re-establishment of democracy in Spain. You should consider the period from 1930 to 1978, as well as the roles of republicanism and Francoism.

3 Highlight the three events you feel were most significant in shaping the country's changing fortunes in the years 1930–78, and write a brief summary to explain why you have made such a judgement.

WIDER READING

Harrison, J. *An Economic History of Modern Spain*, Manchester University Press (1978) provides some informative figures and statistics about the nature and extent of Spanish economic growth during the historical period in question.

Joll, J. *Europe since 1870: An International History*, Penguin (1990).

Muro, D. *Ethnicity and Violence: The Case of Radical Basque Nationalism*, Routledge (2008) assesses the growth of Basque Nationalism and focuses on its radical and violent aspects during the 1960s and 1970s.

Payne, S. *The Franco Regime 1936–1975*, University of Wisconsin Press (1987) is a rigorous coverage of the Franco administration, with use of statistical data and detailed information throughout.

Sánchez, A. *Fear and Progress: Ordinary Lives in Franco's Spain, 1939–1975*, Wiley-Blackwell (2010) highlights the contrasting themes of 'fear and progress' as experienced in the daily lives of ordinary Spaniards under the Franco regime.

Preparing for your AS Level Paper 2 exam

Advance planning

1. Draw up a timetable for your revision and try to keep to it. Spread your timetable over a number of weeks, and aim to cover four or five topics each week.
2. Spend longer on topics which you have found difficult, and revise them several times.
3. Above all, do not try to limit your revision by attempting to 'question spot'. Try to be confident about all aspects of your Paper 2 work, because this will ensure that you have a choice of questions in Section B.

Paper 2 overview

AS Paper 2	Time: 1 hour 30 minutes	
Section A	Answer 1 compulsory two-part sources question	8+12 marks = 20 marks
Section B	Answer 1 question from a choice of 3	20 marks
	Total marks =	40 marks

You should familiarise yourself with the layout of the paper by looking at the examples published by Edexcel. The questions for each section are followed by eight pages of lined paper where you should write your answer.

Section A question

Each of the two parts of the question will focus on one of the two contemporary sources provided. The sources together will total around 300 words. The (a) question, worth 8 marks, will be in the form of 'Why is Source 1 useful for an enquiry into…?' The (b) question, worth 12 marks, will be in the form of 'How much weight do you give the evidence of Source 2 for an enquiry into…?' In both your answers you should address the value of the content of the source, and then its nature, origin and purpose. Finally, you should use your own knowledge of the context of the source to assess its value.

Section B questions

These questions ask you to reach a judgement on an aspect of the topic studied. The questions will have the form, for example, of 'How far…', 'To what extent…' or 'How accurate is it to say…'. The questions can deal with historical concepts such as cause, consequence, change, continuity, similarity, difference and significance. You should consider the issue raised in the question, consider other relevant issues, and then conclude with an overall judgement.

The timescale of the questions could be as short as a single year or even a single event (an example from Option 2C.2 could be, 'To what extent was Russia's involvement in the First World War responsible for the fall of the Provisional Government in 1917?'). The timescale could be longer depending on the historical event or process being examined, but questions are likely to be shorter than the those set for Sections A and B in Paper 1.

Use of time

This is an issue which you should discuss with your teachers and fellow students, but here are some suggestions for you.

1. Do not write solidly for 45 minutes on each question. For Section A it is essential that you have a clear understanding of the content of each source, the points being made, and the nature, origin and purpose of each source. You might decide to spend up to ten minutes reading the sources and drawing up your plan, and 35 minutes writing your answer.
2. For Section B answers you should spend a few minutes working out what the question is asking you to do, and drawing up a plan of your answer before you begin to write your response.

Preparing for your AS Level exams

Paper 2: AS Level sample answer with comments

Section A

Part A requires you to:

- identify key points in the source and explain them
- deploy your own knowledge of the context in which events took place
- make appropriate comments about the author/origin/purpose of the source.

Study Source 6 (Chapter 1, page 302) before you answer this question.

Why is Source 6 valuable to the historian for an inquiry into the reasons for the outbreak of the Spanish Civil War in 1936?

Explain your answer, using the source, the information given about it and your own knowledge of the historical context. (8 marks)

Average student answer

This source offers some insight into the mindset and attitudes of the Republicans before the outbreak of the Spanish Civil War, particularly as internal tensions within the country had significantly grown by the mid-1930s. Azaña was a leading Republican. In this speech he is expressing his views in public to his own supporters, so he is more likely to be honest in these views. The speech was delivered less than a year before the civil war broke out, and it is a reasonable assumption to believe that it reflected what many Republicans were thinking.

When delivering his speech, Azaña's choice of words appears to be quite dramatic in its effect. Words such as 'tyranny' and 'dictatorship' are possibly used in order to make his Republican supporters more fearful and concerned about what their political opponents had in store for the country if they gained political power. At this point in time Azaña was in a fairly powerful political position and had some significant influence among Republicans. He was therefore ultimately seeking to exploit this power in order to get his own supporters more focused and aware of what Nationalist and conservative politicians were aiming to do if they had political control of Spain.

Overall, the source is interesting and valuable due to it being a primary source from the build-up to the Spanish Civil War. This was likely to be a typical view of many Republicans, and it therefore suggested that a civil conflict in Spain was highly likely to occur in the near future.

> A reasonable opening summary that identifies some basic aspects and features of the source and who the speaker is. It does provide some limited background context to the civil war, although the issue of Azaña speaking to supporters needs to be clarified and explained more fully, as it is slightly simplistic to claim that such speeches will involve 'honest' views.

> This section pays some attention to the terms and words used in the source, although the interpretation of them needs to be fuller and more developed. The final point about Azaña being in a powerful position is too general and not completely accurate, as his position in Spanish politics had been weakened since his time as prime minister.

> This conclusion offers some valid summary comments about the value of the source. It does, however, assume that the source is typical of all Republicans and that war was highly likely.

Verdict

This is an average answer because:

- it has some focus on the source, but many of the comments require further explanation and support in order to demonstrate understanding
- there is an attempt to use own knowledge, although it is not developed enough and some information is inaccurate; the contextual information is too thin

- the answer sets out what the source is saying and provides some evaluation of how this might be valuable to a historian, but makes too many assumptions to credibly support this view.

Use the feedback on this answer to rewrite it, making as many improvements as you can.

Paper 2: AS Level sample answer with comments

Section A

Part B requires you to:

- interrogate the source
- draw reasoned inferences
- deploy your own knowledge to interpret the material in its context
- make judgement about the value (weight) of the source.

Study Source 10 (Chapter 1, page 307) before you answer this question.

How much weight do you give the evidence of Source 10 for an enquiry into the reasons for the attempted military coup of July 1936?

Explain your answer, using the source, the information given about it and your own knowledge of the historical context. (12 marks)

Average student answer

The source offers some value in trying to understand the motives of the Spanish military when they organised a coup against the Republican government in the summer of 1936. The source features a speech by General Franco who would go on to be the leader of the Nationalist forces and the eventual ruler of Spain. He expresses some powerful and strongly held views to his troops about why the coup is taking place and there is great enthusiasm among his troops for his demands for conflict to occur. This source is therefore an attempt to justify the actions that he and other officers were taking at this point in time. The speech is likely to be an accurate summary of what Franco felt in his role as the leading military figure in Spain.

Franco uses words like 'anarchy' and 'obscene', all of which seem to highlight the difficult conditions facing the country in the summer of 1936. It is therefore safe to believe that Franco was accurately highlighting the desperate situation that the Spanish people faced during this period, and why he and his officers had to try to overturn the Spanish government. The military officers like Franco believed that any war would be over fairly quickly, and they did not believe that the Republicans had much popular support.

The source is only one person's viewpoint from one side of a major historical conflict. It is therefore not the full picture of how things were at the time, and to get a complete picture you would need to consider other viewpoints as well. However, it should be noted that Franco was a respected military figure with a good reputation so his views and arguments would carry some weight.

> This introduction offers a reasonable summary of what the source is saying and why the coup is taking place. However, there is no clear explanation of how much weight the speech given by Franco would have in explaining the attempted military coup. The contextual knowledge is also inaccurate as Franco was not the dominant military figure at the outbreak of the civil war.

> There is some valid identification of the language used by Franco as a means of highlighting the difficulties facing Spain at the time. However, it is simplistic to assume that Franco's words were an accurate summary of the current situation, and the notion that he could be exaggerating matters to justify his actions and motivate his troops needs some consideration. The assertion that the army believed the Republicans had little popular support is not accurate on the basis of this evidence or wider contextual knowledge.

> That Franco's speech is only one viewpoint is a valid point to highlight and deserves some credit, although a clearer judgement concerning how much weight should be given to the source is required as part of the conclusion.

Verdict

This is an average answer because:

- it offers some limited interrogation of the source and makes a number of subjective and assertive comments that are not justified by the source information
- it indicates some knowledge of the significance of Franco's role, although wider contextual knowledge about him is weak

- it highlights some historical value of the source, but lacks focus and accuracy in its evaluation.

Use the feedback on this answer to rewrite it, making as many improvements as you can.

Paper 2: AS Level sample answer with comments

Section A

Part A requires you to:

- identify key points in the source and explain them
- deploy your own knowledge of the context in which events took place
- make appropriate comments about the author/origin/purpose of the source.

Study Source 6 (Chapter 1, page 302) before you answer this question.

Why is Source 6 valuable to the historian for an inquiry into the reasons for the outbreak of the Spanish Civil War in 1936?

Explain your answer, using the source, the information given about it and your own knowledge of the historical context. (8 marks)

Strong student answer

The source is of immense value to our understanding and analysis of why the Spanish Civil War broke out in the summer of 1936. Azaña was a former prime minister of Spain who remained a popular figure within Republican circles, although he was less powerful than he once was. However he still carried some influence, and in making this public speech to political supporters he was attempting to highlight the perceived dangers of recent political developments in Spain. By the autumn of 1935 when this speech was made, tensions between the left and right of Spanish politics were reaching boiling point after years of simmering hostility.

When making this speech, Azaña uses language very much designed to rouse his audience into action and to make them more vigilant with regard to opposing political activities. He dramatically makes reference to the emergence of 'a battlefield between democracy and its enemies', while also warning the crowd of the imminent dangers of 'tyranny with all its horrors', 'dictatorship', 'intolerance' and 'physical violence'. Such words conjure negative and alarming images about the condition of Spanish political and civic life, as well as about the aims of their political opponents. In this sense the speech summarises how prominent Republicans acknowledged what they believed were extremist and distasteful elements emerging within the country's Nationalist political opinion.

This source therefore provides some relevant and significant evidence for any historian seeking to gain an understanding of why the Spanish Civil War erupted in mid-1936. It captures the tensions and political antagonism of the period most effectively, and although it is only one political viewpoint, the nature and tone of Azaña's comments and rhetoric suggests that Spanish society is polarised and highly vulnerable to a civil war developing. While it should be acknowledged that Azaña was speaking to a crowd of supporters and may have sought to exaggerate matters to generate further support for his viewpoint, the sentiments that he expresses are consistent with other developments and political conflict of this period.

> A very strong opening, which is sharply focused on the question and indicates a clear understanding of who is speaking and the significance of what they are saying. There is excellent and clear use of own knowledge, providing context of the kind of political environment in which the speech was made.

> This section develops the answer further and offers some good focus and attention on what Azaña specifically says and the type of language that he uses. It is a valid and well-made argument to highlight how the words used appear to heighten tensions that already existed, and this is evidence of some accurate source analysis.

> This is a good attempt to draw a conclusion and to directly answer the question. The candidate summarises and identifies some aspects that arise from the source, while still retaining a focus on how the source indicates the likelihood of future civil war.

Verdict

This is a strong answer because:

- it has sharp focus on the question and provides specific and precise arguments to a good standard
- it deploys appropriate own knowledge accurately and

effectively, with a clear historical context included throughout the written content
- it makes use of evidence from the source, with some particularly good analysis of the language used within it, to evaluate the value of the source.

Paper 2: AS Level sample answer with comments

Section A

Part B requires you to:

- interrogate the source
- draw reasoned inferences
- deploy your own knowledge to interpret the material in its context
- make a judgement about the value (weight) of the source.

Study Source 10 (Chapter 1, page 307) before you answer this question.

How much weight do you give the evidence of Source 10 for an enquiry into the reasons for the attempted military coup of July 1936?

Explain your answer, using the source, the information given about it and your own knowledge of the historical context. (12 marks)

Strong student answer

The source provides some excellent historical value to a historian seeking to assess why the Spanish military launched a coup in the summer of 1936. Such value stems from the fact that the source is a speech by one of the leading figures involved in the coup (Franco), who went on to lead the Nationalist forces during the civil war and the country afterwards. The speech is addressed to Franco's troops that are being called to action, notably while they are still located in Morocco. It appears to be intended as a rallying cry to justify why they are taking the course of action that they are, against the country's elected government. This somewhat extreme response by the Spanish army arguably justifies the strong language and emotive rhetoric within Franco's speech.

The language used by Franco within this source provide a useful indication of why he took such an active role in the coup. They also illustrate the urgency he feels is needed to challenge the Spanish government, as well as the manner in which he aims to motivate his troops and justify his actions. He patriotically calls his fellow soldiers 'Spaniards' in an attempt to stir their nationalist instincts, while depicting a bleak picture of Spain under Republican rule, using words such as 'anarchy', 'revolts', and 'revolutionary hordes'. Such words and phrases are negative in tone and give an impression of severe unrest and social upheaval across the Spanish nation. Recurring references to insurrection re-enforce his message that the army needs to restore order. He emphasises the 'savage' environment and the disorder which exists within parts of Spain. In terms of wider historical context, the country's armed forces were particularly alarmed at the radical influences that were active within the elected Spanish government at this time, and this was a major factor in Franco's return to the mainland to participate in the coup.

The source is a one-sided viewpoint offering a single perspective on the reasons and justifications for how and why the military coup occurred in June 1936, paving the way for the Spanish Civil War. Franco's views are subjective and aligned with a nationalistic and conservative political agenda. A left-wing historian from the time would dispute many of the comments and assertions made. However, the source does capture the frenetic and frenzied mood of the time.

Comment boxes:

This is a clearly focused and well-balanced introduction which provides effective and relevant comments about the nature of the source, as well as illustrating the wider political environment in which Franco is speaking.

Provides some strong and specific analysis of the language used by Franco, and examples are effectively referenced to explain and describe the mood of the speech. This attention to the key words used is combined effectively with some strong contextual knowledge of the environment in which Franco was speaking.

A well-rounded concluding summary that retains a good focus on the source material's content. Addresses some potential flaws of the source, at the same time re-emphasises its key values.

Verdict

This is a strong answer because:

- it shows detailed understanding of the question by interrogating the source, commenting on key points within it
- it makes effective use of contextual background information to support points made about Franco and shows a good

understanding of the historical environment of the time, bringing in own knowledge in support of arguments made
- it makes an overall judgement about the value of the source, while acknowledging both its strengths and weaknesses.

Paper 2: AS Level sample answer with comments

Section B

These questions assess your understanding of the period in some depth. They will ask you about the content you learned about in the four key themes, but may not ask about more than one theme. For these questions remember to:

- give an analytical, not a descriptive, response
- support your points with evidence
- cover the whole time period specified in the question
- come to a substantiated judgement.

To what extent were Franco's economic policies successful in the years 1959–75? (20 marks)

Average student answer

Franco won the Spanish Civil War in 1939 and then tried to stay out of the Second World War, eventually taking a neutral position. Such events damaged the Spanish economy and meant that it didn't develop as fully as it could up until the late 1950s. This in turn led to poor social conditions and people began to protest, which put Franco under pressure. However, after 1959 efforts were made to improve Spain's weak economic position, and Franco introduced a number of new policies during this period that attempted to deal with the country's long-term problems. The policies introduced brought about a lot of change to the country's economy by the 1970s.

Franco had originally followed economic policies that were supported by the Falange Party. These included autarky and corporatism which aimed to put Spain's national interests first. There wasn't much trade with other countries as a result, and this didn't help Spain's overall position. These policies therefore did not create enough growth and the country's position struggled in comparison to other countries in Europe. Franco's government later tried to join the EEC but this move was blocked and people's living standards remained low. This showed that his government's policies were not working when it came to the economy, and as a result it made his own position a lot weaker. This is why Franco decided to look into new methods of improving the country's economic position after 1959.

Because of these continuing economic problems, after 1959 Franco's government decided to follow different policies. He did this because he was concerned about his own power base and there were signs of social unrest. He therefore wanted to improve Spain's economic output and bring it up to the standards of the rest of Europe. One of the main changes that came about was that Franco brought new people into his government, and quite a few came from the 'Opus Dei' movement. This pushed the Falange Party out of the picture and they now had less influence, with new ministers being seen as clever and open minded. They did not agree with many of the Falange policies when it came to the economy, and they have been described as 'technocrats'. This provides some clear evidence that Franco was willing to develop and introduce new policies to improve the Spanish economy.

This opening paragraph is vague and the points made are too generalised. Most of the focus is on the period outside the question's timeframe (1959–75) and there are a number of imprecise comments made. It needs to briefly provide specific reasons and evidence as to why the Spanish economy was so weak prior to 1959 and then introduce the policies Franco's regime put in place to revive it. There is no clear or explicit reference to the question, nor is there any initial judgement here.

Various points in this paragraph are valid, but they are not adequately developed. For example, 'autarky' and 'corporatism' need to be explained more fully and their impact on the Spanish economy backed up with supporting evidence.

There is again a series of relevant facts covered here, but many points and definitions are insufficiently explained and lack depth, for example, Opus Dei, technocrats, etc. This section also fails to adequately explain what the new economic policies were and how they differed from those supported by the Falange Party.

The 1960s were generally seen as a positive period for Spain's economy and tourism was a massive factor in this. The government was keen to encourage holiday makers to visit Spain, but some people were put off by the country's strong Catholic values. Despite this, lots of resorts became extremely popular due to the warm weather, and this made lots of money for the Spanish population throughout the rest of this decade and into the 1970s. This was a boost for Franco's government and made him more popular.

Spain also began to have more dealings with Europe on a financial and trading level, and lots of foreign investment came into the country. The USA also contributed to this, and all of this income made the country far more prosperous. Franco believed that his policies were the reasons for all of this success, but he could not have achieved what he did without the money that came in from abroad through trade and tourism. The whole country benefited from this economic growth and before long Spain was no longer classed as being a poor nation. Lots of Spaniards also went to work abroad and they sent their wages back home to their families which also boosted Spain's wealth. These developments seemed to prove that the new policies introduced after 1959 were a success.

All of these developments meant that by 1975 Spain had become a much wealthier country with a growing economy. Franco could take great credit for this in the way that he had recognised that things needed to change in the late 1950s and the difficulties of recovering from the country's various conflicts. He had introduced appropriate policies to deliver economic growth and he had rejected the failed policies of the past. By the 1970s Spanish people generally had better quality of life with more consumer goods being sold and a greater number of jobs being developed in the country's tourist industry.

This paragraph contains some accurate material, but there is limited development of the points made. Figures and data relating to tourist numbers would be helpful, and the comments about the Catholic Church need greater clarification. The country's population didn't equally share the benefits of tourism either, but the final sentence fails to clarify this. The answer would be greatly improved by developing the argument that not everyone shared this economic growth.

This paragraph again contains some fairly basic factual material, which while again relevant is not sufficiently explained or developed. The issue of American and European investment is brushed over too quickly. There are further inaccurate generalisations made about tourism, and the specific economic policies of Franco aren't explained at all. The answer should have included reference to the free market policies established by the technocrats and foreign investment, both as part of the economic miracle.

This final paragraph attempts to round up and conclude the question. There is some focus on the question, but much of the information repeats what has already been said in the answer. There is also an overall failure to acknowledge the negative aspects of Spain's growing economy, such as the continued poverty in parts of the country and the fact that all citizens didn't benefit from the economic boom. In omitting this, the answer has failed to reach a reasoned judgement on how successful Franco's economic policies were in the years 1959–75.

Verdict

This is average answer because:

- there is some attempt at explanation, but it does not analyse both sides of the argument about how Spain's economic growth benefited some parts of the country, but not others
- the material included is accurate but basic and supporting evidence to back up key points is lacking in depth
- it offers some judgement, but the reasoning is unbalanced and vague
- there is too much focus on events outside the timeframe of the question; the answer could be improved with more defined links to the question overall.

Use the feedback on this answer to rewrite it, making as many improvements as you can.

Paper 2: AS Level sample answer with comments

Section B

These questions assess your understanding of the period in some depth. They will ask you about the content you learned about in the four key themes, but may not ask about more than one theme. For these questions remember to:

- give an analytical, not a descriptive, response
- support your points with evidence
- cover the whole time period specified in the question
- come to a substantiated judgement.

To what extent were Franco's economic policies successful in the years 1959–75? (20 marks)

Strong student answer

Between the years 1959 and 1975, Spain experienced significant economic progress and recovery from the damage caused by its past internal unrest and international isolation. Its rate of economic development was such that some have described it as nothing less than an 'economic miracle'. By the late 1950s, Franco found himself under significant social and political pressure due to falling living standards and rising unemployment, which in turn led to growing levels of unrest among certain sections of Spanish society. Realising his own long-term position was perhaps at risk unless social and economic improvements were made, the Spanish leader initiated a significant review of his government's economic policies and embraced a new political direction as a result. The long-term outcome of this process was that by the mid-1970s Spain had one of the world's fastest growing economies, although it must be noted that not all Spanish citizens shared in its growth in equal measures.

By the final years of the 1950s Spain's key economic indicators were in a poor condition, with unemployment at approximately 35 percent, inflation rising rapidly and the country facing bankruptcy. This situation had arisen primarily because of the failure of existing economic policies, broadly shaped by the doctrines of 'autarky' whereby the country tried to be self-sufficient and minimise its trading links to other nations, alongside 'corporatism' whereby trades unions and employers were actively involved in government economic policy-making. Both policies involved a pivotal role for government economic management, and both were closely linked to the political agenda of the Falange Party. The Falange had been the dominant force within Spain's one-party state and a loyal pillar of support to Franco over many years. However, the Falangist economic model had produced sluggish and disappointing levels of economic growth. As a consequence, in early 1957 Franco boldly replaced a number of Falange ministers with politicians who were members of the religious Opus Dei movement. This was an organisation that was committed to promoting the interests of Catholicism within political life but its supporters also advocated free market economic policies that would significantly limit the government's role in the management of the Spanish economy. These new politicians were highly educated and were known as 'technocrats' due to their support for policies that were more likely to work on a practical level, as opposed to supporting a policy for purely ideological reasons.

This is a strong opening paragraph, which clearly addresses the question and focuses on the chronological period under scrutiny. It summarises the key background factors in an effective way, providing some useful context. It also offers some judgement and balanced analysis from the outset in relation to the underlying theme of how economic growth was not evenly shared across Spain during this period.

This is a well-developed paragraph. The points made provide further contextual information that is relevant to the question, and arguments and terms highlighted are backed up with clear and specific factual information. The argument being developed is well substantiated, with sufficient explanation and analysis.

The free market policies that were allowed to flourish in Spain during the 1960s proved to be the catalyst for the country's economic revival, and in subsequent years Franco sought to take the credit for this turnaround in the country's fortunes. The Spanish government's new economic approach sought to significantly improve and develop trading and commercial links with other countries, and this was symbolised by its failed attempt to join the EEC in 1962 which was a clear sign of its more ambitious and expansive intentions. This more outward and welcoming approach to the rest of Europe came to its ultimate expression in the rapid growth of Spain's tourist market, which Franco and his ministers promoted as being an area of significant economic potential. The warm weather and idyllic beaches were major attractions, and the relatively cheap package holiday deals were appealing to the increasingly affluent middle classes of Western Europe. By the mid-1970s an estimated 30 million holiday makers a year were visiting Spain, generating average annual income of $3.5 billion and making tourism a vital component of the Spanish economy. This booming industry fuelled a surge in private investment in projects such as building new hotels, and in turn this created enhanced employment opportunities for Spanish construction workers as well as within the thriving tourist and leisure industry, improving ordinary people's lifestyles in the process.

> This is a very detailed section that contains lots of precise and relevant supporting evidence about how the Spanish economy was transformed during the 1960s and into the 1970s. There is some effective use of data, and good evaluation and analysis in terms of why such specific information is of significance to this particular question.

This arrival of different European cultural influences (often symbolised by the bikini), also played a part in modernising Spain's previously rather conservative social attitudes and moralistic 'Catholic' culture. However, it was not just Europeans arriving in Spain that had a positive economic effect, but also the increased opportunities for Spanish workers to find employment in more affluent parts of Western Europe. Thousands of Spanish workers took up such opportunities provided by a more accessible and outward-looking Spain during the 1960s in particular, and some of their earnings from working abroad were sent back to further boost the spending power of their families at home. American investment was also vital to the country's economic recovery, and improved links with the USA saw high-profile visits by US presidents and a significant amount of trade and business links developing between Spain and the American superpower during this period, which again had positive effects on the Spanish economy.

> This section provides a further dimension of Spain's economic recovery, highlighting more specific and wide-ranging examples of how the country's economic performance was boosted by foreign investment and employment. It also acknowledges and analyses some social implications of economic growth, which enhances the sophistication of the overall argument.

Despite such positive indicators, it should however be noted that there remained some negative aspects of Spain's economic performance between 1959 and 1975. Income from tourism was not evenly spread and those living in rural areas away from tourist resorts did not share in the prosperity that it created. Shanty towns were therefore still prominent on the edge of many large cities as a further reflection of ongoing poverty, while the oil crisis of the early 1970s brought a reduction both in the number of tourists and Spaniards working abroad, suggesting that Spain's economic status was far from stable or secure. However, despite such undercurrents to the country's economic performance between 1959 and 1975, the long-term developments and more liberalised and positive trading relations with the outside world provided ongoing opportunities for Spain to boost its commercial and economic position, and it is for this reason that Franco's economic policies deserve credit.

> This is a strong evaluative conclusion which acknowledges that the country's economic performance between 1959 and 1975 was far from positive in all areas. This provides some important balance to the answer, while also offering some valid judgement in response to the question.

Verdict

This is a strong answer because:

- relevant issues are explored and analysed throughout the answer, while a good focus on the question and its timeframe is retained
- it demonstrates in-depth knowledge through the use of a wide range of accurate and precise material
- it offers judgement based on a well-developed, balanced argument in relation to Spain's economic performance during this period
- the answer is well organised, coherent, logical and persuasive.

Preparing for your A Level Paper 2 exam

Advance planning

1. Draw up a timetable for your revision and try to keep to it. Spread your timetable over a number of weeks, and aim to cover four or five topics each week.
2. Spend longer on topics which you have found difficult, and revise them several times.
3. Above all, do not try to limit your revision by attempting to 'question spot'. Try to be confident about all aspects of your Paper 2 work, because this will ensure that you have a choice of questions in Section B.

Paper 2 overview

AL Paper 2	Time: 1 hour 30 minutes	
Section A	Answer 1 compulsory source question	20 marks
Section B	Answer 1 question from a choice of 2	20 marks
	Total marks =	40 marks

You should familiarise yourself with the layout of the paper by looking at the examples published by Edexcel. The questions for each section are followed by eight pages of lined paper where you should write your answer.

Section A question

This question asks you to assess two different types of contemporary sources totalling around 400 words, and will be in the form of 'How far could the historian make use of Sources 1 and 2 together to investigate…?' Your answer should evaluate both sources considering their nature, origin and purpose, and you should use your own knowledge of the context of the sources to consider their value to the specific investigation. Remember, too, that in assessing their value, you must consider the two sources, taken together, as a set.

Section B questions

These questions ask you to reach a judgement on an aspect of the topic studied. The questions will have the form, for example, of 'How far…', 'To what extent…' or 'How accurate is it to say…'. The questions can deal with historical concepts such as cause, consequence, change, continuity, similarity, difference and significance. You should consider the issue raised in the question, then other relevant issues, and conclude with an overall judgement.

The timescale of the questions could be as short as a single year or even a single event (an example from Option 2C.2 could be, 'To what extent was Russia's involvement in the First World War responsible for the fall of the Romanovs in 1917?'). The timescale could be longer depending on the historical event or process being examined, but questions are likely to be shorter than those set for Sections A and B in Paper 1.

Use of time

This is an issue which you should discuss with your teachers and fellow students, but here are some suggestions for you.

1. Do not write solidly for 45 minutes on each question. For Section A it is essential that you have a clear understanding of the content of each source, the points being made, and the nature, origin and purpose of each source. You might decide to spend up to ten minutes reading the sources and drawing up your plan, and 35 minutes writing your answer.
2. For Section B answers you should spend a few minutes working out what the question is asking you to do, and drawing up a plan of your answer before you begin to write your response.

Preparing for your A Level exams

Paper 2: A Level sample answer with comments

Section A

You will need to read and analyse two sources and use them in tandem to assess how valuable they are in investigating issues. For these questions remember to:

- spend up to ten minutes reading and identifying the arguments and evidence present in the sources; then make a plan to ensure that your answers will be rooted in these sources
- use specific references from the sources
- deploy your own knowledge to develop points made in the sources and establish appropriate context
- come to a substantiated judgement.

How far could the historian make use of Source 13 (Chapter 3, page 353) and Source 10 (Chapter 4, page 372) together to investigate the extent to which Spain improved its international relationships in the Cold War environment?

Explain your answer, using both sources, the information given about them and your own knowledge of the historical context. (20 marks)

Average student answer

The two sources offer differing views about Spain's international relations during the Cold War and cover different periods of Franco's rule. Source 13 is a United Nations General Assembly Resolution from 1946 which clearly highlights the level of hostility felt towards the Franco regime in the immediate years after the Second World War. This could be linked to Spain's unwillingness to side with the Western Allies against Hitler. Source 10 is dated from 1970 and is a speech by US President Richard Nixon on a state visit to Spain. This offers a different view of Spain's international position and suggests the country is now in a much stronger position due to the unwavering support of its long-standing ally, the USA.

Source 13 offers primary evidence that Spain was very isolated after the Second World War. It had lost its former alliance with Germany and Italy, as both of these nations had been defeated in the war and had seen their powerful leaders removed. Franco had remained very loyal to Hitler and this had damaged both him and Spain once the war was over, and many other countries were not likely to forget this. This explains this viewpoint of the UN resolution which condemns the country as being fascist in nature and actually refers to its links with 'Hitler's Nazi Germany and Mussolini's Fascist Italy'. The source therefore places clear blame on to Franco's Spanish government for supporting such unsavoury allies, and the new organisation of the United Nations took a very dim view of Franco's regime as a result.

> A reasonable opening summary that identifies and explains the basis of each source. Some of the contextual information is, however, a little vague and needs clarification. For example, Spain's neutrality during the Second World War needs to be emphasised, and the nature of American support to Spain was more complicated and less straightforward than these comments suggest.

> This paragraph offers some further explanation of the source material, but as in the first paragraph, the nature of Spain's relationship with Hitler needs clarifying. The fact that Franco did not formally join with Hitler and remained neutral needs to be explained, as to say he 'remained very loyal' is not wholly accurate. There are, in fact, alternative historical viewpoints that would claim he did not support Hitler for the majority of the wartime period, and this needs to be explored in more depth.

Source 10 is another piece of primary evidence but is dated almost a quarter of century after Source 13. This is a significant period of time and the source is of value as it features a powerful American politician speaking to Franco at an official state dinner in Madrid. The USA had been Spain's firm ally for many years, supporting Franco's regime and what it stood for. This shows how much progress the country had made since the UN's negative resolution of 1946, with the leader of one of the two major superpowers being willing to visit and speak so highly of Franco and his government. Nixon positively refers the country's 'vigorous people, proud people, a young people, a dynamic people'. This attitude of the USA was a reflection of the much more supportive view of Spain among Western nations in particular by 1970, and this boosted the country's position, status and importance during the Cold War.

During the Cold War, Spain was not one of the major players but its position within Europe meant that it could not avoid some kind of involvement. In the early part of the Cold War the country had few allies and lacked international support, and this is clearly evident in Source 13. However as the years progressed it built up its reputation and became closer to other nations, and this is certainly supported by Source 10. By the 1970s it was therefore a key player and an ally of the USA, having taken sides because a number of American presidents liked Franco and supported his domestic policies. There was also long-standing Spanish hostility to the Soviet Union which dated back to Spain's civil war during the 1930s.

By 1970 Spain had moved on from its past position as an outcast in foreign affairs and was fully welcomed back into the intentional community once again. This indicated that it had certainly improved its position on the world stage and had a significant role to play in the ongoing Cold War. The only country it was still on bad relations with was the Soviet Union, but with the support of the USA this did not appear to be a major problem.

> Source 10 is commented on in more detail here. The differing timespan between the sources is fairly relevant and worth a brief mention. Evidence from both sources is used well, but it is the additional and contextual information which is weak. The USA's relationship with Spain is far too simplistically explained. It is inaccurate to say that the USA had been Spain's 'firm ally' and that the USA had 'supported Franco's regime and what it stood for'. Likewise, Western support for Spain was far from 'positive and supportive'. The candidate has yet to address the question, which asks to what extent Spain improved its international relationships during the Cold War.

> Much of this paragraph repeats what has already been said earlier in the answer and there is no analysis. There are again some inaccurate and generalised comments, for example, that the USA supported Franco's domestic policies (which was not the case). The reasons why the USA was willing to have such dealings with Franco requires more refined explanation to provide a clearer overall analysis of Spain's international position. Spain's hostility to the Soviet Union is correctly identified but again not fully explained.

> The conclusion does attempt to answer the question, as it is valid to suggest that Spain had improved its international position between 1946 and 1970 on the basis of these sources. However, that the country was 'fully welcomed back into the international community' was not true. To reach a substantiated judgement, the answer should consider the extent to which much of Western Europe and indeed the USA continued to have major concerns about Spain's political system well into the 1970s.

Verdict

This is an average answer because:

- it demonstrates some understanding of the source material and shows some analysis of the key points, but the supporting comments are not developed or explained in enough detail
- the use of wider contextual information is weak and inaccurate in various places, particularly in relation to Spain's relationship with the USA

- there is some focus on the question and valid links made between the sources. However, a number of key points and arguments are imprecise and vague. The overall judgement is therefore not entirely secure or convincing.

Use the feedback on this answer to rewrite it, making as many improvements as you can.

Paper 2: A Level sample answer with comments

Section A

You will need to read and analyse two sources and use them in tandem to assess how valuable they are in investigating issues. For these questions remember to:

- spend up to ten minutes reading and identifying the arguments and evidence present in the sources; then make a plan to ensure that your answers will be rooted in these sources
- use specific references from the sources
- deploy your own knowledge to develop points made in the sources and establish appropriate context
- come to a substantiated judgement.

How far could the historian make use of Source 13 (Chapter 3, page 353) and Source 10 (Chapter 4, page 372) together to investigate the extent to which Spain improved its international relationships in the Cold War environment?

Explain your answer, using both sources, the information given about them and your own knowledge of the historical context. (20 marks)

Strong student answer

The two sources certainly provide contrasting perspectives of the status of Spain's international relations during the Cold War. Source 13 dates from 1946 and is a resolution passed by the fledgling United Nations General Assembly. It is highly critical and negative in its attitude towards the Franco regime. Source 10 dates from nearly a quarter of a century later and features US President Richard Nixon voicing his fulsome praise and enthusiastic support for Franco and the Spanish government. The varying timescale is of significance to a historian, as on a fundamental level it clearly indicates that broader international attitudes towards Spain have shifted during the intervening period between the sources. However, to what extent the comments by Nixon totally eclipse the previous view of the United Nations is unclear, and further analysis is required to assess whether there remained any lingering hostility and criticism towards Spain by the start of the 1970s.

Source 13 is a resolution passed by the United Nations General Assembly during the very early stages of this organisation's existence, and it explicitly condemns Franco's Spanish government. It employs some bold allegations to support this position, describing Spain as a 'fascist regime' with close links to the discredited and defeated regimes of 'Hitler's Nazi Germany' and 'Mussolini's Fascist Italy'. To be associated with these two countries and their authoritarian and dictatorial political structures gives Spain an image of being different and detached from the rest of the Western world and particularly Western Europe. This is because the majority of its neighbouring countries were liberal democracies, and Spain's specific political system is therefore the focus of much criticism. However, the primary focus of criticism in this source is ultimately its activities during the Second World War, with the resolution claiming that Franco 'gave very substantial aid to the enemy Powers'. This is the main element of the criticism of the Spanish government in the immediate aftermath of the Second World War, although it should be noted that for the majority of the wartime period Spain adopted a position of neutrality and Franco did not embark on any kind of formal alliance with the defeated powers of Germany and Italy. However, Source 13 ultimately does not acknowledge or recognise this point, possibly because its advocates believed that Franco's support for the defeated powers existed on an informal level.

This is a strong and well-focused introduction that identifies the origins and provenance of both sources. It also starts to develop the analysis of the sources, effectively highlighting the significance of the differing timescale of each source, as well as identifying the key phrase in the question, 'to what extent', at this early stage.

This is a very detailed and rigorous analysis of Source 13. It clearly explains the historical context of the source and highlights some of the language and vocabulary used within it to re-enforce its rather harsh and critical tone. It then develops some detailed and quite sophisticated commentary and analysis of Spain's position of formal neutrality during the Second World War, and raises the question as to whether the tone of the source can be fully justified in the light of wartime events. This is a confident approach to take in questioning the source's overall message.

Source 10 features a public speech by US President Richard Nixon at a formal state dinner in Madrid in 1970. In relation to the negativity of Source 13, the fact that Nixon is attending such a dinner with Franco and expressing such warm words could be viewed as something of a surprise. This therefore clearly indicates that in the years between 1946 and 1970, something significantly changed to make one of the two great superpowers and a key figure at the United Nations take what appears to be a more conciliatory attitude towards Franco's regime. A key factor in this changing position of Spain had been the evolution of the Cold War and the need for the USA to cement its position via a number of key alliances across Europe in particular. This led the Americans to sign the Treaty of Madrid in 1953, which saw them provide some significant financial investment into Spain in return for the use of Spanish air and naval bases for US forces. By the Americans taking this step for pragmatic reasons as much as anything else, Spain was brought out of virtual international isolation, with the US government putting the Cold War struggle against the Soviet Union above any concerns it had for Spain's domestic political status. This was the starting point for a constructive economic and financial relationship between Spain and the USA, which led to a formal visit by President Eisenhower in 1959 and this further visit by Nixon in 1970. Nixon's comments about Spain by this stage are very positive; praising the country and its 'dynamic people – the people that have been responsible for Spain having the fastest growth rate of any country in Europe over these past few years'.

> This is a detailed analysis of Source 10, and its offers a comprehensive and perceptive assessment of Nixon's comments. It also provides some strong and accurate historical context for the source, offering clear and accurate arguments as to why Spain's international position by 1970 was so markedly different from its position in 1946. The broader personal knowledge and understanding of Cold War dynamics that is evident is excellent. This could be developed further to consider Spain's perspective of international relations in addition to the American viewpoint.

Looking at both sources together it is clear to see that attitudes towards Spain had changed over approximately 25 years. However it would be wrong to interpret Source 10 as a complete rejection of the views and sentiments expressed in Source 13. Even in 1970 there were ongoing concerns about the nature of the Spanish political system, its lack of democracy, its poor civil rights record and Franco's dictatorial status. Spain remained different to the vast majority of the Western world in this respect, and the Americans did express concerns about this matter. The Americans attempted to influence change in Spain by working behind the scenes, adopting the view that by developing trade and economic links they could perhaps influence eventual political reform in the country.

Overall therefore, it is clearly apparent when comparing both sources that Spain moved from a position of isolation and detachment in 1946 to a more integrated international position by 1970. Between the dates of each source Spain had joined the United Nations and developed closer links to the USA, but it remained outside the mainstream of European politics and Franco continued to resist significant political reforms. However, due to the development of the Cold War Spain had managed to strengthen its links with major powers like the USA, and this suggested that Franco had exploited superpower tensions to his own country's benefit. However such links and gradual moves away from isolation evident in Source 10 highlight long-term factors that explain how Spain eventually embraced liberal democratic reform in the latter part of the 1970s. This ultimately highlights how improved international relationships had a major impact on the country's domestic position.

> These two paragraphs round off the question very effectively, with an important recognition that Spain was not completely welcomed back into the international community by 1970, and that problems with its political status remained. The answer goes on to further clarify the various factors and dynamics in Spain's relationship with the USA, and offers clear judgement that Spain was certainly less isolated in international terms in 1970 than it was in 1946. It concludes with a valid long-term and synoptic angle, by identifying elements within Source 10 that can be linked to Spain's eventual transition to democracy in the late 1970s.

Verdict

This is strong answer because:

- it is rooted in the sources and identifies and illustrates their key features, integrating references to them throughout the answer
- it deploys an excellent range of knowledge of the broader subject matter to support arguments made and to provide some strong historical context, although it perhaps gets diverted towards an American rather than a Spanish viewpoint in places
- it sustains a strong focus on the demands of the question, providing rigorous and detailed source analysis and cross-referencing. It also indicates a high level of understanding and develops a clear and balanced overall argument with strong judgement evident.

Paper 2: A Level sample answer with comments

Section B

These questions assess your understanding of the period in some depth. They will ask you about the content you learned about in the four key themes, but may not ask about more than one theme. For these questions remember to:

- give an analytical, not a descriptive, response
- support your points with evidence
- cover the whole time period specified in the question
- come to a substantiated judgement.

'The extent and scale of international support was the decisive factor in determining the outcome of the Spanish Civil War.'

How far do you agree with this statement? (20 marks)

Average student answer

The Spanish Civil War took place between 1936 and 1939 between the Republicans and Nationalists. This was a conflict that involved much of the Spanish population, although there was some intervention from other countries also. It must be stressed however that foreign involvement was fairly limited and it was ultimately a war which the Spaniards resolved between themselves.

The civil war broke out in the summer of 1936 following an attempt to seize power by some of Spain's senior military officers. This followed a significant period of violence, unrest and tension, and had seen the country's more right-wing figures become more and more concerned about some of the policies of the more left-wing Republican government. Both sides of these different political viewpoints had different ideas of how Spain should be run and this was the root of why the civil war occurred. In this sense, it was mainly a domestic dispute, and other countries were not that interested in the war's outcome and only got involved towards the end.

It can be argued that the powerful leadership of General Franco and his knowledge of military affairs was really the major factor in determining what happened during the Spanish Civil War. Franco had lots of experience of leading the Spanish army and he successfully motivated his troops. He knew how to plan and prepare for battles and this was a major advantage of the Nationalist forces in the civil war. The Republicans were not as experienced in warfare and had fewer military officers in their ranks, and were therefore less effective on the battlefield. They also had a divided leadership and no one with the same sort of skills who could lead their troops. On this basis it can therefore be argued that the skills and experience of the Nationalist leadership, and Franco in particular, was the major factor in determining the outcome of the Spanish Civil War.

> While there is some focus on the question, this is a weak and limited opening summary. It does acknowledge some basic factual points about the Spanish Civil war, but it is brief and more contextual detail is needed. It also makes some inaccurate and undeveloped assertions about the scale and extent of foreign involvement in the conflict.

> There is some attempt to provide a general background to why the war occurred, although this is again a little thinly developed and needs more historical context. There is another attempt to address the issue of international involvement, but it again lacks accuracy as foreign intervention was evident and significant from the war's earliest stages.

> This paragraph features an attempt at some judgement and analysis in response to the question. It offers an argument that it was internal domestic factors that shaped the outcome of the civil war, namely the effective leadership of Franco. However, some of the points are too generalised. More detail is required about Franco's strengths and Republican weaknesses, and some analysis of how they influenced the outcome of the civil war.

In contrast to the position of Franco, the role of other nations and the international community was less significant. Hitler and Mussolini had shown some sympathy with Franco, but they were reluctant to get too involved in Spain's domestic affairs. Hitler took some persuading to support Franco, but he did eventually provide the Spanish Nationalist leader with arms and aeroplanes in particular. Mussolini was also cautious about getting too involved, but he did send some troops that boosted the overall size of the Nationalist army. Therefore, while both countries did get partly involved in the Spanish Civil War, they tried to keep their distance and offer only limited support because they were fearful of upsetting the wider international community. The Republicans tried in vain to get Britain and France to take their side, but this was unsuccessful. Apart from a small trickle of volunteers who made little impact, the Republicans received hardly any international help or assistance other than from the Soviet Union, based on shared left-wing sympathies. However Soviet involvement was also quite restricted and didn't really affect the war's outcome.

Overall therefore, the main factor in determining the outcome of the Spanish Civil War was that the Nationalist forces possessed better and stronger leadership, in particular due to the important role of Franco. The Republicans could not compete with his military expertise and success. While there was some interest in the Spanish Civil War on an international level, the level of intervention was relatively low key and not that significant on the outcome. The Nationalists would have been triumphant even without the limited support they received from Germany and Italy, while the Republicans had little international support as it was. It can ultimately be concluded that while there was indeed some foreign intervention in the Spanish Civil War, it did not have a major effect on the outcome which was largely decided by internal Spanish factors.

There are some valid points within these final paragraphs, and the answer retains its focused argument that the Spanish Civil War was decided almost entirely by internal factors rather than international involvement. However, the supporting evidence for this is thin and weakly developed, and much of the information has already been mentioned earlier in the answer. Meanwhile, the evidence for foreign involvement and intervention is superficially covered, generally overlooked and inaccurate, notably the extent of German and Italian involvement. There is no mention of the International Brigades and the extent to which non-intervention influenced the outcome. This failure to address the significant scale and extent of foreign intervention weakens the quality of the answer and makes it rather one-sided.

Verdict

This is an average answer because:

- there is some attempt at explanation and a reasonable focus on the question, but the overall argument is imbalanced and fails to fully address what is being asked
- some of the material included is accurate, but is lacking in clear historical context; arguments and supporting evidence lack depth in several places
- there is an attempt to reach an overall judgement, but it is not entirely convincing as the response has not thoroughly considered all aspects of the question, particularly the impact of foreign intervention
- it is fairly well organised and has some structure, but the argument is too simplistic and one-dimensional. There needs to be more use of appropriate evidence in order for all aspects of the question to be properly covered.

Use the feedback on this answer to rewrite it, making as many improvements as you can.

Paper 2: A Level sample answer with comments

Section B

These questions assess your understanding of the period in some depth. They will ask you about the content you learned about in the four key themes, but may not ask about more than one theme. For these questions remember to:

- give an analytical, not a descriptive, response
- support your points with evidence
- cover the whole time period specified in the question
- come to a substantiated judgement.

'The extent and scale of international support was the decisive factor in determining the outcome of the Spanish Civil War.'

How far do you agree with this statement? (20 marks)

Strong student answer

The Spanish Civil War was a major historical event of the 20th century that had both significant domestic and international dimensions to it. On the one hand it represented the culmination of a prolonged and bitter struggle between the left-wing and right-wing ideological factions of Spanish political life, which was reflective of a divided and polarised broader society. On the other hand it indicated an opportunity for various foreign powers to wield a degree of influence over Spain's future direction, while also strengthening their own positions within an increasingly tense and unstable international (and specifically European) community. During the course of its duration between 1936 and 1939, the war saw extensive involvement from not only Spanish combatants and participants, but also from various international groups and armies. To what extent this foreign intervention was decisive and significant to the war's outcome has been a key area of debate among historians in the years that have followed.

Although the initial spark for war stemmed from deep-seated domestic tensions between Spain's left-leaning government and its various conservative critics, from the very outset there was prominent foreign intervention in the country's civil war. This was evident in Hitler's offer to Franco to allow him to use German aircraft to transport Nationalist troops from North Africa within the first week of the civil war in July 1936, while also providing various arms and military equipment during the conflict. By the end of 1936 a further influx of Italian 'blackshirts' had begun to arrive in Spain in support of Franco's Nationalist army, and by the time the war was over a considerable 75,000 such Italians had been estimated to have been directly involved in this Spanish civil conflict. Such blatant and explicit support for Franco from these two 'fascist' dictators indicated that there was a broad ideological alliance with Franco's Nationalists, and it appeared to be in the interests of these other European leaders for Franco to triumph. This explains why their support was so significant, and it occurred despite there being a Non-Intervention Pact signed by the majority of Europe's nations once the war had broken out. The fact that it was so flagrantly ignored says a lot about how ineffective the pact was.

Such high-profile foreign support for Franco was further evident in the ruthless bombardment of various Republican strongholds by the German air force 'Luftwaffe' during the civil war. The most notorious example of this was the destructive 'carpet bombing' of Guernica by the 'Luftwaffe''s Condor Legion in April 1937. In the civil war's latter stages of 1938–39, the Italian air force was active in bombarding the coastal cities of Barcelona and Valencia on behalf of Franco, and such activity was arguably decisive in delivering Franco's overall triumph within a quickened timescale. Given this obvious foreign support for Franco's Nationalists, the Republicans sought to draw in some international support of their own. The Soviet Union was

This introduction has a clear focus on the question and provides a good historical context to the various elements involved in the outbreak of the Spanish Civil War. From the outset it acknowledges that there were both domestic and international dimensions to this war, and that both aspects had some significance. It then directly addresses the historical debate connected to the question in terms of how decisive international factors were in the war's eventual outcome.

This paragraph is a very detailed assessment of how foreign involvement and intervention in the Spanish Civil War was evident from its very early stages. It specifically focuses on the support given to Franco's Nationalists by both Germany and Italy, and provides good supporting evidence in the process. This paragraph sets out an argument in support of foreign involvement during the Spanish Civil War influencing the outcome.

an obvious sympathiser due to their shared left-wing ideologies, and from late 1936 various military supplies and resources were provided from Moscow. However, Stalin was keen to keep this support fairly discreet so as to not antagonise other powerful nations within Europe committed to non-intervention, and the volume of such Soviet supplies were less numerous than those received by the Nationalists from their European allies. However the fact that two such powerful leaders as Stalin and Hitler were keen to actively involve themselves in the Spanish conflict indicated just how significant it was viewed by the big European powers, with each country wanting to secure Spain as a long-term ally. The Republicans received little encouragement when they sought the support of Great Britain's National Coalition and France's left-wing government, and as a consequence of this, thousands of volunteers from a wide range of nations formed 'International Brigades'. These unofficial battalions arrived in Spain to fight in defence of the Spanish Republic. While the quality of such irregular troops was not always great, their arrival did boost both Republican numbers and morale.

> This paragraph develops the extent of foreign involvement in the Spanish Civil War. There is some excellent and substantial evidence that indicates the full range and scale of foreign intervention in the conflict, and the varied examples are relevant and appropriate. This section clearly focuses on the question in terms of the significance of how the wider international community was heavily involved in this primarily Spanish conflict.

A focus on international influences does however run the risk of ignoring the significant domestic factors that shaped the outcome of Spain's civil war. Regardless of foreign support, there is strong evidence to suggest that Franco provided the Nationalists with exceptional leadership which played a key role in how the war finally ended in their favour. He had the majority of Spanish military officers within his ranks; by contrast, the Republicans had fewer experienced soldiers. Franco's charisma won him the admiration of other international leaders, and he had few to challenge him at the head of his army. By contrast, Republican leaders were less dominant and focused, and their forces lacked the same level of unity. Franco's tougher approach to keeping order also meant that the Nationalists generally had better control of their zones than those occupied by the Republicans. Franco's military powers therefore saw him secure a stunning series of military victories with few setbacks along the way, steadily taking over the country at a fairly swift pace. The Republicans were generally unable to deal with his more skilled and experienced soldiers and better overall military strategy.

> This paragraph offers a clear counter-argument that domestic factors should not be overlooked and were also significant in the war's development. There are, however, a few weak assertions which suggest that Franco's skills made the war more successful for the Nationalists than it was. The final point about the 'swift pace' of his victory overlooks the lengthy timescale of the war and the fact that the Republicans refused to be overrun and held firm for many years in locations such as Madrid.

In conclusion, therefore, it is quite clear that significant international activity from a wide range of sources was certainly evident throughout the Spanish Civil War. Key nations such as Germany, the Soviet Union and Italy had visible and high-profile presences during the three-year conflict, while a wider range of other nations saw their citizens contribute to the International Brigades, who also participated in many of the war's key battles. While Franco was certainly an effective leader with strong military skills and experience, he faced a fairly daunting task of trying to remove an established and democratically elected government. It is therefore open to question as to how much success he would have enjoyed during the war if he had not been supported by significant amounts of weaponry, military equipment and personnel from Hitler and Mussolini's regimes. It is notable and significant that the level of international support received by Franco was of a higher quantity and better quality than his Republican opponents, and this factor certainly consolidated his existing strong qualities. It is in this sense that it can be argued that international support was the decisive factor in determining the outcome of the Spanish Civil War.

> This concluding paragraph provides a solid and focused attempt to address the question. It offers a solid summary comparison of international vs domestic factors, and provides a clear and effective judgement in the process.

Verdict

This is a strong answer because:

- it puts both sides of the argument, looking at both the international and domestic factors that helped to shape the outcome of the Spanish Civil War

- it offers a wide range of substantial evidence, which is used to support the various points and arguments made
- it reaches a secure and convincing concluding judgement
- it is well organised and communication of factual material is clear and precise.

401

Index

abdication, definition 12
abortion, and the Catholic Church 367
  in Germany 96–97
Adenauer, Konrad 30–32
anarchism
  in Italy 169, 171
  in Spain 288
Anschluss 11, 115, 125, 127, 130, 243–44, 245
anticlericalism in Spain 290, 291
anti-Semitism
  anti-Semitic decrees in fascist
    Italy 222–23, 237
  anti-Semitism in the Weimar Republic 106
  Nazi racial policies 107–9, 119
appeasement policy 331
armistice 12
Aryan racial theory 92, 93
  in Italy 223
  influence on Nazi foreign policy 119
autarky
  aim of the Nazi regime 72
  in fascist Italy 229, 230
  in Franco's Spain 347–49
authoritarian government 332, 336
Azaña, Manuel 287, 290, 294–99, 302, 305

baby boomers 83
balance of trade 346
Basque Homeland and Freedom
  group (ETA) 369–70
Battle of Vittorio Veneto (1918) 186, 188, 192
Bauhaus movement 99
Berlin Wall 82
  fall of the wall (1989) 34–35
black market 63, 70, 347
blackshirts 198, 201–3
Blitzkrieg 78, 79
bourgeoisie 325
Brandt, Willy 33
Bundesrat 9

Cardorna, Luigi 185
Carlists 310, 312, 330, 337–38, 374
cartelisation 229
Catholic Church
  Clerical Laws in Spain (1938) 336
  conservative force in Spain 292
  disestablishment in Spain 291, 294
  educational provision under Franco 344
  influence in Franco's Spain 367–68, 341–42
  influence in Italy 168–69, 170, 176, 179–80,
      196–97
  red clergy in Spain 369
  relationship with Mussolini 229, 234–38

Caudillo 336
censorship
  in Spain under Franco 341
  in the Italian fascist state 219
  under the Nazi regime 48–49, 102–3
  under the Weimar Constitution 100
co-determination 81
Cold War 27, 353–56
collectivised economic model 312
Comintern 130, 133, 322
concentration camps 25, 49, 79, 107, 109
concordat 342
confessional schools 9, 98
consent
  de-Nazification policies of the
    Western Allies 57–59
  support for the Nazi regime 56–57
  supporters of democracy in the FRG 59–61
  supporters of the Weimar Constitution 53–55
constitutional monarchy 286
control
  FRG response to political extremism 51–52
  Nazi censorship and repression 48–50
  of the Italian population by the fascist
    state 217–23
  Weimar government response to
    extremism 47–48
corporatism in Franco's Spain 346–49
Council of Europe 85
cult of personality 334
  Franco 334, 343
  'Führer myth' (Hitler) 56–58
  il Duce (Mussolini) 220–21, 236
cultural experimentation in the Weimar
    Republic 99–100
cultural tensions in the FRG 104–5
culture
  influence of fascist culture in Italy 221
  Nazi cultural policies 102–3
currency devaluation 69

D'Annunzio, Gabriele 194–95
death camps 107, 108, 109
deflation 69
democracy
  collapse under the Weimar government 17–19
  referendum and elections in Italy (1946) 263
  supporters in the FRG 59–61
  transition from dictatorship in Spain 378–81
de-Nazification policies of the Western
    Allies 57–59
depression *see* Great Depression
devaluing a currency 69
devolution 296

dictatorship *see* Franco; Hitler; Mussolini
dissidents 340

Ebert, Friedrich 12, 14, 39, 47, 67
economic development
  FRG (1945–89) 79–85
  Germany (1918–89) 62–87
  Mussolini's policies in Italy 227–33
  Nazi economics 72–78
education
  in Spain under Franco 344
  in the FRG 103–4
  in the Weimar Republic 98–99
  indoctrination of youth in the Italian fascist
    state 217–18
  Nazi education policies 100–1
  post-war de-Nazification policy 103–4
Erhard, Ludwig 31, 32, 80–83
ethnic minorities
  attitudes in the FRG 111–12, 113
  historical prejudices in Germany 105
  Nazi racial policies 107–9
  status in the Weimar Republic 106–7
  see also Gypsies; Jews
eugenics 92, 106
European Coal and Steel Community
  (ECSC) 85
European Economic Community
  (EEC) 62, 85, 366
European Monetary System 62
expressionism 99
extremism
  response in the FRG 51–52
  Weimar government attempts to
    control 47–48

Falange-Española 302, 305–7
  see also Spain under Franco; Spanish
    Civil War
fasci, definition 197
fascism, definition and origin of
    the term 166, 197, 199
  see also Italy, fascist state; Italy, rise of
    fascism
fascists, definition 39
Federal Republic of Germany (FRG)
  attitudes towards ethnic
    minorities 111–12, 113
  Basic Law (1949) 28–29
  consolidation under Adenauer and
    Erhard (1949–65) 30–32
  creation of 1945–49 26–30, 80
  cultural tensions 104–5
  currency reform 80

economic challenges (1966–89) 83–84
economic miracle (1955–66) 81–82
educational policy 103–4
effects of the Berlin Wall 82
fall of the Berlin Wall (1989) 34–35
generational tensions 105
integration into the European economy 84–85
maintaining political stability (1965–89) 32–35
outbreak of terrorism (1980s) 34
political dissent and active challenge (1949–89) 43–46
response to political extremism 51–52
social market economy 79–81
supporters of democracy 59–61
terrorist attacks 46, 51–52
women's role and status 95–97
feminism 345
First World War (1914–18)
effect on Nazi foreign policy 119, 120–22
state of Europe following 8
Franco, General Francisco
as *Generalissimo* 312, 329
see also Spain under Franco; Spanish Civil War
free market economy 32, 348
Freemasonry 235, 339
Freikorps (Free Corps) 12, 13, 39, 47
Futurist movement in Italy 195

General Agreement on Tariffs and Trade (GATT) 85
general strike in Spain 299
German Democratic Republic (GDR)
creation of 30, 80
effects of the Berlin Wall 82
erection of the Berlin Wall (1961) 30
fall of the Berlin Wall (1989) 34–35
women's role and status 97
Germanising policy 26
Germany
changes after the First World War 8
economic development 62–87
expression of opposition 36–46
government pre-First World War 9
political and governmental change 10–35
revolution from above (1917) 10
terms of the Treaty of Versailles 11
types of divisions within 9
see also Federal Republic of Germany (FRG); German Democratic Republic (GDR); Nazi Germany; Weimar Republic
Gestapo 21–22, 25, 49–50
ghettoes 56, 108, 109
Giolitti, Giovanni 166, 168–69, 171, 174–80, 182–84, 187, 197, 200–2, 204, 208
Goebbels, Joseph 23, 24, 25, 26, 48, 102
Great Depression
effects on women in Germany 92
impact on the Weimar Republic 68–69
response in fascist Italy 228–29, 232
role in the outbreak of war 137–38

Green Party 33, 34
Gross Domestic Product (GDP) 347
Gross National Product (GNP) 348
guerrilla warfare 312
Gypsies 105, 106, 107, 109

Hallstein Doctrine (1955) 30, 31, 32
Hemmingway, Ernest 323
Hindenburg, Paul von 10, 16–21, 38, 40–41, 47–48, 67, 69, 119, 120
Hitler, Adolf
aims of the Third Reich 119
as Führer 20, 23
attempts to assassinate 42
decision to invade Poland (1939) 128–32
decision to use political power 121
'Führer myth' 56–58
influence of the fascists in Italy 39
influence on Nazi foreign policy 122–32
Mein Kampf 38, 40, 119, 121, 126
Munich Putsch (1923) 39–40
rearmament and expansion of Germany 127–32
rise of 18–19
suicide 79
views on his intentions 114–15
views on provoking war 127–32
see also Nazi Germany
Hitler Youth movement 41, 101
Holocaust 58, 107–9
hyperinflation 64

Ibárruri, Dolores (*La Pasionaria*) 326–27, 379–80
inflation 62, 346
International Brigades 315, 323–24, 327
International Monetary Fund 85
irredentism 172–73
Italy
referendum and elections in 1946 263
struggle to be a 'great power' 172–73
the Roman Question 170, 176, 196, 235–36
unification issues 166–67, 168–69, 170
Italy, as fascist state (1925–46) 166–67, 216–38
agricultural policies 230–31, 232
Allied invasion of Italy 258–59, 262
Allied invasion of Sicily 257
anti-Semitic decrees 222–23, 237
autarky policy 229, 230
Battle for the Lira 227
campaign for 'reform of customs' 223
challenges to 240–56
changes between 1943 and 1946 258–61
control of the Italian population 217–23
creation of the Vatican City state 235–36
cult of *il Duce* 220–21, 236
drive for population increase 229–30
fall of Mussolini (1943) 257–58, 259–60, 262, 263
fall of the fascist state 256–63
foreign policy aims and results 240–52
German invasion of Italy 259

German surrender in Italy 262
goes to war on the side of Nazi Germany 253–56
implementation of the Corporate State 227–28
indoctrination of education and youth 217–18
influence of fascist culture 221
Italian antifascist partisans 260–61
Kingdom of the South 261
military weaknesses 253–55
neutrality (1939–40) 251–52
Pacification of Libya (1929–32) 242
press control and censorship 219
propaganda 219–21
relations with Nazi Germany 243–44, 245, 247–52
relationship with Italy's elites 224–26
repression and persecution of opposition 221–23
response to the Great Depression 228–29, 232
results of Mussolini's economic policies 227–33
role of women 229–30, 237
Salo Republic 259–60
support for Franco in the Spanish Civil War 166, 247
totalitarian rule 222–23
war economy 255
Italy, as liberal state (c1911–18) 168–90
cost of First World War 187–88
declaration of neutrality (1914) 180–81
defeat at Caporetto (1917) 185–87, 189
economic and social problems 171–72
foreign policy under Giolitti 178
growing instability (1912–14) 178–81
impact of franchise extension (1912) 179
impact of the First World War 181–90
impact of the invasion of Libya 178–79
influence of Giovanni Giolitti government 174–80
influence of the Catholic Church 168–69, 170, 176, 179–80
intervention crisis 181–84
irredente lands 172–73
mass emigration (early 1900s) 172
military stalemate (1915–16) 185
north–south divide 172, 173
political system after unification 170–71
rise and growth of nationalism 176–77, 179–80
rise and growth of socialism 175–76, 179–80, 187
significance of victory 188
the Roman Question 170, 176
war economy 187–88
Italy, rise of fascism (1919–26) 166–67, 192–213
adoption of the 'New Programme' (1920) 199
Biennio Rosso period (1919–20) 196
change to proportional representation (1919) 196
creation of a fascist dictatorship 206–13

creation of the Partito Nazionale Fascista
(PNF) 199
disappointed expectations at Versailles
(1919) 193–94, 195
dispute over Fiume 193–94
establishment of the dictatorship
(1925) 211–13
Fasci di Combattimento 192, 197–98
fascist ideological confusion 199
growth of the Catholic political party 196–97
growth of the PSI (socialist party) 196–97
impact of the 1919 election 197
March on Rome 203–5
mistakes by Mussolini's political
opposition 206–13
'mutilated victory' account 193–94
nature and extent of fascist support 199
occupation of Fiume 194–95
political legitimacy of fascism 198–99
post-war social and economic crisis 196
problems following the First
World War 192–97
repression and constitutional amendments
(1925–26) 212–13
role of King Victor Emmanuel III 203–5, 261,
263
role of Mussolini 200–5
squadristi culture of extreme violence 198–99,
201–3
violence against socialists 198–99

Jews see anti-Semitism
Juan Carlos, King of Spain 378–81
junta government 311

Kapp Putsch (1920) 39, 42
Kiesinger, Kurt 32
Kinder, Küche, Kirch 88–89, 92–96
Kohl, Helmut 33, 34
Kristallnacht ('Night of Broken Glass') 107, 108

labour camps 79, 107, 109
Länder 9
Largo Caballero, Francisco 312–13, 322
Lateran Pacts (Italy, 1929) 235–38
League of Nations 134–45, 194
Lebensborn programme 92
Lebensraum 25
left-wing political viewpoint 290
living standard changes in Germany
(1918–89) 69–72, 76–77, 86–87

Marshall Plan 27, 80, 85, 354
martial law 325
Metropolis (Fritz Lang film) 99
military coup in Spain (1920s) 286
militia, definition 300
modernism 99
Munich Putsch (1923) 39–40
Mussolini, Benito 39
appointment as prime minister 204–5

colonial ambitions 244–47
controlling the PNF 206–8
cult of il Duce 220–21, 236
deposed and imprisoned (1943) 257–58, 259
dual approach to achieving power 201–2
early career as a journalist 179
execution (1945) and burial 262, 263
Fasci di Combattimento 197–98
fascist ideology 198–99
foreign policy aims and results 240–52
from radical socialist to pro-nationalist 183
influence of the occupation of Fiume 194–95
March on Rome 203–5
Matteotti crisis 209–10
mistakes by his political opposition 206–13
plan for the fascist state 216–17
relations with Britain and France 243, 244,
245, 247–48
relations with Nazi Germany 243–44, 245,
247–52
relationship with Italy's elites 224–26
relationship with the Catholic
Church 229, 234–38
rescue by the Germans 259–60
results of economic policies 227–33
rise and fall of 166–67
role in the rise of fascism 200–5
taking advantage of political unrest 200–1
use of violence as a political tool 198–99
see also Italy, as fascist state; Italy, rise of
fascism

National Socialist German Workers' Party
(NSDAP) see Nazi Party
nationalisation of property 291
nationalism
and fascism in Italy 166–67
in Italy 176–77, 179–80, 183, 187
in Spain 310–12
see also Nazi Germany
Nazi foreign policy
and the outbreak of war 114–32
historical influences on 119–22
influence of Aryan racial theory 119
influence of Hitler's ideology 122–32
influence of the First World War 119, 120–22
influence of the Treaty of Versailles 120–22,
127–32
Nazi Germany
attitude to women 92–95
changing living standards 76–77
command economy 74–76
cultural policies 102–3
economic impact of war 77–78
economic policies 72–78
education policies 100–1
establishment of a dictatorship 20–22
foreign policy and the outbreak of war 114–32
government in wartime (1939–45) 25–26
government structure and features
(1934–39) 23–25

invasion of Italy 259, 262
opposition and dissent (1933–45) 40–43
racial policies 107–9
relations with Mussolini 243–44, 245, 247–52
supporters of 56–57
use of censorship and repression 48–50
Nazi Party
rise of 18–19
Negrín López, Juan 322–23, 329
Neue Sachlichkeit (New Objectivity)
movement 99, 100
neutrality 334
North Atlantic Treaty Organization
(NATO) 85, 354
Nosferatu (first vampire movie) 100
November Criminals 17, 120
Nuremberg Trials 58

oil crises (1973 and 1978) 83
one-party state 325
opposition
active challenge in the FRG 43–46
antifascist organisations in Italy 222, 260–61
to the Nazi government 40–43
to the Weimar Government 39–40
Opus Dei 360
Organisation for European Economic
Cooperation (OEEC) 84, 85
Orwell, George 323, 324, 325, 330
Ostpolitik 32, 33, 34, 61

pan-Germanism 119
Picasso, Pablo 323
Pius XI, Pope
relationship with Mussolini 235–38
Pius XII, Pope
dealings with fascist and Nazi regimes 237
support for Franco 341
plebiscite, definition 236
political spectrum ('left' and 'right') 290
Popular Front in Spain 302–8
proletariat 300, 301
propaganda
in Spain under Franco 341
in the Italian fascist state 219–21
use by the Nazi regime 56–57
proportional representation in Italy 196
protectionism 347
proxy war 315

rationing 26
reactionary, definition 298
realpolitik 350
refugee problem after the Second World War 79
Reich, definition 9
Reichstag 9
repression
in the Italian fascist state 212–13, 221–23
terror tactics in the Spanish
Civil War 328–29
under the Nazis 49–50

White terror of Franco's regime 340
republicanism 288
  in Spain 284, 286–308, 310, 312–13
  Italy becomes a republic 263
  see also Federal Republic of Germany (FRG);
    German Democratic Republic (GDR);
    Weimar Republic
right-wing political viewpoint 290
Risorgimento 169

Salandra, Antonio 169, 171, 179, 180–82, 185, 188, 203–4, 205, 209
Schmidt, Helmut 33
Schutzstaffel (SS) 21–22, 25, 49–50, 108
Second World War
  attitudes of individual countries 136–37
  changing views of historians 114
  evaluating interpretations of history 116
  German surrender in 1945 79
  historical influences on Nazi foreign
    policy 119–22
  impact on women in Germany 94–95
  influence of economic depression 137–38
  influence of international politics 133–35
  interpretations of Hitler's foreign
    policy 117–18
  interpretations of Hitler's intentions 114–15
  neutrality of Franco's Spain 350–52
  resentment of the Treaty of Versailles 120–22, 127–32
  role of Nazi foreign policy 114–32
  summary of causes 115
  weakness of the League of Nations 134–35
  see also Nazi Germany
social democracy 364
social market economy, development in
  the FRG 79–81
socialism
  in Spain 288
  rise in Italy 175–76, 179–80
  variants of 289
soviets 12
Spain
  accession of King Juan Carlos 378–81
  anarchism and syndicalism 288
  class-based conflict 286–87, 299–300
  end of constitutional monarchy
    (1920s) 286
  military coup (1920s) 286
  military dictatorship (1930) 287–88
  modernisation (1956–75) 358–81
  political and social instability
    (1930–78) 284–85
  socialism 288
  transition to democracy 378–81
Spain, Second Republic (1931–36) 284, 286–308
  assassination of Sotelo 306
  Asturias uprising (1934) 301, 304
  attempted military coup (1936) 306–8
  economic and social problems 292–93
  Falange-Española 302, 305, 306, 307

forces of conservatism 291–92, 298–99
impacts of the 1936 general
  election 303–8
political unrest 292
Popular Front 302–8
'years of reaction' (1933–36) 297–308
'years of reform' (1931–33) 293–97
Spain under Franco (1938–75) 334–77
  attitudes towards women 344–45, 367–68
  Basque Homeland and Freedom group
    (ETA) 369–70
  censorship 341
  changes during 1939–56 350–56
  Clerical Laws 336
  Cold War international relations 353–56
  conservative social policies 336
  control of the Spanish people 339–45
  cult of personality 334, 343
  death of Franco (1975) 377
  development of corporatism 346–49
  economic and social change
    (1956–75) 358–65
  economic performance 345–49
  education policies 344
  establishing Franco's dictatorship
    (1938–56) 334–55
  Franco as *Caudillo* 336
  growing opposition (late 1960s) 368–70
  impact and growth of tourism 362–63, 364
  implementation of autarky 347–49
  influence of the Falange 336–38
  neutrality in the Second World War 350–52
  political change (1956–70) 366–72
  political terror and repression 340
  post-Franco succession planning 337–38, 374–77
  Prince Juan Carlos named as
    successor 374–77
  propaganda 341
  relations with the Catholic Church 341–42
  return to monarchy (1969) 374–77
  transition to democracy 378–81
  White terror of Franco's regime 340
Spanish Civil War (1936–39)
  atrocities by both sides 319, 323
  attitudes towards women 326–28
  bombing of Guernica 319, 323
  course of the war 317–24
  factors in the outbreak of war 307–8, 310–16
  factors influencing the outcome 329–31
  impact on ordinary Spanish citizens 324–29
  International Brigades 315, 323–24, 327
  opposing ideologies 310–16
  Republican political divisions 322–23
  role of Franco 329–31
  significance of the international response 247, 310, 314–15, 330–31
  use of political terror 328–29
Spartacists 12, 47
Sturmabteilung (SA) 18
syndicalism 226, 288

technocrats 360
terrorism, attacks in the FRG 34, 46, 51–52
Third Reich, aims of 119
totalitarian government 331
Treaty of Rome (1957) 85
Treaty of Versailles (1919) 11
  contribution to Second World War 120–22, 127–32
  impact on German politics 37–39
Trotskyite ideology 322
Turati, Filippo 175–76

underemployment 346
United Nations (UN) 332, 353

Vatican City state, creation of 235–36
Victor Emmanuel III, King of Italy 203–5, 261, 263
Volksgemeinschaft 23, 101
Volkssturm (Nazi Home Guard) 25
Volkswagen (VW) 77, 81

Weimar Republic
  Article 48 of the Constitution 16
  attempts to control extremism 47–48
  attitude to women 90–92
  challenges faced by 15–17
  changing living standards 69–72
  collapse of democracy (1930–33) 17–19
  creation of 12–13
  creation of the Weimar Constitution 13–15
  cultural experimentation 99–100
  economic challenges (1918–32) 63–69
  education system 98–99
  impact of the Great Depression 68–69
  Kapp Putsch (1920) 39, 42
  Munich Putsch (1923) 39–40
  nature of support for 53–55
  political extremism and crises
    (1918–33) 39–40
  political impact of the Treaty of
    Versailles 37–39
Wilhelm II, Kaiser of Germany 9, 10
women in fascist Italy, role and status 229–30, 237
women in Germany, abortion rights 96–97
  attitude of the Weimar Government 90–92
  effects of the Great Depression 92
  impact of Nazi rule 92–95
  impact of the Second World War 94–95
  Kinder, Küche, Kirch role 88–89, 92–96
  new women 91
  role and status before the First World
    War 88, 90
  role and status in the DRG 97
  role and status in the FRG 95–97
women in Spain
  attitude of the Franco regime 344–45, 367–68
  attitudes during the Spanish Civil War 326–28
  influence of the Catholic Church on 367–68
women's liberation movements 96

Acknowledgements

The authors and publisher would like to thank the following individuals and organisations for permission to reproduce photographs and text in this book.

Photographs

(Key: b-bottom; c-centre; l-left; r-right; t-top)

akg-images Ltd: 41, 44, 82, 89, 337, Album/Oronoz 355, IAM 13, picture-alliance/dpa 113, ullstein bild 62, 65, 88t, 120, World History Archive 375; **Alamy Images:** INTERFOTO 327, Lebrecht Music and Arts Photo Library 289, Mary Evans Picture Library 334, 343, National Geographic Image Collection 6, PARIS PIERCE 326, The Art Archive 189; **Bridgeman Art Library Ltd:** Private Collection/De Agostini Picture Library 88b, 99, Private Collection/The Stapleton Collection 73; **British Cartoon Archive, University of Kent www.cartoons.ac.uk:**/ Solo Syndication/Associated Newspapers Ltd 126, David Low, Evening Standard, 4 October 1935/Solo Syndication/Associated Newspapers Ltd 246; **Corbis:** Alinari Archives/F. Slocovich 195, Berliner Verlag/ Archiv/dpa 8, 131, K.J. Historical 168; **Getty Images:** DEA Picture Library 177, DeAgostini 285, General Photographic Agency 175, Hulton Archive/Galerie Bilderwelt 80, Keystone-France/Gamma-Keystone 218, Popperfoto 371, Roger Viollet 231, 237, Rolls Press/Popperfoto 308, Universal History Archive 167; **Mary Evans Picture Library:** 10, 22l, 22r, CAGP/Iberfoto 303, Iberfoto 341, Sueddeutsche Zeitung Photo 36, 49, 287, 319, Weimar Archive 93; **Punch Cartoon Library:** 323; **Rex Features:** A.Bruni/Alinari 204, 221tl, 221bl, Image Broker 220, Roger-Viollet 221br; **TopFoto:** AP 172, Keystone 11, 34, The Granger Collection 210, 251, ullsteinbild 54

Cover image: *Front:* **Getty Images:** FPG

All other images © Pearson Education

Tables
Tables pp. 14, 17 and 19 from *The Weimar Republic* by John Hiden, Longman Seminar Studies in History, Pearson Education Ltd, 1974, p. 78, Copyright © 1974, reproduced by permission of Taylor & Francis Books UK; Tables pp. 31, 33 and 60 from *Germany since 1945* by Pól O'Dochartaigh, Studies in Contemporary History, Palgrave Macmillan, 2003, Appendix 1, Copyright © Pól O'Dochartaig 2003, reproduced with permission of Palgrave Macmillan; Tables pp. 54, 55 based on data from *Election in Europe: A Handbook* edited by Dieter Nohlen and Philip Stover , Nomos Verlagsgesellschaft, 2010; Table p. 65 from *The Encyclopedia of Money*, 2nd edn by Larry Allen, ABC Clio, 2009, p. 219, reproduced with permission of ABC-CLIO in the format Republish in a book via Copyright Clearance Center; Tables pp. 68, 73 and 82 (second table) from Table 18, p. 284, tables pp. 70 and 76 (second table) from Table 25, p. 290, table p. 82 (first table) from Table 10, p. 279, tables pp. 82 (third table) and 84 from Table 12, p. 280, table p. 87 from Table 29, p. 292 of *Modern*

Germany: Society, Economics and Politics in the Twentieth Century, 2nd edn by V.R. Berghahn , Cambridge University Press, 1987, reproduced with permission from Cambridge University Press; Tables pp. 75, 76 (first table) and 78 from *Nazism 1919-1945*, Vol. 2, State, Economy and Society 1933–39 by J. Noakes and G. Pridham, Exeter Studies in History No. 8, University of Exeter Press, pp. 292, 323, 298, reproduced with permission from Liverpool University Press; Table p. 173 from *Modern Italy 1871-1995*, 2nd edn by Martin Clark, Longman, 1996, p. 36. Copyright© 1996, reproduced by permission of Taylor & Francis Books UK; Table p. 299 based on data from http://www.historiaelectoral.com/e1931.html; Table p. 304 from *The Collapse of the Spanish Republic 1933-1936,Origins of the Civil War* by Stanley Payne , Yale University Press, 2006, p. 177, reproduced with permission; Tables pp. 346,362,368 and 369 from *The Franco Regime 1936-1975* by Stanley Payne, University of Wisconsin Press, 1987, pp.246, 485, 555, 560, Copyright © 1987 by The Board of Regents of the University of Wisconsin System. Reprinted by permission of The University of Wisconsin Press; Table p. 361 from *An Economic History of Modern Spain* by Joseph Harrison, Manchester University Press, 1978, p. 156, reproduced with permission from Manchester University Press; Two tables p. 363 from *An Economic History of Modern Spain*, by Joseph Harrison, Manchester University Press, 1978, reproduced with permission from Manchester University Press.

Text
Extract p. 18 from *A History of Germany 1815–1945* by William Carr, Edward Arnold, 1969, pp. 343-344, Copyright © William Carr 1969, Bloomsbury Academic, an imprint of Bloomsbury Publishing Plc; Extracts pp. 24, 25, 29, 56, 'Source 9' p. 50, p. 75 from *Nazism 1919–1945*, Vol. 2, State, Economy and Society 1933–39 by J. Noakes and G. Pridham, Exeter Studies in History No 8, Exeter University Press, 1984, pp. 138-39, doc. 138, doc. 138, p. 568, p. 459, p. 291, reproduced with permission from Liverpool University Press; Extracts pp. 28, 34 from *Germany since 1945* by Pól O'Dochartaigh, Studies in Contemporary History, Palgrave Macmillan, 2003, pp. 11, 188-189, Copyright © Pól O'Dochartaig 2003, reproduced with permission of Palgrave Macmillan; Extract p. 32 and Extract 4 p. 47 from *A Concise History of Germany* by Mary Fulbrook, Cambridge Concise Histories, Cambridge University Press, 1990, pp. 215-216, p. 158, reproduced with permission from Cambridge University Press; Extract p. 35 from *The Wall: The People's Story* by Christopher Hilton, The History Press, 2011, pp. 346-347, Copyright © Christopher Hilton, reproduced with permission; Extracts pp. 37, 137 from *From Versailles to Pearl Harbor* by Margaret Lamb and Nicholas Tarling, Palgrave, 2001, pp. 29, 184 reproduced with permission of Palgrave Macmillan; Extract 'Source 1' p. 38 from *Mein Kampf* by Adolf Hitler, translated by Ralph Manheim, published by Hutchinson, 1933, pp. 91-92, reproduced by permission of The Random House Group Ltd; Extract 'Source 2' p. 38 from 'The Stab in the Back' by Paul von Hindenburg, November 18, 1919 in *The Weimar Republic Sourcebook* edited by Anton Kaes, Martin Jay, and Edward Dimendberg, University of California Press, 1994, pp. 15-16, reproduced with permission of UNIVERSITY OF CALIFORNIA PRESS in the format Republish in a book via Copyright Clearance Center; Extract p. 42 from *Nazism 1919-1945*, Vol. 1: The Rise to Power 1919–1934 by J. Noakes and G. Pridham, University of Exeter Press, 1998, pp. 14-16, reproduced with permission from Liverpool University Press; Extract 2 p. 45 from *Germany 1933–1990*,

Vol. 2, The Long Road West by Heinrich August Winkler, Oxford University Press, 2007, p. 232, By permission of Oxford University Press; Extract 3 p. 45, p. 59 from Katherine Bagley, Ronald Bruckmann, Peggy Fiebig, Christopher Fields, Richard Hallenback, John Lamont, Sarah Mielke, Russell Miller, Caitlin O'Donnell and Alexandre Rourk, Washington & Lee University GLJ Seminar Fall 2008, 40/68 – Germany's 1968 and the Law – Part II/II, *German Law Journal*, Vol. 10, No. 3, pp. 223-260 (2009), available at http://www.germanlawjournal.com/index. php?pageID=11&artID=1089 reproduced with permission; Extract 'Source 6' p. 47 from *The Weimar Republic* by John Hiden, Longman Seminar Studies in History, Pearson Education Ltd, 1974, p. 93, Copyright © 1974, reproduced by permission of Taylor & Francis Books UK; Extract 'Source 8' p. 50 from *Inside Nazi Germany: Conformity, Opposition and Race* by Detlev Peukert , B.T. Batsford, 1987, reproduced with kind permission of B.T. Batsford, part of Pavilion Books Company Limited; Extract p. 57 from *Backing Hitler: Consent and Coercion in Nazi Germany* by Robert Gellately, Oxford University Press, 2001, p. 15, By permission of Oxford University Press; Extract p. 69 from *Modern Germany: Society, Economics and Politics in the Twentieth Century*, 2nd edn by V.R. Berghahn, Cambridge University Press, 1987, p. 74, reproduced with permission from Cambridge University Press; Extract p. 70 from *Rethinking the Weimar Republic: Authority and Authoritarianism 1916–1936* by Anthony McElligott, Bloomsbury Academic, 2014, p. 86 © Anthony McElligott 2014, Bloomsbury Academic, an imprint of Bloomsbury Publishing Plc; Extracts pp. 87, 104 from *A History of West Germany*, Vol. 2 by Dennis L. Bark and David R. Gress , Blackwell, 1989; Extract p. 91 from 'Anticipating the Future in the Present: "New Women" and Other Beings of the Future in Weimar Germany' by Rudiger Graf, *Central European History*, Vol. 42 (4), pp. 647-673, 2009, reproduced with permission from Cambridge University Press; Extract p. 94 from *From Nurturing the Nation to Purifying the Volk* by Michelle Mouton, Cambridge University Press, 2007, reproduced with permission from Cambridge University Press; Extracts pp. 95, 96 from *War Wives* by Colin and Eileen Townsend, Grafton, 1989, pp. 260, 139-40, Copyright © Colin and Eileen Townsend 1989, reproduced by permission of Sheil Land Associates Ltd; Extract 3 p. 97 from 'Non-German Minorities, Women and the Emergence of Civil Society' in *The Cambridge Companion to Modern German Culture*, Vol. 1 edited by Eva Kolinsky and Wilfried van der Will, Cambridge University Press, 1999, pp. 129-130, reproduced with permission from Cambridge University Press; Extract 4 p. 97 from 'Lysistrate geht um. Kein Pilenknick, sondem die Emanzipation der Frau lehrt die Gesellschaft das Furchten' [Lysistrata on the Move: The birth rate is not dropping due to the pill; it is women's emancipation that is teaching society fear] by Viola Roggenkamp, translated by Allison Brown, *Die Ziet*, 22/04/1977, reproduced with permission; Extract p. 98 from 'The German Evangelical Churches and the Struggle for the Schools in the Weimar Republic' by Frank J. Gordon, *Church History*, Vol. 49 (1), p. 49, March 1980, reproduced with permission; Extract p. 101 from *Hitler and Nazi Germany: Questions and Analysis in History*, 2nd edn by Stephen J. Lee, Routledge, 2013, pp. 54-55, Copyright ©2013 Routledge, reproduced by permission of Taylor & Francis Books UK; Extract p. 106 from 'Letters to "Der Sturmer": The Mobilization of Hostility in the Weimer Republic' by Dennis E. Showalter, *Modern Judaism*, Vol. 3 (2),p. 183, May 1983, By permission of Oxford University Press; Extract p. 111 from *Encyclopedia of Contemporary German Culture* by John Sandford, Routledge, 2013, p. 244, Copyright © 2013, reproduced by permission of Taylor & Francis Books UK; Extract 1 p. 118 from 'The Origins of the Second World War' by Georg Franz Willing, *The Journal of Historical Review*, Vol. 7 (1), pp. 95-114, 1986, http://www.ihr.org/jhr/v07/v07p-95_Franz-Willing.html. This paper was first presented by the author at the Seventh IHR Conference, February 1986; Extract 2 p. 118, Extracts pp.124, 134 from *The Origins of the Second World War in Europe* by P.M.H. Bell, Pearson Education Ltd., 2007, pp. 348-349, 49-50, 58, Copyright © 2007, reproduced by permission of Taylor & Francis Books UK; Extract p. 119 from 'Misjudging Hitler' in *The Origins of the Second World War Reconsidered* by Richard Overy, Routledge, 1999, p. 34, Copyright © 1999 Routledge, reproduced by permission of Taylor & Francis Books UK; Extract p. 120, Extract 5 p. 123 and Extract p. 128 from *The Origins of the Second World War* by A.J.P. Taylor, Penguin, 1973,pp. 97-98, reproduced by permission of Penguin Books Ltd.; Extracts pp. 122, 'Source 3' p. 123 from *Nazism 1919–1945*, Vol. 3: Foreign Policy, War and Racial Extermination by J. Noakes and G. Pridham, University of Exeter Press,1995, pp. 628-29, 673, reproduced with permission from Liverpool University Press; Extract p. 125 from 'Germany' from *The Road to War* by Richard Overy and Andrew Wheatcroft, Vintage, 1989, p. 47, Copyright © 1989, 1999 by Richard Overy & Andrew Wheatcroft, reprinted by permission of The Random House Group Limited and of Viking Books, an imprint of Penguin Publishing Group, a division of Penguin Random House LLC; Extract 8 p. 126 from *The Foreign Policy of the Third Reich* by Klaus Hildebrand, B.T. Batsford Ltd, 1973, pp. 23, 28, reproduced with kind permission of B.T. Batsford, part of Pavilion Books Company Limited; Extract 9 p. 126 from *How War Came* by Donald Cameron Watt, William Heinemann, 1989, p. 32, reprinted by permission of Peters Fraser & Dunlop (www.petersfraserdunlop.com) on behalf of the Estate of Donald Cameron Watt; Extract p. 128 from *Hitler: A Study in Tyranny* by Alan Bullock, Odhams Books, 1965, p. 471, reproduced with permission of Curtis Brown Group Ltd, London, on behalf of The Beneficiaries of the Estate of Alan Bullock. Copyright © Alan Bullock 1965; Extract p. 131 from *War and Economy in the Third Reich* by Richard Overy, Oxford University Press, 1994, p. 24, By permission of Oxford University Press; Extract 13 p. 132 from *Germany: Hitler and World War II*, Essays in Modern German World History by Gerhard L. Weinberg, Cambridge University Press, 1995, p.111, reproduced with permission from Cambridge University Press; Extract 'Source 6' p. 132 from *Documents on German Foreign Policy*, Vol. 6, 1918–1945, HMSO, 1956, pp. 574-75 and Extract p. 136 from *Documents on British Foreign Policy, 1919–1939*, 2nd series, Vol. 12, Doc. 651, HMSO, 1972, Contains public sector information licensed under the Open Government Licence (OGL) v3.0.http://www. nationalarchives.gov.uk/doc/open-government-licence; Quote p. 166 from *The Last Days of Mussolini* by Ray Moseley, Sutton Publishing, 2006, p. 3, reproduced with permission; Extract 1 p. 174, Extract 3 p. 180, Extract 1 p. 252 and quotes pp. 176, 230, from *Modern Italy 1871–1995*, 2nd edn by Martin Clark, Longman, 1996, pp.35, 156, 284-85, 146, Copyright © 1996, reproduced by permission of Taylor & Francis Books UK; Extract 'Source 4' p. 174 from *Selection from Prison Notebooks of Antonio Gramsci* edited by Q. Hoare and G. Nowell Smith, Lawrence & Wishart Ltd, London, 1971, p. 263, reproduced with permission; Extracts pp. 177, 178, 'Source 11' p. 184, 202 and quotes pp. 192, 193 from *The Force of Destiny: A History of Italy since 1976* by Christopher Duggan, Penguin, 2007, p. 368, 382, 389, 436, 432, 413, 415, Copyright © Christopher Duggan, 2007, reproduced by permission of Penguin Books Ltd.; Extract 2 p. 180 from 'State and Society, 1901–1922' by Paul Corner in *Liberal and Fascist Italy* edited by Adrian Lyttelton, Oxford University Press , 2002, pp. 27-28, By permission of Oxford University Press; Extract p.182 from 'Italy in the International System, 1901–1922' by Thomas Row in *Liberal and Fascist Italy* edited by Adrian Lyttelton, Oxford University Press, 2002, p. 93, By permission of Oxford University Press; Extract 'Source 12' p.184 from *Gabriele D'Annunzio* by P. Alatri, Utet, 1983, p. 343-344, reproduced with permission; Extract p. 190 from 'Consequences of World War I' by Paul Corner in *Liberal and Fascist Italy* edited by Adrian Lyttelton, Oxford University Press, 2002, p. 36, By permission of Oxford University Press; Extracts pp.207, 211, quote p. 241 from *Mussolini* by Denis Mack Smith, Weidenfeld and Nicolson, 1981, pp. 57-58, 85-86, 173 reproduced with permission from the author; Extracts pp. 211, 238 (Ext. 2), Extract 2 p. 252 and quotes pp. 220, 223, 227,236, 240, 243, 244, 252,254, 258 from *Mussolini* by Richard Bosworth, Arnold, 2002, pp.202-203, 238, 370, 428, 16, 226, 238,184, 267, 301, 368, 306, 325, Copyright© Richard Bosworth 2002, with permission from Bloomsbury Academic, an imprint of Bloomsbury Publishing; Extracts pp.212, 213 from *Mussolni: A New Life* by Nicholas Farrell, Weidenfeld and Nicolson, 2003, pp.155-156, 143, reproduced with permission from the author; Extract p. 223 from 'The Origins of the "Manifesto of Racial Scientists"', *Il Gionarle d'Italia*, 14 July 1938, translated by Aaron Gillette, *Journal of Modern Italian Studies*, Vol. 6 (3), pp. 318-320, 2001, Routledge, reprinted by permission of the publisher (Taylor & Francis Ltd, http://www.tandfonline.com); Extract p. 225 from 'Dictators Strong or Weak?' by R.J.B. Bosworth in *The Oxford Handbook of Fascism* edited by R. Bosworth, Oxford University Press, 2009, pp. 271-272, By permission of Oxford University Press; Extract p. 233 from *Sawdust Caesar: The Untold History of Mussolini and Fascism* by George Seldes, Harper & Brothers Publishers, 1935, pp. 364-365, Reprinted by permission of Russell & Volkening as agents for the author. Copyright © 1935 by George Seldes, copyright renewed 1963 by George Seldes; Extract 3 p. 238 from *The Vatican and Italian Fascism, 1929–1932* by John Pollard, Cambridge University Press, 1985, pp. 48-49; Extract 'Source 1' p. 246 from *Fascist Voices* by Christopher Duggan, The Bodley Head, 2012, pp. 276-277, Reprinted by permission of The Random house Group Ltd and Felicity Bryan, Copyright © Christopher Duggan 2012; Extract 'Source 2' p. 246 from *Christ Stopped at Eboli* by Carlo Levi, Penguin Books, 2000, pp. 131-132, © 1945, 1963, 1975, 1990, 2010, 2014 Giulio Einaudi editore spa, Torino, translated by Frances Frenaye Lanza. Translation copyright © 1947, renewed 1974 by Farrar, Straus & Giroux, Inc. Reprinted by permission of Farrar, Straus and Giroux, LLC. CAUTION: Users are warned that this work is protected under copyright laws and downloading is strictly prohibited. The right to reproduce or transfer the work via any medium must be secured with Farrar, Straus and Giroux, LLC; Extract p. 247 from *Spain and the Great Powers in the Twentieth Century* by S. Balfour and Paul Preston, Routledge, 2002, p. 161, Copyright © 2002 Routledge, reproduced by permission of Taylor & Francis Books UK; Extract p. 261 from *The Fascist Experience* by John Pollard, Routledge, 1998, p. 113, Copyright © 1998, reproduced by permission of Taylor & Francis Books UK; Extracts pp. 284, 330 from *England, Your England and Other Essays* by George Orwell, published Secker & Warburg, 1953, reproduced with permission of The Random House Group Limited; Extract p. 287 from *The Spanish Civil War, Reaction, Revolution and Revenge* by Paul Preston, HarperCollins, 2006, p. 17, Reprinted by permission of HarperCollins Publishers Ltd. © 2006 Paul Preston; Quote p. 290, extract p. 306 (partially) from *The Collapse of the Spanish Republic 1933–1936, Origins of the Civil War* by Stanley Payne, Yale University Press, 2006, pp.1, 177, reproduced with permission; Extracts pp. 292, 'Extract 3' 297, 311, 338 from *The Spanish Civil War* by Hugh Thomas, Penguin Books, 1965, pp. 87, 84, 239, 774, Copyright © 1989 Hugh Thomas, used by permission of The Wylie Agency (UK) Limited; Extract 4 p. 297 from Julián Casanova, *El Pais*, 12/08/2012, reproduced with permission; Extract 'Source 2' p. 298 from *The Coming of the Spanish Civil War: Reform, Reaction and Revolution in the Second Republic*, 2nd edn by Paul Preston, Routledge, 1994, pp. 65, 71, copyright © 1994 Routledge, reproduced by permission of Taylor and Francis Books UK; Extract 5 p. 298, Extract 1 p. 314, Extract 3 p. 379 from *Europe since 1870: An International History* by James Joll, Penguin Books, 1990, p. 352, Copyright ©James Joll 1973, 1976, 1983, 1990. All rights reserved. With permission

from The Orion Publishing Group, London, and by permission of Peters Fraser & Dunlop (www.petersfraserdunlop.com) on behalf of the Estate of James Joll, PFD aka Peters Fraser & Dunlop; Extract 'Source 3' p. 298 from *The Courier Mail*, Brisbane (Australia), http://trove.nla.gov.au/ndp/del/article/1136745, 01/11/1933, Newspaper articles found in Trove reproduced courtesy of the National Library of Australia; Extract p. 302, 'Source 8' p. 342 from *Edexcel AS History Unit One: Republicanism, Francoism and Civil War in Spain, 1931–75* by R. Bunce, P. Callaghan and L. Gallagher, Pearson Education Ltd., 2008, p. 25, 79, reproduced with permission; Extract p. 306 (partially) from *Right-Wing Spain in the Civil War Era: Soldiers of God and Apostles of the Fatherland, 1914–45* by Alejandro Quiroga, Bloomsbury, 2012, p.77 © Alejandro Quiroga, Miguel Angel del Arco and the Contributors, 2012, Bloomsbury Continuum Publishing, by permission of Bloomsbury Publishing Plc; Extract p. 307 from *The Spanish Civil War: A Cultural and Historical Reader* by Alun Kenwood, Berg Press, 1993, p.56, by permission of Bloomsbury Publishing Plc; Extracts pp. 318, 'Extract 2' p. 342, 348 from *Franco* by Paul Preston, Fontana, 1995, pp. 200, 585,585 reprinted by permission of HarperCollins Publishers Ltd ©1995 Paul Preston; Extracts pp. 320, 329 from *The Battle for Spain: The Spanish Civil War, 1936–1939* by Antony Beevor , Phoenix, 2006, pp. 90, 103, Copyright ©Ocito Ltd. 2006, reproduced with permission from Orion Publishing Group, London and Andrew Nurnberg Associates; Quote p. 324 from *The Spanish Republic at War 1936–1939* by Helen Graham, Cambridge University Press, 2002, p. 425; Extract p.324 from *Homage to Catalonia* by George Orwell , Penguin, 1938, pp. 148-49, Martin Secker & Warburg 1938, Penguin Books 1962, 1989, Penguin Classics 2000. Copyright ©1938 by Eric Blair. This edition copyright © the Estate of the late Sonia Brownwell Orwell, 1986; Extract p. 327 from Marxists Internet Archive; Extract p. 340 from 'Franco's Victims' Relatives Relive the Horror' by Fiona Govan, *The Telegraph*, 01/02/2012, Copyright © Telegraph Media Group Limited; Extract p.341 from Pope Pius XII speech translated by Rorate Caeli blog, http://rorate-caeli.blogspot.com/2011/07/passion-of-spain-75-years.html, reproduced with permission; Extracts pp. 349, 350, 362, 369 from *The Franco Regime 1936–1975* by Stanley Payne, University of Wisconsin Press, 1987, pp. 389-390,273, 463, 561, Copyright ©1987 by The Board of Regents of the University of Wisconsin System, reprinted by permission of The University of Wisconsin Press; Extracts p. 351 from The Avalon Project, http://avalon.law.yale.edu/wwii/sp13.asp; Extract p. 353 from United Nations General Assembly Resolution A/RES/39 (1), 12 December 1946, http://research.un.org/en/docs/ga/quick/regular/1, © 1946 United Nations. Reprinted with the permission of the United Nations; Extract p. 364 from *Fear and Progress: Ordinary Lives in Franco's Spain, 1939–1975* by Antonio Cazorla Sánchez, Wiley-Blackwell, 2010, pp. 116-17, reproduced with permission of Wiley-Blackwell in the format Republish in a book via Copyright Clearance Center; Quote p. 367 from Spanish Press Law 1966, translated by William Chislett in 'The Foreign Press During Spain's Transition to Democracy, 1974–78: A Personal Account', http://www.transicion.org/90publicaciones/ForeignPressDuringTheTransition.pdf, reproduced with permission from the author; Extract p. 377 from 'Crown Prince Juan Carlos Steers Spain towards Democracy' by Peter Niesewand, *The Guardian*, 7/11/1975, Copyright Guardian News & Media Ltd 2015; Extract 'Source 14' p. 379 from *The Best of All Possible Islands* by Richard Frederick Maddox, SUNY Press, 2012, p. 40, reproduced with permission.

Every effort has been made to contact copyright holders of material reproduced in this book. Any omissions will be rectified in subsequent printings if notice is given to the publishers.